My Life Is in Your Hands
&
Take My Life

Praise for Eddie Cantor's
My Life Is in Your Hands
(with David Freedman)

&

Take My Life
(with Jane Kesner Ardmore)

"I had the thrill of interviewing Eddie Cantor on radio and television. He remarked that he was as proud of his literary achievements as his show-business prowess. This book is a 'must' for an era and the man for whom the word 'superstar' could have been created." —**Joe Franklin**

"[An] extremely well-written autobiography." —*Library Journal*

"[Cantor's] story is presented articulately and with considerable charm." —*The San Francisco Chronicle*

"If you knew Eddie like I knew Eddie, oh oh oh what a star. Take his life in your hands and read and laugh at the odyssey of one of show business's greatest personalities." —**David Brown**, producer, on *My Life Is in Your Hands*

"Cantor was more than a star—he was a galaxy. Nobody shone brighter on Broadway or in Hollywood and his life is as rich as his talent. Take his life and enjoy it." —**David Brown** on *Take My Life*

"This book, for all its personalized saga, will contribute to the definitive history of show business from the turn of the century through the 1950s." —*The New York Herald Tribune*

"Eddie Cantor was my father-in-law. Not only was he a great entertainer and a wonderful storyteller, but he was a great humanitarian, unselfishly giving his time and money for worthwhile causes. I am proud to have known him. Read this magnificent book." —**Robert Clary**, singer and actor

"[This book] is never dull; often funny; always, in its own way, 'human.'" —*Saturday Review*

My Life Is in Your Hands
&
Take My Life
The Autobiographies of Eddie Cantor

Eddie Cantor
with David Freedman (*My Life Is in Your Hands*)
& Jane Kesner Ardmore (*Take My Life*)

Foreword by Will Rogers
New Introduction by Leonard Maltin
New Preface & Addendum by Brian Gari

First Cooper Square Press edition 2000

This Cooper Square Press paperback edition of *My Life Is in Your Hands & Take My Life* combines, for the first time in one volume, unabridged republications of *My Life Is in Your Hands* (co-written with David Freedman and first published in New York in 1928) and *Take My Life* (co-written with Jane Kesner Ardmore and first published in New York in 1957). This special edition has been supplemented with a new introduction by Leonard Maltin, a new preface and addendum by Brian Gari, a new recording history (songs, LPs, CDs, and hits), a new filmography, and a new index by Vince Giordano and Brian Gari. It is reprinted by arrangement with the Estate of Eddie Cantor and Jane Kesner Ardmore.

My Life Is in Your Hands copyright © 1928, 1956 by Eddie Cantor
Take My Life copyright © 1957, 1985 by Eddie Cantor and Jane Kesner Ardmore
New introduction copyright © 2000 by Leonard Maltin
New preface and addendum copyright © 2000 by Brian Gari
Special edition copyright © 2000 by the Estate of Eddie Cantor and Jane Kesner Ardmore

All rights reserved.
No part of this book may be reproduced in any form or by any electronic or mechanical means, including information storage and retrieval systems, without written permission from the publisher, except by a reviewer who may quote passages in a review.

Published by Cooper Square Press
An Imprint of the Rowman & Littlefield Publishing Group
150 Fifth Avenue, Suite 911
New York, New York 10011

Distributed by National Book Network

Library of Congress Cataloging-in-Publication Data

Cantor, Eddie, 1892–1964.
    My life is in your hands ; and, Take my life : the autobiographies of Eddie Cantor/Eddie Cantor with David Freeman and Jane Kesner Ardmore.—1st Cooper Square Press ed.
    p. cm.
    Originally published : 1st work. New York : Harper & Bro., 1928; and the 2nd work. Garden City, NY : Doubleday, 1957.
    ISBN 978-1-59393-634-1
    1. Cantor, Eddie, 1892–1964. 2. Entertainers—United States—Biography. I. Title : My life is in your hands ; and, Take my life. II. Freeman, David, 1941– III. Ardmore, Jane Kesner. IV. Cantor, Eddie, 1892–1964. Take my life. V. Title: Take my life. VI. Title

PN2287.C26 A3   2000
791'.092—dc21
[B]   00-034542

The paper used in this publication meets the minimum requirements of American National Standard for Information Sciences—Permanence of Paper for Printed Library Materials, ANSI/NISO Z39.48-1992. Manufactured in the United States of America.

TO
MY FATHER AND MOTHER
WHOM I NEVER SAW
AND TO ESTHER
WHO WAS BOTH
TO ME

CONTENTS

Introduction by Leonard Maltin	ix
Preface by Brian Gari	xiii
Warning by Will Rogers	xv
My Life Is in Your Hands	1
The "Lost Chapter"	301
Take My Life	1
Addendum by Brian Gari	289
Recording History (Songs)	291
Recording History (LPs)	294
Recording History (CDs)	295
Cantor on the Charts	297
Filmography	298
Index by Vince Giordano and Brian Gari	303

INTRODUCTION

Several generations of Americans knew and loved Eddie Cantor—on stage, in movies, on radio, on records, and eventually on television. A star on Broadway in the second decade of the twentieth century, he was still a headliner forty years later in people's living rooms.

One doesn't think of careers lasting forty years or more in today's show-business environment. The pace of life has accelerated so much, and the audience has become so fragmented, that it may not be possible to sustain that kind of success any more. But Cantor was canny enough to know how to reinvent himself, in subtle ways, and how to sustain his stardom through decades of change—not only in society, but in the means of reaching an audience. From vaudeville to the Broadway stage, from silent movies (where his expressive "banjo eyes" had to take the place of his voice) to early talkies, from the pioneering days of network radio to the infancy of live television, Cantor was there—and he was a headliner.

In the 1950s, the erudite television comedian and host Steve Allen wrote a wonderful book called *The Funny Men* in which he analyzed the personas and techniques of many top comedians, young and old. In characterizing Eddie Cantor he said, simply and perceptively, "Eddie Cantor sells yesterday."

One doesn't think of nostalgia being a relevant commodity as far back as the 1950s, but in fact both Cantor and his

INTRODUCTION

pal George Jessel made ample use of it throughout their careers. When Eddie played Carnegie Hall in 1950, he regaled his audience with songs and anecdotes of the past (as well as making timely comments about the present).

What's even more remarkable is that as early as 1928, Eddie Cantor decided to set his thoughts down on paper. Telling his own story would be one thing, but Eddie also enjoyed painting word-pictures of his famous friends, from W. C. Fields to Will Rogers.

Thus, at the height of his fame, Eddie Cantor took on the mantle of show-business chronicler. If only others had followed his example.

There is no doubt that Eddie had a healthy ego, but he also had a healthy respect for talent. Perhaps that's why he enjoyed sharing stories and observations about his Ziegfeld costars, his movie leading lady Clara Bow, and the many others he encountered in his colorful career. One certainly can't picture Al Jolson—if he had sat down to write his memoirs—devoting a paragraph to anyone but himself!

What's also impressive about Cantor's stories is that he calls 'em as he sees 'em. He tells of his failures and disappointments (such as his second silent film, *Special Delivery*, which, as he indicates, isn't nearly as good as his first, *Kid Boots*), not just his successes.

Yes, there is a heavy layer of sentiment in these pages, but it's what I like to think of as *honest* sentiment. Surely, Eddie was not above a bit of exaggeration for dramatic effect, but there is no question that his was a genuine rags-to-riches saga. No one handed him anything; he and the other chil-

INTRODUCTION

dren of immigrants who made it to the top of the show-business ladder (from Irving Berlin to Jimmy Durante) earned every bit of their success, and with it I suppose they also earned the right to pontificate a bit.

While Eddie Cantor made use of professional writers as his "ghosts," (first David Freedman, who became an indispensable Cantor collaborator on his 1930s radio show, then Jane Kesner Ardmore), he was professional enough to acknowledge their existence—and they were professional enough to acquire Eddie's "voice" in their writing. You never doubt for a moment that you're listening to Eddie Cantor himself, spinning his show-business tales.

These books provide a window through which we can see another world, a look at show-business as it no longer exists. They also remind us of the American dream at the dawn of the last century. Eddie Cantor personified that dream.

LEONARD MALTIN
Toluca Lake, California
September 1999

Leonard Maltin is best known as the film commentator on television's *Entertainment Tonight*. He is also the author of many books, including *The Great Movie Comedians, Movie Comedy Teams,* and *The Great American Broadcast,* and editor of the popular paperback reference *Leonard Maltin's Movie & Video Guide.*

PREFACE

A few years ago, while feeling proud that I had helped to reestablish my grandfather to his rightful place in the recording and video marketplaces, I also felt something was missing. What about his writing? In particular, what about his autobiographies? I immediately set out to see if I could fill that gap by getting his wonderful 1928 autobiography republished. I recalled reading it while on an airplane and feeling so deeply absorbed in his ability to communicate his incredible life story (up to that year) in such a literate fashion considering his severe lack of education. (I must, at this point, acknowledge David Freedman's contribution to this process.) I had very little experience in the book world and knew it would probably be an uphill climb. It was and it wasn't. What certainly helped were the hundreds of letters that members of the Eddie Cantor Appreciation Society sent to me to arm myself for battle. When I walked into the office of Michael Dorr at Cooper Square Press, I gave him a copy of *My Life Is in Your Hands* as well as the hundreds of letters. A few weeks later, he told me of his interest to republish the book. I casually mentioned Cantor's 1957 autobiography *Take My Life*. Michael was surprised that there was another. He asked to read it and to my astonishment came back to me asking if Cooper Square Press could republish not only *My Life Is in Your Hands* but *Take My Life* as well. I have included the rarely seen additional chapter from 1932 that fan club member Stephanie Goldberg alerted

PREFACE

me to some years earlier. I would like to personally thank all of the members who wrote letters, as well as Stephanie Goldberg, Leonard Maltin, Milton Berle, Jerry Stiller, Joe Franklin, David Brown, Robert Clary, Christopher Clay, Jane Kesner Ardmore, Vince Giordano, my mother Janet Cantor Gari, and Ross Plotkin at Cooper Square. And finally, to Michael Dorr for his dedication and belief, I offer heartfelt thanks from me and all the fans of the immortal Eddie Cantor.

BRIAN GARI
New York City
June 2000

For more information:
The Eddie Cantor Appreciation Society
14611 Valley Vista Blvd.
Sherman Oaks, CA 91403
website: *www.eddiecantor.com*

WARNING
By
WILL ROGERS

Eddie wants me to write a "Foreword" to this life of his, that he has lived up to the time that the Publishers said, "Thats enough for one life, We cant end the life, but we can end the book". I told Eddie there wasent any use of having a "warning" that the people maby wouldent read the book even if it dident have a foreword or warning.

You see Eddie being an Actor, (I think he mentions it somewhere in here) He was smart enough to not want to start right off with his own stuff, No Actor likes to "Open the Show", that is start off first, They like to have something on ahead of them, They dont care how bad it is, in fact the worse it is the better it makes their stuff look, So that is just the reason I am here, I am the "Dumb" act, or animal act, that starts the show.

Some books have been made by these preliminary "Warnings", But that was when they were awful clever, or were kept awful short.

Its hard to get good writers to write these first page "Warnings", You see you dont get anything for it, and the better writer you are the harder it is to write for nothing, They are generally done out of what is called friendship, But they say "Friendship and business dont mix" and as all of your good stuff that you are able to

WARNING

sell to some publisher yourself is business, why you dont like to mix it with your friendship.

I never read this book, and am writing this with the distinct understanding I am not to read it, in fact thats the pay that I am getting for the warning, I know his life personally, If this is his real life, Why neither I or any of us ought to read it, and if its not his life I dont want to be dissalusioned, People are like a Cat when it comes to their lives, they have at least nine, and they can pick out the one to write about that they think will look best. I do know that Eddie has had a pretty checkered career, (I will never know why they always speak of careers as "Checkered") He is the only person I know that got to the very top of his profession without going the usual American Magazine route, (Hard work, perseverance, and taking advantage of his oppurtunities).

Knowing how to pick good Lyrics had more to do with it than hard work. I think Eddie has one of the youngest lives that has ever been published, If its a success there will be a great demand to get Autobiographies while they are young, In fact get em before there has really been a chance to learn anything that shouldent be in a Life story, Now his next book will be called "My Life after you read my last life", I may read it, for he will be wealthy during it and thats when a man becomes unconsciously funny is when he becomes rich. When I first met Eddie, neither of us knew whether Zeigfeld had a "Follies" or whether he was maby a Livery stable keeper.

WARNING

I liked him as a kid, right from the start, I was getting just enough more money than him to feel that I could advise him, I happened to have been with two or three Zeigfeld shows when Eddie joins us in a new one for the first time, He made a bigger hit than either W C Fields or I either one, But still somehow we couldent feel jealous of him, It seemed like the bigger he went the more we liked him, and by the time he was asked to write this, why we are thinking quite a bit of him, But you know I believe that if this fellow hadent got over so big on the stage I would have had about the same regard for him, for it was what happened off the stage that I always liked about him, as much as his wonderful entertaining, There is a lot of sentiment about Eddie, and a lot of fine qualaties, For instance the proceeds of this book all goes to a Boys summer camp that he is interested in and works for and looks after, for poor Kids on the East side that never saw a stretch of country in their lives, So I advise you all to buy this Book, for you will be helping some poor kid to get poisen ivy that would never in the World have had the oppurtunity otherwise.

This Book will fill up just as much space in a book shelf as the life of pretty near any of those other fellows, unless it was Napoleon, or Washington or some of those far sighted old boys that carried writers right with em to make up their lives as they went along.

Now if you want to read any further than this, why go ahead, I have warned you, Stop now! and go get the life

WARNING

of Josephine, or Peggy Joice, or somebody who has had a life.

But dont say I havent fullfilled my purpose in this book, I have warned you, and I dont think Shakespeare could write a better "foreword" than that, I know he couldent for nothing.

My Life Is in Your Hands

with David Freedman

MY LIFE
IS IN YOUR HANDS

Introduction

WHILE most biographies are written about people whose lives are almost ended, I thought I would be original and write about mine, which has hardly begun. It is true I am the father of five children—mostly daughters—in fact, I have as many daughters as I have children; but that is scarcely a sign of infancy. It is rather a sign of a one-track mind. Still, I am only thirty-six, and in these days when science is trying to prolong life indefinitely we will soon reach a point when a person in the thirties will be just old enough to wear bicycle stockings and eat pop corn. If science continues its great work, the only way a man will be able to die a natural death will be to cross the street and be hit by a truck.

However, I have dug up evidence from the Talmud in defense of the old idea that the human span is only three score and ten, or seventy years. Like most defense evidence, it is in the form of a legend. The legend tells that every seven years the individual changes and that in one's life one passes through ten completely different personalities. And now that I am thirty-six and halfway over, I have a strong curiosity to look back and see who the other five Eddies were that I left behind. As I look

MY LIFE IS IN YOUR HANDS

back I am fond of every one of them—although some of them ought to be ashamed of themselves—and after you hear what they were up to, you may wonder, as I often do, how I turned out to be myself instead of a ukulele or something.

In order to make the story a true and complete one I shall conceal nothing. If I thought it would help I could reproduce a set of X-rays I recently took that reveal my innermost self. But besides revealing a patch of pleurisy and the image of my suspender button, these X-rays shed no light on how I became a singing waiter at Carey Walsh's and why I didn't remain one.

I feel that no man's life is sufficiently interesting in itself unless it is in some way a pattern or design created out of the times and reflecting in it bits of other personalities. I have always felt like a part of other people and that other people were a part of me. The dim, brief images of my father and mother have formed an unforgetable picture in my mind, although I never really had the opportunity to know them or even to speak to them, for as my lips were forming into words they were gone. It was through my grandmother that I learned to know them and it was she who reared me through the early years. Grandma Esther is one of my proudest figures before the world.

In trying to recall and restore the five Eddies I have been, I snatch at outstanding bits, high spots that glitter out of the background of the past like the points of stars. Little episodes, long faded, come to life again.

MY LIFE IS IN YOUR HANDS

I see myself as a young trouper with Gus Edwards' "Kid Kabaret." Georgie Jessel, Leila Lee, Eddie Buzzell, and George Price were all youngsters in the show. Jessel and I began a friendship then which has lasted to this day, sincere, whole-hearted, always anxious to help each other to succeed—a unique thing in the show business. I was a few years older and big-brothered him. I used to bathe him then, lay out his clothes for the morning, watch over him and being older than the others, I took charge of the railroad tickets when the show traveled. The boys all put on short pants for the train ride and I gave the conductor half-fare tickets. After a while he came back fuming and angry.

"What the hell is the idea?" he growled at me. "Those fellers half fare?" I looked up, innocently surprised.

"What's the matter, conductor?"

"Why," he cried, "they're in the smoking-car, each with a big black cigar in his face, and by the language they use they're older than I am!"

"Boys will be boys!" I murmured with a sigh.

It's wonderful how the most trifling incidents cling to the mind. But it's not wonderful with me. I've got to have a good memory to remember the kind of jokes I tell. As I begin to assemble incidents and experiences I am astonished to find how little I have forgotten. In fact, I can remember the story of my life from about two years before I was born, and I think that's pretty good.

MY LIFE IS IN YOUR HANDS

At different stages I see clusters of interesting personalities who were my friends and colleagues. Some of them are celebrated people whom you know, like Will Rogers, W. C. Fields, Marilyn Miller, Fannie Brice, Benny Leonard, Florenz Ziegfeld, Jack Dempsey, and a host of others, among them world-famous figures with whom I had interesting experiences like the late Presidents Wilson and Harding and the Prince of Wales; others are humbler figures of whom you probably never heard but who are just as human, interesting, and important to me. A meeting I once had, in a summer-school recreation center with a little girl, exerted a far greater influence on my life than my signing a contract for five thousand dollars a week which made me the highest-salaried comedian in the musical show business. And that's no lie. For that little girl later became my wife.

It was very hard to make her believe that I would ever get paid for acting. For even when I got my first chance on the Amsterdam roof in the Midnight Frolics, entertaining the four hundred and becoming sociable with the Vanderbilts and the Stotesburys, my wife and I would go back after the show to our bedroom in her sister's flat, where we lived with our two little daughters, Marjorie and Natalie, four people in one room. After the glamour and glitter of the Frolics we would sit in that one room up in the Bronx and wonder whether we'd ever be able to afford a home of our own. Some years later we had the home, but she still doubted. The world of the four hundred was still a far-away dream.

MY LIFE IS IN YOUR HANDS

One night I received word in my dressing-room from Rodman Wanamaker to come to a party at his home after the show and meet the Prince of Wales. I had no chance to notify my wife, and when I finally got home it was five o'clock the next morning.

"Where have you been?" she asked with a chilling calm.

"I was with the Prince of Wales."

"Oh, get into bed!" she muttered, angrily. "I suppose tomorrow you'll come home at six in the morning and say you were out all night with President Coolidge!"

While I intend to relate some of my experiences with a number of your favorite celebrities, I wouldn't write a whole biography for that. Nor would I write a book about myself just because I happen to be one comedian who's made a million dollars and has still got it—though that isn't such a bad reason for writing a book—but because I think the story in itself with its human aspects should make a good picture, not only for Fox or Famous, but for a lot of people who would like to follow me through, behind the scenes, in the toughest performance I ever gave in the biggest show I ever played that has had a continuous run for thirty-six years, produced under my personal direction, written by myself and entitled, "The Life of Eddie Cantor."

The curtain rises on chapter one.

Chapter I

MY FATHER, Michael Cantor, was not a successful man as measured by the usual standards. Most successful men devote themselves to a serious life-work and in their spare moments encourage a hobby. My father encouraged only his hobby and overlooked the life-work. His hobby was a slightly damaged, second-hand fiddle which he fingered rather deftly and from which, by the aid of a horse-hair bow that was always shedding, he could on occasion call forth really musical tones; sometimes sprightly, more often plaintive, but always appealing, soothing, like little trickling rivers of memory from a life he might have lived, a life he had built around him of music and dreams to shield him from this strange city he didn't understand, from all the harsh tumult and clatter of iron and steel that were flying up around him.

It never occurred to my father that with such playing he could join the musicians' union and get a job and possibly work up to be a bandmaster like my friend, George Olsen, and run a night club. But that would have made things too easy for me. Besides, I was not yet on the scene to give him the idea. The mere thought of a regular job would make Michael Cantor put his fiddle away for a month and idly walk the streets for weeks to wear off the shock. For my father, in his dreamy, half-dazed fashion, loved life too well to make a business of it, and being a youth of only twenty at the time, he still cherished illusions.

He must have imagined that the thin voice of his fiddle would some day be heard above the rumble of engines, that his youthful fancies and folk songs would catch the harsh city's ear, and that tenements, tunnels, and skyscrapers would tumble and dissolve into a sweet, country setting like his native village near Minsk and he would sit and serenade the city which had declared a legal holiday just to listen to his song. He was only twenty and married and lived on Eldridge Street, a great street for stables, and he needed dreams like these to keep the smell of his equine neighbors from his nostrils and to justify his idleness, his poverty, and his incurable optimism.

And so in his two-room flat over a Russian tea-house, he lived with Maite, a young, wan creature already sallowed by premature hardships, her face tarnished by the fine yellow dust of the great city, and her young brow perked in pain with thoughts too old for her. Perhaps Maite had hoped to see her Michael some day as the grand maestro leading an orchestra on a gilded platform; perhaps she had secretly aspired to be one of those fine ladies in shiny silks that fluttered like colorful butterflies on the gay white way in New York's midnight sun. She was only one year removed from Michael and still at the time of life when music and laughter are food and air, but she was already approaching motherhood, and all her thoughts and features settled to the gravity of that prospect.

Cares grew upon her like weeds. Hardly surviving the burden of an early marriage with no resources, she would soon have this new responsibility. She would have to prod the dreamy Michael on, awaken him from his stupor, and hope for the dramatic day when he would shoulder his fiddle like a sack of tools and go out to work. For herself she had never demanded anything. The daily portion came from Providence, not the city, and was often delayed in transit. But for the child it would have to come more regularly. Michael Cantor could not feed an infant on music. Not an infant like me, anyway. Nature provides its newborn with their own capacity for song—I'll tell the world. But Michael seemed oblivious to all necessity. To every complaint of my mother he would set a bar of music and to every entreaty for work he would play a rhapsody.

Work was made for subway-diggers and beam-riveters, but not for Cantors. He had been ordained by a mystic power to play the city's tune, and though the city failed to recognize the tune and though his family would writhe with hunger listening to it, Michael was impelled to play doggedly on.

Maite's mother arrived from Russia to help her only daughter. Maite's mother was one of those rare, precious women born for perpetual toil and perpetual devotion. From the age of thirty she had been a widow and labored to support her three sons and Maite. In her native

Russian province she was known as Esther the Cigar-maker and while Russian cigars never won gold medals at international expositions, Esther's products could be smoked safely and had been lit right after drinking vodka without exploding the smoker. With such modest fame, Esther had managed to build up a small cigar establishment. But when her daughter appealed to her, Esther sold the business cheaply, realizing enough to pay for her passage and bringing a little bag of silver rubles just as the young Cantor couple was sinking into destitution.

For a time the Cantor home brightened up. Esther took care of the house, prepared the meals, and secretly slipped my father a few dollars each week, that he might turn them over to Maite and pretend he had earned them himself. And when young Maite, now twenty-one, took to her bed upon the midwife's advice, the little flat had an air of holiday.

It was the last day of January, 1892, in a small, gas-lit bedroom on Eldridge Street, on a biting cold night usually good for theater audiences, at about the time that the regular overture begins, that I made my début before a packed house. The excited voices of relatives and friends, the clamor of street wagons, the sounds of the Russian balalaika from the tea-house, the muffled groans of my mother and my father's plaintive fiddle, all joined in a strange ovation on my first appearance.

Esther, now a grandma, bustled about, running from the living-room into the bedchamber and back—a matter of two steps—assisting the midwife, serving cakes to the guests, refilling flasks as fast as they were emptied, while the party of neighbors and well-wishers got sick drinking shlivivitz to my health. Later Grandma Esther, beaming, breathless, perspiring, came to tell them that all was well and, while there was not very much of me, I was the image of my father, only I didn't have a fiddle. At this news all glasses were drained and refilled. Michael cleared the dream mist from his eyes, seemed to realize at least for a moment that he was a father, a progenitor, a man whom the world owed a debt for his accomplishment, after which he was rightfully entitled to spend the rest of his life in undisturbed revery and occasional fiddling. The balalaika below burst into new merriment, the friends and relatives drank again, danced and laughed, as if each had come into a separate fortune, and even Michael felt that a turn had come in the tide of affairs; only I, in the next room, cried with the unfailing instinct of childhood that everything wasn't quite so rosy as they cracked it up to be.

While the guests crowded the little flat it was warm, but after they left it recaptured its dank and chilly atmosphere, and through the cold, hard winter my mother almost never let me out of her arms, wrapping and huddling me close to her to keep me warm. But my father failed to respond to the supreme test. Instead of buckling up and knuckling down, he slumped aside into deeper dreams. I must have been six months old then, but even I turned a pair of big, popping eyes on him with a questioning look, as if to ask, "When do we eat?" But my father had wasted his years wondering, "When do we play?"

Grandma Esther's little fund had given out, but the good woman took a huge basket of candles, matches, safety-pins and knick-knacks and began to peddle among the housewives, canvassing the tenements from door to door. She walked each day with her load from Cherry to Division Street, through Henry and Madison, until permanent knotted lumps formed on her arms where the basket handle rested.

Maite had hoped that Michael would change. In fits of self-discipline he would get a job, but it never lasted. He could not understand why a man had to work who was born to play the fiddle. Why did a man of twenty-two have to carry the weight of the whole world—we two were the world to him—on his frail, stoop shoulders? But Maite had given up urging him on. Once we had slipped over the brink, we didn't need Newton's law of gravity to figure out how fast we would fall. When I was a little over a year old my mother died in childbirth.

My father was a stunned, distracted man. Grandma Esther, calm in her stoic grief, thought only of his suffering, comforted and cared for him like her own son. But he suddenly grew restive, nervous, excited. He wandered through the streets constantly now, gaping, staring like a man who had lost his way. Somewhere in the midst of the crowded, tangled city he would find her again. He could not believe that she was gone. He would surely come upon her, standing alone on a street corner, waiting for him, and he would lead her beyond the city limits to a patch of green and sky where they could walk a little in peace, and chat and laugh and have their first real outing. For in spite of all the years of lolling and dreaming, for some reason his life had always been crowded and rushed, and Michael felt that he had never been quite alone with Maite, that he had never had a chance to tell her what she really meant to him and how deeply, genuinely he was fond of her and how much he would like to do to make her happy. But where would he look for her? The streets turned and twined upon each other like a wriggling wilderness of snakes.

The relentless, brutal majesty of fate was wasted on my poor father. He did not understand it; he was afraid to understand it. He only heard voices without faces taunting him, shouting at him, "So you idled and played and to what purpose?" If he could only see who spoke to him and assure these heartless forces of fate that he had meant no harm. But an invisible hand slapped him full in the face and he slumped into bed with a chill and a sharp pain in the chest. His cheeks flushed in indignation and he lay in feverish excitement, mumbling in protest and defiance.

The local lodge doctor held his thin, clammy hand and diagnosed his emotional turmoil as pneumonia. But Michael, who had begun to understand, smiled a dry, yellow smile. "It's not pneumonia, it's music," he murmured, huskily. "It's music!" A rattling wagon clattered by over the cobblestones. Some children blew on rasping horns. I was then two years old and toddled about, trying to wind the cat's tail around its neck while it howled pitifully. "I tell you it's music," whispered my father, grown old and haggard at twenty-two.

"Mamma Esther, let me play," he entreated, and the sad-faced toil-worn old woman brought the second-hand fiddle from its peeling fiddle-box. Michael took the plaything from her like a child, the wooden instrument with strings that held his secret which the busy, proud city had refused to hear. He tucked the violin under his chin, shakingly moved the bow across the bridge, pulled a few reluctant, complaining tones from its hollow box, and for the moment he was lost in the dreams of song that trickled like little rivers of memory from the life he might have lived. I stood holding my victim cat in a grip around the throat and clutched it tighter, almost strangling it, as with wide, staring eyes and open mouth I watched my father play.

"What's papa doing?" I wondered. "Gimme it!"

"It's music, mine child," said Grandma Esther, stroking my hair.

"Minuzick!" A strange new word with magic meanings. My father was too weak to play and the violin dropped mutely across his chest. Grandma Esther tried to take it from him, but he held it firmly.

"Gimme it!" I cried. "I wanna play too!"

"Not now," pleaded my grandmother, softly. "Some day you'll play like your father."

My father lay back on his pillow, still clinging to his

violin, his eyes slowly closing in that mist which shut the world from his thoughts.

"Michael," murmured Grandma Esther, bending over him tenderly. "Michael!" Then she cried with the muffled anguish of a thousand groans. "Michael! Michael! Answer me! Answer your Mamma Esther!"

"Why don't papa play no more minuzick?" I whimpered, uneasily, clutching at the old woman's dress.

"He's asleep, mine child," Grandma Esther sobbed, and her tears streamed down on my upturned face. "You're an orphan, woe is me! Alone in the world!" And sobbing and weeping, she kissed me through her tears.

Chapter II

I WAS two, and Grandma Esther sixty-two. We were a couple of lonely creatures at the opposite poles of life, one looking forward, the other backward, to the same welter of poverty, adversity, and toil. Other women at her age had earned a brief vacation from their labors, if only to be sick and lie in bed. But my grandmother could not afford the luxury of illness. Her years had been a ceaseless treadmill, grinding, churning, without hope, without end. She had married in her youth to snatch a few years of domestic happiness and leisure. But her young sickly husband needed her help and Esther's only rest from work was on those occasions when she had to be confined. Her husband, soaked with the nicotine and tobacco fumes of his trade, soon died and the burden of support fell with its full weight upon her. When at last her three sons and only daughter married, her duties as a mother and provider ended, only to start again with me. She could not earn enough from peddling candles and matches to rear me as she would like. So from carrying baskets Grandma Esther took to lifting steamer trunks on her back and lugging them up three and four flights as part of her duties in furnishing servant girls to private families.

She conducted a humble employment agency of her own and supplied maids and nurse girls to households, and cooks, dish-washers, and waitresses to small restaurants. She rented two rooms in a basement that were combination office and home, as well as temporary lodging-house for the unemployed. Here eight or nine Polish immigrant girls would eat from the common caldron and sleep on the kitchen floor, sprawled over mattresses and covered with brightly patched quilts. And when a Polish maid was provided with a job, Grandma Esther would lift the girl's trunk upon her shoulders and lead the way. Her brokerage fee for each servant was one dollar, later increased to two, but that included the cost of maintaining the girl before she was placed. As my grandmother could not afford the price of a license, she conducted this sadly unlucrative business without it and stood in constant fear of city officials whom competing agencies sent to spy upon her. When a stern-looking inspector quizzed her she would explain that the girls, while of a different nationality, were her blood relations, and overnight I used to get as many as seven sisters and eight first cousins. But finally she amassed the snug fortune of twenty-five dollars to pay for a license so that she could struggle and starve officially.

Even then the agency was obliged to shift its headquarters frequently. Sometimes for a detail like non-payment of rent and more often because the landlord, who had let the flat for a family of two, visited us and found ten or twelve. But moving was not very expensive, only a little bothersome. The sole cost involved was the hiring of a pushcart. This my grandmother loaded herself with a chest of drawers, a half-dozen mattresses, an iron bedstead, a few stools, some kitchen utensils, and with me perched on top of the load she would push her cart to the new abode and was ready to do business once more. If 127 Madison Street had grown too tony and swell to have a dozen people in two rooms, she would settle down at 11 Market Street, where they were glad to accommodate seventeen people in one room. The main thing was that I should have a congenial home and pleasant surroundings.

At first Grandma Esther, for my sake, settled with me at the home of her daughter-in-law, who then had only three children, Minnie, Annie, and Irwin. This she did to provide me with playmates. But I was at the time a rabid woman-hater—a prejudice I have since outgrown—and I decided to do away with all little girls of my own age or thereabouts, so that Minnie and Annie were found in a badly wounded and partially unconscious condition after a few friendly and playful encounters with me. But while I beat the little girls in true cave-man fashion, Irwin beat me, and this I resented at the top of my voice.

Still, the only systematic musical training I ever received dates from this time, and I originated it myself. I would take my aunt's modest supply of silver, and from the fifth floor, where we lived, I used to drop forks and spoons, one at a time, through the steep shaft of banisters, and by the clang I could tell on which floor the silver had landed. It required quite a little skill to send a knife clear down the five flights and detect by the sound that it had landed in the hall. Afterwards I tried this trick with plates. These cute ideas completely horrified my poor aunt. She was afraid I would try to throw the dining-room furniture down next, so she put me to bed without food; but Grandma Esther, indignant that her darling little Eddie had not been properly appreciated, smuggled some cookies in to me and hid the leg of a chicken under my pillow. Kissing and soothing me, she decided then and there that we would live together and alone.

And so all day, while the good woman delivered Polish girls and their baggage at a dollar a head, I grew up on the sidewalks of New York, with an occasional fall into the gutter. Grandma Esther had failed to take scientific courses in mother-training, but in her simple, bungling way she did the best she knew. If I banged myself against a stone slab and came into the house with a lump bigger than my head, she pressed the cold steel of a carving-knife against the swelling, mumbled some strange incantations to drive off the evil spirit, and pretty soon the lump subsided. If I was laid up with fever she covered my face with a damp cloth, sprinkled some herbs and red pepper upon it, then uttered a prayer to my departed mother to intercede on my behalf with the powers of heaven, and immediately the heavenly wheels of influence were set in motion and I was saved.

Only the ignorant, according to my grandmother, depended on doctors. She considered it a sacrilege the way the woman on the top floor of 13 Market Street would constantly call the neighborhood doctor, with the result that her child was constantly ill. And the doctor, a stout asthmatic with a red face, would not even climb the four flights to look at his patient, but carried on his examination from the sidewalk, shouting up to the woman who leaned out of her window to answer him.

"What is it, Mrs. Lefkowitz?" cried the physician.

"Mine child, it hurts him his belly!" complained the worried Mrs. Lefkowitz.

"Give him castor-oil!" shouted up the physician. "And throw down a dollar!"

Grandma Esther looked on, her head nodding sadly. Here was a man walking from house to house, bellowing up medical advice to the women and getting money thrown at him from every window. And she felt she had cured more people with her mysterious herbs and incantations than all the doctors ever would. But one day her sacred magic failed.

I was an excited umpire on the side lines of a gang fight when a jagged, flying brick struck me, cleaving my forehead almost in two, and I fell unconscious on the curbstone in a pool of blood. My grandmother, wailing and distracted, tried with her prayers to revive me, but finally carried me into the nearest drug store. The druggist on the East Side was in those days a factotum of science. If you came in with a prescription from a professor, he usually frowned and asked in deep concern, "What is this for?" You told him it was for your stomach and he laughed pityingly. "Why, then he gave you the wrong thing. This medicine is only for tonsils. Besides, he gave you a dose that could kill a horse!" And you wound up by taking the druggist's prescription instead. And if you came in for liver pills, the chances were you went out with a camera, a hot-water bag, a box of stationery, and a carpet-cleaner. This druggist in particular had acquired a wide reputation as a surgeon because he had once bandaged a badly cut leg. He always prided himself on the fact that the bandage never came off, though the leg did. Reassuring my grandmother that there was nothing to worry about, he put five stitches into my forehead, omitting the perfunctory routine of first washing out the wound, and then he made one of his perfect bandages. In two days my head was swollen to a size that no success in later life could swell it again.

My grandmother, now really frightened, carried me to the Essex Street dispensary where the wound was reopened and carefully treated. For three months she carried me in her arms each day to the Good Samaritan Dispensary, watched over me tenderly, soothing me through the nights of fever and pain, until at last the wound was healed and I could walk again. To this day that scar cuts across my brow and I sometimes wonder why I haven't invented a romantic story about it, to tell people that a hand wielding a saber suddenly appeared and slashed across my forehead to set a stamp of eternal sadness which the comedian always conceals beneath his mask of make-up. Now that I've made it up, maybe it's true at that.

As I grew older my grandmother left a standing order at the corner grocery that while she was away on business

MY LIFE IS IN YOUR HANDS

I could choose my own meals from the menu of canned herrings, sardines, and the various barrels of olives and cheese. And after a light diet of kippered herring I would wander among the pushcarts for my dessert. I developed a knack for slipping bananas up my sleeve and dropping apples into my blouse while the peddler was busy filling some housewife's market bag. I used to pack a peach into my mouth with one snap of the jaws and look deeply offended when the peddler turned suspiciously upon me. With steady practice I got so that I could gulp a banana at one swallow and appear absolutely famished with a plum in each cheek.

One of my earliest achievements which I feel would have won me a place in history even if I had never met Ziegfeld, was that, between the ages of six and twelve, I became the world's supreme delicatessen eater, absorbing more salami, pastrami, bologna, and frankfurters in that short span than most families do in a lifetime. That's a fact. Even now as I daintily dip my zwieback into a cup of lukewarm milk I shudder as I think of my early prowess. I was the trusted emissary, or maybe ambassador, of the Isaac Gelles Wurst Works in those years, and carried their daily supply of pickled meats from the factory on Essex Street to their big store at 14 Market Street. I used to start out with an empty stomach and a full basket and wind up *vice-versa*.

I often watch my own children now, eating their careful diets of orange juice, gelatine puddings, coddled eggs and custards, nicely caloried and vitamined, and I can't help wondering how any of the old East Side herring-tearers remained alive at all. Still, we had our own ideas of training then. We believed that if practice makes for progress, then a stomach trained on bologna can in later life digest nails, and a head banged often enough on pavement can later buck granite. I guess both methods are partly right. It's the age-old issue that will never be solved, between the coddled egg and the hard-boiled one.

At the age of six I began to keep late hours. At midnight, after my grandmother had retired, I would crawl on to the iron bedstead beside her, and if she happened to wake up and ask me where I had been, I appeared to be sound asleep and even gave a snore or two to convince her. But in reality I had been out with a band of boys two and three times my age who spent their nights in a revelry of song. For the East Side at night is not only menaced by the caterwauling of cats, but by gangs of youngsters who sit on the stoops and the corner stands, singing all the popular songs with all their might at an age when their voices are changing. In a choir like this my voice stood out to advantage.

While children of six usually sing all their songs on one and the same note and that note for some reason is usually flat, I managed to follow the tune pretty well and if a note was very high I made it, if I had to climb a pole to reach it. The other boys, in recognition of my ability, would let me sing a solo; but some unappreciative listener on the third floor once drowned out the concert with a pail of water, giving an impromptu black-out to my act.

But I wasn't discouraged by this icy reception. Only a jealous man, I thought, would pour water on a performing artist. And if my voice could arouse such envy, I must develop it at all costs. So I sang under the same window the next night and twice as loud.

I grew lean, big-eyed, eager, eating from grocery barrels, singing in back yards, playing in gutters and on the roofs of houses, and combining with it all the smatterings of a public-school education. I was not introspective—whatever that is. I simply took to life as a darky takes to rhythms, and vibrated with it. In short, I was a typical New York street boy who, by a peculiar and deft twist of fortune, eventually lands either in the Bowery Mission or in a bower of roses.

Chapter III

ONE day I learned about parents. They were mysterious people who bought wonderful things for other children, but never thought about me. Little Jonah Goldstein had a wagon and said his parents bought it. Young Ira Atkins paraded with a popgun and a wooden tomahawk. The street-corner club met and boasted of the rare gifts they would get for the holidays. One dark, stern little lad, Daniel Lipsky, not only received presents, but at the age of nine already carried a pad and pencil in his pocket to calculate his savings and set aside a small sum to buy tokens for others. He was born with an infallible instinct for figures and if the club planned a joint enterprise he quickly concluded, "Boys, this will cost a dollar twenty and we've got to chip in eight cents a piece." The moment one uttered a number Daniel would say, "Six per cent of that" and give you the answer. It was a kind of magic to me. And when Daniel marched down the block in a new birthday suit and revealed a fire-engine he had gotten for Channukah, I realized that parents must be marvelous things. I'd have to get myself a few.

"My father bought me this," remarked Lipsky, impressively. "That fire-engine must cost four-ninety-eight!" But I was not to be outdone.

"You call that an engine!" I sneered. "That's a peanut! Why, my father is a fireman! He rides the hook-and-ladder and everything!"

"You ain't got a father," retorted Benny Shulberg.

MY LIFE IS IN YOUR HANDS

"I have so!" I insisted. "And any time I want I can go down to the fire house and ride the engine with him!" For a moment the other boys' features darkened and their lips drooped in envy.

"Say, fellers, is he really got a father?" asked Benny, waveringly. But I was determined. If every other lad had a father, I had one, too, and a real live father—a father who was a fireman one day, a cop the next day, and on another occasion the biggest chief the Indians ever had!

"Well, if you got one," snarled Jonah Goldstein, who had a wagon and a legal mind even at that early date, "then why don't we ever see him and where's the presents he brings you?"

This stumped me, but only for an instant.

"You think my father would hang out with you guys! But Danny seen him and he seen all the presents. Didn't you, Danny?"

This was too speculative a proposition for Danny to underwrite. He always believed in safe, conservative investments and I'll come to that when I explain the million dollars which ultimately appeared upon the scene, after Dan put the brakes on me and muzzled me with a budget. In the meantime he let me plunge into Father Preferred without margin.

"Aw, you're lying!" chorused the boys.

"I'm not!" I said, grimly. "I'll take you down to the fire house and you can meet him!" Tears had come to my eyes and the boys felt they had pressed me too hard. "Well, maybe you got one," said Ira. They knew I was an orphan. But if I had been only a little taller I'd have impersonated my own father and shown those wiseacres!

Still, this same imaginative technique applied to my school lessons did not work. I could not picture the answer to a problem in arithmetic, and no matter how vividly I exerted my fancy, my dates in history were wrong. But I had to get promoted in some way and the way I could talk myself out of an answer established me as a star in rhetoric. At least, if I didn't answer correctly, I recited well, and teachers loaned me to one another to serve as general reciter in the assembly. As one of them observed, naïvely, "It doesn't matter what he says, but he says it beautifully." I never could learn the exports of South America, but when I recited, "Benedict Arnold—The Traitor's Deathbed" and "The Soul of the Violin" the assembly applauded and the geography teacher forgave me. I was the star at every graduation but my own. My own didn't materialize.

While Benedict Arnold pulled me through four terms, the "Address of Regulus to the Romans" dragged me through an additional three terms. And it looked as though Antony's oration over the body of Cæsar would sweep me through the last year and graduate me with honors. But a narrow-minded schoolmaster of the old birch-rod type insisted on treating me like one of the class and refused to promote me for a little thing like failing in all my subjects. I was young and impetuous, so I struck the teacher on the jaw with a board-rubber and left the school while he was still being counted out.

The way I figured it at the time, the teacher was jealous because I could recite better than he could, just as the fellow with the pail of water had been jealous of my singing. That gave me confidence and I resolved, as summer approached, to do a real singing-and-reciting act at the boys' camp which I had been attending every season from the age of nine.

There had long been a movement on the East Side for fresh air. But the East Siders were not clear on the subject of air and could never quite distinguish it from food vapors. Each street had its own favorite flavor which it cherished with a certain local and civic pride. If, for instance, the tang of herring was missing from Hester Street, the Hester Streeters thought they were walking in a vacuum. Similarly, the Italian quarter had its air pockets filled with garlic; under Williamsburg Bridge blew strong fish breezes, and no rich supply of ozone was complete without the ingredients of a dozen stables and the thousand and one fumes arising from vegetable pushcarts, poultry and meat markets, pickle works, and refuse cans. If one walked down Orchard Street toward Rivington, one knew definitely that here air was literally cheese, sometimes fragrant cream cheese blended with cottage, and sometimes it was stale Roquefort with a dash of Gorgonzola. Subtract the cheese from this region and people would die for lack of air.

Under such circumstances the uninitiated uptowners

who knew nothing about air and described it as a tasteless, odorless, colorless, meaningless substance that hovered about anywhere and nowhere, and could never be smelled, tasted, or even touched, were a crowd of visionary reformers who were trying to tamper with the fundamental laws of nature. Their insidious propaganda that windows should be opened and air allowed into homes was an obvious plot to destroy the home. For each little flat manufactured a thick, tasty atmosphere of its own like gravy, which must never be allowed to escape or mingle with the aromas of the street. And when I slipped into the two-room apartment to sleep in my grandmother's iron bed, with ten other roomers scattered on the floor, all problems of insomnia were instantly solved, for the atmosphere knocked me into slumber with one blow. I didn't sleep in those good old days; I lay unconscious. Nor would the fall of a building or a feeble fire alarm disturb me.

Fortunately, I had a faithful waker in the person of my school chum, the punctual Lipsky. This boy, to whom I was drawn by the sheer force of opposites, made it first a duty, then a passion to come every morning at seven-fifteen and begin the waking operation, which usually lasted three-quarters of an hour. It was as serious a process as waking a man out of ether.

The first step was to shake me gently with a kick that rolled me clear across the bed. This was a signal for me to yawn and turn over on the other side. Then Lipsky took a firm grip of my long, black hair like a handle and pulled my head off the pillow, forcing me into a sitting posture, at which I opened one eye, said, "What the hell is the idea?" and promptly dropped my head back on the pillow. Lipsky pulled it up again and this exercise was repeated ten times.

Then the relentless Daniel rolled me back and forth, massaged and pummeled me like a rubber at the bath, bent me up like a jack-knife and pulled my legs and arms out of their sockets, folding and twisting me in all possible shapes and positions, until he was covered with perspiration, exhausted, and ready to fall asleep himself. It was the routine of this morning waking that years later gave me the idea for my osteopath scene in the Ziegfeld Follies. It went over so well that I've had a mauling scene in almost every show since, and I've been thumped, thwacked, and twisted into a cruller on the stage by masseurs, chiropractors, bonesetters and fight-trainers.

The first time I did this scene, Bert Williams, the great negro comedian, suggested that while we were not on the stage we should stand in the wings and count each other's laughs. He did a very funny monologue then, and when it was over I told him, "Bert, you got twenty-nine laughs." That was like telling a man his stock had doubled in a week. Then I went on for my osteopath scene, and when I came back-stage Bert shook his head.

"How many?" I asked.

"You got just one laugh," he said.

"What do you mean, one laugh?"

"Well, it lasted from the time you got on till the time you came off."

But in the days when I rehearsed that scene with Lipsky it was no laughing matter. I needed a pulmotor to bring me to. Yet no one suspected that it might be lack of air.

So a new experience awaited me the first summer that I and my faithful alarm clock, Dan, were dispatched to the country for two weeks' vacation by the Educational Alliance, the community welfare center on East Broadway. For one dollar and a half to cover the fare, the Alliance sent poor lads from the tenements to a delightful boys' camp at Surprise Lake, Cold Springs, New York. Grandma Esther, thankful to be rid of me for two weeks and have me out of harm's way, paid the fare, and I went for my virgin trip to the country. I was thrilled with the awesome prospect of meeting Nature face to face. But the first deep breath of country air made me hiccup and gave me chills.

Cold Springs was a strange place. There wasn't a horsecar or a delicatessen store in it. It didn't have a single tenement house or a back alley. It was not a network of brick walls covered with patches of sky like metal ceiling. It had no walls of any kind and it was all sky. Sky, sky, sky, as far as the eye could see. A rich, blue-silk sky with islands and castles and ships painted on it in silver and gold tinted silhouettes. And green stretches of grass rolled like plush carpets over wide, endless playgrounds.

MY LIFE IS IN YOUR HANDS

My first breathless impression of wonder was mingled with anger. Why had the city folk held out on me and not told me of this "bunk" sooner? Why, this place had Seward Park and Pitt Street Park backed into a flower-pot! I hadn't seen so many trees in one place except on the wall paper in the Lipskys' front room. And Lake Surprise, brother, was a flabbergasting astonishment!

The nearest I had ever got to a lake was the fountain at Rutgers Square where the kids used to duck for pennies in hot August days. But here was a lake that was first cousin to an ocean. Besides, look at the color of the water! I didn't know that water one swam in could be transparent. Off the East River docks, where the boys went for a dip, there was always a blue film of oil from passing tugs, and a boy who didn't come out of the river looking dark brown hadn't bathed!

But if Surprise Lake was for bathing, they must have champagne springs for drinking. And they had! Pure champagne sparkling out of the natural rock. A strange, magic world I had stumbled into, with fruits growing on trees instead of pushcarts, soda water bubbling out of stones, air that was sharp and tasted like peppermint, and beautiful scenery like in the geography books.

I wandered out of the camp along the dirt roads banked with rich green and golden foliage, my eyes popping at all the flying, hopping, dancing fragments of beauty that darted in shining streaks out of bushes, over trees, into the sky. I wondered whether in this heavenly place there were cops and gangsters like in the city of smoke and walls, or whether little boys put on white shirts and wings before they went to bed. I absent-mindedly picked up a nice round stone. Ah, if I had that in the city to throw at Epstein the tailor's window!

I passed a pretty row of freshly painted cottages. Each with shiny windows glittering in the sunset and dressed in gay, beribboned curtains like little picnic girls. How could I resist throwing that stone and watch the angry faces appear and chase me down the road? I knew those calamity cries: "You loafer! You bummer! You wouldn't never come on this block again!" It would feel like home to be cursed and maltreated in this strange, almost inhuman paradise. I threw it! There was a loud, sharp crash of splintered, screaming glass, and then there was silence. No angry face appeared. Only the hole like a gash in some live, breathing form gaped at me and I ran frightened back to the camp.

Here amid the clatter of evening dishes I joined the group from my own district, shouting and laughing, eating my fill of fresh, wholesome food, fondly hoping that this life would last forever. That night, chilled with all the health and vigor that had suddenly broken through my skinny, underfed body, I went in advance of the others to the sleeping tents, and knowing I would be cold through the night, I glanced casually about to see that no one was watching and appropriated two blankets from the cots of other boys and wrapped them around my own. I knew I would be punished for this theft and as I lay warmed by three blankets I expected the camp cop to come after me and poke me with a club. But nothing happened and I was allowed to sleep comfortably on.

The next day the camp director, Morris Berk, smiled genially at me and I smiled back, happy that all was well.

"Come here, my boy," said the director, kindly. I approached in anticipation of something pleasant and Morris Berk patted my cheek in a fatherly fashion. "You're a nice lad, Eddie, and I know you feel chilly at night and like to keep warm, but when you steal two blankets from the other cots that means that two other little boys lie all night without blankets and feel very cold. Now, is that right?"

I felt hot waves of embarrassment mount to my face. I had never been reprimanded quite so gently and no one had ever appealed to my innate sense of justice. Instead of a scowl I got a smile; instead of a blow, a pat on the cheek. Yes, life was totally different in this marvelous boys' heaven. I would never throw a stone at a window again. I would never do wrong. This was a great turning-point in my life. The next night I stole only one blanket.

Chapter IV

LIFE at Surprise Lake Camp was a glorious dream to the scrawny, underfed lads of the Ghetto, but after two weeks they were parceled back to the dungeon streets and towering caves, while new boys with yellow faces and blue lips arrived. My problem was how to stay on permanently in this miraculous land where the parks never ended and the city streets never began. Every Saturday night there was a roaring camp fire and the hardy backwoodsmen from Orchard and Hester Streets gathered around the crackling logs, told blood-curdling tales, and burned marshmallows on match-sticks.

Here I used my ingenuity. "The Traitor's Deathbed" and "The Soul of the Violin" had all but pulled me through school. Perhaps they would prolong my stay at Cold Springs. Anyway, it was worth trying, and I recited them as I never did before, determined to wring their hearts and make them put out the fire with their tears. I made such terrifying grimaces, rolled and bulged my eyes, and wrinkled my face so fiercely that my youthful audience involuntarily made faces after me; but the older fellows and directors thought my violent dramatic effort was a corking good parody and they broke into gales of laughter. The younger boys joined them, and very much to my dismay I was hailed as a great comedian. Of course, I agreed that I had intended the recitations as a parody, but I wondered to myself, "Could I make them laugh if I wanted to?"

MY LIFE IS IN YOUR HANDS

The boys clamored for an encore and cried, "Let it be as funny as the last one!"

I gave impersonations of the Polish servant girls whom my grandmother placed on jobs. I had often done this at home to amuse the girls themselves, and at least they thought it was funny, so I took a chance. I burst into a protest in Polish gibberish that had no meaning at all, and it went over. I've found that comedy that has no message is always delivered. Then, with a kerchief wrapped around my head like a shawl, and a shrill voice, I posed as a grand and haughty servant girl interviewing and cross-examining her miserable mistress. I got what I was after. I was kept over for an extra week as an amusement feature of the camp.

I became well known among the boys and was called "Happy" because I tied a little can to my head and looked like Hooligan. One summer I managed to stay on for seven weeks. But it was not always easy to get the initial fare to Surprise Lake. Lipsky, who was methodical and thrifty, would be all set with his fare for the summer by the previous November, while I never had anything but the desire. My grandmother, to teach me thrift, refused to pay my fare unless I earned it, so a few weeks before vacation I suddenly became industrious, and offered to collect her oustanding accounts for candles and safety-pins, a side line she maintained along with her agency.

"And where is the money from Mrs. Pincus?" she inquired as I failed to turn over the collection.

"She'll pay next week," I said, carelessly.

"And what's about Mrs. Gartel and Mrs. Finkel and Mrs. Bendelbloom?"

"Everybody next week!"

And next week when she asked, "Well, what's about Mrs. Pincus and Mrs. Gartel and the rest of them?" I became impatient. "Don't you remember they all paid you last week, grandma?"

Grandma said nothing, but as I was preparing to leave the house triumphantly she called after me, "Now remember, use that money for fare! And next time, don't think you're so smart!"

I felt rather awkward, but I was happy, for I had to get to Surprise Camp by whatever road I could take.

At the camp the directors would eat their meals after the boys were served, and though I usually avoided work, I vied for the privilege to wait upon them. I became a surprisingly efficient and diligent waiter, and in my industrious, preoccupied manner I always managed to take away their desserts before they were half finished, and the directors, ashamed to grapple with me to retain their dishes, let them go, and I finished the desserts myself.

Still, while I probably ate more desserts than all the directors combined, I often came late for meals, and after the last bell sounded, the iron rule of the camp forbade food to the delinquents. At times like these I put on my most famished expression and went guiltily to the back door of the kitchen, where the beaming Mrs. Bloomer, a buxom, benevolent matron, would never let me go hungry. She took such a motherly delight in conspiring with the late comers that it was a wonder anybody ever came on time. To this day—it is twenty-five years since—camp alumni still come at any hour and find a hearty welcome at her table.

When I was ten, twenty-nine boys and myself formed a camp club at Cold Springs which still exists. In these twenty-five years not a member has been added and not a member has been lost. We solemnly resolved at that time to give to other half-starved city boys the same pleasure we had shared, and though we have grown to manhood, drifted into various pursuits, some married, others still eligible, all are active members of the camp club and contribute to its work. We continue to meet in a different member's home each month, planning improvements and extensions for the camp. And Daniel Lipsky, the first president of the club, is the president to this day.

Recently, by the action of its directors, the name of Surprise Lake Camp was changed to The Eddie Cantor Camp but greatly as I prized this honor, I asked them to retain the original name for the sake of its memories and associations. For along with my work on the stage the pleasure of helping city-saddened boys to health and recreation has absorbed the best impulses I have had in life. The Eddie Cantor Camp Committee of which our early club formed the nucleus, has through the years with its own funds, transformed the old tents to modern bungalows, of which we now have one hundred. From a summer resort we turned Cold Springs into an all-year home for boys, and the sicklier ones were toned up in the winter. In the neediest cases we have even eliminated the charge for fare—because I know what it meant for me to raise that dollar and a half—and we have often prolonged the vacation for some from two weeks to a month. Our camp takes a boy from the door of his home and brings him back there, giving him all the comforts of nature, science, affection, and good food without taking a penny from him.

It seems a matter of fate that I, who am the father of five girls, should have a whole campful of boys on the side. But that's not why I did it. I am really devoted to the boys, without any ulterior motive. Every year I arrange one affair for the camp with an all-star bill that makes Ziegfeld and Dillingham wish they had a camp for every day in the year to be able to line up such an array of talent on a single stage. Two years ago while I was in Hollywood making a picture I had an attack of pleurisy, but in spite of it I made the trip to New York to attend the camp benefit, and returned the next day.

Once my overzealous affection was misunderstood by the boys of the camp. I visited Surprise Lake and wanted to entertain the boys as I had done twenty years before around the camp fire. A couple of camp instructors with megaphones went out on the ball fields and playgrounds announcing, "Eddie Cantor will sing a few songs for you. Everybody come to the auditorium!" I was sitting under a tree, waiting for my public to be corralled, when a group of red-faced lads hot from a ball game passed by, dragging their bats and gloves with glum, sullen faces. One of them grumbled, "Aw, Gee! We come out here to have some fun and now we got to go in and listen to this guy, Eddie Cantor!"

But I'm far ahead of my story. It was a long time before I, a skinny, hollow-chested son of the slums, could lend a hand to a new generation of starvelings. Nice and simple as it looks on the whole, it was complicated in its details, and during the vague, formative years I vacillated, drifted between impulses to act and amuse and a desire to slouch around street corners, hang out in poolrooms, join guerilla gangs, and become a gangster's tool. Who could tell, by looking at a group of East Side youngsters, which would become a Gyp the Blood or Lefty Louie and which a Marcus Loew or Irving Berlin?

What would become of me I knew least of all. For this is a fact. All those grappling, struggling little lives that swarm upon the sidewalks of New York and overflow its housetops and its gutters like the millions of crawling, flying, creeping creatures of the forest, are endowed with a similar mixture of spirit, vitality, ambition, and cunning; each gifted with an abundance of wild energy like the thousand streams that feed a waterfall, and it is hard to say which of these forces will assert itself—which shall aspire to the lion's throne, which acorn shall rise to the prowess of an oak, which flying egg shall hatch to be an eagle, and which sorry blend of life essence shall be the worm.

Thrown indiscriminately into the maze and tangle of

skyscrapers and lowly tenements, like seeds cast over rocks and fields and seas, these countless thousands rise and grow and pass through what is broadly the same school for all. Poverty clamps them down to narrow limits, desire urges them on to new ambitions, necessity whets their natural cunning and teaches some to steal, others to lie, and encourages all to deception; then sad experience makes them kind and tolerant; those who are weak, adversity makes weaker; those who are strong, success makes stronger; and in the last selection and arrangement of their lives, those who were at first together are now far apart and some have traveled up the river to the chair and others traveled up the ladder to the throne.

At twelve I sizzled with purposeless energy. If it could have been properly chained, and Ford had retracted sooner, he might have hitched me to his factory and saved a power-plant. But it was allowed to run wild and my energy took on every shape except work. As a boy of thirteen I felt my first urge to power. I pulled a cap down over my eyes, donned a big red sweater and flourished a bat, looking for all the world like the chief of a gas-house gang, when in reality I was flat-chested, underweight, frightened at my own bluff, and ready to be blown over by a breath. Still, when Pock-faced Sam, chief terror of the local strikers, had to hire guerillas to guard the strike-breakers, he was so impressed by my formidable appearance that he engaged me as one of his strong-arm men. I pushed my cap down lower so they couldn't see how my teeth chattered and swung my bat, nearly falling over with the effort, and pulled down three bucks a day for the pose. I didn't realize then that it was the actor in me that earned me my pay.

I was all for the rough life, spat sideways, and carried a gun for a regular gangster, but if the gun had ever gone off I'd have gone with it. In a gang fight I did all the acting and made enough facial contortions to scare away all the opponents my pals couldn't lick. Being the skinniest and most agile of the younger boys, I was employed to crawl through narrow bars and fanlights to open doors and secret passages for the marauders.

One of the gang's prize loots was a bicycle shop. I was lifted on a big chap's shoulders and slid in through the transom over the door. After I unlocked the door, the whole gang mounted bicycles and rode them to 110th Street near Central Park, where the leader assembled the booty and made sure that none of his loyal crew had cheated him. The other youngsters and I were rewarded with a cup of coffee and two doughnuts apiece, and we got a nickel each for car fare home. The distracted storekeeper knew who had committed the theft, but dared not squeal, and the next day the leader came down to see him and sold him back his own stock of bicycles.

It was high adventure. But what displeased me about these otherwise thrilling experiences was that they were too secret and confidential. If I was going to crawl through a transom or climb a drain pipe, why not first call a crowd together and at least get applause for it? My instinct for the footlight must have been greater than for

MY LIFE IS IN YOUR HANDS

the searchlight. I longed for an audience. Regardless of what I did, I wanted to do it before the multitude, and so in my fourteenth year I turned to politics as the natural outlet for my talents. I had noticed that politicians, even when they had nothing to say, had listeners.

Those were busy years for me. I was too occupied a man now to take vacations or even think of the little strip of woodland at Surprise Lake. I threw myself enthusiastically into the midst of the political conflict. I didn't know at first that I had to belong to a party or fight for issues. I fought and argued purely for the fun of the fight and the sound and fury of the argument.

I got on a soap box and attacked the first candidate whose poster I noticed in a butcher shop. It happened to be Morris Hillquit, a Socialist. I told my audience in strict confidence that Socialists were bomb-throwers and that Hillquit ate ham, even though his picture was in a kosher butcher shop. I worked havoc on the unfortunate candidate and some of my more susceptible listeners made a definite resolve to go out and commit murder. It thrilled me to find that I could influence the moods and emotions of people. "I've got them going," I thought. "Now let's see if I can get them going the other way."

The next night I spoke in praise of the man I had attacked. I championed Hillquit's cause and hailed him as a leader of the working class. I ripped off my own shirt in tattered strips to show the blood stains on my back from the lash of my brutal boss in the sweatshop. "Down with the capitalists," I cried, "and up with Hillquit!" I had never been in a sweatshop, but I knew how to slap on red paint, and the act went over big.

But the next time out I stumped for Hillquit's opponent. I held my audience so spellbound that pickpockets found easy pickings among the engrossed listeners, and whenever I paused for effect or for breath they would urge me to talk on. "Go on, kid! It's great stuff!" they pleaded, and I went on more and more excitedly while they frisked the crowd. I was doing fine and so were they.

Once in a while a charitable pickpocket would interrupt me in the middle of my speech and say: "All right, kid, you can go home now! We got enough!" It was not till later that I learned what an invaluable asset I had been to the pickpocket industry.

My passion for talking was a labor of love and while other distinguished orators of my day belonged to the Spellbinders' Club and got two dollars a night and spoke for only one candidate, I got nothing at all and spoke for and against everybody.

It was only when I attacked a Democrat whom I had praised the night before, that some self-appointed representatives of the party knocked the soap box from under me, dispersed my audience with a few well-aimed beer bottles, and gave me such a beating that I solemnly swore that if I cared to have a future as a public speaker and remain alive, I would henceforth be a loyal Democrat. That is how I was enrolled in the party.

One of my first assignments was to speak for a young

Assemblyman running at the time, known as Alfred E. Smith. I decided to make a great speech because this was the first candidate I really knew personally. For young Mr. Al was a popular and lovable figure on the East Side. When I lived on Henry Street, Alfred Smith lived on Oliver Street, two blocks away. From the poolroom around the corner where the other boys and I spent edifying hours, Mr. Smith would call the whole crowd over to Bassler's saloon and blow to drinks. But Al always picked the youngsters out of the crowd, separating them from the rest, and he would order nothing but sarsaparilla for the kids and schooners for the young men.

He would lead us in song, protect the weaklings from the bullies, and add that bit of kindliness and sunshine to the dingy gloom of our lives which would be reflected on our faces for many days. We idolized young Mr. Al, and all the boys stood loyally by him like a recognized and unanimously appointed guardian of our destinies.

When tough, heavy-set men of the alleys, with big, square jaws and shifty eyes, would throw a rock at an old peddler merely because he had a beard, Al Smith would come to the old man's aid and put his arm around him like a brother. It was the downright, simple heroics of the thing that struck the slum boys with wonder, and I can never forget the picture of this young and handsome Mr. Al coming among the ragged, hairy, bearded people of the abyss, extending a hand of welcome and friendship to all of them, as if the lady of the Statue of Liberty had sent her own son to receive these poor, bewildered immigrants on her behalf. So when I took the stump, my first words were, "This man who is running for Assembly now will some day sit in the White House, and the present Assemblyman is the future President, Alfred E. Smith!"

After words like these I felt I had suddenly become a man, and I secretly resolved that the next time Al Smith invited the boys to Bassler's saloon I would refuse the sarsaparilla and insist on the schooner. Al Smith, however, told me, "Kid, you may be old enough to prophesy, but you're too young to drink beer."

Last year, while playing in the Ziegfeld Follies, the doorman came to my dressing-room and said there was a Mr. Smith downstairs who wanted to see me. I was busy making up for the opening scene and hadn't the time to be disturbed. "It's one of those song-pluggers," I told the doorman. "I guess he wants to sing me one of his new songs. Tell him to come back after the show." As the doorman turned to go, the door opened and Mr. Smith appeared.

"Say, what's the idea telling me to come back after the show?" asked Mr. Smith. And he got down on one knee and began to wave his hands in a mammy posture *à la* Jolson. "I've got a great song and I'm going to sell it to you right now!"

"Why, Governor!" I exclaimed, running to meet him. "Why didn't you say it was you!"

"I did."

"But you didn't say 'The Governor'!"

"I left him in Albany."

Outside of his official capacity he was plain "Mr. Smith." A marvelously human fellow, modest, unassuming. A really great man. Always taken up with his duties, he rarely goes to amusements and he probably sees no more than ten or twelve shows a year, but he makes a holiday of them like a child. Generally when some prominent official or personage is in the theater, the management has been notified in advance and most often the tickets are complimentary. Alfred E. Smith always buys his own tickets and you never know when he's there. He simply sends out a man to any agency to get the best he can for the money, and the man never says, "The tickets are for the Governor."

It was a great thrill to me when I made my bow on Broadway to have the young Mr. Al from Oliver Street applaud my efforts from the Governor's chair.

But when I first stumped for him on soap boxes in the open air, while it made me happy, it also made me hoarse. Grandma Esther nursed me and poured me full of raw eggs and milk. She was puzzled at my sudden tonsilar activities.

"How much do you get for making all these speeches?" she inquired.

"Nothing," I rasped.

"Then what are you doing it for?"

"For pleasure!"

"Pooh! Maybe it's a pleasure to the public, but it's a pain in the neck to you!" she observed, unconsciously coining a gag, and she hinted to me that a less talkative job might yield more silent but solid returns. I was still one of those simple children of art who thought that to get paid for work was a sin. Besides, I felt there was only one kind of work in the world—play; and to get paid for playing was a new idea. I suspected it wouldn't last long, and it didn't.

I got a job with an insurance company at 100 William Street, handling the postage of their correspondence department. In the two brief weeks that I handled this postage the company's correspondence increased, but nobody knew why. The officials of the firm, judging by the reams of stamps consumed, began to wonder who was writing to every person in the country and a few in Europe. They had their suspicions and decided on an experiment. They were curious to see, if I left the firm, whether the stamps would stick. So I was asked to leave, the stamps stuck, and the experiment was a success.

This left me without a job and it took me two years to decide that I wanted another one. I returned to the old block, a happy-go-lucky free lance, the envy and the ideal of all those boys who had to work. As I stood with my hands in my pockets at the corner stand I could contemplate life with a broad philosophy. I had been a politician, an entertainer at the camp, a member of the local gangs, a strong-arm man in labor agitations, an assistant to my grandmother in placing domestics; I had even socked a teacher and lost a job, and now, with this huge background of life, I felt ready at the age of thirteen to retire and spend my remaining days in leisure, comfort, and advice to the young.

Like my father, I had developed a hobby. I liked to make funny faces at passers-by. At first they started and then they laughed. This encouraged me and I played such pranks that people would gather about me in the street and wonder when I would pass the hat around. Some of them asked, "Poor boy, whose is he?" They didn't know I was having a good time and trying my hardest to be funny. They only shook their heads and made stormy-weather forecasts about me. But occasionally somebody would say there was hope and that I'd turn out all right. In fact, I had a secret admirer who built symbols around me and thought I was Puck himself. But I found out afterward that she had designs on me.

One of the domestics lodging with my grandmother was a young Russian girl with large, black, sad eyes that reflected all the gloom and sorrow of her oppressed people. In her native town nobody had ever laughed, except the Cossacks. She had learned to associate laughter with bloodshed. So to her my comedy was not a joke, but, as she said, "It was a new world, a revelation." I should have become suspicious right then and there, but I didn't. I asked her to tell me more. I liked it.

She said, "I long to be always in the presence of your warm, pure humor. It's a new kind of sunlight."

She became jealous when I made the other girls laugh. She tried to save me and my jokes all for herself. It was the first time anybody had made a fuss over me and I fell headlong, like down a flight of stairs. But when she finally managed to be alone in the house with me and gave me those earnest, longing glances, I began to feel uneasy. Being a Russian, she took even comedy seriously.

Fanya was only sixteen but she acted like much older. She urged me to sit beside her and hold hands, but I pleaded with her to let me go because the boys were waiting for me. It was my first rehearsal in life of a scene I have since used on the stage in many diverse forms—the seduction of the bashful boy by the bold, bad lady. It was always funny, except this time. I was hardly fourteen and had my code of honor to defend. For I knew that if the fellers on the block found out that I had held a girl's hand, I'd be branded as a "sissy" for life. But Fanya was very serious about her little comedian and I got scared.

"The boys are calling me," I pleaded, weakly. "Let go my hand! Listen, I'll tell you a joke if you let me go! P-l-e-a-s-e!" I cried, horrified, as she put her arm around my waist. "Listen! What's the idea?" I bawled as she dragged me to her in real apache style. And then she kissed me. "Oh, my God!" I groaned as if lightning had hit me. But she mangled me in an embrace and I couldn't even breathe. These Russians are certainly a serious people.

But Grandma Esther had a habit of coming into my life at crucial moments. "Fanya!" she commanded, sternly, appearing in the doorway. "Put the child back in his cradle!"

This made me rise to the dignity of the situation.

"Cradle!" My grandmother had wounded me deeply. "I'm a man!" I cried, and was tempted to stand up on a chair to prove it.

"Leave my house!" exclaimed Grandma Esther to Fanya, and Fanya turned her large, appealing eyes to me, the man in short pants and bicycle stockings.

"If she goes, I go with her!" I cried, completely losing my sense of humor.

"Keep quiet, before I spank you!" warned the old woman. I backed away, but Fanya flung her arms about me.

"My hero!" she murmured, adoringly.

Grandma Esther, until now angry and menacing, at the sight of this spectacle could restrain herself no longer, and burst into laughter.

"What's so funny about it?" I inquired, beginning to perspire.

"Why don't she get a feller her size?" taunted grandma, amused but still angry.

I treated this slur with the silent contempt it deserved. I took Fanya by the arm and we marched out of the house.

"Stop! You—you—you baseball-player you!" scolded grandma, hurrying after us into the hall. That was the worst name she could call me. To the pious people of the Ghetto a baseball-player was the king of loafers. I wavered, looked back, and tried to release my hand from Fanya's arm, but she held it as in a vise; and though I led her out she led me on.

"I'll follow you to the end of the world!" she cried pulling me down the stairs.

Grandma Esther, despite her wrath, could not imagine how such a ridiculous situation could develop into anything serious.

"Pooh!" she sneered, shouting after us. "Look what's eloping! If he gets tired, Fanya, carry him! And remember, Eddie, be back for supper! Tonight I got meat-balls!"

She knew that not even love could interfere with my love for meat-balls.

Chapter V

IT WAS more than twenty-two years ago, when I was fourteen, that Fanya and I left my grandmother's house and I failed to return for the meat-balls. I was blissfully ignorant of all economic and domestic matters, but Fanya, who seemed to have had some previous training, rented the back room of a flat for eight dollars a month and arranged for my meals with the woman of the house. She explained to this woman that I was her frail young brother just out of the hospital, and told her to feed me cookies with cocoa and other nourishment good for growing children. Fanya departed. I ate heartily and made plans for a new life of independence and leisure when my grandmother, who had soon located the place, came to box my ears and take the infant Casanova home. But I had apparently caught the tang of adventure and refused to be rescued from captivity.

"Shame on you!" Grandma Esther chided. "What'll become of you? Wait! At home I'll give you already!" But even in the midst of her anger she could not resist the question, "Does she give you at least good food to eat?" But after her alternate warnings and wheedlings failed to budge me, she suddenly decided that I had been bewitched and her manner became sad and resigned.

"I was going to scold you," she said, and tears started to her eyes, "but maybe it has to be like this. It's a saying, 'The angels look after all children, but God Himself watches over the orphans.' For my part, Eddie, you can do what you like, but remember, I hoped some day you'd become a big man and I should live to be proud from you!" The good woman kissed me as if she never expected to see me again. She sobbed and departed as if mourning after the dead. I had a hollow feeling in my heart. I was sorry my grandmother hadn't dragged me along by the scruff of the neck.

Impulsively I made the decision to change my whole mode of living. I would write Fanya a letter and leave before she returned. But I didn't know how to begin and I couldn't find a pencil. Besides, I thought it would be better to break the news to her myself. I would tell her that my grandmother and I had definitely decided that I was to become a big man and she would have to forget me. But by the time she returned I decided not to tell her just yet and things drifted on as before.

In the meantime, my old friend Lipsky, whom I hadn't seen for a long while, was devoting himself to courting my cousin Anne while escorting her to school, and he learned through her of the catastrophe that had befallen me. With characteristic thoroughness he suggested that a detective be hired to investigate and track down this mysterious girl who had kidnapped me. My grandmother backed the idea, and one day Dan arrived triumphantly on the heels of a sleuth, to get me out of her clutches. But now that the experience was getting so exciting, I was more than ever determined to stick. It was destined, however, that a few months later I should find my own way out of this peculiar situation in a most unexpected and surprising manner.

It happened like this. Living the life of a man of means with a strange Lady Beautiful caring for me, I cherished the secret idea that I was one of the four hundred. While I belonged to no golf club or social set, I managed to perfect my game of pool and attended the summer-school recreation grounds of P. S. No. 1 and P. S. No. 177. Here I hobnobbed with the *élite* of Market and Oliver Streets, jumped the buck, played basket-ball, and engaged in all other activities befitting a man of my station. Though I could beat most of the boys at feats of sports, I found, to my embarrassment, that there were athletic girls who far outshone me.

One girl in particular won every prize for sports and dancing as fast as it could be unpacked and offered. She had become the main attraction of the recreation center and every youngster who could comb his hair neatly and wear a necktie proposed to her. Ida Tobias was the belle of Henry Street. Despite her athletic prowess she possessed a soft, girlish grace; a frank, bright countenance mellowed by two caressing eyes; but a sensible, aloof air inspired by her mother, who from an early age had warned her against all the potential good-for-nothings of the East Side who could make wonderful love but a very poor living.

I, the secret conqueror of a Russian housemaid, felt that all women must wither and succumb beneath my bulging, dominating glance. But Ida, queen of the summer school, didn't seem to notice that I was alive. She was too much sought after to seek, too busy making conquests to surrender. For me to try and win her by competing with her in high jump, broad jump, vaulting, ladder-climbing, or tango would have meant defeat and disgrace. There was only one chance for me to emerge from increasing obscurity and decline—the chance I had played at Surprise Lake Camp, the chance I had played with the little servant audience in Grandma Esther's agency, the chance to entertain and amuse.

There was a cheap brass band in the playground which the recreation director, Mrs. Ray Schwartz, had introduced to lend a note of harmony to the wild discord of the center. I must confess that I was her all-star nuisance at the time, and I instigated most of the wild discord by pulling girls' braids, breaking up their dances, and running rough-shod through the games. But I made some retribution for this conduct twenty years later when I met Mrs. Schwartz in Paris and the little boy she ran out of school ran her down to Deauville. She had since established a magnificent girls' camp and I was glad to send my two daughters, Marjorie and Natalie, to spend a summer with her under entirely different circumstances from those in which their old man had spent his summers.

But at P. S. No. 177, Mrs. Schwartz tried her best to get on the right side of this rascal, and she discovered that all that was ailing me was a desire to sing at the playground concert, accompanied by the band. I was given the chance and rendered the big hit of the moment, "My Mariuch she took-a de steamboat!" The song was not directed to the large and rather skeptical assembly of youngsters, but to her, the dainty little queen of sports who won all the silver-plated loving cups and athletic medals and didn't know till now that I was alive. Now she knew. But even more than the applause of the hard-boiled youngsters, I longed to hear the voice of her approval. I guess no performance in my life before or since had quite the significance of this one; for Ida Tobias, the belle of Henry Street, who for me was to be the belle of the world, came over and congratulated me.

It was a triumph. The next night I sang again and she allowed me to escort her home. With a victorious leer that swamped the other boys in one flood of humility, I marched out with the lovely Ida on my arm. But a block away from her house she stopped me. "You mustn't walk me up to my stoop," she said. "My parents must never see me with you. . . . You have a bad reputation around Henry Street," she added, bluntly. The news cut me like a saber.

Can she know about Fanya, I wondered? I've made a mess of everything, I thought. That night I spent in restless resolves and nightmares of shame. How could I expect Ida, whom all the boys of the neighborhood worshiped, to single me out for her favor in the light of such a reputation? Yes, everything would have to be different from now on. The old Eddie of the gangs and backroom flats must pass away and a new Eddie be born. The

MY LIFE IS IN YOUR HANDS

next time I saw her I was greatly encouraged, for she smiled and even seemed amused at my poor attempts to be funny. "I guess she doesn't know, after all."

We were sitting alone on the steps of the school with the moon slyly peeping over the tenements, and I felt that the big moment had arrived. I fidgeted nervously and finally blurted out, "You are the only girl of all the girls of the school who are the girl that I love, if you don't mind." There was an awkward pause during which I tried to swallow my Adam's apple; then Ida looked sadly at me.

"I'm sorry," she said, "but my mother expects me to marry some one with a good, reliable position. A man who is somebody, if *you* don't mind." And Ida proceeded to tell me of two handsome young twins, Louis and Leo, who courted her and her sister Minnie, methodically, assiduously, relentlessly. They wore high white collars, brought boxes of candy every Saturday night, took out Ida and Minnie with their mother's permission, and they had steady, permanent positions as Post Office clerks which they could never lose. In fact, they still have them.

My head drooped and brow puckered. Could I get a job in the Post Office? This was the second time stamps had come into my life and stuck me. "What future is there in that?" I argued, pretending to be scornful. "Even after you learn the trade, you can't open your own post office!"

"But you haven't any future at all," reminded Ida, as tenderly as she could. "People say the worst things about you. Some of my friends told me you tied yourself to a lamp-post by your necktie, stuck out your tongue and made believe you were dying!"

"Oh, that was just for a laugh," I said, trying to be modest. "And I fooled them, too. They really thought I was hanging!"

Ida looked at me severely. "And they told me you started to cry and howl at a street corner, saying your stepmother would kill you because you lost a quarter she gave you to buy bread, and the people chipped in pennies and nickels and told you not to cry! Will you do that after you're married, too?"

"Aw, a little stunt like that!" I mumbled, beginning to feel embarrassed.

"A stunt? Why, even the cops laugh at you!" Ida was on the verge of tears. To think that the cops didn't take me seriously enough to arrest me at least.

"Anyway, they know good comedy when they see it," I protested, coming to the defense of the force.

"Well, I'm not going to marry a man," said the thirteen-year-old belle with determination, "who hangs himself on lamp-posts and cries on street corners to make cops laugh!"

"I don't blame you!" I thought, helplessly. Today I might explain these youthful impulses as the urge within me to be myself—but who was I? Judging from Ida's glances at the time, I'd rather not answer the question. I had a feeling it was all over between us, but it wasn't. She continued to meet me often after that. Perhaps she pitied me. In her eyes this funny, gawky fellow who'd stop at nothing for a laugh, was, after all, a skinny, lonely orphan, ill-fed and neglected. That seemed to have an irresistible appeal to the mother instinct of some girls and I felt inclined to reverse my dear grandmother's saying, for it seemed that God watched over all children, but a special troupe of angels looked after me.

On Sundays, when all the girls of the block went out with their beaus to parties, picnics, and Coney Island, Ida would turn down the invitation of Louis Rosner and spend the long, lonely holiday sitting on the school steps with me. "Look at all the fun you're missing," I'd tell her. "You could be riding the Chute the Chutes and Virginia Reel!" But she smiled kindly. "I enjoy listening to you better than a combination ticket to Luna Park!" And that was long, long before I had signed a contract with the Shuberts.

Then she would open the box of candy which Louis had faithfully delivered the night before, and we ate the candy, glancing stealthily about as if we were doing something terribly wicked but enjoyable. When there were no more candies left I got pangs of conscience and decided to earn lots of money so that Ida wouldn't have to accept gifts from somebody else. In the meantime I hadn't a cent, and I often discovered, on leaving her, that she had slipped a quarter into my pocket. It was humiliating to realize how well she knew me. I resented her considerateness, but I appreciated the quarter.

Ida not only sacrificed the pleasures of Sunday. She

soon lost the peace of the other six days. Stormy, quarrelsome times brewed in the Tobias home, streaked with paternal threats and drenched with her tears. For Hattie Immerman, a girl from the block, confided to me that Ida had definitely broken off with Louis Rosner. There had been a terrible scene at the house, and Ida's father had sworn to shut the door on his daughter. But Hattie assured me that even through her sobs Ida had insisted, "I'll marry no one if I don't marry Eddie Cantor!" Yet when I saw Ida she betrayed none of this, sitting as usual on the school steps, encouraging and enjoying my efforts at nonsense.

The time was ripe to break off with Fanya, but I didn't know how. The dingy little room on Cherry Street had grown oppressive and haunting. After all, who was this girl who had taken me out of my grandmother's house and undoubtedly thought that she owned me? Perhaps all that Lipsky had suspected was correct? I would have to assert my rights and reclaim myself. But she seemed so kind and particularly gracious that day. Maybe I ought to wait for a better occasion, I thought.

She told me in her sweetest manner that she had gotten a raise in her pay and gave me four dollars to buy two tickets for a holiday matinée of "The Talk of New York" at the Grand Opera House on Twenty-third Street and Eighth Avenue. It would be the first real play I had ever seen and she wanted me to get the best two seats. I did. But then something strange happened.

I waited for Ida that night to come home from work.

She looked tired and wan, but tried to smile, and I felt a sudden deep compassion for her. She had sacrificed so much pleasure for me. I owed her an outing in return. But I had never had the money to give her a real treat. Now I had two of the best seats for "The Talk of New York," by George M. Cohan, starring Victor Moore.

"Would you like to see a matinée tomorrow?" I asked, casually.

Ida was thrilled but careful.

"Where did you get the money?"

"Oh, I'm coming up in the world," I remarked, with a nonchalant wave of the hand.

"It's wonderful!" Her faith in me had been vindicated.

That night I explained to Fanya that I had lost the four dollars. "Then we can't go," she said, very logically.

I could hardly sleep in anticipation of the next day's glory. I brushed my faded clothes meticulously and hurried eagerly to meet Ida. She let me come right to the doorstep and take her. A young man who could spend four dollars on two seats made a mere supplier of candy pale into the shadows. We reached the theater.

But I did not suspect that the gloomy-eyed Fanya was waiting in front of the Grand Opera House to give me a royal reception. She had probably wondered of late at my air of estrangement and suspected that a strange force was drawing me from her. Now at last she was face to face with my iniquity. She unsheathed a huge hat-pin from her bonnet and with a fierce cry pursued her deceiver down the avenue from Twenty-third to Twenty-first Street. The chase, the scandal, and the screams of startled passers-by were certainly the talk of New York.

One thing, however, the incident closed—the double life was exposed and died of exposure. Fanya was no more. But there is an interesting souvenir of memory that this Eddie of the earlier days has left me; for to this day Fanya, who is happily married and prospering, never fails to attend every opening night of Eddie Cantor's shows. I imagine the sad-eyed Russian girl still longs for the fourteen-year-old comedian to make her laugh. But when the alarming episode occurred she was far more anxious to make him cry.

Perhaps I shouldn't be telling these things. The modern tendency in autobiographies seems rather to conceal and gloss over than to reveal and lay bare. It would be far more pleasant for me to describe my youth as spent in a library or in a garden studying flowers. But I am trying to tell the story of the five Eddies as I remember them, unadorned and unexplained.

Luckily for me, I escaped the hat-pin, but I had still to face Ida.

Chapter VI

THREE years ago, while playing in "Kid Boots" at the Earl Carroll Theater, I felt the first symptoms of temperament. I don't know why, but I couldn't sleep while blasting was going on around me. We lived at the time in Mount Vernon, and as my sleeping hours were from three in the morning to about twelve, noon, I was suddenly torn up at seven-thirty by the infernal noises of dredges, steam-shovels, electric pile-drivers and dynamite. Mount Vernon was being built that year.

The next night I went directly after the show to the Pennsylvania Hotel to make up two nights' sleep in one. At seven-thirty I imagined it was Mount Vernon calling me, for I was rocked out of bed by the same deafening racket. I later discovered that the foundations for a skyscraper were being laid on the next block. "This will never do," I thought. "No sleep, no show."

I happened to meet Georgie Jessel that day and he suggested a nice, private hotel on Central Park West, where I arrived the same night more dead than alive. "This place is so quiet," said Georgie, after settling me in my room, "that you can hear a spider spin. But don't listen for it."

"Don't worry," I said, "I could fall asleep in a trice or even in a taxi." And I promptly submerged.

At about seven in the morning I began to dream that the coal-miners had taken me down with them into the shaft and left me alone while they went out to blow up the mine. Before I could escape I exploded. I was very frightened and went to the window to find that they were digging the new Eighth Avenue subway. This was too much. Why should progress and construction companies follow in my footsteps? Another sleepless night and there would be a bootless Kid Boots.

It was my good fortune, however, to run across my friend Harry Ruby that day, and he recommended the Gedney Farms, a fine old-fashioned farmhouse in White Plains. There I drove as a desperate man is driven to drink. And I found the Ideal. I slept so long I almost missed the show. All night on the stage I looked forward to that blissful slumber in store for me at this new-found paradise of rest. I couldn't wait to hop into the car and speed on my way to the farmhouse. As I drew near, I noticed a bright light through the trees. I was suddenly stopped by a cordon of police.

"What's up?" I asked the officer in charge.

"You can't pass!"

"But I live here!" I protested.

"Oh no! You *lived* here!" he replied.

Just then a rocket of fire spouted into the air. The Gedney Farms was in flames and my two trunks burned with it.

I recall this hectic experience in connection with my early days when insomnia was never a problem. When I was asked, "How do you sleep?" I would rest my head gently on my clasped hands, roll my eyes, and say, "Like this." But now, after the scandal in front of the Grand

Opera House, the problem was, "Where?" I could not very well return to Fanya and her hat-pin. I was too proud to slink back to my grandmother, a disappointing prodigal. But it was getting dark and tiresome walking the streets. Besides, I didn't enjoy the exercise on an empty stomach. A hotel and a meal, on the other hand, involved the question of money, and money was out of the question.

It was really surprising that a night's lodging should be such a problem in a city overhung with pillows and mattresses. Featherbeds and blankets flapped from windows and fire-escapes. Carved bedsteads with satin spreads stood invitingly in orange-lighted furniture stores. I tried to figure out the bed production at Grand Rapids. I estimated that there must be a hundred million cots, sofas, couches, four-posters, Morris chairs, divans, and yet, come to think of it, there wasn't one I could count on. Even the park bench was spitefully partitioned by four iron arm rests, so that I could lie on it only in the form of the letter S, with my head under one iron bar and my legs coiled over another.

At any rate, fresh air would be good for me, so I wrapped myself around with the chill autumn winds and froze into a rigid form indistinguishable from the iron bars. I fixed my imagination on the meal that I might have had at Fanya's and the soft bed at Grandma Esther's, and soon my mind numbed into confusion. Once or twice I started, thinking I heard Ida's voice, "I'll never forgive you for that!" Then I felt Fanya piercing me all over with a thousand hat-pins, and the cutting, unpleasant ecstasy of hunger made me squirm.

At dawn a cop's club poked me out of my ossification. My eyes were heavy and pasty, my mouth sour and dry. "Go on, get along or I'll pull you in!" I stared measuringly at the club and thought, "Why argue?" So I resumed my pointless wanderings. I met another homeless fellow, but he had at least perfected bumming into a science. The first few available pennies, he taught me, must go for cigarettes, not for food, because cigarettes had the supernatural quality of killing hunger pangs. "Dream of a feed, then smoke a butt," he said, "and you'll get the same symptoms of indigestion like after a banquet." The next point was not to be stingy about the size of a bed. "If you want plenty of elbow room, sleep on a roof!"

So the next day went as I was eagerly taking in the mysteries of the free and open life. "In our game, we're like kings—we get everything for nothing," he confided. "Can we get something to eat?" I suggested, feebly. "Leave it to me!" And he made a pass with his hands like a magician. We stopped in front of a lunch-room where the big captains of industry from the fish markets and crockery stores ate a seven-course meal for fifteen cents. "Now watch!" he said, and bravely led the way into Max Sander's exclusive Hungarian dining-hall.

The diners had all finished eating, and a gray, pouchy cat went about clearing remainders from the tables. I trailed timidly behind my friend as he made his heart-rending appeal to Sander. He told him we hadn't eaten for three days. "You don't sound it," said Sander, "but this guy looks it." He went into the kitchen and brought out the largest piece of cooked meat I ever saw. It was brown and fibrous like the side of a boat. He slapped it down in a huge platter and we fell upon it and it disappeared.

After the repast we retired to a tenement roof and stretched out under the stars. The jagged metal roof felt pretty comfortable after the park bench, the brick chimney was a sort of pillow, and with the sky as a blanket, I felt like a true child of nature. At last the problem was solved. I had the meal, the fatigue, and the roof. It was perfect and I slept. At least for the first five minutes I was so completely stunned that I sat up and just stared while the rain came down in buckets. My pal tugged and pulled me, but we didn't get into the hallway until we were soaked.

We managed to find a deserted flat in the building and lay down on the floor. My pal, to dry out his chill, lit a cigarette, but it was damp and needed constant relighting. Somebody who was up at that hour noticed the dancing, flickering lights in the empty flat and decided that the house was haunted. A red-headed janitor armed with a poker and a broom came up to fight the spirits. We were banged and beaten mercilessly and thrown out into the street.

There was no use. I returned to my grandmother. She received me as I least deserved or expected, with every show of kindness and emotion. She knew that her long-lost darling would come back, and tucked me into a fine warm bed, with all the windows tightly shut so that I could sleep to asphyxiation. In the morning there was hot milk and eggs, and I said, enthusiastically, "Well, grandma, now everything will be like old times!"

"Yes," she agreed, "except you got to go to work."

"Why, certainly!" I exclaimed. I had really never thought of that. But I tracked down the want ads, marking a smudgy trail with my finger as I mumbled, "Boy, boy . . . butcher, butcher . . . clerk!" I stopped. The Weir Brothers of 25 Broad Street, a broker's office, spoke out of the page, offering a golden opportunity to youth at five dollars per week. I moistened my hair under the kitchen faucet, combed it back with my fingers, rubbed the dusty shoes against my stocking-legs to work up a shine, and got the job. It was the beginning of resurrection. In a very short time, possibly a half-year, I'd save up enough to buy a derby, a suit that would shine like oil-cloth, and shoes that buttoned on the side. Then perhaps I might be able to face Ida.

It felt like a long time since I had seen her. I had left her rather hastily that day of the hat-pin, but I could remember, in one fleeting glimpse of her face, the indescribable look of hopelessness and sorrow that flashed from it. A four-hour parting in anguish and tears could not have been more fertile of finality. She must have built a noble image of me in her heart, to suffer so when it crumbled. I was through as far as she was concerned, and my only chance to conquer this defeat was to go out into the world, make fame and fortune for myself, and then perhaps some night at the opera I would nod coldly to her from my box, and she would drop her lorgnette in thrilled delight and invite me over. I would approach, kneel, kiss her hand, and offer her a platinum jeweled bracelet as a trifling token of my devotion, murmuring, "Ida, you know, about that hat-pin, now really, it was all a mistake—eh—that girl, she wasn't after me at all —eh ——" And she would say, "Eddie, I've been dreaming only about you through all these years. I loved you —I still do." And getting up gallantly but skillfully, without dislocating my tuxedo or the stiff shirt front, I'd snatch her in my arms and carry her away. In the meantime, like in all the success novels, I was pasting envelopes and forgetting to put in the inclosures.

On my second day in the broker's office I thought it was time to write Ida a letter on the firm's stationery:

We parted so suddenly that I forgot to tell you that here's where I've been working all the time. They like me very much around here and are making me all kinds of offers. It looks like I may soon be a member of the firm. If I could meet you I'd explain that whole mistake about the show and everything. Hoping you're not sore, I'm very sorry, EDDIE.

I didn't get an answer, and thought it was a post-office plot to ruin my romance. Louis Rosner might have come across the letter while sorting the mail. Or maybe he had been reinstated and was back with his candy boxes every Saturday night.

There was nothing left to be done but to work on with Weir Bros. until such time as I could drive into Henry Street with a chauffeur and footman. I was about to complete a week at the new job and it felt like a long time. At last it was Saturday—pay day. The five dollars would look big in singles. I grew giddy at the thought of so much money and hopped up on the desk to do a jig for the other clerks. J. C. Weir walked in to ask why the market letter which usually went out to all customers on Friday wasn't mailed yet and why I was dancing on it. He didn't want to hear my reason and I caught myself as he pitched me through the door without my hat. Ten years later J. C. came into the star's dressing-room of the Ziegfeld Follies to visit a black-face comedian—I give you three guesses.

"How about my hat?" I asked.

J. C. apologized. "We haven't found that hat yet. But you owe me more than a hat. You owe me your whole future."

"How's that?"

"Didn't you learn how to dance on my desk?"

But when it happened I didn't realize how lucky I was to be fired. Neither did my grandmother. And on Monday I marched out at dawn, determined to get work if I had to walk from store to store to Yonkers. I was hired as a stock clerk by the National Cloak and Suit Company at seven dollars a week. Already I was making more money. After twenty-five years of faithful service hanging up coats and dresses in the stock and show room I could see a banquet in my honor as world's champion clothing hanger, receiving a beautifully inscribed coat-tree as a token of appreciation and letting in all the promising young coat-hangers on the secret of my success. This vision inspired me to great industry, and after I was there three weeks the head of the firm himself saw me at work. Mr. Rosenbaum brought some important stockholders into the showroom to impress them with the system and discipline of his organization.

"Everybody's on the job here. We stand for no fooling," he explained, pointing with pride to his staff which had not seen him enter and was grouped around the model's revolving platform, where I stood, decked out in a lady's fur coat, wriggling my body with exaggerated feminine grace while all the employees laughed.

"Get that pop-eyed guy outta here!" roared the captain of industry. And my dreams as a stock clerk died.

I didn't seem to fit in. I was always trying to be funny even in the midst of such grave matters as mailing market letters and hanging clothes. I thought it would amuse my employers, but instead, they cried as with one voice, "Can that guy; he makes us laugh!" The world was a serious place. I'd have to put on big glasses and a chronic frown, wear a pencil on my ear and growl.

In the meantime I heard definite rumors about Ida. She had erased me from her life. She had been seen walking arm in arm with a respectable, serious-looking boy friend. He had a hard white collar and a hard black hat. A steady, reliable young man whom no happy-go-lucky comedian could safely scorn as a rival.

It was time to act and act swiftly, decisively. Any day I might hear that Ida had agreed to marry this persistent, methodical suitor. I went to the corner poolroom to meditate. Here I met the brainiest billiard-players of the district. Fellows who could put English on the ball, reverse, draw, shoot at any angle, and make the little ivory spheres behave like tiny Golems charged with life. They could do the same with bullets.

One of them, Kimel, could shoot with the unfailing precision of a minute-man, and he could pull a gun from more places than a magician could produce rabbits or flower pots. His advice to the love-lorn would make Beatrice Fairfax admit she's a man and resign in his honor.

"They's only one way to fix them guys what's sweet on your baby," counseled this student of broken hearts and fractured skulls. "Shoot the bum!"

My mouth parched. "But he may object," was the only argument I could think of.

"Are you gonna ast him?" sneered Kimel, already clapping a pistol into my hands that he had conjured out of nowhere.

"S-s-say! Wha-what's th-this!" I stammered, starting in terror. "I-I-I-wha-wha-wha ——"

"Aw, go on, hurry up! I'll wait for you, and bring back the gat!"

MY LIFE IS IN YOUR HANDS

He shoved me, palpitating and frightened, out of the poolroom, holding me and the gun together lest we fall apart.

"There he goes!" roared Kimel as we reached the street. "Pump him full of lead or I'll pump you for being yeller!" He was beginning to take a deeper interest in the affair than I did. "Shoot, you sap!" And he gave me a hearty kick, propelling me part way down the street. I was quivering with fear, unable to drop the gun held in a paralyzed grip, and, anxious to escape from the devilish Kimel, I began to run, while people shrieked at the sight of an armed maniac and fled to cover.

Ida, walking with Louis Rosner in peaceful dignity, turned at the cries of alarm from passers-by, beheld the frantic Romeo with wild hair and shivering hands dashing down the block, and she warned Louis to run for his life. Louis, believing he was being hotly pursued by a demon, took to his heels and disappeared. Kimel's hoarse shouts could be heard high above the general confusion, urging the heart-broken lover on to swift justice. "Get him, kid, and aim straight!"

I was running for dear life myself, but I gave the semblance of a chase, and as soon as I could turn the corner, I dropped the gun, sneaked off ashamed and completely bewildered. I had ruined everything now. I could never show my face on that block again.

What would Ida think! And I had dreamed some day to nod to her from a box at the opera and give her a jeweled platinum bracelet! What a hopeless, entangling mess my life had turned out to be! The incident was the gossip of Henry Street for many days. The Tobiases would never live down the disgrace. That their daughter should ever have associated with a rough-neck like that! Ida was definitely, irrevocably through with me. The world had shut its doors and I was left naked and alone outside.

Chapter VII

MY ATTEMPTS at comedy seemed to get me into many serious situations. Friendly neighbors tried to explain my conduct on the theory that my head had hit the pavement once too often. In reality, I was unconsciously trying to inject humor into the cheap melodrama of life around me. Poverty, drudgery, ignorance, petty struggles, all of these entangled me in a mesh of disappointment and bewilderment. But fortunately, when everything failed, I still returned to acting.

Dan Lipsky and I formed an amateur team. We played at private affairs, weddings, bar mitzvahs, club socials, local theatricals. At first the somber Lipsky did all the comic bits while I recited the tear-and-sob-producers. Gradually we shifted rôles. I glued on a beard and put over wise cracks taken liberally from vaudeville acts I had seen. Joe Welsh's line always served as a handy opening. It appeared funny for a young boy with a beard to shake his head gravely and say, "If I had my life to live over again I wouldn't be born."

One night I'd play little Lord Fauntleroy with a blond wig and no front teeth; the next night Dan and I were both dressed as dwarfs in a dramatized fairy-tale "Snow-White." But we left in the middle of the performance when an enterprising booking agent offered us fifty cents apiece to go up to a club and do our beard-and-joke act. It took so well that the manager of a downtown music hall on Clinton Street invited us to play there for two dollars. We went on, and every gag we tried fell flat like eggs on a cake of ice. We watched the other acts and discovered we had been the only ones who spoke English on an all-Yiddish bill. By the next night we had translated our entire act into Yiddish, induced the manager to give us another chance without the two dollars, and were received by the audience with laughter and shouts of approval. We had simply talked to them in the wrong language, and this in a general way is every actor's problem in adapting himself to his audience. Drifting as I did into every conceivable type of crowd, I trained myself to the fact that "the audience is never wrong," and if a performance failed to go across it was either the fault of the material or the manner of presentation. By carefully correcting the one or the other or both with an eye to the peculiarities of the audience I could never fail a second time. I proved this to myself on many occasions later on, when in the same night I'd perform at the Vanderbilt home and then rush down to Loew's Avenue B Theatre and be a hit in both places.

After Clinton Music Hall, however, we weren't rushed quite so hard and Lipsky deserted the stage for a job in an engineer's office, while I began to flounder once more. I still didn't suspect that I was an actor, and nobody else suspected it for me. Again I marched the streets, slept on roofs, loafed on the corners, and dreaded the want ads. I couldn't return to my grandmother's without a job and I couldn't hold a job long enough to return. I reached the point where I begged for little loans—my credit wasn't very big in those days—and anything upward of a nickel was a large financial risk. All the other boys had definitely found their avenues in life. This one drove a baker's wagon, that one studied telegraphy, the third had a city job. Only the funny chap who rolled his eyes and made smart cracks was hopelessly befuddled and sinking fast.

"Say, Marty, will you lend me a dime? I didn't eat in two days."

"Why don't you get a job?"

"Have a heart, Marty. I'm trying to get one," I pleaded, too faint from hunger and disappointment to think of stronger arguments. "I'll get one soon and pay you back."

"I heard that before," said the capitalist. "Hey, fellers, look at this guy! He's been sponging on us long enough!"

"You ain't fit for nothing!" snarled another successful plutocrat who was a big man among errand boys.

"I betcha I can imitate Cliff Gordon better'n you can!" I cried, defiantly, my eyes moistening with chagrin.

"Say, if you're such a great actor, why don't you go on the stage?" inquired Marty. A very simple question hard to answer.

"Well, there's lots of great actors can't get a job," I argued in vague self-defense.

"Aw, can that!" sneered Harry, another creditor. "If you're so hard up for a dime and you're such a great actor and you say you ain't had any food in two days, I'll show you how you can make a dollar. But you wouldn't lift a finger to raise a gold eagle!"

"How can I make a dollar?"

"By working!"

"Aw, that's an old one!"

"I mean it! Go up to Miner's Bowery Theatre. It's Amateur Night tonight, and even if you get the hook, you get a dollar along with it!"

The hook! I can picture young Eddie, scarcely sixteen, but already more battered and calloused by adversity than many an older lad, still clinging to the last illusion of his life, faith in his own powers. Now he might have to surrender that, too—for a dollar. The risk was too great, it was inhuman. And yet, he hadn't eaten regularly in days. He hadn't eaten at all in the last fifty hours or had a bed to sleep in. He'd have to get something somewhere or fall flat on his face. Still, to get the hook! That would mean the end.

"We'll go up and watch you!" said Marty, with a trace of malice in his tone.

They wouldn't miss a spectacle like that. They wanted to be there and jeer along with the rest.

"No, I'm—I'm not going."

"Aw, you're yeller; you're a yeller coward and we're through with you!"

"I'm not yellow! I'm just sick and—and hungry and I'm ready to faint. Won't one of you guys lend me a dime so's I can get a bite to eat?"

"We're off that lending stuff. We work for our money! Go and work for yours!"

"All right! I'll go!" Eddie felt a flush of defiance, and perspiration broke out upon him in cold drops. He'd show them! But his trousers were badly torn. He couldn't appear on the stage like that. They'd give him the hook before they gave him a chance. One of the boys weakened. "All right, I'll change pants with you," said Herman. "But out of that dollar I get fifty cents for the loan of my pants."

"O. K."

"But how'll you look in these torn ones?" Marty objected out of a sudden concern for Herman.

"Nobody'll see. I'll be sitting on them in the theater."

We changed trousers. I went to the stage door, and the boys went up to the gallery to watch the performance. It was my first appearance on a regular stage; it marked a big moment in my life. But all it meant to the Eddie of that time was a hook and a dollar. The hook would make a scar in his heart that would never heal, but the dollar would keep him alive. I can see him distinctly as he stood trembling and chilled in the wings, watching the acts go on, listening with terror to the rough, brutal clamor of the audience that drowned out the feeble efforts of the performers. He felt like an early martyr soon to be thrown to the lions.

Once or twice he heard the jingle of coins on the stage and cries from the gallery, "Take the muzzler off! . . . Go to work, you bum!" And Eddie turned in alarm to a

MY LIFE IS IN YOUR HANDS

hardened amateur-night performer beside him. "Gee! they're giving the poor fellow the works, aren't they?"

"Oh no!" said the old hand. "He's making a hit! That's how they praise you. When they don't like you they don't say a word, but just scream."

"Have you ever tried this before?"

"Oh, I work the amateur-nights regular. I'm at London's every Thursday and at Miner's every Friday. There's a dollar in it."

So there were chronic amateurs who made a business of it, got hardened to the hook and took it as part of their performance!

I shuddered. Two players had already been yanked in by the huge iron hook and the audience let out a bloodthirsty howl. But I dared not retreat. Starvation would be the least of my sufferings if I turned back now. I watched for some sign, some miracle. It seemed to me that the next few acts, while obviously mediocre and even pathetic, were received with a certain amount of mercy. Maybe somewhere behind that frightening mass of hissing faces there was a human heart-throb, after all! Maybe, as soon as I got on the stage, I should tell them that I hadn't eaten for days, that I hadn't slept, that I was an orphan without home, without friends, without hope; maybe they'd all weep and perhaps put padding on the hook. But, no, I'd just dive on the stage the way I'd plunge off a bridge, open my mouth, shut my eyes, and get the hook. That would be the quickest, easiest, dirtiest dollar I had ever earned.

MY LIFE IS IN YOUR HANDS

The last performer came off with a smile that seemed triumphant, then he returned for a minute on the stage to pick up some coins thrown him by uptowners who were slumming. For some reason I felt a little better. I was too green to realize that it was harder to follow a good act than a bad one. I heard the burly announcer with protruding jaw and heavy, stubbled face cry out, "The next number on the program for your approval is Edward Cantor ——" There was a loud derisive laugh from the audience. "Edward" in those days was as unfortunate a choice as "Galahad" now. Any man whose name wasn't John, Jim, or Harry had no right to live. And here was a thing coming out under the perfumed misnomer of "Edward" and it probably wore embroidered garters.

The announcer lifted a hand, "Just a minute!" he roared, gruffly. "Mr. Edward Cantor, Impersonator!" The word "Impersonator" stunned them. They were accustomed to song-and-dance acts, to recitations and acrobatic stunts. But "Impersonator"? What was that?

I, too, am a spectator now as I watch young Edward Cantor step for the first time on a regular stage in 1908. His face was pinched to a tight green and his eyes fairly popped with fright. The first menacing rumblings of booes and howls began to ferment. Isham, the mighty announcer, put a heavy but friendly hand on the skinny lad's shoulder and raised his other hand to calm the crowd. "He's a new one, boys. Give him a chance." The audience had a great regard for this master of ceremonies. At one time or another he had beaten and tamed each one of the savage listeners, throwing them out when drunk and clapping them down when too rough. Isham's request was respected and the audience granted a moment of silence to get its second wind.

Edward began. "I'm going to give a few first-hand impersonations of the leading stars without make-up." Most of the stars he impersonated he had never seen, but he had seen their imitators and gathered his materials from them. His first was of Cliff Gordon, the German Congressman, and the lean, starved young fellow began to puff and blow in a flagrant dialect, as if he were bursting with food and good living.

"The House of Representathieves," he thundered, "giffs Admiral Perry a medal for discovering the North Pole and vat did he find dere? He finded out dat it vass cold! He could haf bought a tearmometer for nineteen shents and stayed home and found out de zame ting! . . . Nowadays efferyvon goes out on shtrike! Soonvile de vifes vill go out on shtrike, too. But can you himachin de scabs coming in to take deir blazes?"

The audience was listening, some even snickered. Remember, these things were funny two decades ago and some of our best comedy writers think they still are—and use them. Murky-looking listeners from the gallery began to shout words of encouragement: "Stick to it, kid, you're lousy!"

After a full embodiment of Cliff Gordon, the impersonator flung himself bodily into the character of Harry Thompson, Mayor of the Bowery, presiding in Essex

MY LIFE IS IN YOUR HANDS

Market Court on a busy day. Eddie dressed Thompson's monologue with extracts from Walter Kelly, the Virginia judge; both Thompson and Kelly were headliners in the days of Tony Pastor.

"Prizzonerr befurr the barr," commenced Eddie, in his broadest brogue, "Pwhat's yer definse?" Eddie assumed the tone and manner of a young faded lass of the Tenderloin, protesting shrilly, "Your honor, I was walking down the street, minding my own business ———" "Tin dollars foin!" snapped the judge! . . . The next culprit was a pretty siren of the sands pulled in by Anthony Comstock's father for wearing too short a bathing suit. "Hild fur furrther examinashun!" glowered the judge. "Nixt! Hurry up thar, Flaherty, I gotta maik a poker date! . . ." A pickpocket came to the bar. Eddie fined him ten dollars but the pickpocket had only three. "Send him loose in the crowd till he gets the other seven," advised the learned pillar of justice. Another victim was hauled up for refusing to pay on her sewing-machine after the first installment. "Pwhat's yer raisin?" inquired Eddie. And Eddie answered with a feminine whimper, "The man told me the machine would pay for itself in time." Bang went the magistrate's gavel.

An eloquent lawyer next appeared to defend a tongue-tied foreign-born gentleman accused of stealing a watch. Eddie made his plea so eloquent that, turning around to impersonate the judge, he broke into tears. Then as the lawyer he pleaded once more, "The poor man can't even speak English," he cried. "He is an innocent victim of a false charge! Send him home, your honor, to his wife and six or seven children!" "He's dismissed!" sobbed the judge. And the bewildered defendant, turning to his lawyer, inquired in college English, "Then to whom do I turn over the watch?"

The audience was warming up to enthusiasm. Piercing whistles and hoarse gallery cries were more numerous now. "Lay down, you're dead!" somebody shouted, offering advice. But Eddie was scoring. He was past the third pole and heading for the stretch. "My next impersonation," he announced, excitedly, "will be Junie McCree," and the audience groaned in anticipation.

Junie McCree always played a dope fiend. He had a chalky complexion, black, close-cropped mustache, and pale-blue, watery eyes. Eddie slumped into the languorous, dope-dazed attitude of the poisoned dreamer. Eddie mimicked McCree's way of uttering his words with a soft, tired drawl, dragging the mounting interest of the hearers to the laugh like a slow-moving vehicle to the brink of a precipice.

Junie McCree was not only a great comedian; he was also an originator. He was the first to bring to the stage that style of fantastic comparison which has now become a fixture of all light comedy. "I'm so broke," he would say, "that if they were selling steamboats for a nickel, I couldn't buy an echo of the whistle." He was the first to call cigarettes "coffin-nails" and matches "sulphur sticks." "Act like a ferry-boat, come across, come across!" he would appeal in his borrowing moments. "Give me three iron men; I want to get a pair of kennels for the dogs." He too originated the notoriously murderous expression, "I wish I had a hotel with a hundred rooms and found him dead in every one of them." A wish that, some say, has since come true in Chicago.

Junie McCree would speak of his son in the same clammy way. "My boy came home, took a jab of the needle, and bought St. Louis. Take another jab, I told him, and pay the rent. . . . Oh, my boy is good to animals. All night in his sleep he says, 'Feed the kitty! Feed the kitty!'"

McCree had a better way than Wallingford to spend a million dollars. "If I had a million dollars," he drawled, languidly, "I'd buy a half a million of hop and a half a million of room rent and leave word not to be disturbed."

All this time Eddie had forgotten about the hook. It hadn't come. Instead there was the rumble of stamping feet, shrill whistling, and a thin shower of coins that pelted the back-drop and rolled toward the gutter of footlights. This was their way of applause, with leather, metal, and siren shrieks; they scorned the effeminate clapping of hands. Isham helped the young impersonator pick up the coins.

After the last act, all the performers who had survived the hook lined up on the stage, and the same hardy Isham announced that the prizes would be awarded. He went from one actor to the other and held a five-dollar bill, the coveted reward, over each head, timing his action to the applause. At first the five-dollar bill lingered over a couple of artistic dancers, then over a singer, then over Eddie. Isham shifted the prize from one head to the other, until all but the dancers and Eddie were eliminated. At first it was hard to decide for which there was a louder and more sustained racket; then the house went Eddie and he got the five-dollar bill.

It was triumph, fairy tale, heaven, all rolled in one. In moments like these one does not measure victory by eternity. All eternity lives in those moments. Who in the wide world cared that I had won five dollars in a cheap burlesque house? But I wanted to laugh and to cry and to shout all at once. There was nothing bigger in the world to me. Herman hailed me at the stage door and we changed pants. I got back my torn ones and gave him his fifty cents rental fee. Then I took the crowd down to Chinatown and treated them all to chow mein and chop suey. A wise guardian might have cautioned me against eating three big bowls of fried noodles and onions after a two-day fast. But my new-found friends and I ate until the night's receipts vanished.

I must say their attitude toward me changed. Marty slapped me on the back and Harry said he knew all along I'd make good. Then they left me and I returned to my open-air quarters on the roof, where my bed was a stretch of cold, rusty metal under the water-tank. I was suddenly seized with the terror of death as my stomach violently rebelled against the Chinese idea of food, and I lay writhing on the roof, utterly miserable and alone.

It was one of those moments of anguish—of which I had experienced many—when the childish, hopeless wish for a father and mother, a home and its warmth of security, broke upon me in all its fullness and regret. I was a very unhappy fellow as I lay there, chilled and sick, sobbing through the night.

But even this sad anti-climax did not wholly obliterate the new vistas opened to me. I felt certain of one thing now: I would be an actor. The next week I entered the amateur contest at the London Theatre, another Bowery palladium, and was offered a regular job with the company. I was too shy to accept, for I still lacked faith in myself. I was content for the time with periodic performances, winning the amateur prizes and building up my little act of impersonations. I Burbanked the best material of such headliners as Harry Thompson and Walter Kelly and soon had as good an act as either.

I learned to please different groups in an audience and never failed to work in a popular old jingle when I noticed enough children among the listeners. Unconsciously I was following a sound principle used by the big department stores who build their clientele from its infancy, and no doubt many of the youngsters who remember the jingle have seen me as adults. The latest children audience to hear this early rhyme were children of my own. It runs like this: Knott and Shott in a quarrel got and Shott took a hot teapot and cracked Knott on his bald spot where he ought not and then there was a pistol-shot and Knott shot Shott and Shott shot Knott, but Knott was shot and Shott was not and the rest of the darn thing I forgot. It didn't compare with Longfellow, but it also rhymed.

I remember one encore in particular that always brought a laugh, though I could never explain why. When my act was over and the audience sustained its applause I would reappear, lift my hand in a lofty gesture, and for no reason at all I would say, "I, too, am a mother!"

Finally I plucked up the courage to accept an engagement with Frank B. Carr's burlesque review called, "Indian Maidens." At last I was a recognized professional, a salaried servant of the footlights at fifteen dollars a week. Out of this salary I had to pay off an elaborate equipment of four changes, as I appeared successively in the guise of a tramp, a Hebrew comedian, a waiter, and a bootblack. The only line of the show I recall was from the bootblack number. A row of pretty girls with pleasing leg surface had their boots shined by the sooty wielders of the brush. As the bootblacks looked up at the shapely, charming legs, they sang out in chorus, "It's a shame to take the money!"

In November the show left for the road. "Indian Maidens" played for four weeks in small towns and I was just beginning to enjoy the free, flashy life of the traveling actor when it closed. We had been gradually reduced to one-night stands, business got worse and worse, and when we opened in Shenandoah, Pennsylvania, on Christmas Eve, nobody was in the theater, not even the manager. He had left for New York.

MY LIFE IS IN YOUR HANDS

I was stranded without a penny. Shenandoah was a nice, cold town with the snow falling in silent, white slivers. The air nipped and stung and swirling winds wound the flakes into ghostly shrouds. All the shop windows were decked with evergreens in sparkling candlelight and holly. Men and women hurried about, laden with holiday packages. And I trudged the streets, silent, desolate, and alone.

Chapter VIII

WHEN I first met Will Rogers on the Orpheum Circuit I used to take him down to the East Side to kosher restaurants where for sixty cents we had a fine meal that took a half a day to eat, and he rather enjoyed the food. But after a number of these trips he turned to me uneasily and said, "Say, kid, if I hang out with you much longer, I'll become a rabbi and you'll become a cowboy." It has nearly come true, for now Will Rogers is a minister of good will and peace, while I, at this writing, am out in California near a ranch.

I regret that at the time I did not initiate him into the wonders of an East Side wedding, for then we'd have gotten bigger meals for less money. In fact, one of the greatest institutions for public welfare twenty years ago was the East Side wedding, where anybody with a clean collar and a quarter could come in shortly before midnight, check his hat, and partake of a twelve-course wedding feast. With a little courage, he could even kiss the bride.

There were public wedding-halls along Clinton Street, St. Mark's place, and near Second Avenue. By a systematic route planned according to schedule I sometimes spent every night in a week at a different marriage celebration. At first the sheriff at the door eyed me suspiciously because of my shabby clothes, and I had to mingle with the wedding guests to get in; later on he had no suspicion at all, he knew I didn't belong, so he simply winked and let me through.

I quickly learned to make myself useful at these affairs. Before the last course was served the head waiter would slip me a quarter to drop into the tipping plate with a loud clang so that every one should hear and follow suit. After the supper it was customary to read messages of felicitation from friends who could not attend. I became a popular telegram reader at weddings, a function that for entertainment and importance ranked second only to the wedding ceremony itself. For nothing was quite so necessary as to impress those present with the numerous and powerful friends that the betrothed couple had in all parts of the world. When there were no telegrams, we got blanks and made up our own.

"Here's to Mr. and Mrs. Louis Pincus," I'd read. "May they live in prosperity—from your Aunt Sadie in Connecticut. . . . I'm sorry I cannot attend wedding of Mr. and Mrs. Pincus—Theodore Roosevelt. . . . As my new show opens tonight, I cannot get away—George M. Cohan."

Occasionally, one of the sheriff's lieutenants and I would lure the groom into a small compartment in the rear of the wedding-hall and get him into a game of seven-eleven with phony dice. At first he would stand aloof and throw his money to the floor, but as he began to lose he became more absorbed, flung off his swallow-tail, and got down on his knees, while his parents and in-laws hunted frantically for him and the blushing young bride stood under the canopy wondering where he had disappeared to and why he was holding up the wedding. He'd be losing ten or twelve dollars when they yanked him away in spite of his protests, and we had to promise him to continue the game after supper. But promptly after supper we sneaked out of the hall.

I got to be a popular figure at weddings, proposed toasts to the bridal pair, led in song and dance, and wound up by kissing the bride and even the bridesmaids. The groom and his relatives thought I was a long-lost brother of the bride and the bride's people imagined I was the principal relation of the groom, but the fact was I knew nobody at all. But there was one wedding where everybody would know me and I couldn't be a crasher. What was worse, I couldn't even be a guest. It was the wedding of Ida's sister, Jennie.

Grandma Esther had salvaged me from Shenandoah, Pa., and I returned to find that Ida and Minnie were going out once more with the Rosner twins. At Jennie's wedding, Ida's and Minnie's engagements would be definitely announced and their marriage would follow within the course of a year. Their father, David Tobias, had warned Ida against me, as if she needed that warning after all the blunders I had made. But knowing my reputation as a crasher, the Tobias clan was organized to keep me off the block of the wedding-hall.

Perhaps it was the severity of her parents that softened Ida's feelings toward me. Perhaps she still had that tender, motherly emotion for this lonely, funny chap, but those we mother we do not marry. Yet she agreed to meet me again near the old school. But she tried to make it clear that it was for the last time. Her first act as we met was to extend a hand in parting.

"Eddie, I'm sorry for you. I'm afraid my parents are right. You'll never amount to anything."

"I'm trying to settle down. Could I help it if they left me flat in Shenandoah?"

"I can't make you out. So far, all I've had from you is heartaches and shame!" There were tears in her eyes. Maybe she did care a little. "When you were younger you hung from a lamp-post and cried to collect a crowd. Now you're chased by a woman with a hat-pin or you run down the street with a gun! You certainly are improving with age! I suppose as you grow older and more settled, you'll jump out of windows and swing from telegraph wires!"

"You don't understand, Ida. I'm making pretty good. I was getting fifteen dollars a week for ten weeks."

"Where's the money? What did you do with it?"

"Well, they took out some of it for costumes, and it's true they took the costumes, too—still, they owe me the rest. But their credit is good."

"There you are! You're letting yourself in for a tramp's life. Knocking around from city to city, living in third-rate hotels, eating stale, bad food, never knowing what a home is like, being stuck in strange places with no friends, no money, and no one to turn to."

"But as long as I can come back to you." I was getting really emotional.

"You expect me to sit around waiting through the years while you go everywhere and get nowhere? We'll never have a home, we'll never have any happiness."

"I—I'll write you nice letters."

"Yes, you'll write—please send railroad fare. Stuck again! Besides, you think I'd marry to be separated? We might as well divorce before we're even engaged. Oh, you were never cut out to be an actor, anyway!" she exclaimed, going in for prophecy.

"Oh, is that so!" I wrinkled my cap into a roll, clenched my lips, and went away. At the corner I turned to see how my dramatic departure had affected her, but she had disappeared.

On the night of Jennie's wedding I stood in the hallway opposite the Tobias home on Henry Street and watched the long procession of automobiles line up in front of the house. As was the custom, all intimate friends and close relatives first visited the bride's residence, drank a few preliminary toasts there, and then set out for the hall. Gradually the guests came down the stone steps, the men in evening dress, the women in glittering, gaudy splendor, laughing and chatting together as they entered the cars and drove away. Ragged children and unkempt neighbors leaned against rails and out of windows to behold the grand manner in which David Tobias staged a wedding. Finally the bride herself appeared in silver white, escorted by her mother, who was weeping softly.

The groom followed with his father, and then came Ida. She looked incomparably beautiful and majestic in her new dress purchased specially for this occasion. Louis Rosner, in a hired tuxedo, escorted her, while his brother Leo held Minnie's arm. They settled cheerfully in a car and something Louis said made Ida laugh. She seemed to be enjoying herself as the motor hummed and they sped away. The last car vanished down the block. It had taken an hour to see this merry party off. After that I wanted to go home to my grandmother's and take gas.

What wouldn't I have given to have a father then, a big, important father who was perhaps the sheriff at the door or the officiating reverend, a man with authority who could say, "Unless Eddie is received here as a guest of honor, I refuse to go on with the ceremony!" Why was I cursed to have no father and no mother? If only I had a mother on whose lap I could rest my head and weep. I went to bed early and cried through the night like a child.

Minnie's engagement was announced at Jennie's wedding. Jennie was a June bride and Minnie would marry in October. Then perhaps would come Ida's turn and all the time I would be standing in the doorway across the street and watch life and love and happiness pass me by. "At the next wedding I'll be the whole show!" I determined, grimly. How, I didn't know. But the following day I looked up a friend, Joe Malitz, who took me with him to Coney Island for a job.

We went to work at Carey Walsh's saloon next to the famous Roseben's pavilion and opposite Diamond Tony's. Coney Island was then, even more than now, a motley medley of social peaks and grottos. Now it is mostly grottos. The whole island was dug into love tunnels and overhung with scenic railways on rickety stilts. People went rushing about with angry faces, looking for pleasure; masses of perspiring and dishevelled men and women poured endlessly out of street cars, elevators, and automobiles; and after having traveled for hours they started at once to ride again up and down crazy tracks and through evil-smelling caves. They were mostly people who could spare only one day in the week for fun, and they had to get it quick and in concentrated doses.

They didn't even have time to laugh or ponder a jest, let alone think. It had to be slash-bang-biff all the time and they had fun pummeled into them with steel pistons and sledge hammers. Revolving in a barrel until all the organs changed places, whirling in a reel till the women lost their corsets and the men lost their shoes, riding at full speed down a vertical wall, eating frankfurters, then rocking on Noah's Ark till they got seasick—that was fun. Blowing horns, munching popcorn, drinking lemonade—that was fun. To the poor, eating is always fun. People went out for a great time and they got it if they had to be knocked senseless to appreciate it. I had never been to Coney Island before, and, working in Walsh's saloon, I didn't even suspect there was an ocean and bathing. I naïvely believed that Coney was an island because it floated in liquor. Afterward I found that my childish belief was correct.

Carey Walsh's saloon aspired to the dignity of a cabaret. While bottles were thrown occasionally, the guests aimed only at one another, never at the entertainers. I received this positive assurance along with three dollars per night that I sang. Only in the height of the season did Carey Walsh do business to sing about. Still, for ten weeks it looked like steady and continuous employment, and nothing was ever more continuous than my singing. On a Saturday night I would sing about one hundred times, and at the beginning, when my repertoire was limited to only four or five songs, I would repeat each number with variations about twenty times. I immediately set to work to replenish and expand my stock of tunes. I spent my nights at Carey Walsh's and my days at music publishers, and while I got thinner and thinner my bank roll got fatter and fatter. But that was all I cared about.

It did not take me long to observe that the waiters averaged more for a night's work than such artists as Joe Malitz and I. For the waiters were given a $5 stack of chips for $4.50, and on every $5 in sales they cleared fifty cents for themselves. In addition to this they received tips, and made on Friday, Saturday, and Sunday almost twice as much as we earned all week. It was a momentous decision. I would have to forsake art for business. I compromised, combined both, and became a singing waiter.

This was too much for Joe Malitz. As an artist he

could not stoop to such exploitation. He quit. To this day, I am told, he regrets it. For he had a sense of comedy that was uncanny and a fine knack of showmanship. And if all singing waiters become Irving Berlins, Joe Malitz certainly sold his Adversity Common at far below par. I clung to the worthless stock, not because I had such faith in the profession of singing waiters, but because at the moment it represented all the stock in the world I had in myself. Perhaps I was just waiting for fate's wheel to turn, and singing while I waited. It would have been nicer to wait under a willow tree instead of over tables, and it might have been sweeter to sing under a balcony than under a tray-load of gin and suds, but the only balcony I'd ever known was at Tony Pastor's, so I took to the napkins and drink-chips with zest. I became Carey Walsh's pet, and years later I got a real thrill when I appeared on the stage of Henderson's Theatre in Coney Island and the old saloon-keeper, suffering from locomotor ataxia and hardly able to move, banged his stick against the box that he sat in, as he shouted to the audience with tears in his eyes: "My boy! He's my boy!"

On the other hand, my memories as a waiter have often given me a haunting and peculiar feeling, and once, sitting at a dinner between Mayor Walker and William Fox, and watching the waiters bustle about with their trays, I wondered, "How do I come to be sitting here?" When the Mayor was almost finished with his fish, I involuntarily got up and bowed courteously, saying, "May I take the dish, sir?"

MY LIFE IS IN YOUR HANDS

It was in those glorious pre-prohibition days that we learned how to cut liquor. Once a customer tippled over the thin line of consciousness every waiter became a prohibition agent. And the way we cut liquor was to cut it out altogether. We had a system. It was each cabaret girl's business to sit opposite a simple, sober earthworm and make a rum vessel out of him; but as soon as he became goggle-eyed and tongue-tangled, he would order gin, pay for gin, and get sink water. How modern that sounds! And what a hot drink sink water can be to a man who looks at a girl and sees quadruplets! He smacked it down with a quaff that would have done honor to liquid fire. And the girl, who had been drinking sink water right along and charging it up to his bill as cocktails, had orders from the house to look delirious and sigh with passion when her new-found gentleman friend staggered toward her and embraced the waiter instead.

At a certain hour of morning, when each guest's head spun like a miniature Virginia Reel and Loop-the-Loop, Carey Walsh's saloon suddenly turned into a soft-drink parlor; every order of whisky was filled with stale ginger ale, and celery tonic flowed for champagne. Yet with each drink the drinkers got drunker, for after the first stiff glassfuls the memory lingered till dawn. It was a great life of make-believe, and what went for the drinks went for the songs.

It was a guest's inviolable right to request a particular song and it was the singing waiter's duty to know it. There were guests from all parts of the country, and each loved his home-town melody and wanted the waiter to sing it. Some preferred organ-grinders' classics, others chose popular numbers, while there were always those who demanded that I sing the songs of their childhood—which was long before I was born. It is to the everlasting glory of Carey Walsh's that no request number was ever refused, no matter whether anybody had ever heard of it or not.

A hardy, ruby-nosed Westerner with big ears like his own corn marched in with a delegation from Parsnip County, Nebraska, and said, "Hey, kid! Let's have good old 'Robin Red Breast'!"

"Righto!" I cried, as soon as I realized it was a song and not a brand of Scotch. "Robin Red Breast? Why, of course!"

My confidence inspired the Nebraskans and they sat down like around a log fire back home, to listen to the sweet ditty.

"Hey, Jimmie!" I shouted to the pianist. " 'Robin Red Breast'!"

"O. K.!" said Jimmie. He never said anything else and he was never at a loss, for Jimmie had the rare talent of making up tunes on the spur of the moment that others take weeks to write. He has since come into his own as the versatile Jimmie Durant of Clayton, Jackson, and Durant. He is also the proprietor of the famous *schnazel*, the nose that knows no end. With him at the piano I could have shouted, "Encyclopedia Britannica!" and he'd have said, "O. K.!" and set a tune to that too.

MY LIFE IS IN YOUR HANDS

"Let's go!" I signaled and burst into melody, uttering whatever words came to my mind first. *"Robin Red Breast in the trees, sits on a bough, amongst the breeze!"* There was one rhyme already. *"Waiting for his mate. What can make her late?"* The Nebraskans looked slightly perplexed but patient, and I steamed full blast into the chorus: *"Robin Red Breast, you're a dear!"* I don't know what gave me the idea that it was a very effeminate song. *"Robin Red Breast, singing here—Oh, you Robin Red Breast, I can tell you by your song. Robin Red Breast, birds like you never go wrong!"* Whenever in doubt, I always finished on a high note, as that brought enough applause to drown out the protests of those who had asked for the number. So I let out a final devastating, *"Oh, you Robin R-e-d B-r-e-a-s-t!"*

"Cripes!" roared the Westerner. "That's not the right song!"

"Oh, are there two of them?" I stared innocently.

This question always planted a doubt in the mind of the guest and he felt compensated, for at least he had heard the mate to his favorite number. It was good drill in extemporaneous acting and had many variations. If a truckman entered the saloon I'd break out, as if finishing the refrain of a popular hit, *"What care I for gold and silver? All I want is a horse and truck! The honest sweat upon my brow, From—from toiling in the muck!"* This brought the truckman beaming to my table and sweating with appreciation.

But as the night wore on and the crowd began to show

[101]

the merrier effects of drink, the songs became sillier in proportion, until the time that the crowd was most giddy and riotous with fun and liquor, when the drinks ceased to have a kick and the songs had no tune, no rhyme, no reason. And the game that was played in Walsh's saloon was played outside along the Bowery, where all the con games and sucker traps of the world were strung out in an endless net to catch the simple urbanite in his quest for pleasure.

On rainy or off nights during July and August, I got permission from Walsh to earn some side money as a shilliber for Japanese ball games, shooting-galleries, and ring-pitching concessions. I would roll Japanese balls and, regardless of the score I made, I would receive a huge, hand-painted set of fine porcelain dishes. "Gee! Look what I got!" I'd exclaim in loud delight, and passers-by would stop, look, listen, and fall. Then I'd go the back way, return the dishes, and get a quarter.

There was a concession in those days called, "Hit the Nigger—Three Balls for Five." I was paid to bounce a few soft balls on the negro's docile dome until a crowd gathered, and the rest was easy. The negro would make a slurring remark to irritate some likely sucker in the mob. This sensitive soul, observing the ease with which I struck the negro's shiny pate, would pay for three hard balls to vent his spleen. He missed because the negro was an expert dodger, but his pride would not let him quit before he struck a blow. The negro kept dodging and insulting him, and the heroic pitcher of wasted balls would spend as high as five dollars in the hope of hitting his tantalizing target.

In another booth I struck down straw-stuffed cats with baseballs. For every three cats that fell I got a five-pound box of candy—to hold. But when an outsider was lured into the game, they always substituted for one of the three innocent pussies a cat loaded with lead that couldn't be knocked over with a sledge hammer.

At the shooting-gallery I took my pay in trade and really became known along the Bowery and at Walsh's as a good shot. Out of sixty wooden birds I could shoot down fifty-two. But the owner of the gallery employing me as booster, insisted that I shoot only at the big gong, which required as much skill as hitting a wall with a truck. But it was this very fact that attracted the crowd. They could not see what was so marvelous about banging away at a bell the size of an iron foundry, and each took a gun-load to prove that he could bang away, too. But my private shooting practice was more skillful, and in time I was so accurate a shot that one might have suspected I was training for future Broadway managers.

In fact, ten years later I had occasion to exercise this skill with Ziegfeld. The Follies was opening in Atlantic City when Ziegfeld, Dave Stamper, the composer of the show, and I were walking on the boardwalk and happened to pass a shooting-gallery. Ziegfeld knew nothing of my marksman's eye inherited from the early days as a Bowery shilliber, and neither did Stamper. I nonchalantly, as it were, invited Florenz to try a gun-load of fifteen shots with me. The producer consented, but before I lifted my gun I remarked to Stamper:

"On whom will you bet?"

"Well, I don't know," Stamper said. "I guess I'll bet on Ziggy."

I smiled. It was a shame to take the money. "How much?"

"Oh, I don't know—five dollars."

"You couldn't possibly make it more than that?" I inquired, kindly, but I really didn't feel right about taking the five; it was too obviously like robbing cradles. So I bet five and began to shoot.

"I'm not so good today," I explained, modestly, as I hit thirteen out of fifteen of the little wooden birds.

Then Ziegfeld took up his gun-load and shot down three of the birds with three consecutive shots. But an accident like that I had made allowance for. Then he shattered a couple of pipes revolving on a cylinder. Then he snuffed out a flame. Then he turned his back to the shooting gallery and fired the gun while taking aim by a pocket mirror. Then he slung the gun over his left shoulder and shot that way, hitting everything and anything and asking me each time whether I could suggest any new way of holding the gun or from what position I'd like to see it fired. My eyes popped. Ziegfeld hit a perfect score. Pipes, ducks, birds, flames disappeared. So did my five dollars.

"Hey! What's this—Jesse James?" I cried.

"Ziggy worked in Buffalo Bill's show as a youngster,"

explained Stamper, "and every morning the company got shooting practice."

I took care not to flaunt my skill as a shot after that. I was pretty good as a shilliber, though. And that summer of 1909 I managed to amass the unprecedented fortune of four hundred dollars, the first savings of my life. But I didn't intend to leave them in the bank. I had endured the hard, grueling experiences of the summer to fulfill a single purpose. Minnie Tobias's wedding would take place in October and I intended to be there.

All summer I had kept in touch with Ida, trying to convince her that at last I was earning good money as manager of a Coney Island restaurant. She probably imagined that some day I would be the proud founder of a chain of restaurants or sell lunch-room fixtures. She managed to find out where I worked, and one evening, to encourage me, she unexpectedly arrived at Carey Walsh's with her sister Jennie and the latter's husband. Fortunately, I noticed them before they caught sight of me, and, quickly throwing off my apron, I assumed charge, giving orders to the other waiters, who thought I had gone out of my mind. Ida looked proudly on. She had undoubtedly brought members of her family to get a better opinion of me. But my obsessing thought was to get them out as swiftly as possible. I told them this was my night off and if they would wait outside I'd join them and we could take in the sights together. As soon as they left I hurried into the kitchen, put on my coat, and sneaked out the back door. We spent a pleasant evening together, but

MY LIFE IS IN YOUR HANDS

I had a lot of explaining to do the next day to Walsh, the manager, and the waiters. But I was invited to Minnie's wedding.

I got the finest tuxedo I could hire. It never occurred to me, even with $400 in my pocket, to buy one. Nobody did. I bought the shiniest patent-leather shoes that buttoned on the side. I donned a glossy silk hat and rented an automobile for the occasion. The fame of my sudden prosperity had spread through Henry Street and Ida's father began to think it was his severity that had finally reformed me and set me on the right course.

I called for Ida in the rented car and we took another couple as our guests as we drove off to the same wedding-hall from which I had been barred less than six months before. I tipped the sheriff at the door, I tipped the coat-checker, I tipped the matron of the wedding-hall. I almost tipped the groom. I wanted everyone to know that Eddie Cantor had arrived.

Ida, beaming, blushing, thrilled with the new hope of my amazing transformation, went about leaning on my arm, introducing me proudly to relatives and friends who had inquired after me in insinuating tones at the last affair, but who were surprised and taken aback to meet me now. "They say he's the manager of a big restaurant," they whispered behind my back, "and soon he may own it!"

I felt the wad of warm yellow bills in my pocket. There were still three hundred dollars left after peeling off one hundred for my outfit and a wedding gift. This was all the money I had in the world, but this was also the only night in the world. A plan formed in the shadows of the doorway opposite Ida's house, on the drear, chilly night of Jennie's wedding, had come through. I was learning the magic of dream-stuff turning into reality. Everything was coming out just as I had designed it. And here I was the lion of the party, but before I got through I would be the whole jungle.

"Come on, folks! Eddie's treating to champagne!" The news spread like a bugle call to arms. All the guests gathered around the bar with military dispatch. The bottles popped, sparkled, and rolled away with a hollow clink. At the fourth glass per guest I seemed to have grown in stature and my face assumed to them a blurred, almost spiritual haziness. "He's a great man," said the befuddled drinkers. "This Tobias knows the kind of boy to pick for a son-in-law!" They were beginning to think it was my wedding. I slapped down the yellow bands of money on the bar and ordered more and more quarts of the glittering water at four and a half dollars a pop.

David Tobias tapped me patronizingly on the shoulder. "Hold your money, my boy," he whispered, as if I were squandering family funds.

"That's all right," I assured him. "There's more where this comes from."

"Eddie," said Ida, tugging at my hired tuxedo, "that's enough."

"This is my night!" I cried. "Another round!"

The drinking ended; so did the three hundred. My reputation as a *bon vivant* and captain of industry was firmly established. Those who knew of my hungry days recalled them dimly as out of a distant past. "I knew him when he didn't have shoes, and look now!" Luckily I had a dollar left in my coat to tip the chauffeur, unless the diligent hat-checkers had already found it.

But I had captured the night. Even during the wedding ceremony somebody mentioned what a wonderful thing it would be if Ida and I were also under the canopy. It seemed to be a propitious time to talk to Ida's father and commit him.

"Well," said Tobias, smiling rather genially at me, "I'm glad to see you settled down to be a business man and you dropped all that foolishness about acting and singing."

"Still, I may go back to it some day," I ventured. Old Tobias frowned.

"What? Now that you got a little capital saved up? All right, you spent a small part of it on a good time, but that's over——"

"Yes, it's all over!" I agreed, staring at the empty champagne bottles that grinned open-mouthed at me.

"The rest of your money you should invest in a nice little business."

I looked helplessly to Ida, but she seemed to like her father's sound, practical view. "Of course. What else can you do?" she asked.

"But—but what business would I be fit for?" I exclaimed, my hands stuck deep into my empty pockets.

"I got just the thing for you!" Tobias's eyes lit up.

He was a born suggester. Only moderately successful himself, he had a remarkable faculty for advising others how to get along. This faculty ultimately consumed so much of his time and thoughts that he gradually neglected his own affairs and retired from work altogether, so that he could dedicate his whole life to making suggestions. "You should buy yourself a nice gents' furnishing store. It's a wonderful business!" And Tobias screwed his eyes up shrewdly.

"Were you ever in it?" I inquired.

"No. But I know all about it," he confided. "You can make thirty per cent profit on a small capital. Besides, you're just built for it!" he said, appraising me carefully.

"How small is the capital?"

"Well, twenty-five hundred dollars is a fair start."

"Oh, that's not so much," I said, carelessly. "But I still think I'm going to be an actor."

"An actor!" David Tobias showed a surprisingly irritable temper when that unworthy calling was mentioned. Even Ida was shocked.

"Young man," cried Tobias, severely, "if you don't forget acting you'll have to forget Ida."

"But, Mr. Tobias," I said, becoming alarmed, "you as much as agreed that Ida and I can get married."

"You better forget about that. What I'm telling you now is final. When you've got the twenty-five hundred dollars and you want to buy a gents' furnishing store and settle down like a man, we'll talk. Not before. Goodby."

MY LIFE IS IN YOUR HANDS

I drove Ida back to her home in the rented car and we scarcely spoke. I didn't mind what the old man said, but I had a feeling that in large measure Ida agreed with him. In a way, I didn't blame her. Acting, at best, was a precarious career, with many hardships and uncertain returns. I was taking a wild plunge in the dark in preference to a life of comparative security behind a necktie counter. But what was Ida's attitude? Was it really a choice between her and the stage?

Chapter IX

IT WAS surely no well-formed plan that urged me on to the stage. I simply followed my nose, and I had a substantial one to follow. Nowadays, with all this higher cultivation that our eyes and ears get through radio and phonofilms, we don't appreciate our noses enough. We imagine all they're good for is hay fever. Some of us think noses are only ornaments and try to remodel them. But for sensing the general direction of life, give me a good old reliable sniffer every time. If you're lost in a thick, black forest with a thousand tangled trails, a telescope and field-glasses are about as useful as a bathing-suit on the Sahara or a ton of bricks on a parachute, but the old Indian pathfinder with nostrils like an English pointer never goes wrong.

And at this stage of the struggle I was tangled up in a lot of trails. The ancient prophets were fortune-tellers compared with the prophets of Henry Street. According to them I was engaged to Sodom and married to Gomorrah and the least they expected of me was to become a train-robber. If I went on the stage, I'd be lost. If I didn't sell neckties, I'd be lost. In fact, if I didn't do a thing, I'd be lost.

The thought that I would have to pursue my career in secret made it the more enjoyable. David Tobias's ultimatum still echoed through my mind, "Either forget about acting or Ida will forget about you." That made the stakes very high. I promptly forgot the warning and set to work. There was a People's Vaudeville Company in those days with a chain of four third-rate houses distributed evenly on both sides of the Jersey ferry—the Lyric in Hoboken, the New Lyceum in Elizabeth, the Royal and the Lyric in Brooklyn. The company also ran a Sunday concert show each week at the West End Theater in New York. It was a modest, struggling amusement circuit organized by a former furrier called Adolph Zukor, another furrier known as Marcus Loew who had previously conducted a penny arcade with David Warfield, and two ex-drug clerks, Joseph Schenck and his brother, Nicholas Schenck. These four partners, newly recruited to show business, had little money and less experience and were mainly backed by enthusiasm. Still, they managed to get on in the world.

The last I heard of them, Marcus Loew was still in the vaudeville business until his untimely death a year ago, and according to reports he had not done so badly. His enterprises had run into many tens of millions. The Schenck brothers had attained the front rank of motion picture production in America. One of them had married Norma Talmadge and headed the United Artists. The fourth, Adolph Zukor, was making a fair living as the president of Famous Players-Lasky Corporation. In fact, in 1926, when I met him again, he thought nothing of paying me a hundred and fourteen thousand dollars for eight weeks, or about fifteen thousand dollars a week, for my part in the filming of "Special Delivery." But in 1909 the four of them thought it a pretty big investment when they signed me up for four weeks at twenty dollars a week, and they were careful to stipulate that the contract was effective only if my first performance at the Lyric in Hoboken met with their approval. Joseph Schenck came over expressly to watch me on the opening night, and, fortunately, he was so impressed that I played a full week at each of the four houses and was permitted to play the circuit again, provided I could change my act.

"It's a limited circuit," Schenck explained, "and we never book the same act twice in one season, but if you'll get up an entirely new line of gags, we'll let you on again."

"That's fine!" I said, eagerly; but it wasn't fine at all. From the time my impersonations had scored in Miner's burlesque I had painstakingly added bits to my act, until now I saw no way of changing a single word of it. On the other hand, I could not surrender this rare opportunity to play the circuit again. It meant another four weeks' pay. I went to the dressing-room that I shared with a couple of acrobats and a bird-whistler and stared glumly at my image in the glass. I saw my opportunity slipping and myself back on the fateful corner of Henry Street out of a job once more.

It would be hopeless to change my act. It would mean the gathering of new material, selecting and perfecting it, spending weeks, maybe months. All the jokes and smart lines I used had been borrowed from headliners of the first-class houses. If I borrowed new stuff it might not be so good. I had already helped myself to the best. There was only one chance. If I changed my make-up. A mere facial disguise might disguise everything. With a different make-up and a different delivery even the same lines would sound different. Great idea!

But, unfortunately, I knew little about the art of make-up. It was easy enough to smear a healthy tan over my face and flourish an eyebrow pencil, but to make a beard look like a natural growth instead of a horse's tail, or to draw skillful lines and create fine facial effects like a Hamlet or Othello—that was out of the question. Besides, it would kill my act. I sat in a blue gloom, toying with a piece of burnt cork that I picked out of a charcoal can on the make-up shelf. I tried a few dark lines around the mouth and they only made me look haggard. I tried to wipe off the marks, and they spread. My eyes fairly popped out of my head. I had it! Quickly I rubbed the cork over my cheeks, my brow, my neck, my ears, leaving an oblong of white skin around the lips to exaggerate their thickness. I was covered completely with burnt cork, as shiny as a lump of coal. Black-face!

My eyes glistened, my teeth gleamed, and because I feared to get the cork dust into my eyes I amateurishly left large circles around them, but out of this blunder was born a new idea. I decided to cover the fault with a pair of white-rimmed spectacles. The spectacles gave me a look of intelligence without straining my face. Unwittingly I had added an intellectual touch to the old-fashioned darky of the minstrel shows. By putting on glasses the sooty spirit of the cotton fields was brought up to twentieth century.

At first I dressed in a battered high hat, a loose-fitting second-hand Prince Albert, and huge pancake shoes, but later I brought my negro friend up North and tailored him nattily in a wasp-waisted coat, white socks, and patent leathers. There was just a trace of cotton fluff in his ears, but the night-club rhythm danced in his eyes. I leaped with both feet into the new creation.

Hiding behind a black mask, I got the booking for another four weeks on the same circuit. That was easy. And the audience, like Schenck, accepted the same act in black-face like a new sensation. Afterward I dressed as a Dutchman and finally as a Hebrew comedian, and each time my booking was renewed, though the act was identical and every line unchanged. I played the circuit so long that the audiences began to learn my jokes by heart. But Old Black-face, caught in a moment of perplexity and soon discarded, returned to serve me and lead me on.

I had worked steadily now for sixteen weeks at twenty per. This news reached home. The big city, cosmopolitan as a whole, is provincial in every part. Henry Street was like Squeedunk. Becker's candy store near the corner was like Squeedunk's country store. I was making good in my home street. Benny and Jonah and Danny and Ira had heard all about me and my fame had spread from the west end to the east end. Of course, I was only a small-timer, but the boys were loyal to home talent and made a big-time fuss. Besides, I wasn't squeamish or bashful about my work and could be called upon to give a performance at any moment, in the candy store, in the hallway, in the middle of the block.

One Sunday, Henry Street needed somebody to be proud about. A neighboring but rival village called Jefferson Street was welcoming one of its famous sons. Roy Arthur had achieved greatness as a member of Bedini and Arthur, a team of jugglers and travesty artists that played the top-line theaters, and when he descended to the slums to visit old friends, the haughty Jefferson Streeters paraded their man of renown along the length and breadth of Henry Street. Henry Street, deeply humiliated, almost buried itself with shame in its own ash-cans, for it had no one worthy of comparison. So they trotted me out.

"Go on, Eddie, do your stuff!"

We were on a stone stoop overhung with bedding, and the audience jammed the steps, overflowing to the curb. I did not wait to be asked twice. I cast one swift appraising eye at Arthur and went into my act as if he and the rest of them had paid for admission. The crowd applauded and cheered lustily. It was a triumph for Henry Street. But I kept my eye on Arthur. What would he say?—the star from a top-line theater. He only nodded, smiling perfunctorily, and talked with his friends of other things, as if to say, "We'll let that pass." But before he left he turned to me and said, casually, "Drop around some time next week and look me up at Hammerstein's."

"Next week?" I thought. "When was next week? Today is Sunday. Tomorrow is Monday. That's next week!" I was there promptly Monday afternoon, and during the intermission Arthur introduced me to the redoubtable Bedini.

"How would you like to join our act?" were Bedini's first words. I had to swallow a lump and speak at the same time, and nearly choked trying to do both.

"How would I like? Say, well, gee!—of course!"

"How would thirty dollars a week strike you?"

"Strike me? It would knock me flat!" I failed to say it, but that was how I felt. Hammerstein's was then the pivot of show business and the thought of stepping on the same stage with all the headliners was too much to believe.

"Well, you're hired," said Bedini, briefly.

I didn't ask when I'd start. I was afraid he'd say, "Never!" I just stayed there. Bedini and Arthur went on for their turn again and came off, and I still stayed there. I expected to get a part at once. I noticed that Arthur made up in black-face, my favorite color, but that didn't faze me and I still stayed there. Finally Bedini threw some clothes into my hands and I trembled in eager expectation. Soon the magic order would come, "Get into make-up!" But he didn't say that. He said, "When the tailor comes, give him these suits to press. I have to wear them for tomorrow matinée."

It looked as if the whole thing was a practical joke. It seemed that Arthur had told Bedini, "This kid is very clever," and Bedini, in recognition of my ability, immediately made me his valet. The whole week I never got beyond the dressing-room. My part was all backstage. I brought up sandwiches, helped to unpack trunks, looked after the make-up and costumes. But at the end of the week I got thirty dollars. I figured they wouldn't carry a joke to the point of paying me money. Maybe, after all, I was one of the act.

I watched my "acting partners" keenly, listened to their careful discussion of every piece of stage business, and while they performed I peeked through the wings and wandered into other dressing-rooms. I was getting paid to inhale atmosphere. Stage life seeped in through every pore.

Dressing-room No. 9, famous for its size, was the clubhouse of the theater and here I got a liberal education. For no matter what rooms the actors dressed in, eventually they all gravitated to this one to be with the "regulars." Here I saw dice games with all-star casts. The big electric-light names of two decades ago would all be chanting the old spiritual, "Come, Seven!" while Bedini sat before the mirror, bronzing up his handsome face. DeHaven and Sidney, dancers; Rice and Prevost, comedy acrobats; Stepp, Mehlinger and King, the Rathskellar Trio, who sang and played the piano; Ferry the Frog, great contortionist of his time—they were all gathered here when Bedini suddenly suggested to them, "I want you to hear this boy and tell me what you think of him."

That was the signal. I plunged into my impersonations as I had done on the stoop in Henry Street, but this was quite a different audience. When I finished it was very quiet and even chilly in the room. All those who watched me knew the originals intimately and turned up their noses at my imitations. I had reached Hammerstein's, but it looked as if I would never see its footlights.

More weeks passed and I continued back-stage. If they'd only give me a chance I felt I could go out there and knock the audience into the aisles, but I was a prisoner in a theater and all doors to the stage were locked for me. I saw actors go on and come off, excited, exhilarated; I heard the applause they received and watched them return for encores; and there I stood right behind the wings, but as far from sharing their life as if I were sitting in the pit.

But down on Henry Street everyone got the impression that I had reached the cross-roads of the world.

"What are you doing now, Eddie?"

"Oh, I'm playing at Hammerstein's," I said, carelessly.

The Henry Streeters were awed. "What! Hammerstein's Victoria on Forty-second Street and Seventh Avenue! Why, that's the greatest vaudeville house on earth! You're made!"

"H'm-h'm!" I agreed, as if that were a matter of course. "I'm playing with Bedini and Arthur. Why don't you drop in and see our act?"

"We sure will!"

"Watch for me!" I warned them. And they did. They watched till they were cross-eyed, and when I met them again they scrutinized me suspiciously and whispered to one another, "This guy must be nuts!"

"Say, who are you kidding, anyway?" one of them sneered. "Maybe you're washing dishes some place, but you ain't at Hammerstein's!"

"Maybe you couldn't see me from where you were sitting," I tried to explain. "But I'm there, all right!"

"Then why ain't your name on the program?"

"Oh, that?" I became earnest and indignant. "Did you notice it? Funny thing! Hammerstein has been complaining about that, too! He told them they're keeping my name off too long!"

"Haw! Haw!"

But I had outwaited my ill-luck. The next day Bedini told me, "I may use you in the act." My heart slurred over a half dozen beats, as if I were sliding downstairs. I could see myself already in the center of the stage with the spotlight on me, going through ten minutes of rapid-fire monologue. "You want me to do my specialty?" I suggested, trying to look calm.

"No. You'll just stand in the wings, and at a certain signal you'll bring on a plate, give it to me, and go off."

"That's all?"

"That's all."

Bedini, being the virtual boss of the act, told me to make up in black-face like Arthur. Two black-face figures would set him off better, while another white-face might detract from his central position. Trifles like these often become vital matters in the world of make-believe. Besides, burnt cork was plentiful.

So my first appearance in top-line vaudeville was to

come out at a certain cue, hand Bedini a plate, and go off without a word. For this I took hours to prepare my make-up, fuss over my costume, and rehearse the various possible ways in which I could hand over the plate. But my chief problem was how to come on and go off so that the audience would notice me and possibly even laugh at my exit, for I had already learned that a laughing exit is often preferable to a prolonged appearance. The first thing I decided was that once I got on the stage I would take my time about handing over the plate. I looked leisurely at each of my partners and then I looked over the audience in a lofty manner, while Bedini and Arthur looked at each other in amazement at my cheek. This brought a laugh, and a hand at my exit. It also raised me a few notches with Bedini.

A week later he asked me whether I knew how to juggle. The only juggling I had ever tried was to roll my eyes in their sockets, but now Bedini showed me how to roll a hat down the length of my arm and catch it as it dropped off. Only after I had mastered the hat did I try the same trick with a plate. I now devoted all my spare time to juggling, and became quite accomplished in every phase of the art. With that my rôle expanded. In addition to bringing on the plate, I had a new piece of business.

After Bedini, who was an able juggler, slid the plate off his arm and caught it, Arthur clumsily tried to mimic him, smashing the dish. Then I took another plate, slid it down my arm, caught it with ease, and snapped my fingers scornfully at Arthur. Arthur pursued me with a hammer and I exclaimed, "He means to do me bodily harm!" It was the first time any audience had heard a negro speak such Oxford English, and it was the first line I spoke on big-time. From that moment on Arthur and I developed into a sissy-bully team, he the boor and I the cultured, pansy-like negro with spectacles, and anything I could devise to enrage him was effective and brought laughs.

Bedini now got an increase of seventy-five dollars a week from the Keith Circuit for the added member to his cast, and he increased me, accordingly, five dollars. Our act finally drifted from juggling to travesty exclusively, so that we began to appear toward the end of the bill, and we parodied all the headliners. This work was mostly extemporaneous and required quick and often inspired thinking. No hard and fixed framework could fit into such an act. Every Monday, with the changing bill, our comedy changed to suit. Once Bedini felt sure of me, he let me have a broad and liberal training. He encouraged me to come on the stage at any time, providing I thought I had something funny to offer. At first I was extremely careful not to abuse this precious privilege, and whenever I entered to interrupt Bedini and Arthur I invariably managed to score a laugh. Gradually I got so that I kept on interrupting them nearly all the time. But Bedini never objected to it and, what was perhaps more important, neither did the audience. In fact, they liked it.

MY LIFE IS IN YOUR HANDS

I became a full-fledged junior member of the firm, but my salary remained the same. However, I got my reward in glory, for the act was now styled on the program,

BEDINI & ARTHUR

Assisted by Eddie Cantor

It was the first time my name appeared in print, and I stayed after the show to help clean up the theater, so that I could collect old programs, cut out the name of our act, including mine, and I mailed copies to all my friends, not forgetting those skeptics who had come to see me while I was hidden back-stage.

Our team burlesqued and parodied most of the famous stars of the time. In 1910 Molasso introduced the apache dance for the first time in America in his act, "Paris By Night." We followed right after him, using his set, and by very seriously imitating the high spots of the dance, we brought the house down with a roar. Here I learned one of the basic lessons in the delivery of comedy, and that was, never to consciously point one's fun, but to do one's comedy very seriously, almost grimly, and let the audience pick the laughs itself. We burlesqued Ruth St. Denis, Mlle. Daisy, Gertrude Hoffman, and I played Salome, an artist's model, and danced to Mendelssohn's "Spring Song" wearing dresses, but always in black-face. By sheer accident I once lost my dress while dancing and the audience screamed. After that, whenever I played a woman I had to lose my dress. In fact, whenever we ran low on laughs Bedini would signal, "Drop the dress!" and it was sure-fire.

It is hard to explain in cold type what audiences consider funny. Gestures, subtle inflections of the voice, fleeting changes of expression, an upward roll of the eyes, may turn a dull line of print into sparkling stage humor. Here, for instance, is a specimen of poetry I used to recite on one of my exits, that never failed to rock the house with laughter. But I took care to look deeply poetic and wistful as I uttered these epic lines:

> "Twinkle, twinkle, little star.
> How I wonder what you are!
> Up above the world so high —
>   Oh, what care I?
>   Oh, what care I?"

Probably in the sharp contrast of pure nonsense and earnest delivery, comedy was born.

This impromptu mode of play was a perfect discipline in ready wit and a more solid training for the stage than all the academic courses in rhetoric and vocal expression combined. I was with Bedini and Arthur for two years, playing three summers at Hammerstein's Victoria for six, eight and ten week periods. Our longest run at the Victoria was when we burlesqued the court-room scene from "Madame X." These were my school days in the theater, and I remember the first time I met the great William Hammerstein himself I felt like a boy facing his principal. In those days the impresario's "O.K." was like a blank check signed by the Secretary of the Treasury. He took a personal interest in all the acts of his show-house and had watched my gradual progress on the stage. He patted me on the head in fatherly fashion, saying, "Son, you'll headline on this corner yet."

It happened, but not quite as Hammerstein had expected. In 1926 at the Rialto, which now stands exactly where the Victoria had been, I accompanied the screen version of "Kid Boots" by a personal appearance at the modest weekly allowance of seventy-five hundred dollars, a mere two hundred times the salary I had earned on that same spot seventeen years before. But I'd gladly have waived the pay check to have Willie Hammerstein sitting in the theater and call out in his hearty voice, "Well, son, what did I tell you?"

In 1910 we were playing at Keith's in Louisville. The theater was short of an act and Bedini offered to oblige the management by sending me out in front of the curtain to do a five-minute bit while they set the next scene. "Go out and sing that song I've been hearing you rehearse," Bedini suggested. I hadn't sung since the days at Carey Walsh's, and this was my first attempt to sing on a stage and before sober people. I had picked up an advance copy of a new song entitled, "The Rag-Time Violin," by a comparatively new writer, Irving Berlin. Its spirit and rhythm fitted in with a peppy, lightning delivery and as I was intensely nervous and self-conscious, I walked rapidly up and down the stage, clapping my hands and bobbing about like perpetual motion. The result was something new and entirely unintentional in jazz interpretation, and the clapping of hands, the quick, jerky step and rolling eyes, have since become my trade-mark. I had to sing encores till I was exhausted, and the little curtain number was afterward retained in the act and expanded to ten minutes of music and monologue.

A few months later, in Atlantic City, we played on the same bill with Gus Edwards and his troupe of young prodigies. This was the first time he saw me perform, and as a judge of juvenile talents he commended my work. The next day Edwards asked Bedini whether he could borrow me for a benefit performance at the Chelsea Yacht Club, one of the select social centers of the Jersey shore, and Bedini agreed. At the affair I teamed up with a couple of Edwards's youngsters and most of my work was impromptu. Edwards was enthusiastic on the way home.

"My boy," he said, "you made the hit of the evening, and if you're ever out of a job, come to me!" After a while he added, apologetically: "You understand Bedini is a very dear friend of mine and I couldn't just take you from him. It wouldn't be right. But if you ever should quarrel with him—it's liable to happen, you know—always remember, you can count on me."

I began to realize that after two years I was still getting only thirty-five dollars a week with Bedini and Arthur. In Cincinnati I suddenly discovered that I had developed a terrible temper and couldn't restrain myself from slipping into arguments with Bedini. But he was such a tolerant and liberal master that it was really hard to pick a quarrel.

We were planning to do a burlesque show for next season, to be called "Dandy Girls," and after managing to intrude my part into every scene I complained that I had no rôle at all. At last Bedini lost his temper, too, and in an unguarded moment he exclaimed, "You do what I tell you! If you don't like it, quit!". I felt like kissing him.

"I quit!" I cried, deeply wounded, and hurried to a drug store to call up Edwards, who was playing at Morrison's Rockaway Theater.

"Gus Edwards?"

"Yes."

"I quarreled!"

"Meet me at my office in New York the first thing tomorrow morning!"

That night I went to consult my old friend, Dan Lipsky, to help me with my new business arrangements.

"I've been getting thirty-five from Bedini, but I think Edwards should do better than that."

"He'll probably give a five-dollar raise and make it forty," Dan opined. "But in order to get forty you say, 'Fifty!' and hold out for it! When it comes to paying salary, they're all alike!"

I went fully primed to meet the new manager.

"Eh—Mr. Edwards," I began, trying to remember Dan's business-like tone, "I —— You understand that in the matter of salary—I've got to get at least—eh—" I didn't have the nerve to pop the fifty.

Gus Edwards interrupted me with a good-natured wave of the hand. "Why, my boy, I wouldn't think of starting you on less than seventy-five dollars a week!"

Chapter X

IN 1912 Gus Edwards produced a vaudeville act called, "Kid Kabaret," with a cast that included Georgie Jessel, Eddie Buzzel, George Price, Leila Lee, Gregory Kelly, and Eddie Cantor. The whole act brought something over a thousand dollars a week and that was considered high. If the same people were engaged today it would cost fifteen times as much, but I don't think the act would be fifteen times better. It might not even be as good. For none of us has remained childlike, simple, and cute.

Eddie Buzzel was then an attractive youngster of fourteen or fifteen, who played straight and serious parts. It was only later, when he found out that comedians got more money, that he decided to become funny. Jessel was a dashing dandy of twelve with a high hat, white vest, spats, and a cane, but at heart he was a child longing to play, and would have traded his whole outfit for an electric train. Leila Lee was a little girl, hardly six, who had "it," but didn't know what it meant. Now she does. Perhaps I, who was nearly nineteen, and played the colored butler in livery, was the most sophisticated of the lot. The whole troupe, in addition to talent, had that rare quality of youth and refreshing naïveté which has never been recaptured on the American playboards.

The story of the act was simple. Young Buzzel's wealthy parents—wealthy with stage money—had gone to a theater and cabaret party, and the youthful host invited all his infant friends to have a little cabaret of their own. The company was well stocked with gifted dancers and singers ranging from the age of measles to early wisdom teeth, and it was my part to furnish the comedy while joining in the musical numbers and doing impersonations. The idea was to show that we would run a better cabaret than our elders, and I think we did. I don't know, for I hardly ever go to a cabaret. If I get the urge for night clubs, I go home, close the windows, blow smoke in my face, and charge three dollars to sit down and have somebody trample on my feet. But Gus Edwards's "Kid Kabaret" was better than that.

It was not only first-class vaudeville, but the best and only acting school of its kind, where poor young boys and girls could learn the art of entertainment in all its forms and get paid for learning. Among some of the Edwards protégées who have grown to fame are the Duncan Sisters, Herman Timberg, Helen Mencken, and Betty Pierce. Gus Edwards has done more for the youth of the stage than any other man I know. He not only schooled a large number of our present-day stars, but composed songs that suited the needs of his youngsters, with the result that he contributed some of the most famous hits of his day to the literature of popular music. "Tammany," "School Days," "Sun-Bonnet Sue," "Good-by, Little Girl, Good-by," "See-Saw," "By the Light of the Silvery Moon," were some of the Gus Edwards songs that now form part of the folk-music of our country.

Behind the scenes, Edwards managed his troupe of

juveniles like a family. Mrs. Edwards always traveled with the company when it started on tour, and often had as many as twelve to fifteen boys and girls under her care. I initiated Jessel into the mysteries of bathing, and practiced my new-found knowledge of dieting on him, so that he never ate a thing he liked. I taught him to save money, but he spent it between lessons.

The most unprofessional kind of friendship developed between Jessel and me, for we always sacrificed personal interest for each other's sake. A friendship like this is rare not only in the theater, but outside the theater as well. To have one's name featured above the rest is the first thing an actor dreams of and craves—even a child actor. Still, while I was the one featured with "Kid Kabaret," I asked Edwards to feature Georgie Jessel equally with me. This made little Buzzel jealous. He balked, spoiled his lines, upset our cues, and tried to throw the act into confusion. That night I went to his room and gave him a good talking to with both fists. When he had sufficiently recovered from my arguments, he came in sheepishly to Jessel and me, apologized, and asked whether he could henceforth room with us. We said he could and he did, and the three of us have remained dear friends and pals ever since.

Throughout my whole career on the stage this was the only fight I had, except when I enlisted for four rounds at Jack Dempsey's training-quarters to give him a few pointers on his coming battle with the French champion, Carpentier. Dempsey crouched and rushed toward me in

MY LIFE IS IN YOUR HANDS

his weaving style, and I began to speak very rapidly through my nose, muttering: "Misericorde! Pas si fort! Pas si violent, monsieur!"

"What's that?" asked Jack, dumbly, coming to a sudden halt.

"I'm talking French so you'll get used to Carpentier."

"What are you saying?" He screwed his eyes suspiciously.

"Have a heart! Take it easy, monsieur!"

When Jessel and I were not acting, we were playing. We had no outside games or diversions, so all our fun had to be born of the theater. On one occasion we ruined a perfectly boring mystery thriller. Just as the distracted father cried, "Where is my daughter?" we walked across the stage behind him, both of us in black-face, with brooms slung across our shoulders. The audience broke into laughter and the actors of the piece were mystified, instead of the audience. On another occasion we found that a newcomer to our act, a little girl violinist, was getting more applause than was healthy for her. The next night when she took her bow we were right beside her, each of us with a violin of his own, and shared the hand. Another time, as she finished her number, I suddenly appeared in one of the boxes of the theater and began a campaign speech: "Ladies and gentlemen, if I am elected the public monies will be safe. I will guard them and keep them. You'll have nothing to worry about!" A distraction like this always brought a laugh and diverted some applause. It was not very ethical, but neither is boot-

MY LIFE IS IN YOUR HANDS

legging. And bootlegging applause is one of the oldest tricks of the show game.

Jessel and I made many plans together. We intended to write a play, but never got beyond the intention. It was to be about the Sons of Potash and Perlmutter, but we found out they never had any children. At Lake Charles, Louisiana, our juvenile company undertook to furnish the entire vaudeville program of the theater. Each of the troupe was featured separately and also teamed for other numbers. Jessel and I did a juggling act, harking back to my training with Bedini and Arthur.

For two seasons I played with the Edwards caravan in many theaters throughout the country, and during those tours I met another actor with whom I developed one of the most cherished friendships of my life. He would often appear on the same bill with us along the Orpheum Circuit. He never opened his mouth on the stage and you could hardly get him to talk off-stage. He did a spectacular lassoing act, and his equipment consisted mostly of anchor rope that others could barely lift but which he whirled with ease. He employed in his act another man and a horse. He received three hundred and fifty dollars a week for the act, and after paying for transportation the horse got most of what was left.

We of the Gus Edwards troupe would stand behind the wings and watch this tall, unknown Westerner who was always grinning and chewing gum while he did the most astounding rope tricks with as much effort as if he were buttering toast. He lassoed the galloping horse and rider, he spun hoops around them, he looped the horse's hind leg and the rider's left arm; he could lasso anything from the horse's tail to the rider's mustache. But he couldn't talk. He tried it once by announcing his feats, and his Western drawl brought unexpected laughs from the audience. This confused and embarrassed him so that he never tried to speak on the stage again. Such was my first glimpse of one of the greatest monologists America has ever produced.

Will Rogers was a true horseman of the prairies. He hailed from Claremore, Oklahoma, and that hardy, outdoor core in his nature gave him a quaint manner and picturesque background. He seemed to be out of place, this lonely cowboy struggling along among a bunch of hoofers and wise-crackers, and he must have felt it. He was probably thinking of his little home town and wishing he were back there, but he found consolation chumming around with the Gus Edwards's kids, for we idolized him from the start, and he must have been very fond of us, too. He introduced us to the outdoors, became the captain of our baseball team, and bought us all our gloves and bats. That made a hit with us at once.

He took a particular liking to me, and whenever we met along the circuit we spent a good deal of time together. I bought him his first kosher meal and showed him strange worlds hidden in the slums that he was intensely interested in but had never seen before. The extreme East and the far West met and liked each other.

His conversation was always flavored with a peculiar

MY LIFE IS IN YOUR HANDS

wit and style of his own, and I often urged him to say the things on the stage that he was saying to me. But he wouldn't. This man coming out of the great silence into the little cities of hubbub was still afraid to talk. It was not until some time later, when Max Hart, the theatrical agent, and I as well as a few others who knew him intimately and enjoyed his excellent humor once it could be uncorked and allowed to flow, persuaded him to try, that he finally opened his mouth and talked his way into fame and fortune.

While the years brought vast changes in Will's position, Will himself never changed. He married a girl as genuine and free from affectations as himself. It was a real love match and will always be, and Betty of the Western plains still handles all his matters. Will's children were born in the saddle and he made them ride a horse before he gave them a milk bottle. Still, if his wife was obliged —as mothers often are—to scold or talk harshly to the youngsters, Big Bill of the lasso would go into a corner to hide the tears that came to his eyes. For this calm, slightly cynical cowboy who chews gum and whips out smart lines is one of the most sentimental and emotional of men, with a heart as big as the country he sprang from. Jimmy, his youngest, is a pocket edition of him.

Will Rogers is the most charitable actor in the business and is never too busy to dispense charity personally. If I told of his many anonymous contributions to the Red Cross during the war I'd probably run the risk of being lassoed tightly around the neck for betraying him now, but I'm sure a lot of people would like to know the full stature of this man who hides behind a piece of gum and a Western drawl. Unfortunately, all this will appear too late for his presidential boom, but here is an interesting sidelight. In all the years that Rogers played for Ziegfeld they never signed a paper between them. Rogers shook Ziggy's hand and that was a contract.

Some outsiders got a different slant on Will. When people finally found out he could talk, he got to be in great demand as toastmaster and after-dinner speaker. He always charged heavy fees for this service, and the captains of big business who paid them thought he was avaricious and grasping. But the fact is he never kept that money. The day after he spoke at a banquet he would always turn over the paycheck to some worthy charity organization.

As a rule he was always reluctant to accept the position of toastmaster, but once in his life he actually asked for the job. It was after my star had risen that the Friars' Club arranged a dinner in my honor, and Will Rogers sent word to the committee that he would like to be selected as toastmaster for the occasion.

I suspected that Will wanted the gavel so he could rap me all night; but Will had poked fun at Presidents and royalty and made them like it, so I didn't mind. It was to be a night of celebration and revelry. For dinners are hard enough to go through, even in one's own honor; but if they're boring, they're absolutely indigestible. So I

MY LIFE IS IN YOUR HANDS

was going to have laughter at any expense, even at my own.

But when I sat down beside Will Rogers at the banquet table I noticed he wasn't in the mood for fun. I looked over the glittering hall studded with celebrities from various fields, and it tickled my pride to know they were all there to do honor to the little colored butler from "Kid Kabaret," and that the master of ceremonies was a lonely cowboy who had once been at the end of his rope. Then in one of those sudden flashes my whole life passed swiftly and vividly before me. I remembered the ragged, hungry nights on the roof, my tryout at Miner's with the big hook looming in the wings, my days as a singing waiter, my good and brave grandmother who used to lift trunks on her back to earn food for us both, and here I was now at the head of a festal board, one of those who had climbed to the top of the heap. There are times like these when I get so sentimental I can cry at card tricks.

Then Will Rogers got up and said the dinner was very good, but he wanted to tell them a story that was better. He remembered the opening night of the Ziegfeld Follies of 1917. It was my début with the Follies and my first big chance. Will watched me that night and was confident I'd make good. I did, and he came into my dressing-room to congratulate me. He expected to find me bouncing around the place with glee and liquor. Instead he saw a skinny young fellow doubled up in a chair, with his head bent over the make-up shelf, crying as if his heart would break.

"What's the matter, kid?" he asked, startled and worried. "What are you crying about? Why, you're the hit of the show!"

But I couldn't press back the tears and my voice was choked with sobs. It was the most wretched moment of my life. Through all the years I had striven toward this goal. Only in my wildest dreams had I hoped to be one of the outstanding hits of the Follies and it had happened. But now it meant nothing, nothing at all to me, for the one person in the world who should have been there to see it, whose heart would have throbbed with a thousand pleasures of pride and love, that person was not there. This would have been the one moment of happiness she had waited and hoped for through eighty-four years of the most abject toil and misery, but she was deprived of it. Shortly before I made my début in the Follies, Grandma Esther's eyes were closed in night.

Will Rogers told the story, and tears streamed down his face. "That's why I wanted to be toastmaster," he said. "You are honoring this boy for what he has achieved and he deserves every bit of it, but I love him for the way he loved his grandmother." W. C. Fields, who sat on Will's left, was crying, too, and all the banqueters sat sniffling and red-eyed. It started as an Eddie Cantor evening and turned out to be a Jane Cowl night. No group of comedians ever presented a sadder spectacle. But I was grateful to Will for the simple, human way he had turned the affair into a tribute to the memory of Grandma Esther.

One incident in her life, however, was a pleasant one,

and mainly because she knew it would bring me happiness. When I left the Gus Edwards troupe I was twenty-one. I returned to New York and confided to my grandmother that I was going to get married. She was glad.

"Now you'll have some one to take care of you. After all, I'm getting old. I'm of little use."

"Don't worry, grandma. Just wait! Everything is going to turn out fine! How would you like to ride around in a car with a nice little great-grandchild?" At least this prediction did come true.

I had worked steadily for four years, and after contributing part of my earnings to Grandma Esther, I managed to save enough to buy a dazzling diamond ring which I even flashed from the stage, cutting a hole in my glove finger for the sparkler to shine through. In addition, I had twenty-five hundred dollars in the bank.

I stared at the little bankbook with mingled feelings of pride and dread. Wasn't this the fateful figure that David Tobias foretold would land me behind a necktie counter? I had been allowed to follow the stage as a makeshift until I should accumulate enough money for a real business. The time had come for me to quit acting and get down to shirts or abandon the thought of marrying Ida.

"You mark mine words," said Tobias, shaking a prophetic finger at me, "if you wouldn't open a gents' furnishing store now, you'll be sorry the rest of your life. And remember David Tobias warned you!" Then he bent over to me in a confidential undertone; "After all, how long do you think people will go on paying their good money for such foolishness like dancing and singing? Some day they'll get wise to themselves, then where will you be?"

But Ida was beginning to waver. A woman sees the immediate, and, after all, how many of us can see that far? I had earned money, that was certain, and I might even turn out to be a fair actor. Anyway, it was worth chancing. We cajoled her father, but concealed our assets, and being out of work anyway and having nothing to do, we got married.

We took no resplendent hall. David Tobias doubted whether I'd open a shirt store even though I promised vaguely, and for that reason he was not so enthusiastic over this match as he had been about the others. "Better not get stuck for too much," he thought, and so there was no splurging for halls, bands, or caterers. We had a quiet little wedding at the Tobias flat in Brooklyn. Only a few close relatives were invited, and when they started to give the presents I realized how close they were.

At Jennie's and Minnie's weddings there was something to rejoice about. These girls had married modest suitors viséd and okayed by their parents. But Ida had picked herself this Eddie Cantor who was only a tolerable sort—tolerable after a great deal had been overlooked and forgiven—and there was no earthly reason why the wedding should be permitted except that the two foolish youngsters loved each other, and what a poor excuse that was! The wedding broke all traditions, for the only ones who were happy at it were the bride and groom. We found an unexpected ally in the weather, for it was June, the 9th of June in 1914, and really, even if nobody else smiled, June smiled and Ida smiled and I just grinned.

Dan Lipsky, in the meantime, succeeded in convincing my cousin Anne that she ought to marry, too. Their wedding was five days after ours, but Ida and I were already off to Europe on our honeymoon and lost out on their supper. From our twenty-five hundred dollars in the bank we deducted seven hundred for the honeymoon. We planned to be moderate and economical in our pleasure. It made no difference that I traveled second class, for I traveled with a first-class wife.

Chapter XI

ONE memorable flop came at this time, fast and early in my career, but I recuperated with profit. When Ida and I arrived in England we found that honeymooning in the fog was a prosaic business. We had to light a match to kiss. Besides, if I laid off a week from work I might lose the habit, so I teamed up with a vaudevillian named Sam Kessler, whom my theatrical agent, Max Hart, had recommended to me, and we played a week at the Oxford in London. It was the gloomiest, coldest, foggiest week I ever spent on the stage, and I am surprised to this day that the audience didn't get up and throw seats at us.

Nevertheless, Charlot, already famous then for his revues, seemed to think it wasn't my fault, and offered me a job at the Alhambra minus Kessler. I played several weeks in his revue, and scored one of the biggest hits of my life with the song, "I Love the Ladies." I had to sing ten and twelve encores with extra choruses of this number every night. My wife sat in the pit at each performance, and in the morning washed clothes, kept house in a modest way, and the trip we had taken to spend, turned into a thrift contest.

Charlot's revue was the *élite* of light entertainment. There were such celebrities on the bill as George Grossmith, Connie Ediss, and the late Lee White. It was my first experience before an ultra-ritzy and meticulous audience, and considering the sorry way I had stumbled on the threshold of England, this was a swift and promising recovery; but then the war came.

Ida and I returned on the *St. Paul*, July 29, 1914. It was the last ship back to America before war was declared and seemed to realize the heavy responsibility of bringing us home. Laboring under this strain, the *St. Paul* trembled all the way, just managed to dock, and, landing us safely, keeled over and died. Throughout the following years, right up to Armistice Day, I was active in war work and enjoyed the distinction of being among the leaders in the sale of Liberty Bonds. I also joined the entertainment forces of the War Department and played hundreds of benefits at soldiers' camps and hospitals.

I once met Benny Leonard at a war camp, and my fighting blood was stirred. We put on a battle to the finish for the boys, but first I made Leonard eat two bananas, and when the gong sounded I aimed for his stomach. I landed such telling blows that every time I hit him the gong rang and he had no chance to strike back. Needless to say, I won, but I couldn't claim the title, as I was underweight.

Some years later, at the Walter Reed Hospital in Washington, Jane Green came with me to entertain the convalescent soldiers who were brought in wheel chairs to the auditorium. She sang them one of her hot, loving numbers, after which I asked the nurses to come and take the temperatures of all the patients. I always framed special gags for the soldiers, and found that the best laugh came from the old one about asking for two-dollar contributions to bury the second lieutenant. They all readily offered ten dollars to bury four more.

In the meantime, Max Hart had joined me in a team with Al Lee, who was considered one of the best straight men in the business. As "Cantor and Lee" we played the Keith Circuit in a medley of talk and song called, "Master and Man." It was a black-and-white act. Black-face had become an inseparable part of my stage presence. Audiences had begun to accept me as the man with the ebony mask, and I feared that the day might come when I could never take it off. I would always be Eddie Cantor, the black-face comedian, but if I ever tore the mask off I'd be nobody at all. The thought began to prey on me, but I could do nothing about it. For the time being, blackface was helping me to success and I rubbed on the burnt cork thicker than ever.

"Cantor and Lee" opened at the Star Theater on 107th Street and Lexington Avenue in August, 1914, and went over from the first. We toured the circuits for two years, getting three hundred dollars a week for our act, and after agent's commission, railroad fare, tips, and laundry were deducted, we had a hundred and fifteen dollars apiece.

The gags of this period show an advance in popular comedy over the days of Walter Kelly, the Virginia judge. I was no longer satisfied with picking up jokes and retelling them. I strove after originality and most of the material in our act was my own. Instead of copying from others I was getting to the point where they copied from me. This is an instance.

In one part of the act I would mention my father and roll my eyes skyward. "My poor father is gone," I sighed. Lee took off his hat and bowed his head in reverence. "With good behavior," I continued, solemnly, "he ought to be out in 1921. After all, no matter how much the boss likes you, you can't work in a bank and bring home samples!" This line was afterward used by a dozen comedians.

I also had the honor of elevating "eczema" to the rank of a vaudeville joke. I told Lee, "I'd go to war for my mother country, Russia—Darkest Russia—for all my relatives are there—General Walkowitch, Itzkowitch, Eczema——"

"Eczema?" he cried, surprised.

"Yeh, that's another itch."

Our patter consisted of many gags thinly strung together and grouped under general ideas, of which love was the most general.

"I caught you hugging and kissing a young girl," I said to Lee, and he replied, evasively, "Oh, that was just my aunt."

"It's good to kiss your aunt, but it's a dirty trick to play on your uncle!"

"Talking of kissing," said Lee, for no reason at all, except to furnish the lead line for the next joke, "I passed your house, old man. Next time when you make love to your wife, pull down the shade."

"When was that?"

"Last night."

"Why," I said laughing, "the joke is on you! Last night I was in Philadelphia!"

In a routine of this kind I attempted to embody types of gags that would appeal to every element in the audience. Sometimes a mere play on words would get a laugh like, "Your neck reminds me of a typewriter—Underwood."

The ideal joke, however, is usually the one built on actual experience, no matter how remotely. I was stopping at the Sherman Hotel in Chicago and couldn't sleep. A crowd was playing poker next door and they must have used horseshoes for chips. I knocked at the wall to quiet them, but they ignored me. I knocked again and again, and finally one of them answered me, shouting, "Hey! It's a hell of a time at night to be hanging pictures!"

We introduced a novel bit of clowning with our act which was much imitated afterward. Lee would sing a soulful ballad that I interrupted with utterly irrelevant and nonsensical remarks. After a heart-rending line of melody like, *"You dragged and dragged me down until the soul within me died,"* I asked him, "If there were any hens around a lunatic asylum would they lay cracked eggs?" He cast me a look of scorn and wailed on, *"You made me what I am today. I hope you're satisfied!"*

"I know where you got that collar," I replied.

"Where?" he started.

"Around your neck."

He loathed me for this and burst with a torrent of

feeling into the crescendo, "*And though you're not true, may God bless you!—That's the curse of an a-a-aching hea-hea-heart!*" It was a pity to see a bald man sweat like that. "I know a great thing to keep your hair in," I suggested.

"What's that?"

"A cigar box."

It was strictly a nut act. If Lee's father was an engineer who made engines, that was nothing, because my father was a commuter and made two trains a day.

With this act I introduced the hit song, "Down in Bom-Bom-Bay," a lively pioneer of the jazz age which swept across the continent from saxophone to saxophone. I also made my début as a poet and rendered a dramatic recitation of an ode I had written to the electric light. For the sake of its beautiful imagery and note of pathos at the end, I reproduce it in full, including the title:

    ODE TO THE ELECTRIC LIGHT.
Oh, you wonderful electric light,
    Light that shines so bright,
When the day is over
    We turn to you at night.
A great man has invented you,
    Edison is his name;
Now you're doing the world a lot of good
    With your magic flame.
For days and days I could sing your praise,
    My love for you isn't sham;
But when I'm sitting in the parlor with my girl —
    Pooh! You're not worth a damn!

MY LIFE IS IN YOUR HANDS

During these years my wife and I lived up in the Bronx. We had sublet a single room in her sister's flat. Early privation and the insecurity of my profession taught us to save and prepare for any emergency. Our one dream was to have a little home of our own, and with that in view we set aside thirty to fifty dollars each week until we could see the foundation and one of the walls beginning to rise. In the meantime, on March 31, 1915, our first child was born. We called it Marjorie because it was a girl.

The need for a home became more imperative, but rather than spend our slim savings on a temporary apartment, we resolved to stay where we were and fight it through to a bigger and better goal. I continued with Lee for ten months after Marjorie was born, then something unexpected happened.

Earl Carroll, who had written his first musical show, "So Long, Letty" was at this time working on a new one, entitled "Canary Cottage," which Oliver Morosco was going to produce. Carroll had seen me with Lee and told Morosco, "This fellow ought to be good for our show. He sings songs like nobody's business and covers that stage like liquid fire."

Morosco wanted to engage us as a team, provided we would come to California, where the play was to be produced. But Al Lee refused to retreat to the sticks. He had set his heart on capturing Broadway and didn't believe in Columbus's idea of a roundabout route. Our paths parted. He stayed East and I traveled West. The new job would yield me one hundred and seventy-five dollars a week, with no commissions or side expenses, which was sixty dollars more than I was making with Lee. Besides, it would be my first entrance into musical comedy.

So I went to the land of grapefruit and joined the inmates of "Canary Cottage." The star of this piece was Trixie Friganza, assisted by the able Charles Ruggles and Herbert Corthell. It was a formidable trio with wide and established reputations. I had a minor rôle that was literally tacked on to the book, smuggling me into the cast chiefly for a song-and-dance specialty. It was the small part of a colored chauffeur, and, as is not unnatural, the star of the show tried to make it smaller.

During rehearsals I'd suggest funny lines for myself that I had stayed up the night before to work out, and both Morosco and Carroll agreed they were funny, but the next day they would be thrown out. Instead of expanding, my part was steadily dwindling, and on the race of opening night I could already see myself among the also-rans. By a lucky chance, however, I met Raymond Griffith, who visited some of our rehearsals, and we became fast friends. He took such a kindly, big-brother attitude toward me that gradually I confided my fears to him. It was the same Raymond Griffith who had left the stage when he lost his voice and was obliged on that account to enter the movies, where he made a sensational career for himself. But at close range he could still talk in a hoarse whisper and talk horse sense.

"Looka here, my boy," he said, "don't let Trixie

Friganza worry you. Write down whatever you think is funny, but don't do it at rehearsals. Let nobody suspect what you've got up your sleeve. But on opening night in Los Angeles, spill it!"

"Maybe I ought to talk to Morosco," I suggested.

"If you do," said Griffith, huskily, "he'll spin you out on your ear and you'll find your heels sticking out of an ash-can in the back alley. After all, Friganza is a big star and you're only a punk! He's staking his dough on her, and if she says thumbs down, you're down, and out, too!"

I was a faithful pupil. I betrayed nothing. When we opened at San Diego for three days to try out the show, I was just fair. I had a few sawed-off bits to do, and two songs, "I'll Marry No Explorer" and "It Ruined Mark Anthony." The songs went well, but the dialogue barely toddled along.

But on the opening night in Los Angeles I sprang the surprise. I had fifteen entrances and exits in the show, and each one clicked with a clang. When I came on to dust the furniture I also dusted the fruit bowl and the fruit, and, taking up three oranges, I did my juggling act from the Bedini and Arthur days. On another exit I worked in my ventriloquist bit that I had developed while with Gus Edwards. A third time, as Trixie Friganza, who was all dressed in white and weighed about two hundred and forty pounds, left the stage, I exclaimed, looking after her: "My God! A milk wagon!" The plan was to make my absence from the stage felt and to win a hand if possible at every exit. I had prepared a number of new extra choruses for my songs, and each went better than the previous one. In the limited domain of "Canary Cottage" I had made a rash but successful *coup d'état*. The singing colored chauffeur was the hit of the night.

After the performance, Oliver Morosco came backstage and visited each dressing-room to congratulate the actors, but he did not come to mine. I was heartbroken, despondent, and realized that my nerve had probably been my undoing. But that night Morosco came to my room in the hotel. "Eddie," he said, "stay one year with me and I'll make a big star out of you. My boy, you're the apostle of pep!"

A week later I received word that another child was born to me. I had planned to call him Michael, after my father. But I compromised on Natalie when I learned it was a girl. Charles Ruggles observed, "I guess you're disappointed it wasn't a boy." "With a fellow like me," I told him, "I'm lucky it wasn't a rabbit."

I stayed on for five more months with "Canary Cottage." Natalie had joined us April 27, 1916. It was now September and I had not yet seen her. I was growing more and more homesick and kept up a steady stream of letters and wires to my wife and Max Hart to get me back to New York if I had to be kidnapped.

Finally my wife, her sister, and Max Hart worked out a plan among themselves. I was sent an alarming wire saying that Ida was in a grave condition. I went to Morosco, showed him the telegram, and wept bitterly upon his shoulder. I was giving up a good job, a fast-growing reputation, only to be near my family once more. He wept with me and let me go.

I was packing my trunk when a message arrived from Hart. "This is your big chance," he telegraphed. "Ziegfeld has booked you for twenty weeks on the Amsterdam Roof in the Midnight Frolics." A season with Ziegfeld! My heart beat a loud tattoo of triumph. The most undreamed-of good fortune had suddenly fallen like manna into my lap. I flew on wings of new hope across the country. Could it be possible? Twenty weeks—a season —signed in advance!

Only after I arrived in New York did I learn that Ziegfeld hadn't signed me at all. He had only agreed to give me a single night's trial and on that trial depended whether he would engage me or not. He bound himself to nothing. And I staked everything on one night.

Chapter XII

WHEN I met Max Hart he was shrewd enough not to tell me beforehand how much depended on my first-night showing. He let me ease along on the assurance of a twenty-week job. Had I suspected the odds I was facing I might not have been able to overcome my nervousness. Instead, I met Ziegfeld with an amazing air of confidence. He wanted to see me rehearse my act, but I startled him with the assertion that I never rehearse.

"What do you do?" he inquired, skeptically, with his characteristic nasal twang.

"Oh, I'm marvelous!" I replied.

"How do you know?"

"Why, Mr. Ziegfeld, I wouldn't lie to you!"

He probably decided right there and then: "This fellow is a queer duck. I'll let him on and take him off and that'll be the end of him!"

The Amsterdam Roof was a unique pleasure center, neither theater nor cabaret, but a blend of both. It was a supper club where it cost a person five dollars just to sit down and a good deal more to get up. A five-dollar cover charge in 1916 makes even our present night clubs look like cafeterias. It was an intimate, yet cold and *blasé*, crowd, composed chiefly of the Four Hundred who thought it banal to be amused and dared you to do it.

There were the Vanderbilts, the Harrimans, the Astors, and other distinguished families of little old New York. They combined with their pleasure a degree of aloofness and aristocracy that made it difficult for a comedian, and especially a new one, to catch just the right note of intimacy that would not be offensive and comedy that would not be common. But strengthened by the thought of a twenty-week guaranty, I felt like one of the partners in the place and went at the Four Hundred like the charge of the Six Hundred.

My first bit of business was to appear with a deck of cards like a sleight-of-hand artist, and gravely ask some of the guests to assist me in my act. I gave a few cards to William Randolph Hearst, a few to "Diamond Jim" Brady, and a few to Charles B. Dillingham, and instructed them to hold the cards up high so that the rest of the audience could see them clearly, and then I began to sing, "Oh, how she could yacki hicki wicki wacki woo!"

Throughout the whole number the three men faithfully held up their cards, not daring to move or lower them, for fear they should spoil my trick. Laughter gradually spread among the other guests as they began to realize that the cards had nothing whatever to do with the song or with anything else, and after I had finished a number of choruses I collected the cards from them and thanked them for their assistance. They were three of the best straight men I ever had.

My nut act scored, and for twenty-seven weeks I played in the Midnight Frolics. After the third or fourth night I discovered that my comedy did not bring the same volume or quality of laughter. The patronage of this exclusive gathering was limited and the same people came several times a week. This required a complete overhauling of my material almost every day. I would have to have something new all the time.

Here I met Will Rogers once more. He had begun to talk now. But it felt like old times to be together on the same bill, though we had risen many rungs in the climb. I noticed that every dawn after the Midnight Frolics, Will would buy the morning newspapers, read the interesting and important items of the day, and build his political and social comedy out of the news materials. Each morning he had his new act completely framed for the following night. He was a tireless worker and taught me two very valuable principles in the craft of acting. One was that a timely joke, even if it is not so funny, is better than a joke bearing no relation to the times.

I had no better evidence of the effectiveness of a timely jest than when I observed, during Wilson's administration, after his second trip to Paris, that, "Presidents may come and Presidents may go, but Wilson does both." This line was afterward illustrated with a cartoon and reprinted in a thousand daily newspapers throughout the country.

Another pet slogan of Will's was that an actor is as good as his material. He followed these thumb rules himself, always built his gags out of the daily stuff of life, and was most careful to select the finest material. With the limited audience of the Frolics very few actors lasted more than two or three weeks, for most of them had a set specialty or fixed routine, and when the novelty passed off they passed on. But Will Rogers always had something new to offer and I took the cue from him.

Finally I received my graduation diploma and went down to the Ziegfeld Follies. My salary was doubled, from two hundred to four hundred dollars a week, and my work was more than halved. On the opening night of the Follies of 1917 I introduced the song hit, "That's the kind of a baby for me," of which I never did less than ten encores. I had adopted a fast, lightning style of song delivery and the audience seemed to lay bets on what chorus I'd drop in and have to be carried out.

Two years later, the Prince of Wales attended the Follies of 1919 as a guest of the Vanderbilts and he sent word back-stage that he would like me to sing, "That's the kind of a baby for me." We didn't have a copy of the song on hand or the orchestrations, but we held up the show till they were dug out of some old trunks and I sang the song again.

While waiting for the music copies to arrive, I tried to explain the delay to the audience in a tactful way. "I've been asked not to mention the fact that a distinguished member of British royalty is with us tonight," I said, and looked toward the Prince. "But I want him to know if he leaves New York without seeing the Bronx, he'll be sorry all his life!"

The Prince leaned over to Mrs. Vanderbilt and I could hear him ask, "What are the Bronx?"

During the intermission I stood back-stage with Eddie Dowling and we plotted together. "If the Prince comes through here," I suggested, "I'll get at his throat and squeeze till he gives Palestine to the Jews; then you squeeze till he gives Ireland to the Irish." A Secret Service man planted in the wings glared menacingly at us and nipped our conspiracy in the bud. But the Prince must have heard us, because both things have happened since.

On January 31, 1917, a few months before I opened in the Follies, my grandmother died. She never had the satisfaction of knowing I had attained a measure of success. I had contributed all I could to relieve her from work in the latter years, but she still labored on by herself, a lonely, quiet woman with suppressed and inscrutable emotions. She had spent eighty-four years of hard, soul-bruising toil upon the earth, raising children, reviving their wounded spirits, fighting for them in the struggle for existence, and when she passed silently away there was no booming of cannon or military honors at her bier. But to me she is still the noblest type of soldier that ever fought for the only virtues in the world worth while—the relief of suffering and the preservation of her dear ones, without inflicting pain or discomfort on any living soul but herself.

I had taxed her love and endurance to the uttermost and was never able to repay her in the slightest way. The irrevocable tragedy of this tore a painful hollow in my heart. Recently I have made contributions in her memory to a home for the aged and have endowed a room in her memory at the Jewish Hospital of Brooklyn. There is a comfort in the thought that some equally poor and destitute soul may get the relief that was denied to her.

Ida and I and our two children still lived in the one-room annex to her sister's flat. My work was now boiled down to seven minutes. Ida would ride to the theater with me, wait while I went on the stage for a seven-minute bit, and then we would go home together. In the last Follies, of 1927, the situation was reversed. I was off the stage about seven minutes, and if I could play an instrument, Ziegfeld would have had me in the overture. As I told Jessel, "Drop around to the Amsterdam Theater whenever you like; I'm always on."

With my début in the Follies things began to change. After my number and sketch with Bert Williams, I was a free agent and took on assignments in the most varied social circles of the city. One night I would entertain at the Vanderbilt home, and the next night at a Bronx lodge dinner. Within the span of four hours I would play at Henry Rea's palatial home in Southampton and cover an East Side wedding in Beethoven Hall. It was excellent drill in impromptu performance and swift adaptation to surroundings.

Earning four hundred dollars a week plus side income felt rather good. We hadn't enough yet for our own home, but we no longer cared. We grew prodigal with prosperity. I bought a car, hired a chauffeur, and motored down to the stage entrance in style. My sister-in-law lost a tenant and we settled in our own flat. There was, of course, the first meal my wife cooked—horse's hip on toast—and the tears and the tragedy that followed her disappointment and my indigestion. Right then and there I resolved that I would have to earn enough to pay for a cook. It would save Ida's face and save my life. Things were breaking in a grand manner. I was beginning to live the life of a successful New Yorker; a car, a chauffeur, a cook in the near future, and money steadily pouring from the tap.

On the stage, things were getting better all the time. I was playing in a sketch with Bert Williams and my association with him was a joy and an education, for Bert was not only a great actor, but a great and liberal teacher. He was the whitest black man I ever knew and one of the finest artists the musical comedy stage has ever had. When high salaries were low Bert got a thousand dollars a week. He was the grand old man of minstrelsy, and on his European tours he appeared before all the royal rulers.

He had a unique way of rendering songs, injecting his talk between rests and catching up with the melodic phrase after he had let it get a head start. His knack for rhythmic timing was inherent and has never been excelled. We were sonny and papsy on the stage and off.

In our sketch he played a porter of the Grand Central Station who had collected enough tips to send his son to a first-rate university, and expected the stalwart youth to return with football honors and at least the weight-throwing championship. After these fond expectations I entered, slight and effeminate, with white-rimmed glasses and mincing step.

MY LIFE IS IN YOUR HANDS

"Daddy!" I cried in a girlish treble, and Bert said, glumly, "Uh-uh! . . . So you been to college!" And he would look me over with a dismal air. But I replied, airily, "Look, daddy, I carry matches!"

At this, the tough old porter fidgeted his fingers nervously into a fist the size of a brick, but I started with a shrill cry of warning, "Remember, daddy, I have a temper!"

Bert growled, "I'll show you where you got it from!"

The last line of the skit represented the perpetuation of the species. The old porter turned to his college-bred son and, putting his porter's hat on the latter's head, he thundered: "Pick up them bags! This is my graduation and your commencement!"

Bert Williams was not only a great comic, but extremely human and possessed of fine sensibilities. It happened in St. Louis that he walked up to a bar and asked for gin. The bartender, reluctant to serve a negro, said, "I'll give you gin, but it's fifty dollars a glass." Bert Williams quietly took out his bill-fold and produced a five-hundred-dollar bill. "Give me ten of them," he said.

Pop Rosenbaum, who had been the manager of the Follies troupe for years, came in at that moment and cried, "Hello, Bert!" The bartender, who knew Pop, now recognized Bert Williams and grew flustered. "I'm awful sorry," he stammered, "but those are my orders—not to refuse, but to make the price prohibitive." Bert asked the bartender to join him in a drink and they became good friends.

On another occasion, Will Rogers, W. C. Fields, Bert Williams, and I, while playing in Buffalo, were invited for supper, after the show, to the home of Jack "Twin" Sullivan, one of the old-time fist-swinging champions. I didn't know that I had been selected by the host and my white friends as the butt of the evening for a practical joke, but I soon noticed that something was wrong.

We were starved and clamored for food, but the first dish set before me was pork chops, which for me was taboo. Jack Sullivan asked, kindly, "Why don't you eat, Eddie?"

"Oh, I'll just have bread," I explained, watching the others enjoy themselves.

"I'm sorry," said Jack. "We'll get you something else." He brought me a nice thick sandwich, but it turned out to be ham.

"I really haven't much of an appetite," I protested, faint with hunger.

"Aw, come on! You'll have some eggs," urged Jack.

"All right."

He ordered them for me, but they appeared all covered with bacon. I was the youngest of the group and looked like a kid who was being bullied. Rogers and Fields rather enjoyed my predicament and Jack gave the trick away with a grin, followed by a loud guffaw. I felt foolish. It had ceased to be a joke. I was hungry to the point of physical pain.

Bert Williams leaned over and whispered in my ear, "Son, there's a package in my coat for you." I suspected that this was a new trap, but decided to be game. I went into the hall and found a package in the pocket of Bert's coat. It was a brown paper bag and in it, Bert, the good old soul, had brought a sirloin steak. He knew of the joke to keep me without food and had come prepared.

"They've had a laugh, now you have a steak," he said, gleefully, and went into the kitchen to broil it for me himself.

Bert Williams was king of the old-time blackface comics and in the Follies of 1919 he headed probably the greatest and most majestic minstrel spectacle of all time. A few years later, while playing with a Shubert production in Detroit, Bert passed away, and with him passed the last and greatest of the Swanee troubadours.

There was a warm, fraternal feeling among the members of the Follies in those years, and the older actors took a personal pride and pleasure in coaching and helping the younger ones along. While playing with the Follies of 1917 I would return for short engagements to the Midnight Frolics. During one of these periods Will Rogers and I played a few small sketches that we worked out together. They were mainly along the lines of light nonsense and travesty. In one bit we impersonated Dillingham and Ziegfeld, rival producers; in another, Will Rogers impersonated me, clapping his hands and dancing up and down while I impersonated him with his rope and chewing gum. We finished our act with a duet entitled, "Oh-oh-oh-oh!" that was, fortunately, not so painful as it sounds.

In return for my early treats to kosher restaurants,

Rogers now broke me in to eating at swell hotels. Things were happening fast and frivolous. But peculiarly enough, though I earned more than before, I was saving less. I had plenty of money, but it was slipping through my fingers like sand. I took stock tips and invested in cream-puff copper, a soft thing. It was so soft, all my money sank into it. I bought shares of no par value, and they were true to name. I was trying to get rich quick, and how Wall Street loves that kind!

On the other hand, the whole of Henry and Madison Streets had been informed of my phenomenal rise to wealth and station, and the whole category of jobless actors made it their business to be informed, too. Every Saturday afternoon when the pay envelope arrived, I was greeted at the stage door by a host of admiring friends eager to congratulate me, patting me and touching me for all they could. One fellow needed fare to St. Paul, Minnesota; another one had to pay back-rent or move to the park; a third one's life depended on an operation. I broke one hundred-dollar bill, then another. Before I got to the corner I was earning little more than my chauffeur. Week in, week out, this startling charity work continued, gaining in popularity and cost.

Some people who-knew-me-when, but whom I hardly knew, were in the clothing line and had to be tided over rough periods. It gave me a genuine thrill to help some old acquaintances, particularly the restaurant man who had given me my first meal after three eatless days in the park. But for the most part, I was breeding an increasing swarm of down-and-outers who had found in me good pickings, and I used to arrive in our six-room flat on 168th Street completely picked to pieces.

The vision of a home and savings, peace and security, had faded into a mad jumble of worthless paper stocks and ragged, hungry, devouring friends. I had succeeded, and yet I was nowhere. My money poured like water through a sieve and I was the sieve.

We were four now. Ida, Marjorie, Natalie and I. The tide of prosperity and reckless living was sweeping us along, with no solid footing anywhere and everything rolling pell mell downstream. While playing in Chicago I got a sudden attack of pleurisy. A doctor offered to pierce my chest with a long needle, but I declined the offer. My chest felt as if a thousand needles were piercing it already, so why add another?

I was confined to bed for many weeks before I could return to New York. My condition was seriously weakened and doctors ordered a protracted rest. I had to quit the show. It seemed as if my whole career had suddenly been cut off. I was a sick man, out of a job, my investments wiped out, no savings left, and all I had done and dreamt and hoped for took on the form of cheaply gilded shares with the mocking words across them, "No Par Value."

Chapter XIII

MY PHYSICAL condition was bad, but my financial condition was worse. My oils and coppers had turned to muddy waters and I had lost eleven thousand dollars —all I had. I lay on my back with a sharp pain in the chest, and don't remember whether it was my pleurisy or investments that hurt more.

While convalescing, I began to make resolutions. I would regulate my life according to a system. I'd save all my future earnings in a bread-box and at dead of night I'd hide it under planks in the floor. Then let the brokers try and get it! On pay day, when the borrowers gathered in convention at the stage door, I would hobble out in disguise with a beard and a crutch, and once I got past them I'd run for my life. But something happened unexpectedly and it changed all these elaborate plans.

One day I got a telephone call from my old friend, Dan Lipsky. He was now working as a stenographer at the Manufacturers Trust Company and had something important to tell me. While I traveled with the Follies, Dan and I had often corresponded, but since each of us had married we had seen little of one another, and I wondered what he would have to say. I remembered him from the earliest days with a pencil and pad, calculating his way through life.

When he quit being my acting partner at fifty cents a performance be became an office boy at six dollars a week. Like the loyal and industrious employe that he was, he held the job for two years and three months before he discovered that stenographers got better pay. Once he discovered this, he promptly bought a Pitman shorthand book and began to study. He made a wager for one dollar with his mother that he would know shorthand in a month. The book had a hundred and fifty pages, so he divided it by thirty days and methodically covered five pages a night. In one month's time he was a stenographer, won the dollar, and got a raise to eight dollars a week, working for a human-hair concern. He became expert at dictation, taking the usual business letters that read in the main, "Dear Sir: Your inquiry to hand and beg to state that we have a special new wig for Sundays to match your spats." Or, "Dear Madam: Under separate cover we shipped you this day three light-brown switches, a half dozen rats, and eight curls guaranteed not to shrink, fade, or unwind in the wash." But this romantic industry was ruined by hair-cuts and Dan Lipsky was out of a job.

He took a city examination in stenography and ranked third out of thirty thousand Pitmanites, getting a position in the Bureau of Licenses. A few years later he became confidential secretary to Edward Riegelmann, then Borough President of Brooklyn. During all this time he was making mental notes as well, and saw his opportunity when the Victory Celebration Committee was appointed to receive the home-coming heroes of the World War. Nathan S. Jonas, a figure of growing prominence in Brooklyn public and commercial life, was chairman of this committee and Dan spent restless nights hatching plans how he could get near the mighty Mr. Jonas and be associated with him in this work.

In the meantime he had married my cousin Anne, when he earned seventy-five dollars a month, and they immediately began to save a dollar a week, having their first fifty dollars at the end of the first year. As Dan is to me a remarkable study in thrift and self-management, I give his career in detail as an object lesson to the other ten million office boys, stenographers, and small wage earners, that they may realize what a lesson it was to me. For when I earned four hundred dollars a week and barely managed to make ends meet, Dan already had comfortable savings and wise investments on something like one-tenth of my salary.

After a good deal of discouragement and difficulty, Dan managed to get the job as executive secretary to the reception committee. Nathan S. Jonas commented favorably on his work and Dan already had visions of entering the banker's huge financial organization. But when the confusion and enthusiasm of the reception were over and the committee's work was through, so was Dan; and one day he found himself out in the chilly atmosphere with no job, and no alternative but to return to the borough president's office and hang his hat a peg lower.

Instead, he wrote Mr. Jonas a letter and won a hearing. Mr. Jonas was very kind but brief, and regretted that he could see no opening in the bank for Dan. This was the big moment. Some one else might have shrunk from view, like cheap flannels in a rain, but Dan didn't.

He remembered our acting days together, and put over one of the most dramatic bits of his career. He talked so fast, so long, and so well that Nathan S. Jonas, who had once been an insurance agent himself, was sold on a Lipsky policy and agreed to invest a small premium on the young man's chances.

Dan was ostensibly hired as a stenographer, but never got any dictation. Jonas already had more stenographers than he could possibly dictate to, and Dan spent his time reading all the magazines and sitting on all the chairs. He suspected that unless he got work quick he'd get the works quicker, and asked for permission to employ himself in his own way. "Oh yes, you're the stenographer I hired," said Jonas, reminiscently. "Well, go ahead. Make yourself useful."

This was Dan's passport. He started on a tour of the organization, spending several weeks in each department, familiarizing himself thoroughly with the work from every angle. A few months later he returned to Mr. Jonas and said, "I believe I am now thoroughly familiar with the business and system of the Manufacturers Trust Company." The rest happened strictly according to the books. Mr. Jonas made him his private secretary, and today Dan is one of the vice-presidents and important executives of the Manufacturers Trust Company—proving again that Horatio Alger did not live in vain.

But when Dan came to see me he was still a stenographer, earning about fifty dollars a week. He offered to handle my finances and regulate my affairs. I showed him

MY LIFE IS IN YOUR HANDS

my copper and oil shares and he said they were wonderful works of art. Then I told him of all the loans I had made to friends who had wept on my shoulder as I left the theater.

"What collateral did they give you?" he inquired.

"Collateral?" I got scared. "Oh, they couldn't stick me with that stuff!" I assured him. "I'll admit I fell for tears and handshakes, but do I look as if I'd fall for collateral?"

Dan took a deep breath. "Let's proceed," he said.

"Luckily," I told him, "I'm not in debt."

"Then we'll put you in debt."

"What? You'll put me in debt?"

I thought that was his way of being funny, but he spoke quite gravely, "That's the only solution for a fellow like you. You've got to be in debt!"

"Say, that kind of financial advice I can give myself!"

But Dan sat unmoved and continued in his dry, quiet tone, "You owe the Manufacturers Trust Company ten thousand dollars."

I started suspiciously, "Since when?"

"And you've got to pay it off at the rate of two hundred and fifty dollars a week out of your four-hundred-dollars salary."

"Just a minute! What kind of a game is this? I owe nobody anything."

"Well, I'll take you down to see Mr. Jonas and you'll find out." I began to get worried. This game of financing didn't look very healthy to me. He hadn't even promised to make me a millionaire in six months. On the contrary, I was in debt ten thousand dollars just for talking to him!

"Listen, Dan," I said, trying to keep calm, "I'd be pleased to meet Mr. Jonas, but what I really thought you'd do is to help me save enough to buy a house."

"Yes," assented Ida, who had joined the conference, "that's been the dream of our lives—to have our own home."

"If you do what I tell you," said Dan, "you'll have your own home within two years. What day is today?" And he looked at his watch.

"That sounds very good, but how? I owe ten thousand already, and now I'll owe for a house, too, that I haven't got."

"How much do you need to live on?" asked Dan.

Ida and I began to track down our expenses. It seemed that all we did was to send things to the laundry, and still that didn't account for the whole four hundred. Gradually, by consenting to sell the car, and the chauffeur along with it, and sticking as closely as possible to eating, drinking, and sleeping, we got the budget down to a hundred and fifty a week.

"That's fine," observed Dan. "You'll get a hundred and fifty dollars a week and not a penny more. The rest you pay on your debt."

"Then how can we save for the house?"

"You don't have to save for it. It comes by itself."

"Gee! This is worse than cream-puff copper!" I thought to myself.

"And furthermore," said Dan, "you get Ziegfeld to pay you by check instead of cash, and I'll come every Saturday and grab the check before the line forms at the stage door."

"And for all these services of putting me in debt and grabbing my check and getting me a house that'll come by itself, how much do I owe you?"

"Ten dollars a week."

"That's the only reasonable part about the whole arrangement. It's too reasonable!" I was inclined to suspect that Dan, in his eagerness, was trying to practice his new-found banking knowledge on me and didn't know how. Still, his authoritative business manner impressed me and I agreed to try. I met Nathan S. Jonas, a man of natural dignity, whose strong, intelligent face was permeated with a warmth of good-nature that made him at once imposing and intensely human. He spoke in a genial, fatherly way that immediately spoiled my pet notion of a banker as I had pictured him. He didn't smoke fat cigars or wear a big chain across his abdomen to prevent him from skidding, nor did he press a lot of buttons so that I should fall through a trap-door after he had my money. In fact, I didn't owe him a thing yet. But I was going to. Oh yes, I was going to!

He agreed with Dan that I should buy ten thousand dollars' worth of Victory Bonds and that the Manufacturers Trust Company would finance the purchase with the understanding that I owed them the money and would pay it off in forty weeks at the rate of two hundred and fifty dollars a week. "The only way you can save," said Mr. Jonas, kindly, "is to be compelled to save. So we're putting you in debt to yourself. You owe yourself two hundred and fifty dollars a week that must be paid."

It was my first real transaction, wise, safe, profitable. I returned to the Follies and every pay day Lipsky arrived at the New Amsterdam Theatre to take the check. It was a real thrill to me the first week when I saw one hundred and fifty dollars come for the household and two hundred and fifty go to the United States Government for Victory Bonds. In forty weeks I owned ten thousand dollars that were working for me night and day in the service of the richest and strongest government on earth. In the meantime I had been raised to six hundred dollars a week, and Dan pointed out that I should buy as many shares as possible of the Manufacturers Trust Company stock. They were at that time a hundred and seventy-two dollars a share. Besides many rights that accrued to me, they are today more than nine hundred dollars a share and proved to be the bulwark of the modest little fortune that I gathered in less than ten years. Today I am one of the large stockholders in the Manufacturers Trust Company.

Dan Lipsky, with his earnings, which at the time were not more than sixty dollars a week, made similar investments to mine on a proportionately smaller scale; and I am convinced that anyone, no matter how modest his income, providing it is regular and budgeted, can and should set aside a sum for sane and sound investment as I did. Regardless of what bank or trust company he may go to, providing it is a legitimate institution of finance of established reputation, he will always receive the most expert advice, and instead of shaky and shady investments, his money will always be safe and the bulwark of his future secured.

A sense of growing security inspired me. I was building my house upon a rock rather than public whim. For the fortunes of my career might vary and the day might come when I'd walk out on the stage and the audience would say, "Cantor, you're through. Go home." And I'd answer, "O.K. We owe each other nothing." I'd go home, sit in the parlor, and read my clippings, not from newspapers, but from bonds.

As far as I could I've influenced many of my actor friends to do as I did. For a time I made Jessel bring me his weekly earnings and follow me. Many an actor, who was suddenly enmeshed in difficulties through unwise investments or problems of necessity, and who failed to receive attention or proper consideration from his bank, has come to me and I've had his case carefully ironed out at the Manufacturers Trust Company, of whose Advisory Board I am now a member. The outstanding policy of my bank is this paramount stress on the human equation and the effort to study individual cases. Hard and fast rules have limited finance so that only the initiated few can profit by its aid. But by solving each individual problem and giving every person the benefit of the highest banking knowledge, money which has been the source of so much evil can be turned to the supreme service of good.

It was in the Follies of 1918 that my new business learning came to the aid of our great melody team, Van and Schenck. I did a little banking all my own and banked mostly on my nerve. We were playing in Chicago at the time and Gus Van came into my dressing-room looking worn and wrung out with cares.

"I invested twenty-five hundred in the market," he said, "and I went clean. My wife don't know and I must get the dough back. Think fast, Banjo Eyes!"

The call boy's voice rang like a bugle through the hallway, "Eddie Cantor, specialty!" and I had to hurry down to the stage.

"I've got an idea, Gus!" I exclaimed, and ran down for my cue.

During my specialty I used a line about Green River lime juice drink. I was paid a hundred dollars a week for fifteen weeks to mention this name, and usually worked it in with a gag. I'd pull out a wire which I said had just come from Ziegfeld. "He's heard that I'm advertising Green River lime juice drink," I told the audience, "and warns me not to use the name Green River lime juice drink in the show. So why antagonize him? I won't mention the Green River lime juice drink."

After my act, I met Van and Schenck and told them of my plan. The next day we would go to the Ostenreider Advertising Company, which was paying me a

MY LIFE IS IN YOUR HANDS

hundred dollars a week, and suggest a new idea to them. Van and I would write a song about their marvelous beverage and the harmony masters themselves would sing it. It would probably become a popular hit and be sung in every home. It was understood that Van, Schenck, and I split the money for the masterpiece three ways.

We went down to the advertisers with the song all written. It was entitled "Green River" and was simply awful. The refrain ran like this:

> For a drink that's fine without a kick,
>   Try Green River,
> It's the only soft drink you should pick.
>   Try Green River!

I sang it to the Ostenreider outfit for all I was worth and Van and Schenck harmonized with all they had. "Can't you see, gentlemen?" I added to the force of the melody. "You'll give out copies. It'll sweep the country!"

"We'll give you five thousand dollars for it," agreed the Ostenreiders.

"Ten thousand or nothing!" I cried, walking out in disgust.

As we reached the hall Van grabbed me by the neck. "I'll cripple you!" he growled. "Now we'll get nothing."

The next day I received a call from the firm. "The best we can do is seventy-five hundred."

"Good enough!" I said. Gus got his twenty-five hundred, Schenck got his, and I got mine. I don't know what they did with theirs, although I have a faint inkling.

MY LIFE IS IN YOUR HANDS

Throughout the season of the Follies there was a famous dice game, a continuous one that lasted from the beginning to the end of the run of the show, and in it were practically all the high lights of the bill.

I was steadily earning more money, and even my father-in-law was beginning to reconcile himself to my occupation, though he always regretted the gents' furnishing store I could have owned. Still, I knew that one day he would capitulate, and he did. It was while he introduced me to an old friend of his that he said, in awed tones: "I want you shall meet my son-in-law, Eddie Cantor. He makes eight hundred dollars a week." But he felt I was not a real business man. He once saw Harland Dixon in our show and asked me, "What does he get?"

"About seven hundred a week."

"What? For a little dancing? You see, if you was a real business man, you'd take that up and make the seven hundred on the side!"

As money came in, I found myself in constant debt, thanks to Lipsky, who bought up large blocks of stock and made me pay them off with earnings that would otherwise have frittered away in silly extravagances. We started a thrift account for each of the children. There were three now. On the night of June 10, 1919, when the Follies opened in Atlantic City, my third child was born. After two girls you would naturally expect a third girl, and that's what it was. Edna arrived when I was on the road, but a week later, on my return, I was properly introduced to her.

MY LIFE IS IN YOUR HANDS

Ever since the day of her birth she and her two sisters have had thrift accounts, putting aside five dollars a week for each. Their savings are invested in bonds, so that they will all have substantial sums when they grow up. I also increased my insurance as my family and income grew.

In 1920, returning from the road, I drove up to 631 East 168th Street, Bronx, where we had been living all this time, and found the flat to let. No one was at home. I called up Dan, surprised and a little alarmed. I could not understand what had happened. Dan tried to reassure me: "It's nothing, Eddie. Ida needed a little rest and went with the children to a place in Mount Vernon." He promised to join me at once.

I had a vague idea about what it might be. "Maybe this time," I thought, "it will be a boy." We drove up to Mount Vernon, and the peaceful suburban atmosphere with rich, embracing trees and lawns of green, aroused a dreamy, gentle feeling in me. I recalled the days at Surprise Lake Camp when I first met nature face to face. We stopped before a beautiful country home with white façades and heaving bosoms of foliage.

"What a lovely place this is!" I exclaimed. I was tired from the long journey east and this seemed the ideal spot to be united with Ida and the children once more.

"This is your home," said Dan.

"You mean—" I was thrilled. Tears came to my eyes.

"The two years are up and you've got what you want."

"You mean it's all mine? My home? My place?"

"Here's the deed to the property. Ida and I picked it. We thought we'd surprise you. Mr. Jonas himself sent up an appraiser from the bank to see that we were getting the right value for our money. And now it's yours. You've earned it."

Chapter XIV

IN THE spring of 1907, a handsome man in the middle thirties, with a rather prominent nose, got off an ocean liner in New York Harbor, and stepped on Manhattan soil flat broke. Three years before he had run a vaudeville show in partnership with Joe Weber at the famous old Weber and Fields' Music Hall on Twenty-ninth Street and Broadway. But he suddenly grew tired of the show business and resolved to quit it for good. He sold his share of the partnership for solid cash, went to Europe, and loafed across the continent for three years until he blew in every dollar he had, and now he was back again, walking up Broadway and wondering how he could get into the show business once more.

For fifteen years he had dabbled in production, and as many times his fortunes had zigzagged up and down. His first show, a musical comedy called "The Red Feather," opened on the night the Lyric Theatre opened in 1892, the year of the World's Fair. It was a success. But he couldn't hold money. He liked the gesture of it. He drifted into many musical and vaudeville enterprises and even produced farces such as "Papa's Wife" and "The Parlor Match." But he never tried to capitalize his successes or organize his finances. He was essentially a brave, bold adventurer of the theater who was only on his mettle when he was on his uppers.

He needed plenty of mettle now. Few remembered him and less cared to, as he strolled penniless and hopeful along the bright White Way. Spring puffed its warm breezes in his face, the promise of a hot, arid summer, the worst possible time of the year to launch a show. Nevertheless, he went up to see Mr. A. L. Erlanger, who was already then the little Napoleon of the theatrical world.

He had a soft, persuasive manner combined with the gambler's cool confidence, and even the cautious Mr. Erlanger was inclined to take a chance. He agreed to back him in the production of a small summer show, not exactly vaudeville, nor yet musical comedy, but something different and entirely new in this country—a revue. It would be a modest experiment for a short summer run, and if it served no other purpose, it would at least keep one of the Erlanger theaters open during the torrid months.

Most of the acts were borrowed from burlesque, but there was a novel and refreshing touch of beauty to the show that distinguished it at once and made it an instantaneous success. It was the first revue in America and the first time that pretty, coquettish girls walked off the stage into the audience. It could have played longer, but the theater had already been booked for another show and the revue traveled to Baltimore and Washington, where it played to capacity houses. This was the first Ziegfeld Follies. It cost thirteen thousand eight hundred dollars for costumes and scenery, and thirty-eight hundred dollars a week in salaries and running expenses. One of the last Ziegfeld Follies cost two hundred and seventy thousand

MY LIFE IS IN YOUR HANDS

dollars to produce and thirty thousand dollars a week to run.

In the past twenty years, the Ziegfeld Follies have become an American institution of international renown. It is the ultimate ideal of every young American beauty, not barring the movies. The Erlanger Circuit that the first Follies of 1907 traveled is the same circuit it has traveled for twenty years, expanding in scope with the Erlanger interests. During that period, many hundreds of girls from all parts of America have been glorified through the Follies' ranks and attained rich husbands or fame on the stage and screen. Lillian Lorraine, Marion Davies, Justine Johnstone started their careers in the chorus of the Follies. The Follies programs of 1917, '18 and '19, listing the girls of the chorus, almost read like an alphabetical arrangement of the headliners of today.

But more impressive even than the famous beauties of the Follies was its cast of stars, staggering in magnitude when measured by the salaries they now command. In the Follies of 1917, the first that I joined, there were Bert Williams, Fannie Brice, Will Rogers, W. C. Fields, Walter Catlett, and Eddie Cantor. Today such a cast would cost twenty-five thousand dollars a week and, counting the celebrities in the chorus, the salary list would be ten thousand dollars more than the gross receipts.

The greatest musical comedy cast ever assembled in a single show, I believe, was in the Follies of 1919. In that production, Ziegfeld had Eddie Dowling, Bert Williams, Ann Pennington, Marilyn Miller, Van and Schenck,

George LeMaire, Ray and Johnny Dooley, John Steele, Mary Hay and Eddie Cantor. The salary for this cast today would just equal every dollar the box office could take in for the week, not counting the chorus, musicians, or running costs. I reproduce the program of the 1919 Follies as an interesting and unexpected development of the little summer show that Flo Ziegfeld innocently started back in 1907 to tide over hot weather.

When Will Rogers first went with Ziegfeld he got a hundred and twenty-five dollars a week for the season. In his last appearance with the Follies, Will received thirty-five hundred a week for fifty-two weeks in the year. During his third season with Ziegfeld, Will was earning only three hundred and fifty a week, and he came to Flo, saying, "When I left Oklahoma I promised my wife and children that some day I'd make four hundred a week, and if I could ever make that the dream of my life would be fulfilled." Ziggy promptly fulfilled his dream, but the next year Will asked for six hundred.

"What's the idea?" said Flo. "I thought your wife and children were perfectly satisfied with four hundred a week."

"They are," replied Will. "But since then I've gotten another child and he's kicking."

In those days Ziegfeld concentrated his whole year exclusively on the Follies and built it slowly, consummately. He conceived it, directed it, and worked upon it with a staff of able lieutenants until it was architecturally perfect. Gene Buck wrote the lyrics, Dave Stamper composed the tunes, Ned Wayburn staged the dances, and Ziegfeld introduced Urban with a new conception of scenic art. Urban has since designed the new Ziegfeld Theatre.

When I say that the Follies of 1919 was the greatest of its kind, I am not judging merely by box-office receipts. For in that respect the Follies of 1921 was unique. It ran for two seasons in New York. But the 1919 show was one of those ideal organizations of entertainment that bespoke the last word in stage generalship and the most perfect harmony of actors and material. Everyone in the cast clicked. Each specialty, no matter what its character, was performed by the acknowledged master of that field.

First of all, there were four big song hits where two would have been ample. "Tulip Time" and "Mandy" by Buck and Stamper; "A Pretty Girl Is Like a Melody" by Irving Berlin; and "My Baby's Arms" by McCarthy and Tierney, who afterward wrote the music and lyrics for "Kid Boots" and "Rio Rita." Eddie Dowling, Ray and Johnny Dooley, played the Bullfight Scene. John Steele and Delysle Alda sang the leading sentimental numbers. Bert Williams and George LeMaire, the best heavy straight in the business, played the Sharp-Shooting Scene. Marilyn Miller, Ann Pennington, and Mary Hay, who later married Richard Barthelmess, held up the dancing end of the show. I played the Osteopath Scene with LeMaire, and also introduced the popular song, "You'd Be Surprised." Then we had Van and Schenck for melody rhythms. If you were a hit in a show like that you were a hit.

I must have made an impression on at least one person, for nine years later he not only remembered the song I sang, but the special slurs and peculiar inflections I had used in its delivery. I met him in a rather embarrassing moment. He was a motorcycle cop and interrupted me at Queens Plaza just as I was about to establish a new record with my car for the trip from Great Neck to New York.

"Get over!" He waved me sullenly to one side and dismounted. "Gimme your license!" I took my license out of a pocket in the car and he read it with a frown. Then he looked up at me suspiciously.

"Are you Eddie Cantor?"

I don't know why I hesitated. At best I am no Adolphe Menjou, but with a two days' growth of stubble and my coat collar turned up I pass for a genuine freight-car resident, and the feeling that I looked grimy and unkempt must have made me self-conscious.

"You got any other identification?" growled New York's finest. I took out a watch that Ziegfeld had inscribed to me. The cop's eyebrows lifted and his eyes fairly popped. He looked at my new Cadillac, then at the inlaid timepiece, then at my hairy face, and thought here was a prize catch. I was not only a speeder, but probably a robber, too. He already had visions of elevation to the detective force. But he tried a last clue.

"You say you're Eddie Cantor," he snapped. "Well, do you know a song, 'You'd Be Surprised'?"

MY LIFE IS IN YOUR HANDS

"Yeh."

"Well, sing it!"

And there in the rain, with my collar turned up and two days' growth of beard, I sang a verse and chorus with the special slurs and peculiar inflections I had used nine years ago; and the cop seemed to listen for just those touches that characterized my delivery. His eyes were screwed in an expression of stern intensity, but gradually they relaxed and a broad grin spread over his face.

"You're Eddie Cantor, all right!" he cried, patting me on the back. "Now run along and take care of yourself!"

In the Follies of 1918 I roomed with Frank Carter, who afterward married Marilyn Miller. For a long time I played as important a rôle back-stage in this romance of the wings as on the stage in blackface. Marilyn's parents strongly opposed the match, and, having had my own experience with Ida's parents, I became a willing and handy Mr. Fixit for the lovelorn couple. I arranged little tête-à-têtes for them at restaurants, slipped notes from one to the other under the nose of Marilyn's watchful parents, and the love-match went through as per schedule.

One day, while we were playing in Philadelphia, Frank Carter bought a magnificent high-powered automobile for his dancing star. He drove it himself to the theater hoping to surprise her with it. The car was struck in a collision and he was killed. For a time it seemed that poor Marilyn would not survive the shock of this tragedy. They had only recently been married and were extremely fond of each other. The grand suite Marilyn and her mother occupied, was now a lonely place with haunting memories, and Marilyn sat all day in a daze of anguish, lapsing from spasms of sobs to blank, morbid moods.

After each performance of the Follies, Van and Schenck and I would go up to her rooms in the hotel and give a special little performance for her, to lift her out of her melancholy and make her forget. Our own hearts were heavy, and we often had lumps in our throats while trying to entertain, but we clowned it through and it was a touching sight to see her smile. Marilyn was as brave a trooper as ever marched the boards, and a little while later she was twinkling gracefully across the stage again. But behind the dancing star that smiled at the audience so charmingly was the little heartbroken widow who wanted to cry.

It was in this Follies, too, that I faced a crisis of my own. I had made the resolve that old Black-face must die. In a moment of emergency I had put on his dark mask and he had helped me to success. Now the audience knew only this cork-smeared face, while I stood hidden behind it wondering what would happen if the blacking came off. I feared that in this lay the seed of a greater tragedy than any I had yet experienced, and I had made my mind up long ago to leave tragedy to the Booths and Mansfields. I was not going to be a slave to a piece of burnt cork for the rest of my acting days. For the Follies of 1918 I prepared a scene in white-face. My agent, Max Hart, asked Ziegfeld to let me try it, and he agreed, but in an evasive way.

I rehearsed my skit with Frank Carter, but on the

opening night Ziegfeld refused to let the scene go on, saying there was no room for it in the show. The fact was, he doubted my chances in white-face and feared to risk the change. But this change meant more than my job to me. It meant my future and freedom from the pale of the black label. The second night I gave him an ultimatum, "Either the scene is in or I am out—altogether." Ziegfeld reluctantly agreed to give the act a trial. This marked my first appearance on the musical-comedy stage in my own face, and, good or bad as that face might be, it was the first time that I felt revealed to the audience and in personal contact with it.

In the scene I played a ludicrous weakling applying for admission to the aviation corps, and I received a grueling physical examination at the hands of Frank Carter. He whacked and banged me, clapped me together and pulled me apart like an accordion, and did everything but twine me around a spool. It was the first physical comedy scene I ever played and turned out to be the biggest hit of the show. In the next Follies I followed it up with the Osteopath Scene, which transplanted the idea of bodily punishment to a new and more fertile locale. A scene of physical comedy has since become a standard element in my repertory of fun.

It seems that audiences love to see somebody knocked and battered about to the point of insensibility so long as they feel he isn't really getting hurt. But if they suspect the punishment has passed the point of fun, they suddenly stop laughing and even show resentment. This happened

MY LIFE IS IN YOUR HANDS

one night at a performance of "Kid Boots," when the burly doctor who mangled me in a variation of the old Osteopath Scene, did it so well that afterward I had to go to a real osteopath to be treated.

In my last Follies, ten years after the Follies of 1918, the aviation scene was new again, and we considered using it as a physical comedy skit. But by a curious freak, in trying to adapt it to the recent developments in the news, the physical punishment took the form of a mental examination, and the laugh effects I once produced by being thrown all over the stage, I now got by sitting quietly in a chair and answering questions.

I played the part of a Jewish aviator from Newark and named my plane "Mosquito—The Spirit of New Jersey." Major Brown, in charge of the flyers at Mitchell Field, said he would like to quiz me. It is interesting to observe how, by stringing our gags together from line to line, we made the quiz take the place of a physical scene.

The major scanned me contemptuously, "You don't look like an aviator!"

"You don't look like a major."

"Sit down!" he growled. "You were in the army? Did you get a commission?"

"No, a straight salary."

"Have you ever flown before?"

"I had flu during the war."

"Flown! Flown!"

But I was adamant. "Flu! Flu!"

MY LIFE IS IN YOUR HANDS

"You must say, 'I have flown.' You can't say, 'I have flew.'"

"Are you telling me? I was sick in bed with it! I ought to know what I had." The major changed the subject.

"Can you name some of the principal aviators of nineteen twenty-seven?"

"Well—Chamberlin, Levine, Ruth Elder, Levine, Commander Byrd, Levine——"

"Who else?"

"Did I mention Levine?"

The major eyed me suspiciously. "What is your name, anyway?"

"Ginsberg."

"Your first name?"

"Gregory."

"Gregory Ginsberg! Is that your right name?"

"My right name is Levey."

"Why did you change it?"

"Well, I was in the South, around the Mississippi, during the floods, and I read headlines in the papers that they were going to blow up all the *levees*."

The officer curled his lip in disdain.

"I have a few formal questions to ask you. Married?"

"No."

"Children?"

"Major!"

He ignored my shocked expression and continued:

"Where were you born?"

"In Chicago. I'll show you the scars."

"Never mind. How do you sleep?"

"Like that." I clasped my hands as a cheek-rest.

"I mean, do you sleep well? Are you disturbed at night?"

"Yes. I'm disturbed terribly."

"What disturbs you?"

"My brother Morris. I sleep with him."

"How does he sleep?"

"Like this." I put my feet in the major's lap and he shoved them off in a rage.

"How long can a man live without brains!" he exclaimed, beside himself.

"I don't know. How old are you?"

When the examination was finally completed, I was to hop off like Lindbergh, with one bottle of water and five sandwiches, but, unlike Lindbergh, I intended to eat on the way, and called off the whole flight when I discovered that all the five sandwiches were ham.

I recall this skit so minutely because in its earliest essence it was my first scene in white-face. And it must be said for Ziegfeld that despite his hesitation he had the showmanship to let me experiment. For in theatrical production precedent is not a safe guide, and the sheer spirit of gamble is often two-thirds of the victory. In this regard Ziegfeld is, without exception, the biggest sport in the business. With a wave of the hand he has often discarded a scene in the Follies that cost fifteen to twenty thousand dollars, where another producer would hesitate and sacrifice the rest of the show to preserve a dull but expensive set.

On the other hand, Flo has many peculiarities that are often bewildering and embarrassing to his actors. He has a phenomenal passion for sending wires, and I have tipped off my friends that, should Ziegfeld happen to pass away, they could sell Western Union short and become millionaires overnight. Ziggy has often stood in back of the orchestra during a rehearsal, and instead of calling out to the actors and telling them his criticism or suggestion, he would go out into the lobby and send them telegrams back-stage.

He once sent me a twelve-page wire and added, "Will write you in detail tomorrow." On one occasion at least I hit upon a temporary cure for this telegraphic flood. I received an enormous telegram from him while playing with "Kid Boots" in Chicago. He made certain suggestions, saying he believed a certain song should go out and certain lines should be changed, while certain actors were slipping up and certain scenes needed watching; and what did I think of this, and didn't I think that was better, and wasn't the other thing as good as the first? The whole was such a bewildering tangle that I knew here would begin the world's longest correspondence in telegraphy, so I simply replied, "Yes." I thought this would cap the volcano, but I promptly received another telegram twice as long as the first, saying: "What do you mean, 'Yes'? Do you mean 'Yes' you will take out the song, or 'Yes' you will put in the lines, or 'Yes' you will fix that scene, or 'Yes' you have talked to those actors?" And so on for pages. To this I answered, "No." That ended the bombardment.

But it seems there was often a subtle purpose in this onslaught of yellow messages. Toward the end of the season, as the contracts with actors began to expire, they would get the most irritating and bewildering reams of wires, scolding and criticizing them, and those who had planned to ask for a raise got worried about their jobs and were glad to sign again on the old terms. But once this method didn't work. Ziggy shot me a couple of stinging messages, and instead of blushing with shame, I flushed with anger and came back with a sudden resignation. He quickly wired me that he was only kidding me, but it was one time I couldn't see the joke. He had to tack on a thousand dollars a week extra as heart balm for the rest of the season, and then the humor of the messages dawned on me. Those were two expensive wires that cost him twenty thousand dollars.

But it is all in keeping with his flourish in the grand manner, which is not affected, but comes natural to him. He lives like a potentate, and his musical-comedy settings reflect his innermost quality of the far-flung and majestic. He has an uncanny sense of lighting effects, color combinations, costume harmonies, and scenic backgrounds. He pays the highest salaries to artists and is the greatest manager for girls that America has ever had. As far as actors are concerned, a man to Ziggy means nothing, but girls!—he has made many girls and girls have made him, and on that principle is based his chivalry, theatrical display, and success.

Chapter XV

ON THE opening night of the 1917 Follies three figures stood back-stage of the New Amsterdam Theatre, looking through the wings while waiting for their cue. One of them was a tall, lean Westerner from Claremore, Oklahoma who chewed gum with the slow, measured rhythm of eternity; the second was a man of medium height, puffy-faced, big-nosed, a juggler with sly, peepy eyes who had come out of Philadelphia; and the third was a thin, nervous chap, younger than the other two and smaller, with dancing, popping eyes and hands that moved all around him. He had arrived from the depths of New York's East Side.

They were three different types of comics who had risen from widely different schools of acting and the most diverse schools of life. The first, Will Rogers, had come upon his stage career by accident. As a youth he went down to South America to teach the gauchos to swing a lasso. When he came there he found that their ropes were too long and their motions were all twisted, but they could lasso like nobody's business. There was no one to teach, so in disgust he embarked on a cattle boat for Africa. When he landed in the dark country he met another man of the open spaces, Texas Jack, who was running a small-time rodeo show, and Will joined the company as a rope-twirler. That was Rogers' first appearance on the stage—a cowboy in Africa.

The second, W. C. Fields, had a totally different development. At the age of eleven he left his home in Philadelphia to take his first job as an actor at Plymouth Park, a little Coney Island near Morristown, Pa. His wages were five dollars a week, out of which he paid an agent's commission of a dollar and a half weekly. From there he went to play at a drinking-garden in Atlantic City for ten dollars a week and "cakes" which meant food, but it was neither cakes nor food, just beans. There was no charge for entertainment, and the proprietors of this fancy saloon did all their profiteering on five cents a beer, pretzels and Fields thrown in. His first real break came in burlesque, where he got eighteen dollars a week when he got it. At one time he was willing to settle all his back-pay claims for fifty cents to ransom his laundry. "If I had fifty cents," growled the burlesque manager, "I'd start a number two company!" This line has since become a catch-phrase in the profession.

While Bill Fields has achieved fame mainly as a juggler and comic pantomimist, many people have the mistaken idea that he never opened his mouth on the stage until four years ago, when he starred in his first big musical-comedy vehicle, "Poppy." At that time the critics united in applauding him as the man who had found his voice, and hailed Bill's larynx as if he had just had it installed. The truth is, Bill had been talking on the stage for over twenty years. He had a speaking part as far back as 1905, when he played in his first musical show, "The Ham Tree," with McIntyre and Heath. But the story of his protracted silence sounded like such good publicity that Bill never took the trouble to correct the critics.

If anything, Bill Fields talked so much on the stage that at least once his talk got him into a serious mess. He was playing at the Winter Garden in Berlin and had translated his monologue into stilted German, using old text-book words instead of colloquial idioms, so that he found himself saying such awkward things as, "I'll break your throat" and "I bit my language." What was worse, some of his innocent wise cracks became, in translation, highly blasphemous and even profane, and instead of the snickers and giggles he expected, he got hisses and boos. In France they laughed at the wrong places, and in Italy he was threatened with stilettos. After that, Bill made his European tours without words, relying solely on pantomime, but back in the States he always talked. As an actor he played the longest circuit around the world twice. It was on his first trip that he met Will Rogers in Africa.

These were two of the comedians who stood in the wings of the New Amsterdam Theatre. I was the third. It was our first night together in the Follies. We had drifted here from strange places through many hardships, and tonight we would be taking turns on the same boards, in front of the same footlights. We felt as if from the very first we had battled every inch of the way together. There was never a thought of rivalry or envy. Though each would try his hardest to excel, he hoped his colleagues would achieve the same distinction. Frank Carter, one of the handsome straight men of the show, passed us as we stood there. He must have thought we were queer, curiously contrasted figures, and he smiled. "As I live!" he exclaimed, jovially. "The Three Musketeers!"

Probably at no time in theatrical history did three comedians in the same show work so harmoniously together. In a business where a laugh to a comedian is life itself and he usually begrudges every chuckle another comic gets, the Three Musketeers of the Follies were ready to lay down their laughs for one another. Will Rogers would watch my act from the wings or W. C. Fields' skit and offer changes in the lines or situations that invariably improved the original material. We tried to do the same for him whenever possible.

One day, Will, Bill and I made a covenant among us and went further back than Dumas' musketeers for our idea of friendship. In fact, we went all the way back to Omar Khayyám, the original old soak of Persia. According to Fields, Omar had formed an alliance with two other tent-makers which provided that whatever might befall, any one of the three could always come to any one of the others and share his tent, his loaf of bread, and his jug of wine. Fields might have had an ulterior motive in telling us this story. Maybe he intended to retire on us. Nevertheless, we gave the pledge. Strangely enough, we have never needed to call on one another. To this day each of us has managed to do a fair business in his own tent.

Only once did all three of us play in a single sketch, and it was one of the worst sketches the Follies ever had. It was Ziegfeld's idea to put his three musketeers in an opening skit and start the show with a bang. It was not only a bang, but a blow-out. Fields was grotesquely made up as the director of a patent office, and many inventors and cranks forced their pet ideas upon him. Will Rogers and I were among the patentees. Each night we changed our inventions and always sprang something new on Fields, who was unprepared for the surprise. He had to keep right on edge to make sure the laugh was not on him.

As neither Will Rogers nor I had to use make-up for this scene, we would rush in from the street the last minute and patent anything we could lay our hands on. It was the first comedy scene in the show, and if Will did not arrive on time I ran on for him, too, and he often served me the same way. Only Fields had to be on hand very early every night, make up carefully, and go down with a heavy heart to his worthless patent office.

But he bided his time and turned a laugh on Rogers in which I was an unwitting accomplice. One night during the war Bill arrived in Rogers' dressing-room with a new joke he had just heard. The Germans had unloosed Big Bertha that shelled Paris at a range of eighty-five miles, but the American wits failed to be impressed. "Aw, that's nothin'," they said. "Uncle Sam's now got a gun that can shoot everybody in Berlin right from Staten Island, and all those it don't kill it takes prisoners!" Will Rogers thought it was such a funny line that he decided to work it in that night as the finish to his monologue.

Hearing this, Bill promptly came to my dressing-room. He knew my act went on ahead of Rogers' and said, "Eddie, I heard a great one today that you could use in your specialty." He told me the same joke, but didn't tell me that Rogers was planning to use it. I thought it was nice of him to give me the gag. During my specialty I put it over and it brought a big laugh. But while I was on the stage, Fields kept Rogers busy up in his room and Will suspected nothing when he went on for his cue. He did his act as usual, and then for a smashing finish he told the gag about the gun.

"Well, how did it go?" asked Fields, eagerly, as Rogers came off, looking rather sullen.

"Strange," muttered Will. "It sounded like a funny line to me, but nobody laughed except the musicians."

When I played in the Porter Scene with Bert Williams, I came on as a college youth just back from the halls of culture with two empty satchels, but one night I nearly broke my neck trying to trip lightly on to the stage with them. They were as heavy as light cannons. Fields had secretly filled the bags with telephone directories and bricks. To reciprocate this courtesy, I invited him the following week-end for a game of golf. Bill takes his golf very seriously and can play very well. I led him to believe that he was in for a hard match, and he came all primed, canceling a real game for this one. When I met him on the links I took off my coat and stood in my pyjamas and bed slippers. Bill laughed, but he didn't enjoy the game after that. He felt foolish following me around in my night-clothes for nine holes. As for me, the way I play golf, I should always wear pyjamas and sleep through the game.

Practical jokes were a part of the theater, and the comedy we started on the stage overlapped into life. No member of the show escaped being involved in some prank, and once or twice there were almost serious consequences. While we were in Atlantic City with the 1919 Follies, Irving Berlin and I stopped at the Marlborough Blenheim Hotel. Berlin got a rush message to return to New York, and he asked Harry Akst, his musical secretary, to pack his bags for him the same afternoon. I volunteered to help Harry, and took a few pictures off the wall, which I tucked into Berlin's satchels. In New York, Berlin's valet unpacked the luggage, and Irving never knew that he had taken along these strange souvenirs from the city by the sea. But he soon received a letter from the hotel sarcastically observing that they thought he was a gentleman and asking why he marched off with pictures from their walls and why he didn't take the walls too!

Berlin was amazed. He grew highly insulted and came back with a snappy denial. Moreover, he demanded an apology or he would have a lunacy commission investigate the management. Other letters followed that consumed a lot of time and temper on both sides, but I don't think the dispute has ever been settled. This is the first light shed on the mystery. The pictures are probably still in Berlin's attic and undoubtedly he has never seen them.

Another jest that took a more earnest turn than we expected was one that Fields and I framed around Will Rogers. If he reads it here, this will be the first time he learns the facts and discovers the culprits. Will would often tell us of the dearest friend he had in the world, a pal of his early days back in Claremore, Oklahoma, called Clay McGonigle. At first we thought the man was a fictitious character, the name sounded so pat; but Will told us so many interesting tales about good old Clay and himself that gradually the feeling came upon us to conjure up Clay and one fine day bring him on to New York. Unknowingly, Will Rogers himself showed us the way.

It was war time and we sat in Will's dressing-room listening to his stories about the old days and his inseparable crony, Clay McGonigle. "Haven't seen him in years," said Will, "but I've a hunch that I know just where he is right now. He's out in France with the doughboys, holding the front-line trenches. He must have gone over the day war was declared—he was that adventurous!"

This was our cue. We'd have McGonigle going over the top. But we had to fashion our material skillfully to fool a shrewd one like Rogers. Luckily, his valet confided to us that Rogers had a nickname which McGonigle had given him and which nobody else had ever heard. When Will and Clay rode the freight trains together, Rogers would often pass a night in a car full of chickens and emerge in the morning covered with feathers, like the last of the Mohicans. Clay grinned at him, exclaiming, "Look at Chickenchief!" and the nickname stuck. With this priceless secret in our possession we were ready to frame a letter that Rogers would have to believe. Bill wrote it out in a clumsy hand:

Dear Chickenchief,
Will be out front tonight watching your show. Will see you for the last time. Tomorrow I'm on my way to France. Whoopee!
Your old pal,
Clay McGonigle.

We relayed this note to Will Rogers, and soon after he came down to my dressing-room with a twinkle of excitement in his eyes. Fields, who dressed in the next room, joined us casually.

"Boys," cried Rogers, with an emotional tremor in his tone, "you'll never guess who's out in that audience tonight!"

"Who?"

"My old pal, Clay McGonigle!"

"No!"

"Yes," said Will. "He left a message for me with the

doorman. Funny, we just talked about him yesterday. Gee! It'll be great to see him again!"

It was a pity that Clay had forgotten to specify where he would be sitting in the audience, but Will Rogers felt sure he could locate him. "I could pick him out of a thousand!"

"Will Rogers!" shouted the call boy. Will snatched a piece of gum he had plastered under my make-up shelf, stuck it into his mouth, and ran down for his cue. He would keep the same four pieces of gum going all season and stick them in strategic places where he could get one at a moment's notice. Gum was as much a prop as his ropes, and he never chewed it off-stage.

Fields and I were consumed with curiosity to know how our joke would develop, and we went down to watch Will's act. He was twirling his loops with more energy than usual and shooting all his gags at Clay. There was no audience for him that night but Clay. Every line he uttered began with Clay and finished with McGonigle. "Remember the old days, Clay?" he exclaimed, hopping into his circling ropes. "What would the folks back home say, old pal, if they knew you were sitting here tonight!" It was a total blank to the audience. But what did Will care? Somewhere out there was his oldest pal and dearest friend, and he was going to give him a good time before he sailed for France. "What do you say, Clay? I'll meet you after the show!" Fields and I had to hold each other not to collapse.

After his act, Rogers told us he wouldn't show up in

the finale that night. "I've got to get out early and stand in the lobby to catch Clay as he leaves the theater. See you tomorrow, boys."

He stood in the lobby watching the crowds go out, certain that he could spot Clay among thousands. But there was no Clay. He waited till remnants of the audience straggled out and the last man left. Then he came back, thinking Clay might have called at the stage door. He grew impatient, swore, and finally called up the William Penn Hotel as the most probable place where his friend might be stopping. But they had never heard of McGonigle. He tried every hotel and club he could think of, and hunted through the night for his pal. It had ceased to be a joke. It was a lesson in devoted friendship that Fields and I never forgot.

For a long time after that Rogers often wondered what had happened to Clay that night. Now he'll know.

But the practical joke is a ruthless weapon with a double edge and I've often had it turned on me. Van and Schenck once took me to a Childs restaurant in St. Louis after the show. While I went to get a table they lingered behind to tell the manager and waitress that I had just returned from a sanitarium, not entirely cured, and that I was still slightly deranged. The manager and waitress looked queerly at me and treated me with caution. Gus Van further confided to them that my whole mental disorder was due to drinking too much milk and that under no circumstances must I get near a glass of it. They knew I was dieting at the time and that milk was my main item of diet. Suspecting nothing of all this, I asked for milk and was surprised to hear the waitress suggest that I take cocoa or tea instead.

"Why can't I have milk?" I asked, getting irritated.

"We haven't any," said the waitress, glibly.

"But I see a lot of people at other tables drink it," I protested, angrily. "How is that?"

"They—they brought it along with them—when—when they came in," explained the waitress, becoming alarmed. This seemed very peculiar to me and I insisted on speaking to the manager. I made such a strong and lucid appeal to him that he almost relented, but Van and Schenck motioned to him as if mortally afraid. "No! No milk! He'll calm down!" Van whispered to him. "But if you give him milk, he'll bust up the joint!" I finally had to drink cocoa.

But sometimes, without anybody planning or anticipating it, a practical joke would be born of itself. We were playing in Cincinnati and Fannie Brice, who was stopping at the Sinton Hotel, acted mother to the troupe. Fannie is the type who, in her spare moments, will sew hats for poor chorus girls, mend stockings, and even wash light underwear. She is a natural-born mother and W. C. Fields, Will Rogers, Don Barclay, and I became her children by adoption.

One night we visited her at the hotel to take her along for a bite after the show, but she insisted on feeding us right there.

"I'll save you boys some money," she said, but in reality she prided herself on her cooking skill and wanted us to sample her master dish. We consented and waited an hour and a half while she busied herself in her improvised kitchenette, preparing the famous spaghetti *à la* Fannie with tomato sauce and all the fixings. Luscious flavors of food tickled our nostrils, and our hunger grew steadily keener. At last Fannie beamed triumphantly as she set the grand steaming platter before us.

We had to admit it was worth waiting for, and began to eat heartily. But before the second mouthful an afflicted expression came over our faces. At first I thought my sense of taste was at fault, but all the others sensed the same fault. It seemed that Fannie's maid had filled the jar of powdered cheese with Lux and Fannie had sprinkled the spaghetti full of it. Our mouths were foaming with soap. We had to go out to eat, after all, and Fannie laughed all the way. But there was a disturbing hysterical note in that laugh.

The Ziegfeld actors formed a happy household in those years. A spirit of genuine fellowship and helpfulness prevailed in the Follies of '17, '18 and '19 that has rarely been equaled by any other troupe. The older members of the cast took it to be their pleasant duty to give the younger ones the benefit of their stage experience. Each actor felt like a guardian over the others and took pride in their success. There was no doubt that such bonds of friendship could stand any test of endurance. And soon came the biggest test of all. In 1919, while the Follies played in New York, an alarm was sounded. For the first time in its history the theatrical profession was called out on strike.

There had been grave abuses in the producing business. Actors would rehearse for ten and twelve weeks without pay; then the show might play a week or two, and they'd have to start rehearsing in a new piece all over again. On the other hand, if the show was a success a manager could play as many extra holidays as he pleased without compensating the actor for the extra performances. On holidays like Washington's and Lincoln's birthdays, the actor played gratis. In fact, whenever the manager saw a flag waving he declared a holiday or an extra matinée, and there were producers who ordered special performances in honor of their own birthdays. Out West, where Sunday shows were permitted, actors played seven nights a week as well as two matinées, and received no extras. Chorus girls particularly were hard hit. They never received a cent during months of such long rehearsals that made the recent dance marathon look like a short afternoon. Besides, when their show finally opened they got as low as twenty-five dollars a week, and out of that had to pay for their stockings and shoes.

It must be said for Ziegfeld that he never deducted the cost for stockings, and his general wage scale for girls was much higher, but the strike was not directed against individuals. As long as he remained apart from the Producing Managers' Association he was unaffected by the strike. The first day of the walkout it was rumored that he had joined the managers' group and I quit. I went to see the Scandals that evening, but Ziegfeld located me there and called me back an hour later with the assurance that he hadn't joined. I promptly returned to the show, and in the second act did my first-act bit. Five days later, however, I discovered that Ziegfeld was a member of the Producing Managers' Association.

That night I took my stand on Forty-first Street opposite the stage door of the New Amsterdam Theater, and as the actors of the Follies arrived I whistled to them. The first to appear were Van and Schenck. They heard the siren call and turned their heads.

"What's up, Eddie?"

"Strike."

Without a word they crossed over to my side of the street and stuck. As the next actors arrived, all three of us whistled. They halted at the signal and turned. They were Johnny and Ray Dooley.

"What's the matter?"

"Strike."

In a short while the whole cast was lined up on our side of the block and we marched to the headquarters of Actors' Equity. Frank Gilmore, who headed the organization, was delighted to receive us. This was the one big show that had held out. After we joined Equity, success seemed certain. At the time, Bill Fields was playing up on the roof. As the Midnight Frolics was considered part of the vaudeville field, its actors were not included in the strike. But Bill heard the clarion call of the Musketeers and left the show to join us.

MY LIFE IS IN YOUR HANDS

None of the Ziegfeld stars had anything to gain by the strike. But neither had Frank Bacon, who after long years of struggle had just hit his stride in "Lightnin'." Yet he quit readily on behalf of his colleagues, even if it meant that he and Mrs. Bacon would have to take up once more the hunger-racking struggle of a lifetime. There was no question of personal profit. It was a spirited movement to elevate the profession as a whole, and the more successful actors made sacrifices freely that their less fortunate associates should gain a measure of protection.

The Actors' Equity Association opened a benefit performance week at the Lexington Opera House, where the greatest vaudeville bill of all time was given on behalf of the cause. The opening day, before the show began, all the actors marched down Broadway, each company bearing its banner, and I carried the colors of the Ziegfeld Follies. It was the first war art ever waged for bread, and it was an inspiring spectacle to see. At the Lexington Opera House prominent actors sold tickets, while other celebrities of the stage acted as ushers. The rest played on the bill, which included such names as Ethel Barrymore, her brother Lionel, Frank Tinney, John Charles Thomas, Eddie Foy, Ed Wynn, W. C. Fields, Frank Bacon, Brandon Tynan, and the Follies cast.

Never were performances given with such enthusiasm and zest. Each actor thrilled with purpose. The comedians were never funnier, the tragedians never wrung such tears. Most of the men dressed together in a grand democracy. They shared one another's make-up, outfits, gave lavishly of all they had. We played twelve performances in six days and were eager to do more. We made bonfires of our emotions and swept our audiences in a blaze of excitement. It was the greatest week in our lives.

Ed Wynn was taken out of the show by a court order. According to his contract with the Shuberts, they had the power to enjoin him. A comparatively new actor, James Barton, just risen from burlesque, took his place. The week at the Lexington Opera House made Jimmy Barton, and soon after, the Shuberts signed him, too.

Some theaters, only partly handicapped by the strike, refused to shut down, and we formed committees to try and keep the public from attending their shows. Bill Fields, Ernest Truex, Frank Fay, and I drove along in a car which we intentionally stalled in front of one of these theaters. We pretended to be fixing the car and clowned around until the prospective ticket-purchasers were attracted by us. We entertained them so well on the street corner that they willingly missed the show inside. The policemen were in sympathy with us, so was the public, and we invariably captured the day for Equity.

The actors won. Most of the abuses were eradicated. Chorus girls were provided with a better wage. No actor would have to rehearse more than four weeks without pay. There would be extras for holidays. While managers retained a free hand in casting, they could no longer try out an actor and make him rehearse for several weeks, only

MY LIFE IS IN YOUR HANDS

to fire him before the show opened. They would have to decide within the first ten days whether he was fit for the part. If they retained him after that he was entitled to the regular two weeks' notice with pay. Irresponsible producers would be required to post a surety. This was as valuable a safeguard to legitimate managers as to the actors. It helped to clear the show business of undesirables. Equity has since developed to be as great a boon to producers as to its own members. It is now recognized by both sides as a monument to the growing dignity and stability of the American theater.

After the victory we all returned to our old posts, but things were no longer the same. Ziegfeld had promised to star me in his next show at a greatly increased salary. Instead, he stalled and avoided the subject. The memory of the strike was still fresh in his mind. I asked for my release and got it. If not for the strike, I probably would have played opposite Marilyn Miller in "Sally." By joining my less fortunate colleagues to aid their cause I had definitely surrendered this opportunity, which, as the figures afterward proved, would have yielded me nearly four hundred thousand dollars. But I had sincerely enjoyed the sacrifice and felt more than repaid for my share in the triumph of Equity.

The Three Musketeers were now separated. Will Rogers had accepted a movie contract. Bill Fields drifted back to the Frolics, and I was alone with no immediate prospect in view.

Chapter XVI

IN 1920, during the season after the strike, the Shuberts were preparing a revue that had all the elements of entertainment but comedy. They lacked a comedian, and as I lacked a management, we soon came to terms.

The Shubert organization operated like a huge industrial plant. The two brothers, J. J. and Lee, had both begun their theatrical careers as ushers in a theater at Syracuse, and the same accurate, methodical system by which they never directed a customer to the wrong seat, they now applied on a larger scale to the efficient conduct of their vast enterprises.

Lee took charge of all the real-estate interests of the firm, while J. J. concerned himself exclusively with production. He perfected his machinery of production to such a degree that he often managed to turn out ten and fifteen shows a year. He is unquestionably one of the preëminent showmen of our time, and has such a canny sense of the theater that he has frequently, by drastic and lightning changes on dress-rehearsal night, transformed a flop production into a hit. He recognized Al Jolson in the raw, and when I made my stage début as a youngster with Bedini and Arthur at Hammerstein's, J. J. had already made Jolson a Broadway star.

Before the new Shubert revue took shape, J. J. asked me to play several weeks in the "Broadway Brevities," a Shubert production at the Winter Garden. In this show I introduced a scene at the dentist's where I got many laughs and the reason I recall it is because I've never got any laughs at a dentist's since.

After four weeks of rehearsal the Shubert revue went down to Philadelphia for its opening trial. As I approached the theater I was dazzled by a mighty blaze of electric lights and beheld my name for the first time in the place of honor above the title of the show. Perhaps nobody else caught the full significance of what the bright bulbs were saying, but I stood and stared until they almost blinded me. The legend read:

EDDIE CANTOR
IN
THE MIDNIGHT ROUNDERS

Instead of thrilling me, the sight of this display made me weak and a sinking fear tugged at my heart. This night would decide whether I could be a star.

"Listen, J. J.," I said, "why don't you hold off the fireworks till after I've made good?"

"Don't be foolish, Eddie," he replied, impatiently. "You'll be a knockout!"

It was a night of high fever and rapid pulse. The "Midnight Rounders" whirled round at a dizzy pace. To add to the speed and confusion of this first wild night, J. J. ran back-stage every few minutes and shouted orders. "Kill the next scene," he cried. "Reverse the dance numbers and put in the specialty after that. The next four songs are out. Call Eddie!" It was long before my cue and I ran down from my dressing-room in a bathrobe, half made up and excited.

"What's the matter, J. J.? Is the show off?"

"Not yet. Just go on and stall," he said, "while we switch the next scene."

"What do you mean, 'stall'?"

"Do anything. Only keep 'em laughing!"

I went on in my bathrobe and told the audience the truth. "Jake Shubert sent me out to stall while they change the show around. It may take weeks." I was wholly unprepared, but the job was to make them laugh, and I did.

A few minutes after I returned to my dressing-room, J. J. called me again.

"What's the matter now?"

"Go on and stall."

This time I went on in my undershirt and did another impromptu monologue. When that was over I went back to my room, sighing with relief. I began to get ready for my regular turn, when the call boy rushed in, breathless.

"Mr. Shubert wants you right away!"

"Say, what is this—a gag?"

I was caught completely unawares and ran down without my trousers.

"What's the matter, J. J.?"

"Go on and stall."

"What! Without my pants! At least give me a hat!"

I put on a derby to feel dressed, and in this ridiculous

outfit I made another unexpected appearance. The three stalling episodes proved so successful that we kept them permanently in the show.

The opening night lasted till twelve. The revue received a stirring ovation. After the show Shubert came back-stage. The whole cast assembled to listen to any comments or criticisms he might want to make. He turned to them, putting his arm around my shoulders. "Ladies and gentlemen of the cast," he said, "I want to introduce to you Broadway's newest star—Eddie Cantor."

"The Midnight Rounders" was my first starring vehicle. After the opening, I had prepared a little party for my friends to celebrate the occasion. There were about twenty of them who had accompanied me from New York, some with their wives, and they all arrived back-stage in full dress, hungrily waiting for me to lead them to the sumptuous banquet they expected. "You're a hit," they said, "and we're entitled to a feast in proportion to the triumph!" I led them to a Childs restaurant, where I had reserved tables in advance. The banquet consisted of a baked apple and cream for each guest.

"What's the idea?" they protested.

"Well," I explained, "this morning, before the show, I thought to myself, 'Which would my friends rather have—a big hit or a big banquet?'"

"A big hit, of course!" they cried, enthusiastically.

"That's what I thought."

They sat down in their evening dress and stiff shirt

fronts and ate the apples with the elaborate formality of a feast.

The full responsibility of my new position grew upon me. It was no longer like playing on a Ziegfeld bill studded with big names. If I got sick in the Follies, I might be missed, but the show could still go on. Now the burden of the whole revue was pivoted on me and if I failed to appear, the doors of the theater would be locked. The welfare of the entire company was in my keeping and I didn't permit even illness to interfere. There were times when I danced and sang through a dozen numbers and encores unable to take a deep breath, because one side of my chest was tightly strapped to dull the pain of pleurisy. I staggered off the stage exhausted, almost unconscious, and a doctor worked steadily over me to get me ready for the next cue. But the show went on.

It was in "The Midnight Rounders" that I first played a scene which proved to be one of the most popular hits of my career. It was called "Joe's Blue Front" second-hand clothing store, and started a vogue of clothes shops in musical shows. The original one, however, is still considered by many as unsurpassed.

I played the assistant to the late Joe Opp, who was the tailor. Our first and only customer, Lou Hearn, came in for a fit, and before we got through with him he took one. My first sales blunder was to touch the material of the suit he wore, thinking he intended to buy it.

"Ah, that's the best suit in the house," I exclaimed, admiringly.

"That's his own!" scowled the boss.

The customer then explained that he wanted a suit with a belt in the back.

"A belt in the back?" By steadily repeating this phrase and lifting my arm as if to strike him every time his back was turned, the audience laughed more and more in anticipation of the moment when I'd haul off and give him the belt he wanted. After I finally got him to compromise on a hunting suit, I showed him a Prince Albert cutaway.

"Is that a hunting suit?" the customer sneered.

"Sure. We been hunting for the pants for two years."

He was hard to satisfy, so I persuaded him to get a nice second-hand suit made to order. He got on the model stand and I took his length right down to the ground, including the height of the stand. Hearn and I then laid him out flat, as if to measure him for a coffin. I sang the numbers off the tape and Hearn sang after me as he wrote them down.

"*Sho-oulders, sixty-two and a ha-alf . . .*" I chanted in the manner of hymns. "*Wai-aist, ninetee-een . . . Slee-eeves, sixty-eight!*"

We proceeded in this singsong way as if we were praying, and the customer who watched us with a puzzled air finally joined in with, "*Swee-eet Adeli-ine!*"

After the fitting, I again tried to sell him a suit. This time a blue one, but he wanted it with stripes. My fingers were covered with white chalk and by running them along the coat I spread stripes over him. "They fit you. You were born to be in stripes!"

"I'd rather have a two-button sack suit," he reconsidered.

"Why, certainly!" As the coat I gave him had three buttons, I tore one off. "How's that?" He still hesitated.

"You look like a different man in that suit," I urged. "Your own wife wouldn't know you. Go out in the light and see for yourself." He went out while I replaced the other clothes on hangers. When he returned I approached him as if he were a new customer "Yessir. What can I do for you, sir?" He started in surprise.

"Why, it's me," he cried. I stared at him blankly.

"Me! Lou Hearn! The fellow who was just in here to try on a suit!"

"You!" I was amazed. "You see? Even I didn't recognize you!" That clinched the sale.

At the wind-up of the skit I had so muddled and confused the customer that he was trying on a boy's sailor suit, though he still longed wistfully for something with a belt in the back. He finally ran out of the store with nothing on at all but his red flannel underwear, leaving his own suit behind.

"Joe's Blue Front" was the only scene I ever played in two consecutive shows. After running for two whole seasons in "The Midnight Rounders" we transplanted it bodily to "Make It Snappy," where it carried on with equal success.

I had a physical comedy scene in "The Midnight

Rounders" that took the form of an examination for life insurance at the offices of the Disreputable Insurance Company. The doctor in charge asked me, "Do you think you can pass?"

"Give me a pair of dice and I'll show you."

Under pressure, I admitted that I had already been turned down by three companies—The New York, New Haven, and Hartford. The examiner then inquired sternly, "Do you drink anything?"

"Anything," was the answer.

These and other gag lines were freely borrowed by vaudeville teams and used in cities on the road before I got there. When I arrived and used the same lines it gave the impression that I had borrowed from them.

"The Midnight Rounders" played for seventy weeks along the Shubert Circuit. In the company were Nan Halperin, Lou Hearn, Jane Green, and Harry Kelly. It was probably the most charitable troupe of boys and girls I ever played with, and on afternoons that we had no matinées we would hunt up some hospital or sanitarium and entertain the patients.

On September 16, 1921, during the road tour of the show, I received word that a fourth child was born to me. Ida and I being already the proud parents of three daughters, I confess that this once we vaguely expected something different. And it was. It looked different, it cried more at night, it took the bottle oftener. It was entirely different from the other girls in every respect but one. It too was a girl. So we called her Marilyn.

MY LIFE IS IN YOUR HANDS

While traveling with "The Midnight Rounders" I often gathered bits of personal experience and worked them into my monologues. The best known of these is a line my daughter Marjorie gave me when she was six. Due to the road tour, my absences from home were long and frequent, but as soon as we played in a neighboring city I hurried home to see the new baby. I rang the door bell, and Marjorie answered. She looked rather strangely at me and ran into the hall, exclaiming: "Mamma! That man is here again!"

Another bit in my specialty grew out of a totally different experience. I was stopping at the Hotel Wolverine in Detroit, and Fronde, the hotel proprietor, urged me to drive over with him and another friend to the races at Windsor, Canada. It was the first time I saw horses that were not hitched to wagons, and I suggested, as a lark, that we place a bet on a horse called Bumpity-Bumps, because its name reminded me of the good old horse-cars. We chipped in ten dollars apiece, thirty in all, but while we chatted in the club-house it became too late to bet. Fronde wanted to run out and bet the money at the pari-mutuel machines, but I dissuaded him. "After all, I hate to see even thirty dollars for the last time!" He bowed to my wisdom. A few minutes later the race was on and Bumpity-Bumps won at a hundred and ninety-seven dollars for two. We could have made about a thousand dollars each, but we didn't. We were true sportsmen, and took the thing so calmly and quietly that none of us talked all the way home.

MY LIFE IS IN YOUR HANDS

That night I told the story in my specialty, and added a sequel. "Considering what we might have won on Bumpity-Bumps," I said, "we decided to play the next race. We bet a horse ten to one and he came in a quarter to six. He seemed to be awfully stuck up and wouldn't run with the others. Then we bet a mudder, but he loved mud so much, he stopped to eat it. Still, we'd have been even for the day if we had played on credit!"

A third experience that told well from the stage was one I had coming in from Pittsburgh. I sat behind two men in the train who happened to be talking about me. One of them was saying: "I saw Eddie Cantor in 'The Midnight Rounders.' You think he's such a nice fellow off the stage?"

"Nice fellow!" said the other with a trace of a sneer. "Why, he's a relative of mine!" I was taken by surprise and tried to get a full view of this new-found kin, but I felt sure I had never seen him before. "Sure!" he continued, glibly, obviously trying to impress his listener. "Whenever Eddie is in Pittsburgh he comes to our house for a good old Friday-night supper, and how he loves that stuffed fish and noodle soup!" He went on to describe intimate details about me and my family that were all wrong and I felt like interrupting to correct him. At last his boastful nerve began to irritate me and I leaned over to him. "You know Eddie Cantor?" I inquired, as if interested.

"Why, sure!" he said with brazen self-assurance.

"You say he's been to your house lately?"

MY LIFE IS IN YOUR HANDS

"Only last night!"

"Is that so?" It was news to me. "Well, I happen to be a pretty good friend of his myself," I said, "and I'll bet you you wouldn't know Eddie Cantor if you saw him."

I knew the fellow was lying, but I knew he had gone too far to back down.

"It's a go," he said. "I'll bet you ten dollars." He must have felt the possibility of meeting me pretty remote.

"And you'd know him if you saw him?"

"I sure would! He even told me he's leaving for New York tonight and if he's on this train he'd look me up!"

What a bluffer! The papers had carried an item about our leaving for New York and he probably had seen girls of the chorus board the train. But he had talked himself right into the trap.

"Well, if he's on this train, who is he?"

"You are," he said, beginning to laugh. The two of them had framed their little chat just to attract my attention, and it had succeeded perfectly.

After "The Midnight Rounders" the Shuberts starred me in a new revue the title for which J. J. picked up from an elevator boy who was rushing the crowd into his car with the whip line, "Come on, folks, make it snappy!" J. J. came up to the office with a grin on his face, "Boys, I just got the name for our next Cantor show. We'll call it, 'Make It Snappy!'"

MY LIFE IS IN YOUR HANDS

It was a snappy show in every sense. We snapped right through it from start to finish, and after a season's run at top speed it snapped altogether. The outstanding innovation of our revue was a harem scene in which I burlesqued Rudolph Valentino as a sheik. After an eloquent description of me as the mighty Sheik of the Sahara, mounted on his fiery Arabian steed that galloped across the desert in a cloud of flame, horses' hoofs were heard, and I came on the stage riding a bicycle.

I had a eunuch managing my business, and the women punched time-clocks as they entered the harem tents. But I was not destined to enjoy this Mormon life for long. A rival sheik from another Turkish coffee-house was hot on my trail and came upon the scene, his face menacing and his head bowed by the weight of his mustache. Fortunately, before he lifted me on the point of his saber he noticed a locket around my neck which looked pawnable. He opened it and beheld the picture of a woman. Then began a most touching scene of recognition between a long-lost father and son.

"My wife!" he cried, pocketing the locket.

"My mother—Sophie Tucker!" I cried, trying to get it back.

"My child, Sarsaparilla!"

"Pop!" And we clinched.

At the close of the harem scene a troupe of skilled Arab acrobats swarmed all over the stage in fantastic somersaults and pinwheels. One day, two of this troupe come to my dressing-room to tell me that the Shuberts had decided to cut down on expenses and let the acrobat caravan go. These two Arabs happened to be nice Irish boys who wanted to work and knew how.

"We're fired, Mr. Cantor," they told me, "but we noticed you've been so good to everybody in the cast that we thought we'd ask your advice. Maybe you could recommend us to some booking office."

They had been getting thirty dollars a week each. Now they wouldn't even get that. I felt a deep sympathy for these boys, still young and facing all the hardships I had known so well. "I've got an idea how to use you in this show," I said. "Wait for me after the matinée." Late that afternoon I made them up as old men in the mock disguise of country yokels with wrinkles and whiskers, and I dressed them in old farm clothes that Lou Hearn dug out of his wardrobe. I then fixed up a little music for their act and put them out in a number by themselves. When these two rickety old men with gray beards and hobbly steps suddenly went into their neck-breaking leaps and somersaults they proved to be a riot and stopped the show. Later on they got three hundred dollars a week from Ziegfeld and are earning double that today. The Kelo Brothers are now a headline act on Broadway.

While passing one of the dressing-rooms I often stopped to listen to two young girls of the chorus who sat in their room harmonizing popular songs in a unique and charming way. One day I told them that I thought they had great possibilities. I took them to music publishers and selected a little repertoire for them. When their singing act was ready I fixed a spot in the revue to try it out. They proved an instant hit. This was the beginning of the rise of the McCarthy Sisters, who have since become a leading attraction of the "Scandals."

It has given me great satisfaction, during my years on the stage, to spy out promising talent and do all I could to encourage it. In 1918, the parents of a young man came to me asking that I do something for their boy. He had been coming around to my dressing-room for a long time and an intimacy had grown up between us that ripened into friendship. He gradually confided to me that he hoped some day to reach the footlights, and I promised to help him. I gave him my own monologue, worked over a little program of songs with him, and made him try out the act in an outlying playhouse of Chicago. His first effort was a little crude but encouraging, and we worked together for some time until he found himself. He got seventy-five dollars a week at the start, began to write his own stuff, and made steady headway. Today, Jack Osterman is one of the big lights in the younger musical-comedy world and commands a salary of twelve hundred and fifty dollars a week. I got a real thrill one night when I watched him on Broadway and he introduced me to the audience as the fellow who put him on the stage.

MY LIFE IS IN YOUR HANDS

While "Make It Snappy" did not measure up to the success of "The Midnight Rounders," it managed to attract capacity crowds in all houses on the road. I remember sitting one night in the box office of the Apollo Theatre in Chicago and the house was completely sold out. I always had four front seats reserved for the use of my friends, but it was getting late and I did not expect to take advantage of them. A little nearsighted man with furry eyebrows came over to the window, noticed the sign, and looked rather crestfallen. He and his wife, both tiny and squinting, could never hope to see the show, even if there were two seats at the rear end of the orchestra. He was about to walk away when I called to him, "I'll let you have two of my seats." He appeared very pleased and appreciative. Before he went in he said, "Some day I hope I can do something for you," and handed me his card. It read, "A. Hutchins, Undertaker and Embalmer."

At the close of "Make It Snappy" the Shuberts asked me to renew my contract, but I had grown tired of revues. I wanted a musical show with a story. I felt that was the logical step upward. Opposite the Apollo Theater in St. Louis, Ziegfeld's "Sally" was playing. Ziegfeld was in Palm Beach at the time. One of the newspapers observed in its theatrical column that "Eddie Cantor at $3.30 a seat is better entertainment value than Marilyn Miller and Leon Errol at $4.40." I was anxious to have Ziggy see this. I reprinted this comment in a full-page advertisement that I took in *Variety* and Ziggy saw it. A few days later he telephoned to me from Palm Beach. I told him the principle consideration for my return would be to play in a musical show with a story. He agreed to star me in my first musical comedy.

Chapter XVII

THE birth of a good musical comedy is like the old alchemist's efforts to produce gold. He would throw a multitude of elements into his caldron, copper and lead, iron and sand, acids and stones, churn them into a molten mass with rods, bellows, and flames, and in the end he either had a pretty mixture that was nothing at all, or, if gold did appear, he never could tell which of the countless things he had tried caused it, or how to repeat the process exactly. That is show business, and particularly musical comedy.

It is true, we are guided by some simple basic rules, but the factors that go into the construction of the musical play are so numerous and often accidental that even those who watch its development most closely and know every step of the way are always surprised at the finished product. Sometimes, not agreeably. And it isn't necessarily one thing that matters, like a song or a setting or a situation. It is that intangible something called "clicking." If a show doesn't "click" it's not there. Sometimes even the story doesn't count. I have seen a manuscript on the strength of which a manager launched the most elaborate production, but when he finally presented it, not a single line or idea of the original manuscript remained and the show was a hit.

"Kid Boots," which has been rated by many as the best all-round show I have played in, and one of the most successful musical comedies of the American stage, started vaguely, gropingly, and with not even an idea. All we had was a desire—my desire to act and Ziggy's desire to stall. With Ziggy, stalling is lifted to the dignity of an art. If he says, "See me Thursday," you can't tell if it's this month or next year. It seemed ages as the weeks creaked by and nothing happened. We were in search of an author with an idea for a real musical show, and it looked as if the authors had conspired to keep in hiding.

One day, Joe McCarthy, the lyric-writer, of the musical partnership of McCarthy and Tierney, who had written the score for "Irene," came around with a suggestion for a play about golf. The novelty of locale is one of the hardest problems in musical-show business, but with this popular game as a background there seemed to be some promise of a new atmosphere. McCarthy had an idea about a bootlegging caddie-master who practically ran an exclusive golf club through his liquor business and intrigues. Ziegfeld and I liked the idea from the start, and the problem now was to get some one to write the book.

We wanted some fresh ideas injected into musical comedy and were anxious to avoid the stiffly patterned, conventional plot. Ziegfeld called in a writer who had never done a musical show before. He had just come into some prominence through a successful comedy he had written, called, "Six Cylinder Love," that was produced by Al Lewis in association with Sam H. Harris. Before this, William Anthony McGuire was comparatively unknown to the theater.

MY LIFE IS IN YOUR HANDS

He had written a play at the age of sixteen, but wisely kept it a secret. In fact, he wrote eleven more before he finally plucked up the courage to submit one. No playwright of recent years has had such a difficult beginning as Bill McGuire, or such a spectacular rise. Because of a frail and sickly childhood he quit public school in the fifth grade and never entered a hall of learning again until he was nineteen, when he returned to Notre Dame for a two-year academic course. The first play he tried to sell a manager was called, "The Soldier and The Cardinal." This manuscript was so stubbornly and frequently rejected that Bill had it printed in book form at his own expense in order to preserve for posterity the most rejected manuscript in history. It was dangerous to smile at young McGuire in those days, for if you did he immediately autographed a copy of *The Soldier and The Cardinal* and presented it to you. He never would get another friendly smile after that.

But it was destined that this much-maligned and despised play should one day, in an altered version, be a Ziegfeld hit and establish Bill McGuire as one of the best book-writers of musical comedy. It happened like this. When Bill went back to Notre Dame to polish up his spelling he picked up a book called, *The Three Musketeers* and found, to his amazement, that it told almost the identical story he had written in *The Soldier and The Cardinal.* Bill modestly concluded that Dumas had plagiarized the whole idea from him. Lucky for Dumas that he wasn't alive. But Bill's hour was drawing near.

MY LIFE IS IN YOUR HANDS

He was beginning to be admitted to managers' offices. He wrote a play called "The Walls of Wall Street," which was acted at a benefit and distinguished society figures took part in the production. Frank Keenan was impressed by the young man's promise and engaged him to write a play. Frank Keenan was one of the greatest character actors of our stage, so it couldn't have been his fault that Bill's play, "The Heights," sank to the depths in a week. On the other hand, Bill claims it's the greatest play he ever wrote.

He had to leave New York after that and try Chicago, where they didn't know him. There he wrote "The Divorce Question," which ran one year and had five road companies, but never got to Broadway. He then came out for race suicide in "The Good Bad Woman," but when that didn't work, he urged more population in "It's A Boy." At last "Six Cylinder Love" arrived and made the grade in high. Hit followed hit. He wrote and produced a melodrama, "Twelve Miles Out," and last year he wrote two of Ziegfeld's biggest successes, "Rosalie" and "The Three Musketeers." The dream to have his first play produced was realized in this curious way, for in adapting the famous French novel for the stage, McGuire incorporated many lines and scenes from his virgin effort, "The Soldier and The Cardinal."

But when Bill McGuire undertook to write the book for "Kid Boots" he had attained none of his present distinction and we had mainly our faith to go by. After many discussions of the golf idea, Ziegfeld suggested that

McGuire, McCarthy, and I get together and plan out the story. New delays set in. McCarthy couldn't meet us Wednesday and Bill couldn't make it Thursday. But Friday was fine for everybody.

"Then it's definitely agreed," I said, "that we meet at the Lambs' Club, Friday at one o'clock."

"O. K."

Ziggy seemed glad that he had got the three of us off his hands and lapsed into pleasant dreams, probably thinking we'd never go through with it. In the meantime he had me tied to a contract which prevented me from accepting other offers. Days flapped their wings and flew away while I idled and waited. At last came Friday. I made sure to eat at twelve, to be at the Lambs' Club promptly at one. McCarthy arrived at one-fifteen and McGuire didn't show up at all. He didn't even phone. He was beginning to display the temperament of a real playwright. The next day we learned that he had been obliged to go out of town, and that week was wasted.

We finally arranged a meeting for the following Wednesday, wiring to Bill in Atlantic City, and he agreed. We met at McCarthy's house in Pelham. Joe served drinks and we liked them. After the fourth drink none of us knew what we had come up there for. So that was done. We stopped over and the next day got down to business. Weeks and weeks had frittered away and something actual had to be accomplished, so we decided on the title, "Kid Boots," which we had had in the first place. We also decided on the subject. It was to be a play about golf.

McGuire promised that in four or five days he'd have a rough draft ready of act one. Ten days passed. No rough draft and no McGuire. McCarthy and Tierney and I became uneasy and went to Ziggy. Ziggy seemed surprised at our complaints and remarked coolly, "I thought the play was all finished by this time." Then we told him what we thought of McGuire in a series of well-chosen adjectives, and he sent for Bill. Bill, we suspected, was working on another play, not on "Kid Boots."

"Give me a few more days," he urged, after we all had pounced upon him. "I've got a new idea."

We left Ziggy, but we didn't leave McGuire. We took him to the Lambs' Club and he recited some lines he had thought up for the show which we believed were great. He might have been working on it, after all. He certainly showed ability and our confidence was restored. But we were a little afraid of his knowledge of musical-comedy technique, as this was his first effort in that line, so we suggested that some one else be called in to collaborate with him. McGuire readily consented to split his royalties with some one capable of aiding him in technical construction. Another week passed and Otto Harbach, master technician, was engaged.

We now started migrations to Harbach's home. Joe, Bill, Otto, and I held a convention there and everybody agreed that we'd have a great show, but as yet there wasn't a line on paper to prove it. I finally had a private little session with myself in my own house and decided that I'd have to start doing a little work myself if I was ever going to star in "Kid Boots."

I submitted a couple of unfinished scenes, suggestions in the raw that started McGuire and Harbach thinking. One of them was the idea of a comedy golf lesson. As caddie-master I could teach on the side, and have some big husky woman as my pupil. The other idea was a physical-comedy scene. We would disguise my old osteopath act and set it in the ladies' locker-room of the club. To make my torture more intense, Ziggy suggested the introduction of an electric chair like the one he had seen at Dr. Khonstamm's where he went for electrical treatments. McCarthy and Tierney got at the piano and started to fake tunes and lines for the entire musical opening of the show, and it sounded fine. Things were beginning in a vague, chaotic way to shape themselves.

A week later, with Harbach, who is an indefatigable worker laying the framework, McGuire brought in the first draft of act one, embodying the locker-room scene and the golf-lesson. While he and Otto furbished up the act, the problem of casting arose. We didn't have the second act until we were almost ready to open.

We came to Mr. Ziegfeld armed with the script of act one, and now it was his turn to stall. "What!" he exclaimed. "Ready so soon? You really going to have a show? What's the idea of rushing me?" We knew he needed a week to stretch and get used to the thought of a production. We let him stretch while McGuire and Harbach continued to go over the act with a fine comb and polish it to a bright finish.

I brought in several lines to them every day, lines that I had used before and were sure-fire. Both playwrights looked bored at my literary efforts, and spurned the lines because they were mere jokes and had nothing to do with the play. I tried to show them how they could be fitted in and finally most of them were fitted in, and they eventually turned out to be among the biggest laughs in the show.

Bill and Otto read Ziggy the first act and I tried to play it for him as they read. I lay on the floor, I kicked my legs, putted golf balls on his desk, hopped onto his lap, and pinched his cheek, and Ziggy was ready to cast. McGuire knew the types he wanted and insisted on them. His ability as a casting and stage director is equal to and perhaps greater than his skill as a writer.

Harbach, on the other hand, is a graduate engineer at dramatic construction. He knows just when the heroine should enter, and at what hour the hero should be broken-hearted, and exactly when the climax should crash down on the house. He has a sense of timing and sequence which is essential to the successful development of a musical story.

McGuire gave his mental picture of the characters and suggested most of the actors suited for the rôles. Ziegfeld had one cry, "Too much money." But the cast on paper looked good to us and we held out, wearing down Ziggy with arguments, cajolery, and firmness until he consented. The cast—Mary Eaton, Jobyna Howland, Harry Fender, Harland Dixon, Marie Callahan, and a few days later, Ethelind Terry and Beth Berri were added. We were confident that we had a great musical-comedy cast. There never was a greater.

When the question of engaging the different actors came up, Mary Eaton's lawyer insisted that she be co-starred with me. Ziegfeld refused, and I objected also. After all, Mary had only been one of the many players in the last Follies and was recently regarded merely as a dancer in the "Royal Vagabond," while I had three seasons of starring to my credit and was considered a drawing card in New York and on the road. There was no personal question involved. I simply considered it poor business to surrender so lightly the one thing I had surmounted so many difficulties to achieve. I persuaded Mary's father and her lawyer that she should be featured in equally large type. Thus, instead of

EDDIE CANTOR and MARY EATON
in
"KID BOOTS"

it was made to read,

EDDIE CANTOR
in
"KID BOOTS"
with
MARY EATON

Actors hold out for such things.

MY LIFE IS IN YOUR HANDS

Mary consented. Our association in the show was of the pleasantest and she afterward appeared in her first starring vehicle, "The Five O'Clock Girl" where she achieved, in proper time, the honor she had so coveted.

McCarthy and Tierney had all the numbers ready for act one. We read the first act to the entire cast, the parts were distributed, and rehearsals begun at a hall on Seventieth Street. I took my part home and upset many a rehearsal by bringing in new suggestions. Edward Royce, who staged the book and dances, willingly paused to receive my ideas and skilfully interpolated them. He was an invaluable man for directing stage action and conceiving dance interpretations. He worked for many hours on Mary Eaton's numbers and ballets.

One of my suggestions opened the way for a new headliner. We had engaged sixteen colored boys for a caddie number, but I felt that these boys would be working against great odds, and to get any recognition would have to be much better than they were. Instead, I suggested a single dancing specialty. I had in mind a young man who was little known but whose dancing appealed to me, and I brought Horton Spur into the show. His appearance in "Kid Boots" established his reputation.

While the rehearsals progressed, McGuire brought in an additional scene for act one that developed into one of the funniest situations ever written for musical comedy. There was a golf match in the show that had the hand of a girl at stake. I attempted to eliminate one of the golfers with a hammer, so that the hero could replace him in the contest. In working up to the hammer blow a situation of comedy suspense was created that produced five minutes of continuous laughter. The situation grew and became funnier the longer I played it.

We were going into the third week of rehearsal when it suddenly occurred to me that there was no second act. I hurried to Ziegfeld, who was occupied with the opening of his new Follies. He sent out an alarm for the delinquent playwrights, and more sessions followed. A week later the tail end of the show began to emerge. The final scene of the second act was to be set in the cocoanut grove, where a ball would be held and I would appear in black-face to do my specialty.

I felt the need for a band in this spot to enrich the scene and accompany my songs, but Ziegfeld had already protested strongly against the increasing expense of the production, and it looked almost impossible to get a band that would be both good and cheap. Fannie Brice, knowing our problem, told Ziegfeld and me of a new band she had heard out West that to her mind would one day be a sensation.

The unique feature of this band was its capacity for playing jazz time in a subdued and dulcet style, getting its effects through subtleties rather than noise. She had first heard it in a hotel at Portland, Oregon, and the last she knew it was playing somewhere along the Orpheum Circuit. I was intensely interested and induced Ziegfeld to wire the leader of this band, a Mr. George Olsen.

MY LIFE IS IN YOUR HANDS

George Olsen had begun his musical career as a drummer, not out of necessity, but as a hobby, for he was always in comfortable circumstances and made good money from a trucking and storage business that he owned jointly with his brother. But he preferred the hobby to his business and organized a small jazz band that he conducted in the main hotel of Portland, his home town. Fannie Brice and other Broadway stars would stop there on their Western tours and urge George to break through the narrow walls of the little hotel and reach out to the rest of the world. He finally migrated with his modest band to California for a trial performance, and on his first appearance in vaudeville scored an immediate success.

Olsen and his band acquired a local reputation, but its scope was limited. When the Ziegfeld offer reached him out of a clear sky, he realized that this was his big chance. The money that Ziegfeld offered him was no object, or at least such a small object that Olsen couldn't see it. But he accepted a contract for eight hundred dollars a week for the whole band, and lost money every week, making up the deficit out of his own pocket.

When "Kid Boots" opened in Detroit it was such a triumph that both Ziegfeld and Ed Royce thought we could get along without the band and save the eight hundred. But I felt it would be a big mistake and insisted that Olsen and his orchestra accompany me in my specialty. A warm friendship grew up between George and me, and on several occasions I championed his cause with Ziegfeld, who for some reason was anxious to make life for the bandmaster particularly hard. At least once I was obliged to tell Ziggy, "If George doesn't play I don't play."

During that year Olsen and his orchestra appeared with me at fifty-eight benefits for charity. One Sunday we played on four different programs, and George with his men rushed through the streets, carrying their heavy, shiny instruments from theater to theater. The wholehearted spirit in which he volunteered his services and the splendid way his band performed won fame for the Olsen orchestra overnight.

Last year his net personal earnings were five thousand dollars a week. He and his band played in "Good News" and at the Club Richman, while two other Olsen orchestras played at Miami and Havana. Endowed with a pleasing personality and educated at the University of Michigan, he lends that dignity and refinement to jazz interpretation that have made him a society favorite. Today Olsen's is the biggest jazz orchestra of the Victor Company and the sale of his records is second to none.

While the finishing touches were being put to "Kid Boots" I attended the opening night of the 1923 Follies. Tickets were selling at twenty-two dollars a seat, and when I found where my seat was I came equipped with a wrench, a hammer, and screwdriver and began to bang and loosen the seat just before the overture started. An usher hastened down the aisle and tried to stop me. "Let me alone," I cried. "I paid twenty-two dollars for my seat and I'm going to take it home!" The audience laughed and so did Ziegfeld. The critics observed that it was one of the best bits of the show that night.

In the same Follies I wrote a sketch for Fannie Brice, called "Snappy Stories of History." It represented a girl seated on a park bench, reading a magazine of *risqué* stories. A fellow would come out and tell her that in his book of history there were far more snappy tales. Then the curtains parted, revealing Fannie Brice in her versions of Queen Isabella, Queen Elizabeth, and Pocahontas. One night as I visited the show I noticed that the man with the book failed to appear on his cue. Fannie stood on the stage in bewilderment, not knowing what to do next. I snatched a program from one of the ushers, walked on the stage out of the audience, and played the man's part.

The time was fast approaching for the opening of "Kid Boots." McGuire revised the second act, improving it substantially. We needed a strong comedy scene toward the finish of this act, and he brought in the famous "Nineteenth Hole," which was one of the high spots of the show. Everything was ready now but the scenery and costumes. I wondered what could be delaying these last and essential elements of the production. I went to see Ziegfeld and stir him to action, but he received me rather indifferently.

"I want to talk to you, Eddie," he said, as if to prepare me for something unpleasant.

"What is it, Flo?" I sensed that something was wrong.

There was a minute of silence.

"I don't think we ought to go through with this show," he said at last.

I was stunned. My lips suddenly parched and I couldn't find my voice. But when I found it, the words gushed in torrents.

"Listen, Flo, after all this tough work and rehearsing five weeks and a cast like that and ———" He cut me short.

"I've made my mind up."

"But why?"

"I think it's a sure flop!"

Chapter XVIII

WHILE probably the greatest producer of hits, Ziegfeld is no optimist. He knows that a show may be sure-fire at rehearsals and look like amateur night when it opens. For that reason, as a production becomes more and more promising, he grows more pessimistic. Only recently, while three of his most sensational triumphs were in the making, he telegraphed McGuire, saying: "Why did I ever undertake so many shows! I am in the worst predicament of my life. I've got three flops on my hands." He was referring to "Show Boat," "Rosalie," and "The Three Musketeers." McGuire was deeply moved by Ziggy's complaint and replied, "Please accept my condolences in this your darkest hour of success."

I therefore knew that Ziegfeld's gloom over "Kid Boots" was a great sign. The problem was how to get him to order the scenery and costumes. I went to his office and reënacted the whole play before him from start to finish. I don't believe I ever gave a better performance of "Kid Boots" than that day. I sang the different numbers and choruses and played all the different parts in the piece, for I have always made it a point, in every show I have acted, to acquire a working knowledge of all the rôles, and have frequently jumped in to play an absent actor's part in an emergency. Ziegfeld's hopes were restored. He ordered the costumes and scenery.

Shortly after that, the whole cast went down to the

New Amsterdam Theatre to hear the entire musical score and see the new sets. Then came the dress rehearsal. Ziegfeld removed his coat, and when Ziegfeld removes his coat the serious part of show business begins. He has often worked through a dress rehearsal for a span of twenty hours, starting at two in the afternoon and still going strong the next morning. The theater is empty and a solemn air pervades the darkened orchestra where only the glow of a lighted cigar betrays his presence. The stage brightens up as for a regular performance and the play begins. No one must sit around in the theater or make a noise, for now comes his part, the rôle Ziegfeld plays in the show.

Numbers are done over and over again and dances are restaged at his request. Spots for certain specialties are switched and musical cues adjusted. He complains that the finale is too drawn out and the scene in one, in front of the drop, does not give enough time for putting up the next set. He hardly interferes with the dialogue or comedy scenes, for he has no fixed ideas as to what the audience will like and waits for the public reaction on the road to draw his conclusions. If the costumes don't harmonize with a particular scene according to his notion, they are discarded as so much cloth, and that's that. His main concern is ensemble effects and the sweeping impression of the whole.

He begins to give instructions to the electricians for the lighting of every scene and most of it sounds like deep Greek.

"Blue foots up on dimmer at start of overture," he says, "and white and amber foots up on dimmer at the end. Next scene, all lamps flood until finish, then dim down to blue and white one-quarter up and palm curtains open."

In this fashion are born those color moods which lend the final aura of splendor to the already lavish production.

"Kid Boots" opened in Detroit, December 3, 1923. It clicked from the first and ran as smoothly as a performance played after six months on Broadway. On the opening night I created a dozen new laughs by impromptu lines and they remained in the show. The audience received the production as a sensational triumph. Ziegfeld and Royce were so elated with my performance that they came to my dressing-room and kissed me. The tension of the first night, always severe with me, broke me down completely this time, and I cried like a child, the tears rolling down my face and ruining my make-up.

We played four weeks on the road, traveling to Cincinnati, Washington, and Pittsburgh, and opened in New York on New-Year's Eve. By that time some of the dancing costumes looked a little smudged to Ziegfeld and he ordered new dresses for several numbers. It was an additional item of eighteen thousand dollars, but he wanted the whole production to be crystal sparkling for opening night. In that respect his gallant gestures to his public are unique.

We opened at the Earl Carroll Theatre, and a little

extemporaneous curtain speech I made that night was kept in the show for three years.

"Kid Boots" contained every type of comedy for which I was best suited. The pattern of its comic scenes and their sequence were skillfully designed and have rarely been excelled. The shades of fun varied from light gags and wise-cracks to human situations, and from great physical hokum to delightful nonsense. My very first entrance was planted for a laugh. I rushed in, jumping about as if to work off an attack of fits.

"What's the matter, Boots?" asked one of the guests, trying to calm me. "What are you jumping around for?"

"Let me alone, will you!" I exclaimed, excitedly. "I just bought a second-hand watch. If I don't do this, it won't go."

In a musical comedy where spoken scenes are limited of necessity, the fact that I was the comedian of the show had to be established quickly, not by announcing it in the program, but by the first two minutes of dialogue. To accomplish this I wove in a half-dozen jokes around the fact that I was the caddie-master.

Thus, when I addressed the caddies, they fell down at the mere force of my authority.

"Get up," I said, sternly. "I suppose you know I'm the caddie-master around here!"

"Yes, ma'am," they replied.

"Yes, *ma'am?*" I was taken aback.

"No, ma'am."

MY LIFE IS IN YOUR HANDS

"No, *ma'am?*" I understood, tore off the red necktie I was wearing, and put it in my hip pocket. "Don't let this thing fool you. I'm a pretty tough guy, I am. When I have waffles for breakfast, I throw away the waffles and eat the irons!"

They stared at me and slunk away, but I called them back.

"How often have I told you guys there's been complaints about golf balls being missing. Now I don't mind you sneaking in a ball now and then, but remember, a golf ball is never lost till it stops rolling. Remember, honesty is the best policy. You've either got to be honest or I get half."

This kind of a scene had the double purpose of getting laughs and introducing my character. This was swiftly followed by a human situation in which I tried to comfort Tom Sterling, the forlorn lover. Against the serious background of his hopeless love for Polly, played by Mary Eaton, my comedy proved twice as effective.

"I've got troubles, Boots," he sighed, bitterly.

"You've got troubles? Lookit. I lost my salary shooting crap, my girl swallowed her engagement ring and I owe two hundred dollars on it. I've got an accident policy and I can't get hurt—and you've got troubles!"

I tried to show him that if there were harmony between him and Polly all their troubles would vanish.

"Do you know my idea of perfect harmony? I'd like to see a baseball game between the Ku-Klux Klan and the Knights of Columbus, with a negro umpire, for the benefit of the Jewish War Relief. I tell you, Tom, everything happens for the best—for some one. Say, if no one got the worst of it, no one could get the best of it."

"Boots, I'm in love."

"In love—that's different. In love everybody gets the worst of it. But, Tom, how can you be crazy about a girl like Polly? You must remember she's a swell girl from a big family, while you're only a handsome bozo. Forget it, Tom!"

"I can't."

"Don't say you can't. Look at me. When I was a kid I promised myself that when I'd be twenty-five I'd have a Rolls-Royce. Well, yesterday I was twenty-six and I put five dollars down on a Ford!"

This line brought one of the biggest laughs in the show. Yet under the guise of comedy we were carrying on the story of the play, which is the ideal method for light entertainment.

After planting the fact that I used crooked golf balls loaded with a little lead on one side so that my pupils could never master the art of putting, the well-known golf-lesson scene began. Jobyna Howland, who had made her mark in the "Gold Diggers," played an eccentric doctor who, in spite of her robust physique, was learning golf to build up. She was proud to let me know that she had played pretty well the day before.

"What did you go around in?" I asked with a professional air.

"A blue skirt and a brown sweater."

"No, no! I don't mean your attire. I mean the score—the number. What number did you make it in?"

"Oh! Seventy-one."

"Seventy-one! Why, that's phenomenal!" I exclaimed. "And the second hole?"

"Seventy." But she quickly retracted, "Oh, I don't remember, I'm so dumb."

"Dumb? You're not half so dumb as Mr. Pillsbury." He was an important member of the club.

"Is he dumb?"

"Is Pillsbury dumb? He thinks General Electric is a soldier."

"Well, isn't he?" We pursued the matter no further.

Then the lesson began. She started to make a little hill of sand for the ball. This exhausted my patience.

"Don't you know that you don't use sand to putt?"

"Well, what do you put to putt?"

"Put to putt? What the ——! Never mind the sand, I tell you. We'll play house later! Let me see you putt. You see, Doctor, you're all right, but that's where you fall down, when you putt."

"I must fall down when I putt?"

"No, you *mustn't*—but you *do!*"

"I mustn't, but I do! What are you talking about?"

"Pardon me. You're not Pillsbury's sister, are you?"

"No."

"All right, then let me see you putt. Come on—putt!"

She was all entangled in the frills of her dress like

MY LIFE IS IN YOUR HANDS

strings of spaghetti, and by the time she could get one hand loose to put around her club the other was waving aloft like a signal.

"Will you please tell me what you're going to do with that hand?" I inquired, severely.

"Oh, you can hold it," she said absently.

"I don't want it. This is a golf lesson. This isn't Central Park. Now putt. Don't look at me; keep your eye on the ball." She was getting cross-eyed trying to look at both of us, so I crawled down near the cup. She started to aim at me. "Wait!" I cried. "Stick in your tongue. You don't putt with your tongue! That's for approaches."

She putted. The ball rolled for a short distance, then turned crooked in its course. I could depend on it.

"That's near enough, near enough—by way of Syracuse."

"That ball always rolls crooked," she complained. "Why can't I get it in that little thing-a-ma-jig?"

"Thing-a-ma-jug? That's a cup! Not a jug!"

"Well, why don't I get it in the cup!"

"You don't bend over enough. You see, Doctor, you must be dressed for golf—that is, there are certain things you can't wear when you play golf. Now, if I wore a high collar I couldn't bend, either."

"Yes, I know, but I don't wear a high collar," she said in her husky, mannish tone.

"Well, whatever you do wear, you shouldn't——"

"Oh, you mean a corset."

MY LIFE IS IN YOUR HANDS

I was shocked. "Oh, Doctor!" I cried, hiding my face. "I couldn't say it!"

To get her set for the game I bent her into a right angle and she couldn't bend back. Aching, twisted, and half paralyzed, she could hardly raise the club.

"That's fine! Now putt!"

She did and the ball rolled crooked. Exasperated, she swung the club at me, but I drew out the flag pole to defend myself. We fenced like that all over the green until she broke into tears.

"Now, Doctor, don't cry," I said, soothing her. "Remember, Rome wasn't built in a day. You've only been putting two years."

She revenged herself on me, however, when she caught me later on in the ladies' locker-room, where I had been hiding bootleg supplies. To explain my presence there I pretended to be sick, and Dr. Fitch, my golf pupil, put me through every torture of electrical science. This was by far the funniest scene of the show and consisted chiefly of action, with only brief snatches of dialogue interspersed. It was the best physical-comedy scene I have ever played, and Jobyna Howland did her part so well that I always had real aches and pains when it was over.

After giving my neck a light wrench, she sat me in an electric chair that sparked and sizzled.

"Sit there," she ordered, "and don't get up until you count ten ——"

"Ten!" I cried, instantly.

MY LIFE IS IN YOUR HANDS

"No, count slowly."

"Five and five."

"No, slowly! For if you count over fifteen it might burn you a little."

"Might burn me a little?" I remonstrated, while the electric current held me in its grip. "1-2-3-4-15-600-900——"

Dr. Fitch went to answer a telephone call while I screamed in the thousands. When she finally turned off the current I rushed to a fire pail, sat in it, and fanned myself with a palm leaf. I tried to steal out, but this was only the beginning. Dr. Fitch insisted on curing me and stretched me out on an osteopath table. She chopped her hands up and down my spine, crushing me with her elbow every time I bobbed up. Then she made a handle of my hair and tried to see if my head was removable. After that she slammed me about unmercifully and swung each of my legs from one end of the table to the other. When I finally got off I staggered over to the electric chair, sat in it, and motioned for her to turn on the switch. She did, with a graceful smile, and the scene blacked out.

In the caddie-shop scene there were echoes of "Joe's Blue Front," and the old clothing-shop keeper came back to stand me in good stead. Once a comedian has struck certain styles of comedy that suit him, it is interesting to follow the many variations he devises, so that he can use the same idea and yet conceal it. But in the caddie shop I introduced a novel trick of dialogue, where by constantly repeating a single word it steadily mounted to a laugh.

Pillsbury, a guest of the club, entered the shop to buy a blue sweater. While in "Joe's Blue Front" I would have bewildered him with a dozen ridiculous sweaters of all colors, here I got the same effects by simply plugging a single word, "blue" and using lines instead of props.

"You want a sweater—blue?" I inquired.

"Yes, Blue."

"Must be a blue one?"

"Yes! Blue!"

"In other words, a blue sweater!" I began to look over my stock. "Don't you want an umbrella?"

"No! I want a sweater—a blue one!"

"A blue sweater!" I mused to myself, searching the boxes on the shelves.

"Yes! Blue!" reiterated Pillsbury, apparently peeved.

"Blue! A blue one. What size?"

"Size thirty-eight—blue."

"Blue. I beg your pardon, you said blue?"

"I said blue!" returned Pillsbury, angrily.

"Just to verify it, that's all," I said, soothingly. "We have some lovely underwear."

"I don't need underwear!"

"Aren't you lucky! Most people do."

Pillsbury started indignantly.

"I'm sorry, sir, but we're all out of sweaters." He

turned toward the door with a dejected air. "Now don't be discouraged. Remember, there's always the river."

I finally sold him a red cap.

The scene in "Kid Boots" that ranked nearest to the Osteopath Scene for laughs was one that rose directly out of the plot and needed no extraneous gags. This is ideal and rare, for if the story can so be turned that its crucial moments are handled lightly and in fun, then the story helps the fun and the fun helps the story.

In this case the situation revolved about a championship golf match to be played by the rivals for Polly's hand and heart. I was trying to help Tom, the hero, get into the match, and the only way was to incapacitate his friend Valentine, who had been selected by the club to represent it.

For more than five minutes I stood behind the counter with a hammer, poising it over Valentine at various times as if to crown him and make way for Tom. The comedy was primarily one of action and stage business. As I got into position for the attack, with the hammer behind my back, I inquired of Valentine, "If you were sick tomorrow you couldn't play, could you?"

"I should say not."

"How do you feel?"

"Why, I feel all right."

"I was just thinking, if anything happened to you, Tom would take your place ——"

"Yes, of course, Tom is my logical successor."

"He'd take your place?"

MY LIFE IS IN YOUR HANDS

Valentine lit a cigarette and I covered my eyes while lifting the hammer to strike him. But I weakened.

"Even—even if you had a sprained wrist you couldn't play?"

"No! The slightest thing would incapacitate me."

I wiped my brow, lifted two hammers, but hesitated again.

"Do you know anything about the law?" I suddenly inquired.

"I studied law—I'm a lawyer."

"Oh, you're a lawyer!" I put down both hammers. "I guess you could tell me what is assault?"

"Assault and battery?"

"I know what a battery is. I mean just plain assault."

"If one person strikes another with intent to injure, that is assault——"

"But if it's an accident?"

"Oh, well, if it's really an accident, then the person can't be punished."

"He can't be punished?" I asked, eagerly.

"No."

"Umph! That's a good law." I lifted the hammer with renewed confidence. "You feel all right?"

"I feel splendid."

"But if you had an injured wrist—*zowie*—the match would be off."

"But—*zowie*—I haven't an injured wrist."

"Ah, but you have an injured wrist!" I dropped the

hammer on his hand and he let out a yell that rocked the caddie shop. "Gosh! What an accident!"

Tom got into the golf match, but one of my intrigues miscarried and the crooked golf ball that was intended for his rival found its way into Tom's bag. He played eighteen holes with the loaded pill and lost the game. But to the very end the comedian was concerned with the vital points of the plot, for when I confessed that the crooked ball was mine, the match was voided and Tom won the girl.

There was one other comedy scene in the show, entirely distinct from the rest in style and conception. It was called the "Nineteenth Hole"—a small drinking bar where I stood deeply grieved at the misfortune that had befallen Tom, due to my crooked golf ball. Dr. Fitch and Pillsbury joined me there and we almost drank ourselves into a coma. This led to the discussion of sex complex.

In a musical show, comedy is timed and graded very much like climaxes. The kind of fun that demands a mental effort from the audience is good at nine-thirty. But at ten-thirty the audience is getting tired and the comedy rising out of situations must bow to good old hokum and sheer nonsense. And the "Nineteenth Hole" is one of the best examples of good nonsense.

I asked Pillsbury, "Do you know anything about sex complex?"

"Do I! I should say I do!"

"I'll try you out. In what part of the anatomy is the jugular vein?"

"What part of it?"

"That's what I said—what part of the anatomy is the jugular vein?"

"What part of it?"

"You know—*I'm* asking *you!*"

"Why?"

I admitted I didn't know why, but just then Dr. Fitch entered and we both felt relieved.

"Ah, Doctor!" we exclaimed.

"Ah, liquor!" she perceived. And promptly guzzled.

"That's to be sold, you know," I reminded her. We decided to ask her. Surely a doctor would know.

"Dr. Fitch, where is the jugular vein?"

"Oh, I don't know—somewhere near the Amazon River."

"No!" We were both flabbergasted.

"No?"

"No!"

"No? Maybe not. I'm very deficient in my geography."

"That's not geography. That's sex complex."

"Don't be vulgar!"

"Oh, it's dirty? Well, well, well!"

"Boots, don't you know what it is?"

"Yes, tell us what is the precise meaning of sex complex," urged Pillsbury.

"You folks don't know?" I inquired.

"No."

"That makes it easier. Sex complex is a scientific—that is—there are two kinds of people—male and female—and deep in the jungle—the lioness—is the mother—give up? Now then, in the wolf family—and ofttimes among the spotted leopards—there is a difference."

"A great difference?" Dr. Fitch asked me, rocking with her fourth glass.

"Oh, sister! Hear ye! Hear ye! Especially among the tigers, and that's why dreams are so important—the subconscious mind is a reservoir ——"

"Huh?"

"A reservoir—reservoir ——" I illustrated by squirting a bottle of seltzer at them. "Of concealed thoughts—secret desires—and any good doctor—any *good* doctor can tell by your dreams just what your secret desires may be ——"

"Oh, Boots," exclaimed Dr. Fitch in her strong basso, "last night I dreamed there were three wild men chasing me."

"Oh, Doctor! That wasn't a dream, that was a wish. But dreams alone don't explain sex complex."

"No?"

"No—deep in the jungle ——"

"Oh, must we go back there again?"

"Everything starts with animal life—even children start in with animal crackers—aminals—aminals—I mean animals are smart—think of how many centuries ago the mother elephant knew that some day there would be circuses!" Here I had to squirt seltzer again to revive my groggy friends and prepare them for this profound observation. "But mark you, animals alone are not vice-a-versa!"

"No!" they readily agreed, but then seemed doubtful, "No?"

"Why of course not! Take a zebra———"

"Zebra?" inquired the learned doctor. "What is a zebra?"

"A zebra is a sport-model jackass. And that's why I say—give me a word—lying down, with six letters—that is the gender of zebra! Do you know why you didn't know? Because that word has no cinnamon!"

My erudition baffled them completely and we concluded this intellectual discourse with the solemn anthem, "We were only playing leap frog!"

"Kid Boots" ran in New York until February, 1925, to a box office of one million, seven hundred and fifty thousand dollars. It traveled on the road until late in 1926 and earned a gross total of three million dollars.

I had now reached what seemed to be the height of my profession. In the old Henry Street days I had never dreamed of such a leap to success and popularity. And often, at the different stages of my progress, I would go down to the old haunts, take a walk around the park in Rutgers Square, or wander along the memory-laden trail of Henry Street. At least for a little while I wanted to meet again the Eddies that I once had been, the toothless Eddie who had climbed through a transom to help loot a bicycle store and the famished one with popping eyes and hollow cheeks who rented a pair of trousers to play the amateur night at Miner's.

Back-stage I now carried on a complete and separate life from the comic caddie in the golf club. And after every exit I had to pick up the thread where I had left it for my cue. I had to answer a great deal of fan mail, I dictated articles, thought up skits for revues, concerned myself with welfare work. Prominent persons from every sphere of life visited my dressing-room now—Governor Smith, Ex-Ambassador Gerard, Ambassador Claudel of France, Marcus Loew, Adolph Zukor, Paul Block, Commander Byrd, Harold Lloyd, Jesse Lasky, Mayor Walker, and, contrasted with them, newsboys, gunmen, sick and destitute, old acquaintances from the East Side—all anxious for a helping hand, making this little room the center of their world and hoping for anything from an autograph to a new start in life.

On June 1st, 1925, my wife and I sailed to Europe for our first trip of rest and pleasure. It was entirely different from our second-class honeymoon eleven years before. That was a contest of thrift and industry. She washed clothes, while I acted, and both skimped. This time it was a contest of spending. Every morning we decided on the best place to eat, the nicest place to visit; only once we went back to a humble spot of memory just to marvel how we were able to endure it. "But remember," Ida cautioned, "no matter how swell you get, your hat must always fit the head of the little boy on Henry Street!"

When we returned to New York the captain of the liner called me up on the bridge, and through his binoculars I could see a yacht approaching, flying the banner of "Kid Boots." The company, headed by George Olsen and his band, had sailed out to welcome us back. As we neared them, the band struck up "Eddie, Behave," and Ethel Shutta, comedienne of the Follies, led the welcoming party in song. It was on this trip that George Olsen and Ethel kindled the romance which later led to their marriage.

"Kid Boots" went on the road again, but I was beginning to long for some new avenue of expression. For some time I had cherished the hope of entering the movies. One day I did a short subject for the DeForrest Phonofilm just to test my chances. When the film played at the Rivoli, Lasky happened to see it and said to Walter Wanger, his manager-in-chief, "There is a screen personality."

Lasky bought the motion-picture rights to "Kid Boots" for sixty-five thousand dollars, with the proviso that I play the lead in the film version. When I went to Hollywood to start my first picture, I found that the man in full charge of its production was an old boyhood chum of mine from Henry Street, Ben Shulberg.

Chapter XIX

WHILE the thought of living in Hollywood thrilled my children, yet they were reluctant to leave our home in Mount Vernon where they had built up pleasant friendships and associations. I tried to comfort them.

"Look who your new friends will be! I'll have Gloria Swanson play jacks with you and you'll skip rope with Vilma Banky!"

Margie, my oldest, was skeptical.

"Yeh! And I suppose you'll get Norma Shearer to wait on us at table!"

But when I suggested that we leave three weeks before school closed, they were promptly converted.

On arriving in Los Angeles, we rented a bungalow in Beverly Hills and left the door open for Chaplin, Fairbanks, and Rin-Tin-Tin to walk in. But Margie says the only regular caller we had was the landlord.

Personally, I looked forward to my Hollywood visit with a good deal of excitement. I had read so much about this hell's kitchen in the newspapers that I brought along a one-piece cutaway bathing suit to wear to banquets. I expected to see a repetition of the old Roman days when emperors threw parties on the street and half-naked men and women caroused on beds of roses. Instead, it turned out to be a small factory town, very provincial and terribly industrious. For the first time in my life I had to wake up at dawn and get into make-up so I could be shot at sunrise.

MY LIFE IS IN YOUR HANDS

Everybody went around in some disguise and you couldn't tell whether the cop on the beat was an extra or whether the bootlegger he was shooting after was a star. The whole population marched out in the morning carrying make-up boxes, and long lines of laborers filed into the picture factories to put in a day's work as villains, kings, pirates, and Indian chiefs.

The town is mainly divided into two huge production plants, and at the head of each of these is a mere youngster. Irving Thalberg, aged thirty, supervises the Metro-Goldwyn-Mayer output, and Ben P. Shulberg, thirty-six, does the same for Famous Players. Each of these factory foremen gets a quarter of a million dollars a year, which I understand is a little more than the union scale. They are thoroughly efficient, shrewd masters of production, and the only thing they carry on the hip is contracts. All the big names, I found, were sober, earnest people who lived on diets and answered fan mail. There are undoubtedly wild scenes in Hollywood, but they only take place when you ask for a raise.

After punching a time-clock I was ready for my début in pictures. In casting "Kid Boots" for the screen, Ben Shulberg selected three of the most beautiful girls in filmdom—Billie Dove, Natalie Kingston, and Clara Bow. I was unused to screen methods at first, and the director, Frank Tuttle, had to cut my stage tempo to half its speed. My style of acting was altogether too fast and made the camera eye blink. Afterward, on my return to the Follies in 1927, it took me several days to regain my original pace.

Clara Bow proved most helpful to me with suggestions and advice. She told me, "What rehearsals are to the stage, spontaneity is to the screen." In this art, more than in any other form of acting, the first principle is to be yourself. She is. She is never camera conscious and acts with the same ease on the set as she would in her home. In some of our scenes together she was supposed to scold me severely. But while the camera ground away at our quarrel and caught all her pretty frowns, she was really saying, "Eddie, you're doing fine! Just flash those banjo eyes and there's nothing to it!"

Frank Tuttle followed the same principle of spontaneity. In several scenes he let me run loose, instructing the camera men to keep on filming regardless of what I did, and to my great surprise, as well as his, some of the funniest bits in the picture were born that way. One of them was an imaginary love scene that I carried on with my own arm. By pulling up one sleeve, powdering the arm, and tying my watch-chain around the wrist like a bracelet, it created the illusion of a woman's arm, the rest of her body apparently concealed behind the side of a door. My own girl, sitting at another table, could see me flirting with this hand, holding it tenderly and finally kissing it, while it gently pushed me aside. She grew jealous, came over to attack the hidden vamp, only to discover that it was my arm. Another bit was an impromptu Charleston that I danced when a chunk of ice slid under my collar and down my bare back.

Tuttle knew that I was accustomed to play before audiences and that their laughter would stimulate my sense of ad-libing. To help me along in these scenes he collected a crowd of onlookers and they laughed at so much per day. I never got so many laughs in my life.

But there were also serious moments in the production. One of them was when I had to kiss Clara Bow. It seems we got everything right but that, and we had to do it over and over again. And when Clara kisses you, you have been osculated! She could kiss a tree and start a forest fire! And what a figure! How it vibrates and quivers! It's like the New York Telephone Company. Every line is busy!

We had mood music for our scenes. The band would set us in an atmosphere of romance or frivolity, and after the shots were taken, Clara Bow, Frank Tuttle, Billie Dove, and others of the company would gather on the set and ask me to entertain them with some numbers. I sang as many songs out on the movie lot as I did in Coney Island long ago, but without waiting on anyone.

There were many daredevil stunts in "Kid Boots," and I was soon initiated into the mystery of doubles. Whenever there is an element of danger the star is exempt. Some stunt man doubles for him, often risking his life for a few dollars. After all, why should the star take a chance when he has a wife or two, three automobiles, and a swimming-pool dependent on him.

In the Cliff Scene of "Kid Boots," which made the movie audiences gasp, doubles were used for both Clara Bow and myself. In most of the hazardous scenes everything was done by doubles, except in the case of the horse, and later on he complained about it. Only once did I double for myself, and heartily regretted it.

The picture showed me being dragged along the ground by a galloping horse, with a rope around my waist. When this shot was taken I was tied not to the galloping horse, but to a slow-moving automobile, the director riding alongside me in a moving camera truck. While I was running, supposedly pulled by the frantic steed, the director told me to skip gracefully. I tried it and fell. The automobile dragged me some distance over the rough road before it was stopped. My knees were bleeding and gravel had cut my hands, lodging deep under the skin. I had to spend several hours in getting the gravel removed. If I needed sand to make good in pictures, I surely got enough then for the rest of my career.

The method of shooting scenes was something new to me. On the stage I had been trained to a strict logical sequence of the story. But here the director jumbled parts of the middle with the end and shot them before the beginning, so that I first ran off with the girl and later was introduced to her. In the same way, Billie Dove was married to the hero, and some time after, I arranged their first meeting.

The reason for this was economy. All bits of action that occurred in a certain set or location were taken regardless of their sequence in the story. The director also bunched those scenes that involved his leading stars, so as to shorten their playing time and save on the payroll. By this means he "killed off" the principals as quickly as possible. Billie Dove, who appeared in the picture right up to the end, was through with all her scenes the first week. And while "Kid Boots" took more than a month to film, Billie Dove got only one week's salary.

On the movie lot I met my old friend, Raymond Griffith, who eleven years before had advised me how to handle my first musical comedy rôle in "Canary Cottage." We recalled the stunts he had taught me to get by the watchful eye of Trixie Friganza. It was a laughing matter now. On the next lot to ours, Emil Jannings was preparing his first American production, "The Way of All Flesh." Though a native of Brooklyn according to press reports, he knew little of the language, and he and I often attracted attention in restaurants as we played our thoughts in pantomime for each other.

One evening I spoke at a dinner in the movie colony and Jannings' wife, sitting next to him, translated my remarks in a whisper, with the result that a few minutes after the audience laughed he would break into a roar. This startled me, and not knowing the cause at the time, I observed: "Emil Jannings isn't German. He must be English!"

On the other side of "Kid Boots" was the lot reserved

for Adolphe Menjou, then working on his picture, "The Man in Evening Dress." Menjou, who, according to my daughter Margie, "chews gum in the most adorable manner," is meticulous not only about his gum. He studies his parts with great insight and care, is as charming and refined off the screen as on and is one of the few movie actors who brings to his work a great amount of education, understanding, and culture.

One day Menjou and I went up in an airplane for the experience, and I took along my colored valet, Benny. When we finally came down to earth again, Menjou remarked, "Why, Benny, you turned white!"

"You wasn't blushing, either, Mr. Menjou," said Benny.

On another occasion, when Menjou visited me in my dressing-room, he asked Benny, "What's today's date?"

"I don't know the date, sir," replied the valet.

"Look at that newspaper," I told him.

Benny dismissed the suggestion.

"Aw, that's yesterday's paper," he said with a wave of the hand. Benny had formerly been Harry K. Thaw's valet. Maybe that explains it.

On another lot, some distance away, the great picture, "Wings," was being filmed and Richard Arlen, who played in it, would come over to our studio after work to meet his sweetheart, Jobyna Ralston. Jobyna had been Harold Lloyd's leading lady and played with me in "Kid Boots." There was only one spot in the picture where I had occasion to kiss her, but every time I noticed Dick

Arlen approaching, I pretended to rehearse the kissing scene with Jobyna. We did it so realistically that Dick began to get worried. This probably had something to do with their early marriage.

Life on the movie lots carried with it a fascination far greater than mere parties or banquets. While huge armies worked in each inclosure to build the flashes of city, country, and far-away places embraced in the gleam of each camera eye, there was a little French restaurant right outside the studios where the most amazing medley of all ages and nations would assemble daily for the midday meal.

Mme. Helène's was the famous rendezvous for the stars of cinema. There you would see Wallace Beery in a sailor costume lunching with Florence Vidor, adorned as a countess. Raymond Griffith in a high hat would be rolling dice for his lunch with young Lawrence Grey. Richard Dix in football togs would be eating pie *à la mode*, and dainty Bebe Daniels would be sitting over her bowl of spinach. It was all she ate. You wondered how she could do all she did on that bit of green grass. She was a hard worker and had a keen practical brain. She bought real estate in her spare time and closed profitable deals. On the lot she was one of the most daring movie actresses, and the easiest job was to double for Bebe, for most of the hair-raising, spectacular stunts she performed herself. Adolphe Menjou, immaculately stenciled in his fashion-plate, might be eating with a hobo who was paying for both, and the hobo would be Chester Conklin.

Later, when the "King of Kings" was filmed, stately biblical figures began to wander into Mme. Helène's little lunch-room, and the rulers of ancient Rome and Judea mingled with the aviators from "Wings" and the train robbers from "Special Delivery." Visitors thronged to this little world of magnificent chaos where time, place, and history were thrown together like the colors in a ball of agate, and they gladly paid the high tariff tagged to each small dish of food. But the joke was on the actors. For though they made the place the attraction it was, they had to pay the same high tariff themselves.

The gala event of Hollywood, however, was not the daily luncheon at Mme. Helène's, but New-Year's eve at the Mayfair Club. Here, indeed, scintillated the entire glory of moviedom. The ballroom needed no candelabra, for it blazed with a million watts of diamonds. The jewels of the profession were assembled in stone and in person. You saw Jack Dempsey in his civilian nose, with Estelle Taylor sparkling on his arm. There was Jobyna Ralston dancing with William Powell, the brutal villain who had killed her in a picture only a week before. Pola Negri, the gypsy vampire, would be floating on the arm of Charlie Rogers, the guileless juvenile. All parts had been abandoned now to play their parts in life. And the world of make-believe receded into the shadows of the vacant movie lots at the dazzle and grandeur of this richer, real world. I sang at the Mayfair Club to entertain my colleagues, and Dempsey and I staged a mock battle.

MY LIFE IS IN YOUR HANDS

That evening left a stirring impression on my mind and I marveled at this new world of iridescent splendor representing many millions, many romances, many miracles more wonderful than Aladdin and Sinbad ever dreamed to see, and it had all come into being through the imagination and business brains of a former furrier, a former druggist, and a former cornet-player—Adolph Zukor, Joe Schenck, and Jesse Lasky.

"Kid Boots" took six weeks to film. It could have been completed in five weeks, which would have established a record for a big picture, but one solid week was devoted to a single stunt scene which afterward did not even appear at the first showing. In this scene I was all set to dive backward from a springboard about twenty-five feet in the air to impress my girl, not knowing that my rival was emptying the pool to impress my skull. While I made elaborate preparations on the springboard the water was being steadily drained, and when I finally took the back dive I was plunging headlong into a pool as dry as Hoover would like it.

The diving illusion into a dry stone pool was accomplished by the use of rollers which the movie audience could not see. I was slid across the full length of the pool on these rollers right into the arms of my husky rival, Malcolm Waite, who received me warmly with two fists. There was a deal of accessory horse-play and slapstick connected with this scene, but when Ben Shulberg saw the picture at the preview he thought it was all too mechanical. He believed that, since I had played such a legitimate character throughout "Kid Boots," it would be best to avoid this lapse into hokum. A week's extravagant labor was erased with a word.

When the picture was finally completed and while it was still being studied in the projection room for cuts and revisions, I lost no time in getting my tickets for New York, figuring that they could never really hurt a man three thousand miles away.

At Chicago I stopped for breath. There I met Georgie Jessel and my insurance agent, Jack Kreindel. It was comforting to travel the last lap of the trip with friends and confide to them my fears about the picture. They tried to divert me with a game of cards, but I lost, and that depressed me more. At eleven we retired to our berths in the compartment. I lay sleepless for more than an hour, and noticed that Georgie was restless, too. It would be nine hours before we pulled into New York. As we lay for a time whispering to each other, Jack Kreindel's deep slumber broke upon us in thunderous snores.

"We've got to fix that guy," Jessel finally decided.

"O. K.," I replied.

We got up and began to dress. It was after one. I nudged Kreindel.

"What'sa matter?" he started.

"Hurry up," I said. "The train pulls into Grand Central in half an hour." Jessel and I continued to dress in the most matter-of-fact manner. We brushed our teeth, combed our hair.

Kreindel stretched happily. "Gee! I slept like a log!" he exclaimed. "The night passed like a minute!"

"You'll be late!" said Jessel, curtly, and Kreindel started to dress. "Boys, I had a great night's sleep!" he continued, getting into his clothes; but we disregarded him as we put on our coats. He was soon dressed and rang for the porter.

The porter arrived, looking drowsy. "Yessir?"

"Hurry up! Take out these bags," said Jack. "We're late!"

"What for?" inquired the porter, opening his eyes wide.

"We'll be in New York in a few minutes!" persisted Kreindel, sternly.

"You will?" cried the porter. "We just pulled out of Cleveland and we got eight more hours to go!"

Three weeks after my return to New York I received a wire from Ben Shulberg. It read:

HOLLYWOOD, August 27, 1926.

EDDIE CANTOR,
New York.

DEAR EDDIE—Previewed "Kid Boots" last night stop Would have done your heart good to see how much audience liked you stop Picture has everything it needs to make it popular entertainment stop Will have print in New York in about four weeks for you to see stop You can accept my honest assurance you have no occasion for any further worry about picture or your screen personality kindest regards.

B. P. SHULBERG.

Two weeks after this one I received another telegram. It was from Jesse Lasky himself.

MY LIFE IS IN YOUR HANDS

Having just seen "Kid Boots" I hasten to congratulate you stop Picture will be success and your performance is outstanding and proves conclusively to my mind you have all qualifications for successful screen career kindest personal regards.

"Kid Boots" opened at the Rialto Theatre, New York, the first week of October, 1926. I was engaged to make a personal appearance with the picture at seventy-five hundred dollars a week. As a compliment to me on my screen début, George Olsen and his band insisted on coming to the Rialto to accompany my numbers.

I played to a new public, the majority of them people who had never seen me on the stage because they could not afford the Ziegfeld rates. In one material respect I had to change my style. For as I improvised and varied the program the same people stayed on after each showing instead of emptying the house to let in a new crowd. It was good for me, but not good for business.

I finally stuck to a single routine, and after that the crowds moved briskly. The picture played an entire month at the Rialto, which was a record for one's first picture. "Kid Boots" ranked seventh among the first ten hit productions of the year from the Famous Players' studio, and earned seven hundred and fifty thousand dollars. I was reëngaged for another picture. I had received only three thousand dollars a week for the first one, but for my work in the new one I received one hundred and fourteen thousand dollars, or eight times as much.

Chapter XX

"SPECIAL DELIVERY," my second picture, was an original story written by myself. I had intended to create a more human, less hoky vehicle only sparsely interspersed with gags. But when the story was rewritten for the screen and finally produced, everything between laughs was cut out, giving the hoppy, hiccupy effect of a comic strip or a stale-joke book. It was one of those sad cases of authorship where I saw my brain-child get its brains knocked out and I had to be an accomplice to the crime.

One incident will illustrate what happened. I had a scene with Mary Carr, who, when the final picture unraveled itself from the mess, was not even in the film. Mary Carr played the mother of a boy who had left home and had never written her after that. Day after day, as I passed with my mail-pouch, the old lady would intercept me, asking, "Mr. Letter-carrier, anything for me?"

"No. No word from your Jimmy," I told her.

Tears trembled in her eyes as she turned back to her house. One day I resolved to bring her a letter from Jimmy. Before approaching her doorstep I sat down on another stoop and wrote a letter to the old lady, saying:

Dear Mother—I'm sorry I ran away from home. I've been ill but I'm well now. Inclosed find ten dollars for spending money. Please write me care of General Delivery, Scranton, Pa.

Your loving son, Jimmy.

MY LIFE IS IN YOUR HANDS

I handed the letter to Mary Carr. She opened it while I lingered on to watch her emotion. She kissed the letter, took the ten-dollar bill with a grateful expression, and went joyfully into the house. A few hours later, passing along the same route, I met Mary Carr going to mail a letter. I knew it was addressed to her lost son and insisted on mailing it for her. From now on I would be her lost son. When she left me I opened the letter eagerly and read,

My dear boy, I was happy to hear from you. Keep well. Thanks for sending the ten dollars. I know you have sent me many a ten-dollar bill, but the postman on our block looks like an awful crook. In the future please send money orders. Your loving mother.

This whole episode was photographed and shown in the projection-room, where it was received with enthusiasm. James Cruz, one of our great motion-picture directors, happened to be there at the time and said it was one of the finest touches he had seen in pictures. Yet the whole thing was not even shown at the preview, and I don't know why to this day.

Another serious alteration in the story was caused by the federal authorities. Our plot centered about a mail robbery, during which I, as a rookie postman, accidentally captured the robber chief single-handed after a series of funny mishaps. This made me undeservedly a hero and won me the girl for whose hand a fireman and a policeman had also aspired.

MY LIFE IS IN YOUR HANDS

It was not until the picture had gotten well under way that we learned the government would not permit the showing of even a comical mail robbery on the screen. Had this been discovered before we started to shoot the picture, it would have altered all our plans and most probably we would have selected a different story altogether. But as it stood it was too late to turn back, and instead of the mail robbery we introduced a bucket-shop broker who used the mails to defraud. This switched the picture into conventional lines and diminished its strength considerably.

With the story weakened and the human element destroyed, we started to gag and almost suffocated. Of the two hundred or more gags that we filmed I liked one particularly. Tired of lugging my load of mail through the streets and up the stairs, I suddenly paused beside a hurdy-gurdy. I asked the organ-grinder whether he could play, "Bye-Bye, Blackbird." He churned out the tune and I began to sing it. A great crowd gathered to see and hear this strange street exhibit, and when the people were all assembled I distributed my mail among them, calling the roll from the letter pile.

In another scene a big bull-dog was supposed to jump for frankfurters that I held. The trainer was not around that day and his assistant had little standing with the dog. The bull thought my leg was the frankfurter and dug his teeth into it. The wound had to be cauterized, or "cantorized," as the men on the lot put it. This was the only realistic bit in the picture and it happened off the screen.

During the shooting of "Special Delivery," Douglas Fairbanks and Mary Pickford visited my lot. "Oh, how we could use both of you in this picture!" I said. But they didn't take the hint.

Another guest was Morris Gest. "You might own this production," I told him.

"How's that, Eddie?"

"If it goes over it's another 'Miracle'!"

Somehow I felt that this was far below the promise born of "Kid Boots," but there seemed to be nothing we could do about it. We just glided along with it, but the glide was downstream.

While the picture was still in the cutting-room, being glued together for the preview, I traveled to New York and back to California, a distance of six thousand miles, to play a single benefit performance for my Boys' Camp. The Camp Committee counted on my appearance, and I did not want to disappoint them. I arrived at the Casino Theatre the night of the benefit, played there, and the next day I was on the train returning to the Coast.

During my stay in California I had an impulse to play two theaters which belonged to a circuit that had turned down Al Lee and myself at a salary of three hundred and twenty-five dollars a week in 1915. This time they gladly paid me forty-five hundred dollars a week and I didn't work half so hard as in the days with Lee.

But the years of ceaseless activity on the stage coupled

with numberless benefits that I always played in spare intervals had accumulated their toll of strain and fell upon me like an avalanche. As "Special Delivery" drew to a close, so did my strength. I had been losing weight, could not digest properly, and suffered from enervating fatigue. I began to visit doctors and read all the magazines in their waiting-rooms back to 1860. I learned the difference between a general practitioner and a specialist. I found out that an ordinary doctor may treat you for pleurisy and you die of a broken leg. But not with a specialist! Whatever he treats you for you die from.

They finally decided it was my tonsils. I planned to go to New York for the operation. Wallace Beery asked me, "Why should you go to New York when you can take them out here?"

"But they're New York tonsils!" I argued. And New York got them.

Even after that my condition showed little improvement. Anticipating the worst, I resolved to increase my life insurance, and Betty, Will Rogers' wife, sent a doctor to examine me for an additional policy. He asked me the usual questions and I gave the usual answers. We were getting along swimmingly when Ida walked into the room. She didn't know it was an examination for insurance and was anxious that the doctor should know everything that would help him make a correct diagnosis.

"Have you been to any doctors recently?" he inquired.

"I haven't been to a doctor in years!"

"Eddie!" my wife exclaimed, surprised. I tried to

MY LIFE IS IN YOUR HANDS

signal her, but the medical examiner kept his eyes riveted on mine.

"Were you ever seriously sick?" he continued.

"Never!"

"Eddie!" my wife repeated, this time more reproachfully. I began to feel alternately flushed and chilled.

"Ever have any trouble in your chest?" he asked.

"My chest? Oh no!"

Ida could restrain herself no longer.

"Why don't you tell the doctor about your pleurisy?" she cried, amazed that I should have overlooked such an important fact. The doctor stared hard at me.

"Ha-ha!" I laughed, uneasily. "Can you imagine, Doc, I forgot that!"

"H'm, h'm!" he muttered. "Anything else the matter with you?"

"Not a thing! I'm perfect!"

"Is that so!" Ida was beside herself. "Why don't you tell him about the rash that came out on your back and your bum knee? You know it sometimes snaps out of place! And that choking feeling you get at night, and how tired you are after the least exertion, and how you can't sleep, and what all those big professors said is the matter with you!"

"It's marvelous how women remember these trifles!" I said, grinning foolishly. "They're not important, doc."

"I wouldn't say that," said the doc.

"Is there anything else you'd like to know?"

"I guess that will do," he observed, kindly, taking his hat. It did do. I was politely rejected.

The time had come for my return to Ziegfeld. He had wired me that he would do no more Follies shows unless I consented to star in the next one. I realized the difficulty of bearing the full weight of a whole revue on my shoulders, but in consideration for this Ziegfeld was willing to shorten the term of our contract. If I starred in his next Follies he would take a year off the agreement, which still had three to run. The deal was arranged. I lost a year from my contract and five from my life. It was the hardest individual work I ever did in any show.

On the train coming east Irving Berlin and I laid out the plans for the 1927 Follies. For his end of the production Irving Berlin received five per cent of the gross, which was the highest royalty ever paid to a composer of musical comedy. It was so high that even Berlin was impressed. One day while crossing Times Square a taxicab grazed my toes and Berlin pulled me back with a jerk.

"For Heaven's sake, Eddie, be careful!" he cried. "Think of my royalties!"

As is customary in a production like the Follies, a large number of extra scenes are prepared with the view to eliminating the dull ones after a tryout. But in this case there didn't seem to be any dull ones and we retained them all. The comedy skits furnished a wide range of humor from an aviation setting to a bird shop. The two sketches that became most popular in New York were the Taxicab Scene and the Mayor Walker Scene. In fact, there was scarcely a musical production after that which did not include an impersonation of the Mayor.

The Taxicab Scene was my newest variation on the old reliable physical-comedy act. It represented a modern he-girl escorting home a modest she-man and trying to flirt with him. The bashful boy resisted and the bold bad lady persisted. At last she exclaimed in disgust, "You're the coldest proposition!"

"I'm sorry," I retorted with dignity. "I'm sorry we're not the same temperature."

The quarrel led to my being kicked out of the cab. I was invited to walk the remaining ten miles or else agree to be mauled with affection.

"I guess I'll else," I wailed, crawling back to my seat.

As Mayor of the City of New York I was kept permanently busy posing for photographers and turning the city over to visiting channel swimmers, athletic champions of tennis and golf, crowned heads, and aviators. The office of Mayor was not new to me. In 1924, in a contest by popular vote for "Mayor of Broadway" conducted in S. Jay Kaufman's column, I was elected by a plurality of eleven thousand. As the Ziegfeld show was always included in a first-night reception to city guests, I had occasion to coin many impromptu lines welcoming actual celebrities who visited the Follies.

The night Colonel Lindbergh attended the show I asked him whether, in flying over Scotland, he found the air-pockets too tight, and when Ruth Elder was in the audience I presented her with a key to the city, saying: "You will go down in history as the only woman who was ever picked up on the ocean."

Impromptu situations are the spice of the stage. They have often yielded my best laughs, but in most cases the situation arises but once. Thus in the Animal Store Scene, a dog I employed happened to scratch himself with his hindpaw in a strumming motion, and I dubbed him "Ukelele Ike." It was a spontaneous laugh, but the next night the dog refused to strum.

A more personal type of impromptu jest was the one I played on Dr. Goddard of Philadelphia. He was the surgeon who had operated on Dempsey's nose. In his office, he maintained a severe dignity, but when sitting in the theater he would become so exuberant in his laughter that his collar always wilted from the excitement. When he came to see me in the show I threw him a fresh collar from the stage after every scene.

On October 8, 1927, while playing in my last Follies, I became a father once more. My fifth daughter, little Janet, was born.

"What's the idea, Eddie?" cried Ziegfeld. Even he was flabbergasted. Not to mention myself.

"It's for you, Flo," I replied. "I'm raising my own Albertina Rasch ballet."

Ida suffered severely after the birth of Janet and required several blood transfusions. For some time her life was despaired of and after each performance I spent the rest of the night by her bedside. She recovered and after a long convalescence regained her normal vigor. One night I returned home with a diamond-studded bracelet, the stones set in platinum. Fifteen years before, when we were engaged, she had gazed at such a bracelet in the window at Tiffany's. It was one of those shining, magic wonders floating in a different world from hers that she never hoped to attain. Now it coiled its gleaming warmth about her wrist. She was delighted as a child. One of Grimm's fairy tales had come true.

I was on the stage nearly two hours every night out of the two and a half. The ordeal broke through my thin resistance and I was taken with a relapse of pleurisy. While playing in Boston I had to quit the 1927 Follies upon the advice of my physicians and submit to a long rest cure. Much publicity attended my illness because Ziegfeld, for some unknown reason, decided I was shamming. He insisted upon an arbitration proceeding before Actors' Equity, and his personal physician, Dr. Wagner, was permitted to examine me and decide whether I was sick or not. Unfortunately, I won. The doctor stethoscoped, fluoroscoped, and X-rayed me and concluded that I was even sicker than I thought. When Ziegfeld heard this, he promptly dropped the rôle of investigator and urged me to go ahead and get a good rest.

I spent six weeks at Palm Springs, California, and then went to the Battle Creek Sanitarium for another six weeks. My health has been gradually restored and today I feel as well as ever. On my return to New York I set to work on the new Ziegfeld musical comedy, "Whoopee!" based on the farce, "The Nervous Wreck," by Owen Davis. My recent experiences at Battle Creek proved valuable training for just this type of show. Out there, every time I saw a man with a white coat I stuck out my tongue and started to undress.

"Whoopee!" is like a family reunion of many of those who helped make "Kid Boots" a ringer. George Olsen and his band are with me. Ethel Shutta, who is now Mrs. Olsen and already has an Olsen junior, plays the leading comedienne rôle, while William Anthony McGuire who wrought the book of "Kid Boots," is the fashioning hand in "Whoopee!"

Along with my work in the new show I have made a few short subjects for talking pictures in the Paramount Studios on Long Island. If they are favorably received by the public I shall soon do my first long movietone picture. Between the talking films and the new musical play I shall find a happy winter's work, providing the public finds it happy, too.

It is my hope, after these efforts, to enter the producing field and perhaps appear in my first straight play where I will not have to depend on singing or dancing or clapping of hands to get my effects, but upon the simple ability of acting, which maybe I have, after all.

Chapter XXI

PERHAPS this thing I am about to reveal is a little too personal. After all, there is a limit even to candor. But I know the readers expect a certain amount of inside stuff, a keyhole look into those hidden corners of one's private life, otherwise they'll want their money back. Well, I admit today I am keeping six women. It is a remarkable experience. You would imagine this slightly complicates my life, and it does. When I kiss one, all the others get jealous, though not violent.

I've got a system. I don't tell them I'll put them on the stage or try to win them with other promises. I just pay their bills. Besides, I carry on no intrigues. A liberal understanding exists between me and my women. I tell each one frankly that I love all the others, and they stand for it. In fact, they're loyal not only to me, but to each other. And they're so sensitive that if I quarrel with one I have to give them all presents.

I have tried a daring experiment. There are men who might think it wiser to keep six women in different apartments in various parts of the city, but I have them all live in different parts of the same house. It saves taxi fares. In the evening I go from door to door and kiss each one good night. They are all beautiful, running the full gamut of ages from the oldest, who is in the early thirties, to the youngest, who is ashamed to admit it, but she is still teething. They represent every type, manner, and mood of womanhood.

MY LIFE IS IN YOUR HANDS

Ida, the oldest, is calm, motherly, staid, and serious. Margie is a lady of thirteen with a weakness for playing Juliet in high-school theatricals. Her ambition is to become a counselor when she grows up, teaching and guiding the young. The other four, ranging from eleven years to eleven months, have decided just to go on eating. Yet they all seem so busy and absorbed in their separate pursuits that I feel like an idler by comparison. Ida goes shopping, Margie reviews movies for the local paper, Natalie, Edna, and Marilyn go to school, and Janet goes to the crib.

Since our return from Hollywood we live in a rented house at Great Neck, Long Island. This is our temporary dwelling until the time when our own home will be erected. It is a spacious, choicely appointed cottage with all improvements, and you can have the lease cheap when our own home is ready. There are big grounds with a nice white fence all around, a vegetable garden and garage space for several cars. It is quite the thing for one who has lived in a two-room basement on Madison Street.

When we gather at the dinner table we are seven—one man among six women. They wait until I come down and always expect me to surprise them in different make-up. I've found that little pranks, funny notions, queer entrances set the house on a roar and help digestion. Ida presses the button under the table and the head waitress enters, followed by an assistant who has another assistant and so they keep on assisting each other. The meal begins. There are many courses, enticing entrées, soups, roasts, elaborate desserts. Our menu changes twice a week with the cook. It is all on a high scale now. But Margie doesn't eat. She looks wistful and peers longingly into space. I finally find out what is stirring in her soul. She would give the meal, the table, and the whole place along with it, for one hot dog.

It brings back memories. Twenty-five years ago I was an errand boy for the Isaac Gelles Wurst Works and used to carry their daily supply of frankfurters and pickled creations from the factory on Essex Street to the store on Market Street, eating half of the output on the way. I guess Margie would have relished that kind of a job. Maybe these children miss a little of the struggle that their old man had. Life may be sweet but not when there's so much sugar that it gets into the blood. One day little Edna, aged seven, got up and walked out of the house. Nobody suspected that she had left except to play on the lawn. But a few hours later we realized that she was missing. We sounded an alarm. She was finally discovered at the other end of Great Neck, on her way to Mexico. She had gone in quest of romance, adventure, and the unknown.

They must be my daughters. This restless longing is not their only point of resemblance to me. I remember during President Harding's administration my family and I paid the President a visit and he patted the little girls on the head genially, saying, "Eddie, you have bright children."

"Yes," I replied, "when they grow up they'll all vote for Al Smith."

"I guess it's hereditary," observed the President, smiling.

Margie's interest in welfare work is another point of resemblance. Merely to be a stage success has never represented to me the fulfillment of my life's desires. As I look back over the five Eddies I have been, I am glad to find that the actor is not the chief among them. There was the boyhood Eddie of the East Side tenements whose spirit survived the struggles of adversity. There was another Eddie, the business man, who achieved economic independence and security. There was a third Eddie with simple, bourgeois tastes who raised a family and built the comforts of a home. The fourth Eddie rose along Broadway in a blaze of electric lights and satisfied the longing of a lifetime to become a star. But there was also a fifth one, the Eddie who always gave of all his energies and powers to aid those less fortunate than he.

I have never stinted on playing benefits or helping worthy causes. While the field of philanthropy has its queer offshoots, it is in the main the worthiest human pursuit. It is true that sometimes a woman whose name has been left off the letterhead of a hospital or orphan asylum will print her own letterhead and start an opposition charity. It is also true that some benefits cost more than they make, like one at which I was asked to appear, where I showed the committee how it could save five hundred dollars by no running the affair at all. But in general I have found charity movements to be worthy and wise and I have always helped them with money and services.

One night I played six benefits, which I think is a record. After attending the ones where I was scheduled to appear, I visited other theaters down the line where I was not expected, and dropped in at the stage-door entrance, asking, "Do you need an actor?" In no place was I rejected.

This service to others has its compensation. As Will Rogers says, "Benefits are great places to try out new material." The audiences are sympathetic and the actor needs just that element of warmth and encouragement to experiment with a novel idea that he wouldn't dare chance before his usual house of cold, critical taskmasters.

Only once was my spirit of benevolence abused. After a performance at the Colonial Theater in Boston, an elderly lady met me at the stage door. She told me how much my performance had touched her. All night she had sat gazing worshipfully at me through her tears. I reminded her of an only son she had lost in the World War. She had spent her last few dollars to see me and would come to see me again, but she hadn't even the money for bread. A lump of emotion gathered in my throat and I pressed a ten-dollar bill into her trembling hand. A few minutes later I met Willie Howard.

"A funny thing happened to me, Eddie," said Willie. "A little old woman with tears in her eyes just stopped me at the stage door and said she spent her last dollar to see my show because I reminded her of her only son lost in the war. I slipped her a ten-spot. It's very touching, isn't it?"

"It touched me too!" I agreed. But I guess it was worth the ten dollars as a lesson in good acting.

I have always been active in the work of Federation and have served as toastmaster at its dinners and aided in its drives for funds. I am deeply interested in the Big Brother movement and have addressed gatherings for it in nearly all the principal cities, helping to organize and launch the Detroit Chapter and the St. Louis Chapter. On the latter charity venture I made a profit. It cost me nothing to make the speech and in return I got a silver cane with the inscription, "To Big Brother Eddie from his Little Brothers in St. Louis." I was also one of the organizers of the Jewish Theatrical Guild and am its first vice-president. In addition to these activities, I have contributed to and worked for temples, churches, hospitals, memorial drives, and charity funds throughout the country without number.

Even when my strength was ebbing and my energies exhausted I cut down on my work more than on my benefit performances. In this feeble way I constantly tried to extend the actor's scope and establish his position not only as a public entertainer but as a public servant in the best nonpolitical sense of the term. My pet activity, of course, is still the Boys' Camp at Cold Springs, New York, where as a boy, emerging from the city's slums, I saw the first stretch of green that was not a pool table.

MY LIFE IS IN YOUR HANDS

And so, engaged in welfare work, secured by sound investments and surrounded by a goodly family, the life of the early Henry Streeter is complete. But there is one thing more. After the children have settled down to their home work and Ida prepares to receive some friends in the parlor, I step out on the lawn. Opposite my house is one of the most magnificent estates in Great Neck. I cross the road and approach its stone gateway. There is a small sign near the entrance reading, "Nathan S. Jonas." As I walk up the wide gravel path I gaze at the unfolding garden plotted majestically across the plain of green and tinted with mellow colors in the last gleams of sunset.

The slum boy of the tenements is learning all about trees and flowers and nature. I gaze at the full-grown elms, white pines, Japanese maples, willows, and beeches. Four years ago this wonder garden was a cornfield. Beyond it were barren tangles of weeds. Now a stately castle rears its armored head upon the hill. It is the story of a modern pioneer, a pilgrim of the twentieth century whose wheels of industry are push-buttons and who accomplishes overnight what it took backwoodsmen many generations to perform.

I ring the doorbell and am admitted to the beautiful château. A stately lady with silver hair and soft blue eyes comes to meet me. She leads me by the hand to a little flower-laden bower at the rear of the house, and there an imposing gentleman with a trace of Southern aristocracy in his manner rises to extend a cordial hand of welcome. I sit down with this elderly couple and a peaceful feeling of well-being warms my heart, but my eyes grow moist and filmy. At the age of two I had floundered in the streets and gutters of New York, fatherless and motherless, and now I am sitting in a flower-laden bower with my parents. Mr. and Mrs. Nathan S. Jonas have become father and mother to me.

When I suffered a breakdown while in Hollywood, Jonas said to his wife: "Come, we will go to California. Our boy needs us." And they came on to comfort me and offer me advice and aid. When physicians decided that my tonsils had to be extracted, Jonas was not satisfied until the biggest medical authorities confirmed the decision. He watched over me through my operation and convalescence as he would over a child.

Through the years he had given me wise counsel in all my financial matters and often guided me in the performance of charity work that it might do the most good. When I planned to build a permanent home he gave me ten acres at cost that I might build it near his. Jonas is one of the pioneers in the development of the Lakeville section of Great Neck. In 1923 he bought a hundred and seventy-one acres of ground there at sixteen hundred and fifty dollars an acre. He intended to use the land for his estate, but it occurred to him and a few friends to form a golf club instead and he turned over the contract to the entire property for that purpose at cost.

In that way the Lakeville Golf Club came into being. Jonas was its founder and organizer and is today its treasurer. It is regarded as one of the most beautiful and exclusive country clubs in America. But it cost Jonas the land for his estate, and when he sought to purchase another parcel he had to pay almost four times the price he had paid in the first place. Now land in Great Neck is worth more than ten thousand dollars an acre, the holdings of the club having risen eight times in value.

I have often wandered with Jonas over his fifty-six-acre estate adjoining the club and shared the joy he takes in this self-made retreat from the business world. Here the banker and the actor go far back to primitive rustic life, but it is idealized and you can detect the magical touch of power and gold in every flower of the garden and every string-bean on the farm. Instead of waiting hundreds of years for saplings to sprout and grow into mighty trees, they rise here in full bloom within the span of a week. Space and time are the slaves that tremble under the wand of wealth. The far ends of the world are gathered here.

There is a giant apple tree from Sea Cliff, dug out with roots and all and transplanted in the Jonas landscape. Next to it stands a weeping beech from Flushing, a Crypt de Maria from Glen Cove, and over there, near an old elm taken from the streets of Great Neck, are white pines recently arrived from Maine. But Nathan Jonas does not depend entirely on the miracle of money. Back of the garden and the castle is a nursery of trees. Here a world of youngsters is being raised and fed from infancy, little peach trees, evergreens, maples, and beeches. In the future, Jonas will not have to go over the wide world for his trees. He will get them all out of his own back yard.

To the south we enter a boxwood garden reminiscent of Southern estates, for Nathan S. Jonas was born in Montgomery, Alabama, and though he came to Brooklyn when only a year old, he still retains a fondness for his native Southland. There is also a pretty rock garden with a wooden bridge. It is all different from the scrawny flower-pots the old Italian used to sell under the Williamsburg Bridge. Here wistaria, orchids, magnolias dazzle over the natural rocks and give the little scene an air of fairyland. Did I ever dream that I'd wind up my stage career as a florist?

Jonas and I go into his vegetable and fruit grounds. He and his wife live solely off their farm as simply and plainly as the ancient people in the land of milk and honey. He takes more pride in the twenty-cent meal of green vegetables that he has invented than in all the great banking institutions he has welded into a single control. We have a hearty feast on the pickings as we pluck ripe berries in season, tackle tomatoes from the bush, and pull young cucumbers off the soil. Through the cycle of grandeur and pomp he has returned to the simple and primitive, and I admire him for it. Many bonds, beside gilt-edge ones, join me to Nathan S. Jonas.

We have mutually, tacitly adopted each other. I have even tried to be helpful to him. Before leaving for the Coast I said to him, "I'll look you up a couple of old banks and you look me up a couple of new gags." And his sense of humor can be depended on. When he served on the Board of Education under Mayors Low and McClellan, he pulled a gag which, if nothing else had happened between us, would have justified my adopting him as my father. It was during the school teachers' agitation for better pay that the spokesman for the teachers exclaimed before the Board of Education, "After all, there is very little difference between men and women!"

"Thank God for the little difference!" observed Jonas.

But the quality that has attracted me most to him is his life-long devotion to charitable service. Even when he was making only a modest income himself he initiated benevolent movements. He founded and organized the Jewish Hospital of Brooklyn, raising its first hundred thousand dollars and developing it almost single-handed into a six-million-dollar institution. Last year, by unanimous vote of the directors and trustees of the hospital, its name was changed to the Nathan S. Jonas Hospital, a unique tribute to a man still living; but at the desire of Jonas this action was rescinded.

He also founded and organized the Brooklyn Federation of Charities as a central agency for the efficient and scientific distribution of funds to all worthy causes. It was after he proved the economy and effectiveness of this organization that the New York charities took the cue and followed suit. During these years that Nathan S. Jonas had risen from an obscure basket salesman and insurance agent to the leading Jewish philanthropist of Brooklyn and had become president of the Manufacturers Trust Company, his younger brother, Ralph Jonas, was also managing to struggle along in his own modest way.

Ralph had become head of the Brooklyn Chamber of Commerce. He founded the Brooklyn branch of the Ethical Culture School, became a patron of the arts, assisting such talents as Max Rosen, the well-known violinist, and aiding Eva Le Gallienne in her plan for a popular-priced Civic Repertory Theater. Ralph Jonas also donated one million dollars to found the Long Island University, which officially opened its portals of learning September of this year. There were only two other donors to this enterprise of culture—James H. Post, who gave fifty thousand dollars, and Nathan S. Jonas, who contributed twenty-five thousand dollars.

This spirit of philanthropy and welfare work fascinates me. My association with Nathan and Ralph Jonas has therefore not merely been one of business and banking, but I have always stood ready to answer their call and coöperate with them in every benevolent enterprise where they felt my efforts might help. It was a happy choice of family for me. It has filled my life with those elements of kindness and social consciousness that mere acting and the theater could never provide.

As I sit on the porch of the Jonas home, inhaling new and rare species of roses and orchids that Mrs. Jonas cultivates in her hothouse, my thoughts fly across the dreary years when I wandered, homeless, hungry, and cold, through the lonely nights in the Ghetto. I think of my poor grandmother who toiled in her dingy cellar, lugging the heavy trunks of servant girls to top-floor flats to earn the meager dollars that kept us alive. And I think of my dream-dazed father torn out of the Russian steppes and suddenly transplanted to a new world of roaring engines and electric energy while he tried to play his plaintive little fiddle through it all, with the flush of a dying fever on his sunken cheek and a gnawing pain of sadness in his heart. And I see my dear young mother, in the tiny two-room flat, over the clattering tea-house, urging my father to work, begging him to go out and grapple with this strange Goliath of industry that only frightened and dismayed him. And those two young, sad people, bewildered and worn before their time, were both killed by adversity when a single light of hope or happiness might have changed the whole course of their lives.

And I sit with these two silver-haired people in the twilight, a rich aroma of nature's luxuriant abundance filtering through my whole being. By what strange, indefinable touch has all that misery and suffering been transformed into something grand and symphonic, something so peaceful and majestic! Why can't I imagine that these two are my parents? That their early death and misfortunes were the dark flashes of a nightmare, and that they really live. That they are sitting with me now in this bower laden with roses riding in happy dignity on the crest of the world!

Nathan S. Jonas takes an accountant's report from a table. "Here, Eddie," he says, "is the latest statement of your finances. It has been a struggle for you, but always upward. I congratulate you, Eddie. Today you are a millionaire!"

I take the statement and gaze at the final figure. One million dollars! While I have been busy building a career, my savings and investments have been busy too, growing in safety and size. In 1924 I won the first prize in a letter contest conducted by a business magazine for the best answer to the question, "What is your bank doing for you and your community?" What better answer could I give than this financial statement? The Manufacturers Trust Company was awarded the banking-service cup and richly merited this distinction.

Plans are now fully under way for my new home. Tunneling for the foundation is well under way and soon the walls will begin to rise. The architect and workmen are constantly on the grounds. The other morning I heard loud blasts and the harsh clatter of derricks scooping up rocks. It disturbed my sleep and I was about to swear at the builders. But then I realized it was my own home they were making the racket about. I went back to sleep with a blissful smile.

The new house will have every improvement, including ceilings, floors, and a motion-picture theater. I am still wondering about a name. I don't know whether to call my new home "The House That Ziegfeld's Jack Built" or "The Cantor Home for Girls."

And now that you have heard the story of my life, let me add the final word—it has just begun.

Chapter XXII—The "Lost" Chapter

No mystery melodrama ever contained the twists and thrills of the year 1929. It was the year of the great massacre when stocks fell from their zenith to zero and millionaires fell from their penthouses to the sidewalk. People who had joint accounts jumped out of windows together, and others, who had even their clothes on margin, went through the streets in pyjamas.

Everybody was "Moanin' Low!" And the Morris Plan was loaning Moe. The only fellow I knew who got a lucky break in the panic was my uncle. He died in September B.C.—Before the Crash. He had a blood pressure of 160. When it reached 250, he tried to split it four for one.

As you can readily guess, I was slightly mixed up in this; but I was not in the market—I was under it. I had taken an unexpected ride in the Otis elevator. They let me in on the top floor. When I ran out of collateral, the cable snapped, I landed in the basement without a shock absorber. They sent a margin clerk and two other interns to collect the pieces.

Besides, I was suffering from Montgomery Ward of the liver, General Electric of the stomach, Westinghouse of the brain, and a severe case of Internal Combustion. I was simply one of the many who were caught short, but luckily, in the midst of my misery I had the presence of mind to write a little book about it, and sold enough copies not to have to sell apples.

Early in 1929, I had thought myself at the peak of my

THE LOST CHAPTER

career with a beautiful home, a happy family and a million dollars. I started the year 1930 with an unhappy family, a mortgage, and a deficit. Strangely enough, however, these very reverses proved something new to me. In spite of my losses and the handicaps of covering margin, my career went forward. I learned the interesting fact that success and happiness had little to do with money and much to do with one's spirit and state of mind. I went to Hollywood and made the picture, "Whoopee," adapted from the stage hit in which I had appeared for over a year. It proved to be my biggest success up to that time. True, the money I earned from it went to pay off obligations, but my position had improved.

In the meantime, general conditions became more serious. The crash of 1929 was a boom compared to the depression of 1930 and 1931. Things became so bad that even those who didn't intend to pay were not buying.

According to experts, our depression was really a kind of inverted prosperity. We were hungry because there was too much wheat. We were broke because there was too much money, and we slept in the park because there were too many houses. We were just perverse, that's all! Other experts said we were merely suffering from overprediction.

In my own case, the depression brought a strange result. Before the crash I had a million dollars, a house, three cars, and four daughters. Now, all I had left was five daughters.

I promptly realized, along with many others, that even more serious than the crash or the depression was the mental attitude of the public. Prosperity might be around the

THE LOST CHAPTER

corner, but nobody knew the name of the street. As long as people admitted defeat, no prosperity in the world could lift them out of the doldrums. I believe I was one of the first to point the new way and cheer the casualties back to a normal and healthy outlook. Laughter and light-heartedness in times like these are the only effective remedies. I therefore decided to run for president at a great personal sacrifice in salary, only to do what I could for my people. Have you ever heard of my people? I've been keeping them for years, but if I'm elected, the government will have to keep them—or there won't be any government!

After "Whoopee" I made another picture called "Palmy Days," because most people had their palms out. On my return to New York I contracted for my first sustained appearance on the radio over the NBC broadcasting system. Every Sunday night at eight o'clock I went on the air for Chase & Sanborn's coffee and for Eddie Cantor's bread and butter. In the brief twenty-one weeks that I broadcast, I established the unique record of becoming the Number One attraction of the air, excelling in point of popularity the oldest and most established features on any program. It isn't nice for me to say this, but it's true. This proved easily to be the peak of my career thus far, and I realized then how foolish it was of me to look back enviously at 1928 and '29. I had much less money now—but I had a great deal more to look forward to.

I was obliged temporarily to discontinue my radio work in order to return to Hollywood and start on my third talking picture. This is tentatively called "The Kid from Spain,"

THE LOST CHAPTER

and is scheduled for appearance in the Fall. After that I shall eagerly return to the radio, and continue my campaign for the presidency. I really think I have a chance, especially if the other two parties stop running—and judging by results, they've stopped running long ago.

I prepared a book called "Your Next President" which has just been published and which fully sets forth my political views and plans for bringing back America to the high level of affluence and well-being which it always enjoyed at a dollar a copy. Every true Cantor supporter should make sure to order this book, containing the Cantor platform, and keep it close at hand. It means a great deal to the voters and a great deal more to me and my publishers.

But all jesting aside, my candidacy for president has enabled me to do a few constructive things. One night, while on the air, I acted as Eddie Cantor, D.D.—Depression Doctor—and one of my distinguished patients was none other than Uncle Sam himself. He came into my office wearing the same old blue coat, red-striped trousers, high blue hat with silver stars—only his white chin whiskers looked a little whiter.

"I don't feel very well, Doc," he said.

"Don't call me Doc—call me Eddie," I told him, offering him a seat with the bottom missing—it was the only chair I had. "What seems to be the matter with you, Uncle Sam? You look rather thin."

"I don't know, I've tried various methods for getting fatter, but I don't seem to have any success."

"Have you tried eating? You know—food?"

THE LOST CHAPTER

"I never thought of that. Besides a lot of my nephews and nieces have been out of work and—"

"I understand. You don't like to sponge on them. Now I'm going to ask you a few questions, Uncle Sam. When were you born?"

"Well, in seventeen seventy-six."

"That makes you a hundred and fifty-five years old. Why, you're just a kid, Uncle. You're suffering from growing pains, that's all."

He smiled kindly at me. "Maybe. But the pains are rather weakening me. I feel terrible."

"Don't be foolish, Uncle Sam. I've been sicker than you, myself. Did I ever show you my operation? Look! Oooo, was I sick! And look at me now! You'll feel better soon. You've had these attacks before, Uncle Sam—remember 1907—1893—1873——?"

"Yes, but this is the worst one yet."

"That's what you say every time. Why, compared to that internal trouble you had in 1865 which nearly upset your whole system, you haven't even got a bad cold now!"

"Well then, why am I getting so thin?"

"You're working off your excess fat."

"But I get these dizzy spells and feel weak."

"Well, your blood pressure is a little too low and your temperature is below normal—but everything will go up soon. Even the market. The worst is over, Uncle Sam."

"Maybe—but I never felt worse!"

"Now let me tell you something. The time you were really sick was late in 1928 and during 1929—that's when you

THE LOST CHAPTER

thought you were feeling fine, but you were really running a high fever. You had enlargement of the spendiorum, speculationitis, and inflationary rheumatism. And you didn't even know it! It seems to me, Uncle Sam, as if you spent 1929 under the influence of intoxicating ideas. You got a drink of that Wall Street cocktail . . . you went up like a rocket and you came down like a stick!"

"Wall Street cocktail?"

"Sure—one drink and you get a seat on the curb with your feet in the gutter. It's simple. In 1929 you went on a spree. In 1930 you had to be put to bed. And 1931 was the morning after the year before!"

"Well, Eddie, you've told me all the things that are wrong with me and now I feel sicker than ever."

"Wait till I give him my treatment. Here, take this smiling jack—you jack up each side of your upper lip till the corners reach your ears. That'll give you a good broad grin."

"And you think that'll pull me through?"

"Sure," I said. "You're soon going to have one of the biggest booms in years—a lot of booms!"

"A lot of booms?"

"Yes—a lot of presidential booms for the coming election. But if you keep cool and pick the right man, you'll be fine."

"But I still feel so weak!"

"You shouldn't! Look at your Standing Army, Uncle Sam. You've got the biggest standing army in the world—yes sir, five million people who stand each morning and each night in the subways, elevators and street cars, because they haven't got seats. And they're all trained because they go in trains and they answer military commands like 'Step lively' and 'Move to the front.' And the beauty of your standing army is that it draws no pay—in fact, it pays for standing!

"Seriously, Uncle Sam, you've got everything! You've got the people, the natural resources, the power and the wealth to be the biggest nation on earth!"

"Well, then, why am I so broken up?"

"You've become a little too high hat—you're not working as hard as you used to. Do the chores around the house. Plain, honest work can't hurt you. And keep cheerful. Get out of the shadows and into the sunshine. Face the sun and the shadows will fall behind you. If you think you're in the soup, get acquainted with the people who would thank God if they could get a bowl of soup into them!

"And be careful about what you read. Keep your eye off the stock market page. Turn to the sporting page and the comic section. Take a look at the radio page and see what's in the air. Listen to Cantor on Sunday nights. And that reminds me. I think you need a little pepping up—have a little more fresh coffee in your diet."

"What else must I do?"

"You must stay at home—stop making those trips to Europe—they can only get you in trouble. Now just stay around the house and attend to your own affairs for a while. Sell that hammer you knock with and start sawing wood.

THE LOST CHAPTER

Don't look back, look ahead, the view that way is a whole lot pleasanter. Keep singing in the rain and tend to business. What business are you in, anyway?"

Uncle Sam handed me his card. "Well, I've got a lot of businesses, but mostly real-estate."

"Yeah, I heard about your real-estate—you own forty-eight states."

"Yes," said Uncle Sam, bowing his head in shame.

"Well, look 'em over, Uncle," I told him. "How can you be sick when you own forty-eight states like that? Just look at the reserve and natural resources you can draw upon! Out West you've got the Rocky Mountains. Let me tell you, the material used in constructing your mountains is of the highest grade—full of gold and silver, and any time you need some pocket money, just go over and break off a piece of mountain! Look at the other things on your property! Don't worry about your banks! You have the biggest and longest banks in the world on both sides of the Mississippi River. You've got the Great Salt Lake in Utah where there's enough salt to put salt and sand into all our backbones! Why, there's so much salt out there that I've seen them drive a hundred head of cattle into that lake and they came out pickled beef!

"Then you've got a nice little park called the Yellowstone National Park. Why, many European kingdoms could move into that park and get lost in the woods. Then you've got the biggest factor in the world for building happy homes— Niagara Falls—and you've got the biggest, deepest, widest place to drop all your troubles—down into the Grand Can-

THE LOST CHAPTER

yon. Why, Uncle, you're the richest, strongest man on earth and you don't know it!"

The old man seemed to brighten up. I noticed a twinkle in his eyes. "You really think so?"

"I'll show you what I think. I think you're such a safe risk that I'll recommend you for a hundred billion dollar life insurance policy to last forever. . . . And I'll write the policy myself!"

THE END

Grandma Esther.

His father, Michael Cantor, who died when Eddie was two.

Eddie in a soldier suit, age eight. This picture was taken by a New York street photographer, 1900.

Three Beau Brummels of the East Side—Jack, Murray, and Cousin Eddie.

Eddie Cantor, 1908, in his first made-to-order suit for stage and street wear.

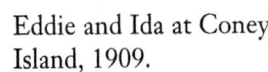

Eddie and Ida at Coney Island, 1909.

Eddie in his first vaudeville act with Bedini and Arthur, 1912.

Georgie Jessel and Eddie Cantor, 1912, traveling with *Kid Kabaret*.

Scene from *Kid Kabaret*, 1912, showing among others, Georgie Jessel, Eddie Buzzell, and Eddie Cantor.

Eddie as the Singing Butler in Gus Edwards' *Kid Kabaret*, 1913.

Eddie and Ida in 1914.

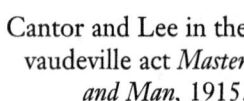

Cantor and Lee in the vaudeville act *Master and Man*, 1915.

Eddie Cantor and Bert Williams, who were Sonny and Papsy on the stage and off, 1917.

Eddie Cantor in black face in the *Follies of 1917*.

Harry Kelly, Eddie Cantor, W. C. Fields, and Will Rogers in the *Follies of 1918*.

Ann Pennington and Eddie in the *Follies of 1918*.

W. C. Fields, Will Rogers, Lillian Lorraine, Eddie, and Harry Kelly in the *Follies of 1918*.

Johnny Dooley, Eddie Cantor, Gus Van, Bert Williams, Joe Schenck, Eddie Dowling, and Ray Dooley in the *Follies of 1919*.

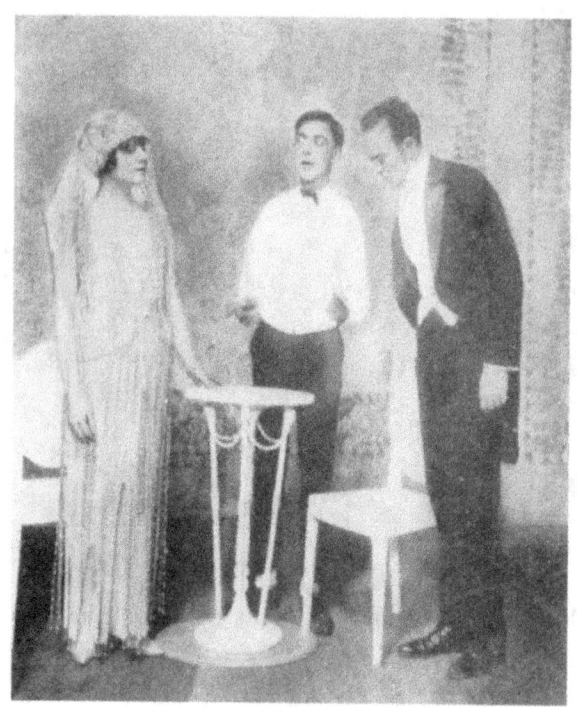

Lillian Lorraine and Eddie Cantor in a scene from the *Follies of 1919*.

Ann Pennington, Eddie, and Brooke Johns in the *Follies of 1919*.

Will Rogers.

Ed Wynn and Eddie picketing for Actors' Equity during the strike.

Eddie Cantor as the tailor's assistant, with Lou Hearn and Joe Opp, in the clothing-shop scene of the *Midnight Rounders*.

Nathan S. Jonas.

Eddie and his boys of
Surprise Lake Camp.

Fannie Brice and Eddie Cantor
in Los Angeles.

Eddie Cantor training Jack Dempsey for his fight with Carpentier, with Jane Green as Referee.

Eddie Cantor in *Kid Boots*.

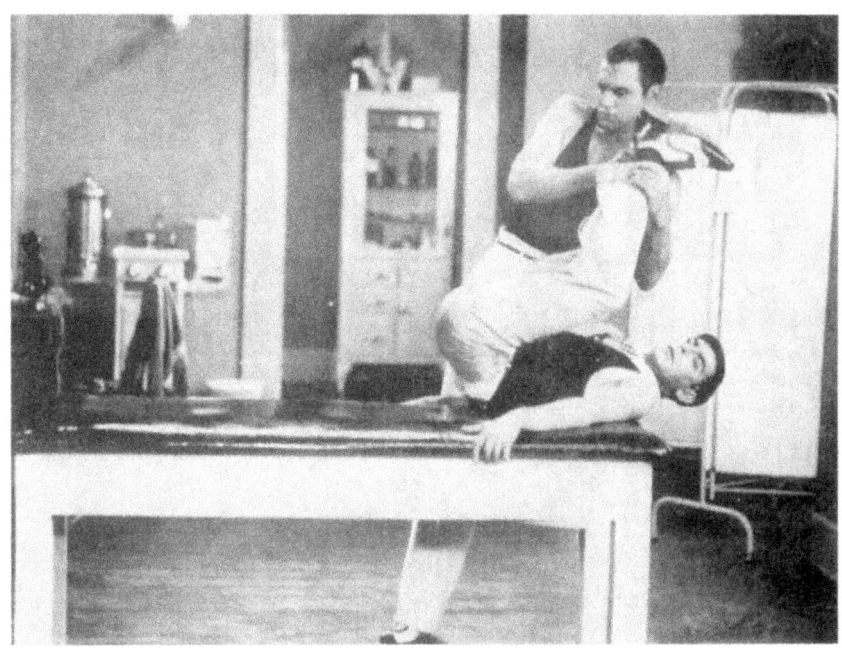

Eddie in the osteopath scene from *Kid Boots*.

Eddie Cantor and Clara Bow, who appeared together in the picture version of *Kid Boots*.

Marie Callahan and Eddie in the "Wedding March" from *Kid Boots*.

Clara Bow, Eddie, and Dorothy Matthews from *Kid Boots*, 1926.

Eddie in blackface.

Ziegfeld Follies of 1927 rehearsal. Eddie, Ziegfeld, Irving Berlin at piano, dance director Sammy Lee.

Frances Upton and Eddie in the taxicab scene from the *Follies of 1927*.

With Frances Upton in the *Follies of 1927*.

Eddie as the mailman in *Special Delivery*.

Eddie Cantor and Daniel Lipsky, his financial adviser.

With James J. Walker, then Mayor of New York, 1929.

William Morris, Sr., Eddie, Sophie Tucker, George Jessel, 1930.

With the Ziegfeld girls in *Whoopee*, 1930.

With Rubinoff, 1932.

Eddie and the Goldwyn Girls in *Roman Scandals*, 1933. At Eddie's right: Lucille Ball.

Eddie and the Goldwyn Girls in *Kid Millions*, 1934. At Eddie's left, Lucille Ball.

Will Rogers and Eddie at a dinner for Eddie by Masquer's Club in Hollywood, 1936.

Florenz Ziegfeld Jr. and Billie Burke.

With Dinah Shore at a Marine base.

With Deanna Durbin, 1937.

With Bobby Breen on stage at the Palace Theatre, Cleveland, 1937.

Eddie and George M. Cohan, backstage at *I'd Rather Be Right*, 1937.

The family—Marjorie, Baby Janet, Mrs. Cantor, Edna, Natalie, Marilyn, and Eddie Cantor at the piano.

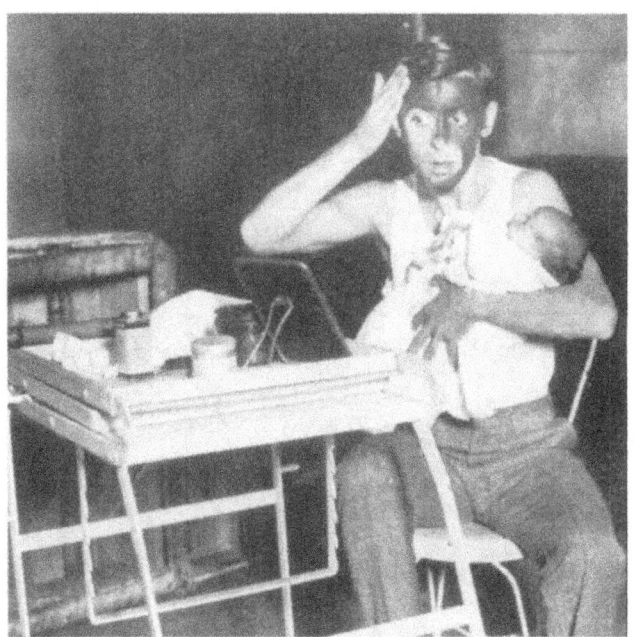

Eddie shows his daughter how he makes up for the stage.

Christmas Eve, 1943, at the Hollywood Canteen: Betty Grable, Bette Davis, and Eddie Cantor Claus.

Eddie and Jolie at broadcast rehearsal, 1947.

Earl Carroll, Eddie, and Bert Parks at Earl's Hollywood night club.

Backstage at a benefit performance, 1947: Danny Kaye, Eddie, Jimmy Durante, Georgie Jessel, Edward Arnold.

Some old friends help celebrate Eddie and Ida's thirty-third wedding anniversary, 1947: (left to right) George Burns on trombone, Groucho Marx with guitar, Jack Benny and his violin, Eddie on bass.

With Fanny at her home, 1948.

Eddie Fisher, Ida, and Eddie, Florida, 1950.

Eddie and Dorothy Lamour at a TV rehearsal on the afternoon of the night he suffered a heart attack, 1953.

Jimmy and Eddie.

Ida and Eddie.

The Cantor family: (left to right) Michael Metzger (Natalie's son); Marjorie; Eddie; Ida; Judy McHugh (Edna's daughter); Edna; Natalie; (front row) Janet; Brian Gari (Janet's son); Marilyn. (Missing is baby Amanda Gari, Janet's daughter.)

Take My Life

with Jane Kesner Ardmore

Contents

PART ONE The WOMEN in My Life
1. Grandma Esther — 11
2. Ida — 24
3. The Girls From Show Business — 33
4. Fanny Brice — 42

PART TWO The MEN in My Life
5. Jimmy Durante — 53
6. My First Agent . . . My First Partner . . . — 62
7. Irving Berlin — 68
8. Georgie Jessel — 77
9. Al Jolson — 86
10. Max Hart, Earl Carroll, Oliver Morosco — 96
11. Will Rogers — 104
12. Ziegfeld — 116
13. W. C. Fields — 139
14. Ben Schulberg, Sam Goldwyn — 150
15. The Song Writers — 162

PART THREE The REST of My Life
16. The Girls — 175
17. Politics and Politicians — 187
18. Audiences — 201
19. Radio Audiences — 213
20. Jack Benny — 224
21. Radio Cast of Characters — 231
22. Television — 245
23. The Beggar — 253
24. The Men Behind the Beggar — 266

PART FOUR   The BEST of My Life
26. With All My Heart   277
25. With Half a Heart   285

October 1, 1952. Night. An ambulance at the door and a guy on a stretcher being carried out. I'm the guy. I'm having a heart attack and I know it. Maybe I'm dying. I know that. You've heard it said that your life passes in review at the very last minute? I'd always thought it absurd but it's true. So help me. The ambulance screams into the night and I see it all . . .

The opening night of the Follies . . . the March of Dimes . . . Ida . . . the girls . . . my Grandma Esther . . . the friends who worked with me, laughed and cried through the years of show business. Did I ever say thank you for all they gave me . . . Will Rogers, W. C. Fields, Fanny Brice?

The purse I stole when I was thirteen . . . the children we saved from death in Germany . . . like a balancing of the books. Will the good things outweigh the bad? What have I lived for, really?

I made up my mind years ago that I'd be a man long after I was through as an entertainer. But have I made it? Have I ever made it?

PART ONE

The WOMEN in My Life

1. Grandma Esther

Everyone on the East Side knew Esther Kantrowitz, a strong, small woman in a worn skirt and blouse, with the traditional brown wig and a kerchief tied over her head, who trudged up and down the five-story tenements, up and down, carrying her great basket of notions from door to door. On the side she ran an employment agency for servant girls. And on another side (I favored this side), she was a *shadchen*—a matchmaker.

There were all the servant girls who came in and out of our house, and my grandmother was a shrewd judge of character. Whenever she met a man she thought might be right for one of these girls, she'd introduce them. The courting was conducted at our house on Grandma's tea and cookies, and if the couple married, Grandma'd get a fee, usually twenty-five dollars. She explained to me that we had to leave the couple alone in our basement flat to get acquainted. If they got married, we'd get some money. Every couple looked to me like a potential pair of shoes or a pair of pants.

Then, of course, she'd go to the wedding, wearing her skirt with the long pocket. She'd come home late, waken me from a sound sleep, and start stuffing me with a leg of chicken, meat balls, lox, wedding cake and other dainties, all wrapped carefully in napkins and hidden in her long pocket. I bet I ate more wedding feasts without attending the weddings than any bachelor on record. She was worried that I didn't get enough to eat. "So skinny," she'd sigh, "such a plucked little owl." My father had died at twenty-two. She worried about that, what might it mean for me. She'd rub the back of my neck and murmur, "Itchik, Itchik, we build this up, make it strong, yes?"

That was my Grandma Esther, "Bubba" I called her, a woman with the saddest face I've ever seen and in it two light blue sparkling eyes, quick to humor, quick to laughter. In the old days in Russia she had been left, a young widow with four children. She supported them by making cigars. Hand-rolled. She never did have enough extra money for the necessary license; and since you weren't allowed to make cigars without a license, she was arrested several times and brought before the judge. On these occasions, she'd pretend to be insane, putting on a great show, dancing, singing, twirling her skirts. Each time the judge was convinced and let her go. She was a great mimic—in fact, that's where I got the idea.

A woman would come to the flat and tell Grandma what she wanted in the way of a servant, "Someone who can cook well, clean well, care for a baby like its own mother, good disposition . . ." all very polite and explicit and of course for as small a salary as possible. The minute she'd leave, Grandma'd take a couple of small mincing steps and imitate her client to a T. "Cook vell, clean vell, care for de babee . . ." Then she'd find the right servant girl—there were always eight or nine of them sleeping and eating in our basement flat—and when the girl went to work at the place, Grandma'd collect a dollar fee. She'd also lug the servant girl's trunk to the new address on her own strong short little back.

That was my Bubba. She had come to this country, already a woman of sixty, to care for her delicate daughter Maite, for Maite's young dreamer husband, Michael, and for the baby who was on its way—me. Two of her sons were in America (later she sent for the third) and she had given Michael the money to come to America in the first place. She didn't dream of gold-paved streets or a ready-made living, she asked only opportunity for young people and this seemed like the right place. All her hope and much of her love was focused on her daughter, my mother. As for Michael, she hoped he would do more in the land of promise than he had done in the old country; but my dad was evidently a lovable ne'er-do-well who played the violin. Thinking people should throw money through the windows, he wouldn't even have gotten up to open the door! With Maite ill and expectant, he sent in desperation for Esther. She arrived to find them both half starved. And when they died, these bewildered young parents of mine, my mother in childbirth when I was a year old, my father of pneumonia a year later, Bubba settled down in a new country to raise me. She was sixty-two, I was two.

It was no easy life. She'd spent her small bag of silver rubles on my parents' illnesses. From then on it was a constant battle to keep some sort of food in our stomachs and a roof over our heads. How vividly I remember that basement of ours on Henry Street: living room, bedroom, and kitchen, so hot in summer, so cold in winter! In November—I give you my word of honor—we'd go around and nail down, actually nail down the windows so no air could get in. We'd go to sleep literally drugged from lack of oxygen, the servant girls on the floor and Grandma and me in the big feather bed, and all about us in the tenements, other people struggling similarly for survival and a breath of air. Any wonder I used to hang myself from the street lamps to make the kids laugh? We *had* to laugh to keep from crying, there was such poverty, such misery and disease. All the things that weren't good, we had.

Only Grandma had no complaints. She loved God and had a heart full of warmth for Him and for everyone else. Having nothing, she always found a way to give part of that nothing to others. For a beggar she'd dig up an apple, an orange, maybe two pennies. She turned no one away. As for the basement, she was proud of living in it. "From here, there's only one place to go," she'd say, "up!" And you had to be patient and go slowly. Everyone was trying to move too fast. "People who go too fast don't see the scenery," she'd say.

All of this in Yiddish, Polish, Russian or a mixture of the three. She spoke no English and understood none. When I was six she got me cleaned up the best she could and hauled me to Public School. I should have been entered as Isidore Itzkowitz; but when the registrar asked "Name?" Grandma, confused, started to give her own "Kantrowitz," and never finished it.

"Kanter," the registrar said, "that'll be enough. Isidore Kanter."

When I left this school for P.S. 2, I altered the spelling to "Cantor," and by the time I migrated to P.S. 1, I changed the Isidore to Eddie. Did I say "*I* changed"? Ida changed, my girl, Ida Tobias. She went around with a Mamie Osteroff who had a brother named

Eddie. Ida thought that was a cute name for me. So I became Eddie. Except to Bubba. To her I was Itchik.

Truant from school, pilferer of pushcarts, hooligan, street fighter, liar—to her I was her Itchik and she loved me no matter what. She was patient. She prayed—that I would come to no harm, that I would grow and fatten. That was no cinch. She was so busy eking out an existence that there were few hot meals. She would leave a nickel on the kitchen sink each morning. That would buy me four cents' worth of salami and a penny's worth of bread. By the time I was thirteen I'd consumed more delicatessen than most people eat in a lifetime. I was also adept at augmenting my diet. Passing a pushcart I would push two plums in my mouth and still look famished. I could shove a banana down my throat like a sword swallower.

Somehow we always got through the summers. But the winters! Our clothes were so thin. I never had an overcoat, and no matter how many old vests, ragged sweaters or shirts I piled on— Grandma was always bringing home some rag for extra padding —the wind from the East River sliced through to the bone. You'd sit in school all day in snow-damp clothes, your shoes stuffed pulpy with wet cardboard.

I must have been eight when the New York *Evening Journal* announced a Christmas fund. The best letter written to Santa Claus would win for the writer whatever he asked. I promptly wrote to Santa Claus in care of the *Journal:* "Dear Santa, I'm an orphan. I have no mother or father . . ." this was the way I started everything. "I live with my grandmother who is very poor. I have no warm clothes. I would like a pair of rubber boots, an overcoat, and a sled. That is all I want for Christmas." I knew I'd win. I'd never really doubted Santa Claus, I'd just figured it was taking him a while to hear about me. All the kids in our neighborhood believed in Santa. Their elders celebrated the Jewish Chanukah, which comes close to Christmas, but the children all believed, I certainly did, in a jolly man in a red coat who *gave* kids something. Grandma, bless her, never disillusioned me.

Now picture this. It's Christmas Day. The kids are out in the snow playing with their sleds. Some of them have mittens and are building snow men. I have nothing—nothing but an unfulfilled hope. The kids scream and holler and bellyflop down the street while I sit on the top of the stoop, too chilled to move, a sodden heap of wet clothes. I hate the New York *Journal*. I hate William Randolph Hearst, whose name is on the paper's masthead. I hate Santa Claus. Grandma tries to make me come inside. Tea she'll make. I keep sitting, frozen on the stoop. And then suddenly, at the end of the day, up drives a truck with the sign "New York *Journal*," and the fellow has a box.

"Where's Isidore Kanter?"

My heart falls into the street. "Me! I'm Isidore Kanter. Me! Me!" I yell.

"You sure?"

"Sure. Ask 'em. Hey, fellas! Ask any of 'em. Who am I?"

They all gather around while I open the box. Boots, overcoat, sled. The first presents I've ever had. I'm so happy I cry. Grandma cries right with me. Now I can believe in Santa Claus again and he has a face like William Randolph Hearst. From that day to this, no one could say anything against Hearst to me. Even the fact that my benefactor's politics and mine did not agree—it's like having a drunken father. He's *your* father.

Then came the day we moved from Henry Street. We'd been paying nine dollars a month. The rent got too steep and Grandma found a place on Market for seven. Eleven Market Street. There was a tenement house in the front, then you went into a yard and in the back of the yard there was a consequently cheaper place. We lived on the third floor; the toilet was in the yard, just one toilet for sixteen families. If you had to wait in line, you skipped it. All of us on Market Street were a laxative maker's dream.

About this time I got my first job. There was a delicatessen on Market that sold Isaac Gellis's meat. My job was delivering a basket of corned beef, pastrami, salami, and frankfurters from the Gellis factory at 37 Essex Street to the delicatessen.

A hungry kid with a job like that? And take-home pay besides? The fellow would pay me three cents or two sandwiches. I took the sandwiches. Salami. I was all salami. When I walked down the street I was a sausage with eyes.

Shortly before Al Jolson died he visited the famous Isaac Gellis factory at 37 Essex Street. A grandson of Gellis mentioned to Jolie that Eddie Cantor used to come with a basket and deliver his meats. Jolson said, "Does Eddie ever come down here when he's in New York?" The fellow said yes. Jolie grabbed a menu and wrote me a note, "Dear Eddie, they tell me your old job is waiting for you. Come at once." (I saw the note for the first time years after Jolie's death.)

Luckily for her peace of mind Grandma didn't know much about digestion and nothing about vegetables or vitamins. Usually on Friday nights she'd cook a hot supper, some kind of stew, using the cheaper cuts of meat which take a long time to get tender. Tender? that's funny. It's downright snobbish. If we'd waited from that day to this, those stews wouldn't have been tender. So she cooked them fast, lighted the candles, and we'd celebrate the Sabbath. I'd stuff down the hot stew in chunks and try to sneak out of the house. If Grandma caught me, I'd have to wash my face and go with her to *shul*, Grandma in her small black hat and black *Shabbos* dress (she wore the same one for twenty years until I started working for Bedini and Arthur). Most nights I escaped and was on my own, and it would be midnight before this man about Henry and Market streets would crawl in.

I went to all the shows, no charge. I'd just hang around until intermission, then the crowds would come out and I'd go in. I never saw the first act of anything. Sometimes I didn't see more than five minutes of the second act, then I'd go flying. There was always the danger of getting turned over to the police.

Grandma had plenty to worry about. For another thing, the constant street fights. If Division Street was at war with Henry Street and you tried running an errand across Division, you'd get backed into a corner by the Division Street boys. They'd threaten to kill you. What's more, they meant it. Sometimes I'd get away by pleading, "Go ahead, hit me. I've got no one to protect me, no father, no mother . . ." Sometimes it worked. Other times . . .

One day I was using the cover of a boiler over my arm as a shield. I waved the boiler cover and yelled, "Come on!" The kid came. With a rock. While I shielded my front he cracked my head. So I went to a drugstore and the druggist sewed it up. He didn't clean it, just sewed it. Two days later my head was out like this, the biggest head I've ever had. Grandma carried me to the Good Samaritan Dispensary on Essex Street and bought the necessary ticket for a dime. We were standing in line when a doctor passed, got one look at my swelled head, and snatched me out of line into an operating room.

My best friend was a boy named Dan Lipsky. He came every morning, shook me awake, and dragged me to school. He didn't fight. He was a good boy, and that gave Grandma hope. Any pal of Dan Lipsky was going to be a fine, bright boy, that's how Grandma figured it. She didn't know.

I've mentioned changing schools several times. There was a reason. The first two schools were very prejudiced. They expected you to do homework and get passing grades. I thought this the most anti-Semitic thing I'd ever heard. Then I got to P.S. 1 and they weren't prejudiced. I could recite and if I'd recite, they'd promote me. Did I recite! I'd always been frightened of being alone. I longed for crowds. To sing or imitate a Polish servant girl for the kids on the street, to hear them laugh, applaud, gave me a sense of power and there's nothing you can't do with power, like a woman with sex.

Now at P.S. 1 I'm in my glory. I live for graduation day. On graduation day, the auditorium is packed. My grandmother has gotten me a pair of knickers, new, and a blouse. When the moment comes, I walk from my seat to the platform. I prolong the walk. I don't want it ever to end. I turn right and left, muttering, "Hi, fellas." Today I'm no orphan. I forget the endless delicatessen, the toilet in the cold back yard, everything. I'm it. I stand on the stage and recite *The Soul of the Violin*. I'm the violinist starving in the garret, remembering the performance in Vienna when a lady threw me a rose from her box—the thorn caught and the petals fell in a shower at my feet. I'm going to have to sell the violin, I tell it farewell. "It has come at last, old comrade, it has come at last, the time when you and I must say good-by." When I finish, there's not a dry eye in the house. The teachers are crying! I'm crying! Talk about stopping a show—I've stopped the graduation.

Can you imagine what that meant to a kid who was cold, hungry and lousy-looking? The sound of applause was heat and food, mother and father, pink champagne. My grandma couldn't be there to hear it, she had to work; but when she'd come home the neighbor women would gather around. "A great boy," Mrs. Horowitz would say. "You can be proud, Esther." Then my grandmother wasn't cold either. She was warm through her thin shawl.

Twice a year, graduation. I never got a passing grade but they shoved me along from class to class so I could recite *The Soul of the Violin*, *The Traitor's Deathbed*, and other heart-rending ditties. I go to school and learn nothing. Comes the opening day of the term, 1905. The new teacher, redheaded, red-mustached Thomas W. Clark, calls me to the desk and says:

"Cantor, I don't care how well you recite. You can turn audiences inside out. You don't leave this room until you learn enough to get passing grades."

I'm thinking fast. "Mr. Clark," I say, "may I leave the room?" I leave; I never return. "Narrow-minded bigot," I think.

Grandma didn't know I'd left school. When the truant officer showed up I explained that I was the only support of my aged grandparent. He took a look at how we lived and let it go. We were back in the basement on Henry Street. The place had gotten "run down" so we were able to afford it again. The truant officer looked around and went away.

Grandma didn't succeed with my formal schooling as she had hoped, but she did somehow get me to a place where I learned more than I ever learned in school. Surprise Lake Camp, a camp for poor undernourished kids who'd never seen a blade of grass or a tree. They scooped us up off the parched summer streets of New York and sent us to heaven, a beautiful spot opposite West Point, where the air smelled sweet, where there were growing things and three square meals a day. Here I ate for the first time. I was crazy about it. I became camp clown in the hope that I'd be held over for more than two weeks. It worked. They'd keep me six or seven weeks each summer. I'd play jokes, sing, anything to keep staying.

One night, lying in bed in the tent, it occurred to me:

"How come we're here? How come it doesn't cost nothing?"

Another kid in the tent, Georgie Sokolsky, had the answer: "Oh, because somebody's interested in kids like us."

For a minute it was quiet. Just the dark tent and the kids breathing. Then half to myself I murmured:

"Thank you, somebody."

That was a rare moment of insight, the closest I ever got to religion in those days. Yet I did read the Bible. It was the one book in Grandma's basement and I read it backward and forward until I knew it by heart. "Look, Ma, no hands." And she saw to it that I was *bar mitzvah*. She paid a dollar and a half a week and I pretended to go to Hebrew school but I never went, not until a short while before the ceremony. Then I spoke with the rabbi and he helped me prepare a speech so I shouldn't disgrace Esther Kantrowitz. I added quite a few things to the speech while the rabbi wasn't looking. In the orthodox shul, the women sit upstairs, so I looked up right at my grandmother, intoning, "There sits my grandmother, she has been my father and my mother." It was the only time she saw me on stage.

Like yesterday, there it is, the synagogue on Pike Street, in my pocket a gold watch, big as an onion. Grandma had scrimped and saved so Itchik should have a watch. Bar mitzvah over, I'm leaving the shul, the watch is gone. I don't say the shamus stole it, but after that he knew the time before anybody. I should be the one to put my finger on the shamus? I was not above suspicion myself. For years, I've been adroit at snitching fruit from pushcarts. Now something much worse . . .

I'm thirteen and I steal a purse. The poor servant girl has no job, she has twelve dollars in the whole world and all I think is, "How dare she have that much money when I'm dying to see Joseph Santley in *Billy the Kid?*" I snatch the purse as the girl washes her face—she'd come to our house so Grandma'd find her a job. I pocket the money, throw away the purse, see the show. Then I'm scared to go home. I stay away a week, see *Billy the Kid* every night, and find a flop in the Bowery for twenty-five cents. When I finally go home I'm scared to walk in.

"I didn't do it!" I cried, opening the door.

"Do what?" screamed Grandma, clutching me. She's been half crazy. Now she laughs and cries. Better a live criminal than a dead little popeyed kid. And I'm to get a job. No more running the streets, she says. A job! (The truant officer must have been there while I was gone.)

The first job was with an insurance company on Williams Street. They were very tough. They didn't like the idea of stamps disappearing from the stamp drawer. I was supposed to mail about forty letters a day. I'd slip twenty twos in my pocket and sell them for a quarter, with this I'd go to Tony Pastor's. One day these snide people tricked me; they counted the stamps. I told Grandma

I had an offer of a better job and went out to find one. I landed at the National Cloak and Suit Company. There I was fired—but by the president.

My friend Herman Walker was working as a runner at Weir Brothers, 25 Broad Street. He got me a job as a runner. Five dollars a week. We delivered stock certificates from one brokerage firm to another. Friday afternoon after the market closed was our big time. We'd send out a market letter recommending a certain stock, say Butte Copper, and suggesting the client sell General Electric. Then Monday, possibly two commissions.

It's Friday night. Four or five of us are getting out the letter. The minute J. C. Weir leaves, I seize a girl's muff from the hatrack, jump onto a table, and am Anna Held, singing, "I Just Can't Make My Eyes Behave." Suddenly a hush. No more laughs. J. C. Weir is in the room and I'm out. Fast. Not even a chance to get my cap.

Eleven years later I open at the *Follies*. After the show the doorman brings up a card. J. C. Weir. He comes into my dressing room with one arm behind him. "Congratulations, Eddie. Here is the hat you didn't get when you left." And he hands me a high silk hat.

I wish Grandma Esther had lived to know about Mr. Weir. All she knew when I left Weir Brothers was that I'd had a job, now I didn't have it, and no cap to boot. I told her I'd changed my mind, I wasn't going into business after all, I was going into the theater. She shook her head. This was the worst. "Actors—nothing! Like baseball players—nothing!" she said. She kept repeating it till I brought her the first ten dollars I won in an amateur night. The ten dollars changed her mind.

Of course, that didn't happen immediately. First Dan Lipsky and I teamed up to play weddings, club socials, and amateur theatricals. Dan did comedy bits and I recited the tear-jerkers. But I couldn't resist some of the wisecracks I'd heard in vaudeville; I glued on a beard and opened with Joe Welsh's line, "If I had my life to live over, I wouldn't be born." Next night at the Educational Alliance, I'd play Little Lord Fauntleroy in a blond wig, no teeth, and an East Side accent, "Does the *oil* want to see me?" When Dan and I stood on a real stage for the first time at the Clinton Music Hall, our beard-and-joke act fell flat—we spoke in English, not knowing we were in a Yiddish theater. Dan gave up acting for banking about then and I started haunting Miner's Bowery Theatre.

I didn't actually get up the nerve to go in at the stage door—not for some time, not until my credit ran out with the boys on the street from whom I constantly mooched. Grandma and I'd had an argument. She thought I ought to get a job, any kind, I was becoming a bum. She had paid the servant girl the twelve lost dollars and I could get a job. There were two nights when I slept on the roof. I'd had nothing to eat. I tried to mooch and the fellows had the same comeback Grandma had—why didn't I go to work? Well, I was looking, I was an actor. Bunk, they said, if I was an actor, I could go on Miner's Amateur Night. Tonight! Even if I got the hook I'd earn a dollar. "How can I go on in these torn pants?" I cried. Herman Walker promptly took off his pants. I could just pay him half the buck I was gonna earn. We'd swap back after the performance.

I'll never forget that night. I was scared to death. I stood in the wings shivering in my pants—pardon me, in Herman's pants—while the regular burlesque show ended and the amateurs went on, were jeered, hooted, and got the hook. Most of 'em were pretty seasoned amateurs too. Then the announcer was saying, "Next, Mr. Edward Cantor. He *says* he's an impersonator." Someone pushed me, rushed me out into a blaze of lights and Bronx cheers. Things were flying onto the stage. Rotten fruit. I ducked. They wouldn't let me say a word. Suddenly I had an inspiration. In the burlesque show was a comic named Sam Sidman who had a stock line. He'd grimace, stamp his foot, put up one hand, and whine, "Oh, dat makes me *so mad!*" In my extremity I held up one hand, there was a slight pause in the clamor, and I whined, "Oh, dat makes me *so mad!*" They roared. They let me go on. There were even cheers from the gallery, "Stick to it, kid, you're lousy!" But coins began to pelt the stage. I won first prize and picked up several dollars besides.

Herman was waiting at the stage door. Then we all went down to Doyer Street in Chinatown and I treated the crowd to chow mein. I had three portions—on an empty stomach, yet. I've never been sicker in my life than that night, sitting on a curb in Chinatown. But I was in show business! I'd had my first baptism under fire and I couldn't wait to get home and give Bubba those ten bucks.

From then on, for a while, I did all right. I played the amateur nights around New York till I exhausted them. Then it wasn't so good. I played a club now and then for seventy-five cents. At least I had that to bring home. Finally I landed a professional job with a burlesque show, Frank B. Carr's *Indian Maidens;* fifteen dollars a week and a chance to go on as a tramp, a Hebrew comedian, a waiter, and a bootblack. We played tank towns for four weeks. I was beginning to enjoy life as a big timer when business, which hadn't been too hot to start with, froze. When we opened in Shenandoah, Pennsylvania, on Christmas Eve, no one was in the theater, not even the manager. He'd left for New York and left us to fold in the snow. Grandma had to send me money to come home.

She didn't say "I told you so." She just took me in and fed me and looked at me with a face full of compassion. I didn't think about it then, but she must have been a lonely woman who suppressed all her emotions but one—love. She kept on loving me, deserving or not. Mostly not. In those early days everything I did that was decent I was doing for *me*. I sang in front of the campfire, not to entertain the boys but to make myself important, a kid with broken teeth and no corpuscles. I'd sing and big boys would put their arms on my shoulders. But sometimes when I did something right, regardless of why, Grandma would say, "*Goot, mein kinde.*" As I've grown older, I've wanted to deserve that. I hope she knows.

She said "*Goot, mein kinde,*" the day I introduced Ida. Ida was just a little kid. She used to walk me home because I couldn't walk her home, her family didn't approve of me. One summer evening Ida and I came along the street and Grandma was sitting on the stoop trying to cool off. "Bubba, this is Ida Tobias." Grandma looked her over carefully. She was, remember, a good student of human nature. Then her eyes smiled with their merriest bluest smile, she loved Ida from the first.

As time went on she hoped for our marriage. Ida would take her place, she said, and do right by me.

Even after I had made some progress in show business Grandma Esther wouldn't move from Henry Street, she just moved up from the basement to the ground floor on a level with the street. When Ida and I would go to visit her I'd run in, kiss her, and she'd drag me to the window so the neighbors could see how I was kissing her.

She was ill for a long time before her death at eighty-four. She had raised a family of her own and then taken on this orphaned hooligan; and she died knowing that she hadn't failed; he hadn't perished of malnutrition, and he hadn't been hung. This was important. Our neighborhood produced one boy who became the greatest song writer in the world, Irving Berlin, and another boy, Lefty Louie, who was electrocuted for the Rosenthal murder. Grandma died several weeks before I opened in the *Ziegfeld Follies*. It was she who had made it possible, who should have been there, but she was dead. When Ida and I went to her house after the funeral we found a hundred dollars in the bureau drawer and a note: "For my funeral, please." She wanted "nothing from no one." Not material things anyhow.

During her lifetime the one happiness I gave her was in marrying Ida and giving Bubba her first two great-grandchildren, Marjorie and Natalie. Maybe that was better than fame, after all. It's been better than fame for me too.

2. Ida

My luck began with Ida the day I met her at P.S. 177 Recreation Center. A basketball game was in progress. Here was this girl shooting baskets from every part of the court, the crowd applauding like mad, and I couldn't stand it. I started to sing. I pulled out my whole repertoire, parodies of popular songs. Ray Schwartz, the supervisor, wanted to throw me out, but Ida said no, she wasn't afraid of competition. Three nights later we met. I couldn't even buy her a five-cent soda, but she had an answer for that. Confectionery stores weren't sanitary, she said, who wanted a soda? (Who wanted one? She did!)

To this day I can't see what attracted her to this homely, dirty, skinny guy with holes in his clothes and shoes Grandma had patched. I think, essentially, she had a mother instinct that reached out to me as it would to a stray cat.

For Ida was the belle of Henry Street. She not only was the star of the basketball team, she did the high jump (in bloomers), played the piano, danced better than any of the other girls, and was the most popular. Best of all, when she laughed you could hear her; and my ambition in life was to make her laugh, to make her notice me. She noticed. I was the *schlepper*, the hanger-on. There was a boys' club that met at the Educational Alliance. After the meeting the boys'd go for a soda. I'd try to promote. "If you'll put up two cents, another guy says he'll give two cents . . ." or, "You're not going to give *one* cent when that guy'll put up *three?*" The only time sodas materialized was when Ida'd maneuver it so I'd earn a dime running an errand for someone. It was always her dime. For Ida, summer nights when the kids were sitting on the curbs, I'd hang myself from the street lamp, sing, crack jokes, stand on my head. Anything for an exhibition. "Happy Eddie." Sometimes it was tough. Fellows would take her skating, I'd have to dig up skates somehow and get out there and make like a skater.

Just to make matters complicated, when I first met Ida I was involved with another woman, one of the servant girls for whom my grandmother got jobs. This girl was nineteen, I was thirteen. One day Grandma chased her out of the house for making advances—to me! I stood up on a chair and shouted, "If she goes, I go." Grandma laughed, but I went. The girl thought I was a good investment, I was going to be an actor. She took me to her place on Cherry Street. A few days later Grandma tracked me down.

"Better come home," she said. "We're having meat balls." I *loved* meat balls, so I left.

A few weeks later the girl gave me money to buy tickets for a show, Victor Moore in *The Talk of New York*. I bought the tickets but—I took Ida. The girl was waiting when we came out; she chased me down Seventh Avenue with a hatpin.

From the day we met, it was always Ida. I went to camp that year and wrote long letters. As the years passed, her parents offered strenuous objections to me because I wanted to be an actor. One of her sisters was being courted by a fellow who had a brother. The family arranged for the brother to court Ida. He brought her big boxes of candy. It was good candy. She brought it all to me. After I got my first job we'd walk from Henry Street to Fifty-eighth, to Proctor's Theatre, more than fifty-eight blocks each way to see the vaudeville show. She used to find out which of her girl friends' mothers was going out, so we could sit in a little parlor and be romantic. From the day we met she lived a double life; but eventually her family caught on to that and for a year we didn't see each other. We were sixteen then. When we started dating again we'd meet at her cousin's house.

Ida worked at Levi Simpsons, designing ladies' neckwear; jabots were very big then. I'd gotten a job with Bedini and Arthur, a juggling act, at Hammerstein's theater. I was supposed to hand the jugglers their props, but as we progressed, they let me do a few bits. One Saturday afternoon Ida came to the theater with a bunch of girls from Levi Simpsons. Just before the matinee my whole closing with the jugglers was cut. Now all I had to do was walk on and hand them a plate. I didn't come around to see Ida for four or five days.

When I went on the road with the juggling team I was earning thirty-five dollars and every week I sent twenty-five home to Ida to save. Then came the big break, with Gus Edwards' *Kid Kabaret*, seventy-five a week! I wrote every day and sent money every week and silver spoons from every town in the USA. I never actually proposed to Ida, but she certainly couldn't have been surprised when, after that tour, I suggested we get married and she go with me to Europe (a straight man, Sammy Kessler, and I had a European booking).

Only one thing bothered Ida. "What can I tell my mother?"

"Tell her we're going to get married and go to Europe."

"Europe!" yelled Ida's mother.

"How much you making?" shouted her dad.

I told him.

"Clear?"

"Well, I have to pay for my own make-up."

"You see?" he said. "Always a catch to it."

Ida's dad said all actors were bums. He didn't want any bums in his family. He wanted me to go into a legitimate business. Gents' furnishings. I kept lying. I said, "Let me stay in show business long enough to make the money for a store." So now I had $2,500; Ida'd saved it for me in the Bowery Savings Bank.

"So what's gonna be?" her dad said.

"A man as big as David Tobias should have a son-in-law with only one store? It should be three minimum. One in the Bronx, one in Manhattan, one in Brooklyn."

Years passed. I am married and have five children. I'm playing the Paramount. Ida's dad comes down to see me. I know what he'll say. So quick, I whisk him in front of the theater, I show him the tremendous sign: EDDIE CANTOR IN PERSON. Then I hurry him down the street to the Rivoli. Another sign: EDDIE CANTOR—ROMAN SCANDALS. I rush him over to Forty-second Street, a revival of *Whoopee*. No comment. Ida's dad takes me by the wrist, walks me in front of Nat Lewis's haberdashery, and says, "*That* sign will always be there."

But the $2500 didn't go into gents' furnishings. Ida and I sailed second class on the *Aquitania*, with the money in a boodle bag around her neck. Sammy and I opened in London and dropped dead. I was scared. I had a wife to support and no job. Luckily Ida *wasn't* scared. She has instinct, this girl, and a great sense of humor. We were painfully economical. In London we allowed ourselves so much for breakfast, for dinner, and supper; Ida washed the skin off her knuckles doing our laundry in the hotel washbowl. We kept right on the economy drive after André Charlot hired me for *Not Likely*. Every night Ida'd climb the stairs to the gallery where tickets were two shillings. It never occurred to us that she could have come backstage. Once we went to Lyon's Corner House for tea. The waitress brought a beautiful tray of pastries; we asked how much and she told us. It was the equivalent of twelve and a half cents. We thought we were buying the whole tray and forced ourselves to eat every crumb. It was twelve and a half cents *apiece!* Ten times twelve and a half—I haven't been able to eat pastry since.

When war broke out we caught the last boat home, the *St. Paul.* We landed in New York, walked down the gangplank, the *St. Paul* got a look at us, tipped, and sank.

Now we were married people back home. We lived in the Bronx with Ida's sister Jennie, Jennie's husband, and her two children. It was their apartment, we had one room and—in short order —our first baby, Marjorie. It was a railroad flat with a long, dark corridor. The sisters alternated on housework and child care. While one cooked and cleaned the other took the children out for rosy cheeks. Marjorie was so used to being with her cousins that, like them, she called her mother "Aunt Ida." It couldn't have been an easy life, I was on the road, we had little money, but Ida took it calmly and in stride. When Marjorie had an earache and it was pronounced mastoids Ida just inquired for the best doctor in New York, wrapped her child in blankets, and took her, on the trolley. She called me after the operation was over.

Not having had a family as a child, I'd made up my mind to build one. The early years were difficult for me too. Let me show you what I mean. . . .

Nineteen hundred and sixteen. Natalie is born. I'm three thousand miles away, in Los Angeles, rehearsing for a show called *Canary Cottage*. The show opens, it's a big hit. I'm a big hit. But I'm unhappy. I'm homesick. I send home all but twenty-five dollars of each pay check, live on Broadway above the Pig'n Whistle for a buck a night. This leaves eighteen dollars for food, laundry and transportation. If I have a soda one day I skip it the next. My wife and two children are living with her sister in one room. I want a home for them; that's my job and my wish, a home. I leave *Canary Cottage*, a hit show and a good job, to gamble, to audition for Ziegfeld back in New York.

This is the second big stroke of luck. First Ida, then Ziegfeld. He puts me in the *Midnight Frolic*, then the *Follies*. Ida's family can't believe it, I've made good. I can't afford tickets for the opening night of the *Follies*, but I arrange for them to see the Wednesday matinee. After the show they're waiting at the stage door. A friend is with them. Ida's dad introduces me, like this—"Meet-my-son-in-law-makes-four-hundred-dollars-a-week."

Even now, playing on Broadway, it isn't an easy life. Ida spends half her time shushing the kids. "Shhh, Daddy's sleeping." She gets them up early, dressed, out to play, fast. I get up at noon, read the papers, have breakfast while they have lunch, read the mail, have dinner at five to get to the theater by eight. Subway to the theater, subway home; at one-thirty, Ida's waiting up with hot chocolate and cookies.

Any marriage should be a partnership. Ours has never been a matter of fifty-fifty. Most of the credit for our success goes to my wife. She accepted show business and put up with it. One situation became a standard joke. If I was on the road I'd try to get home for Sunday, my time with the youngsters. I'd take the midnight train after the Saturday-night show and get in Sunday morning. Then I'd sit quietly in the living room, reading the paper until they got up. As if I'd been there right along. One Sunday morning Marjorie went running to say, "Mama, that man's here again."

We'd always felt that we should set ourselves goals, family projects. Our first project—an apartment in her sister's building. Then a house at Mt. Vernon, a miniature colonial house with four bedrooms and a maid. We had three children now, Marjorie, Natalie, Edna. The maid was essential. I remember the first meal Ida ever cooked, horses' hips on toast, I think it was. One bite and I knew I had to make money—we needed a cook for survival. Now we had the maid and an enclosed back yard where the children could play. Until then the only trees they'd seen were in Van Cortlandt Park where I'd take them Sundays. Song Writer Harry Ruby took his Toby and I'd take my girls and we'd spend the day. I was a fiend for outdoor exercise. Harry and I'd play baseball, the children ran on the grass, Ida'd bring a big box lunch. We had a Maxwell and I drove, terribly they tell me. But now we didn't need Van Cortlandt Park, we had our own back yard.

I wasn't there enough. I was on the road. Once, while I was away, Ida had her hair cut, her beautiful jet-black hair. Once, while I was playing Chicago, Marilyn was born. Ida's wire read: *Another girl excuse it please.*

Two weeks later she brought Marilyn to Chicago to show me. We've talked of it often, wondering how she had the nerve. A two-week-old baby! She put her in an open suitcase to sleep, so she wouldn't roll out of the berth. Up until now, since our marriage, Ida'd been constantly pregnant. Now we felt our family complete and she was able to travel with me part of the time. She loved her children, she was a devoted mother, but she was a wife first. Often she'd bring the four children with her, with Sterno to heat the bottles. Wherever I was at Christmas, they came en masse. Natalie was the jinx, she had a knack for catching diseases at the wrong time. We were playing *Kid Boots* in Pittsburgh, they were all coming for Ida bought them each an outfit at Best's and had the bags packed. That morning Natalie came down with measles.

But many's the time Ida left the children in her sister's care and joined me. She was always knitting, teaching the show girls how to knit mittens, sweaters. Once when she was traveling with me, there was a dog act on the bill and Ida fell in love with the dog. He was a Boston bull with big eyes, like mine. His name was "Poonelo," and that's been her pet name for me ever since. It's a pet name, it also means "Schnook." When I promise too much she sighs, "Oh, that Poonelo." Someone will call from downtown; they're coming to see us. "I'll send the car," I say, forgetting that the chauffeur has errands to run all afternoon. In the end I hire a car to fetch the people who were perfectly able to get out under their own power. "Poonelo," Ida says.

She's the practical one, the balance for all the impulsive crazy things I'm likely to do. The first trip to California, July 1926, five nights and five days on a train with four small children, one still on the bottle, no air conditioning. And she still has her sense of humor!

California living meant a lot to us all, and one of the things that made California for Ida was Fanny Brice. In the old days in New York, Ida would call for me at the theater. She'd sit out in the car, matinee days, watching Fanny swing down the street in her riding habit, slim and chic. She adored Fanny from a distance, but Ida at that time weighed a hundred and eighty pounds and she was too shy, too self-conscious to speak. In California they became fast friends.

Ida and Fanny were much alike, completely real, completely frank, great entertainers. Fanny entertained the audience, Ida entertained Fanny. They came in out of the sun one day, I heard Fanny shriek from the bedroom. Ida had just stepped out of the shower and was singing, with a bath towel wrapped around her, "Nature Boy." When Fanny designed our house on Roxbury Drive (she was a talented decorator), she was terribly concerned about the color of the walls in the living room. The painters mixed and mixed but couldn't get exactly the color she wanted. Fanny went home and brought an ash tray the right color. The next day the painters tried again. All day. Finally they called Ida to show her what they had—a good color but not the color of Fanny's ash tray. The painters were scared. "No problem," Ida said, "just paint the ash tray."

You see what I mean? Practical. She's saved my life more than once. In 1927 I was plagued with pleurisy. I'd always feared tuberculosis (my father had weak lungs) and I took a leave of absence to go to Palm Springs. Ida knew how depressed I was and she hit on a solution of her own. What I needed, she decided, was a new baby. Janet, the only planned one of the five—planned, that is, by Ida—was just what the doctor should have ordered. She became everybody's favorite, simply because we hadn't had a baby for four years. And she was so little. She was born two months ahead of schedule. I was at the theater and the chauffeur was lost for two and a half hours trying to get Ida to the hospital in Brooklyn. I rushed to Brooklyn, stayed through the night, watched Ida's color come back with a blood transfusion, and was thrilled to meet my fifth little girl. Ida was right; a new baby, a new challenge, something to live for.

Some people have the ability to love but they think of themselves first. Ida has the kind of love that thinks first of the ones she loves. She has always done things to make life easier and happier for me. We built a home in Great Neck, 1928. A big home, too big, a mansion on ten acres, but what a thrill for me who'd lived in a basement with out-of-work servant girls sleeping on the floor! Ida met with the architects, made the plans, everything was made special, even the doorknobs. When it was finished she opened a door upstairs, "your suite." Shut off from the rest of the house was a bedroom, a den, a bathroom as big as a dance hall. In it you press a button, a massage table swings down from the wall and a sun lamp lights up in the ceiling overhead.

So now we have the house and it's furnished and we've spent sixty-five thousand dollars just on shrubbery. We're on easy street. Ida has fixed it so I live like a king.

When the stock market is crashing, every night Ida picks me up, I have to tell her . . . today we lost one hundred thousand dollars . . . today, one hundred and twenty-five thousand dollars. Finally one night, I say "Ida, we have nothing. Not a cent." I feel in my pocket and pull out sixty dollars. We drive on in the dark, the chauffeur guiding the big car expertly through traffic. Ida is pressing something into my hand. A little bracelet, a trifle I'd given her for her birthday.

"Poonelo, see what you can do with this," she says.

That night we have a big meeting, Ida and I. We talk all night. There are two things we can do. We can sell the house, get rid of the help, stop spending. Ida is willing to go back to an apartment. Or we can go ahead as if nothing's happened. I'm still working in *Whoopee*. Maybe I can find a way to earn more money.

Ida says, "It'll do something to your personality to cut down. After all you've only lost money. You still have your sense of humor. That's the one thing you didn't have on margin."

Immediately she has made everything right. If you're not frightened of being frightened and have the ability to sell something . . . isn't this the land of opportunity? Two days later I start a book, *Caught Short*. Simon & Schuster publish it, sell one hundred thousand copies the first day. It's a funny book about the stock-market crash. It grows out of a curtain speech I'm making at intermission. At first I'd talked for about three minutes, trying to kid the audience out of their depression. I told about the man walking into the Biltmore Hotel, asking for a room on the nineteenth floor. The clerk says, "For sleeping or jumping?" The three-minute speech gets longer and longer until it takes the whole intermission, the book sells a half million copies. I begin to pay back on the $285,000 debt to the bank that had covered calls for more margin.

Before this when someone asked me to appear at private parties I'd laugh, now I go. One evening Walter Chrysler has people in for cocktails and gives them their choice of entertainment. I sing all the choruses of *Whoopee* and Chrysler hands me five one-thousand-dollar bills.

Whoopee ran until May thirtieth that year. It could have gone on and on, but Ziegfeld was broke too and was glad to sell the picture rights to Goldwyn. Ida and I talked it over, saw the financial possibilities of the movies, and came to Hollywood. After having been much worse than broke in 1929, the years 1930 to 1935, the worst of the depression, were my most fruitful. Working in pictures, I earned in six or seven weeks what I'd earned in a year, plus radio for Chase and Sanborn and 50 per cent of the gross of any theater engagement. The credit is all Ida's. She kept me from getting scared.

While I was making money Ida was losing weight. Did I heckle her? I made her life miserable. She's naturally a tiny person, all the weight she'd put on during pregnancies wasn't good for her, and I told her so. Love has nothing to do with it. I'd love her if she weighed three hundred. Ida with me is a permanent thing. It's like going to Vegas and gambling, or buying United States bonds. But I haven't begun to tell you about Ida. You'll have to read the whole book.

3. The Girls From Show Business

When I was in Gus Edwards' *Kid Kabaret* in Knoxville, Tennessee, 1912, I had laryngitis and was sent to a local doctor. He sprayed my tonsils, gave me a gargle and some advice.

"Do you know Sophie Tucker?" he said.

I did not. Sophie was a headliner, a star.

"She played here last week," the doctor said, "and let me tell you, son. She doesn't know how to use her voice. That's what you have to learn. She's ruining her vocal chords. That woman won't last five years."

Four years later I met Sophie and tried to tell her what the doc had said. She screamed with laughter. "These are no vocal chords, kid, these are bands of steel."

Forty years later, she's still laughing and she's still never needed a mike. Sophie can't imagine being sick, and you can't imagine it either. She's like granite—all but the heart. Sophie'll do an hour show in a night club, give it all she has, and in between that show and the late one she'll sit in the lobby talking her head off, selling her book or records or an album for one of her charities. At times like this she hates to give change. Give her a five or a fifty and she'll say, "Great, you can spare it." She's an indefatigable worker for charity, an indefatigable entertainer, and an indefatigable friend. No acquaintances for this red-hot mama; everyone's her friend to the point where every year she sends personal birthday greetings to three or four hundred people, in her own handwriting. You can call on her for anything at any time: money, advice, unquestioning loyalty; she'll do anything in the world for you except stop a card game when she's losing.

How many times she and Ida and I have gotten together when

Sophie finished work at 3 A.M. We've had a bite to eat, gone home, I've gone to bed, and when I wake up at 10 A.M. I'll hear Ida pleading:

"Sophie, I've got to get some rest. You should too."

And the answer: "Sophie never leaves a loser. Deal, Ida, deal."

Our friendship started in 1916 when the Solax Club gave a party at Reisenweber's at Columbus Circle. Sophie was one of the big hits of New York, and Reisenweber's was something like the Latin Quarter today, but noisier—Sophie *made* it noisier. This Solax Club was organized by a group of grown-up East-Siders, trying to help East Side kids get off the streets (we thought Solax had something to do with sunshine). The members were all my friends and they asked Sophie if she'd mind my taking part in the show. I didn't start work on the New Amsterdam Roof until midnight.

"Bring him down!" said Sophie. She not only worked with me, she helped me. We sang a song, "Put Your Arms Around Me, Honey," yes, that must have been the song, because I remember saying, "I'll have to make a second trip!" That made Sophie laugh and I tried another line, "Sophie, I love to see you laugh. When you laugh, so much of you has a good time." We clowned around and, of course, never did anyone have such a stooge. (Stooge, incidentally, was our slang for "student," the guys in show business who were learning the craft, second bananas.)

We've clowned around together many times since at benefits but never in shows. Actually Sophie's stints in theaters came early, she was in the *Follies* and in Winter Garden shows, but for those her stuff had to be toned down. Sophie's entirely a night-club singer. Her style and material are hardly what you'd want at a Holy Name breakfast. But in the night clubs she's queen, she has no inhibitions and needs none, she sings the words we used to write on the sidewalks of New York. And you *hear* her. The voice was robust even when she was a kid, singing around her family's kosher restaurant in Hartford. She could audition in New York, she says, without ever leaving Hartford. There's never been anyone who could get over lyrics with such potency, that's why song writer Jack Yellen has been writing for her for thirty years. He knows what he writes will get a demonstration.

Sophie's generous to other performers, and her maternal instinct is a mile wide. She gave me her friendship immediately;

she gave me plenty of good advice, and introduced me to her agent, who's handled me for more than twenty years. And the laughs we've had! Sophie came back one time from England after scoring a triumph. I met her at the dock. As she came down the gangplank she spied me and in a booming voice yelled, "Eddie, I went over big—*very big!*"

"Sophie," I yelled, "you came back the same way."

On her fiftieth anniversary in show business she was given a public dinner at the Waldorf and on the dais was seated the Who's Who of show business. There was never a greater tribute to a performer. A half century is a long time in any business, and to stay on top in show business—that's an eternity. But like so many of the top gals, Sophie paid for her success with a tremendous price personally. Love and marriage, a family, Sophie's the original woman who pays. Perhaps that's why she gives so willingly of herself to her friends, why she works her heart out for that other family, the needy.

It's strange how many personal tragedies lie behind the successful women of show business. Let me tell you about Marilyn Miller. ("Lumpy," we called her, meaning lump of sugar.) She was probably the most beautiful girl I've ever seen and she didn't have to depend on that beauty; she could sing, she could dance like a nymph. We worked together in the *Follies of 1918* and *1919;* and during the first of these shows, Frank Carter—our singer, dancer, juvenile, and straight man—fell in love with Marilyn and she with him. But for some reason Marilyn's mother took a dislike to Frank and would not permit Marilyn to date him.

Marilyn and Frank had taken me into their confidence, and my job was to play cupid. Marilyn's mother had no objections to Marilyn's having dinner after the show with *me*, a married man with children, very safe and "he makes her laugh to boot." So after the show I'd put on my dinner jacket and take Marilyn—to Frank. Then I'd go to some delicatessen and kibitz with the boys until it was time to pick Marilyn up and take her back to her mother.

In 1919 Marilyn and Frank ran off to Maryland and got married. Marilyn was still in the *Follies;* Frank had joined the cast of *Two Little Girls in Blue.* They were married in the morning and went back to their shows that night. They were supremely happy, and after a while Marilyn's family forgave Frank.

Comes the time when we go on tour—Marilyn and Frank spend all their money on phone calls. When they have a Sunday off they fly to each other. At the end of the season both our shows play Chicago and the two kids continued their honeymoon. One afternoon Frank takes Marilyn to the auto show and she sees a Packard car with a custom-built body. It costs eleven thousand dollars—in 1919.

"Frank," Marilyn says, "I must have that car. Please, Frank."

"Lumpy, I love you, but that car's too expensive." Marilyn's disappointed. She's crazy about that car.

At any rate, we leave Chicago the next week to play St. Louis, Columbus, and Philadelphia. While we're in Philadelphia *Two Little Girls in Blue* closes for the season. Frank buys the Packard and starts off driving to Philadelphia to surprise Marilyn. He never gets there. An accident takes place en route and Frank is crushed to death.

Now someone must tell Marilyn. The theater manager said, "Eddie, you're such a close friend of Marilyn and Frank . . . you."

I washed up faster than I've ever washed in my life, to catch Marilyn before she left the theater. I walked into her dressing room. "Marilyn, you're a terrific performer. You sing, you dance, you have youth. No matter what ever happens, you'd be the kind of trouper who'd go on."

Marilyn whirled around from her dressing table. "Eddie! Frank is dead!" Not a tear, she was too shocked. She got up like a robot, put on her coat and we went back to her hotel. Then it started. Frank's pictures were on the wall, three or four of them. She went around the room, looking into Frank's face and crying hysterically. I had to get a doctor to give her a shot and put her to bed. From then on we devoted ourselves to Marilyn. Van and Schenck and I would put on impromptu shows in her living room, before the show, after the show. We couldn't make her laugh, but we could keep her from sobbing herself sick. One night I put on a pair of shorts and a tam-o'-shanter, took my golf clubs, and about 2 A.M. went out into the hall. I sent Van and Schenck to tell Marilyn to come right out. She came.

"Eddie what are you *doing?*"

"Well, Marilyn, I want to get out on the golf course before it gets crowded."

Marilyn laughed and laughed until she was tired enough to sleep. This went on day after day until the season closed, and somehow this gallant girl managed to get through every performance.

We met again in 1936. I was recuperating from surgery and a note came from another patient in the hospital, a Miss Miller wanted to see me. I got a wheel chair and went over to her room and stayed until one in the morning. Marilyn had been married twice since, but that's not what we talked about. We talked about Frank. Marilyn cried, "Eddie, what's happened to my life? I was so happy! And now, all these years and I'll never see Frank again."

She was having a minor operation the next day, a sinus operation, and she said that the moment it was over she'd come to my room and pay back the visit. She died during that operation from complications—of the heart, I'm sure.

And then there was Ruth Etting. We were together in the *Follies of 1927* and in *Whoopee* and *Roman Scandals*. Ruth was a country girl from Nebraska, married to a semi-gangster, "Colonel Gimp" Snyder, from Chicago. We'd met at Henrici's over hot chocolate and *kuchen*, this sad-eyed girl and this man—so like Jimmy Cagney in *Love Me or Leave Me*, a so-called tough guy with a very soft spot. The soft spot was for Ruth and no one ever tried any harder for a girl than the Gimp did. But Ruth was with him not because of love but because she felt completely in his debt.

She was a girl who minded her own business, learned her songs, gave a performance, and went to bed early. No night clubs, no pretense. She was an excellent singer and that was that. All the ambition was the Gimp's. The night *Whoopee* opened . . . I'll never forget him, bursting into my arms after Ruth had spoken her first lines on stage. She had maybe six lines altogether, but the colonel embraced me, kissed me, almost choked me. "I knew the dame could sing," he said, "but to *act* . . . to *act!*" You'd have thought Ruth was Ethel Barrymore or Tallulah. And, of course, Ruth just went her way quietly.

An actor in the show was crazy about her; but any sort of conversation between them was difficult with the Gimp constantly backstage. So in the first act, when this actor and I shook hands, I'd hand him a note from Ruth. In the second act, he'd slip his answer into my pocket, and I'd pass it on to Ruth as we went up in the elevator after the show. If the Gimp had ever caught us, we'd have wound up, in his favorite phrase, "DSF"—dead stinking fish.

Ruth stayed with the colonel out of loyalty, she even laughed at his jokes out of loyalty, with her mouth but not with her eyes; and eventually Ruth was to have her freedom and her happiness.

I don't mean to imply that all these glamorous talented girls were hiding broken hearts. There was Mary Eaton, my leading lady in *Kid Boots*, who was completely lighthearted. She never even knew what was going on in the world outside the theater. Many nights, after the show, we'd go to Child's for cocoa and wheat cakes or a plate of rice with a poached egg on top. One night I picked up the paper and read where the Ku Klux Klan was riding again.

"Eddie," she said, "Are you for them or against them?"

"Mary, don't you ever read the newspapers?"

"Only the reviews the morning after we open," she said innocently. And you had to laugh because the girl was a doll, she was natural and charming and had talent. She once made a picture in which I was merely a guest star. When the director heard that Mary was going to be in the picture, he said, "Oh no, not that dumb blonde. She has nothing!" A few weeks later, he married her.

And there was Jobyna Howland, one of the great comediennes in the theater who almost turned *Kid Boots* into a tug of war. She had a wonderful part, the part of the lady physical-culture expert and her lines were sure laughs, but that wasn't enough for Jobyna. Every time I had a line that was funny she'd fan herself furiously with a large feather fan. This is old and cheap stuff, an attention distracter, and it went on week after week until I told her, "I don't mind competition, Jobyna, but that fan's too much for me." She stopped making like a fan dancer but she got even. In the osteopathic scene she had a chance to rough me up and she did. She'd actually come out with tufts of my hair in her hand, when all she had to do was let me move slightly and it would look as though she was pulling my hair.

Jobyna's trouble was that she had been in a big hit show, she'd been the star, and she couldn't forget it. After a year of *Kid Boots*, sure she was indispensable, Jobyna said she was exhausted and asked for a vacation. She was certain we'd have to call her back in a week; but the fact was, Cecil Cunningham in the same part never lost a laugh and Jobyna discovered "I'm not as tired as I thought I was," cut her vacation short, and came running back. After that, we became good friends, and I managed to hang on to the rest of my hair. We were together at Ziegfeld's funeral, clinging together as bereft as any brother and sister.

And Ethel Merman. I first saw Ethel on Broadway when she sang "Delilah" and "I Got Rhythm" in Gershwin's *Girl Crazy*. I became a mad Merman fan. She has some of the quality of Sophie Tucker, some of the quality of Fanny Brice. Can you say more? Berlin always said that if you write a song for Ethel you'd better make sure the words are good because everybody in the audience is going to hear 'em. She has the greatest confidence on stage of anyone I've ever met, including Jolson. And she's honest, with herself and with everybody else.

We had a ball working together in Hollywood, making *Kid Millions* and *Strike Me Pink*. (In the first of these, despite the fact that I'm so much older, she played my mother or at least, in cahoots with some racketeers, pretended to be my mother.) While she's serious about her work, Ethel's never serious to the point of being tense. She comes on the set knowing everything, the words, the director's instructions, everything—her memory's terrific. But if you start to ad lib, she'll ad lib right with you and her sense of fun is incomparable.

While she was in California she'd be out at the house a great deal. She's crazy about kids and my kids were crazy about her. She never talks down. With her own kids now, she's always on the level. "Hey, stinker, I want to tell you something . . ." She blamed me because her first baby was a girl. We met one day at "21," Ethel so pregnant it looked as if she might drop the baby between courses. I gave her a little pat and Ethel jumped.

"Oh, now it's going to be a girl," she wailed.

Ten minutes after the baby was born she phoned me at RKO. "Eddie, I told you. It's a girl!" In that voice of hers, that Merman voice.

Like Sophie, Ethel has never needed a mike. And that's why, for my dough, she's always greater on the stage than on the screen.

She thrives on an audience; and the shock, the absolute, bombastic style which is so right in the theater isn't as good in pictures where she's projected right into the audience's lap. The first time Ethel was with me on radio, 1934, I pointed to the microphone and said, "Ethel, radio's wonderful. Think of it. Through this little device you'll be heard in millions of homes throughout the country."

"What's the matter with those bums," laughed Ethel, "too lazy to open a window?"

Obviously, if you're a comedian, there's nothing like working with a top comedienne, a gal with an innate sense of fun, who can ad lib, who can spark you: a Sophie Tucker, an Ethel Merman, a Joan Davis. Joan and I made several pictures together, the first of them an idea of mine called *Show Business*, the story of four people who meet early in life, their marriages, their struggles and their ultimate goal to be in a Ziegfeld show. Joan Davis, George Murphy, Connie Moore, and I were the four. We all loved the idea and were excited about it. Joan, one of the greatest ad-lib comediennes in the business, put in many of her own lines and pieces of business and was an outstanding hit.

We had a burlesque opera in the picture in which we mouthed words to a real operatic recording. Joan wore a dress with a long train. As producer of the picture, I'd seen the dress and thought I knew the scene; but Joan showed up with a pair of trick falsies that were so outstanding they made Jane Russell and Marilyn Monroe look like boys. These bosoms went out and out as she held a high note. It was hilarious. And there was a scene in a restaurant when we were still small-timers trying to get a break. Joan and I were talking about our plans, how the four of us would do an act together. All the time she talked she was dropping sugar in her coffee, and more sugar. Finally she lifted the cup and took a sip. You expected her to wince. She didn't. "Needs sugar," she ad libbed.

A funny dame. And I think, too, that the audience enjoyed the idea of two homely people getting together. It gave the rest of the people in the audience hope.

The picture was a great success, so much so that I was engaged to produce and star in another picture with Joan, *If You Knew Susie*. Again she kidded through the whole picture; and when you have people doing that in a comedy, you have a better chance for success because the mood gets on film. That's why the Hope-Crosby "Road" pictures have always been so gay! Bing and Bob try to top each other, the book is of little consequence, the fun is there between them. It was that way working with Joan. She does the best physical comedy, she can slide halfway across the floor and not take a pratfall if she doesn't want to. But far above that, you can rely on her to have an answer to anything you say that's not in the script. We did the same thing on radio, guesting on each other's programs, Joan was among the top names in radio at the time.

One of the wonderful things about show business is that all your life you work with people who are the most talented, creative people in the world. And this brings me to my dear friend who needs a chapter all her own, Fanny Brice.

4. Fanny Brice

Fanny was the most honest person I ever met. She was a sophisticate, a great star, with the simplicity of a peasant. Crude, almost vulgar, she had a sharp intellect and a sure taste for all the best things in life. She couldn't abide falseness in an object or a person, and it showed—in the beautiful homes she decorated for her friends, in her own painting, the blending of color, in the art, jewels, clothes, and people that surrounded her. Katherine Hepburn brought her every script and read it aloud. If Fanny didn't like a script, Hepburn didn't play it. Moss Hart read her his plays, so did Ben Hecht; Sylvia Kaye tried out every song she wrote for Danny.

Fanny's artistic integrity was instinctive. So was her nose for people. She had no qualms telling someone, "I don't like you too much and if you never come around again it'll be all right with me." But if she loved you she loved you. And being with her was like visiting a perfumery, you *had* to come away smelling better. We were friends for thirty-four years, from the day we met until the day she died. From her I learned a good many of the tricks of show business. I learned the power of concentration, and if I had to learn it, she taught me the joy of simple pleasures, a cold chicken leg at midnight, sitting in a kitchen with friends.

Fanny had worked her way up from a childhood where she stole in order to eat and landed in the big time via the burlesque circuit. She started with Ziegfeld in 1910, and by the time we met in the *Follies of 1917* she was an established star. She and the lovely dancer, Ann Pennington, were close friends—Fanny with her funny face and Penny with her beauty, Fanny the kind of a girl who was a man's best pal, Penny so sexy that every man wanted to protect her or else . . . But the two girls had a lot in common. They were both talented, creative people, but, forgetting their talent, they had heart and understanding and the ability to give. They'd both been in show business long enough to know the ropes. They'd lived in the best hotels, they knew the top restaurants, they had stunning clothes and an assured femininity. There was nothing coquettish about either of them. They were competing in a man's world and they didn't expect any odds. We were great pals. Fanny and I would ride for hours on top of busses with Penny for the "fresh air" she felt was indispensable. We often dined together and we'd split the check three ways and the tip. I couldn't afford to take them out and they didn't expect it. Part of their sophistication was the ability to stand on their own feet and be friends—with stagehands, stars, and with each other. Long after Penny was out of show business she was Fanny's house guest and Fanny'd buy her expensive clothes, rip out the labels, and sew in some lesser marking so Penny'd not feel in her debt.

But to go back . . . I'd known Fanny's brother Lew in vaudeville. I'd asked him to team up with me before I teamed with Sammy Kessler for the European fiasco of 1914. Lew turned me down because he frankly didn't think we had a chance. Later, Lew *didn't* have a chance. He was a clever entertainer, but because he was Fanny's brother too much was expected of him.

When I showed up at *Follies* rehearsals Fanny promptly put a protecting arm about me. She was only a year older, but she was a star and she didn't have an envious atom in her whole anatomy. She just had plain talent. Her sense of humor lay at the core of it. She could burlesque what other people were doing seriously and be a riot. As a ballet dancer her movements were hilarious. As Mme. Du Barry she'd come out gorgeously attired, wave her fan, and with a thick Jewish accent say, "I'm a bad voman, but I'm dem good company!" And of course her singing voice had something else. All the persecution of a race was in her heart and in her throat; when she poured out a ballad you cried.

Her first advice to me was, "Kid, don't push yourself here. You're up against top competition and you don't have to push." She sensed the brashness in me and she didn't want me to get slapped down.

For a minute I resented the advice, but gradually I understood what she was saying. She was saying that I was now on stage with the best in the business, Rogers the top monologist, Fields the top pantomimist, Bert Williams the greatest blackface comedian, herself the top comedienne—and none of them was trying to steal the show. Theirs was a camaraderie I didn't know existed in show business. I never heard of it before, I never have seen it since. They were a family and they wanted the *family* to be a hit. They helped each other. "Your finish isn't good in that scene. Try this tonight."

And I quickly saw that what Fanny was giving me was more than lip service. She'd watch me rehearsing with Bert Williams and give me tips. "You don't take bows the way you took 'em in vaudeville, kid. The *Follies* audience is wiser." In vaudeville you'd always have a trick on your bow, something to milk a little extra applause. Here, she showed me, you wanted reserve and poise, "You mustn't have the attitude that you're an interloper; you belong."

She went to Gene Buck and Dave Stamper who wrote the songs for Ziegfeld and suggested that she and I do a number together. *She* certainly didn't need *me*, she just wanted to give me a break. The number was "Just You and Me," and to match my blackface, Fanny tanned up. She asked me if I could dance. I lied of course I could, but I kept stalling when she wanted to rehearse. Finally, the day before we left for Atlantic City to open the show, Fanny dragged me onto the stage. I hoped I could follow her and get away with it, just a simple soft-shoe dance; but after a dozen steps she turned her head sideways, muttering as she danced, "You sonofabitch, you can't dance a lick!" And she never missed a step, she just called over Ned Wayburn, the choreographer. "This guy can't even do a time step," she moaned. "Teach him something he can pick up in the next few hours."

We had a lot of fun with this song-and-dance number. Once Fanny and I stopped speaking. Driving in Fields's car, we'd hit a bump and I'd hit the top of my head. Fanny roared with laughter.

"Fanny," I said indignantly, "I'm in pain."

"If your eyes weren't popped already, they'd pop now, kid," howled Fanny.

I stopped talking. I was hurt. That night we got on and started singing our number. I was telling her how much I loved her and here we were not speaking. I looked at Fanny, she looked at me, we both laughed so hard we couldn't get out the lyrics.

How could you stay angry at Fanny anyhow? She couldn't stay angry at anyone. She had a maid, Adele Moon, she'd fire at the rate of two or three times a week. The maid was with her for years. Fanny'd say, "You go, Adele, and never come back." The next day the Moon showed up as usual.

"Shall I run your bath, Miss Brice?"

And Fanny'd say, "Of course."

Once Adele got fired on our account. Fields's and mine. Fanny was always cooking for us, saving us money. Usually we traveled in Fields's car, but once when there was a blizzard we had to travel to Cincinnati by train. We're all set to eat in the dining car but Fanny won't hear of it. "Ridiculous. We'll be in in an hour, I'll cook your dinner." She was a great cook; no one could make goulash and spaetzle like she could, and spaghetti. So we come in to Cincinnati hours late, Fanny rushes around and buys spaghetti and starts cooking. She carries all the equipment with her in suitcases: hot plates, pans, everything. Here she is, saving us money, smelling up the Sinton Hotel (Suite 607–609) with spaghetti sauce, and splashing around expensive perfume to drown the essence of garlic and olive oil. The spaghetti is finally finished, we dive in, and Fields starts foaming at the mouth. Me too, and Fanny. We look like we all have hydrophobia. The grated-cheese jar had been filled with soap powder by mistake! Fanny gathered up all the spaghetti, put it down the toilet, then had to pay a plumbing bill to have the plumbing unplugged.

"This time I'm going to fire Adele!"

Which, of course, she didn't. She loved people and enjoyed them. If she was telling a show girl a story and was called for her cue, she'd holler back "Just a minute," and finish the story. Our opening night in Atlantic City, with all of us jittery, the callboy had to literally pull her out of the dressing room where she was trying one of her hats on a chorus girl. She kept right on talking until he dragged her out. As soon as the number was finished she came back and picked up where she'd been so rudely interrupted. She was always giving clothes to girls who didn't look smart enough.

Fanny's clothes were beautiful and she had the figure to wear them. Her jewels were fabulous. She bought them partly because she loved them and partly because she couldn't resist a bargain. Someone would come to her with an $8000 bracelet for $5000 and she'd buy it. Quick! Nobody in the world had the genuine affection for a bargain that Fanny had. If she could get something worth $50 for $22.95, her day was made. In her later years she hounded small shops for rare objects to put in the homes she furnished. (This interior-decorating stint was a labor of love, she differed from others in that profession in that she accepted no money from her "clients," nor a word of interference.) Her taste was exquisite. She did our home and she'd hunt for weeks to find not only what was right, but a bargain to boot. A desk, a chair, a vase. One day she brought a Chinese silk painting and hung it on my wall.

"Fanny, that's wonderful," I said.

"Cost you three hundred dollars."

"It's worth it, it's beautiful!"

You should have seen her face light up. Radiant! "Ten bucks is what I paid for it!"

She was a shrewd businesswoman and money was important. She'd scrambled up to adolescence without it. During the years she was with Ziegfeld they fought constantly over it. No matter what kind of a contract Fanny had, she wanted more money. One day Ziegfeld and I were having lunch and he complained to me. "That Fanny Brice. She won't go on the road unless she gets more money." And one thing Ziegfeld couldn't stand—he hated anyone who even hinted not going on tour. He wanted his show the same in Cincinnati as it was on Broadway.

"Fanny's associated with crooks and she's becoming one," he said.

"Then why do you want her?"

"But, Eddie, she's so good!"

And she got the raise and she went on tour.

But there came a time when even a raise couldn't keep Fanny in the show. She was about to give birth to her first child and had to drop out of the *Follies*. Flo was outraged, he regarded the actors in his troupe as members of his family. He wired the expectant mother: *"How can you do this to me?"* Later on, when Fanny was having her second child, Flo wanted her husband to sign an agreement that there'd be no more interruptions of his *Follies* while it was on tour! But no one ever ruled Fanny!

Through the years I often asked her advice. When I left Ziegfeld I asked Fanny what kind of a contract to get from the Shuberts. She said, "From the prestige standpoint you can't get the kind of a contract you had from Ziegfeld, so don't work for a salary. Get a per cent of the gross." It was a brand-new idea to me and I didn't think it would work, but it did. Just as Ziegfeld kept hiring Fanny. It doesn't matter what a producer thinks of you personally or what his policy; if you hold a full house, he'll raise the ante.

Fanny was the business adviser, the mother confessor, the doctor, the marriage counselor to everyone. She could advise expertly on everyone's life but her own.

From the time I knew her, Fanny was in love with Nicky Arnstein, a man with the most disarming charm, who just wasn't kosher. To be polite about it, he was a confidence man. In 1918 Nicky was doing a stretch in jail and Fanny was courted in Chicago by a very successful architect, a man who had built some of the finest theaters in the Middle West. He begged her to marry him and stop jumping around the country like a gypsy. When she said she couldn't give up show business, he offered to travel with her. He appealed to me, asked me to talk to Fanny. And it was true, this fellow had everything I should think a woman would want—looks, money, humor—except he was not "My Man." Fanny was rehearsing for the song already.

She married Nicky and many times Nicky traveled with Fields, Fanny and myself as we went from one city to the next. Fanny carried a case with her jewels in it, always. One bitterly cold day a fellow waved us down on the road. "Can you give me a lift? My car is stuck up here about two miles." Fields told him to hop on the running board and off we went. Without moving his lips, Nicky, who could recognize one, muttered, "This guy's a stick-up man."

"What'll I do with my jewel case?" whispered Fanny.

"Drop it on the floor. Bill, slow down and tell the guy to jump."

Fields slowed down and started swearing, Nick leaned forward threateningly, and the fellow jumped. There was no doubt Nicky was right. He knew what he knew about crooks and we never questioned it. That would be like talking about maps to Rand McNally.

Fanny adored Nicky and during their marriage had two children, Frances and Billy. She raised the children, kept them close to her, and still stayed in show business. But she would not have Fran and Billy growing up in her image, and when they were old enough she sent them abroad to study. Fran married one of the most astute artists' agents in the business; Billy became a fine painter. In her later years Fanny lived primarily for Billy, for the abiding faith she had that he would become one of the great painters of our time. As he may very well be.

While the children were small and Nicky found her amusing, Fanny had a full life. She stuck to Nick through jail sentences and a federal trial. She handed over a fortune in money and gladly pawned her jewels and faced the press with her head high. What broke her heart wasn't that Arnstein happened not to be honest— but that he happened not to be honest in love either. There came a time when so many appointments were keeping him away that she realized no one could have that many appointments. She checked. He was meeting a dame. That was always the cross of Fanny's life, another dame. It happened again with Billy Rose. She'd always thought that she and Billy were such good friends that he'd have come to her honestly and *told* her. Instead, a newspaper reporter phoned and asked for her comment on the romance between Billy and Eleanor Holm. Just like that. "I can do everything better than she can except swim," quipped Fanny.

She was fascinated with Berlin's song, "You're Laughing At Me." "What a song! How can he be so smart?" she'd say. "'You have a sense of humor and humor is death to romance.' That's the story of my life."

In a way it was the story. There was show business, and for thirty years she charged it like a battery—vaudeville, theater, movies, radio. But if she had been a happy woman she could have kept on with show business, because she had something to offer until the day she died. A loved woman, I believe, is less aware that she is growing older. Fanny grieved. She'd study the mirror. "Ida, look at me, I'm getting wrinkled. I'm through."

She felt that television was her enemy. On radio the Baby Snooks character was convincing, on stage for a scene it was great. Fanny felt it wouldn't work on television, she thought she looked old. Sometimes at our house, fooling around in the living room, we'd ask Fanny to sing. "I can't sing any more," she'd say. The hell she couldn't. She *could* sing, she could dance too. Once in a while we'd get her to dance, and her grace was unbelievable. Fanny was foolish to feel she had nothing more to give. Of all the people in show business, comedians suffer least from age. How you look doesn't matter if you're making people laugh. In every theater audience of fifteen hundred, there must be forty or fifty or more who are not there to be entertained, they're there to forget. The comedian is their Nembutal, their Miltown, whatever medicine they need.

Fanny was a tonic for more than forty years, and even after she stopped her public career her personality was a tonic to those around her. My girls adored her, especially Edna, who also paints. With Fanny's kids and ours, we were like one big family. Fanny would drop by every day to chat and to raid the icebox. She hated to eat alone and Ida keeps an icebox stocked the way an icebox should be. Every day Fanny wanted to play gin. Ida made me do the playing because Fanny took two hours to play a game. She hated to give up a card, especially an ace. She'd soliloquize. "He took a ten of spades. What's he got—six-seven-eight-nine-ten? Impossible. I have the nine. Maybe three tens. Maybe . . ." ad infinitum.

One day I say, "I can't play long today, Fanny, I'm going away." I was going to New York. My bags were packed and in the car.

"Just one game," Fanny says. So we sit down and start.

"Well, come on, Fanny, play."

"I'm thinking."

"Well?"

"Now let's see. He took a queen of diamonds. What's he got with the queen?"

Finally I say, "Fanny, excuse me just a minute . . ."

I go to the car, drive to the station, catch the Chief. Two days later I wire her from Chicago, *"Well, Fanny?"*

Many's the time we'd gather in our kitchen for a midnight snack and listen to Fanny until 5 A.M. Many's the time we'd go to her house in the middle of the night when she felt lonely. She couldn't bear loneliness. The phone would ring at 1, 2, 3 A.M. and Fanny'd say, "Whatcha doin', Eddie?"

"Nothing," I'd lie, and pulling pants over my pajamas, I'd waken Ida, and off we'd go to yak with Fanny. She called me at

3 A.M. the night she heard again from Nicky Arnstein. He was "Arnold" then, a man of seventy. Fanny was fifty-eight; but the old voice on the phone had brought back the old excitement. She didn't tell me that. She just said, "Can you come right over, Eddie? Don't ask questions. I have to see you."

I never rushed faster in my life. Fanny was sick again, she was, God forbid, dying. I rushed upstairs three at a time to find her high up in bed, her eyes shining.

"So tell me something!" she said.

"Fanny! It's after three, I was sound asleep, I thought . . ."

"Nick's coming tomorrow," she said and giggled. "Kid," she said, "remember that spaghetti in Cincinnati?"

She knew intuitively what Nick was going to want, he wanted to get back together after all the years. He had come a-courtin'. But this time, even though it was good to be wanted, she saw Nick as he was; handsome, charming, and a bum. He couldn't fool her again.

No one could. Her observations about life were so apt, her wit so wry, no wonder the intellectuals of Hollywood sat at her feet: Constance Collier, George and Ira Gershwin, George Cukor, S. N. Behrman. The guttersnipe now reigned over an atelier, and every new talent was brought to her throne for an estimate. Once it was a new writer. This fellow was being enthusiastically received and her "fans" couldn't wait for Fanny's verdict. The verdict: "He's a silk herring." In Fanny's book, charm was no longer enough.

I want to give you one more picture of my irrepressible friend. She was in the hospital and, deeply saddened, terribly worried, I rushed to see her. Fanny didn't have time to talk to me. Under the oxygen tent she was figuring out the racing form, having just discovered that under an oxygen tent in the next room was the biggest bookie in Los Angeles. She couldn't talk to me till she'd finished picking a sure winner for the sixth.

That was Fanny Brice. She made millions of people laugh in her lifetime, she made them forget their troubles, she gave them her love. It must give her a great standing in front of God as it did in front of God's children.

PART TWO

The MEN in My Life

5. Jimmy Durante

I've mentioned my first professional engagement, the road tour with the burlesque show *Indian Maidens* that left me stranded in Shenandoah in the snow. Grandma Esther came to the rescue and I returned to New York the way I'd left—broke. And just in time to witness, from a cold doorway across the street, the wedding of Ida's sister, Jennie. Ida felt sorry for me, but the truth was it looked as though her dad was right, at seventeen I was nothing.

To prove he was wrong I went out one night early in June 1909 to look for a job at Coney Island. A boy named Joe Malitz went with me. He had a good voice, this Joe, and a great sense of comedy, but no nerve. I supplied the nerve. We hooked rides out to Coney and wandered into Carey Walsh's saloon, next to the famous Roseben's pavilion, across from Diamond Tony's. Carey was in, he looked us over and asked what kind of voices we had. I promptly offered to sing.

Carey sent me over to the piano player, a thin homely kid with some brownish hair and a good-sized nose, and the show was on. I sang "Put Both Hands Up," "Wild Cherries" and "When I'm Alone I'm Lonesome." Joe sang a few songs, and we were hired. It wasn't hard to get jobs like these; the boss had nothing to lose, the singers who hung around a saloon worked for twenty dollars a week and tips. On Friday, Saturday, and Sunday you'd sing a hundred and fifty to two hundred songs; the more you sang the more you were likely to make. It didn't take me long to notice that the waiters did better than the singers and I decided to double in brass as a singing waiter. This way, every night when you came in, you'd buy five dollars' worth of checks for which you paid four-fifty; every time you sold five dollars' worth of drinks you made fifty cents, plus tips. And being a singer, you might have a customer who felt mellow enough to tip fifty cents for a sentimental song. If he was good and drunk, you might get more. You got smart about your repertoire. If you saw a guy sitting alone, you'd go right into "Melancholy Baby" and maybe get a dollar, or even two. My pal Joe wouldn't go along with the gag. He thought waiting on tables pretty undignified and after a week he left.

But I stayed on for the three summer months and not only made the first money of my life but one of the best friends of my life, the guy who played the piano. He was pretty good at it too, nothing to make Horowitz kill himself, but a guy with a sure beat and a great improviser. He was young, sixteen; he was shy, but he had a flare for showmanship, he could fake through anything and make it sound like music. And generous! He was the kind of guy —if you brought him in a sandwich he'd want to give you a whole roast beef. His name was Jimmy Durante.

We got along from the first night, and from the first night we never turned down a request. Jimmy tells the story this way: "Say a guy asked for 'Springtime in Kalamazoo,' which neither of us even ever heard of . . . I'd fake a melody and Eddie'd turn to the customer and sing 'Oh, it's springtime in Kalamazooooo,' then turn away and double-talk softly, 'My thoughts go wanderin' back to you, I'll never ever be *no*thun but blue . . .' All the time I'm pounding away fortissimo, then Eddie'd swing back to the customer and moider 'em with *When it's springtime in Kal-a-ma-zoo.* Sometimes the guy was so drunk he wouldn't notice. But sometimes he wasn't that drunk. 'What the hell you singing, kid?' Eddie'd get a bewilderin' look and say 'Why, "Springtime in Kalamazoo."' 'That ain't the song I know,' the guy'd say, and Eddie'd open his big eyes innocent-like and say, 'You mean there are *two* of 'em?'" There were plenty of songs we did know, more all the time. Afternoons I haunted the song publishers in Tin Pan Alley. Often I'd find unpublished songs, dusty on the shelf. I'd sing 'em, so would other guys around Coney. Afterward, the publisher'd decide to publish. The songs were getting around!

Jimmy and I didn't start working until nine. Earlier in the evening we'd wander around Coney having fun. I was a shillaber, a guy who works in cahoots with the concessionaire. We'd walk past a shooting gallery; I'd pick up a gun, shoot, and hit the bell. It's easy to do, you could do it blindfolded, bang, bang, bang. At this moment, a guy walking past with his girl decides it's pretty easy and stops to watch. He sees me shoot the bell or maybe knock down a row of bottles with a baseball and he steps up and lays down his cash. But when he tries to hit the bottles, they've substituted some bottles so heavy you couldn't knock 'em down with a brickbat.

Jimmy and I'd have our laugh, I'd collect a quarter for my job as front man, and we'd go over to Feltman's for a couple of hot dogs and a glass of beer. Then to work. At 4 or 5 A.M. Carey Walsh's called it a night and we'd start for home on the Brooklyn L. We'd discovered the first day that we were neighbors. Jimmy had grown up on Catherine Street near Madison, his dad owned a barbershop. I lived on Henry, a block away—but we'd never met! So we'd ride home together every morning. We never did visit each other's homes, we were both too poor, too ashamed of what home was like. But the world was a better place that summer because we'd met. As Jimmy says it, "Eddie and me had lots of fun, we seemed to match."

Ragtime Jimmy and I talked of many things on the Brooklyn L. We'd compare notes on the happenings of the evening. The other singing waiters had a trick. Say I'd have a party that was drinking fast. That was good, it didn't take long to drink up five dollars' worth. But while I'd be hustling drinks for them from the bar, another waiter'd stroll over and say, "Get this kid to sing, 'To Arms,' he's great." While I sang, on the stage "To arms, to arms, there's a ring around the moon . . ." the other waiter would take over my table. Jimmy set me straight on that.

We were both crazy about Carey Walsh, who suffered from locomotor ataxia. The poor man couldn't get out of his chair unless he held on to someone, then he walked jerkily, stiff-legged so if you let go of him he'd fall. However, when he was drunk he could get up and walk by himself. He was Jimmy's and my best fan. Nights like Mondays and Tuesdays when the place was practically empty we put on our best performances for him, and he'd applaud us to our hearts' content. Six years later when I played Henderson's vaudeville house at Coney with my partner, Al Lee, Carey came early, sat in a box, and hitting the chair with his cane by way of applause, he'd yell, "That's my boy." He gave Jimmy and me a lot of encouragement when we worked for him.

But Jimmy wasn't ambitious. He had taken music lessons as a kid; he didn't need them, his playing was spontaneous and it was just a way to earn spending money. Even when everyone would gather around to watch his wonderful left hand, he didn't get big ideas. The most he dreamed of was having a band, playing the piano in his own band. I used to say, "Jimmy, you could be a piano player all your life, until you're a hundred. You've got to do something different if you're ever going to make a big hit. The audience likes you. Why don't you get up on the floor and say something to them, or just sit at the piano and make remarks while you play?"

"Gee, Eddie, I couldn't do that," he'd say. "I'd be afraid people would laugh at me."

He was so right; they were going to laugh and keep on laughing for a lifetime. But he didn't start talking until 1923 when Lou Clayton joined him at the Club Durant. Jimmy'd had a band of his own, all right, but the bosses would never let him talk. Now he and Clayton were their own bosses, and Clayton, as president and treasurer, put Jimmy on the floor between him and Jackson for a routine of songs, jokes, and impromptu fun that caused an immediate sensation. The underworld and the upperworld discovered Clayton, Jackson, and Durante at the same time.

Because the trio had no material, they had to depend on the impromptu. Lou would stamp out on the floor yelling, "Where is he, where's Durante?" Eddie, from the kitchen, would come, yelling, "Where's Jimmy? Where's the Schnozz?" They'd look in the men's room, in the ladies' room, in the kitchen, then one of them would shout, "We've struck oil," and they'd come in leading Durante by the nose. He'd point to his schnozz. "Dere it is, folks, de real thing. It ain't gonna bite 'cha and any famous personages in the dump can come up and autygraph it." They'd aim their quips at the Walter Winchells, the George M. Cohans, the Owney Maddens, the Damon Runyon characters of Broadway. At the end of the evening a fellow like George M. Cohan would leave a hundred dollars on the register and say, "Ring this up. I've had too much fun just to pay the charge on the check."

Lou Clayton was the most important person in Jimmy's life. A tough little guy with a sledge-hammer punch, he'd wandered into the Club Durant one night after dropping ninety-eight thousand dollars in a floating crap game. He was a great gambler, he was also a great dancer. He did a little soft-shoe number at the club that night and Jimmy asked him to come in and join him. When Lou asked how much he was making, Jimmy said he was good for "ninety, a hunnert dollars a week."

Clayton turned down the offer, but not long after, Jimmy suggested they buy out the owner and they did, Clayton borrowing the money from another gambler for his share. Lou gambled his own money. He became one of the most fabulous of golfers; he'd play for ten dollars a hole and was known to run this up to fifty thousand dollars a year, but he was scrupulous about business money. And from the day they started their partnership he handled all Jimmy's business and was responsible for bringing him up into the big time. There was never a contract between them, just a photograph of Jimmy autographed, "To Lou, my dearest pal and partner until death do we part."

And that's how it was, despite the intense antagonism of Jimmy's wife, Jeanne, for Lou. Jeanne was a singer and Jimmy made a mistake by having her give up her career. She was lonely at home nights, and from the time Clayton entered the picture she was lonelier because there was more and more work for Jimmy. As he moved up into the status of a star personality, Jeanne resented Lou, feeling he'd taken Jimmy away from her. She didn't want to share her husband with the world, she didn't even want the luxuries his success gave her. She just wanted Jimmy. And not having him (he seldom got home before four or five in the morning), she began to drink.

It was Lou who finally landed their act at the Palace and at a price neither Jimmy nor Eddie Jackson had dreamed of, because Clayton kept holding out, kept saying no. They were a sensational hit at the Palace, where they introduced their famous number "Wood Wood Wood," in which they brought on stage everything from a picture frame to an outhouse, until the stage was piled with lumber.

They were always rowdy, always roughhouse. People think that breaking up a piano is new for Jimmy; but when I see him take an instrument apart I'm back in 1925 again. We're having the annual benefit for Surprise Lake Camp where I was sent as a kid. Clayton, Jackson, and Durante play the show and Durante demolishes the piano. Wrecks it. The theater charges me four hundred dollars. Next day, when Jimmy and I lunch at the Astor, I say, "Thanks for coming to the benefit, Jimmy. Next time, do me a favor, stay home." I tell him about the piano and Jimmy sends me a check for four hundred dollars and a note; "This'll take care of the piano I'm gonna bust at the next benefit!" To this day, he's the biggest single contributor to Surprise Lake Camp; and Clayton, Jackson, and Durante played all our benefits.

The trio of friends never broke up. When Jimmy got too big for the act, Clayton stayed on as his business manager and Eddie stayed on as his friend. Both the boys were on the payroll of every Durante picture, but they were backstage. No man in show business ever had the intense loyalties Jimmy has had. He gave the word loyal a new dimension. To this day he pays Clayton's widow, Ida, a commission for every job he does. The cruelest blow in Jimmy's life was Lou Clayton's death. He had grieved for Jeanne when she died, but when Clayton died he retreated from show business. All of his friends tried to talk to him, it did no good. I tried. Eddie Jackson tried. Clayton had entrusted Eddie with the job of "looking after the Schnozz. Anybody does anything to him, I'll be back to settle the score."

What finally jolted Jimmy out of his apathy was television. We talked about it one day. "I'm gonna take a crack at it, Eddie," he said. "This is what Lou'd want. He told me before he died, he told me this thing was comin' along big and it was for me. Better than radio, he said, cause they'd have the schnozzola to look at." His faith in Lou was so great even death couldn't shake it, and Lou was right, the TV audience loved Jimmy.

You see, there's something that comes through the camera onto the screen—it's not just a photograph, it's a fluoroscope. Someone at NBC, discussing a certain comedian, once asked me, "Why doesn't *this* guy make good with the people? The columnists like him, he has a great reputation, and he's funny. The people laugh but they don't really care about him. They *care* about Durante."

To me the answer is simple. This other comedian hates people. He's up there performing because he gets paid for it and he thinks it's the thing to do. But Jimmy loves people. The minute they see that kisser they know he loves 'em. And that's why the end of his program, where he walks away into the smaller and smaller pools of light, tugs at their hearts and brings tears. It's like Jimmy was leaving for good. They know instinctively that he'd rather be up there entertaining them than anything else in the world and they're right. Even if he wasn't getting paid for it. If he had to pay to do it.

Let me show you what I mean. On New Year's Day 1943 Ida and I were down at Palm Springs. I'd gotten up early to take a walk, and of all the people to meet in the village, suddenly around the corner comes that nose.

"Eddie!" he yells.

"Jimmy! Happy New Year!" And we throw our arms around each other as if we hadn't met in years.

"Eddie," he says, in the middle of the embrace, "I'm just thinkin'. This must be a tough time for the guys over there in that hospital." The government had taken over El Mirador Hotel and made it into Torney General Hospital. "Here it's New Year's Day, they're sick, some of 'em have amputations. What da ya say we go over and entertain 'em?"

I thought it was a great idea and suggested we stop off at his bungalow first and rehearse. His place is always full of his pals: Jules Buffano, his piano player through the years, Eddie Jackson, who's been with him for thirty-five years, Jack Roth, his drummer from the old Club Durant, and Lou Cohn, who since Clayton's death has handled most of Jimmy's business. They're not at all surprised when we start in rehearsing at 9 A.M., New Year's Day. Then we call the hospital and ask if they mind if we come over. Do they *mind!* We get over to the hospital about ten-thirty and stay till five. We sing every song we ever sang in the days at Coney Island. Through the years Jimmy and I have appeared many times together at benefits, on radio and now on television, and we always go back into the old routine and have a ball. We clown, we kid, we reminisce about the time I convinced him we should run for President and Vice-President. "We should be together, Jimmy, in Washington. Think of it—with my eyes and your nose, what I couldn't see, you could smell!" By five o'clock it's time for the patients' dinner and we say good-by. We're both so hoarse we can hardly talk, especially Jimmy, who starts off hoarse. As we walk down the street, he can barely croak, "Eddie, tell me, don't a t'ing like dis make ya feel *good?*"

Is it any wonder that all the big stars Jimmy's had on his programs—most of them start out being frightened—all end up falling in love with him? Helen Traubel, Margaret Truman, Greer Garson. If any of his guests dislikes a line in the script, he doesn't try to sell them on it. He says to his writers, "Look, fellas, let's change this. It isn't good." Being a guest on his program is like being a guest in his home.

One time his writers, looking for someone with stature and dignity to play opposite Jimmy, came up with Greer Garson. The first rehearsal is always at Jimmy's house. The day Greer was to arrive Jimmy told the gang: "Now look, this is a fine lady, fellas. And none of that obscurity you're throwing around goes while she's here. I want you to be gents."

Greer Garson came. They sat around, the writers, the staff, while Jimmy and Greer read the script. When they'd finished Jimmy said,

"How do you like it, Miss Garson?"

"Well, I don't know," Greer said. "Is this going to be funny?"

"Oh yes," Jimmy said. "This is funny stuff. These boys, these writers are the best."

"I've never done comedy like this before," Greer said. "Suppose we do it and it isn't funny. What then?"

"Then, Miss Garson," quoth Jimmy, "we're all gonna be in the terlet together."

Even being a super gent for Miss Garson's sake, he can screw up the English language as no one else can. He's always talked this way. He actually doesn't know the words, I'm positive he doesn't, and it's become a stock in trade. True, a few of the choicest plums like "catastastroke" he's hung onto knowingly, but I've seen him many a time at rehearsals, reading a script, handing it back to his writers and saying, "Break dat up into some small ones, will ya?" when he doesn't understand a word.

He has a built-in humility which doesn't keep him from hobnobbing with the world's elite. One time when we were at Palm Springs, Jimmy was summoned to meet Albert Einstein. The great scientist was staying at the same hotel. Einstein wanted to know if Jimmy would care to play with him, he played the violin. Jimmy said sure, and sat down at the piano. Einstein gave him a little run on the violin, Jimmy gave him a little run on the piano. Einstein gave another little run, Jimmy began to improvise. The great scientist accepted defeat at this moment, conceded the duet, and kept right on being a Durante fan.

Jimmy Durante

I know of no one as interested in giving of himself as Jimmy Durante. No one. And it shows. He hasn't an enemy in the world and his friends don't just love him, they worship him. He sums up his philosophy this way, "I figger there are more good people in the world than bad ones. I don't mind if a gent scratches a match on my furniture so long as he's careful to go with the grain."

He has a quality of tenderness you seldom see in a man. If you're sad, he's sad. When I was in the hospital with a heart attack, Jimmy came every day. I was allowed no visitors and he knew that, but he came every day and sat in the corridor outside my room.

After I was well enough to go out he invited me down to Del Mar. He spends part of every summer vacation there, playing the horses. "Ya gotta come, Eddie. It's wonderful for ya. Down here nobody bodders ya, nobody bodders ya at all." So I went.

The first day at Del Mar he and I both lose on the first three races. Jimmy doesn't bet big, neither do I, but of course we like to win. So after the third race I run into a man I know from Louisville, Kentucky. This fellow owns a stable and he doesn't give tips; but he does tell me that they have a horse today and the horse is ready. I tell this to Jimmy.

"Jimmy, I'm going to bet ten dollars."

"Eddie," he says, "ya mortify me. On this kind of a FBI inside I'll bet fifty bucks."

The horse comes in and pays twenty-two dollars. Jimmy sends me to look again for my friend from Louisville. This time he tells me about another horse. I bet twenty, Durante bets a hundred. The horse comes in and pays ten dollars. From then on we don't lose. We win on every race. Jimmy's elated, he's clowning, then suddenly he gets serious. He claps one hand on my shoulder and says, "Eddie, promise me one thing. No matter what happens today—we go back to show business."

We both went back. It would be a great loss if Jimmy ever abandoned show business. There's just no one else who can send out those currents of fun and love. I, for one, never have missed (unless I've been on a plane) a Durante broadcast or his TV show. For me it has an added meaning. I hear and see this guy today and all the time I'm seeing double, another guy, a kid sixteen with brownish hair, playing the piano like a son of a gun for the customers at Carey Walsh's and dropping his tips in the cigar box.

6. My First Agent...
My First Partner...

When I was working at Coney Island I didn't tell Ida that I was a singing waiter. I told her I was managing a restaurant, *and* making good money. Somehow she found out where I was. To my horror, one night, into Carey Walsh's saloon walked Ida, her sister Jennie, and Jennie's husband. I saw them before they saw me, tossed off my apron, and started giving loud orders to fellow waiters. They thought I'd gone crazy. I had. I had to get Ida and her relatives out of this place and fast. I rushed over to greet them, explained that this was my night off, if they'd wait outside I'd join them immediately and we'd take in the sights. Then I hurried to the kitchen, put on my coat and sneaked out the back door, AWOL. We had a pleasant evening and I was invited, as I'd hoped and planned, to her sister Minnie's wedding.

Loaded with the four hundred dollars I'd accumulated at Carey Walsh's, I got the finest tuxedo I could rent, bought shiny patent-leather shoes that buttoned on the side, donned a silk hat, and rented an automobile for the night. Six months before, I'd watched Jennie's wedding from across the street; tonight, I was able to call for Ida in style, and electrified Henry Street with the evidence of my success. I tipped the sheriff at the door, tipped the coat checker, tipped the matron of the wedding hall, and almost tipped the groom. I wish you could have seen my Ida, how proud she was. "They say he's the manager of a big restaurant," people whispered. "Soon he may own it!"

As soon as the bride and groom were safely married I ordered champagne for the crowd. When they'd drunk enough of the champagne they began to think it was my wedding. So did I. Ida's dad whispered I should hold on to my money but I told him there was more where this had come from. By the time the night was over my bank roll was about over too and I was once again an unemployed would-be actor.

I had cards printed: "Eddie Cantor, Dialectician," and spent my last twenty-five for my first new suit. Up until now I'd worn secondhand suits from the Bowery. The new natty gray striped number was made to order, and in it I set out to rock Broadway. Broadway managed to withstand the shock. Then I heard of an agent named Joe Wood and I started hanging around his office.

"This is a business for professionals," Joe told me.

"No one's born a professional," I told him.

We repeated this conversation ad boredom. Joe got tired of my hanging around and told his girl to say he was out. I'd wait for hours until he *had* to come out of his office to eat or sleep. And I finally won. Joe said go ahead, show him what I could do.

"Ladies and gentlemen," I began and went into the comedy-dialect routines I'd done on amateur nights.

Halfway through, Joe shook his head but he gave me a card and sent me to Gaine's Manhattan Theatre on Thirty-fourth and Sixth Avenue (the theater was later torn down to make way for Gimbel's). Now there were no unions in those days and the gimmick was this: three or four agents would send down four or five acts. The theater would only be good for seven acts, but they'd put on all twenty, pick the best, and send the rest home. The ones who were sent home didn't get paid. They'd say you were "canceled." That's where the word "canned" came from. You'd go on, give a first performance, and the manager would tell his secretary, "Can that guy before he stinks up the place."

I went on at the matinee and did my best. I was the most novel act of the show. No laughs. No applause. But instead of canning me the manager called Joe Wood. "We're keeping this boy, Cantor. He hasn't made good but he's different and I think you ought to come down and see him."

That night I went on the seven-o'clock show and was a riot. *With* the same act. It was the same every day. I flopped every afternoon and was a hit at night. Joe Wood came down to the second matinee and told me, "You're O.K., Eddie, you have a good act. Don't worry about an agent, you've got one."

From then on we became friends. Joe booked me into theaters

in Schenectady, Troy, Mechanicsville, and points north and south. The pay was roughly twenty a week or $2.85 a day. Out of the twenty Joe got two dollars. Then of course, traveling to Troy and Schenectady I'd have to pay my own fare and hotel bills. Did I say "hotels"? I'd find boardinghouses where you'd get two meals a day and a bed for two dollars, and I'd wind up at the end of the week with a buck. But, I was working. Then one time, he booked me into the West End Theatre, Harlem, just to play Sunday. This was a movie house, on Sundays they also put on several acts of vaudeville. After the opening matinee, a man walked backstage and handed me his card. "Joseph M. Schenck, president, People's Vaudeville Company." The officers of the company were also listed: Joseph Schenck, Nicholas Schenck, Adolph Zukor, and Marcus Loew. I'd never heard of them.

"Where do you go next?" Mr. Schenck asked.

"Oh, I've got a lot of things in the fire," I lied.

"That's too bad, Cantor. I'd book you tomorrow for the Lyric in Hoboken and then the New Lyceum in Elizabeth, New Jersey."

I accepted promptly.

"You'll get the same salary you're making here, two shows in the afternoon, two shows at night. Come in tomorrow and we'll sign the contract."

The People's Vaudeville Company had a chain of third-rate houses distributed on both sides of the Jersey ferry—the Lyric in Hoboken, the New Lyceum in Elizabeth, the Royal and the Lyric in Brooklyn and I closed at the Amphion on Sunday, rounding out two weeks and one extra day. Schenck called me in and told me they liked me.

"If you could do a new act, we could play you around the circuit again."

"I *have* a new act," I said.

"Fine, when can you open?"

The next day I was back in Hoboken, scared to death. I didn't have a new act. It had taken me years to work up this one and I'd already borrowed all my jokes and smart lines from the headliners at first-class houses. I decided to take a chance. I glued on a little chinpiece, stuffed a pillow in my front, and went on as a Dutch comedian. The same gags, a different dialect. Instead of the little Italian in the subway, it was now a Dutchman in the

My First Agent . . . My First Partner . . .

subway. Harry, the Mayor of the Bowery holding court, was now Harry with a Dutch accent.

After the Dutchman I did a Hebrew comedian around the circuit. The fourth time around I was really stumped. I sat down with a piece of charcoal to put a few lines on my face. The lines only made me look haggard. I tried to wipe off the marks, they spread. Blackface! I quickly rubbed cork over my cheeks, neck, ears. Afraid of getting it in my eyes, I amateurishly left large circles around each eye and to cover that fault, donned a pair of white-rimmed spectacles. The glasses gave me a look of intelligence, a new touch to the old-fashioned darky of the minstrel shows. And I played the circuit again! By now the audiences had heard my routines so many times they knew every joke by heart, but the fourth time around Schenck told me, "You know, Eddie, I like this last act of yours better than the other three."

I had now worked eight weeks, *in a row*, and the news considerably enhanced my reputation on Henry Street. One Sunday, after I'd gotten home, some guys from Jefferson Street came walking along parading a famous son, Roy Arthur, of the team of Bedini and Arthur, jugglers and travesty artists who played the top-line theaters. The guys on Henry Street promptly trotted me out and insisted I do my stuff.

I didn't wait to be asked twice. I went through my whole repertoire as if it were a tryout, keeping my eye on Arthur. The crowd applauded, but that didn't matter; what mattered was this man from another world, the world of top-line theaters. He didn't burst into cheers but he did say, "Drop around sometime next week and look me up at Hammerstein's."

I was there the next afternoon and Arthur introduced me to Bedini, who was actually his boss. Bedini liked what I did but he couldn't see any room for me in the act. Arthur thought that the act would be bigger if I were in it. For a while we were at an impasse. Bedini and Arthur kept on working and I kept hanging around. They'd send me out for laundry, send me to the tailor's, I brought up sandwiches, helped unpack trunks, I'd pick up a dollar for this errand, a quarter for another. This went on for some time. My specialty was no good for the big time because all the meat of it had been cadged from big-time acts. But Bedini couldn't get rid of me. Arthur kept touting me, and finally I was hired. The pay was thirty-five a week, my job was to make up in blackface (Arthur also wore blackface), walk on stage, hand Bedini a plate for his juggling act, and walk off without a word. I'd made up my mind that when I did get on stage I'd take my time about handing over that plate and I *did*. I looked leisurely at each of my partners, then looked at the audience in a lofty manner, while Bedini and Arthur exchanged amazed glances at my cheek. This brought a laugh and my exit got a hand. Bedini now showed me how to roll a hat down the length of my arm and catch it as it dropped. After I'd mastered the hat I tried a plate. I devoted every spare minute to juggling so that I could be in the act. We worked out a routine. After Bedini slid the plate off his arm and caught it, Arthur would try clumsily to do the same thing and he'd smash it. Then I'd take another plate, slide it down my arm with ease, and snap my fingers scornfully at Arthur. Arthur'd chase me with a hammer and I'd scream, "He means to do me bodily harm!"

It was the first time any audience had heard a Negro speak such Oxford English and it was the first line I spoke on the big time. From that moment Arthur and I developed into a sissy-bully team, he the boor and I the cultured, pansylike Negro with spectacles. Neither Bedini nor Arthur uttered a word on stage but Bedini was very liberal and allowed me to say all the impromptu things that entered my head. He told the musicians they could drop to pianissimo whenever I came out. We changed our routines every week with the changing bill. Bedini allowed me to come on stage whenever I wished, providing I had something funny to offer. At first I was careful not to abuse the privilege and not to interrupt Bedini and Arthur too often. After a while it got to the point that what Bedini and Arthur were doing was an interruption to me. Bedini got seventy-five dollars extra for the addition to his act and this defrayed my traveling fare, which he paid. Best of all, the act was now styled "Bedini and Arthur, assisted by Eddie Cantor." I stayed after the show to help clean up the theater so I could collect programs and mail copies to all my friends.

Our team burlesqued and parodied most of the famous stars of the day. When Molasso introduced the apache dance for the first time in his *Paris By Night*, we followed right after; using his set and seriously imitating the highlights of the dance, we brought the house down. Working with Bedini and Arthur, free to utter lines at will, I learned the basic lesson—the trick is to deliver your lines seriously, almost grimly, and let the audience pick the laughs itself. We burlesqued Ruth St. Denis, Mlle. Daisy, Gertrude Hoffman. I played Salome (still in blackface of course) and danced to Mendelssohn's "Spring Song," wearing dresses. Once I accidentally lost the dress and the audience screamed. From then on, whenever I wore a dress I lost it. If we were low on laughs, Bedini would signal, "Drop the dress," and it was sure-fire. Seriously, looking spiritual and wan, I'd recite:

> "*Twinkle twinkle, little star*
> *How I wonder what you are!*
> *Up above the world so high*
> *What care I?*
> *What care I?*"

and run off stage. It was the contrast of nonsense and earnest delivery that was funny. And the impromptu mode of play was wonderful discipline. It quickened your wits.

Joe Wood had said this was a business only for professionals. Thanks to him and to Bedini and Arthur, I was becoming one.

Strangely enough, Joe ceased to be my agent when I went with Bedini. He hadn't gotten me that job and I had an idea that it was just great to make 100 per cent of my salary, no 10 per cent to anybody. A lot of actors are like that. They figure they can get a job themselves and save the agent's commission. Actually they never save anything, for a good agent will get you much more salary than the commission amounts to. It took me a long time to learn this. When I made movies years later for Samuel Goldwyn I had no agent. And while I made good money I'm sure a good agent would have gotten me a half a million more. I know he would, for I did have an agent for the next pictures, the William Morris office. And you know who handled me at the William Morris office, as recently as ten years ago? Georgie Wood, Joe's son.

7. Irving Berlin

My first big break came in 1910 when Bedini and Arthur played Buffalo. Roaming around Tin Pan Alley, I'd picked up a song called "Ragtime Violin" by Irving Berlin. I'd sung Berlin's songs before at Carey Walsh's, one ditty entitled "Next to Your Mother Who Do You Love?"—music by Ted Snyder. It was a good song but "Ragtime Violin" was even better. I rehearsed it every Monday, sang it for Bedini, but never had a chance to sing on stage.

When we hit Buffalo the manager wanted to put Bedini and Arthur next to closing, but that meant they'd have to be able to close "in one" (close for say three or four minutes before a curtain while the scene was being set for the next full-stage act). Bedini and Arthur had a full-stage act themselves and they never had been able to close "in one." Now with "Ragtime Violin" I could go out and sing for the three or four minutes and we'd fit in next to closing.

I'd never sung on a theater stage before, and never to sober customers. I bought a big professional violin case and a funny little dime-store fiddle and ran out for the opening matinee as nervous as a witch. I scratched a few awful chords on the fiddle, took out an oil can, oiled it, and started to sing. Luckily the spirit and rhythm of the song fitted with a lightning peppy delivery. I was so nervous I walked quickly up and down, clapping my hands as I sang, rolling my eyes, and bobbing like the red, red robin. The audience went crazy. After three encores I started adding catch lines so they'd bring me back. By Wednesday, the song was running close to seven minutes.

Roy Arthur and I shared the same dressing room, divided by a partition from Bedini's. When we got back to the dressing room after the Thursday-night show, Mike Shea, the theater owner, was talking with Bedini and I could hear him.

"If that little guy in blackface could do five more minutes, we'd get rid of you and Arthur," Shea said.

The minute he walked out I knocked on Bedini's door.

"Mr. Bedini I'll have to have a raise."

He gave it to me too, an extra five which brought my salary up to the fabulous forty a week!

A song writer whom I'd never met had started me on my way. He was going to have a lot to do with my career. One year later I started singing his brand-new "Alexander's Ragtime Band," and seventeen years later he was to write the *Ziegfeld Follies of 1927*, the first time one writer ever did music and lyrics for a whole *Follies;* and I was to star in the show, another first, the first time any actor had been starred in a *Ziegfeld Follies*. That Berlin would become America's top song writer was no surprise to me. He had an amazing versatility and a true punch, the quality of schmaltz which makes a song last.

We met in 1915 at Waterson, Berlin and Snyder, Music Publishers. I was singing a song of his, "Araby," at the Colonial Theatre. In those days singers were very important to song publishers; that's how their songs got around. Today, with thousands of disc jockeys, a new tune gets around fast and dies fast. "Young Love" or "The Banana Boat Song" may last ten weeks. But in 1915 a publisher depended on stage singers. If Jolson sang a song, other singers would run to the publisher asking for the Jolson song. In vaudeville you played only a week in one place so it took three or four months before the song got to the point where the public started buying sheet music. Song pluggers went out and sold the song to a popular performer. But I wasn't exactly a hit yet and Berlin acknowledged our introduction as if he'd never heard of me, which of course he hadn't.

We began to be friendly in 1916, the opening night of *The Midnight Frolic*. Then, early in the days of the first World War, Berlin asked me to come to Camp Upton where he was writing *Yip, Yip, Yaphank*. It was the first of the morale-builder shows using the boys in camp as actors and presented to a regular theater audience. What a great show it was! Such lyrics, such music, I could sing you every word of it after all these years. Berlin not only wrote the show but appeared in it. There was a scene where the curtains parted and you saw a *nebbish*, forlorn little private (Berlin, himself) leaning on a mop, doing K.P. duty.

> *Poor little me*
> *I'm a K.P.*
> *I scrub the floor upon bended knee*
> *I wash the dishes against my wishes*
> *To make this wide world safe for*
> *Democracy . . .*

Then there was the greatest comedy song of any war, "Oh, how I hate to get up in the morning," and Irving sang it and was a riot.

The serious part of the show started with a boy sitting at a desk in the YMCA, writing a letter to his mother. At the close of the second act soldiers marched up from the audience and embarked on a ship. The ship moved away and the soldiers sang. Now, picture this . . . In the middle of one of the performances on Broadway the soldiers actually got their overseas orders. They marched up the aisle onto the ship, they couldn't say good-by to their folks in the audience, they were embarking for France with the stage boat pulling away and a thin voice singing,

> *"Don't you worry, mother darling,*
> *Cause when the skies are gray*
> *I can always find a little sunshine*
> *At the YMCA."*

But when the show first started rehearsals for its run on Broadway, Berlin still was writing and rewriting. I used to go up to his apartment on West Seventieth Street and we'd work until three or four in the morning. My part was a small one, I was helping with the minstrel jokes used in the first part of the show. I'd go to sleep around three and when I'd waken at eight, there Irving would be, sitting at the piano where he'd been all night. It was swelteringly hot weather. He'd have a towel wrapped around him and he'd still be working, trying to clean up one line.

He looked then in his bath towel as he looks today in a bathing suit, like the picture on an ad that reads: "Help send this boy to camp!" But he had and he *has* more guts than any man in the business. There have been other great song writers—Cole Porter, Frank Loesser—but what makes Berlin tops is that no one else is such a perfectionist. He can turn out music like a one-man factory, but if he gets stuck he'll spend three weeks on such a line as "But you forgot to remember." He had been a singing waiter at a place in Chinatown called Mike's, but he was bound to succeed, he was born with a brass self-confidence that eclipsed even mine. Berlin had his heartbreaks too; his first wife died on their honeymoon. His memories of her were the basis for "When I Lost You." But the talent went on, so great that the stream of songs seemed never-ending.

Rumors developed that he didn't write it all himself. When he came over to London in 1913 to play the Hippodrome reporters questioned him. "Mr. Berlin, it seems that all the songs that come over here have words and music by Irving Berlin. How do you write it all? Do you write it yourself?"

"Give me a subject," Irving said. "I'll write you a song right now." They were incredulous but they gave him a title. They all went to lunch together; after lunch Irving presented "International Rag" scribbled on the back of a menu.

Still, along Broadway the whisper persisted that Berlin had a little Negro boy in Harlem who wrote at least half his stuff. Then came a period of two years when he couldn't strike a hit. One night at Lindy's he said, "If anybody can find that little colored fella, please send him around, I sure can use him." That was before he reached the era of "How Deep Is the Ocean?" "Say It Isn't So," "Easter Parade," and "Cheek to Cheek." He hit his stride again and wrote whole shows with hit upon hit.

Irving's amazing productivity has been possible because he is one of the few ever able to compose words and music simultaneously. One day he walked into Billy's barbershop at the Strand. The place was humming with talk about Dorando, the Italian runner, supposedly the fastest thing on feet, who'd been beaten the night before at Madison Square Garden by an American runner, Hayes. Every Italian in New York had bet on Dorando, and while Irving was being shaved he could hear their outraged comments. By the time he got out of the chair he'd written a funny, peppy dialect number that I sang.

Then in 1919 Berlin gave me the only song I ever recorded that was a million-copy hit—"You'd Be Surprised." I introduced it in the *Ziegfeld Follies of 1919*. Berlin went with us to Atlantic City to break in the show. We lived together in the hotel that week. The hotels were so crowded that when the Dolly Sisters arrived for the opening they couldn't get a hotel room. Irving and I gave them our bedroom and slept in the living room on couches.

What an exciting week it was! Ziegfeld had a singer, John Steel, who could have been the McCormack of his day, except that he didn't take care of himself. Steel was going to sing arias from several popular operas while beautiful girls paraded past, dressed as the operatic heroines. Ziegfeld asked Irving to write a little introduction. The next morning Irving and I were rolling down the boardwalk in a chair and he started humming a tune to me, then he sang the words.

"Is this any good, Eddie?"

"I don't know, but it'll certainly serve the purpose," I answered sagely.

The song was "A Pretty Girl Is Like a Melody," and it was *so* good and *so* big that all Steel had to do was sing it and forget about the arias.

Can you imagine Berlin's "A Pretty Girl Is Like a Melody" and "You'd Be Surprised" and "Mandy"; Buck and Stamper's "Tulip Time"; *and* McCarthy and Tierney's "My Baby's Arms"—all in one show? Then imagine the sentimental songs sung by John Steel and DeLyle Alda, Van and Schenck for melody rhythms; Bert Williams and George LeMaire playing the sharpshooting scene; Marilyn Miller, Ann Pennington and Mary Hay, the leading dancers; and you'll see why the *Follies of 1919* was the greatest. I did the osteopath scene with the best straight man the theater has ever known, George LeMaire. If you couldn't be funny with him you'd better quit. He was not only sincere in his acting, he played high comedy as if it were *Macbeth*.

Long before we rehearsed the show in Atlantic City I had my own rehearsal of the rehearsal. I'd started a procedure that set a pattern in the business. You see, Atlantic City was only a few hours from New York and I knew that there'd be critics sneaking down to see the show. To be sure my stuff would be good in Atlantic City I'd get bookings under assumed names in theaters uptown, play all my material three and four times a day, spot the deadwood and eliminate it. Songs that proved flat were taken out or changed. More than that, I could ad lib and expand new material and try it out on an audience.

George LeMaire and I played "The Osteopath" with two girls, one a patient, one a nurse. Kathryn Perry, who later married Owen Moore, played the nurse, so we called the act "Kathryn Perry and Company" for the uptown run. "Joe's Blue Front", the clothing scene, was broken in under the name "Joe Opp and Company".

Ziegfeld knew what was going on and thought it a great idea. I'd excuse myself from regular rehearsals in time to get to the uptown theater. "But please don't come, Mr. Ziegfeld, not until I tell you." The last two or three times, when the thing was pretty well rounded into shape, Ziegfeld would catch it. So would Irving. Occasionally he made suggestions and he was always right.

I tried out "You'd Be Surprised" at a theater in the Bronx. At this time I still sang every song running up and down the stage. Irving caught the show and said, "Eddie, for this one you don't have to move. You don't have to get the song over, it'll get you over." So I stood still until I got to the end; then I'd run like hell.

Irving watched every rehearsal, how it was directed, who was to sing. He didn't play for rehearsals, no. Actually he's a very bad piano player, he plays in only one key and his own piano has a lever that changes the key for him. But the slim, sensitive Berlin is full of melody and showmanship—and usually gets what he wants.

Not once, however. Not concerning the hit song he gave me in 1925. He had his own publishing house by this time, the Berlin Music Publishing Company; and song plugger Harry Akst came on to Pittsburgh where I was playing *Kid Boots*. By this time, I was the second best "plug" in the business, right behind Jolson. Harry Akst caught the show, waited for me afterward, and on the darkened stage, with just a pilot light, he played me a new song by Irving Berlin. It was awful. I didn't exactly say that, I just said it wasn't for me, that maybe someone else would like it. Harry was disappointed. He came back to the William Penn Hotel with me to have a bite to eat before he caught the late train.

There was a piano up in the hotel suite and Harry started noodling around, pretty soon he was playing.

"Hey, *wait* a minute, what's that?" I said.

"Oh, just a little thing of my own."

"Well, this I like, this I can do!" I said.

"You mean you want me to tell Berlin you don't want *his* song, you want *mine?* And what do I do for groceries?"

He was working, you understand, for Berlin. But I insisted that Harry stay overnight, I'd phone Irving in the morning. We'd try the song in the show tomorrow, if it was as good as I was sure it was, we could have an orchestration in time for the Saturday matinee. Harry was dubious, but in the morning I phoned Berlin and told him the truth. Berlin said:

"Sure, Eddie. If it's Harry's, we'll publish it. Let him stay over as long as you need him."

That night I sang the song for the first time, without music, just the piano, and the song was such a smash that by Saturday night it had become the finale of the show. The song was "Dinah."

Two years later Berlin and I traveled east from California together. En route, we laid out plans for a show that was to mean a great deal to both of us, the *Ziegfeld Follies of 1927*. Irving, who is probably the best businessman in show business, was receiving 5 per cent of the gross. Now in most *Follies* there were many stars; in this one, I was it. I was on all the time and an understudy was out of the question. One day, after we were a smash hit, he and I came out of a barbershop and started crossing to the New Amsterdam Theatre. A taxi flew past, so close it literally grazed my nose. Irving grabbed me, pulled me back to the curb. "Eddie, my royalties!" he cried.

While we were still rehearsing the show we lived together at the Ritz-Carlton in Boston. He had already written "Shaking the Blues Away," "I Want To Be Glorified," "Ribbons and Bows," "Maybe It's You," "Rainbow of Girls," "It's Up To The Band," "The Jungle Jingle," "Learn To Sing A Love Song," "Ticklin' the Ivories." But he wanted to write another song for me. I'd been very successful with a number called "Ain't She Sweet." It was such a hit that when Lindbergh returned from his great flight and attended a performance of *Rio Rita*, Ziegfeld asked me to come over to the theater and he stopped the show while I came on stage to sing "Ain't She Sweet" for Lindbergh.

Berlin wanted to write a new song of the same kind, and came up with "It All Belongs to Me." Before we even tried out the show, he wrote seven encores. And what happened? I never got to sing the second chorus. The song was a flop and we dropped it. Irving was hysterical. "How're you gonna tell?" he said.

On the other hand, "You Gotta Have It" murdered 'em in the same show. There's a funny story about this song. Like everyone else who ever tried to warble, I'm a frustrated song writer. When a song caught on, like "That's the Kind of a Baby for Me," I'd make up three or four extra choruses. In 1926, coming back from Hollywood, I wrote a song of my own, "I'm So Brokenhearted 'Cause I Haven't Got It." Clara Bow had made "It" famous, I'd just made a picture with Clara, the song seemed a natural. I opened at the Rivoli, sang my new composition, and came off knowing that it was just so-so. At that moment, in rushed Irving Berlin. He'd caught the show out front.

"Eddie, who wrote that God-awful song?"

"I did."

"Do I try to be a comedian?" he roared. He took the thing and sat down at the piano. By next show, he'd converted it into "You've Got to Have It." That night it was a riot.

"Irving," I said, coming off stage, "what can I ever do to thank you?"

"You've done it. I was in pain, now I'm out of pain," and he left the theater.

Not that this really taught me a lesson. I've written songs from time to time—not very good, my royalties from ASCAP are probably around eighty dollars and I've never shown my songs to Berlin. He's had his laugh.

My admiration for Irving has been akin to my admiration for Jolson: two men with top talent. But where Jolson was an unhappy man, an insecure man, Berlin has been a happy man. He started out to be, wanted to be, and became the greatest American song writer. It doesn't happen to many to receive medals of honor from their government for contributions to their country. He got the Congressional Medal of Honor for "God Bless America," for "This Is the Army," for "Yip Yip Yaphank." And in addition, he's had the blessing of a happy marriage.

I was playing Chicago when Irving married Ellin Mackay, and the Jewish newspapers in town called to find out what I thought of the match about which there had been so much publicity. I told them I believe and have believed all my life that the most important religion is love. These people have that, therefore they have everything.

At least half the credit for all the love songs should go to Ellin Berlin, for theirs has been a real love match, and out of the partnership has come a stream of songs that set America singing. Jolson, Crosby, all the great entertainers scored some of their biggest triumphs with this music. And of course, Cantor got started with "Ragtime Violin." I told Berlin that years ago. The son of a gun, he feels I haven't paid the debt yet!

8. Georgie Jessel

I always remember the night I stopped Jessel from going to a house of ill repute. We were in New Orleans with Gus Edwards' *Kid Kabaret* and I was saying, "Georgie, a boy twelve years old is too young!" Georgie begged me. Everywhere we went on that tour we saw the sights. In Washington the White House, in New Orleans . . . Georgie cried so bitterly I finally said, "O.K., O.K., Friday."

Georgie was a witty kid with a mop of curly hair. The girls adored him even then and the feeling was mutual. This was a boy destined to make a career of alimony. He was destined, too, to be the great jester of our time, a jester to kings.

You saw the spark as early as 1910 when Georgie and I met at the Brighton Beach Music Hall. I was with Bedini and Arthur, he with Gus Edwards. I was eighteen, Georgie ten, but Georgie was never young. He'd been born old and at ten he was a miniature man—all but the sense of humor, there was never anything miniature about that. We met several times, then landed on the same bill in Atlantic City. By now, I was singing "Ragtime Violin" in the Bedini and Arthur act and was on my way.

One night Gus Edwards was taking his troupe to a midnight engagement at the Chelsea Yacht Club and asked me to go along. On the way, I framed some gags with Jessel and when we got on we were pretty funny. We imitated Smith and Dale in *The New Teacher*. I played the German teacher, hit Georgie with a bamboo stick, and Georgie danced up and down screaming, "Hit me again, teacher, I'm seeing diamonds!"

Edwards was pleased. This man was truly the kids' best friend. The first Columbus of show business, he went out and looked for talent, then gave that talent a showcase. His kids included Jessel, Groucho Marx, the Duncan Sisters, Hildegarde, Phil Silvers, Ray Bolger, to name only a few. Oh, and me. That night coming back from Atlantic City he had me ride along in his car. "You're a funny boy, Eddie. I don't know what kind of a contract you have with Bedini, but if anything ever happens, call me."

This was all I needed. I had a contract with Bedini, but to go with Gus Edwards! There was nothing to do but goad Bedini into firing me. It took a few months, although I was so fresh I don't see how he held out that long. We were playing Proctor's Fifth Avenue when finally his patience came to an end:

"One more word out of you and I'll fire you!"

"You wouldn't dare," I taunted.

Five minutes later I was phoning Gus Edwards at Rockaway.

The following Monday my salary had jumped to seventy-five a week, and to make it all perfect I was working with my little pal Georgie. We roomed together, and in nothing flat I'd taken over as the big brother I'd probably always longed for. I actually used to bathe Georgie, he'd been a long-time fugitive from soap and a scrubbing brush. I bathed him and scoured his ears and laid out his clothes, clean ones.

He was just an urchin actually, a poor kid who had no father, whose mother worked as wardrobe mistress with the Edwards show, and they'd had tough going. That was another thing that brought us together, a knowledge of poverty. Georgie had started in show business at the Imperial Theatre at 116th and Lenox Avenue where his mother was cashier. He, Walter Winchell, and a boy named Jack Weiner (who became an agent) were a singing trio. Jessel sang loud, so much louder than the other two that theater-manager McKibbon fired Winchell and Weiner and hung out a sign saying, "It's worth five cents to hear Georgie Jessel sing alone." In the 30s Winchell printed the story with a tag line—"and that still goes."

Now that he'd begun to make money Georgie didn't know how to hang on to it. He thought we should have a joint bank account, so if ever either of us got in trouble, we could draw on it. This arrangement didn't last long, Georgie was always in trouble. Besides, I had Ida on my mind. I sent my money home to her.

Georgie had to depend on the little diamond stickpin he wore. Whenever he was in trouble the stickpin disappeared.

"Where's the pin, Georgie?"

"On the dresser."

"You'd better go back and get it."

He'd grin, showing me the pawn ticket. He could always raise a fin on the little pin and it made every pawnshop on our itinerary. One night, many years later at a banquet, the banker sitting next to Jessel confessed, "I haven't been to a theater in ten years."

"Don't apologize," quipped Georgie, "I haven't been to a bank in longer than that."

In the *Kid Kabaret* days I tried to set him straight about money but he only laughed, he's been laughing ever since. Money *has* always been important to me. In those days it meant the possibility of marriage and security. Then it became a measure of success. Today it's a matter of what you can do with it. Years ago, for example, I started a series of contests with a prize of a five-thousand-dollar scholarship to a university. There were fifteen of these scholarships and I thought I was doing something important, giving fifteen youngsters a chance at an education. But Georgie thinks I'm the original tightwad. If you don't take a dozen people to dinner, order champagne by the magnum, and tip the hat-check girl five bucks, you're a tightwad. He kids me.

Many years ago when we moved into a house without a swimming pool, someone suggested we build one. I insisted that we didn't need a pool; besides, they were expensive.

"But, Eddie," the friend said, "what are you gonna do with your money? You can't take it with you."

"If Cantor can't take it with him, he'll send it on ahead," piped up Georgie.

So he's been laughing and I've been lecturing since he was twelve. The lectures I've given on security! The effect—nothing. He's been the fastest guy with a doll or a dollar I've ever seen. And he says I'm the only one on record who gets off the Chief at Albuquerque and sells blankets to the Indians. I was the big brother? He was the sophisticate.

In the Gus Edwards days I had charge of the railroad tickets for the troupe. I bought white knickers for the boys and short skirts for the girls and got them all on for half fare even though some were fifteen or sixteen years old. En route from Portland to San Francisco I gave the conductor the tickets, herded the kids on board, and a half hour later the conductor came looking for me.

"You gave me these half-fare tickets?"

"Yes, sir."

"You point out the half fares, buddy."

I walked through the cars identifying my charges. All went well until we hit the club car. There sat Georgie, in his white knickers all right, but also in a derby hat with a big cigar in his mouth amusing the car with a stream of dirty stories.

We were always trying to maneuver it to get meals for nothing. If we saw some salesmen on the train who looked like New Yorkers, we'd sidle up to them in the club car, start talking about our New York childhoods, and frequently they'd invite us to dinner. We'd been in San Francisco all of two hours when Jessel came bouncing into the dressing room. "Eddie, our worries are over. I just met a girl whose father owns a restaurant. From now on, we *eat!*" And we did, for two weeks. How we ate! But you know something? You can get awfully tired of chow mein.

It was quite a tour. On stage I played the butler, blackface. Eddie Buzzell, now a movie and television director, played the little boy who, after his parents left for an evening of cabareting decided to have a kids' cabaret of his own. Mine was a good part, there's always sympathy in the theater for anyone in a servile capacity; and when I'd talk back to my little Master Buzzell the audience loved it. Just as they love hitting a swell's high hat with a snowball. I had a chance, too, in blackface, to do imitations of Al Jolson and Eddie Leonard. But off stage I had problems.

We noticed that one of our pretty dancing girls was getting fatter and fatter, until at last we realized she was pregnant. Very. Now remember these are all kids. The only fellow older than I was the one who'd gotten her in trouble. But even as kids we had sense enough to know we had to protect her. She couldn't be sent home where her family would know. We had to keep her traveling. I phoned Gus Edwards and explained the situation, and Edwards was wonderful. We replaced the girl, but kept her with us. Luckily we played San Francisco and Oakland for a period of four weeks. She was hospitalized there and able to go on with us when we left.

Taking care of this little girl was a cinch compared with trying to keep Georgie on the straight and narrow. I aged considerably. But nothing has ever altered our friendship and three days have never passed that we haven't been in touch through the years. The big-brother relationship persisted. There was a time when Georgie wasn't feeling too well. We were both starring on Broadway then, he in *The Jazz Singer*, I in the *Follies of 1927*, and after every performance I'd pick him up at his theater and see that he went back to his hotel to bed. Nights I couldn't call for him, he was to phone me. He phoned every night for four nights. Each morning I'd pick up the papers and read of his escapades at the Paradise or other night spots. And *I'm* the one who eventually had the heart attack!

We've never seen eye to eye. Georgie's way of life would scare me to death and mine would bore him; but essentially we each admire in the other what we lack. Georgie has a certain respect for my family life, my five children—he keeps right on trying to find the same; and I admire his happy-go-lucky tomorrow'll-take-care-of-itself attitude, his complete audacity, spontaneity, and lack of fear. We used to have great times playing benefits together, trying to break each other up. And we know we could call on each other for anything.

I was playing Detroit in *The Midnight Rounders* when a telegram arrived between the first and second acts. It's an unwritten law of show business that no telegram is ever delivered to an actor during a performance. The news could upset the show. But manager Jack Reed was a good friend and he came to my dressing room with the little yellow envelope.

"Eddie, should I read it or save it?"

"Read it, Jack, it's O.K.," I said.

The message: *"Wire me fifteen hundred dollars immediately. Desperate. Love. Georgie."* Desperate, he said. Immediately, he said. It could mean he was sick, that a bookmaker was after him or a girl . . .

"Jack," I begged, "take the money out of the box office immediately. Wire it to Georgie at the Dorset Hotel, New York."

The money was wired. No acknowledgment. The next day I phoned him. He wasn't in, but he wired:

"Received money. Grateful. Will talk to you next week."

By next week I was convinced that Georgie was in trouble. "Georgie, what is it?" I said, when he finally called.

"I can't talk now," *sotto voce*. "You're coming back in a few weeks, aren't you? I'll tell you all about it when you come."

I was so worried I went right from the train to Georgie's hotel. He took one look at my worried face and burst out laughing.

"Eddie, don't worry. Everything's great. And did I pick up a bargain in a bracelet for Florence!" (Florence Courtney, his first wife.)

"But, Georgie, you wired *'Desperate'!*"

"Well, you certainly wouldn't have shelled out fifteen hundred if I'd said to buy a bracelet!"

He's so dramatic he frightens you. But once he *was* in serious trouble. Jobs were scarce at the moment, he owed money, and he was ill. He was staying at the Sherry-Netherland and they were dunning him for the bill. He was borrowing money to eat. This time he didn't tell me. I was in Hollywood and he didn't want me to know. With the last thing he could pawn, Georgie bought a gun and decided to end his life.

He wrote a long farewell letter to the world. When he'd finished it and signed his name he phoned George M. Cohan. Georgie had a great respect for Cohan's judgment and he wanted to be sure his last words were right. Now Cohan was crazy about Georgie. When Georgie read the farewell letter Cohan said, "Georgie, I'm sure you can do better. The construction is bad and I'll show you why. Bring the letter over here. We'll kick it around."

So Georgie took the letter to Cohan and Cohan helped him fix it up. Suddenly Cohan said, "You know, Georgie, this is too good for a farewell note, it would make a great radio show."

"It *would?*" Georgie said and forgot all about suicide. Out of the note came a song, "Roses in December," and a radio show. Three or four months later, when we met on the coast, Georgie was able to tell me all about it and laugh at his former woes. He's never down for long. How could he be with that sense of humor?

Early in 1933 Jessel and I, accompanied by a band and several vaudeville acts, made a tour of the country. We played thirty-five cities in thirty-six nights, holding over for a second night at Miami Beach, Florida. (While we were on stage that night, an attempt was made in Miami Beach to assassinate President-elect Roosevelt, the bullet killed Chicago's Mayor Cermak. When we heard the news backstage, Georgie suggested we cut the intermission so the audience wouldn't hear of the tragedy when they got out to the street for a smoke.)

Georgie and I were working together and close again as we'd been in the days of *Kid Kabaret*. It was fun playing with him to packed houses, going from city to city, meeting old friends and making new ones. Before we got to New Orleans we learned that by presidential order the banks had closed. We postponed New Orleans and were ready to disband the company when the William Morris office decided we should play a week in Washington at a motion-picture house.

I readily agreed because it meant keeping the acts together, knowing we could pick up where we'd left off on the tour.

Georgie absolutely refused to go on. "It's silly," he said. "Why knock ourselves out playing five shows a day for a couple of lousy thousand dollars? I'm going to Palm Beach and enjoy myself." Which he did. He left us flat and went to Palm Beach while we played Washington. During the week I received a picture of Georgie on his yacht, the *Norma J*. He was wearing his yachting cap, blue coat, brass buttons, white flannels, and on the picture he'd written, "Sucker, why aren't you doing this?"

Three days later came a telegram: *"Please wire a hundred bucks. Need gasoline for the boat. Georgie."*

There's nobody like him for dash. He loves a public life even at the expense of a personal life. Lois Andrews once told me that their marriage went on the rocks because Georgie couldn't bear to stay at home, they always had to be out, on stage at Romanoff's or Chasen's. He's an extrovert de luxe, always seeking, always on, always dramatic. Most people who can't see well wear glasses. Georgie wears a monocle. I introduced him once as the Bronx Disraeli. We lunched with a group at Romanoff's and Fred Allen, watching him scan the menu through his monocle, said, "What's the matter, Georgie, doesn't the other eye *eat?*"

He carries off the monocle as he carries everything. With less education than almost any entertainer (by comparison I'm a college graduate), Georgie gets up and speaks English that would do justice to a professor. There is no one in the business who doesn't shut up when he's around, and I mean the top comics.

He'll lunch at the Hillcrest Country Club with Danny Kaye, Jack Benny, Groucho and Harpo Marx, Lou Holtz, George Burns and Danny Thomas, and they all *listen* to Georgie.

If he could be as good on stage, where it pays off, he'd be the wealthiest man in the world. And he's good on stage, but he's *great* at a banquet table. Here his ability to ad lib, his wit, and his audacity make him tops. His nerve is incomparable. There's a Jewish word, "chutzpa," that best expresses the quality of nerve Georgie has, and he has it beyond anyone in the world. At a luncheon at the White House, for example, he once cracked about the chicken salad—"Never before has so little chicken served so many!" One time Joe Schenck preceded him at a dinner. Schenck had been married to Norma Talmadge, now Jessel was. "Joe Schenck is a hard guy to follow," said Georgie. "This isn't the first time I've had to do it."

The one time his nerve temporarily deserted him was the night he was to emcee the inaugural dinner for President Truman. Truman had named him Toastmaster General of the USA. In the cocktail room before the banquet the President approached Georgie and asked him if he'd like a drink. Georgie would.

"What's the matter, Georgie, are you jittery?"

Georgie was, for the first time in his life. "I can't help thinking," he told Truman, "here I am, a guy who dropped out of grade school at the age of eight, about to emcee a dinner for the President of the United States. What am I doing here?"

"How do you think I feel?" Truman cracked back. "A guy who played piano in a Kansas City joint?"

Actually Georgie comes from fine forebears. His dad was a playwright and the Jessels are of good English stock; there was a Sir Jessel in Parliament. Georgie could do anything in the world he wanted to do. His problem is doing too much. He has so many irons in the fire, he puts the fire out. I said that one night in introducing him and Georgie was hurt.

"But isn't it true, Georgie," I said, "that as a producer at Twentieth Century-Fox you just flew to Chicago to emcee a banquet, just spent two weeks in New York doing a night-club stint, and aren't you starting your own TV company? And benefits. You play benefits, benefits, benefits, never stopping to find out who benefits? Don't these things cancel each other out?"

Georgie Jessel

Georgie just swings his arm in a deprecating gesture. "You and your preaching!" he says.

I only preach because I love the guy and I'm still trying to play big brother. I don't know why I worry. He's got the greatest wit in the world, and don't think he can't live by it!

One time a little rabbi on Pico Boulevard in L.A. came to Jessel. "You and Cantor raise money for everyone. Why can't you do something for me?" he said. He wanted twenty thousand dollars for an addition to his temple. So we arranged a dinner at the Biltmore and Georgie and I raised sixty thousand dollars.

The rabbi was deeply pleased and two weeks later he brought gifts to Georgie's office at Fox—a *mazzuzah* for each of us, encrusted with a little diamond and rubies. The rabbi made the presentation, blessed us, and left. Jessel opened his desk drawer, brought out a pack of cards, and said, "I'll play you one game, double or nothing."

You see why, when a newspaper man once asked me how I'd like to spend my last night on earth I could answer unhesitatingly, "With Georgie Jessel. It would be nice to die laughing!"

9. Al Jolson

While I was still a stooge for Bedini and Arthur, still rushing around backstage at Hammerstein's taking suits out to be pressed or seeing that Jean Bedini's laundry was back on time—a fellow in blackface wandered onto the stage one day. He was from Lew Dockstader's Minstrels. Now he was doing a single and there was something electric about him that sent a thrill up your spine. He sang and talked; but he was more than just a singer or an actor—he was an *experience*, and he was to become the most romantic figure of a romantic era, the King of it. Al Jolson.

From the time I heard him at Hammerstein's, he was my idol. I somehow saw every show he was in, and always, for minutes after he'd left the stage, you sat still, knowing that a great presence had been there. And I saw him at the Winter Garden where he was at his best, a real one-man show. Oh, there were some other people occasionally on the stage; a line of dancing girls, enough of a company to keep the thing going while Jolie took a glass of water or mopped his brow off stage. But he was the show and many's the night he'd look at the audience about a quarter of eleven and say, "The girls are waiting backstage and they have some songs and dances, but they've worked pretty hard tonight, let's let 'em go home, huh? I'll stay here as long as you want but let the poor kids go home, huh?" And he'd send everybody home while he stood there maybe another hour, singing, clowning, giving the audience the time of its life and having the time of his own. For this was Jolson's big love affair. Through all the years, the love of his life was—the audience.

In 1912, when he was vacationing from this first smash hit at the Winter Garden, our *Kid Kabaret* hit Oakland. Georgie Jessel and I were as excited as if en route to play the Palace. Jolson was in Oakland! He was then married to his first wife, Henrietta, and she was an Oakland girl. The minute we hit town we turned into a couple of amateur sleuths. We found out where he ate, where he shopped, we haunted all his haunts. No luck. Then one matinee after our show at the Orpheum, the doorman came back to say that Al Jolson was waiting to see us.

I laughed. This had to be a joke of Georgie's. Georgie laughed. This had to be a joke of mine.

"Let him wait," roared Georgie.

"Sure," I laughed, "let him wait." I took off my make-up, we dressed and went outside.

My God! There was Jolson!

He told us we were a couple of talented kids and invited us to have dinner. He took us to a kosher restaurant on Turk Street in San Francisco. It was the craziest dinner you ever *heard*. Georgie and I, the two bigmouths, couldn't think of a thing to say. Jolson did a monologue. When he went to the men's room Georgie and I flipped a coin to see who'd follow him. I won. A few minutes later I came running out to tell him, "Georgie, that Jolson! He does it like anybody."

Jolie and I were friends from that night. He didn't like actors, actually, but of all actors he minded me least, maybe because he knew I worshiped him. The song "If You Knew Susie" was given me by the minstrel man himself. He introduced it, then handed it to me, saying, "Eddie, I think this would fit you better than it does me." A while later when we appeared on the same benefit show he listened to the applause that followed "Susie" and slapped my shoulder, "Eddie, if I'd known it was that good, you dirty dog, you'd never have gotten it." When I scored a hit in *Canary Cottage,* Jolson read a review in San Francisco, drove more than four hundred miles to catch the show, and never did come backstage. He told me about it later. It was tough for him to compliment any actor. Years later when I was with Goldwyn in the movie version of *Whoopee,* he took a paid ad in *Variety* to congratulate me. He couldn't *tell* me, but he took an ad. The one time he ever showed his affection was in 1927 when I was sick and Ida took me to Palm Springs. Jolie came to see us. "God sent me down here. I have to take care of you, Eddie. Ida, don't you let him eat any greasy stuff now, we've got to get this boy well."

And he meant it. We were good friends and competitors. During the years when Jolson was with the Shuberts and I was with Ziegfeld it would sometimes happen that we'd open in the same town the same night. This was tough. We'd stay at the same hotel, take our meals together, and send spies to each others' houses to find out the grosses. I should add here that Jolson would have been a sellout if all he'd done was read the telephone directory. I had to have a show, and my shows were better than Jolie's because it was Jolson people went to see, and the rest of his show didn't matter.

The rivalry was at its height when we opened day and date in Chicago, he in *Bombo* at the Apollo, I in *Kid Boots* at the Woods. We both did fine. Professionally, that is. Personally, we were both hypochondriacs and for once both had reason to be. We'd been playing for about sixteen weeks when that cold Lake Michigan breeze caught up with me and I developed my old stand-by, pleurisy.

As the days went by, the pain was such that I could scarcely breathe. The doctor strapped me with adhesive tape and the show went on. *Kid Boots* was a rough show. I bounced all over the place, and it got to the point where I could barely bounce through a performance. The doctor wanted to drain the fluid, but I wouldn't let him. Ida begged me to close the show. Jolie talked to me like a big brother.

"Eddie, show business ain't worth it. You need sun, kid. Go to Miami, close the show, get some rest and heat and get well."

I thanked him sadly, but the show must go on. Why? Because in my mind's eye I could see the headline in *Variety:* JOLSON DRIVES CANTOR OUT OF CHICAGO. Finally one night between the first and second acts I quietly collapsed. The doctor stepped in, the show was closed, and I was trundled to the train for New York.

"You're doin' the right thing," Jolie said. "Get a rest, Eddie. *No show has to go on.*"

I arrived in New York, picked up the New York *Times,* and on the front page read: JOLSON ILL, CLOSES SHOW.

What I hadn't known—all the time I was suffering with pleurisy, Al was sicker than I was, with a throat infection. But Jolie wouldn't close the show, because in his mind's eye he could see a headline in *Variety:* CANTOR DRIVES JOLSON FROM CHICAGO.

He won that round.

Once, however, I was the winner. We were both playing in New York at the time. One night a fan waited for Jolie outside the Winter Garden. She was a sweet little old lady, at least seventy. She held Jolson's hand and wept as she told him, "Mr. Jolson, you're my idol. I'm just a poor old lady and have nothing in the world, but when I hear you sing you bring real happiness to my heart. I save my pennies, save my nickels, and when I get enough, I buy a balcony seat, I come here to the Winter Garden to hear you. Mr. Jolson, if I had all your records, I could sit at home and play them and be utterly contented."

Jolson handed her a fifty-dollar bill. "Why, bless your heart, you go out and buy all my records," he said.

That night, after our shows, we met at Reuben's.

"Jolie," I bragged, "today I met the hottest fan a performer could possibly have. After the matinee a little old lady, with tears in her eyes, told me she loved *me* so much that just hearing my voice made her happy. Would you believe it, Al? She saves pennies and nickels and when she gets enough, spends the whole business on a balcony seat to see *me*. She said that if she only had my records she could sit at home and her life would be that much easier and brighter."

Jolson started to chuckle. "I suppose you gave her money to buy your records?"

"No, I told her to go see you, your records are so much better than mine."

How he laughed! I think his main affection for me stemmed from the fact that I could make him laugh. Like one time in Boston. He called me in the morning to give me a tip on a horse. He was going to bet five hundred dollars, it was a sure thing. I told him to bet fifty dollars for me. The horse lost. That night I paid Jolie a visit. I had a fifteen-minute break in my show, so I walked over to his theater right out onto the stage and handed him the fifty, saying, "Here, Al . . ." We clowned for so many of the fifteen minutes that they were late ringing up the curtain on my second act.

Gay one moment, morose the next, the King was unpredictable. I'll say this. No one has ever had the drive and confidence of Jolson. I'll never forget the Liberty Bond benefit at the Century

Theatre during World War I. Highlight of the evening came when the great Enrico Caruso sang and the audience almost tore down the building. The applause was thunderous and you didn't think it would ever end. Jolson was scheduled to follow Caruso. It wasn't a spot anybody'd envy, but Jolie rushed out onto the stage, loosened his tie, and said, "Folks! You ain't heard nothin' yet."

On the other hand, in a show of his own he couldn't stand for anyone else to be a hit. Did I say in his own show? In any show. He could sit in his Winter Garden dressing room and read that somebody'd been a hit in Detroit—and he'd take it as a personal affront.

In one of the Winter Garden shows there was a dog act, Meehan's Dogs; and they were good. Opening night the dogs got a tremendous ovation. Jolson paced backstage and said he wouldn't go on, he wasn't gonna follow any old dogs. He went on, all right, but he hated and resented their hit.

Right after he and Ruby Keeler were married Ziegfeld signed Ruby for *Whoopee*. It was a wonderful break for Ruby, who'd been a night-club dancer, and she was delightful in the show. We opened in Pittsburgh and after a triumphant first night we all got together to celebrate. Ruby, Ethel Shutta, George Olsen, Gus Kahn, Walter Donaldson, Ziegfeld. Ruby was so excited she phoned Al, who was making a picture in California. I was with her at the phone, planning to say hello too; but hearing what she said, I knew what he was saying.

"Oh, but, darling, I couldn't!" she said.

"Oh, but Al, dear, how could I do that to Ziegfeld, and to Eddie?" she said.

On the other end of the line Al was saying, "Honey, I need ya, I'll give ya all the money in the world, you come on back to your daddy, honey."

And Ruby never opened with us on Broadway. She went back to California because the King, who was such a great star himself, couldn't bear to have her make a hit on her own.

This was what earned him few friends, few lasting relationships in his personal life. His first wife, Henrietta, was a fine girl approximately his age. But when he scored a success at the Winter Garden he somehow felt that Henrietta didn't belong to that success. He sent her back home to Oakland. After a month or so he

Al Jolson

got lonesome and brought her back, bought her some clothes, then sent her home again. He couldn't be with her or without her; and for some time this was the pattern.

Finally he decided to divorce her, so he sent a lawyer to Oakland to see what she'd demand as a settlement. The lawyer returned with the word, "I don't want any of Al's money, I just want to be free." Jolson couldn't understand it. He took the first train to Oakland. Henrietta was waiting for him at the station. He rushed up to her and discovered she wasn't alone. "Al," she said, "I want you to meet the man I'm going to marry." Al got on the train and went right back to New York.

Now he was free. He didn't fool around. He wasn't interested in the girls around the theater; he was wrapped up in his career. One night at a party someone took a swing at a girl. He picked her up and said, "Why, little lady, that man shouldn't have done that," and he took her home. The next week he married her; Ethel Delmar. The marriage was a brief one. Jolie was restless. One time he got tired of his Winter Garden show. He told his friend Buddy De Sylva, "Buddy, I've got to get away." So he closed the show and he and Buddy went to Atlantic City. After three or four days of lying on the beach, watching the water, Jolson said, "Buddy, I'm tired of lookin' at the Atlantic. Let's go to California where we can look at the Pacific." He was soon to be in California for something more than seeing the Pacific. He was to make *The Jazz Singer*.

Oddly enough, I came close to making this first talking picture myself. Georgie Jessel was the one originally signed; he'd played *The Jazz Singer* on Broadway. When Warners got hold of Vitaphone and decided that in one part of the picture they'd actually record Jessel's voice, Jessel wanted more money, and Warners resented it. It was the week before Lindbergh flew the Atlantic. I was playing the Orpheum in San Francisco when Darryl Zanuck and Jack Warner phoned asking me to do *The Jazz Singer* because they were having trouble with Jessel. I said they weren't having any trouble with Georgie that couldn't be ironed out. I'd be back at the L.A. Orpheum the following week; together we could certainly persuade Jessel. The next day they phoned Jolson in Denver. He said sure he'd do *The Jazz Singer* and he did, going on from there to a much greater success in *The Singing Fool*.

I remember sitting in the Winter Garden seeing *The Singing Fool* at a matinee. Jolson had married Ruby a few days before. When he came on the screen and sang "Sonny Boy," there wasn't a dry eye in the house. The woman in front of me suddenly stopped sobbing and turned to her sobbing friend. "What are we crying about? Here he is, married to beautiful Ruby Keeler, they're on their honeymoon, he's got fame, fortune, and love—and we're killing ourselves crying!"

But there came a time when his picture popularity slipped. Up until now Jolson had been a one-man show; all he'd ever had to do was get up and sing. Now the era of the story had come in. On the stage, on the screen, you needed a story. He decided to try radio. "Eddie, why can't I get on radio? You're on—why can't I?" So we sat down and I framed a show for Jolie and arranged an audition. He was delighted.

"Eddie, if I should get this job, I've got no agent, I'll send a check to your boys' camp every week, like a commission." He auditioned, he got the job, he never sent a quarter to the camp.

He was not big on radio. Another type singer had come in, men like Bing Crosby who crooned a song, very different from the bombastic Jolson style. The Crosbys treated radio as if it were an instrument of introduction to your living room. Jolie treated it like an imposter. He played to the studio audience rather than to the listening audience.

In the old days he had never played the Palace and one night at Lindy's when we kidded him about it he said, "I can tell you the exact date I'll play the Palace—the day Eddie Cantor, Groucho Marx, and Jack Benny are on the bill. I'm gonna buy out the house, tear up all the tickets but one, and sit there yelling, 'Come on, slaves, entertain the King.'"

Now the King had fallen on evil days. He wasn't in pictures, or in the theater, he just was no part of show business. He said he'd retired; that was the story. "Money, who needs it?" he'd say; and it was true, he was a millionaire many times over. But he was eating his heart out. Ida and I used to spend a lot of time with Al and Ruby. We'd go up to Arrowhead for weekends. We'd sit around the table after dinner and Al would say, "Ida, tell her, she's a kid, she doesn't know. Tell her about the Winter Garden. Tell her how I used to send 'em all home and do my stuff." It killed him that Ruby'd never seen him in his heyday. It killed him to be passé.

One afternoon he was sitting in his suite at the Sherry-Netherland in New York with his accompanist, song writer Harry Akst. They heard martial music and Harry looked out the window. "Look, Al, it's a parade." Al didn't move. "But you love a parade, Al!"

"Not when it passes me by," said Jolie. He came sadly to the window and watched the marching men on Fifth Avenue. When it was over, he went to the phone, called Washington, and then told Akst, "We're going overseas, Harry, to entertain those boys." They did, and Jolie was back in the parade. His tremendous popularity with the boys overseas led to *The Jolson Story*.

The Jolson Story was not an undiluted joy to Jolie. He wanted to play the part himself. He kept saying, "So I'm older, so I'm a little fat, they can fix it." Nothing would do but that he make a screen test, and even he knew that he didn't look good. He was at the studio every day, long after the songs were recorded. The bigger success Larry Parks was, the more Jolie resented it; but the picture gave him the biggest comeback in the business. His record sales zoomed to fantastic heights, and still he was insecure. We were neighbors in Palm Springs. We walked together, talked together, ate together, and I knew him better than I had ever known him through the years. What amazed me was that this great personality had never learned how to live. He couldn't; there was something chemically wrong. The minute the curtain rang down, he died.

With his own record sales so high, he ran into our house one day in a state of the greatest agitation. He had a record in his hand and I must play it at once. The recording was Frankie Laine's "Mule Train." Jolie listened to it glumly.

"Isn't that only the greatest?" he kept saying. "This guy'll run us all out of the business."

That was the year he was voted "Man of the Year" by a Los Angeles organization and feted with a banquet at the Biltmore Bowl. Jolson insisted I be master of ceremonies. It was a soft assignment. I had only to introduce most of the greats of show business; Jack Benny, Bob Hope, Danny Kaye, Dinah Shore, Red

Skelton, etc. Jolie was in his glory. His young wife, Erle, was there and I addressed myself to her.

"Erle, this is really your night. The applause and laughter you're hearing is an old thing to Al. It happened at every performance wherever he played through the years. But Al is proud because it will give you an idea of his biggest love—before he met you."

Jolson was so pleased that the next day he told his agent, who was also mine, "There isn't a thing that guy Cantor ever wants he can't get from me." A week later I took advantage of this emotion. I told him I had a funny idea for one of my radio programs. Would he like to do it with me? I explained the idea and he was enthusiastic.

"What about money?" I asked. "What will I have to pay you?"

He was hurt. "Don't talk about money or I'll spit in your eye."

"No money?" I thought. This was too good to be true.

We did the show, one of the best programs I ever had. The next day our agent called me.

"Eddie, I hate to tell you this, but Jolson has ordered six suits at two hundred and fifty dollars a suit and says please send fifteen hundred dollars to his tailor right away."

That was Jolson, hot and cold.

But there was one place where he was always hot—on a stage, making love to his audience. And his favorite audience of all time were the servicemen overseas. He never forgot 'em. Although he almost died of malaria in North Africa, despite the crowded schedule of his days after the overwhelming success of *The Jolson Story*, he insisted on being the first to entertain the boys in Korea. Al was as much a casualty as any soldier who died in battle. He was sixty-four when he took off for Korea, a tough age to go traveling through insect-infested jungles in a jeep. But he felt it was worth it, and whether he was playing to forty or four thousand he gave it all he had. His songs, his quips, his personality, these were his ammunition, his way of fighting a war—and who's to say he didn't win?

This was where he counted, where he was *great*, and his death left a real gap in the heart of show business. I was in Mobile, Alabama, when NBC in New York phoned at 4 A.M. They had just received the news of Jolie's death and were paying tribute to him on a special broadcast. Could I be at the studio at 6 A.M.?

They'd cut me in from Mobile. That night I went on with my one-man show. Everything went along as usual until I got to the spot for my regular parody of the King.

"Ole man Jolson, that ole man Jolson
He's older than Johnson, together with Olsen
But ole man Jolson, he just keeps goin' along.
He don't plant cotton, he don't plant 'taters
He just plants corn in the picture theaters.
But ole man Jolson he keeps on going along.
Al gets down on bended knee, sings that 'Mammy' melody
Can't get up from off the ground, his moneybags just weigh him down . . ."

The music started, but I couldn't sing it. Instead, I talked to the audience of the Jolson I knew. I was crying, and so were they. The King was gone, the greatest minstrel of them all.

10. Max Hart, Earl Carroll, Oliver Morosco

When Ida and I returned from our European honeymoon in 1914, I sent her home in a taxi and went right from the dock to the office of Max Hart, then the top theatrical agent in the world. He not only handled the biggest money-makers in the business, he had so many next-to-closing acts that he was once able to threaten the Keith circuit—they'd meet his demands for increased pay for his clients or he'd bring vaudeville to a halt by yanking out his next-to-closing acts.

I had cabled Hart from London when Sammy Kessler and I flopped, asking for advice. He put me in touch with producer André Charlot and Charlot hired me for his revue, *Not Likely*, a big show and a big break for me, a change of pace. Until now, with Gus Edwards, I'd relied on imitations and dialects. I'd tried the same pattern with Kessler but the English audiences didn't "get" the imitations. I knew that no one can go far as a mimic anyhow. You have to stop and be yourself. Martin and Lewis, two of the greatest mimics in show business, stopped mimicry overnight for the same reason; they knew that to go farther they'd have to become themselves. So, with Charlot's revue, I came out and kidded the other acts. There was a burlesque of *Kismet* in the show, with a tattered beggar asking alms.

"Ladies and gentlemen," I said, "don't be fooled by this beggar. I know for a fact that he backs André Charlot. He owns several apartment buildings and his chauffeur picks him up after the show." I sang a song, "I Love the Ladies," that got encore after encore. Soon the audience knew the words and sang along with me. As a result, my first real notices were from the English press. I showed the clippings to Max Hart in the hope he'd book me as a single.

Max wasn't impressed. To a man who handled Fanny Brice and Frank Tinney, I looked pretty thin. What I needed, he said, was a good straight man and he provided one—Al Lee, who'd worked with Ed Wynn. The team of Cantor and Lee was formed at once, and since neither of us had any money for a writer, I wrote an act. *Master and Man* was the title. It didn't mean a thing. We thought it sounded good and fitted in with Lee's whiteface and my blackface. To my knowledge, this was the first time audiences had seen someone in blackface playing without dialect and without comedy clothes. I wore something close to street clothes, but a shade tighter to increase the impression of slightness. We opened with three or four minutes of patter. The war was on and I told Lee:

"You'll have to let me go."

"Why?"

"To fight in the war, to fight for my mother country, Russia."

"Russia?"

"*Darkest* Russia."

"I didn't know you were Russian."

"Oh yes, my relatives are all in the war. My father's General Petrovitch, my uncle's General Ivanovitch. Then there's eczema —another itch . . ."

Lee would sing a ballad which I'd interrupt with zany comment; then I'd sing three or four songs in a row. Before we showed the act to Hart we tried it out "on the dog," the Star Theatre, 107th and Lexington in uptown New York. This was a tough crowd and we figured if we made good there, we'd be sensational before a more genteel audience. When Max saw the act he said, "You can use some better material, but I'll keep you working till you get it." We read every copy of *Puck, Judge,* and the *Literary Digest* and switched the jokes around. Max kept us going for about a year and a half. Some places we did all right; we had a good reception in Chicago. Then we played Milwaukee, the Majestic Theatre. I'll never forget it. We opened at a Monday matinee, fourth on the bill. Now usually the opening act is either an acrobatic or an animal act, the second act builds a little, and around the third act, you get to a big full-stage deal. This bill was different. Brent Hayes, a banjoist, opened the show in one (a short act before the curtain). He was followed by Weston and

Fields, a piano act also in one. Then came my friend Will Rogers, who at that time also worked in one. By this time the audience was ready for something big, a full stage of performers. When Cantor and Lee appeared in front of a street drop, the audience wondered what the hell was going on, they'd been robbed. They gave us strictly silence, no laughs, no applause.

After the matinee the stage manager revised the show and who do you think now *opened* the bill? Cantor and Lee. This was the insult supreme. While the audience was still getting settled, the late-comers struggling through to their seats, we were on stage trying to be funny. We didn't get a laugh all week. I wanted to quit, but on the Monday morning of our opening Al had married Lilyan Tashman and he wanted his week's salary. (Lilyan later turned out to be one of the best-dressed women in pictures, a big star.)

I was heartsick but not as sick as I was going to be. Before the week ended, Mr. Higler, who managed the theater, called me in to his office. "You're a nice young man, Eddie, personable, easygoing, and you're taking your failure here this week with good grace. That's why I want to give you a piece of advice. In this business there are people who have it and people who haven't. You just haven't got it. You're a married man; get out of show business and into something else where you can possibly be a big success. Believe me, I've been in this business for years, I know what it takes to make it and you haven't got it. Take my advice and get out as quickly as you can."

I didn't cry in front of him. I held it until I hit the street. Then I prayed that I'd be run over by a beer truck. I didn't have the courage to kill myself, but oh, for one big Milwaukee beer truck!

Eleven years later I played Milwaukee again in Ziegfeld's *Kid Boots*, the Davidson Theatre. The show was a tremendous hit in New York and Chicago; Milwaukee ate it up. We were not only sold out for weeks in advance, they had put as many extra seats in the aisles as the fire laws would permit. Opening night the manager came back to say there were a lot of flowers, ushers could hand them up over the footlights at the final curtain, but one piece was so huge it couldn't be lifted up. What should be done? I suggested they bring it backstage so I could take a look, then we'd send it to a nearby hospital. The thing was an eight-foot horseshoe of flowers. The little card read, "Aren't you glad you took my advice? Higler."

But in 1915, after Al Lee and I'd left Milwaukee, I often thought of Higler. Even when we played the Palace our salary wasn't staggering, and by the time we paid Max Hart his commission and our traveling expenses we were still very small time. What we didn't know was that Max was throwing us in as a bargain on deals he made for his headliners.

Occasionally we picked up extra change playing a club date. In Rochester some visiting firemen were having a stag and we went right from the theater, I in blackface as usual. Seeing the nature of the event, I dropped our usual act and went into the dirtiest routine you ever heard. Al fed me lines and I used everything I'd learned as an urchin in the streets where you knew about sex before you got to the first reader. We went over big. The men yelled with laughter, I washed up, went back to the hotel, and found a crowd from the stag at the desk getting their keys. They were discussing the show, so I eavesdropped.

"Pretty funny, wasn't it?" one said.

"He seemed to be such a young fellow though, even under the burned cork. How could a fellow that young have such a filthy mind?"

That's what he said—a filthy mind. I took my key, slunk off to my room, and took an oath that jokes obscene should not be heard —I'd never tell an off-color story the rest of my life. It wasn't hard to stick with. Telling a dirty story is like seeing a couple of hundred pigeons flying and firing into the flock. It's too easy, there's no sport to it. And it isn't necessary. During the war many chaplains wrote letters following our camp shows, thanking me for keeping it clean. It made me glad I'd learned my lesson back in 1915, traveling with Al Lee.

Master and Man eventually played the L.A. Orpheum and opening night there was something very special. The *crème de la crème* of picture business were the regulars in this audience and among them, Earl Carroll. Carroll had written words and music for the Charlotte Greenwood hit, *So Long Letty*, and he had just written words and music for a new show, *Canary Cottage*, to be produced by Oliver Morosco. Carroll, catching our act at the Orpheum, thought I'd be good for Trixie Friganza's chauffeur-cook-

and-man-of-all-things in *Canary Cottage*. But he didn't tell me that. He and his arranger, Al Goodman (later my orchestra leader on the Colgate Comedy Hour) came backstage and told me Oliver Morosco wanted to see me.

Next afternoon I went to Morosco's handsome office and faced an impeccably groomed man who wore all the assurance of his own success. He offered me the job in *Canary Cottage*, but without Lee. Without Lee, I turned it down. Feeling a little heroic, I went to that afternoon's matinee and told Al Lee what had happened. He told me I was crazy. If I wanted the job, go ahead, take it. Far from feeling slighted, he explained, "I wouldn't be tied up in a town like this at any price. I'm Broadway." So Al went back to Broadway and I started rehearsals for *Canary Cottage*.

Earl Carroll had written two very good songs for me, "It Ruined Marc Anthony" and "I'll Marry No Explorer"; but my part as the chauffeur was nothing. I felt I should build it up so I'd have something more to do than just wait around for two acts to sing the songs. So at rehearsals I'd ad lib whenever I had an opening. Earl Carroll would laugh, Elmer Harris, the author, would laugh; the next day when I'd start to repeat the business, I'd be told "That's out." Trixie Friganza, fine comedienne that she was and star of the show, didn't think much of my comic intrusions.

Raymond Griffith used to drop in at rehearsals and he gave me some good advice. Griffith and I had become friendly when I was at the Orpheum with Al Lee. He had been a stage star, had lost his voice, and was now a success in silent pictures. In his hoarse croak he took me aside and whispered, "Don't be a fool, Eddie. Everything you try at rehearsal, she'll cut. Just make notes of what you want to do and save it for opening night."

I listened to Griffith. Came the trial run in San Diego, I still bided my time and was nothing. Opening night in Los Angeles I sprang the surprise. Why I didn't throw the whole show off cue, I'll never know. And I didn't care. I just wanted to be seen. When Miss Friganza said, "Bring the car around," instead of leaving the stage I'd grab oranges off the fruit bowl and start juggling. I picked a yellow shawl from the piano and danced off in it. I added extra choruses to my songs. You should have seen Friganza's face and you should have heard her screaming after the show! Mine still wasn't a big part but it was socky enough to make the audience laugh, and the next morning Guy Price, who wrote for the Hearst papers and for *Variety*, headed his review, "Vaudevillian Romps Home with *Canary Cottage*."

But that night I didn't know. I figured I'd be fired. Griffith took me up to his apartment and we opened a bottle of champagne. "So maybe you'll *be* fired," Griffith said, "tomorrow there'll be a hundred jobs waiting."

The next day there was a matinee. As I came into the theater the doorman said, "Just a minute, Mr. Cantor. Don't go to your dressing room until you see Mr. Morosco." His office was seven or eight minutes from the theater and every step of the way, I *knew*. That was it. Good-by *Canary Cottage*. His secretary ushered me right into the august presence.

"Eddie Cantor," he said, "what you did last night is the most unforgivable thing that can happen in the theater. Now you go back to the matinee and do everything you did last night, exactly the same way."

At the next afternoon's rehearsal Trixie Friganza advanced to the footlights and made a speech. Elmer Harris, Morosco, and Earl Carroll were sitting in the third row and she said, "Mr. Morosco, either this amateur goes or I leave. I'll give you my two weeks' notice." Mr. Morosco never flinched, "We intend to keep Eddie Cantor for the run of the play," he said, and that was that. After a while Trixie began to simmer down. She was still the star; after a while she even asked me to write some material for her for club dates she was playing. She paid me two hundred dollars for the material, ten twenty-dollar gold pieces.

After about five months in *Canary Cottage* I was so homesick I couldn't stand it. Natalie had been born and I hadn't seen her. I finally had my brother-in-law send me a telegram to the effect that Ida was very low—I was to come at once. I showed the telegram to Morosco, wept crocodile tears, and after a few days understudy Lew Cooper went on and I went home.

But there are overtones from the associations of *Canary Cottage*. Earl Carroll and I were to be associated again. When I was in *Whoopee* Earl wanted me to write a show for him to be staged under the title *Sketch Book*. I wrote at night and brought him the show in about ten days. It opened with a number "Legs Legs

Legs." The curtain rose just high enough to reveal a line of gorgeous gams and girls' voices were singing, "Why do the men come to see the show—legs, legs, legs." Then the curtain went up and there were no girls, just phonographs with silk-stockinged well-padded legs. I was working for Ziegfeld so, of course, couldn't be in *Sketch Book*, but we had in the show a filmed scene of Earl Carroll and me in his office. I talked about what a big man Ziegfeld was, how he'd given me a handsome watch when I was in his show; so Earl proved he was a bigger man; he gave me a grandfather clock.

Sketch Book opened in Atlantic City with Will Mahoney doing a bathroom scene. The scene flopped and Carroll phoned me from Atlantic City, asking if I could write another; after all, the Crane people had given him the bathroom set. I sat down at once and by six the next morning sent Earl twenty pages of Western Union blanks with a new sketch. It's been used many, many times since, but originally Patsy Kelly was in the bathtub while Will Mahoney was shaving and the plumber, William Demarest, walked in.

"My wife is taking a bath!" cried Mahoney.

"So what?" answered the plumber, "I *took* my hat off." And he went to work with his tools. Patsy got out of the tub, the plumber got in, Mahoney got in, Patsy sent for a cop, the cop got in, recognized the plumber as pitcher for the plumbers' union who'd beaten the policemen's team the week before, Patsy brought in tea and served it. Oh, a wild bit. Earl Carroll thought it very funny.

More overtones. Max Hart. When I was first rehearsing for *Canary Cottage* I ran short on funds and needed two hundred dollars to pay the premium on a life-insurance policy. I wrote asking Max to lend me the money. "I'm an honest representative," Max wrote back. "I book acts. I'm not a loan agency. Sorry." He continued to be my agent until I came to Hollywood to make films, and long after that I sent Max a check every month of his life.

For Max had run into trouble. He sued a booking office for five million dollars. They beat him and from then on, the Keith office would have nothing to do with him. I owed a big debt to Max. He eventually brought me to Ziegfeld and it was he who told me, "You can't keep on being a blackface comedian. You must hold out for whiteface." He was right. Facial expressions are limited under the burned cork. What can you show—joy, sadness, fright?

On Max's advice I finally did hold out for one skit in whiteface and won. So I was grateful, even though Max had once let me down with, "I book acts. I'm not a loan agency. Sorry."

Overtones. Oliver Morosco. Successful when I first met him, he became one of the biggest producers in the business. He did *Abie's Irish Rose, Bird of Paradise*, and he had umpteen companies of *Peg O' My Heart* touring at the same time. When he had an argument with the Shuberts he had the nerve to buck them and build his own theaters in New York, Chicago, and Los Angeles. There was a time when he was earning fifty thousand dollars and more a week. What a sport the man was! And through a woman and a lot of alcohol he lost his theaters, lost his shows, lost his pride, and eventually lost his life. But before he did . . .

During the time I was making movies for Goldwyn someone told me of a comedian in a burlesque show on Main Street who might be good for my Chase and Sanborn Hour. I went down to Main Street, left the car in a parking lot, started toward the theater, when I was approached by the foulest, dirtiest bum you've ever seen. Torn shirt, filthy pants, a face covered with beard and spittle. He lurched toward me, mumbling about a dime for a cup of coffee, drooling as he talked. And suddenly I stared aghast.

"Oliver Morosco!"

He sprang back, not knowing me, dazed with booze, but he knew his name and it *was* Oliver Morosco, the dapper executive who had called me to his office on top the Morosco Theatre building in 1916. I gave him a bill, but not before I'd torn a sheet from a scratch pad and written on it, "Call Eddie Cantor at Granite 5111." I never went to the burlesque show. I couldn't. I went home to tell Ida and plan what could be done for Morosco. First, a place to live. I went to a hotel, gave them money for his rent for a couple of months and cash which they could give him at the rate of twenty-five dollars a week for spending money. Morosco phoned my office all right, went to the new hotel, to a new beginning, I hoped. Four or five days later he disappeared. He had made life so miserable for the desk clerk that they'd finally given him all the money and he'd left. He was run down and killed by an automobile one day, a drunken bum, the man who'd bucked the Shuberts and built a theatrical empire of his own.

11. Will Rogers

The happiest engagement I ever played was at the Orpheum Theatre, Winnipeg, Canada, 1912. *Kid Kabaret* closed the show and fourth from closing was a cowboy who did the best roping act you've ever seen. He carried with him a man and a horse. He'd toss two lassos and rope the man's head and the horse's hooves at the same time. Once he missed. He came ambling off the stage with that grin of his, chawed his wad of gum and said, "If that horse'd been smart enough to stick out his tongue, I'd have gotten him." He didn't talk on stage, he was still a little too nervous to try that, but his off-stage talk was the wittiest, his interests the broadest. This cowboy was the first guy I'd ever met from west of the Bronx and I worshiped him—Will Rogers. We called him Bill.

He started teaching me a few simple roping tricks and briefed me about Oklahoma and his Indian heritage. His dad had been one eighth Cherokee and his mother one fourth; and he was proud of the fact that his ancestors hadn't come over on the *Mayflower* but were there to meet the boat. His big ambition was not to let Oklahoma down. He wanted his state to be proud of him.

Until I met Rogers my world was the stage, my idols were the headliners, my ambition was to be rich and famous. Knowing the man from Claremont, Oklahoma, was to gradually change all that. He was an entertainer and a great one, but his ambitions and talent went far beyond the theater. To him success meant being a good citizen and he opened a new world to me, a world in which you took major pride in being a working member of the United States of America.

Rogers was my grammar school, high school, and college. He taught me that the world doesn't end at the stage door and that politics are every man's business, actors not excluded. He kept on giving me an education as long as he lived; and since his death his writings are still my source book.

You understand, Will Rogers didn't set himself up as any teacher, he just lived the way he believed. As early as 1915 he was preparing for his future career. He'd joined the *Ziegfeld Follies* that year after a success with Blanche Ring in *The Wall Street Girl*. He'd added a monologue to his act and he wasn't satisfied to joke, the jokes must have substance. Every morning he read the papers, the *Morning World*, the New York *Times*, the *American*, the *Tribune*. Then he'd sit down at his little portable typewriter and peck out his commentaries on the news. He'd never had much education; he used to kid about it. "Eddie, I stayed in fourth grade so long I got to know more about McGuffey's Reader than Mr. McGuffey." But he had a built-in shrewdness and he worked at it, edited it, until it became 99.9 per cent pure wisdom.

When we were reunited in the *Follies of 1917* I found a great change in Bill. Not only had he become a top star, the only comedian who actually outdrew Ziegfeld's girls—he had begun to be a spokesman of the people. He never looked up to the mighty or spoke down to the masses. He called a spade a spade and made the spade like it. To a troubled world he brought a little peace of mind with a little piece of rope. Night after night, Bill Fields, Fanny Brice, Bert Williams and I would stand in the wings listening:

"Don't worry if a man kicks you from behind, it only proves you're ahead of him."

"Congress is so strange. A man gets up to speak and says nothing. Nobody listens. Then everybody disagrees."

"I know an Oklahoma rancher who's so rich he doesn't brand his cattle, he has 'em engraved."

The opening night of the 1917 *Follies*, I did what every actor dreams of—stopped the show. "That's the Kind of a Baby for Me" was the song, and the audience applauded and kept on applauding; Tom Richards, who came on next, had to play through the din. Rogers wasn't on until next to closing and he dropped by my dressing room to pat me on the back. I didn't see him. My head was down on the dressing table.

"What are you crying about, Eddie? They're still clapping downstairs."

But my grandmother had died a few months before and I was wondering why, of all the people in the world, why couldn't my grandmother have been there tonight to see me finally make it?

"Now, Eddie, what makes you think she *didn't* see you?" Bill said. "And from a very good seat?"

I've never forgotten that. In fact, I've come to think the same way. We were together in the *Follies of 1917* and *1918;* and Rogers, Bill Fields and I were such buddies, Ziegfeld called us his three musketeers. Three such different guys! I the fresh East Side kid, Rogers the homespun westerner, Fields the man of the world. He used to love to kid Rogers. There was a girl in the show named Allyn King. A gorgeous face, a gorgeous figure, she could sing and act, she was a big thing in the *Follies.* Well, Allyn had one change that was so fast, she couldn't even stop to close her dressing-room door. Fields would see her running in and roar, "Hey, Injun, come out here quick!" Rogers would dash from his dressing room, Fields would put an arm about his shoulders and turn him so he was in full view of Allyn in panties and garters, struggling into costume. Rogers bit on that gag a dozen times, always turned red and fell all over himself escaping, while Fields'd bellow, "What's the matter, Bill? A very pretty girl!"

But one joke of Fields's, meant in good fun, became a cruel jest. We were in Pittsburgh, the Wednesday before Thanksgiving, 1918, the Nixon Theatre. There were probably never three people who loved the theater more than Rogers, Fields and I. Days we had no matinee, we'd go to the theater anyhow to practice. Over at the Nixon this afternoon, Rogers started talking about his old friend, Clay McGonigle. They'd been pals in Oklahoma; they'd gone together on a cattle boat to Australia. Rogers had told us the same story a hundred times and he always ended with, "I don't know what's happened to old Clay but if he were around, there's nothing I have in this world he couldn't have half or all of. That's how I feel about Clay McGonigle." Rogers left us about five-thirty and Fields and I went to an Italian restaurant for spaghetti.

"Eddie," Fields said, "we're gonna fix up that Oklahoma cowboy but good." He called over a waiter and dictated a note which the waiter transcribed in a crude hand.

"Bill I'm going to see your show out front tonight and it's

gonna be a thrill to know my old buddy is in the Ziegfield Follies. Clay McGonigle."

Fields deliberately had the waiter misspell "Ziegfeld." We put the note in an envelope, and back at the theater Fields handed it to the doorman with a dollar tip.

While we're dressing Rogers comes in choked with emotion. "Whitey, Eddie, guess who's in town and catching the show tonight—Clay McGonigle!"

He goes out on the stage this night and for once in his life doesn't stop the show. He addresses his ten-minute monologue to one man, Clay McGonigle. The audience doesn't know what he's talking about. "Clay," he says, "do you remember Mrs. Hennigan's pies?" No one in the theater knows who Mrs. Hennigan is! "And, Clay, when we were on that cattle boat, remember . . ." On and on.

Then Rogers rushes backstage, takes off his chaps, slicks his hair, and when the show breaks he's in the lobby waiting for Clay McGonigle. The people file out. No Clay. Rogers rushes to his hotel to see if there's a message. He checks every hotel in town where his friend might be registered. At 2 A.M. he's at the railway station still hunting for Clay. When he gets back to the hotel, he's white-faced and miserable.

"Fellas, you heard me tonight. Did I say anything that could possibly have offended Clay McGonigle? I can't understand . . . I wouldn't have said anything to hurt him."

We assured Bill he'd said nothing that could've given offense. By now we were so sorry for Rogers we could have killed ourselves; but if we'd told him the truth, he'd have killed us. Eight years later he walked into the Astor Hotel dining room and slapped me on the back of the neck so hard I almost fell into my soup. He'd just read a story of mine in the *Saturday Evening Post* and in the story was the truth about the note from Clay McGonigle.

The incident shows the sort of affection Rogers had, not only for Clay, but for every one who ever was his friend. He used to wire me every time I got a good notice: *"These critics are a little late. I knew this in Winnipeg."* Once his friend, you were his friend forever. He was very close to Flo Ziegfeld. In all the years Rogers worked for Flo, they never had a contract between them.

Rogers had asked for five hundred dollars in the *Follies of 1915*.

"Flo, when I left Oklahoma I promised my wife and children that someday I'd make five hundred dollars a week. That was our dream." Ziegfeld fulfilled the dream, but a few months later Rogers asked for six hundred.

"What's the big idea?" Flo said, "I thought your wife and children were satisfied with five hundred dollars."

"They were, but since then we've had another child and he's kicking."

Bill was a family man and he worked at it. He was deeply religious and absolutely straight. From time to time his wife Betty would come on to visit him, and whenever he had a few days layoff, he'd fly home. He often came home with me to our little apartment in the Bronx, and at the first opportunity he dragged me back to Oklahoma to meet his family. His wife Betty was one of the darlings of the world; you never saw a couple more compatible. Betty understood that Rogers belonged to the public and she was willing to share him. She brought the children up to understand this too. They lived in a simple home adjoining that of his sister, Mrs. Spade, in Claremont. It was a warm and happy family and I enjoyed knowing them. But Oklahoma and the West, of which Bill had bragged so much, left me cold that first trip. All I saw was a very big, empty, lonesome place. And to him our Bronx apartment must have seemed like a jail.

When we were on tour we always palled together, and gradually Bill got wise to me. Having been brought up by a very orthodox grandmother, for me certain foods were forbidden: pork, lobster, crab, oysters—so I'd try to find kosher restaurants. Bill'd ask me to have dinner with him, I'd always have an excuse; "I've got friends in this town." Bill finally figured that nobody could have that many friends. One night when I was turning him down, he said, "Eddie, you kosherin' up some place?" I confessed that I was.

"Well, why don't you ask me to go with you?"

Half an hour later we were seated across the table at a kosher restaurant on Euclid Avenue in Cleveland. Bill scanned the menu a little puzzled and I translated for him. He tried chopped chicken liver first, asked for a second portion and then a third. All the time he kept muttering, "Too late, I guess it's too late."

"Too late for what, Bill?"

"For me to turn Jewish," sighed the cowboy.

Years later when he was operated on for gall-bladder trouble, he blamed the whole thing on me. "That's what I get for going to all those kosher restaurants with Eddie Cantor."

But the truth was it was tit for tat. I introduced him to liver and herring, but he introduced me to his favorite food—chili. I used to tell him it was an internal hotfoot; but the fact remained that this man who dined with presidents and kings, even when he was earning twenty thousand dollars a week, loved nothing more than to eat in the most awful-looking chili joints. I remember going with him to one near the depot in Pittsburgh. It was the worst, I was afraid to go in it looked so spidery. But Rogers was crazy about chili and I was crazy about Rogers. There was a place in Chicago run by a Hungarian! That tickled Bill. "Think of it, Eddie, a Hungarian, and he makes the best Mexican food in the world!" With it, he'd take a bottle of beer. Sometimes, if he were devilish, out on the town, he'd drink two bottles. He never drank anything stronger.

The night the *Follies* opened at the National Theatre in Washington, Rogers was invited to the White House. From midnight until sunrise he talked with Woodrow Wilson, with Secretary of the Navy Josephus Daniels, Secretary of War Newton Baker, England's Lord Balfour and France's M. Viviani. Finally he got up to take his leave. "Mr. President," he drawled, "Congress is gonna ask you how you can train an army so fast. Well, sir, you tell 'em that when you teach an army to go one way, you can do it in half the time." With America in the war, his shrewd comments gained more and more attention. Henry Ford had sent a peace ship of diplomats to Europe. Rogers said, "I think Henry made a big mistake sending those long-hairs over. What he ought to have done was fill up that boat with Ziegfeld's pippins. He'd have the Kaiser and Mohammed V shooting crap over who was going to be first in the receiving line."

When we opened in Baltimore the evening papers carried a story of how the Kaiser, standing up in a small boat, had fallen overboard and they'd had to fish him out. "Well," said Bill, "I see where the old Kaiser tried walking on the waters. Guess he heard that someone else had once done it very successfully."

The beauty of Rogers' quips was that everything he said was basically true, and the great men of the world came to respect that. As time went on, there were few big men whom Rogers didn't know well: Mussolini, the Pope, the royal family of England, the Prince of Japan, Lady Astor, the Prince of Wales, the presidents: Wilson, Harding, Coolidge, Hoover, Roosevelt. He was perfectly at home with all of them because he was always exactly himself.

Alice Longworth once bet Will Rogers that he couldn't make Coolidge laugh. That was before Bill'd met the President. Alice wagered a box of candy against a modish new hat. Rogers went to the White House, was introduced to Coolidge, and said, "What was that name again, please?" He won the bet. Coolidge was to hear more of Rogers. Most astute were his published *Letters of a Self-Made Diplomat to His President*, in which he told Coolidge what he was hearing and seeing in foreign countries.

Rogers' comments had common sense and something more, the quality of prophecy. I went with him to not less than a hundred dinners just to hear him speak, to watch him analyze and psychoanalyze people and events. You see, I'd never enjoyed school, I'd never cared about dates or facts, I just wanted to know if I was going to have something to eat at night. But by the time I met Rogers and Fields (Fields educated me in a different way, I'll tell you about that), I knew I was going to eat and I was learning, not by having facts pounded in my head but by enjoying the wisdom of men whom I loved. Rogers reached me on politics because it was wisdom with a smile.

"The United States is a great country, Eddie; we never lost a war and never won a conference."

"Everyone knows the world is round, but if it weren't for the United States, the world'd be flat."

"Talk about presidential timber [this in 1924] . . . Why man, they have whole lumberyards of it here at the convention. There were so many being nominated that some of the men making the nominating speeches had never met the men they were nominating. I know they hadn't from the nice things they said about 'em."

He begged Alfred E. Smith not to accept the nomination in 1928. He wrote in his column: "Al, give it four more years. Then the Democrats will definitely be in. But now . . . the day after election, you and the Democrats are going to find out how big a country this is west of New York." And when Smith did run he urged him to take off his derby while campaigning. "It makes you look like a city slicker, which you certainly are not." Bill tried out these lines on me. He'd often type out a column or a speech and then read it to me for a reaction. I was New Haven, New York, Atlantic City, and the Bronx. He wanted to see how a westerner's point of view would register.

They once made him mayor of Beverly Hills. "I guess I'll make a good mayor," he said, "because I'm for the common people. And inasmuch as there are no common people in Beverly Hills, I'll make a good mayor."

The one speech from which I can't quote was one he made in 1925 at the Solax Club in New York. This is a Jewish charitable club and they were giving me a testimonial dinner. Rogers asked to be toastmaster. He was, at that time, the most talked-of humorist in the world. Imagine everyone's surprise when Rogers got up and started speaking—in Yiddish. It was the most hilarious evening I ever spent. It seems the minute he asked to be toastmaster, he got hold of a young student who in six weeks taught him enough of the language so that he could conduct the program.

What a great guy he was for benefits! He was always there, always on time, always the hit of the show. Once when I was handling the annual event for Surprise Lake Camp, the house was packed at eight-thirty, but Rogers was the only actor backstage. Actors hate to go on first, so they stall and arrive after a benefit has started. At eight forty-five, with the audience stomping and clapping, I asked Bill if he'd mind opening the show. He went on and stayed out there until the other actors started showing up at nine-thirty.

At a benefit in 1925 I told how, a few nights earlier, I'd entertained the Prince of Wales out on Long Island. It was after midnight when I'd arrived and everyone was very jolly, they'd had a few drinks, I said. Rogers followed me on the benefit. "The only difference between little Eddie and myself is—the Prince of Wales sends for me when he's sober."

The personal jokes between us were endless. When I opened in *Kid Boots* he presented me with a gorgeous silver gun and holster. I had to wear it, too. When Ida gave birth to Janet he sent us a

Western Union telegram, but in gold, a gold plaque. In raised letters it said, "*If you want a boy, send for Western Union.*" This, in 1927, started a gag that became classic.

When we built the mansion in Great Neck, Bill came out to see it. Now this place wasn't just a house. The man who'd built it specialized in *banks;* the steps he had leading up to our library had the sweep of a public monument. Rogers took one look and started to laugh. "You sure you want me in here?" he said. "Is this a reservation for Indians?" Later, when he built his beautiful home in California, he could have put the whole Great Neck place in his bathroom.

Rogers started writing his column in 1921, and it became the most widely read printed word in the country. In 1929 Brisbane asked me to write a daily column for the Hearst papers. There'd been a second fire at the White House and I'd cracked, "Golly, I didn't know business was that *bad.*" Brisbane decided to have me do a commentary on finance. I'm no columnist, but with Bill as inspiration I agreed to try. Rogers, in his column, welcomed me to the ancient and honorable profession. "Eddie and I spent our literary apprenticeship in the same school of hard knocks, Mr. Ziegfeld's *Follies.* We eked out a bare existence among the bare backs . . . Eddie specializes in Wall Street and the financial news. He's another Roger Babson . . ."

"Roger Babson" Cantor kept advising Will Rogers to get into the stock market. But he couldn't understand why any company would take in a total stranger, let him be partners in the business, and give him a share of the profits when they didn't know him. I tried to explain the facts of life about Wall Street and finally, in desperation, said:

"Bill, let me buy you a couple of hundred shares of stock. You don't have to spend a penny. I'll buy it, we'll let it lay and watch it climb. I'll sell at any time you say and give you a check for the profits."

He didn't object too strenuously, so I did exactly that. The first day the stock went up five points. Then it went up three points, then four. For ten days. On the eleventh day the stock dropped two points and Rogers phoned.

"Hey, I thought you said that stock was going up!"

"It's gone up, Bill. It's just dropped a couple of points."

"Get rid of it. I don't want any stock that drops."

I sold the stock and sent him the profits. A few nights later we both spoke at a dinner and Rogers slipped the same check under my plate. "For your boys' camp, Eddie." Sixty-five hundred dollars.

He kept on distrusting the stock market: "A holding company's an arrangement where you hand an accomplice the goods while a policeman searches *you*." And he had the last laugh again because in a matter of months "Roger Babson Cantor" was financially a bum. Those were the days when comedians had such long faces, barbers charged them double for a shave. I was no exception. I couldn't eat or sleep, the blood pressure was high and the stocks low. One day I ran into Rogers on Broadway. He gave me a big bear hug.

"Eddie, saw *Whoopee* again last night and you're pretty lucky, you know. You're young, you're healthy, you'll get all that gravy back—just keep workin'." I must have looked pretty doleful. "Look here, Eddie," he said. "You have a *salable commodity*. It's as good as jewels or government bonds—you can make people laugh!" It was the best of advice. Ida'd told me the same thing; but a wife is always trying to smooth things for you and you feel she's prejudiced. Getting it from Rogers was different. It gave me renewed confidence.

In his scheme of things, what was money anyhow? Just something to do something with. He'd never given a damn about money and he was the most generous man I ever knew. I'd learned this back as far as 1917 when the *Follies* hit Detroit. We took a walk one day shortly before Christmas and dropped in at the Detroit Free Press. Rogers walked up to the Good Fellow Fund window and laid down ten one-hundred-dollar bills.

"Get some toys for the kids," he said, turning away.

"Wait a minute," the girl said. "What's your name?"

"My name won't help the toys any."

In the thirties when acting jobs were scarce I'd meet actors at Bank of America in Beverly Hills—and they weren't taking out, they were putting in—checks from Will Rogers. He was sending out weekly checks to down-and-out actors as if they were relatives. There were actors who turned down extra jobs because they were getting better pay from Rogers for nothing.

When Ziegfeld was ill and broke he was Bill's house guest. No one actually knew where Zieggy was, but he and Billie Burke were living at the Rogers' big ranch in the style to which they'd always been accustomed.

When Bill'd walk out of the commissary at the studio he'd leave enough money to pay for lunch for a group of secretaries or a group of extras.

This is just how he was. He was a guy who really meant: "I've never met a man I didn't like." He believed in people and he had a great hold on people. I think that if Bill had lived, Hitler might never have become the menace he was to the world. Rogers, with his great influence, would have fought the persecution of German Jews from the beginning. He would have appealed to the Christians of America. There would have been no breakdown of Christianity, no timorous laissez-faire policy. He tolerated no intolerance against any people. Of first importance to him always was his role as Mr. Citizen. The minute he wasn't needed before the cameras, you'd find him out in his car, glasses perched on his nose, one earpiece always busted, pecking at his typewriter. He had a voice, he was using it.

Once Bill and I ran against each other for President. The citizens of the District of Columbia can't vote, so they had a gag election. I won, but the fact is, Rogers could have *been* President. If he'd lived he might have been.

So strange, his tragic death. He'd been an enthusiastic air traveler since about 1915. He even got me up in a plane as early as 1919, an open cockpit. He did more flying for this country than anyone save Rickenbacker, Lindbergh, and Wiley Post. He believed in flying to the extent that when Knute Rockne was killed in a plane crash Rogers, in the middle of a picture, begged permission to take off at once to prove that flying wasn't dangerous. He had no interest in parachutes. "If the plane goes, I want to go with it."

He did. Unbelievably, the world was still here and Will Rogers wasn't.

The governor of Oklahoma phoned me soon after. "Would you speak for us at Skelly Stadium in Tulsa? Your friend Will Rogers was to do it, we feel he'd want you to take his place."

It was Citizenship Day and I tried to speak as Bill would have.

To this day, I so often stop and think, "What would Bill do in this situation?" You see, I feel that to live and let live is not enough. You've got to live and *help* live. That's the meaning of citizenship in a democracy. That's what I learned from Mr. American Citizen himself, Will Rogers.

12. Ziegfeld

Rehearsal time on the New Amsterdam Roof. Ford Dabney and his band are playing—I don't hear them. Beautiful girls in short panties are dancing and prancing—I don't see them. Electricians play with lights, carpenters bang on scenery—all I see is a distinguished, gray-haired man with quick discerning eyes. He wears a blue shirt and is chewing a long unlit cigar. He looks to me like all the gods rolled into one. Florenz Ziegfeld! The greatest name in show business and he's just signed me for his unique supper club, The Midnight Frolic—at least that's what *I* think.

My agent, Max Hart, had wired me in California to come at once for a season with Ziegfeld. I left *Canary Cottage*. I'd been dying to leave. I'd been away from home twenty-four weeks, Natalie'd been born, I was so homesick I could hardly stand it. And now I was coming back to this, to Ziegfeld! Like being born again. I rushed from the train to our apartment in the Bronx and told the news to Ida.

"Ida, we've no more worries. Max says Ziegfeld is crazy about me. He says I'll probably go from the Roof to the *Follies*."

So now it's rehearsal time on the New Amsterdam Roof and I'm walking in for the first time, on air.

"Mr. Ziegfeld, I'm *Eddie Cantor*."

He stops talking to the man beside him and grants me a cool, blank look.

"Eddie Cantor," I repeat. "Max Hart . . . my agent . . . Max Hart . . ."

"Oh yes, Max Hart," he says vaguely. "And what do you do?"

"Mr. Ziegfeld! Do I ask you what *you* do?"

He smiles slightly and Gene Buck, his right-hand man, laughs.

"Really, Mr. Ziegfeld, I'm wonderful, you'll see." All this with the audacity of belonging, one of his troupe, a guy who's been signed . . .

"You have music with you?"

Do I have music!

"Give it to Ford Dabney. Girls, relax, take five," he says.

Two minutes later I'm singing, "Oh, How She Could Yacki Hicki Wicki Wacki Woo!" I don't stop. I swing into "Honolulu, America Loves You." I'm twanging a ukulele with two broken strings. It sounds terrible.

"You wouldn't believe it, last week I couldn't play this thing at all." I've swung a string of garlic around my neck. "An Italian lei," I gag, "the breath of a nation."

Mr. Ziegfeld's face never changes. He has a real poker face, something he'd acquired years before, playing poker, roulette . . . but I notice that Gene Buck keeps nudging him, and when I finish the girls applaud. So does the band. I wait.

"Mr. Kiraly'll tell you what time you go on tonight, he'll assign you a dressing room," says Mr. Ziegfeld. That's it.

I rush for the subway, back to the Bronx, tell Ida Ziegfeld thinks I'm a riot, pack my alpaca suit, my straw hat, white glasses and burnt cork, and rush back to the New Amsterdam. I have hours to wait. Part of the time I stand down on the sidewalk, just breathing the air, watching the swells ride up in their Rolls-Royces. The broadcloth gleams, the jewels shine. These people are all going up to the Roof. They're my audience! Let me at 'em!

It wasn't until a quarter to one the next morning that I was on. I stood in the wings watching Joe Frisco and W. C. Fields and Lillian Lorraine. Everyone was wonderful to me. They'd pat my shoulder in passing and say "Good luck, kid." At a quarter to one I heard my opening bar of music and burst out like a fire horse at the four alarm. I wasn't afraid. When you have nothing you can lose nothing. Besides, on the way back from California on the train I'd written ten good minutes of stuff and it was fresh. Very. That's how they billed me, "Eddie Cantor, Fresh From the Bronx."

I started by telling the audience, "Ladies and gentlemen, I'm not a regular actor. I work for a plumber in Hastings and yesterday something went wrong with the plumbing at Mr. Ziegfeld's house. He heard me singing in the bathroom and thought this would be a good gag. So, it doesn't matter if you applaud or not. Tomorrow I go back to plumbing."

The audience smiled. And what a thrill for me after all the cheap bowery theaters to be playing now before the *crème de la crème*, the Vanderbilts, the Harrimans, the Astors! This was the supper club of the Four Hundred, where menus were printed on silk, where it cost the customer five dollars to sit down, and no one could afford to stand up. Here was café society, blasé and *intime*, deigning to be amused; here were Mr. Ziegfeld and Billie Burke sitting at a table with friends. I'd have died to amuse them. But it had to be just right, intimate but not offensive and, my God, not common!

I whipped out a deck of cards and shuffled them like a sleight-of-hand artist. Then, gravely, I approached several guests and asked if they would help me with the act. They were to stand and hold the cards high over their heads so the audience could see them. I didn't even know who the men were. I picked the first because he was so tall—William Randolph Hearst. Another was Diamond Jim Brady. A third, Charles B. Dillingham. They held up the cards, and, ignoring them completely, I started to sing, "Oh, How She Could Yacki Hicki Wicki Wacki Woo . . . She had the hula hula yacka bula in her walk . . ." The men still stood there holding the cards and the audience began to howl, realizing that the cards had nothing to do with the act. After I finished a number of choruses I collected the cards and thanked the gentlemen for their assistance. They were three fine straight men and they were kind enough not to get angry at the gag. I'd taken a big chance; it'd worked. As I gathered up the cards the greatest thing in the world was happening—applause! I had stopped the show! I held up my hand for quiet.

"I may not go back to plumbing after all," I said. "Still, it might be good to have two jobs. Mother needs me now that Dad's gone." I looked sad. "With good behavior he may be out in ten years. You know how it was with Dad. When you work in a bank you just can't take home samples."

That was my first night for Ziegfeld. Next morning I received the first of hundreds of telegrams I was to receive from him: *"Enjoyed your act, you'll be here a long time."*

I went down to see my agent.

He said, "I think you'll be with Ziegfeld a long time."
"Sure. Twenty weeks."
"Longer than that," he said.
"We have a contract, though, for twenty weeks."
"Listen, Eddie, we never had *any* contract until one hour ago."

It was just as well I hadn't known. I played twenty-seven weeks on the Roof and went from there into the *Ziegfeld Follies*. I saw Mr. Ziegfeld constantly and the more I saw him the more I admired him. He was the ultimate, that rare thing, a man with perfect taste. Others gave shows, he gave productions. He was everywhere. He hired actors, okayed songs, selected fabrics, created the ideas for costumes and scenery, found the top people to execute those designs, was an expert on lighting. I watched him but did not know him. His was a reserve that I, with all my audacity, dared not penetrate. Later, ours developed into a warm and close relationship. Billie Burke once told me that of all his boys, Ziegfeld regarded me as a son; but in those early days of the *Follies*, I was frankly in awe of him. He was, in a way no other man ever achieved, a man whose daring and finesse changed the whole picture of Broadway. There was a time when his earnings were fifty thousand dollars a week—that was when *Show Boat, Kid Boots, Annie Dear* and *The Three Musketeers* were playing at once. There were times when he was broke. Money meant nothing to him; it was to spend, and with the taste to spend it, he introduced into the American theater an era of lavishness and glamour that has never been surpassed.

Let me tell you a little about his beginnings. Florenz Ziegfeld came to New York in 1893 when comic opera was neither comic nor opera. The chorus girls were aged wrecks and the boldness of the period was represented in the music halls, where women exposed themselves in long black cotton stockings, tights down to the knees, ruffled petticoats, and billowy skirts. He came to New York not in search of girls but in search of a giant. His dad, Dr. Florenz Ziegfeld, head of the Chicago Musical College, had organized a company to bring continental orchestras to the Chicago World's Fair. Ziegfeld, Sr., was a graduate of the Leipzig Conservatory of Music and a colonel in the Civil War, a man of culture and of discipline, and he expected his son to adhere to both the culture and the discipline. Later Flo was the first to introduce classical music into the American revue, he persuaded Victor Herbert to write all the ballets and finales for the *Follies;* but in those early days he turned a deaf ear to the classics. When his dad introduced the World's Fair series with Hans von Bülow's orchestra from Hamburg and it flopped, Flo wasn't surprised. The backers wanted to withdraw their money before any more orchestras arrived from Europe, but young Flo had another idea. What was needed in the crisis was a strong man. He came to New York to sign up Eugene Sandow, the strong man of Europe, then appearing during intermissions at the Casino Theatre. Abby, Schroefel, and Grau asked a thousand a week for Sandow, Flo had five thousand in the world, so he offered Grau 10 per cent of the receipts and hauled the giant off to Chicago. Dr. Ziegfeld, aghast at this desecration of his temple of art, insisted his name be removed from the front of the house. "Doctor" was removed and "Junior" added. Florenz Ziegfeld, Jr. With Sandow, Junior tried what was to become a magic recipe: one third glamour, one third merit, one third advertising. His wasn't the strongest man in the world, but with the right publicity, with society ladies coming backstage to feel the big muscles, Ziegfeld turned Sandow into another Samson. The giant's 10 per cent amounted to three thousand a week; after the Fair closed Ziegfeld took him to Ringling Brothers.

Florenz Ziegfeld had had his first taste of show business. With more money than he'd ever dreamed of he sailed for Europe, visited Berlin, Paris, and—Monte Carlo. When he arrived in London in 1895, twenty-seven years old, he was broke. He had a sumptuous dinner, tipped the waiter with his last shilling and walked through the fog to meet Charley Evans, formerly of the comedy team of Evans and Hoey, who was taking him to the Palace Music Hall. The show was dreary, the settings poor, the acts humdrum. Then suddenly the stage was transformed. A beautiful girl with soft brown hair was out there alone against the corny backdrop singing "La Marcheuse." She had the quality of a French chanteuse. She sang in Polish, German, Spanish, French, and ended with an English ditty, "Won't You Come and Play Wiz Me?" She was enchanting. Ziegfeld sat transfixed.

"Listen, Charley," he said, when she finally vanished. "If I get this girl to come to America and put her in a show with you, will you team up again with Hoey?"

Evans laughed. Every top producer had tried to sign Anna Held. Ziegfeld was an unknown and he was broke. Yes, indeed, if Flo could sign her, Evans'd go back to Hoey. An hour later Ziegfeld was cabling Diamond Jim Brady for money; he had Anna Held under contract. He'd gone back to her dressing room without a dime and had come out with the contract and much more—with Anna's heart.

Flo's instinct had been exactly right. This girl not only captured the American public, she kept them captured for a generation. His introduction of her was masterly. He didn't star her in her first show. No, indeed. He starred Evans and Hoey, featured Miss Minnie French and Miss Allene Carter, introduced three new faces, and then almost as an afterthought, announced "Also Mlle. Anna Held singing French songs entr'acte." He let the audiences discover Anna, and as they did he let loose a storm of publicity ballyhoo. There was, for example, a lawsuit instituted by a Brooklyn milk dealer for Anna Held's failure to pay for fifty cans of milk delivered two cans daily to the Hotel Marlborough. Who was drinking so much milk? No one, the milk was for Anna Held to *bathe* in. And Ziegfeld refused to allow her to pay for it. The milk was sour, he said, and might injure her exquisite skin.

Thanks to Anna's success, by 1904 Ziegfeld could have retired. He went abroad again—Paris, Biarritz, Trouville, and . . . Monte Carlo. He arrived home broke. Being broke always meant the beginning of something for Zieggy. Once broke, he had found Anna Held. Twice broke, Anna, now his wife, suggested the idea for the *Follies*. "Your American girls are so beautiful, the most beautiful in the world. If you could dress them up chic, charmante, you'd have a better show than the *Folies Bergère*."

On June 9, 1907, the Jardin de Paris, a small variety house perched on the roof of the New York Theatre, announced its weekly vaudeville bill and in small type, "Very soon—the Ziegfeld revue—*Follies of 1907*." With Erlanger to foot the bills, the first *Follies* cost $13,000 for costumes and scenery, $3800 in salaries and overhead. One of the last *Follies* cost $200,000 to produce and $30,000 a week to run. There have never been shows quite like these. This was Ziegfeld's true métier. He was the glorifier of the American girl. His beauties went on to become leaders on stage, screen, and in society. At a time when chorus girls were being paid thirty a week, he paid a hundred and seventy-five and the salaries climbed with the girls' growing glory. And look at the girls! Marilyn Miller, Gladys Glad, Ruth Etting, Evelyn Laye, Marion Davies, Helen Morgan, Ann Pennington, Norma Terris, Marion Shannon, Nita Naldi, Dorothy Mackaill, Lilyan Tashman, Harriet Hoctor, Justine Johnstone, Ina Claire, Peggy Hopkins, to name a few. He would pick one girl for her exquisite form, one girl for her grace, one for her glorious red hair. The redhead would be the only redhead on the stage, her beauty set off like a torch by the surrounding pale silver blondes against a black velvet drop. The magic of his lighting, the elegant costumes, the effects of his ensemble gave the girls something of magic, of spirituality and angelic loveliness.

Veronica, chief costumer who furnished over two and a half million dollars' worth of Ziegfeld dresses, used to reproach him for extravagance. "The audience can't see or appreciate what you spend on the lining of a gown!" And all Ziegfeld dresses were lined, that was the first rule. He'd turn a gown inside out to see how it looked inside. "My girls know," he would answer Veronica. "Beautiful materials, the beautiful feel, makes them more beautiful!" He insisted on the finest ribbons, the most lavish accouterments. He might see the finale and decide to change all the costumes, throw away sixteen thousand dollars' worth of gowns for material of another color.

The beginning of every great Ziegfeld show was a roll of cloth and a strip of canvas. Even before the girls were selected or the performers engaged, Flo would be fingering samples of silk or studying sketches prepared by the great Joseph Urban, his scenic designer. During the production of *Whoopee* I had constant opportunity to watch his methods. Most producers think of a finale in terms of the story or the actors. It's always a perplexing business, the finale. Flo thought of it only in terms of color. "We're going to have a pink finale. Pink and silver." Even I was to be dressed in pink. He loved pink and silver, he loved gold. His sensitive feeling for fabric and color was unique in show business; he handled materials the way a musician would handle his instrument. He spent weeks selecting hats for the chorus of the Wild

West number in *Whoopee*, looking over thousands of shapes and styles and deciding, finally, on the ten-gallon hats which the girls eventually wore . . . although the hats would take three months to be made up and might have delayed the opening.

His feeling for talent was a sure one. Gene Buck had once taken him to see an Andersen fairy tale, *The Garden of Paradise*. It was not much of a show, but the settings were remarkable. They were the work of Joseph Urban, a refugee from war-torn Europe, now in Boston. Ziegfeld wired Urban: "*Can you see me in New York to fix my roof?*" A slightly confusing message to a gentleman who understood no English to start with. The first set Urban prepared for the *Midnight Frolic* consisted of two huge vases and a glittering curtain of pearls. Ziegfeld had asked Urban for "wunderbar"; he got it. Every pearl looked genuine. Urban had designed the curtain using large capsules and spraying them with silver which gave the luster of pearls. He did twenty-nine *Frolics* and then started on the *Follies*. He introduced bridge lights and spotlights. He would set a statue or a vase against a curtain and by playing light on it create a three-dimensional quality. One of his outstanding scenes was the Grand Canyon scene in *Whoopee*. Ziegfeld changed revues from a cheap deal to a rich art and scaled the tickets accordingly, up to $4.40, $5.50, $6.60. He'd auction tickets for *Follies* opening nights; for the *Follies of 1915* Diamond Jim Brady paid $750 for ten ducats.

Flo was equally spectacular in his personal life. He and Anna Held had been divorced in 1913. Shortly after this, at a New Year's Eve party given by the exclusive Sixty Club, he met Billie Burke, newest and youngest of the Frohman stars. Billie today is still one of the most beautiful women I have ever seen, and Ziegfeld was a connoisseur of beauty. On this New Year's Eve he had gone to the party in his favorite disguise, the Harry Watson tramp suit, made up with a pudgy red nose. Gene Buck, who went with him, wore a tin suit he'd been given by Dave Montgomery, the famous Tin Woodman of Oz. As they arrived at the party, there stood Billie and her manager, waiting for their table. Billie's manager murmured the introductions, so Billie didn't even know who this was; he didn't want her to know the "dangerous charm" of Ziegfeld. But the band was playing a waltz, and Ziegfeld took Billie by the hand and led her to the floor. He was one of the best waltzers of his day . . . and the music went on and on, Ziegfeld having slipped the band leader a hundred-dollar bill.

Next day he bought out a flower shop, not only the flowers and plants but even the decorative orange trees in the window. It took a moving van to convey the flowers to Billie's home in Hastings. A week went by and he didn't hear from Miss Burke. When he phoned finally, she said she had tried to reach him but the line was busy. "That will never happen again," Zieggy assured her. "I'm having a private line installed, exclusively for you." He did. The Frohman office was determined to quell the romance, but Ziegfeld finally hired away the manager of her show, Victor Kiraly, and put him in charge of the *Midnight Frolic*. Then he could send notes to Billie, they could meet. Two months later, April 1914, they were married.

He was a great spender; for his daughter Patricia he had a replica of Martha Washington's home built as a playhouse. When free buffaloes were given away in Montana, he ordered one and paid a freight bill of several hundred dollars. When he crossed the ocean in 1922 he paid five and a half thousand for his suite on the ship. In Paris, in a rare fit of economy, he asked American Express to get him four railway tickets to Monte Carlo. When he found the train was sold out he drew a sigh of relief. "Have them put on a private car!"

Budgets were the job of bookkeepers; he was only interested in results. When he put a *Follies* together he assembled top talent regardless of cost: Will Rogers, Fanny Brice, W. C. Fields, Bert Williams—all in one show. As a newcomer to show business, I had seen two *Follies* and regarded them as the best entertainment in the field, something I could never personally dream of. And then one day, there I sat in Mr. Ziegfeld's private office with my agent Max Hart, discussing what I could do in the way of specialties for the *Follies of 1917*. My head was hammering. Mr. Ziegfeld's writers would supply the sketches, but the specialties were my responsibility.

"Mr. Ziegfeld, you'll never regret this," I stammered. "I'll never let you regret it. It's frightening, but, but, I'll do my darnedest."

I did. Bert Williams helped me a great deal. I'd expected possible resentment from Bert. How would he react to another blackface comedian? I couldn't have been more wrong. We had a

Ziegfeld

sketch together in which I was to play his son. We became "Pappy" and "Sonny" on stage and off. He took me right to his big heart and taught me many things. In the matter of timing: "Don't be too anxious for the next line, let 'em laugh." He showed me how to get a hand on an exit. I ad libbed a line—"Mr. Ziegfeld has a method. You make good upstairs on the roof, he brings you down here. Make good here, next year the subway." I had a song— "That's the Kind of a Baby for Me,"—that was good for as many as eleven or twelve encores. Victor had me record it two days after the show opened.

So now I was in the really big time. The *Follies of 1917*, with Will Rogers, W. C. Fields, Fanny Brice, Walter Catlett; the *Follies of 1918*, the *Follies of 1919*, the biggest hit of any *Follies* thus far, with Ann Pennington, Marilyn Miller, Bert Williams, Van and Schenck, Eddie Dowling, Ray and Johnny Dooley; George LeMaire. I introduced "You'd Be Surprised," and other songs of the show were: "Mandy," "Tulip Time," "A Pretty Girl Is Like a Melody." Mr. Ziegfeld was pleased. He began talking to me about a musical comedy in which I would co-star with Marilyn Miller. I'd get one thousand dollars a week and 25 per cent of the profits. But in the middle of the *Follies of 1919* something happened to change all that.

Actors' Equity, of which I was a board member, called a strike. For three or four weeks every show on Broadway was shut down. There was a good reason for the strike. From the beginning, unscrupulous producers had made a practice of rehearsing shows which then flopped. The actors would rehearse for twelve or fifteen weeks without pay, then the play would flop in the first week. Some show girls actually became prostitutes because they were starving. One show rehearsed for fifteen weeks, opened in Atlantic City, moved into New York, and closed two weeks later. As a special favor, the producer "hired" the cast for a new show, rehearsed that for fourteen weeks and flopped the first week. Actors went on like this, sometimes twenty-six weeks without pay! Equity now demanded that no play rehearse more than four weeks, no musical more than five, without pay. They further demanded one eighth salary for extra matinees—anything over eight performances a week. It was customary to schedule extra matinees every time a band played on Fifth Avenue.

A producer like Ziegfeld was not guilty of these sins, but he stood with the other producers in their association against these demands and Equity finally called a strike.

From the *Follies of 1919,* Johnny and Ray Dooley, Eddie Dowling, John Steel and I were the ones who walked. The *Follies* had to close. Even if they could have put on a show without us, the AF of L had joined the strike and tied up the stagehands and electricians. When the strike was over we went back to work. The *Follies of 1919* went on every night as usual, but Ziegfeld didn't speak to me again. He spoke to my agent. He told him the Marilyn Miller show was off. For me, that is. He'd have no more to do with me. He felt that because I was a member of Equity Board I'd had more to do with the strike than the others. When the *Follies* ended, May 1920, I was out of a job. Ziegfeld never even told me good-by.

I went to work for the Shuberts. They had a show, *The Midnight Rounders* playing on the Century Roof. There had been no comedy in this. Now they proposed that I join the *Rounders* and take it on tour while they readied a Winter Garden show for me. It was a trick. We didn't just take the *Rounders* on tour; we played it until the scenery fell apart—ninety weeks. Financially this was a big bonanza for me. I was on a percentage that ran my salary to two and three, four times what I'd made with Ziegfeld. But I'd have gone back gladly. Mr. Ziegfeld was class. The Shuberts were just show business. Sometimes I'd put out a feeler to Max Hart, but he'd say, "Don't be silly. Ziegfeld won't have you."

My next Shubert show was *Make It Snappy*. We snapped right through this one from start to finish and after one season at top speed, it snapped, period. Still the show attracted capacity audiences. When we played Chicago, Ziegfeld's *Sally* was in a theater across the street. One of the reviewers wrote, "Eddie Cantor at $3.30 a seat is better entertainment value than Marilyn Miller and Leon Errol at $4.40." I tore that out of the paper and read it again. This was something I wanted Ziegfeld to see. He was in Palm Beach. I took a full-page ad in *Variety* and ran the comment in big type. The ad ran on Friday; I figured it would reach Palm Beach by Monday.

"Ida," I said, showing her the ad, "Ziegfeld'll call me, Tuesday the latest."

"Eddie! How do you know?"

"I know. The idea of a fellow of his working for someone else and getting that kind of a plug in opposition to a show of his own'll burn him up. Even if he doesn't like me. Besides, time's a great healer."

Tuesday at noon the phone rang. I was at the Congress Hotel, Chicago. December 3, 1923. "Eddie Cantor, Palm Beach calling." I did a shuffle beside the phone and gave Ida a high sign. Then a high nasal voice came on the wire:

"Eddie, Ziegfeld. How are you?"

I was fine.

"What are your plans for next season?"

"I've a couple of things in mind. What about you?"

"I'll stop by Chicago next week on my way back from Florida," he said. Not a word about the strike or ill-feeling. He wanted me for next season and we discussed ways and means of finding a show for me, a musical comedy, which is what I wanted. No more revues, a musical comedy. I was leaping. As soon as I closed with the Shuberts I leaped back to Broadway.

One day I ran into a song writer named Joe McCarthy (no relation to the guy from Wisconsin), a great song writer. "Eddie," he said, "I hear you're going back with Ziegfeld. I think I have a show for you, not really a show, but an idea and a song. The title—*Kid Boots*. The show is about a caddy master at a country club who bootlegs on the side; but they can't fire him because he's got something on every member of the club." I left Joe and ran to Ziegfeld's office. He was intrigued. The idea was good and Joe McCarthy had quite a reputation; he'd written "Alice Blue Gown," "I'm Always Chasing Rainbows," and the lyrics for "Irene." We got hold of a playwright, William Anthony McGuire, and he started writing. After two weeks he got stuck, so we got someone to work with him, Otto Harbach, one of the top librettists and lyricists in the business. Harbach and McGuire worked on the book, McCarthy and his composer, Harry Tierney, worked on the songs; they turned out a wonderful show. And then, something terrible happened . . .

Ziegfeld, who knew all about production and scenery and lighting and girls, knew nothing about comedy. We'd been rehearsing for three weeks when Ziegfeld came up to me after a rehearsal.

"Eddie," he said, "let's call it off. The show's no good. We'll find something else for you. Before we go to the expense of costumes and sets, let's call it off."

I argued. He was insistent. And right then and there I gave what I'll always consider the best performance of my life: I did the whole show, *Kid Boots*. I jumped on sofas, rolled on the floor, went through the hilariously funny scenes, crying, really crying—the scene where the golf pro plays in a match and gets the crooked ball the caddy master is in the habit of slipping to customers when they are beginning to play too well. (The caddy master did this so the customers would take more lessons, but now the pro, Kid Boots's pal, gets the crooked ball by mistake.) Scene after scene, until it was time for the imaginary curtain and I stood there waiting for the verdict. Ziegfeld still wasn't sold. But it obviously mattered so much to me that he gambled, still thinking it a flop.

We opened in Detroit to the damnedest first night you've ever seen. When the first-act curtain fell to cheers, Ziegfeld, director Edward Royce, and I took hands and danced "ring-around-a-rosy" like three kids. The second act was better than the first. Usually an opening night runs till midnight, then the work starts: the cutting, realigning, smoothing the thing into final tempo. But that night in Detroit *Kid Boots* ran like a dream. The curtain rang down at eleven twenty-five. Two encore dances were to be cut, that was all; a perfect show.

Ziegfeld assembled the entire company and addressed them gravely. "I want to warn you against wiring or phoning anyone in New York. We don't want anyone to know what kind of a hit we have. It will only make it harder to live up to expectations. Let's just surprise 'em." Then he added, "If a single telegram is sent to New York about the show, it will mean instant dismissal." Despite the admonition, I called Ida. But true to my boss, all I said was, "You were worried about buying the new coat? You can get it!" (Later that same night Ziegfeld phoned and wired all the critics in New York.) After dismissing the rest of the company he asked Harland Dixon and Marie Callahan to wait. Their comic dance hadn't come off as it had at rehearsal when they'd rolled all over each other on the stage. He grabbed Dixon and started showing him how it should be done; he rolled all over the stage like a baggy-pants clown until the routine was just as he wished it. Then he gravely dusted off his trousers and he and I went to a Chinese restaurant for supper.

"Well, Mr. Ziegfeld," I said, "you should be pleased."

"Eddie," he said, "from now on I'm not Mr. Ziegfeld. I'm Flo. I'm Zieggy."

Our close friendship started from that night. Because I'd believed in *Kid Boots* and it was a hit, there was never a thing I said to him from then on that he didn't accept seriously. We sat in the Chinese restaurant waiting for our food. Ziegfeld took out a pencil and started figuring on the back of the menu. Suddenly he started to laugh. Mr. Poker Face, Mr. Ice Water began to laugh uproariously.

"Look, Eddie." He laughed. "I just figured—if we sell out every performance, I'll only lose twelve hundred dollars a week."

It was true. I've already said that he spared no expense in production and he paid fantastic salaries. For one scene in *Kid Boots*, the scene in the ladies' locker room, he wanted a tall, handsome woman to play the part of Dr. Fitch, the club physical director. The gimmick for the scene was this: liquor was being stolen from the lockers and no one could find the culprit.

As the scene opens, Boots, the caddy master, goes through the ladies' locker room, opens a locker, takes out a bottle, opens another locker, takes out a bottle. Just then, enter Dr. Fitch.

"Boots, *what* are you doing here?"

The audience howls.

"I'm sick," I mutter.

"Where?"

"In the ladies' locker room!"

"Get on the table," commands the lady doctor. Boots climbs up on the osteopathic table and Dr. Fitch proceeds to take him apart. For the small part of Dr. Fitch, Ziegfeld hired Jobyna Howland, a star in her own right, and paid her about fifteen hundred dollars a week. The same with every small detail all the way down the line. So now with a smash hit, he stood to make less than anyone in the show; he stood to lose twelve hundred dollars a week. The only thing to do was to make another deal with Carroll for the theater where we were to open in New York. I should mention here that after the New York run was under way and *Boots* a tremendous success, Flo threw out the scenery and costumes of the first-act finale and replaced them at a cost of twenty thousand dollars!

He made a change in my clothes before we ever got to New York. For the Detroit opening I'd played Boots in exaggerated knickers, a huge sweater, and a funny cap. Over the chow mein he said, "Eddie, let me get you some other clothes for tomorrow. You don't need funny clothes. You're funny. The words are funny. Don't try to help it." He was right. He bought me a pair of cashmere knickers, a sweater that fit, a good-looking cap, and the laughs were not only just as big, they were bigger. (The well-dressed Boots called the caddies together and told 'em off. "We've had a lot of trouble with lost balls. Balls are always getting lost and people think you steal 'em. Remember, a ball is never lost until it stops rolling!")

We opened in New York on New Year's Eve; the seats were priced at $16.50. Flo said he didn't scale them higher because for the 1923 *Follies* he charged twenty-two dollars a seat and I attended the première equipped with a wrench, a hammer, and saw. Just before the overture started, I began banging and hacking at my seat and when an usher rushed to stop me, I cried, "Let me alone, I paid twenty-two dollars for this seat and I'm taking it home!"

At any rate, we opened on New Year's Eve. Flo and Billie were going to a party afterward, so Flo left his tux in my dressing room and dressed there. When he walked out that night he put his arm around my shoulders. "I won't see you at midnight, Eddie, Happy New Year." There were tears in my eyes. All my life I'd longed for a father, and now, of all the men in the world, Ziegfeld was treating me like a son. On my make-up shelf he'd left a bottle of fine old wine and a note. The night *Kid Boots* played its one thousandth performance Flo gave me a shell-thin platinum watch.

Which doesn't mean he didn't heckle me. I've mentioned that he was a great writer of telegrams. As a matter of fact I'll go further, he fought the battle of show business, against comedians, costumers, scene designers, authors, composers, press agents and rival producers, armed with the telephone and the telegram. At 6 A.M. he'd start phoning his press agents, managers, actors, and authors who had probably gone to sleep an hour before. He'd want an Indian scene written so that his girls could walk in trailing feathers four yards long . . . There'd be a picture in the paper of a girl with superb legs. Find her . . . Earl Carroll had been named to judge the beauty contest in Atlantic City. It should be Ziegfeld. Fix it (forgetting that he had publicly stated that the contest was fixed and the judges were furious with him). Other revues were springing up and stealing his girls. He was sensitive about his position as dictator of the revue world and fought to keep his girls at any price. And always and always he bombarded girls, actors, everyone, with telegrams.

He often stood at the back of the orchestra during a rehearsal, and instead of calling out his criticisms or suggestions, he'd go into the lobby and send actors telegrams backstage. His wires had a style of their own. He often would start a wire: *"Dear Eddie, yours of the seventh received . . ."* If his first words were, *"I don't want to annoy you,"* you could expect a message loaded with complaints. If he ended with, *"This closes the incident,"* you'd be sure to get daily telegrams on the same subject for the rest of the season, beginning, *"There's no use crying over spilt milk but . . ."*

While we were playing *Kid Boots* in Chicago, I received a twelve-page telegram with suggestions about changing certain lines, taking out a song, certain scenes needed watching, certain actors were sloughing their lines, the whole message such a jumble of ideas that I knew here could begin the world's longest correspondence in telegraphy. So I wired back, simply, *"Yes."*

Instead of stopping the avalanche I prompted one. Next came a telegram twice as long, ending, *"What do you mean 'yes'? Do you mean yes you will take out the song, or yes you will put in the lines, or yes you will fix that scene? Or yes you have talked to those actors?"* To this I wired back, "No."

Toward the end of every season, as the actors' contracts began to expire they would get bewildering reams of telegrams from Zieggy, scolding and criticizing them so that anyone who was planning to ask for a raise would be glad to sign again on the old terms. Once he shot me a couple of stinging messages and I wired back my resignation. He wired immediately that he was only kidding, but I didn't see the joke. The next thing I knew, my pay had been boosted a thousand a week for the rest of the season, twenty more weeks. That one telegram had cost him twenty thousand dollars. Then I did see the joke!

The one real argument we had concerned my playing benefits. He felt that by working so hard and playing benefits I was jeopardizing a million-dollar show. "You'll peter out," he said. I'd promise not to, and then play the benefits anyhow. Once he caught me.

"I understand, Eddie, that you're going to appear at the Waldorf ballroom midnight tomorrow."

"Me?" I said. "Don't be silly. After a show like this? I'm going home to bed."

Comes midnight, I walk out on the stage at the Waldorf and there sitting right in front, are Zieggy and Billie Burke. Zieggy looks pretty grim. I kill myself to make him laugh and finally get a smile. How? I look down at him and say, "It's not me!"

I was with Flo the night *Show Boat* opened. I'd been with him at many dress rehearsals and openings. I loved to be with him and he seemed to like having me. He certainly knew he could always get an honest opinion. On such a day we'd get to the theater early and stay all day. Coffee'd be brought in, more coffee, no food until after the show. I've seen him work twenty hours through a dress rehearsal, from two in the afternoon until the next morning, his coat off, his cigar glowing. Numbers were done over and over at his request. Spots for specialties were switched, musical cues adjusted. If costumes didn't harmonize with the scene, they were thrown out. He would call instructions for the lighting of scenes; "Blue foots up on dimmer at start of overture . . . white and amber foots up on dimmer at the end . . . all lamps flood until finish . . . dim down to blue and white one quarter up and palm curtains open."

In *Show Boat* he had sacrificed his own ideas of glorification and used the realistic effects urged by Kern and Urban. It was something different from what he had done. There was an electric quality about *Show Boat*. It was a combination of so many talents. Jerome Kern had been crazy about the book from the day he read it, and wanted to meet Edna Ferber. Hammerstein introduced them and the first thing Kern asked was had Edna ever considered her book as a play? Edna had. The three of them put their heads together, they'd gone South to get the feel of the atmosphere, and now here it was. There was a feeling of excitement—messengers with telegrams, flowers, electricians adjusting lights, actors rehearsing last-minute bits, wardrobe women mending last-minute tears, the stage manager shouting orders, the orchestra tuning up. Only one man unperturbed, as if he were alone in the theater. Ziegfeld's sure eye was watching every detail, a dress too short, a spot too blue. Finally the performance itself. We stood at the back, as he always stood, the only calm person in the place, and as the curtain went down to a tremendous ovation, he said, "I think that's gonna be all right."

When *Kid Boots* closed Ida and I went to Europe for our first vacation. How different from our honeymoon when we were afraid to spend a cent! This time, when we came home a yacht steamed out to meet us flying the banner of *Kid Boots*. The company, headed by George Olsen and his band, had sailed out to give us a welcome. As we drew near, they struck up "Eddie, Steady" and Ethel Shutta led the company in song. I went on the road with *Boots;* after it closed, Hollywood.

My next show for Ziegfeld was the *Follies of 1927*. I wasn't feeling well, the years of activity had suddenly avalanched and I found myself with pleurisy and unable to get any life insurance. I still had three years to run in my contract with Flo and he agreed that if I'd star in this *Follies*, he'd cut a year off my contract. I lost a year from the contract and five from my life. I was the only star in that show. I was on all the time. One night I stepped outside to get a breath of air. The doorman looked at me and laughed. "Don't let Ziegfeld see you, he'll have you selling programs in the lobby." The two most popular skits in the show were the "Taxicab" skit and the Mayor Walker take-off. It was a very funny show but the toughest. Imagine carrying two full hours of a two-and-a-half-hour revue!

In the middle of the *Follies* run I developed a relapse of pleurisy and my doctor insisted I leave the show. Zieggy was at his Canadian camp on Lake Edwards and when I wired him, he wired back: *"If you're tired take a few days off."* When I explained that it wasn't a matter of being tired but of being ill, for some strange reason he didn't believe me. He seemed to think I was shamming. He knew that both Zukor and Lasky had made me film offers and he somehow got it into his head that I wanted to go back to Hollywood. He sent me a long indignant wire, bristling with reproaches. Then his mood changed and he wired: *"I* have always treated you like a father who dearly loved his child but you are a naughty expensive child trying to ruin me. Now Eddie, before it's too late, be a good boy. Your brokenhearted father."

I suggested to Actors' Equity that they send me to Ziegfeld's own doctor and they did. The doctor examined me and said, "If he were my patient, I'd send him away for six months." Now Flo believed. He was willing to close the show and bid me Godspeed. He wired: "*Caught a little bear at six this morning. Shall I bring him for your kids? Love and kisses. Your father, Flo.*"

I had a good rest, cut up touches at Battle Creek Sanitarium, Ziegfeld welcomed me back with open arms, and we started hunting for a show. This was when I suggested putting *The Nervous Wreck* to music. I felt completely qualified to play it, I'd been rehearsing in doctors' offices and sanitariums for over a year. But the beginning of every production was a time of uncertainty, doubt, and indecision for Flo. So many factors are involved in a show, and like an alchemist mixing elements, he never seemed to know which elements had caused the gold to appear.

Often he thought shows sure flops. He once wired Bill McGuire that he was in the worst predicament of his life, he had three flops on his hands. These were merely *Show Boat, Rosalie,* and *The Three Musketeers*. McGuire wired back; "*Please accept my condolences in this, your darkest hour of success.*" At first he thought the part of the Nervous Wreck too "straight" a part for me, then he finally agreed that it was the thing and, true to his tradition, started out with a lavish hand, paying more royalties than for any three other shows combined, for authors, song writers, dance director, and the original owners of the play.

Bill McGuire was to adapt the book. He had promised Zieggy a rough draft in three weeks. Ten weeks passed and no book. On the first day of rehearsal he brought in the first scene and we rehearsed ad tedium. Bill came in with the second scene just before we died of suspense. For the next three weeks Bill directed the book by day and wrote new scenes by night but he never did catch up, and two hours before we opened in Pittsburgh we still didn't have a finale.

Mad excitement! While McGuire was trying to finish the show, I walked around Pittsburgh with two featured players, trying to appease them about their billing. I talked so much in the damp, cold air, I lost my voice.

Ziegfeld had been completely immersed with scene designer Urban and the pink and silver finale. Now he dropped everything, rounded up the leading throat specialist of Pittsburgh, who was just recovering from an automobile accident, helped the doctor dress, and all but carried him to my hotel at 2 A.M. The specialist worked over me most of the night and my voice was back in time for opening night. Despite the confusion, *Whoopee* was a smash from the start. It was much too long, but no one wanted to relinquish a line, and Zieggy was easygoing. We played it that way for two weeks until in desperation, after seeing the audience come at eight-thirty and leave "two days later," we cut forty-five minutes from the show.

In *Whoopee* Flo produced one of his most magnificent scenes, the Indian reservation, with beauties in long feather headdresses, riding down the mountainside on white horses. We had two hit songs, "Makin' Whoopee" and "Love Me or Leave Me." We had a fine new singer, Ruth Etting, and a lot of fun. The Pittsburgh opening was on Election Eve, 1928, and while we played that town Flo was in the audience every night with friends. This was always an added incentive to me. I wanted to panic him as much as I wanted to panic the audience. One night when he was out front I started improvising in a scene with Spencer Charters. I asked him if he'd ever had an operation.

"Yes," he said.

"Where?"

He pulled up his shirt. I pulled up my shirt. We compared scars. "I paid a thousand dollars for this operation," I said.

"I paid two thousand," he said.

"Two thousand! Let's see it again." Peering more closely. "Oh, no wonder, you got hemstitching. And a zipper!"

The scene became very funny. Now Flo had a poker face and he seldom showed enthusiasm or emotion of any kind. That night was the only time I ever saw him rock with laughter. He came backstage, wiping his eyes. "Eddie, you ought to do more of that. It's the funniest thing in the show."

We moved into New York, into our biggest joint success. One

spring day we were being massaged on adjoining tables when Flo said,

"I was just thinking, Eddie, how lucky you are. You have a family, you have money. You're in the biggest hit in New York, working for the biggest producer in the world. You've got everything."

I thought a minute. "No, Flo, not everything. I haven't a Rolls-Royce."

He laughed but I was serious. "Remember, when I was first working for you, thirteen years ago on the Roof . . . I used to stand downstairs and watch people drive up in their Rolls-Royces! I'd dream how it would feel to have one."

That was Tuesday. After the Saturday matinee Zieggy said, "Let's have dinner at Dinty Moore's, I'll meet you out front."

I washed the black off my face, met Zieggy, and we started down the street. At Forty-sixth, against the curb, was a brand new Rolls-Royce, gray, convertible . . . It was gorgeous, you couldn't help but notice. An orchid was tied to the handle of the door, and a card.

"Read the card," Flo said. So I did. The card said,

"Eddie, now you have everything. Flo."

I had a chauffeur and I rode in the jump seat, breezy but great, like the rich people, even when the stock market was crashing.

Whoopee could have run on indefinitely, but Ziegfeld had been hurt by the crash, too, and was glad to sell the movie rights to Sam Goldwyn, and himself as part of the contract to act as an advisory consultant on the picture. There was little for him to do. We moved out to the studio in Hollywood, virtually rang up the curtain, and did the same show we'd been doing. It was my first talking picture and an exciting experience for me. For Flo it was a letdown. Here was a man who was a potentate, who had created a domain and ruled it. Now, suddenly, he had little to do. But the advent of talkies had interested him in Hollywood as he had never been interested before—to the extent that he allowed me to call in a friend of mine to act as his agent and help promote a position for Flo in a major studio. Any studio would have engaged him save for one thing—they feared his fabulously expensive tastes. They missed a bet. Flo Ziegfeld would have been a great movie producer, and if his hand was lavish, it had the taste to make the money count.

In Hollywood he was temporarily reunited with three of his "favorite boys"—Will Rogers, Bill Fields, and myself—"The Three Musketeers" he had named us back in 1917 when we all became fast friends working together in his *Follies*. Outside of that, for him the Hollywood interlude was a bust.

We previewed *Whoopee* in San Diego. En route to the theater Flo said, "Eddie, this isn't the place for you. Come back to New York with me. We'll do another show." "Wait till we see the picture, Flo. If I squeeze your hand, you can start getting a new *Follies* ready." But the picture was a success. And working in pictures I could make in six weeks what I'd made in a year—important to a guy who'd recently lost his shirt.

Flo loved New York and went back to it, but he never recovered from the crash. He'd been broke before, yes, but there were always men who would back him to the hilt. After 1929 and 1930 no one had that kind of money.

And there was no more credit. Costumers charged him twice as much as they charged anyone else. "If he pays half," they figured, "we'll break even. If he pays a fourth, we'll at least have the prestige." I came in from the coast one time, went to his office, opened the door—and found him at his desk with his head in his arms. He was broke, he said, he was at the end of his rope. Then he told me all about it. He had a show in rehearsal and no money to take it on the road. While we talked, the music was playing, the girls were kicking, but . . . $84,000 was still needed for scenery, costumes and expenses.

"Eddie," Flo said, "I'm through."

I rushed out to the telephone in the hall and called Ida.

"Ida, don't ask me why. Go to the Bank of Manhattan, take your safe-deposit key with you. You'll find a hundred thousand-dollar bills. Bring them to me at the theater."

When Ida came backstage she was trembling. She couldn't imagine . . .

"Ida, this is what Flo needs to put on his show. We may never get the money back, it depends on how the show goes."

"Well," she said, "just figure it's a hundred thousand less than you got from Mr. Ziegfeld, through the years."

I blessed her and ran in to the theater where the rehearsal was going on. The show was *Hotcha*. Flo paid us back five thousand dollars a week for twenty weeks and closed the show.

The Great Glorifier was getting tired. Behind the scenes of his last *Follies* tragedy was lurking. Employees contributed money toward the production. Billie Burke did all she could to relieve the financial strain. Radio might have saved him, but it came along too late. He did present the *Follies* on the air, a half hour every Sunday night; and with Eddie Dowling as master of ceremonies and program arranger, it was a fine show. Most of the old stars appeared on the program from time to time; and all of us listened in, hearing his thin voice with deep feeling.

He became gravely ill and when he was partially better, was sent West to recover. He never did. I was working in *Roman Scandals* when word reached me that he had arrived and was at Cedars of Lebanon Hospital. I rushed to the hospital to be greeted by his man, Sidney. The boss was resting, Sidney said. The next day he was dead. All of us who had known, loved, and venerated him, were stunned. Will Rogers and I helped with arrangements for his funeral and sat there, with Billie Burke, surrounded by Ziegfeld beauties and Ziegfeld friends, all united in a sense of loss. A great man of the theater had passed from the scene and no one would ever take his place. As if to make the moment more unbearable, the minister used his name every two seconds and pronounced it *Zigfield!*

I have always treasured the last note from Flo, written in pencil on three sheets of plain pad paper, twenty-five days before his death. He had triple-color embossed stationery but he always wrote personal notes in his large angular scrawl on slips and scraps of paper or on a telegraph blank. He wrote:

"Dear Eddie . . . what are your plans? *Show Boat* is doing wonderful." He was referring to the revival at the Casino. "And my cast with Dennis King and Paul Robeson is perfect. Doctors demand I take eight weeks' rest—no business. I may come West. You could go into the Casino and get big dough. Wire me your intentions." And then he added, "Would like to do another show with you before I pass on. Love to all . . . Flo."

13. W. C. Fields

Most people learn to read in school. Not me. I didn't discover books until I was twenty-five, and the self-made scholar who introduced me to the classics of literature was "Professor" Wilbur Claude Dukenfield. W. C. Fields to you.

We met in 1917, my first day of rehearsal for the *Ziegfeld Follies*. I was pretty cocky. I'd tasted blood. I'd been good enough on the Roof to make the big show and I reported for rehearsal in jig time. But when I was introduced to a sandy-haired fellow with a nasal drawl, I was so scared I shook. Fields had been big in vaudeville for some time. I'd seen him with McIntyre and Heath in *The Ham Tree*, or rather, I'd seen McIntyre and Heath with *him*, for Fields in whiskers and a tramp suit managed to dominate the show. And he was always sort of a miracle to me, a pantomimist who could make audiences scream without a word.

What he saw in me, I don't know. Perhaps the fact that I, like himself, had been miserably poor and miserably hungry and had scrambled into show business from nothing. Fields had been beaten so by his father that he left home at eleven. He'd had a bitter and unhappy youth, but now he had nothing left to be bitter about. He was a success, he knew it; and his cynicism about life was balanced by a wonderful warmth. He and Will Rogers were friends and they took me in from the first.

At every rehearsal Fields'd call me aside and make suggestions. "You don't have to bang that line over, boy. When you're on stage with Bert Williams there's no other place for the audience to look except at you and Bert. You don't have to grab the audience by the collar." He told me enough about pantomime so that sometimes I could get a thing over with a gesture, a technique that stood me in good stead when I got to the *Follies of 1919* with a skit called "The Osteopath." Here for the first time I was able to depend on pantomime.

Whenever I made a grammatical error Fields would correct me. He briefed me, too, on Ziegfeld and money. "When we play Columbus at the end of the run, Ziegfeld'll start sending you critical telegrams, he'll criticize you to the point where you'll be glad to work next year for the same money you got this year. Don't be fooled like I was. You're working for four hundred dollars this year, hold out for six hundred."

When the 1917 *Follies* went on tour he suggested we share hotel accommodations on the road. Don't think I wasn't proud! We opened in Boston, the Colonial Theatre. The show was a hit, we went back to our suite at the Touraine Hotel, and in the living room were three buckets of champagne. Fields brought out a couple of glasses and said, "Here you are, son. Let's drink to your health." We kept drinking to my health till we damn near ruined it. By 3 A.M. I was the sickest-looking owl you ever saw. Fields was fine. I never did see him drunk. From that night on, whenever we'd go into a restaurant he'd tell the waiter, "Give the boy with the big eyes a little milk. He's got a weak constitution." From that night, too, he gave up trying to teach me the refinements of drinking and turned his attention to another phase of my education.

In his room at the hotel were three huge theatrical trunks. I'd noticed them and wondered, for Fields wasn't a dandy about dress. A few nights after we got to Boston he started talking to me about literature. Books were the keys to another world; you didn't know anything until you'd started to read. He went over to one of the big trunks and flipped back the lid. Not a thing in it but books! What he was looking for wasn't in that trunk, so he flipped the lid of the next one, fished out a copy of *Oliver Twist* and gave it to me. The next night when we got back after the show and had ordered up some food, he sat and questioned me about what I'd read. "Just why did Nancy feel any loyalty to Bill Sykes?"

Night school had started. After *Oliver Twist*, *Les Miserables*. We traveled together with the 1917 *Follies* and again with the *Follies of 1918* and I kept on reading: Dickens, Hugo, Dumas, Eliot, the works; and discussing them with Professor Fields. In the morning we'd have a session with the newspapers. It wasn't enough to read the story; what was behind it? The man had an amazing reading background. He was up on science, he was up on history; if he were alive today he'd murder them on the quiz programs. And he'd never had formal schooling. One time I asked him how he'd done it.

"Simple," he drawled, "simple, my boy. Started making some money and bought this trunk. Drove up to a bookstore with the trunk on a truck, carted the trunk into the store, and told the clerk to fill it up. 'With what?' the clerk asked. 'With whatever a fellow like me should read.' Two hours later I was on my way with a trunk full of knowledge." Using the same patience with which he'd acquired his skill at juggling, he acquired an education. He read rapidly and had a retentive memory. The first time he went to Australia he stopped off in San Francisco and bought every available book on Australia. In those days it took three or four weeks to get across. By that time Fields was equipped to be a hero before they'd even seen his act. One reporter wrote, "This American knows more about us than we know about ourselves."

The independence of the man made itself manifest in everything he did. He didn't need teachers, he was his own. And his own doctor. As a young man playing the European circuit he'd developed tuberculosis. The verdict—he'd have to quit working for at least a year or he'd be dead. "If I wasn't working I'd starve to death anyhow," he rasped; so he took over on the medical front. His first prescription was an open car, and with the exception of the time he was sleeping or on stage, he was in this car. His second prescription was good food. The third prescription, good wine. He not only cured himself of tuberculosis but established a pattern of behavior that lasted all his life. In his later years the third prescription got out of hand. As he once said, when he'd donated a pint of blood to the Red Cross, "The doctor opined my blood was very helpful. Contained so much alcohol they could use it to sterilize their instruments."

When we were on tour we never traveled by train. It was always in Fields's open Cadillac. Sometimes we'd have Fanny Brice with us and, Bessie Poole, Fields's girl during the *Follies* years. When the weather was mild Bill'd have the luggage compartment loaded with groceries and we'd stop in an open field and have a picnic. He had all the equipment Lewis & Conger stocks, the baskets, the thermos jugs. He'd build a fire and fry potatoes and broil steaks. It was fine traveling in good weather, but he didn't care what the weather, rain or shine. You don't know what cold is until you've traveled across country at seventy miles an hour in zero weather in Fields's open car. Fanny, Bessie, and I'd turn blue with cold while our host drove on, admiring the rigors of nature, declaiming on health and the state of the nation, all wrapped up in his big fur coat and heated from within. When my knees started knocking he'd wrap newspapers around my legs and fasten them with rubber bands. There was to be no talk about trains; fairies rode on trains. We'd stop for dinner along the way and Fields would have a couple of martinis. In him a couple of martinis had the same effect as one usher in Radio City Music Hall!

He could be genial; he was quick to fury. Leaving Washington we came out of the theater carrying suitcases. I came out first and a couple of college boys standing at the stage door shoved me one to the other so I fell over the bags. Fields emerged like a lion. He seized one fellow by the collar, lifted him off the ground, and shook him to a roar of expletives not printable. Then the other.

Everything about him was robust—the voice that had cracked when he was a kid sleeping in winter in the open, the heart, the mentality and the sense of humor. He'd been a man of the world for so long that beside him everyone else was a square.

My favorite of all his stories is this: He told me how, when he'd been in Europe in the early 1900s, it was customary for an act to play a theater not just for a week but for two, even three months. There was the Wintergarten in Berlin, the Folies Bergère in Paris, the China Theatre, Stockholm; the Palace, London. When you finished at one place you'd go on and get bookings at the next. However . . . it often happened that a local actor would catch your act, watch every performance, practice, and while you were still at the Wintergarten in Berlin he'd beat you to a booking in another theater. The only redress was to break the guy's jaw if you ever caught up with him.

Fields, at that time, was doing his famous pool-table act, one of the funniest ever seen in show business. He would come on stage, chalk up his cue, hit one ball, and immediately every ball on the table would go right into a pocket. This was something that had grown out of his experience working in a pool hall when he was thirteen years old, his first job after he'd decided to "go straight." He had studied the solemn manners of the pool-hall habitués, the cautious choosing of a cue, the religious chalking, the holy hush before the shot—all of it had struck him funny. Also, he had become an expert at the game. So now he's playing the Wintergarten in Berlin. He's in his third or fourth week and he walks into the theater one afternoon to pick up his mail. What does he hear—the clicking of billiard balls! He peeks in on the stage and there is another actor from the same bill, a fellow who worked with a very pretty girl, his wife, practicing Fields's act. Fields watches for an hour while the guy goes through his routine with the billiard balls. Of course he knows what's going to happen.

"What did you do?" I asked. "Did you hit him?"

"No, Eddie, no, that seemed not at all polite. I thought the matter over and decided what's fair is fair. He took my act, I had an affair with his wife."

He was a great practical joker and several times I was the butt. The first time, I rushed into the theater late, started to dress, and discovered I couldn't get into the trousers of my black alpaca suit. Bill'd had the wardrobe woman sew up the fly. That was nothing. When the *Follies of 1918* hit Buffalo, there was a party after the show at the home of Jack "Twin" Sullivan. The ex-prize fighter was a good friend of Fields and of Rogers. We got out to the house starved and clamoring for food. Sullivan said, "Here it comes," and out came a steaming platter of pork chops. Everyone started to eat but me.

"Come on, Eddie, dig in," roared Fields.

I muttered something about never eating late at night.

"He's a damned liar," said Fields.

So I admitted I never ate pork chops.

Sullivan ordered the cook to bring out something else and I waited hungrily. When the cook emerged with a plate of eggs scrambled with *ham* I shook my head again and begged off.

"Let the boy starve," drawled my friend.

And I probably would have if Bert Williams hadn't whispered, "Sonny, look in my overcoat pocket. There's a package for you." It was a steak and Bert cooked it himself. He'd heard Fields and Rogers framing me that afternoon, so he had come to the rescue.

Fields's second joke on me was far more successful. We were

playing Boston, the World Series was on, and I bet everyone in the company on the New York team. We won the Series and when I walked in that night I collected from the conductor, the chorus boys, several of the principals, everyone. I must have collected six or seven hundred dollars. As we're changing, Rogers is yelling across to Fields, "Whitey, remember when Sam Hardy won that bet, the party he threw?" Fields yells back, "Yes, that was an elegant soiree indeed. And remember when Sam Hardy bought champagne on his ill-gotten gains?" They keep on hinting, asking where am I throwing the party, until I finally get to thinking maybe I should. So I ask Bert Williams, Rogers, Bill Fields, and Bessie, about ten people all together, to a little party at the Georgian after the show. Fields says, "Son, I don't want you to spend your affluence foolishly, but I think it would be handsome to post a notice on the bulletin board and invite the whole company."

"That's sixty people, Bill!"

"At five dollars a head, three hundred dollars. Not half what you have accrued."

I think about it, decide Bill's right, it's a nice gesture, so I put the note on the bulletin board, inviting the company. At the end of the show the manager calls everyone around and says, "You all know Eddie's giving a party. Everybody be there or there'll be an early-morning rehearsal." That surprises me a little, but I'm glad people are getting into the spirit of the thing. Bill Fields says, "Entrust it to me, Eddie. I'll make the arrangements."

I'm the last to get to the Georgian because I have to remove my blackface make-up. As I come in, they give me a big hand and I'm feeling pretty good about it, like a sport. Just then, a bellboy pages me, I'm wanted on the phone. I go to the booth and a voice says . . .

"Mr. Cantor, I'm with the Goodyear Rubber Company. As you may know, we're having a convention here next week and we want you to come and entertain us."

I explain that I'm doing a show, it's late when we finish, and I don't usually go out afterward.

"You understand, we'll pay you, Mr. Cantor."

Still I'm not eager. I have to bring a piano player, I'm a pretty high-priced fella . . .

"Would five hundred dollars be all right?" he says.

When I'm making six hundred dollars a week? Five hundred would be just fine.

"We'll expect you at the Copley-Plaza ballroom at midnight Wednesday."

When I return to the party every table has a bucket of champagne, they are toasting me, and the party is getting under way. My bill that night runs high enough to take all the money I'd won on the Series, but what do I care? I'm a hero and I'll collect this extra five hundred from Goodyear.

Comes Wednesday, I'm hurrying to get away from the theater and Bill Fields offers to go with me. I explain I'm entertaining a convention, I have to dash. By midnight exactly, the piano player and I are at the Copley-Plaza. The place is dark, the ballroom empty. No one at the hotel has heard of the Goodyear Rubber convention. I get back to the hotel, still puzzled, wondering if I've gotten my dates mixed. And then suddenly Fields starts talking, not in his usual nasal style, but in another voice entirely, the voice I'd heard on the phone, "Mr. Cantor, I'm with the Goodyear Rubber Tire Company . . ." I laughed even though the joke was on me. Everything he did was so funny.

The first time I heard him talk on stage was in the *Follies of 1918*. He was doing his great golf routine and was standing, poised to putt. A gorgeous girl in a riding habit passed by, stopped, and snapped her fingers. She went back off stage and he got all set again to putt. The girl came in, paused, snapped her fingers and said, "Oh, I forgot something."

"Must've forgot her horse," Fields ad libbed in his nasal drawl. The audience howled. The minute he came off, Rogers and I ran to him and insisted he keep the line in. He protested, but he kept it and began adding more. From then on, you couldn't shut him up. He had accidentally found the format for stardom. Once I heard him try to help a less fortunate fellow man.

We were playing the Colonial Theatre in Chicago (on the site where the Oriental now stands). Fields was doing one of his drawings. The doorman came up to say a fellow would like to see him.

"Tell him to go to hell." And Fields went on with his drawing. He drew constantly and expertly, portraits of everyone.

"The man's an actor, a juggler out of work," the doorman said.

"Ah—then send the poor bastard up."

The fellow ran into the room, grabbed Fields's hands and kissed them. "W. C. Fields," he muttered, "W. C. Fields!" Like a down-and-out violinist meeting Heifetz.

"What can I do for you, my man?" Fields said, offering two twenty-dollar bills.

"No, I don't want money. It's my act. I know it isn't good. I play one week and am out of work three. If you could give me one idea for my act . . ."

"Simple," Fields said, "simple, my man. I want you to start by juggling some objects no one before has ever juggled. Spend four or five minutes with sensational tricks, then, as you talk, get funny. Get the audience in hysterics. As you close, do something that'll get the people talking. They'll go out and tell everyone they meet to come and see you."

The man grabbed Fields's hands again, kissed them, and ran out wild with excitement. He was probably downstairs before he realized that Fields hadn't told him a thing. I was on the floor.

"Not funny," Bill said. "May take him seven, eight years, but he'll finally do this kind of an act."

"What kind?"

"You don't think it's good? Get everybody hysterical and then send them out talking?"

I was still laughing. "But how do you *do* it, Bill?"

"How? If I knew I'd do it myself!"

Is it any wonder that he was successful as Micawber in *David Copperfield?* Fields *was* Micawber! Except, of course, for the improvidence. Where Micawber was always in debt and waiting for something to turn up, Fields was loaded both ways. There wasn't a city he ever played where he didn't have a bank account or a safe-deposit box or both. As soon as we'd arrive anywhere we'd walk to the bank and make a deposit. I used to argue that his money should be drawing real interest, that he should be buying stocks and bonds. But he'd been so poor, he was always afraid that when he got to Chicago or Cleveland or Detroit he wouldn't have enough cash. At one time he had several hundred bank accounts in various cities under various names.

Of course when the stock market crashed he had the laugh on those of us who'd been so wise. Did he laugh? He was hysterical!

After he'd finished laughing he offered me any amount of money I wanted, but I was enough in debt without incurring more. I'll say this about Fields's money. He lived well. No man I've ever met had such a happy faculty for knowing what to order in a restaurant. Where Rogers could get by on chili and I could feast on salami, Fields was a true gourmet. He knew what temperature wine should be and he knew what year was the good year for each vintage. He never *dressed*, but he spent money on good living, always had a valet and always had a stable of cars, Pierce Arrows and Cadillacs.

The anecdotes about his driving experiences are endless.

One hot summer day he called and suggested a ride to Long Beach. Not that he was interested in swimming. He never went near water. When he was a young juggler one of his first jobs was at a beer garden on Fortescue's Pier in Atlantic City. In addition to juggling, his duties included swimming out in the brine and pretending to drown a dozen times a day, thus attracting a crowd who might then invade the restaurant. He drowned twelve times a day for two weeks and got so waterlogged he could scarcely juggle. So when he mentioned Long Beach I knew that this was just the usual open-air routine. We were going along, doing probably sixty, when a motorcycle cop pulled up and waved us to the side. He began a lecture on the evils of speed while Fields got slowly out of the car, went to the side of the road, selected a big rock, put a twenty-dollar bill under it and returned to his seat.

"Wouldn't it be funny," he said, "if, when I returned in a few hours, that twenty-dollar bill was *gone?*"

The cop laughed and we went on.

Another time Fields was driving, with his valet, Shorty, in the back seat. Shorty was custodian of a cocktail shaker of martinis. Along the way they stopped to give a man a lift. "Shorty," Fields said, "give the gentleman some healthful libation."

The passenger lifted his hand quickly to halt the hospitality. "I'm a minister of the gospel," he said. "I feel it my duty at this moment to preach you my sermon, number four, on the evils of drink."

"Shorty," Fields said, "get up here and drive. When we come to the first ditch push him out, put two bottles of gin beside him, and deliver my sermon, number three, on how to keep clean in a ditch."

He had a fine disdain for ministers of the gospel and for religion in general and he used to kid me about my faith. If I argued in favor of God, he'd say, "Where was God when my father was beating me?" He wasn't an immoral man but an *un*moral one. He made his own rules. He'd been married when he was very young, twenty-one, I believe, but the marriage didn't work out and his wife and son lived another life.

I didn't agree with Bill or he with me, but our friendship remained close through all the years. When we were both making pictures at different studios we'd meet halfway at Chasen's Restaurant, at a table always reserved for Bill. With him would often be Bill Grady, his close friend and agent in the old vaudeville days. Fields's drinking had increased; it had become a necessity. He was essentially a shy man, a man lacking confidence. Gin gave him not only confidence but bravado. By now the drinking had become a legend and so had his irascibility, and it is true he was suspicious of people and wary. But that didn't go for old friends. He would have trusted Bill Rogers or myself with his life. With more than that, with his cash. He continued thoughtful and loyal. He never forgot my birthday, or Ida's and my anniversary, he never missed a radio show.

"Well, Rabbi," he'd say, "I heard your radio show last night. Pleases me to see you're still knocking them over."

We yakked as we always had about politics, economics. His reading was as prolific as ever and his humor as sardonic. Mae West he described as "a plumber's idea of Cleopatra." Life was a joke and constant drinking spiked the joke. He drove the movie makers wild. Once, when he was becoming unsteady, he was told he couldn't finish a picture unless he straightened up.

"From now on, orange juice," he promised.

So he brought a big thermos bottle to the studio, filled with orange juice. He drank the stuff all day until they found he had gin in the orange juice.

I saw him during his last illness. We reminisced about the *Follies*, about Bill Rogers and Fanny Brice, the party at Jack "Twin" Sullivan's.

"Eddie," he said, "I've often wondered how far I could have

gone had I laid off the booze." And, for the only time, I saw a tear drop off his face. Two days later he was dead.

But with all the drinking he'd gotten to the top and stayed on top and enjoyed his own irascibility to the full. The big sums of money found at his death were immediately the cause of dissension and lawsuit, but what must tickle him is that to this day the bulk of his fortune must be lying in bank vaults all over the world, listed to a variety of incredible names. I can just see the old boy rubbing his hands and musing, "Well, it all worked out neatly indeed. Buried nice and neat and they'll never cast a finger on it."

14. Ben Schulberg
Sam Goldwyn

I came to Hollywood first in 1926 to make the film version of *Kid Boots*. The world of show business was changing. There was something besides Broadway, the great medium of the camera offering entertainers a vast new audience. The man who gave me my first chance at that audience was head of Paramount Studios, B. P. Schulberg, with whom I'd grown up on the East Side. Benny and I had known each other as kids on Henry Street, had both gone to P.S. 1. But Benny had studied his lessons; he'd been so bright he stuttered because he couldn't get out fast enough all he thought, all he wanted to say. He'd gone on to college, become a newspaper man, and then gone out to Hollywood to become one of the two top men in the industry—he and Irving Thalberg. ("Berg" means mountain and Schulberg and Thalberg were tops.)

The train pulled in, I rushed to Benny's office, and we met again for the first time since we were a couple of ragged kids. "Eddie," he said, "I'm giving you Frank Tuttle, our best comedy director. Your leading lady will be Clara Bow." Benny had discovered Clara, she had just made "It." They called her "the IT girl," they called her "the Brooklyn bonfire," and finding her scheduled as my leading lady somewhat eased the shock of reading the movie script of *Kid Boots*. The title was there but that was all. This Boots wasn't even a golf story but a story of marriage, divorce, etc.

Working with Clara made up for that. She had the most electric personality I've ever seen. She knew every trick of the trade. After we'd worked from 8 A.M. until 6 P.M. Frank Tuttle would be dead, everyone would be, except Clara. She hadn't been working—this was fun. She taught me some of her tricks, not to dissipate energy for a long shot but to wait until the camera came up close. "What rehearsals are to the stage, Eddie, spontaneity is to the screen. Be yourself," she told me. In a scene where she was supposed to be scolding me severely, she'd be saying, "Eddie, you're doing fine. Flash those banjo eyes, boy." In love scenes she was hilarious. She could have kissed a tree and started a forest fire; but how she kidded those love scenes, trying constantly to break you up. She knew all the words, and lip readers must have found those love scenes of ours very funny.

Her sense of humor never flagged. There actually was one scene where I had to hit a golf ball. We'd just come back to the set after lunch, I took a swing, keeping my eye on the camera, hit the "ball," and egg splattered all over me and everyone else. Clara'd brought an egg from the commissary and replaced the golf ball.

That was nothing . . . Benny Schulberg had gone out of his way to make me feel at home in Hollywood. I'd spend a lot of time at his home, we'd play cards, we'd reminisce, we'd talk the future of movie business. He got a great boot out of the fact that his small son could beat me at ping-pong. I was a tricky ping-pong player and had won cups, but this kid could trim me. (Budd Schulberg, who turned out to be even a better writer than a ping-pong player.) I'd felt completely at ease and secure in Ben's friendship until one day I found a note in my dressing room.

"Eddie," it read, "what's the matter?" Signed "Ben."

I hadn't known *anything* was the matter; but evidently I wasn't doing so well. The next day another note, and the next. Finally, this:

"Dear Eddie, saw the rushes yesterday. You're not giving the performance you should give. You'd better wake up! Ben."

I left the set. I burst into Benny's office.

"Now let's have it out," I yelled. "What am I doing wrong?"

Ben looked up with a little frown. "Don't you know?"

"No, I don't. I'm not happy and you'd better tell me why."

"You'd better tell *me* why, Eddie."

We got into the damnedest double-talk conversation you ever heard; and I left his office angry and confused. Here were four notes he'd sent me, all sharply critical, and yet when I went and asked him, he didn't have any answers for me. What kind of a boss was that? What kind of a friend? I was so upset that I talked it out with the director, Frank Tuttle. I didn't see how I could go on when something was wrong and I didn't know what. He didn't know either; he mentioned to Clara how upset I was and Clara doubled up with laughter. She had just written me another note signed "Ben." She'd written *all* the notes.

The picture took six weeks to make; if they'd given me my head, we could have done it in three! I had to cut my stage tempo in half and I was never completely at ease because I was used to doing things in a play with growing momentum and here was a picture done in tiny pieces, some of the last scenes first and not a chance to sing a song!

While the picture was still in the cutting room I left for New York, certain I had flopped. I couldn't face the preview. Benny wired me three weeks later to tell me the picture was a hit and that I needn't worry further about my "screen personality." When I saw it myself I realized that the picture *was* a success, thanks not to me or to Clara but to Frank Tuttle, who wasn't taking chances on either of us and had given us business that was sure-fire . . . one scene, for example, where I was trying to make Clara jealous, standing beside a door making love to myself with my own bared and powdered arm around my neck.

Benny made me come back to Paramount and make another picture, this one, *Special Delivery*, a story I had written. I'd started out to create a straight narrative interspersed with some gags, but by the time it was rewritten for the screen and then cut all that was left were the gags. It *was* a flop and I was glad to go back to Broadway and Mr. Ziegfeld's *Follies*. When I returned to Hollywood three years later the industry had changed. Sound motion pictures had come in and I was coming to work for Sam Goldwyn. I was always glad Ben had given me a chance in silents because I'd reached a new audience, I was no longer camera shy, and it's a good thing I wasn't.

The toughest man in the world to work for is movie-maker Sam Goldwyn. I made pictures with him for seven years, fought with him for the same amount of time, and can only say that the end justified the means. It's far better to fight with Goldwyn, be friendly enemies, and come up with a hit, than to work for a producer who puts his arm around your shoulders, takes you out to lunch, is happy-days-in-Dixie, and then comes up with a lot of film that should be left in the can.

This man Goldwyn is all business. Nothing and no one matters except the picture he is making at the moment; and if this concentration militates against personal amity, it pays off at the box office. Goldwyn has developed an intuitive sense about motion pictures far greater than that of anyone else in the industry. He's never made many movies, he just makes the best. He knows what audiences will accept. He lives in a mansion and has a butler, valet, and good cars, and still knows how a plumber would talk to his lady friend in a script. If a scene puzzles him in any way, he knows it will puzzle millions of others and the scene is rewritten.

When we were making *Roman Scandals* we shot one scene eight or ten times until Sam felt it was right. He didn't think people would understand my going to museums and talking to the statues. He didn't dig it. Frank Tuttle, George S. Kaufman, and Robert Sherwood wrote and rewrote the scene until Goldwyn was convinced and the scene was right.

Our association began in 1930 when I was called to Ziegfeld's office, where the top man from Hollywood was persuading the top man from Broadway that his was the studio to film our production of *Whoopee*. Ziegfeld had already been approached by the Paramount people, who wanted to make the picture at their studios in Astoria, Long Island. Goldwyn argued that if a picture could be made well in Long Island it could be made ten times better in California, where there was greater experience, top technicians, and the natural scenery (horses and Indians) indispensable to a Western—which *Whoopee* in part was.

Goldwyn had never made a musical, and this was at the end of the cycle of musicals that followed the advent of talking pictures. He took a risk, of course; a million and a half on a picture starring a guy who'd never made a talking film. On the other hand, the play *Whoopee* was a success; Goldwyn could sit in the theater and see what he was buying.

He talked with complete confidence and know-how. He was Ziegfeld's equal—the first man I'd ever met who was—a member of United Artists, selling exhibitors Chaplin, Pickford, Fairbanks. A man is known by the company he keeps, also a man is known by the company that keeps him; and I made up my mind that if I was going into talkies, this Goldwyn was for me.

Ziegfeld closed the deal and with the deal went the entire cast. I made one other suggestion Mr. Goldwyn accepted. I suggested he hire Busby Berkeley to do the choreography. I had seen Berkeley's show, *Fine and Dandy*, and thought he had a great flare for design, a real picture eye.

The night that *Whoopee* closed in Cleveland we went to Child's Restaurant and Busby sketched out designs for the major dance numbers on the back of a menu. The next day we left for Hollywood, where he was to revolutionize the making of musical films. With us were Goldwyn's writer, William Counselman (he later did the comic strip, "Ella Cinders"), and Goldwyn's director, Thornton Freeland. We talked our way across the country, for there were many changes to be made in transposing *Whoopee* to the screen. Counselman and Freeland knew so exactly what they were doing that the entire movie was shot in thirty-six days. They explained points of movie technique to me. Certain scenes had to be condensed, the choreography had to be changed completely. Present a line of thirty-two girls on the stage and you have something highly effective. Present the same line on the screen and the camera has to move so far back the girls become inch-high midgets. Berkeley, in doing the Stetson-hat number, decided to open with the camera on just one pretty girl wearing a Stetson and twirling a rope. The girl he picked was fifteen-year-old Betty Grable.

My one problem was the novelty of recording songs in advance, then appearing before the camera in costume and make-up, and mouthing the words to a playback. My big advantage was that, having played in the show, I knew where the laughs were and didn't talk over them. There were very few arguments with Goldwyn during *Whoopee*. To begin with, Ziegfeld was on the set as technical adviser, and if Sam did decide something was wrong, we'd remind him that where he'd seen the show seven or eight times, we'd played it seven or eight hundred. Goldwyn was a little in awe of Ziegfeld. Later he enjoyed being called "the Ziegfeld of motion pictures," and he was. (You saw the lavish hand in *Whoopee*, in the costuming, the scenery.)

We filmed outdoor sequences at Palm Springs, and Freeland had the desert blooming with flowers he planted. We used to get up at 4:30 A.M. on the desert to start shooting at 6 because this was June and by 11 A.M. you were falling down with the heat. The first morning as I came on the set, our ingénue, Eleanor Hunt, who was playing her first part, came rushing up with a hundred poppies in her arms and presented them to "my leading man"—me! Freeland almost fainted. He'd had a crew out at five o'clock in the morning, "planting" these poppies and now this dizzy kid had picked 'em!

Expense was no object. When an extra song was needed for me, Goldwyn called in Gus Kahn and Walter Donaldson who had written the original score for *Whoopee*. Gus was a dependable writer and Walter was almost a genius, but they found it hard to actually sit down and get to work. Goldwyn was worried. "Where's the song?" he'd ask Gus.

"I have to get the melody from Donaldson."

Finally Goldwyn gave an ultimatum. "It better be here this afternoon."

Gus finally located Donaldson on a golf course and brought him up to the office. We sat around while Donaldson played and Gus more or less sang, "My baby don't care for shows, My baby don't care for clothes, My baby just cares for me . . ."

Now Gus was hardly Mario Lanza, and Goldwyn listened a little dubiously. "Is it good for dancing?" he said.

"Great," said Gus.

"Wonderful," said Donaldson.

"Play it, Walter," Sam said and, taking Gus, he started dancing around the office, humming the tune. It was quite a picture, big six-foot Sam and little Gus bobbing along at chest level.

Goldwyn keeps his finger on everything. On several occasions we'd sit in a projection room looking at rushes and he'd drive me frantic.

"What happened to this scene?" he'd say. "It was so funny on stage."

"Sam, how can it be funny here with three of us sitting in a room? In a theater it plays to an audience of hundreds and they *laugh*."

He was unconvinced until the picture was previewed in a real theater to a real laughing audience. Like Ziegfeld, he didn't know what was funny and what not. Most of the men who star comedians don't know. They can tell what's funny when an audience laughs. But give 'em credit, they hire us.

Our original contract was for *Whoopee*, with an option on one more picture. I had an idea for a story called *The Kid from*

Spain where I would have to enter an arena and fight a bull. Goldwyn didn't think the public would go for anything Spanish at the time; I didn't agree. *Whoopee* had proved we had a good European market for me, and besides, to make a picture in which we did a ten-minute bullfight in pantomime—a universal language —how could we lose?

So we did a picture called *Palmy Days*. In this I played a fellow who worked for a mind reader and made his prophecies come true. The mind reader would say, "Tonight a young man will come up to you at the corner of LaBrea and Wilshire, he'll take your hand and change your life." Standing behind the curtain, I'd hear the message, rush out to LaBrea and Wilshire and take the client's hand. It was a funny enough premise, but there was no preparation on the script. It took forever to make the picture, while the story line was changed, while Goldwyn hired writers and fired them.

You see, Sam knew when something was wrong and on most of his pictures he never stopped until he made it right, even if production was held up for a half dozen rewrites. The one time he didn't obey his own good judgment was in making a picture called *The Unholy Garden*, written by Ben Hecht. Sam didn't like the story, he didn't like the rushes, and it proved one of his biggest flops; but a man like Hecht, with his stature, his reputation, and his salesmanship, had been able to keep selling him on it.

Goldwyn had a great respect for top talent and the feeling was mutual. Every star of the literary, newspaper, and business world visited at the Goldwyn home and paid him homage. His closest friends were Irving Thalberg, Charlie Chaplin and Joe Schenck. His stars included Ronald Coleman, Anna Sten, Vilma Banky and Miriam Hopkins. The guest list at a small dinner party read like the social blue book of the town. At the Goldwyn home Ida and I met all the stars.

One of Sam's great assets was his wife, Frances, now actually a partner in his business. She has everything Sam might lack. She also had a wonderful flow of stories from her days in the theater as Frances Howard, and a sure way of drawing out the best from her guests.

It always interested me that Goldwyn started life as a glove salesman. He never handled any of his employees with kid gloves. He fought with writers, directors, and actors. But . . . I began to grasp Sam's caliber of showmanship when we made *The Kid from Spain*. He turned this down after *Whoopee;* but after *Palmy Days* he changed his mind. "Let's see that Spanish thing, Eddie." And once he decided on it, he gave *The Kid from Spain* a Ziegfeldian treatment. He hired the best writer Ziegfeld had, William Anthony McGuire, and at my suggestion, hired Harry Ruby and Bert Kalmar to do the music. Instead of getting an actor to play the bullfighter, Goldwyn got one of the greatest bullfighters in the world, Sidney Franklin. When Franklin explained that ordinary bulls wouldn't do, that he could only fight a bull that was truly ferocious, Sam sent to Mexico for four or five great bulls. And whereas for the first two pictures he'd picked a chorus girl out of the line to be my leading lady, he now gave me a talented comedienne, Lyda Roberti.

I've never been so scared in my life as I was during the bullfight sequence. First Franklin did a true bullfight. Chaplin and Pickford, the top stars, came to the big bull ring erected at the studio to watch Franklin's performance. At one point the bull barely missed him, the horn grazed Franklin and plunged into a fence board four inches thick. The next day I "fought" the bull. It was the same breed of violent animal, but two men stood on each side of the bull out of camera range, holding a charged wire between the animal and me. The story idea was that I'd met a bull who understood a certain code. I'd say "Popocatepetl," and the bull would lie down. But in the actual arena the bulls were switched. I'd say "Popocatepetl," and the bull would keep right on thundering toward me. Finally I was supposed to chloroform him, and we did a slow-motion bullfight that was virtually a ballet.

The wire was always there between me and the bull; but I was a happy toreador when that part of the picture was finished. Did I say "finished"? When we previewed the picture in San Diego, Goldwyn insisted my bullfight be reshot. Yes, the audience had howled, but he felt the fight was jumpy, a series of gags, and he wanted an easier flow. Director Leo McCarey argued that this could be done in the cutting. I argued louder than McCarey. So we reshot the scene. It cost Goldwyn sixty or seventy thousand dollars—which may sound like a lot of bull, but the scene *was* better.

In another sequence I was supposed to leap over a fence and the bull was to leap after me and chase me down a corridor. Actually we reversed the shot. We made the bull jump first. At least we *tried*. For four or five days Leo McCarey, with the utmost patience, tried everything imaginable to make the bull jump. The bull would not.

The set is crammed with extras, Goldwyn's getting mad. He comes on the set and says:

"Leo, why doesn't that bull jump?"

"I'm trying to get him to jump."

"Well, you're the director, aren't you?"

"Yes," Leo says, "but the bull isn't a member of the Screen Actors' Guild. You're the boss, Sam, you tell him."

Goldwyn wasn't too happy with McCarey and for a while wanted to take his name off the picture. But McCarey had written half the picture or rewritten it, as well as directing. McCarey is another individualist with a tremendous comedy sense and he'd rewrite a script done by Paddy Chayefsky or Eugene O'Neill. One Saturday morning we got to a scene that didn't play funny.

"Why don't you get sick, Eddie?" McCarey said. "We'll go to Santa Barbara, rewrite the thing, and shoot Monday morning."

"I'm not only sick, I'm almost blind," I cried and went into a sick-headache routine. An hour later we were en route to Santa Barbara. Monday we shot one of the best scenes of the picture. Goldwyn, seeing the rushes, was amused and baffled. He couldn't figure out where the scene had come from.

As you gather, our chief difficulty was in not having finished scripts to start with. After *Palmy Days* I had signed for five pictures with Goldwyn, one a year. I'd go back to New York in between and do my radio series and we made the pictures in the summers. Sometimes while we were still on the air Goldwyn would insist that I come West at once, even in early spring. I'd come and sit for two or three months while he dug up a story. He didn't care that I was losing ten thousand a broadcast. As a matter of fact he discounted radio completely.

When I was at my height on the air he constantly was telling me to get off the air, a waste of time. Why be seen or heard in anything but a Goldwyn vehicle? He was serious. Every time we'd meet he'd say, "You're still on the air, huh?" and shake his head. I would stick our radio rating under his nose.

"Sam, one out of every four people in the United States was tuned in last night."

He was unconvinced. One night at a party we met William Paley, head of CBS.

"Bill, what do you think of this Eddie Cantor? I can't get him off the air."

"Try to get him off NBC, Sam, we could use him," Bill said.

Sam couldn't understand the big openings our pictures got in the hinterlands, Dubuque, Iowa; Lubbock, Texas; towns where the Ziegfeld shows had never played. I'd plug the hell out of our movies on the air. I'd do an entire hour about leaving for California to make a picture. I'd come back from California and sing the songs. Our pictures had a big opening in these small towns because the people were radio fans. If you play to forty million people on Sunday night and tell them about *The Kid from Spain* you're bound to have a Monday opening in Des Moines. Today Sam himself goes on Ed Sullivan's program to plug a picture; but in those days he felt that a Goldwyn picture was the thing and the only thing.

One time I was on stage at the Stanley Theatre in Pittsburgh when Sam called from Hollywood, wanting me to come at once.

"I can't, Sam, I'm booked into Chicago and Cleveland."

"Cancel it!"

I explained that this was impossible.

"Well, fly out as soon as you finish Cleveland."

I flew. I didn't know what he had cooking for me, but it must be important. I had lunch with Goldwyn. The minute we finished the last mouthful he hurried me to a projection room and showed me a Leon Errol sequence from a picture starring British actress Evelyn Laye, something I had nothing to do with. He just wanted my opinion. That was what the rush was all about. Then we got down to the usual argument about my next picture.

Actually I was with Goldwyn too early. He was learning about musicals through experience and I was the experience. Later he proved what he'd learned, in top musicals with Danny Kaye, and he's gone right on. *Guys and Dolls*, for example. But the lack of material on our early efforts drove me wild. I hollered loudly enough so that by the time we got to *Roman Scandals* we had a real book. The writers were Robert Sherwood and George S. Kaufman. They gave us a script that *was* a script. It was a great picture to work in, and driving a chariot with two chargers was exciting, especially the day that one horse charged to the left and the other charged to the right, leaving the poor photographer, his camera and platform in the middle.

The picture took two months longer to make than we'd planned, and as it came to a close, Goldwyn's manager handed me an envelope. There was a note from Sam thanking me for my cooperation and enclosing a letter of credit for twenty-five thousand dollars. "Take Ida and the girls to Europe and have fun."

I made two more pictures for Sam, *Kid Millions* and *Strike Me Pink*, both with Ethel Merman. Ethel was a circus to work with. She played my mother in *Kid Millions* and we had fun kicking that around. We were on location part of the time at Calabasas, California, for the camel sequences. (Eve Sully of Block and Sully was my princess and she and I rode camel-back.) Now you must never get in the way when a camel expectorates; it's as unwise as getting chummy with a skunk. Ethel didn't know that the first day. The second day she walked right to the camel and spit at *him*. "I'm gonna get you first today." Then in *Strike Me Pink* there was a scene where I ran into a fellow demonstrating shampoo and I mean I ran into him. I was a walking effervescence. Before we started, the cameraman and I rehearsed the sequence carefully so it could be done in one take and I wouldn't have to wash up, get made up again, and go through all that. The scene went like clockwork. As I finished, in ran Ethel, breathless, she'd missed it. "Oh, Eddie, I didn't see it. Do it again!" I'm hysterical. I'm covered with shampoo and Ethel talks me into doing it all over again.

That was the only laugh I got on *Strike Me Pink*. As a matter of fact, the months we sat around waiting for a script left me quite another color. Two months missing my radio show. I felt Sam selfish, I felt him spoiled. *Roman Scandals* had been such a hit he thought we could keep rolling along on the strength of it. I told him, "It's like Babe Ruth up at bat. The fact that he made a hit yesterday has nothing to do with today."

Still no script. Fred Kohlmar, Goldwyn's representative, was in New York hunting material for me and came up with a new play that was obviously sure-fire. He phoned Sam, told him about it, and explained that he could have 25 per cent of it for twenty-five thousand dollars. Goldwyn would then have first crack at it for pictures. It would have been a great vehicle for me. The play was sent out, Goldwyn never read it. He had someone else read it who turned it down. I was furious. Later he saw the play on Broadway and offered one hundred and fifty thousand dollars, but that wasn't enough. The play was *Three Men on a Horse*. Goldwyn and I argued over that while I sat around waiting for a picture.

I begged Sam to let me out of our contract and he kept telling me not to worry. How could I *not* worry? Finally he came up with a script and as soon as we finished the picture I started business proceedings, paid my way out of our contract, and for a while forfeited Sam's friendship. I was hopping mad and so was he. I can't blame him. One day he came on the set and I stopped working. I told the director I wouldn't do the scene until "that man" left the set.

For a long while we didn't speak; we met on several occasions and passed each other by. Then one time I was speaking at the Ambassador for some charity, he came up afterward, told me what a fine job I'd done and that we should always be friends. We have been, and I've watched with admiration and respect his growing wisdom, courage and supersalesmanship. He has shown the industry that to make money you must spend it and, given an equal product, he knows how to get eight times as much for it as anyone else could.

Even when we weren't friends I resented stories about Goldwyn's idiosyncracies of speech. "You must shoot this picture in Arizona, you need Indians and there you can get 'em right from the reservoir." Certainly he says something like that once in a while. But the people who think it so funny—if they don't make the linguistic breaks he does, they don't make the kind of pictures he makes either!

I was eager to leave him, eager to make pictures on my own, and I did. But they never came up to the caliber of the Goldwyn pictures. If Sam gave me nervous indigestion while I waited for a script, he also eventually brought out something that *sold* and that established me in pictures as Ziegfeld had established me in the theater.

15. The Song Writers

Some of my best friends have been song writers: Harry Ruby, Bert Kalmar, Gus Kahn, Walter Donaldson, the Tobias boys, a score of others. As a group these men are bright sparks of show business; in themselves they're not only smart, they're brilliant men of wide interests; and even those whom you've known less well have a soft spot in your heart because they gave you something important.

Eddie Leonard, for example. Eddie in 1903 wrote a song which he himself sang in vaudeville, but which was to become almost a theme song for a guy who loved a gal named "Ida." I started singing the song even before Ida and I were married. During *Kid Kabaret*, we had an "Imitation" number. Jessel did David Warfield, another kid did Raymond Hitchcock, I impersonated Eddie Leonard singing "Ida," and the song's stuck with me just as the girl.

Then there is L. Wolfe Gilbert, who wrote the words to "Waiting for the Robert E. Lee." And here's how that song came to be written . . . Gilbert was a critic for *The Billboard* and when Lewis Muir wrote "When Ragtime Rosie Rags the Rosary," critic Gilbert took Muir *and* the song apart. Muir answered back.

"It's easy to criticize," he said. "Maybe you can write a better song yourself."

"If I couldn't, I'd quit," retorted Gilbert.

Before the argument was over, the two men got together and wrote "Waiting for the Robert E. Lee." What a lucky break for me! I found it one day when I was hanging around the song publishers in 1912 and Gilbert gave me permission to sing it in *Kid Kabaret*. I wore blackface, of course, and a battered high hat, a Prince Albert coat, white gloves, and carried a book under my arm. Sometimes I lapsed from southern accent to Jewish accent. The audience loved the song and it became my first hit.

Years later Gilbert handed me another song, "Oh, Katharina," which I sang in *Kid Boots.* He gave me "Camp Meeting Band," "Lily of the Valley," and "Down Yonder" for *The Midnight Rounders.* In 1933 he became one of my writers on the Chase and Sanborn Hour. He wrote some memorable episodes including, in rhyme, the trial of the author of "Who's Afraid of the Big Bad Wolf?"

And there was Con Conrad, best known for "The Continental." For me he wrote the music for "Lena, She's the Queen of Palesteena," and "Ma, He's Making Eyes at Me," and "Barney Google," and—"Margie," which I sang first on a Sunday night at the Winter Garden and then took into *The Midnight Rounders.* Con wrote "Margie" with Benny Davis and J. Russel Robinson and the minute they finished it they brought it over to "plug" it to me because I had a daughter named Marjorie.

All good song writers are song pluggers and one guy who started out as a plugger was to become a successful writer—I'm speaking of Harry Ruby. Harry and I met in 1915 in Toledo, Ohio. He was a song plugger for Waterson, Berlin and Snyder and they'd sent him on to teach me a song. He came backstage, started hitting the piano, and it was love at first sight. I told him I'd introduce the song if he'd come on with us to Dayton. So Harry went on with us to Dayton, taught me the song, sent for orchestrations, and stayed with us until the song was launched. Oh, and it was a hit, "Back Home in Tennessee." *It* didn't need *me* but I've always blessed "Back Home in Tennessee" for bringing Ruby my way. We've been the closest of friends ever since. This was the most honest man, the most principled man, the most literate man I'd ever met, a gentle, rough-looking guy whom Woollcott dubbed "the dishonest Abe Lincoln."

There are three things that have kept Harry alive (outside of ASCAP): Lincoln, astronomy, and baseball. He knows all about the stars, he's an authority on Lincoln, he's nuts about baseball. I lived in Mt. Vernon in the early twenties, he in Pelham, so we were neighbors; and on Sundays he and I would take the kids to Van Cortlandt Park, our wives would bring lunch over, and before you knew it, he'd turned me into a baseball player (not a very good one but anyhow a baseball player). Harry was great; he could pitch or catch, he had me playing first base or shortstop. At one time (in spite of me) we had a pretty good team, playing three, four times a week. Baseball's always been his one relaxation and his big enthusiasm. Somebody once said to him, "If you were in a boat and it was sinking, your father and Joe Di Maggio were on board and you could only save one, which would it be?"

"My father couldn't hit .360 in a million years," Harry said.

Back in 1917 when I got my first car, a Maxwell, Ruby was one of the few who'd risk their necks riding with me. I took a lesson one morning and when the instructor said, "What time tomorrow?" I said, "Never mind tomorrow. I learned the whole thing today." Ruby's dad warned him not to ride with me, but Harry said, "Look, Eddie's working for Ziegfeld, I'm just a song plugger at Waterson, Berlin and Snyder. He's got more to lose than I have." And after that wonderful speech and after several near misses with my car Ruby suddenly asked me to stop, drop him on the corner, he had a date—with the subway!

I knew from the first how comical this guy could be, because while I was still on the road we corresponded; and around 1918 he wrote a song with Edgar Leslie that was one of the best war songs ever, "The Dixie Volunteers." I introduced it in Baltimore during the *Follies of 1918* and it tore down the house. I kept heckling him to write because I knew he could, and then, around 1920, I introduced him to a fellow named Bert Kalmar who'd been a vaudeville headliner (the team of Kalmar and Brown, Brown being Mrs. Kalmar). Bert had hurt his knee and it looked as though he'd never dance again, but he had ideas for lyrics and he knew the fundamentals. The first song he wrote was "Where Did You Get That Girl?" A hit!

The meeting place for all writers at that time was the Strand Theatre Building, the headquarters of Waterson, Berlin and Snyder. Everybody used to gather around Ruby when he played a song, because he made them laugh, and Kalmar detected in Ruby the possibilities of a good commercial song writer. The two teamed up. They didn't click at once, but in a little while along came "My Sunny Tennessee," which we introduced in *The Midnight Rounders*, "When Those Sweet Hawaiian Babies Roll Their Eyes," "Three Little Words," "Thinking of You," "I'm Sorry I Made You

Cry"; Harry collaborating on the lyrics and writing the music.

Ruby and Kalmar got to be a very prolific, very successful team and Kalmar joined us in the baseball stint. He couldn't run but he could hit the ball and Harry'd run for him. The story of their lives was made into a movie with Fred Astaire and Red Skelton —"Three Little Words." They went out to California to write for movies early in the thirties and our friendship continued out there.

Everyone who's ever known Ruby has loved him, so they'll understand what I mean when I say he gives always to everyone more than he gets. I've learned from him patience and tolerance. In all the years I've known this would-be baseball player I've never heard him say an unkind word about anyone. He's the greatest plugger for other people's music you ever heard. Which doesn't conflict in any way with his sense of humor. When I was hospitalized he wrote me a note every day for six weeks and there was a laugh in every one. He'd want to know "Are you going to do my song, 'I'm Sorry I Made You Cry but Your Face Looks Cleaner Now,' or shall I take it to Tony Martin?" He wrote always as if he were still a song plugger, *circa* 1919. And there was one hilarious letter about the ugly secret on his conscience. He must confess about the "Berlin Myth."

"One day a dark, lean boy came into our publishing house with a song called 'Alexander's Ragtime Band.' I listened and smothered a laugh. It was awful and Irving sang it so badly. But I called in another song plugger and said, 'Let's pretend it's great, let's get headliners to do it for this kid—just for a gag.' So we did and that's what happened. It's time to confess, to tell you the truth, this guy Berlin has no talent. It was all just a gag."

There are a couple of other song writers with great senses of humor that they incorporated into a song, "Yes, We Have No Bananas"—Frank Silver and Irving Conn. I found that song in manuscript back in 1923 when *Make It Snappy* was playing Philadelphia. We were holding over in Philadelphia, people were coming back to see the show a second time and we needed some new material. So I wandered up to Shapiro, Bernstein & Co. and here was this song in manuscript. I sang it first at a Wednesday matinee and the reaction was so tremendous, I kept going back everyday for more choruses. There was a time when Victor Recording Company was doing nothing but recording that song; and when

Jimmy Walker came home from Europe a year later, he insisted that the Europeans thought "Yes, We Have No Bananas" was our national anthem.

And another great song-writing team: Gus Kahn and Walter Donaldson. They wrote top songs with other people, they wrote top songs together: "Carolina in the Morning," "Yes Sir, That's My Baby," "Makin' Whoopee"; in fact all the music for *Whoopee*. I introduced "Yes Sir, That's My Baby" in 1925 and it was an especially big kick because the song was written in our living room at Great Neck. My little girl Marilyn had a little toy mechanical pig; and after dinner Gus sat on the floor and wound the tail so the pig would waddle for Marilyn. There was a funny whiny noise that came out when the tail unwound, and the next thing you knew, Gus was making up words to the whine. When they got their first royalty check, Gus showed it to me. "Remember that night at your house, Eddie? This is a lot of money for a Jewish boy to make out of a pig's tail!"

Gus was a very funny fellow. Opening night of *Whoopee* Ziegfeld was so elated that he invited Gus and Walter, who'd written the music, William Anthony McGuire, who'd written the book, and a few others of us up to his suite to celebrate. In *Whoopee*, of course, I was on all the time and when I came in to the party Gus ran to get me a drink and a plate of food. He shoved me into a chair, drew up a footstool, and hoisted my feet.

"Hey, Gus, what is this?"

"Listen, Eddie. You may be Ida's husband, you may be Ziegfeld's star, to me you just represent my 2.5 per cent of the gross. What time do you want your massage in the morning?"

During the three months of getting *Whoopee* in shape, Gus and I were inseparable. He was a hard worker and his talent was continually amazing. We'd leave rehearsal at five-thirty and Gus'd say, "I'll see you at six-thirty with the second chorus." He'd not only be there with the second chorus, he'd be there at six-fifteen. The show opened. You'd sing a number of encores in act one. The audience demanded more and more. Gus'd say, "I'll see you with new choruses for the second act," and he'd go to the men's smoking room and write them. He knew comedy as few song writers know it, as witness: "Ain't We Got Fun?" "Toot, Toot, Tootsie," "Charley, My Boy," "My Baby Just Cares for Me," etc. But he knew pathos too. . . . Once Jolson had gone to California and Gus sent him a wire. When Gus's wife saw the wire she told him it was too good for just a telegram, it should be a song. It *was:* "My Buddy." But nothing he ever wrote was any better than Gus Kahn's own conversation about anything. He had a German cook who was with him a lifetime, and when you went to visit Gus in Chicago he'd speak the whole evening with her accent. He was a top song writer, a successful song writer who knew his business and was strictly business.

Walter Donaldson was just the opposite. Donaldson was a musician, a lovable, irresponsible Irishman who could write hits like "My Blue Heaven" and "Mammy" and was always in hock. He was constantly in debt to ASCAP, against himself, and when that ran short, he'd go to a friend, look you in the eye, tell you the saddest story you ever heard, borrow a thousand dollars, and go straight to the race track. The same night he'd told you about some new and dread disease which meant money for doctors, he'd go to the Edgewater Beach Hotel and pick up the tab for forty people.

Whoever wrote with Walter had to keep him on the ball; but his talent was so great that a music-publishing firm was organized around him; Donaldson, Douglas and Gumble. Walter wrote "My Blue Heaven" in 1927, and I sang it in the *Follies* of that year—with some added lines. Janet had just been born and the extra lyrics were:

> *But five is a crowd,*
> *For crying out loud.*
> *We're crowded in*
> *My Blue Heaven.*

And once Walter and I wrote a song together, "My Dixie Pair O'Dice." Other songs of Walter's that I loved to sing: "How Ya Gonna Keep 'Em Down on the Farm?" "My Best Girl," and, of course, "Yes Sir, That's My Baby."

I was so crazy about song writers, I married into a song-writing family. Ida's cousins, Harry, Henry, and Charlie Tobias, started composing during World War I. Harry was in the army but the other two would sing their songs at recruiting stations, and if things weren't moving fast enough, they'd step up and be recruited. Charlie says he was recruited sometimes fifteen or sixteen times a day. They always gave me first crack at their new material and during World War II their "Don't Sit Under the Apple Tree" and "We Did It Before and We Can Do It Again" were great morale builders when we were making the rounds of the camps. This last, Charlie wrote with Cliff Friend and when it was first sung, two days after Pearl Harbor, you can imagine the impact on the audience!

The show was *Banjo Eyes*. We had a drill scene with sixteen soldiers. I'd gotten involved in a routine that made me late and finally, having had no breakfast, came running onto the parade ground in long underwear, my pants over my shoulder, just as the general arrived for inspection. As the general came down the line, I'd sneak a hard-boiled egg out of my pocket, a salt cellar. I'd salt the egg and gulp it down. We started having trouble keeping the necessary sixteen fellows in the scene, the boys were being drafted and every day there'd be new faces. One matinee I came running on and there was a new boy down the line that looked so like Danny Kaye that I maneuvered over next to him, and it *was* Danny Kaye! I took out my hard-boiled egg, cracked it on my knee, salted it daintily, and took a bite. Then I shoved the rest of it in Danny's mouth. While his mouth was still wide open I shook salt in too. Then a banana. I took a bite of the banana and fed Danny. By now the audience had recognized him and as I fed him, they roared. The drill scene ran eight minutes over that day, and if the audience had had their way, the guys and Danny would still be drilling. This was the scene that ended with "We Did It Before and We Can Do It Again."

But to go back to Charlie Tobias. He and his wife were at our house for dinner one night and I asked Charlie how he wrote. Did he wait for an inspiration? No, Charlie said, he just sat down and wrote. Inspirations were everywhere. At that moment a substitute maid came in to serve the salad. None of us knew her; she'd been called in when our regular girl'd become ill a few hours before.

"What's your name, honey?" asked Charlie. She told him. "Now, you start with that," he said; and within a half hour he had the rough draft of a song that was to become another hit, "Rose O'Day." Just before Edna and Charlie left that night the maid came in again.

The Song Writers

"I want you to know, Mr. Tobias, that my name is not really Rose O'Day. O'Day's my husband's name. I'm Rose Shapiro."

"'Rose Shapiro' wouldn't sell ten copies," Charlie said. "To me you're 'Rose O'Day.'"

So many song writers . . . There are Gene Buck and Dave Stamper, who wrote the scores for many *Follies*. They wrote hits like "Tulip Time" and "Hello, Frisco!" There are Al Lewis and Al Sherman, who wrote "Potatoes Are Cheaper" and "When I'm the President." There are Jack Yellen and Milt Ager, who did "Ain't She Sweet?" and "Lovin' Sam the Shiek of Alabam'." There's Buddy De Sylva who gave us "If You Knew Susie," "Alabamy Bound," and "It All Depends on You." Joe McCarthy and Harry Tierney did the score for *Kid Boots* and the show was Joe's idea. And Jimmy McHugh and Harold Adamson gave me "Comin' In On A Wing And A Prayer," which I sang over the radio and at camps during World War II.

The list of men who influenced my life with the songs they wrote could go on and on; but I must tell you about one who was far more than a song writer, one of the few authentic geniuses I've ever known—George M. Cohan. A man who could write the book, lyrics, and music for shows like *Forty-Five Minutes From Broadway, Little Johnny Jones,* etc. and then star in the shows, a man who could turn around and play a dramatic role in O'Neill's *Ah, Wilderness!* I include him here because he wrote the first song I ever sang.

Remember "Harrigan"? I sang this before a bunch of boys huddled around a campfire when I was a kid at Surprise Lake Camp. In later years I'd meet George M. at the Plaza, at the table that was always reserved for him, his "office"; and he'd introduce me to whomever was there as the song plugger who'd sold "Harrigan."

We met in 1916. He used to come up to the New Amsterdam Roof. He asked me to play a benefit at the Liberty Theatre and we were close friends for several years. Then, during the Actors' Equity strike in 1919, I made a nasty crack which it took him some time to forgive. Cohan was bitterly opposed to the idea of actors forming a union. He told reporters, "If actors win this strike, I'll run an elevator." I retorted, "Somebody'd better tell Mr. Cohan that to run an elevator he'd *have* to join a union."

He didn't talk to me for three years. Then his *Little Nellie Kelly* opened in Boston, I walked into the theater with a friend, bought two tickets, and was about to hand them to the ticket taker when someone snatched them out of my hand. Cohan tore up the tickets, handed me back the money and put his arm around my shoulders.

"You popeyed cocker spaniel, you can't buy tickets for this show," he said, took us in and sat with us. From then on, all was well.

He didn't like the Lambs Club and with his friend William Collier formed the Friars Club in opposition. We would meet there many's the time, and I'd sit enthralled with his stories. In 1924 Willie Collier was out of town and George asked me to do *The Friars Frolic* with him. I was to be responsible for the first half of the show, minstrel stuff, and he was to do the second half. Then we'd finish together.

George was the biggest man in show business and I thought it would be very funny if I kidded him. He thought so, too. I worked up some gags, he wrote a song about Willie's being away, then we did a dance together. Finally Cohan said:

"It was nice of you, Eddie, to come here tonight and work with me."

"That's all right, George. I like to help you boys who're just getting started. I've got mine!"

We worked up eight or nine minutes of kidding around in dinner jackets and straw hats and then discussed what we'd do for a finish.

George sang a song from *Little Nellie Kelly*. The night of the *Frolic* this got a great hand. When the applause was over, I looked at George and said, "You're not kidding, are you, *this* for a *finish?*" Then I turned to the orchestra and said, "Give me that in 2/4 time." And I did the same song but fast, prancing up and down in my usual style with the eye-rolling hand-clapping bit. And then Cohan started imitating me. You've never seen such a thing, George M. Cohan making like Cantor. When it was over, the audience at the Manhattan Opera House wouldn't let the curtain drop, one of those performances you never forget. Or as Cohan would say, "No complaints, kid, no complaints."

This was a great line of his. When he was awarded the Congressional Medal of Honor for "Over There," he came out of the

White House and the reporters flocked around to ask him how he felt. He said, "No complaints, no complaints." The only time he ever complained was when I was playing Loew's State and he dropped in four or five times to catch the act. We were doing such good business he had to stand up. Finally he came backstage. "I understand you're getting 50 per cent of the gross. How about my half buck back, Eddie? Loew's can keep their half."

Actually, money to him was something to *give*. He once gave his mother and dad a present of his theater, the Cohan Opera House in Chicago; and he had a list of pensioners, people who'd worked for him, to whom he sent money regularly. Once we were sitting yakking at the Plaza and he was called to the phone. When he came back he said, "Some actors have audacity. If they had talent as big as their audacity, they'd own the world." He went on to explain. "This on the phone is a guy I've been giving fifty bucks a week for five years. He's met a girl, he wants to get married, but he wants me to raise the ante. He can get married on seventy-five but not on fifty."

"You going to give it to him, George?"

"Seventy-five? I should say not. *Sixty* a week's the most he'll get from me."

Running theaters, running shows, he usually worked without an office; he had as he said, "everything in my hat." Someone said, "You've got two shows running and everything in your hat? Suppose you have another show, what then?"

"I'll buy another hat!"

And then, after his long and successful "run," tragedy. His lifetime partner, Sam Harris, developed cancer. Cohan spent as much time with him as he could; Sam Harris slowly died. Then a little while later Cohan saw the same symptoms in himself. He became embittered. The Broadway he used to know, the Broadway that knew him, was no longer there. Shooting galleries and doughnut stands had replaced the old landmarks. His family was falling to pieces; and, the irony of it, as this is happening, Warner Brothers is making the big success story, *Yankee Doodle Dandy*.

Jack Warner comes to see Cohan. The picture is great. They'll rush it East the minute it's finished.

"How long will that be?" Cohan asks weakly.

"Three weeks."

"Too late, Jack, too late."

But as it turned out, Cohan did see the picture three weeks later. When it was over he asked his nurse to take him to Broadway for one more look. They rode down Broadway, he looked right and left, memorizing everything. As she helped him from the car, the nurse said, "How do you feel, Mr. Cohan?" He turned, he looked back.

"No complaints, kid, no complaints."

And that was his last ride, his last look at the street that had been his home. For many of us it was the end of an era.

PART THREE

The REST of My Life

16. The Girls

Our five girls are as different as the first five days of the week. Marjorie is the family adviser, the sage, the philosopher; she has the best common sense in the family. And while she gives everyone else good advice, she herself is impulsive, generous and honest to a fault. Natalie is the kindest person I know and a born mother. Her boy, Michael, is six feet two, and you should see tiny Natalie up on tiptoe, shaking her finger at him and saying, "You do this or I'll take you across my knee!" Edna is the artistic one, a talented painter, a pianist, and reminiscent of Ida when she was young, very much the mother to her daughter Judy. Marilyn is our stage-struck child. Talented too. She's better on the off-the-cuff stuff than any girl I've seen on television or anywhere. Marilyn and Janet are the New York branch of the Cantor family. We miss 'em and keep the phones busy. Janet, the youngest, is the practical one, the only one who can make a dollar talk; and probably because she *is* practical, she's the one with a beautifully successful marriage, not to mention two darling youngsters, Brian, four, and Amanda, a year old—the first one in the family to look like me!

Janet knows I like meat loaf the way she makes it. So for my birthday she'll send me a frozen meat loaf. Or, she'll bake a cake and send it air mail. Edna will buy me a shirt of some neutral color so that no matter what I wear with it (and I am color-blind) it'll blend. Natalie finds something of mine that's just worn out or used up and she replaces it. (Now where can she find a good secondhand gall bladder?) Marilyn'll borrow money (she's always either flush or broke), go to Saks, and buy something I wouldn't *think* of buying for myself, it's too expensive. When any of the family goes to New York, Marilyn takes over; it's strictly "be my guest." She is show business and lives the show person's life. At 2 A.M. she'll send out to the delicatessen near her home for food. She signs for it with every intention of paying, but when Marjorie's in New York, she'll dash over to the delicatessen just before she leaves for home and pay the bills, which makes Marilyn furious. "I wonder if you realize," she'll write Marjorie, "that you were here as my guest?" When I'm in New York she tries to take my taxi bills. When I protest she says, "But, Daddy, you forget, I'm teaching three or four classes a week" (diction, drama classes). "I *have* money and I'm your hostess!" The female Grover Whalen!

What the girls all have in common is their devotion to each other, to Ida, and to me. I've never seen girls as unselfish, as helpful and companionable, so close that all their joys and all their pain are community property. They have big hearts, not only for the family but for any underdog. Not long ago they discovered a delicatessen on Sunset. A young couple from New York had come West and put every cent they owned in this little place which they keep open most of the night to accommodate show people. The girls wandered in one night, tasted the pastrami, and promptly made phone calls to everyone in town. Now the delicatessen is so successful the girls have a tough time getting a table.

They're a team. Of them all, Marjorie's the scrapper. If she sees something that needs correcting, she *must* do something about it right away. She'll tell a friend, "It's important for you to go to New York. Go. I'll take care of your household till you get back." She'll step in where angels fear and the others right with her. When Marjorie and Natalie were kids Marjorie's the one who would fight for going to the movies. They hadn't seen one for two weeks, they'd behaved, their homework was finished . . . and when she won the battle, there'd be Natalie all ready with her coat and hat on. Natalie never had to fight, she rode the gravy train.

Oh, and another thing they have in common—a sense of humor. Sitting around our dinner table has always been a comedy riot—there isn't a straight man in the house. Back twenty years ago agent Bill Perlberg, now producer of such movies as *Country Girl, The Proud and the Profane*, etc., was at dinner and suggested a booking for me in San Francisco. I was already booked pretty solid and didn't see how I could make it.

"We'll fly," Bill said. "We'll just hop a plane, Eddie."

"All of a sudden he's a flier," Ida said. "Take the train, Eddie."

"There's nothing to flying," Bill insisted. "I flew in from Chicago yesterday, tomorrow I'll fly to New Haven. Then I fly to Dallas—and home to L.A."

"Close the window, Mother," Natalie said, "before he flies out."

There were years when I didn't think I could sleep. I didn't sleep a wink. One morning the girls ganged up on me. I came down to breakfast and was greeted by a chorus of, "Well, Daddy, how did you sleep?"

"Not a wink."

"Poor Daddy," Edna said.

"Oh, and wasn't that a terrible thunderstorm we had about 2 A.M.?" said Natalie.

"Pretty bad," I agreed, falling into the trap. There'd been *no* thunderstorm.

There was many a practical joke. Like Edna's sweepstake ticket, the one that paid off. And in case a sweepstake ticket makes Edna sound like a gambler—she isn't. What she's lost in a lifetime you could put in an elephant's eye. However, she's on friendly terms with the slot machines at Las Vegas, she's dabbled with the daily doubles, and she's a sucker for sweepstakes. We were living in California at the time and Edna bought several tickets from our Irish maid, Clara. I knew about this and couldn't resist. I had a friend in New York send Edna a telegram in the name of a law firm saying that her ticket was worth seventy thousand dollars—she could collect at their Los Angeles office, 712 Spring Street.

I made sure that the telegram arrived on a Saturday morning when I'd be on the Goldwyn lot filming a picture. Edna received the wire and went out of her mind. She couldn't wait to rush out shopping. She bought Clara a gorgeous new outfit: suit, hat, shoes, bag, stockings, gloves; she bought three or four outfits for herself, presents for her sisters, for Ida, and several handsome sweaters for me. When I got home that night she threw her arms about my neck and told me of her windfall, and about the car she'd seen and . . . I simply had to tell her that *I'd* sent the phony telegram. She cried bitter tears. After she told me about her shopping, all she'd spent and what I had to *pay*, I cried right with her!

I gave them a bad time, too, because I was a food faddist, but they gave me a bad time ribbing me about it. Marjorie still insists that there were years when the family ate nothing but liver and tomatoes in every form. "Juice, salad, aspic," Marjorie moans, "tomatoes became a family gag."

There were many family gags. In the *Follies of 1927* we had a dog-shop scene. There was one lousy dog in this shop that we could never sell. Whatever a customer asked for, I'd drag out the same dog. He was a spitz, a poodle, a shepherd; if they asked for a police dog, I'd put a cop's hat on him and drag him out. But no one would buy him. I'd look at the dog sadly and say, "Morris, we'll get rid of you yet."

The girls loved that. When we'd have the same dessert for dinner twice, it was, "Morris, we'll get rid of you yet!" During the time on the Chase and Sanborn Hour, I had a song rehearsed that I wanted to introduce and I never did get a chance. Every week we'd run out of time before I could get to it. "Morris . . ."

When we were staying at the Desert Inn in Palm Springs one year, with the rates over a hundred dollars a day, including meals, I'd wake everyone early so they'd get to the dining room before it closed at nine. Marjorie's quite a sleeper and one morning she just wouldn't be roused.

"But, Marjorie, it's expensive, this is American Plan."

"Tell me, Daddy," she sighed. "How rich do we have to be to sleep through the American Plan?"

No early rising and out to play tennis, golf, or take a dip. Not my girls. The only exercise they get is with a knife and fork. When we were in Switzerland at St. Moritz, Christmas, 1934, I bought each of them a ski outfit—not to go skiing, just to get them outside the hotel into the crisp cold air. They never budged. Finally I got angry. "I bought the suits, you're going to wear 'em," I said. So they put on the ski suits and I had a sleigh waiting at the hotel door. It started to snow as we pulled away, just a light delicate little snow, and these dames all start to cry, especially Edna. As the bitter tears froze, she sobbed, "We came here to have a good time, Daddy, not to get healthy."

They're more at home in the half-dark of a theater, always have been. As soon as they were old enough they'd come to watch. When I was in *Kid Boots*, Marjorie and Natalie came every Friday night and every Saturday matinee. They'd stand in back because the houses were always sold out. The same routine for *Whoopee*. Before these two Ziegfeld shows I worked for the Shuberts. With the Shuberts there were no sellout houses, so the girls could sit in the back row. Natalie wanted me to go back to the Shuberts so she could sit down.

They were on the sets constantly during the summers when I was making movies. They're all hep on show business, they're the most loyal fans any entertainer ever had, they're wonderful critics and they let me have it, both barrels. The minute a radio show was over, or a television show now, they're on the phone with comment. Once, after a Chase and Sanborn broadcast when I'd introduced a song that was a real flop—the words ridiculous—Edna, just a kid, answered the phone when I called.

"How did you like the show?" I asked.

"Oh, Daddy, you were so *clever*, singing a song without any lyrics."

For such good critics, you'd think they'd all have wanted to take a stab at the business themselves. The answer: they didn't have to. Marjorie could be a top TV writer, no question about it. Edna could be commercially successful in the art field. They tried various jobs at one time or another, but they lacked the great incentive poor kids have—they didn't have to make a living. Marjorie got very wistful the other day talking with Jane Ardmore about career girls. Jane was telling Marjorie the thrill of earning your first cashmere sweater, your first alligator shoes. Marjorie sighed. "We've missed something," she said.

They've missed a number of things by being junior Cantors. Some things were too easy and some were too hard. Romance was hard. Nice guys who met them at school were hesitant to ask for dates. They figured these girls went out to big Hollywood parties every night, drank champagne and ate caviar and wore formal clothes. It wasn't true, but a lot of the nice fellows thought so and were afraid to intrude. The not-so-nice ones weren't hesitant at all. Sometimes they had a song to sell or an ambition dramatic, or they just thought it would be fine to be in the family. One of these anglers fell "in love" with each and every one of them, Marjorie through Marilyn. He handed them each the same line and the girls compared notes and thought it terribly funny. "You have such lovely hands, my dear, you should model them."

When he started phoning Marilyn to ask her for dates she balked; but Marjorie, Natalie, and Edna made her go, just to see if she'd get the same line. She did.

And I made mistakes. For instance . . . when we were in Beverly Hills the first time, we realized we couldn't drive a black car in California, it just isn't done. So we had the Lincoln painted yellow. That winter we were back in Great Neck, and the first day the girls were driven to school in the yellow Lincoln the kids jeered until the girls couldn't stand it. They got out and walked the last block. From then on they walked, period.

When Marjorie was eleven I discovered she was saving theater programs. Every time she saw a show she took the program home and added it to her collection. The minute I found out I had my agent send her every program for every show in town. They came. Marjorie thanked me. But the look on her face! All the kick had gone out of it.

And yet they had no delusions of grandeur. I can recall a Monday afternoon in Atlantic City in 1929. Marjorie was with me, we were spending the weekend and would return to New York for a Monday-night performance. In the dining room of the hotel Marjorie watched the waiter serving dessert at the next table. When I asked her what she wanted she said, "I'd like what that woman has over there." The waiter said it was a chocolate cream pot and immediately Marjorie refused it.

"Go ahead, have it, Marjorie."

"I can't," she whispered. "It costs a dollar, I'm sick just thinking about it." And I couldn't tempt her.

We left the dining room, walked down the boardwalk, and stopped at a brokerage house.

"Marjorie," I said, "while we were eating lunch today we earned fifty thousand dollars. Think of it."

She thought. She took me by the hand and walked me back to the dining room, found the waiter, and ordered her chocolate cream pot.

Because she was the eldest, Marjorie traveled with me a great deal. After she was out of school she came to California with me several times, a month or so ahead of Ida and the other four who were in school. On those trips she acted as my secretary and took care of all my paper work; and to this day I lean on her heavily for research on any and every thing. Behind those bright brown eyes, there's a built-in encyclopedia of show business. And there is nothing she couldn't write if she put her mind to it. Times when I was stuck for a serious spot on a radio show, she'd walk into the other room and come out an hour later with an episode for my Night Court of the Air. Something so good we'd never have to change a syllable.

The talent's there, and her critical judgment is right and I listen. She has told me that I do too much reminiscing on my programs, and the other night, watching Betty Hutton on TV, Marjorie came up with a top idea. "Daddy, the next time you're on television, you could make such a hit with a song like this: 'I'd like to stroll down memory lane but the darn place is too crowded now. Youngsters with their teeth still missing are at it selling their reminiscing. Betty Hutton—who's thirty-five—give me a chance while I'm alive.'" More than anyone I know, Marjorie knows what will get over and what won't. Plenty of people can tell you—when it's finished. Marjorie can tell you when it's still on paper. And she could score for herself if she would. As I tell her—you can't *flop* in a dressing room but you can't score either. She doesn't care. She loves her life, her little apartment, her new Volkswagen, her mother, her sisters and me.

And we couldn't do without Marjorie up in Ida's room. That's where all our family conferences are held. Never in the living room, never in the dining room, always in Ida's room. It's the Supreme Court. A child runs away . . . a child wants to leave college . . . or wants to get married . . . or is having a baby . . . or there's trouble in paradise and talk of a divorce. All in Ida's room.

When Janet was fifteen I went to work one day and found the movie studio surrounded by a picket line. And who was on this line, walking back and forth with a big UNFAIR sign? Our baby, Janet! That night in Ida's room I asked Janet if she thoroughly understood the issues and the petitions she was signing. "It's fine to express yourself, but you must know the issues. Do you, Janet?" Her answers were a little vague. I gave her some material to read that treated of the issues, the first stuff she'd read that wasn't slanted. We talked it over again, all the girls having their say. Janet dropped out of the picket line.

But Janet always had a mind of her own and stood on her two

feet. She dropped out of UCLA and took a job as secretary with a theatrical agency—under another name. It was tough to do, what with Social Security, but Janet tried it. One day at lunch a fellow employee made a crack about—guess who—me! Janet arched up. "Who makes *you* such an authority?" she said, and gave herself away in five minutes. Then she ran away. She left a note, she was going to New York. We stopped her in Chicago and brought her back. We sat her down in Ida's room, discussed the move—she was pretty young to live so far away—then gave her the money to go.

Natalie was seldom any trouble. She'd been an obedient child, her ambition was to be a wife and mother. She married a childhood sweetheart and when he grew up he was not the boy she'd thought he was. It was hard for Ida and me to imagine divorce. All we could do was love Natalie and keep her and Michael close to us.

And then Edna. She married a boy who thrust everything else aside in favor of ambition. He started as an office boy with MCA and never stopped until he was a vice-president. It reached the point where on New Year's Eve he and Edna would go out, at midnight the bells would ring, everyone else would kiss and say "Happy New Year," and Edna's husband would be off in a corner trying to sign a client. So it was Edna's turn in Ida's room.

Natalie and Edna were always docile, Marilyn always a bombshell. She'd met Ethel Merman when Ethel and I were working together, and Marilyn was crazy about Ethel Merman. One morning Marilyn zoomed in to breakfast. "Daddy," she cried, "I want to go on the stage." Not even "Good morning"!

"Don't you think you'd better finish your eggs first, Marilyn?" That night we continued the discussion in Ida's room. Marilyn was still in her teens, I saw no signs of talent, actually, but she was dead serious, so we sent her to the American Academy of Dramatic Arts in New York. When she earned her diploma she earned the right to go out and look for a job. She used a number of names; and she's had the usual tough struggle to get into the theater. If you use another name you wait outside. If you use your dad's name they expect too much.

Now I can see that she *does* have talent. She took a disc jockey's place from twelve midnight to 3 A.M., interviewing people, and she was just great. I've seen her since, on dozens of programs, and she is always absolutely sure of herself, a matured performer who knows what she's saying and how to say it. But there's no telling Marilyn or advising her. We're too much alike and she's so positive in her views that five minutes after we've said hello, we're drawing fire.

A few years ago I was asked to play a fair at Reading, Pennsylvania, and it seemed a good spot to put Marilyn on. I asked her how much she wanted and she said three hundred dollars. When she discovered she'd be getting seven hundred and fifty dollars she was enthusiastic and we worked out a good act. She was to sit in the audience and come running up with an autograph book. While we were rehearsing I pointed out to Marilyn that she should stand a step behind me. She's a pretty girl, I wanted the audience to see her face; and if one of us had to turn, I wanted it to be me. So, we're on . . . Marilyn comes running up and stands—in *front* of me, so that when we speak she's turning her back to the audience. I take her arm and try to pull her back. I keep right on trying to pull her back until she's black and blue.

As we go off Marilyn turns on me furiously.

"Daddy, what'd you think you were doing?"

"You were standing with your back to the audience, I was trying to turn you so they'd see your face."

"Daddy!" says Marilyn, "I graduated from the American Academy of Dramatic Arts!"

She's been with me on television with great finesse; but in working with me she's likely to tell me what's wrong with the whole thing (and, let me admit it, she's often right). She wants to run the show, direct and produce, and she can do it. She did a musical for Broadway called *Curtain Going Up*. It wasn't a good show, but she proved her ability to pick talent. She picked an unknown named George Axelrod to write sketches for her—the same boy who later did *The Seven Year Itch* and *Will Success Spoil Rock Hunter?* A couple of her songs later scored in *New Faces*. She found good singers and choreographers, and when she's sold on someone there's no resisting her enthusiasm. She makes you see them and hear them and give them a chance. Her big trouble as I see it—she's fought harder for other people than she ever has for herself. Marilyn hasn't quite found herself yet, but she will!

But to go back to Ida's room.

In the summer of 1956 Ida suffered a small coronary and was hospitalized. On the instant, Ida's room moved from our house to the Cedars of Lebanon. Even when the girls couldn't see her they were there, waiting in an anteroom with me, a little older, a little graver, until the moment when they could see Mother—and always with gifts, a glass of jelly, a bed jacket, a book. Marjorie organized us, finally, so that Ida wouldn't have too much excitement each day, staggered the visits, arranged each one's calendar so I'd never be eating alone. We're always *together*, but an illness like this makes us aware *how* together. Mother's room has always been the center of our house and wherever she is, that's still the center.

Above all, in Ida's room, we've respected each other's right to live his or her own life. Marjorie and Edna always stood up for me when *my* problems were being aired. When I wanted to leave Goldwyn Ida and the other girls urged me to stay, Goldwyn's name had prestige; and they wanted me to stay with Chase and Sanborn. But more important, on matters of principle Marjorie and Edna are likely to side with me where Ida might think I shouldn't butt into something out of my province, shouldn't jeopardize my bread and butter, while I think it might be better not to eat and be able to live with yourself.

We each have our say, but in the long run we respect freedom of choice.

Take Janet's marriage. It isn't easy to have a child phone from New York to tell you she's in love, she wants to get married, and you don't even know the boy. Ida and I wonder, is the fellow earning enough to support her? And maybe a baby or two? Ida and I waited until I had twenty-five hundred dollars in the bank. Janet just said, "We'll get along. Gari'll work" (he's a talented painter and a fine commercial artist), "and I'll work" (she was secretary to the president of American Guild of Variety Artists). You mention all the cautious things and you know they'll go ahead and get married anyhow. And Marilyn, who introduced them, and Marjorie, who knows him, think it's fine.

We needn't ever have worried about Janet. She's proved herself from the beginning. I mentioned her running away. She went to New York, still a youngster, got her job with AGVA, shared a Greenwich Village apartment with Miriam Marx (Groucho's daughter) and this was strictly the army. Sundays, these girls swept, cooked, cleaned and washed. Janet paid $1.50 a week for a used sewing machine, so old it had a foot pedal. She didn't know how to sew but she learned well enough to make slip covers for all the worn furniture in this Greenwich Village flat. She was in New York for a year and a half and proved her independence, so what could we say when she wanted to marry Bob Gari? We said yes. He's Italian, and Janet's become a fine Italian cook and an excellent housekeeper.

Quite a girl. When she was pregnant the second time, out to here, she cooked five days of food and stuck them in the deep freeze, so that while she was in the hospital having the baby there'd be good meals for Gari and their little boy, Brian. Janet always had a respect for money and we kid her that she's the richest in the family because she's always had a file drawer with dollar bills washed and ironed under M. When Macy's has a sale she's the first one standing in line for the doors to open.

She's tried to help Marilyn because Marilyn has budget trouble. One night Janet sat down and itemized every expense Marilyn has. She switched her from a laundry to a laundromat (Marilyn is enchanted with the laundromat), she cut on every item, and still Marilyn was spending more than she was earning. Janet solved it. Marilyn was coming to her house once a week for dinner; she'd have to come twice.

I never have gotten used to the kids not being at home. Ida and I sit down to dinner and I say, "Where are the kids?" None of them lives at home; but Marjorie, Natalie, and Edna all live near us in California and are in and out of the house. Janet was here this spring with Gari and the children. Marilyn's the one we can't lure home often. You have to bribe her with a part on your sixty-fifth birthday TV show. As far as she's concerned, we live in the woods. If you haven't a subway next door to your house and eight picture theaters and a half dozen all-night drugstores in the block, you're camping out.

But even to Marilyn the most important thing in life right now is Janet's baby, Amanda. You'd think no one had ever seen a baby before. They're on the phone to Janet constantly. When Janet was out here in California, Marjorie, Natalie, and Edna were on tap night and day—Amanda's everybody's baby, just as Janet was. The four older girls named Janet—she was theirs. And now Amanda.

How Ida adores that baby! She'll sit for hours just watching the sleeping child. Such a little pussycat. And I must confess, I'm Amanda's slave with the rest of them.

Why not? It's the habit of a lifetime. I've made with a lot of jokes about these girls but I wouldn't have missed them. I'm just sorry I missed as much as I did when they were little and I was on the road. I've made up for this with my grandchildren. To see Edna's Judy confirmed, to hear Natalie's Michael sing with the *a capella* choir at high school—to have all our girls milling around the house taking care of Brian and Amanda—it gives you a sense of life, a sense of fulfillment—more than you could have dreamed of when you were a hungry ragged orphan on Henry Street.

17. Politics and Politicians

My interest in politics started with a sarsaparilla at Bassler's Saloon in 1903. A young Irishman named Al Smith used to gather up all the boys hanging around Catherine Street and take them in to Bassler's. We'd line up at the bar and he'd go down the line. If you were wearing short pants he'd order "sarsaparilla," another short pants, "another sarsaparilla," he'd come to a boy in long pants, "one beer." What a guy! Everyone in the neighborhood loved him. If you had no coal and he found out about it, he'd get some organization to give you coal. If somebody needed a job, if a kid had no clothes . . .

He was a ward heeler and a do-gooder, the first I'd ever known, the nearest thing to a knight in armor that ever showed up around Catherine, Oliver, Madison, Monroe or Henry streets. Call it politics, call it whatever you want—it was still coal or clothes or a job for people who needed it. A young good-looking guy in a jaunty straw hat, and he was our hero. When he showed up in front of Bassler's, the kids came running, the grownups slapped his shoulders and shook his hand. No one called him "Mr. Smith." He was Al. There were placards in the store windows: Al Smith for Assemblyman. Vote for Al Smith.

I'd never heard a political speech in my life. I didn't know a Democrat from a Moose. As for Assemblyman? I took the stump. It wasn't just the sarsaparilla, it was the chance to spiel before a crowd. I got up on a box and let my voice out full. Better than *The Soul of the Violin* . . . "No other person ought to represent this district in our Assembly but *Alfred E. Smith*. He knows the district. He knows the people. The people love him." Pause. Applause. "Let's show him how *much* we love him!" Most of my audience were crazy about Al. How could I miss?

There was one kid who always encouraged me. I was great, he said. I was too good for the dopes on Henry Street and he kept urging me along into better neighborhoods where the crowd could "appreciate" me. What I didn't know was that *he* was appreciating the crowds. His name was Louie and he was picking pockets. The better the neighborhood, the better pockets to pick. (This Louie was later electrocuted for murder.) But me, I knew from nothing. I'm up there intoning, "You won't be sorry you've elected this man to the Assembly. He knows the people. Someday he'll run for the highest office in the land!" I got a little carried away.

I kept right on being carried away. Al Smith won his election, but that didn't stop me. The next time there was an election coming up I made some more speeches, this time for Morris Hillquit, a socialist. I had no idea who he was, I just wanted to show the boys on the block that I could sway them any way I chose. That night I got beaten up by a bunch of hoodlums representing the local Democratic party, Tammany Hall. They gave me a "D.A.," a dental assist, they knocked out some teeth, roughed me up, and gave me my first lesson in the great spirit of the Democratic party—from now on any speeches I was going to make I could make for their candidates, or else. I've been a Democrat ever since. I wanted to keep what teeth I had left.

My next speeches were for Al Smith, then running for sheriff. Some of the boys took me up to party headquarters and introduced me, "Al, you should hear Eddie Cantor, what he says about you!" He shook my hand and said he'd heard of me. He was probably kidding, but that winter he got me an overcoat, it came through some organization with a note from him. I'd long ago outgrown the overcoat from "Santa Claus" and this was a godsend. From then on I never quit making speeches for Smith. (He ran for president of the Board of Aldermen, he ran for governor.) After a while I began to understand what I was talking about. The man did know about legislation, and about people. He was scrupulously honest and he was wise. He was the first who ever said, "Let's look at the record," and his record was something you could look at.

We became close friends as the years passed. He used to come to the *Follies* and tell his guests, "See that little guy jumping up and down and rolling his eyes? He used to put on an act like that for me!" In 1924 I was at the Earl Carroll Theatre in *Kid Boots* and the doorman came up while I was making a change between the first and second acts.

"There's a Mr. Smith downstairs."

"Sammy Smith, the song plugger?"

"I think so."

"Send him up." There were only ten minutes between changes, my clothes were soaking wet, but . . . someone was standing outside the dressing-room door singing, "I wo-o-onder what's become of Sally . . ."

"Come on in, Sammy!"

The governor poked his head in the door, "You mean there's another song plugger named Smith?" he said.

He had a quick humor. One night someone said, "You must get tired, Cantor, the way you run up and down the stage when you sing."

"That's been a lifesaver for Eddie," quipped the governor. "He learned early it's harder to hit a moving target."

He was a good governor and a happy man, married to his school-days sweetheart. I visited him often at Albany. I'd say he had two big disappointments in his life—his disappointment in his protégé Jimmy Walker and, of course, losing the presidential election.

His running for President was a natural. He had the respect of leaders in both parties and he'd been a successful governor. What shocked and disillusioned Al Smith was that religion was brought into the campaign, that he was beaten largely by the silly rumor that if he were elected, the Pope would run the United States government. I was playing in Pittsburgh on the night of that election and the returns were coming in fast. In one scene I was captured by Indians and they were explaining about Pocahontas and how she had saved John Smith. So she saved John Smith. "Why couldn't she have done something for his brother Al?" I said sadly. It became one of the big laugh lines of *Whoopee*.

Al Smith could stand a laugh at his expense, but there were things he could not stand. He was a devout Catholic and what's more, he felt that a man in public office owed a debt to the public. He had loved Jimmy Walker, had had a great part in furthering his career, but while Jimmy was mayor of New York, Al Smith broke with him because Jimmy forgot or wouldn't accept such a thing as closed doors on his personal, romantic life. For a man in his office, the chief executive of a city, to flaunt immorality, Smith could not condone, and they broke. Smith never spoke to him again. Gentleman Jimmy went his way and a fabulous way it was.

Here was a politician who could have easily have been one of our top actors. He was a combination of George M. Cohan, James Cagney, and John Barrymore. He had the most charm, his was the greatest wit, he was the best off-the-cuff speaker I'd ever heard. A born orator, his choice of words was apt, he knew when to pause, when to cock his head, his gestures were entirely his. When he was mayor the first time and toastmaster Louis Nizer introduced him at a dinner with a virtual eulogy, Jimmy Walker got up and said, "After listening to your toastmaster, I can hardly wait to hear what I have to say"—a line widely used since.

What a quick study! At the Pennsylvania Hotel the Manufacturers Trust Company was installing new officers at a dinner. Nathan Jonas, president of the board (of which I was a member) heard that Mayor Walker was in the hotel making a speech, and asked me if I could get him to come up for a moment and address our newly installed officers. I went down to see Jimmy. He had finished speaking and said he'd be glad to. From his meeting on the second floor to our banquet on the fifteenth floor—how long does it take an elevator to go that far?—I told him what the meeting was about, and for the next twenty-five minutes he made the most brilliant speech about banking, what it meant in the financial life of the country—as if he'd spent days preparing.

He was interested in everything. In his early days he'd been keen about sports and was the father of the Walker Boxing Bill, which permitted boxing in the state of New York and of a baseball bill which permitted play on Sundays. He was against censorship of all kinds. When some group urged the banning of a book he said, "Never in my life have I heard of one girl who was ruined by a book." He loved the theater and was always backstage.

In the *Ziegfeld Follies of 1927*, I played "Jimmy Walker." I stood on the steps of the City Hall and "Lindbergh," "Gertrude Ederle," "Ruth Elder," all the celebrities came streaming past. To each I gave a key to the city. Finally I refused to see any more people because I'd run out of keys. Before the show opened Jimmy took me to his tailor, a little fellow on Fifth Avenue, who made me a morning suit exactly like Jimmy's; and I dropped in at the Knox Hat store for a high silk hat. I never did have to pay for it because I suggested that they use as a slogan, EVERY KNOX—A BOOST. So in Jimmy's clothes, I burlesqued Jimmy. He loved the show and saw it time and again. One night I introduced him to the audience and gave him a key—to my dressing room. He made a speech from his seat in the first row. He ad libbed and we started to kid around. A top actor.

And an honest man, but he was lax in his duties. He was more interested in play than in work, and people took advantage of his friendship. You can be such a good fellow that people think you *must* be bad. No one has ever proved Jimmy took anything, but when you don't lock the door someone will take something. With the chips down, Jimmy went up to Albany to see Roosevelt, but Roosevelt could only say, "You must answer the charges. You must stand trial." Even when it was all over and Jimmy had resigned, he polled more votes in a straw vote than any other candidate. But he was a broken man, a man suddenly old, and he went to Europe to live.

We met there in London in January, 1935. He and Betty Compton were now married and they came to visit Ida and me at the Dorchester House. Jimmy was broke, he looked weary. The man who'd been Mr. Broadway, who'd worn New York in his lapel! Ida and I were deeply touched. We were in Europe on a letter of credit and any of it, all of it, was at Jimmy's disposal. But what he wanted was a job, "a twenty-pound-a-week job." He wrote a column for a British newspaper and then came back to this country and worked for the clothing industry.

He'd lost some of the dash, but he was still Jimmy. In 1943 when I did a radio show at Mitchell Field Army Base he spent the day with me. On our way across the Post Jimmy said, "Eddie, an old friend of mine from Fordham University is the Catholic chaplain here. Let's drop in and say hello." We did. A few minutes later, going across the field, we noticed a Jewish temple. I looked at Jimmy, he nodded, we went in and paid our respects to the rabbi. Further along the route the driver pointed out a Protestant chapel and we stopped there, too. "Eddie, think of it," Jimmy said . . . "we just played God across the board."

He visited us once in Palm Springs a few years before his death, and Ida invited him to stay to dinner. "Of course I'll stay. You don't think I'd miss those little meat balls?" He was referring to little meat balls Ida had made for a wedding fourteen years or more before. I don't remember whose wedding—I want you to know I've gone to other weddings besides Jessel's.

But to go back. I mentioned being in Europe in 1935. This was my first opportunity to meet a couple of foreign politicians. In London I did several broadcasts for BBC on "Safety in Traffic," at the request of Leslie Hore-Belisha, who had heard about some of the work done over here for the National Safety Council. The first show for BBC started out with songs and comedy and ended up with a plea for safe driving: "Remember, children should be seen and not hurt." After the broadcast we were having dinner at the Savoy when Vic Oliver came over to the table. Vic, an American comedian, was married at that time to Winston Churchill's daughter Sarah. He introduced himself and said, "Eddie, the old gentleman would like to see you." Winston Churchill! He greeted me very warmly. We chatted. "Eddie, how many choruses of *Whoopee* do you know?" I thought back. I remembered five or six.

"I know *all* the choruses, my boy." And then and there he started to chant . . .

> "*Take Peggy Joyce, with little voice,*
> *She soon became, the nation's choice!*
> *I tell you, buddy, she's made a study*
> *Of making Whoopee.*"

And on and on through countless choruses he went, bald, smiling, charming. During the years, reading every word he's written, following his career as it became part of the history of our time, I've often thought back to that evening at the Savoy.

The other European politician I met at this time was different indeed—Mussolini. As president of the Screen Actors' Guild of America, I had a business proposition on my mind and an interview was arranged through the American Embassy in Rome by a man named McBride, a former Long Islander. McBride told me what to expect. Mussolini had a trick. His office was probably the longest office in the world; it took minutes to walk the length of it, and at the far end Mussolini would sit at a desk on a raised platform. The only furniture in the room was this desk and the chair he sat on and one other chair. Therefore, as one walked toward him down this long empty room, the dictator could size you up and under his gaze you were to feel smaller and smaller.

I go to the meeting. The door opens, it's all as McBride has told me, the endless room, Mussolini on the platform. But I have a trick of my own. The minute I come in I start to talk. Talk, talk, talk, whatever comes into my mind. Now he tries to hear what I'm saying and it isn't easy at that distance. He even strains a little forward to listen and he doesn't stare me down after all. He stands up and shakes hands. Then he pulls a handkerchief out of his pocket and starts waving it. "El Toro!" he says. "Cantor. El Toro!" He'd just seen *The Kid from Spain*.

Then we get down to business. I am proposing that we send English-speaking actors, directors, writers, and even crew to film pictures in Italy. I say it doesn't mean competing with Italian films but that if we could use these Italian backgrounds, it would do this for Italy: the American people would see the Forum, Mount Vesuvius, the Colosseum, the beautiful fountains and streets and buildings, it could be great tourist propaganda. Mussolini stands up to his five feet nothing, points his finger at me, and says, "And what is in it for you?" I said nothing except that it will give members of my union, the Screen Actors' Guild—he doesn't like the word union, the only union he is interested in is with Hitler—anyway, it will give them another outlet. It's not good being confined in one little place, Hollywood; it restricts actors to working always for the same few bosses. This could mean some independent production.

Mussolini thought it sounded good and turned me over to his son-in-law Count Ciano. Ciano did not speak English. I spent a long evening with him, with an interpreter. We might have gotten somewhere too, but something else was brewing, a major war. *Three Coins in a Fountain* had to wait.

I remember asking Ciano, "What is this unholy alliance between Mussolini and Hitler?"

"When the time comes," he said, "Mussolini will take Hitler and . . ." He zipped his finger across his throat.

Any wonder that years later on a Thanksgiving it occurred to me "Isn't it wonderful to live in a country where on a day like this the leader of the nation sits down to carve up a turkey instead of a map?"

I was alluding, of course, to Franklin D. Roosevelt, then President of the United States, whom I had become privileged to know and value as an executive and as a friend.

I met Roosevelt first in Washington thirty-seven years ago when he was Assistant Secretary of the Navy. Will Rogers took me to a dinner at the Mayflower Hotel. "You know little Kosher here," he said, introducing me. Mr. Roosevelt was a good-looking fellow in a dinner jacket. He was genial, urbane, and in excellent health. (This was before infantile paralysis changed his life.) I saw him some nights later at a benefit at Walter Reed Hospital. We had a chance to talk. I found him a better-educated man than either Smith or Walker, after all, a Harvard graduate. He was a classier man but not smarter than Smith. Al Smith was smart. That Roosevelt became a greater man was partly because the office of President inspires you. Any man who occupies the White House must sometime look around, see the portraits of Washington, Lincoln, and Jefferson, and realize that he too can go down in history. But in those early meetings I didn't think of Roosevelt as a history maker. He had a nice personality but I never dreamed he'd become President of the United States.

I believe that infantile paralysis *made* him President, that Roosevelt was compensated for this dread disease by gaining insight, wisdom, judgment far exceeding anything he'd have had living a normal life. When you sit in a chair—and you *have* to sit there—or lie in a bed—and you *have* to lie there—you have time to think and your thoughts are different, more penetrating than the thoughts of normal, busy, hurrying people. Once I said to him,

"Mr. President, it must be hard for you to do all the things you have to do in these precarious times."

He said, "No, Eddie. You see, I don't get about and so everybody has to come to me and this saves me a great deal of time and energy."

There was a tremendous change from the man who'd been Assistant Secretary of the Navy to the man who became governor of New York and then President. He knew pain; I believe he suffered constantly, that every time he got to his feet the muscles of his leg screamed. I never saw him take a step. I've driven with him in a car, Mr. Roosevelt doing the driving with manual controls, but I never saw him walk again. He had not only aged, he'd taken on the face of a sage. And the heart. I felt then and I feel now that with the possible exception of Dr. Albert Schweitzer, this man had the greatest feeling for the human race that I've ever known. What eventually was to kill him—in my opinion—were the casualty lists, the lists of dead soldiers. He died a little with each new list.

It has become popular in some circles to scoff at do-gooders. Pegler has made the word a sneer. So let me explain that I believe in do-gooders. Christ was one, Schweitzer is one, and many other men of many occupations, even if they're not full-time do-gooders, are doing it part time. Roosevelt, like Smith, was a do-gooder and his enemies could laugh and call it good politics. His friends knew better. They knew the heart was there too.

I remember when he first became President, there were so-called race riots in Harlem. The newspapers called them "race riots"; but when La Guardia sent Morris Ernst to investigate, Ernst found that these people had broken into stores, yes, into groceries and bakeries, but they did not take money, they did not touch a safe, they were stealing *food*. Morris said to me,

"Eddie, how far is Harlem from here?" I lived then on Central Park W. and Seventy-fourth.

"About twelve minutes."

"There was a revolution twelve minutes away from your house."

I mentioned this one day to Mr. Roosevelt. He said:

"Eddie, I wish you and all the other comedians would lay off jokes about boondoggling. When you put a shovel in a man's hand, even if he is leaning on that shovel, he hasn't got a gun in his hand sticking it into your back. And when young people are learning to dance and sing and paint pictures—and we're paying them for it —they're not going to have to rob for food." He lit a cigarette. "What allowance do you give Ida?"

I told him.

"Does she account for every penny?"

If he'd known Ida he wouldn't have asked that question. I explained that Ida accounts just so far, then she can't remember.

"If Ida as an individual can't remember," he said, "then this government shouldn't be criticized for dollars that are spent to help some needy people even if we can't account for every cent. If you walk down Hollywood and Vine, Eddie, you may be stopped by four or five actors who are down and out and ask for money. Maybe two of them are phony, but you give to all of them, don't you, to be sure that the two or three who aren't phony will eat? That's exactly what the United States government is doing."

Once I went to see him, representing the Screen Actors' Guild, in the matter of the proposed limiting of actors' incomes to twenty-five thousand dollars. "You're a stamp collector, Mr. President. You can buy a stamp with Washington's face on it for three cents, but there are a few rare stamps worth five thousand dollars and more. There's only one Marie Dressler. If her pictures make two or three million, why shouldn't she earn one hundred thousand dollars?" I knew he and Mrs. Roosevelt were crazy about Marie Dressler. He laughed. Then he grew serious.

"No one wants to take Ida's fur coat away from her, Eddie, or your car. But if the man around the corner is out of a job, his kids still have to eat. If we have to cut from the top to give them food, we'll cut."

If all this sounds like a big case of hero worship—it is. I believed in Roosevelt. Before the 1940 election I campaigned for him. There had been no need to do so in 1932, a change in party was inevitable because of the depression. In 1936 he was a cinch because he had done such a good job, saving the economy of the nation, lifting the hearts of the people. But in 1940, there was the matter of a third term and the bugaboo that a President might stay in office a lifetime. At such a crucial time internationally, it seemed desirable to me to keep in office someone who knew his job and was doing it well, rather than bring in someone who would first have to learn the job. And a third term couldn't destroy the two-party system. A man doesn't have to be re-elected. In fact, my feeling has been that we don't usually go to the polls to elect a man but to defeat one.

Campaigning for Roosevelt was easy because you could say, "Look at the record." With Ellin Berlin, Irving's wife, I walked into the lion's cage of Pasadena, a stronghold of Republicanism, to speak for Roosevelt's re-election. Ellin was a serious and moving speaker. I was comedy relief. I said I knew there must be many

Politics and Politicians

Republicans in the audience who used tooth paste and they might not use my sponsor's tooth paste if they didn't like my speech. But I knew that with Mr. Roosevelt in the White House, we would have something to chew with those teeth. If I joked, I was dead serious; and the audiences, wherever I went, knew it. There are those who feel that an actor has no right to speak his piece politically. I can't see it. We're citizens, aren't we? We pay taxes and have families and as much right to free speech as a doctor, a lawyer, or a columnist. The very columnists who criticize actors for doing it use their columns to express their own political views! Plenty of actors are afraid to take a stand, afraid of alienating part of their public. But are you any happier living with fears? One of the few actors with guts is Frank Sinatra. He was told that speaking his mind politically would ruin his career. Do you know anyone in show business today more successful than this same Sinatra? And he'll never have an ulcerated fanny from sitting on fences.

I knew Roosevelt had the strength and acumen and heart you seldom find, even at the top. I knew he loved America and I knew he hated nazism. I was at the White House in August of 1938 when Henry Ford accepted a citation from the Nazi consul in Detroit. "How can he," stormed the President, "accept a citation from the hand of the world's bloodiest gangster?"

Respecting this man for his convictions was one thing; you were equally charmed by his lighter side. No one—Walker, Smith—no one ever had the devastating sense of humor Roosevelt had. He could laugh at himself. He was an egotist; yet he could deflate that ego with one line.

At Warm Springs, Georgia, one day, he was in a wheel chair being pushed around the porch, stopping to chat with each of dozens of other patients.

"Mildred, did your mother get the bag of walnuts?"
"Yes, Mr. President. Thank you. She's baking cookies to send down this week."
"Alice, that's a pretty ribbon in your hair. I like that . . . Fred, how's that boil? I want to tell you about a salve . . ."

Down the line, forty or fifty people, and a personal message to each, and each name. I was confounded.

"Mr. President. How do you do it? How do you remember all those *names?*"

"Why it's easy, Eddie. I'm a politician!"

He could clown. . . . In the Little White House, there was an anniversary of the City of Baltimore. It is Wednesday before Thanksgiving, 1933, and he's going on the air. An engineer is standing by. "Two minutes, Mr. President." The President is smoking his cigarette in its long holder. "Eddie," he says, "let me show you how to handle these microphones." He pulls over a mike and starts "When the blue of the night meets the gold of the day," more like Crosby than Crosby. Then at a sign from the engineer, his serious talk.

I used to kid him. I'd say, "Suppose Joe Penner, Ed Wynn, and I, suppose we got ourselves two or three little White Houses and went into business for ourselves?" When he was running the second time, I introduced a song, "When I'm the President," and after the election, another song, "Roosevelt, Garner and Me." The first time that went over the air it got a telegram right back. "*Hail the new Triumvirate. Franklin Delano Roosevelt.*"

My real closeness with the President came about through the March of Dimes. We had talked many times about polio and its dread consequences. He knew that it must be fought. "Just because you know nothing about it, you don't quit," he said. "We have to learn. We have to make it something as comparatively harmless as scarlet fever." Once I went to him with the idea for a red, white, and blue billboard that would read, "We cannot stay neutral in our fight against infantile paralysis."

"It's very fine, Eddie, but I'm having so much trouble here now with the word 'neutral' I'm accused of being a warmonger." This was when he asked for ninety million dollars to fortify Guam, the amount a bellboy earned later in Washington for bringing up a pitcher of ice water.

One day I'm summoned to the White House.

"Eddie," Mr. Roosevelt says, "we have to do something to fight infantile paralysis. Can you organize a million men for me who'll give a dollar a year?"

I think about it. "Mr. President, I could get you a million men but they might dwindle down to two, three hundred thousand if you aren't re-elected." The President smiles. "Why not let everyone in on this for ten cents? Let me do some broadcasts, I think I can get you ten million dimes faster than a million dollars."

"How would we do it? Where would they send the dimes?"

"Just give me the use of your name and address, Mr. President. You have a lovely address here! I'll bet you the American people flood the White House. You may lick infantile paralysis with this march of dimes."

The President slaps my knee. "Eddie Cantor, you've just given us our slogan, 'The March of Dimes.'" Then he calls in Marvin McIntyre to ask if he could handle a little extra mail. Seventy-two hours later the White House is all but buried under sacks and sacks of letters and their dimes.

That was just the beginning. We did a lot of broadcasts. The response of the stars was wonderful. Only once I asked an advertising agency for an actor to appear on a March of Dimes broadcast and got turned down.

"We're not going to have any part in building up Roosevelt," the agent said.

"You know," I told him, "I just learned from an authoritative source that the germs of infantile paralysis can't distinguish between a Democrat and a Republican."

The broadcasts went on. One night Cagney played one dime and Bogart another. Cagney was bragging that he was new and shiny but that Bogie looked so thin. Bogie said it didn't matter, he could still join the March of Dimes. He taunted Cagney for looking bright and shiny. "You've never been around!" And Cagney explained he'd spent years under a mattress, a guy from Waukegan had brought him to Hollywood years ago and . . .

Always, after the broadcast, the minute we'd go off the air the phone would ring. Not a secretary, but the President himself to say, "Bless everybody and thank you."

Right after the Cagney-Bogart broadcast the phone rang again and a man from Texas roared, "Gggggggreat show. I'd like to send you a little check. Where do I send it?"

"To the White House."

"Hell, no," bellowed the gentleman. "It'd get lost in all those damned dimes."

I thought he was a joker or a drunk but I suggested he address his contribution to Marvin McIntyre marked "personal."

Several days later McIntyre called. "Do you know So-and-So from Texas? He just sent us a check for fifty thousand dollars. What'll I do with it?"

"Run to the nearest bank, cash it!" I yelled.

And it didn't bounce. It was good.

These were exciting times. Mr. Roosevelt was deeply thrilled with the response to the March of Dimes. He would have been more thrilled with the way Basil O'Connor's carried on. How I wish he could have lived to hear the report on the Salk vaccine! But he knew, he knew. He was a man of conviction and courage.

I'll never forget the time at Warm Springs when Harry Hopkins came rushing in, very perturbed. A senator had that day made a great tirade against the President and his policies on the floor of the Senate. Mr. Roosevelt listened to Hopkins, took out a cigarette, and very calmly lit it.

"Chief, you're not upset?"

"Harry," drawled Mr. Roosevelt, "when one has defeated the angel of death, one doesn't become frightened of a mere senator."

That, to me, sums up Franklin Delano Roosevelt. As a guy who's looked death in the eye himself now, I've learned to understand what he meant.

18. Audiences

I've told you about the men in my life and the women in my life. Now let me tell you about the men-women-and-children in my life, a great family of a different sort—the audience!

There is no such thing as a bad audience. The minute people come into a theater or wherever else you're playing, they have done their part. They didn't come to buy an overcoat or a bowl of soup, they've come to be entertained. And I mean entertained, not insulted. I've never used a mother-in-law joke in my fifty years of show business, because the audience is full of mothers-in-law! What's more, every mother-in-law is someone's mother, so you're insulting most of the audience. You owe those people out front your best taste, your best—period.

If you don't make good, they are the losers. You get paid anyhow; but if you don't entertain them, the audience has lost time and money and something more—some of their happy faith in show business. So every performer should play to an audience as if it were the last performance of his life, as if this is what he'll be remembered for. It doesn't matter whether you're on Broadway or in the smallest tank town, on coast-to-coast television or in a local theater to a half-filled supper show.

One time I told Ziegfeld about a comedy dancer I'd seen in Brooklyn. I thought he'd be great in the *Follies*.

"I should go to Brooklyn?" Ziegfeld said. "Wait till he plays the Palace."

"When he gets to the Palace it'll cost you a lot more money to get him."

"It's worth it," Flo said.

But I was so insistent that he finally did go to Brooklyn. He got there for a Friday matinee. The audience was small and that day the discouraged dancer cut his main dance and left out half his jokes. Ziegfeld came back disgusted. "Eddie, you must've gone crazy! He's nothing." It took four more years for this fellow to get to Ziegfeld: Jack Donahue. If he'd given a good performance on a certain Friday in Brooklyn, he could have saved himself four years of hoofing in vaudeville, because the talent was there, he was the finest comedian-dancer of his day.

You are stealing, you are cheating, you are completely dishonest unless you give at every performance of your life the best performance that you can. Shakespeare has said it much better. "To thine own self be true."

On board the Chief, in March, 1940, I told this to a group of youngsters who were traveling in vaudeville with Ed Sullivan. I told them never to let down, that anything less than their best was not only an insult to the audience but an insult to themselves. Sullivan printed my remarks as "The Ten Commandments of Show Business," and these "commandments" were hung on the wall of every dressing room in every vaudeville house in the country. Actually the kids in show business need to be told all this less than some seasoned, successful performers.

I happened to be in St. Louis with *The Midnight Rounders* when Richard Bennett was playing there in Eugene O'Neill's *Beyond the Horizon*. It was a superb production and I caught it several times at matinees. On my second visit they were playing to half a house. Bennett was a fine actor, he gave the performance everything he had; but between acts he came out and made the most vitriolic speech you ever heard. He told the audience that they were hopelessly provincial, that it was wasting a good play and expert actors to ever come to St. Louis. I went back to see him after the show and told him frankly:

"If you want to bawl someone out, Dick, stand in the street and scold the people who didn't buy tickets. Don't bawl out an audience who've proved their loyalty by coming to the theater. They should have gotten up and walked out." It is depressing to see a half-filled house, but you've got to do your best for the half who are there.

I'd learned this the year before when I faced my first "unpacked" house. I'd left Ziegfeld and the *Follies*, where I was one of many, to be a star for the first time with my name in lights:

EDDIE CANTOR IN *THE MIDNIGHT ROUNDERS*. We opened in December, 1920, at the Shubert Theatre, Philadelphia, and did very well. There was plenty of publicity, Eddie Cantor's first starring vehicle; girls, girls, girls, and we scored a hit. And in Baltimore and in Boston. Then we played Newark, New Jersey. This is only a short ride from New York. We got in late, went right to the theater and started to dress. Company manager Jack Reed came to my dressing room.

"Eddie," he said. "Don't be too disappointed. There's nobody out there. I don't know why. Maybe not enough promotion, maybe . . ."

"What do you mean, *nobody?*"

"I mean just about nobody."

I put on my robe, went out to peek through the curtain, and I give you my word of honor, there were not nine rows of people! I called the company together and told them the truth. "Now, we're going out there and give the damnedest show we've ever given," I said. "I want every mother's son in the theater tonight to be our press agent tomorrow!"

We went out. We gave our best performance, better than to all the packed houses that had gone before; and the audience sensed what we were doing. They were so appreciative that about eleven o'clock, I said, "Ladies and gentlemen . . . you're a bunch of dolls, and you're not going to leave the theater until one of us is exhausted." There was a list of my songs on the back of the program, and I told them to shout for what they wanted. There were twenty songs on the list; I sang all twenty. Then I said, "If you think we're worth it, that we deserve it, please, each of you, send four or five of your friends to see us tomorrow." They almost cheered.

The next night was not sold out, but it was better. Our Wednesday matinee played to two thirds of a house, by Thursday we were packed, and on Friday and Saturday we turned away seven or eight hundred people. The next time I came back to Newark, we took in ninety thousand dollars in two weeks—it stands as the world's record for a gross in any city this size. You see, while Newark is a large city, it has the warmth of a small town; one person tells the other the news over a back fence.

The audience in Newark that first night wasn't the smallest I'd ever faced. No indeed. When I was with the *Follies,* various people, socially prominent, would ask entertainers to come out and play private parties. Many times I went to Mrs. W. K. Vanderbilt's and sang and clowned for a large number of guests. But one night when I got there I was ushered into the dining room, where Mrs. Vanderbilt and one gentleman sat at the dinner table. I looked up and down the long room. Just Mrs. Vanderbilt and her guest. She introduced him.

"Well," I said, "this is no place to say 'ladies and gentlemen . . .'" I pulled up a chair, sat down, and for three quarters of an hour I talked—about my childhood, my grandma Esther, the salami, our basement apartment, and my grandmother's humor and heroism. I talked about Ida and her dad and Al Smith, about life on Henry Street.

A small audience but a good one. Fifteen years later I ran into a big audience that was far harder to sell. It was a personal appearance at the Fox Theatre in San Francisco. Sam Behrman, the playwright, was in town with a play starring Margalo Gilmore; and he and Margalo came back with me to the Fox for my midnight show. This was the sixth performance of the day and I knew that sometimes on a Saturday midnight the audience was a little rough. Young fellows and their girls would arrive with a bottle and they'd what you might call "participate" in the performance. It happened that way this night. Our show started and several acts got hooted off. Now it was my turn. I walked out, the star of the show (getting 50 per cent of the gross), and I couldn't get out my first line. They yelled, screamed, and hooted. I walked to the wings, pulled out a chair, sat down and gave a signal that they should go ahead, whoop it up. Finally they grew quiet. I waited. After about ten seconds of dead silence I leaned back in the chair and said, "Imagine getting paid for *this!*" That did it. I was on—for almost an hour. They hadn't let me get on, now they wouldn't let me get off.

An audience loves an ad lib. It's the something extra, like a curtain speech, that makes them feel they're getting a bargain, like buying things wholesale. What made the Palace so good years ago was the fact that often at the end of a bill many of us would get together and join each other's act, in what was commonly called an afterpiece. This *made* the Palace. In 1931 Kate Smith, Lou Holtz, Bill Gaxton, and an all-star bill established such a camaraderie that they were held over for ten weeks. As soon as they finished, the Palace booking agent invited me to come in and try for a run. I agreed, if I could pick my own acts: Georgie Jessel, a couple of friends of his whom I hadn't seen yet—Burns and Allen—Janet Reed, the Rhythm Boys ("Tip, Tap, and Toe"), Benny Meroff and his band, and Serge Flash.

Georgie and I took a room at the Edison Hotel, a block from the Palace, and for three days and nights mapped out the show. Serge Flash opened, then Jessel and I came on and started kidding each other. We got in each other's acts, played in sketches with Burns and Allen, and everyone was in the finale. It started with me blacking up in front of the audience, one of the Rhythm Boys holding the mirror and kibitzing with me.

"There's one thing Jessel can't do," I said and started singing "Dinah." As I turned, there was Jessel in back of me, blackface, then Burns and Allen, blackface, then Janet Reed. Everyone blacked up but the audience.

We played the Palace for nine weeks and most of that time the only way you could get tickets was through a speculator. The furor had nothing to do with what we each did individually. It was the bargain—the bargain of plenty of talent plus the seeming spontaneity of having the performers get in each other's acts. We could have gone on for fourteen or fifteen weeks, but it seemed smart to quit while we were still playing to "standing room only."

Jessel and I went on from the Palace to the Paradise Theatre on the Grand Concourse in the Bronx. What a contrast in audiences! Only the best play the Palace, so this is a sophisticated audience; but playing the Paradise is like playing in a big kitchen, a strictly homey place where the audience doesn't merely applaud, they virtually clasp your hand. There were people in that audience who hadn't been inside a theater in years. They came because of loyalty and nostalgia for a couple of local boys who'd made good. Some of the women brought us homemade soup! (They left it at the stage door.)

For this audience we added and subtracted material and changed the act. We were doing big business and the management kept coming back suggesting we cut a few more minutes. Our act ran fifty minutes. Cut ten minutes of that four times a day and you have an extra show to take care of the mob in the lobby. One day the manager asked us to cut another five minutes. We figured that I could cut a medley of songs and Georgie could cut his "Chazan ov Shabbas" ("The Cantor on the Sabbath").

We're on, we're winding up the act, when suddenly a fellow shouts from the audience: "Just a minute. Just a minute. What's the matter with Jessel's 'Chazan ov Shabbas'?"

"How did you know about that?" I said.

"I heard it at the last show."

"So you've heard it."

"I want to hear it again. There's a law against it, I shouldn't hear 'Chazan ov Shabbas' again?"

There was no law. Jessel had to sing it before this customer would let us finish the act.

I don't know how many shows he stayed for; a good part of the audience stayed indefinitely. A woman would come backstage and say, "Mr. Cantor, do me a favor. My two children have been in the theater since twelve noon. They haven't eaten for six hours. Will you give 'em these sandwiches?" So I'd call their names and they'd come up on the stage and get their dinner.

Sometimes as I'd go off I'd look at a familiar face and say, "Weren't you here for the last two shows?"

"Yes," he'd say.

"Well, aren't you hungry? What kind of a sandwich would *you* like?"

The customer'd specify corned beef or chicken, and while Jessel was on I'd have a stagehand run next door and get the sandwich. I'd come back on carrying the paper sack. "Oh yes, and a pickle," and I'd pull a big dill out of my back pocket. Sometimes a fresh guy'd say, "What, no coke?"

Audience participation reached its height the day a man stood up and signaled for attention.

"Mr. Cantor, I've long been a fan of yours. May I come up and get your autograph?"

Strictly off-beat; but the audience applauded, so I said that if the rest of the house wouldn't try to follow suit, yes, he could. The man came up and I signed a card for him. Then Georgie said, "How about me?"

"You are Mr. George Jessel?"

"I am!"

"Well, *I* have something for *you*," and he handed Georgie a subpoena.

There is a big difference, of course, between a vaudeville audience and a legitimate-theater audience. There is an aura of expectation attached to the theater, an aura of glamour. The audience has waited often a long time for their tickets and they come with a top-hat feeling. This is true whether the theater is on Times Square or not. Through the years there's been a lot of hoop-de-do about the special caliber of a Broadway audience. It's the bunk. Take a poll of a Broadway audience, you'd find that two thirds of them were out-of-towners in New York seeing the sights. That's why it's no different playing Dubuque or Broadway. Who's in a Broadway audience? Dubuque!

As for opening night on Broadway—that's the worst night of all. Will Rogers offered Ziegfeld his entire salary for a week—he'd have worked seven performances for nothing—not to go on opening night. Why? Because he felt that "these people don't read the papers" and Rogers's act depended on how well they'd read 'em. Rogers was so right.

A smash hit opens on Broadway, a *My Fair Lady* or a *South Pacific*, a show destined to stay right in that theater for two or three years. Now, who is there opening night? All the scenic designers and their assistants (the designer who did the show and all those who wanted to). They don't watch the show, they watch the scenery. They don't care about the music or lyrics or jokes or acting. They're looking at the shade of blue in the first backdrop and wondering why anyone had such a crazy idea for a background. . . . All the costumers are there. They hear nothing, they're interested only in the costumes. "Ruffles?" they mutter to each other. "Ruffles, *now*?" The girls come out, the costumers don't see their faces or their legs, they see just the disembodied costumes. . . . Song writers and publishers are there, not to applaud but to hiss mentally because they didn't do the score.

Then there are playwrights and their agents, the moguls of the networks and the movie representatives, at least forty of these, knowing perfectly well that Paramount has already bought the show and each thinking, "Remind me to fire Wienberg or O'Hara tomorrow, we could have had this thing!" . . . And there are the regular first-nighters who have come not to see but to be seen.

Many of them haven't looked at the stage for the first three quarters of an hour, they're too busy looking at each other; the gowns, the furs, who's who and who's whose. A show unanimously acclaimed by so disinterested an audience *must* be great!

What really matters in the opening-night audience is the critics whose word will go out tomorrow to the reading public. So much depends on them! And let me tell you about the critics: I haven't met more than three or four who ever start out to be malicious or to write a brilliant column at the show's expense. Most of them are pulling for you. They want you to be a hit. It hurts them to write honestly that you're weak in this department or that. Take a hundred critics throughout the country, you'll find ninety-six of them honest and fair; if you listened to their suggestions and followed them you'd have a better show.

The excitement of a Broadway opening is created by the critics and by the presence in the audience of your personal friends and other producers. I've never seen a performer who didn't react to this excitement except two, Fanny Brice and Ethel Merman. Ethel says, "I know the words, I know how loud I can sing. If they could sing as loud and as good, they'd be up here." She and Fanny have been the most confident, least scared performers Broadway's ever known.

There's no *apprehension* about the Broadway opening, because a show has been tried out elsewhere. Apprehension goes with the tryout, in Pittsburgh or Atlantic City or Boston. Then you are really on edge, not knowing how the show will click, and sometimes you don't know even after the opening because the audience is so enthusiastic, they constantly stop the show with applause. A girl will get a reception opening night and never another during the entire run.

But once a show is established you lose your apprehension, you know what you have. What changes is the audience; and the charm of being on stage before live people is that you can respond to them and change, too. I've had my flops, plenty of them; a picture called *Forty Little Mothers* that did nothing; a picture, *If You Knew Susie*, that was nothing. But on stage you're 99 per cent in control of your situation. If you find that a certain attack isn't right, you switch, you don't have to flop. When Ethel Shutta and I were working together in *Whoopee* she was on stage first.

I made my entrance leading a little calf. I was playing the part of a hypochondriac. Ethel would say:
"Henry Williams, what is that?" pointing to the calf.
And I'd say, "Condensed milk."
From the type of laughter, the reaction to the words, "condensed milk," I'd turn to Ethel and whisper, "Eleven tonight," or "Eleven-ten." By the length of the laugh I'd know what time our show'd break. If it was a sharp audience, we'd jump certain things, work a little faster; if they weren't so sharp, we'd slow down to give them time to catch the jokes.

And let me say that as time has gone on, audiences have gotten sharper constantly. When I played in *Banjo Eyes* in 1941 I found that a great change had taken place since my last stage appearance in a legitimate theater. They knew more, they were on to all the tricks. Drop your voice to make them lean forward—old stuff! Radio had helped educate them; personal appearances in movie houses had helped. In big cities the fans had seen all the headliners.

And today! There's no such thing as a "small-town audience" left in America. Television brings them in thirty-nine weeks what they'd have seen traveling to Broadway for ten years! Audiences are hep and they're demanding. It's like this . . . People attending a smash hit in the legitimate theater walk in excited, they practically applaud the usher who seats them. In a movie house the audience accepts headliners as if they were nylons for fifty-nine cents and two performances for the price of one if they wish to stay. But on television you're not only free, they can switch you off with a twist of the dial. The television watchers sit back in their easy chairs and say "O.K., entertain us," and if you don't, and quickly, you're off, brother, and another channel is on.

But to go back . . . Audiences began to get hep when they saw the headliners in the movie theaters; and as the depression reached its height more and more big names played the movie circuits. Curiously enough, entertainers were in this position— theater owners wanted you for personal appearances if you made a very small salary or if you got a fortune. You had to be so cheap it meant nothing, or so expensive you'd bring people in.

Sophie Tucker had introduced me to the William Morris office and to Abe Lastfogel, who has been her agent for life. Lastfogel is more than an agent, he's a psychologist. He was the first to sell an entertainer at 50 per cent of every dollar that came into the theater box office. I was the entertainer. In June 1939 he booked me into New York's Loew's State, where no one had ever received a percentage. The theater averaged nineteen thousand dollars weekly, a lot of business, but Nicholas Schenck was willing to gamble on my earning my 50 per cent over that.

It's June 29. I'm to do my first show at noon and I've left word at the hotel desk that I'm not to be disturbed until ten. At eight-fifteen the operator wakens me with an urgent call. It's manager Rosen at Loew's State.

"I hate to waken you, Eddie, but it means money in your pocket as well as ours. You can come right down, open the doors and give them a show. The crowd's down Forty-fifth Street from Broadway to Sixth."

I rushed to the theater, took a sip of orange juice in the dressing room, and at nine sharp went out to start the show. When it was over I said, "Ladies and gentlemen, the management tells me that more than a thousand people are waiting in the lobby and outside. They've been standing for an hour and a half. You look like a lot of good sports to me and I'm sure if you were standing outside you'd want someone to get up and give you a seat." It worked pretty well, we'd have an exodus of 80 to 90 per cent after each curtain speech. Even so, during the day, ushers from all Loew's theaters and twenty-six patrolmen tried to cope with the crowds that lined Seventh Avenue on both sides of the theater between Forty-fifth and Forty-sixth streets. During the rush people waited two to three hours to be admitted.

Total receipts for the week were $50,317; total attendance, 115,038. I still have framed the newspaper clippings: "EDDIE CANTOR BREAKS ALL EXISTING BOX OFFICE RECORDS FOR RECEIPTS AND ATTENDANCE FOR THE ENTIRE 19-YEAR HISTORY OF LOEW'S STATE THEATRE."

How can you help loving audiences? They not only pay your salary, they give you applause, understanding, and affection. They're as important to an entertainer as his life's blood. Without them, he's no entertainer. And the ultimate for any ham is to face his audience alone, head on, without anything or anyone to help him. It's one thing to be one of many stars in a show or a star with a big show to back you up; but to warrant applause all by yourself is the greatest of all ego inflators.

One of the big gambles of my life and the greatest satisfaction I ever had in the theater was the one-man show, *My Forty Years in Show Business* that I tried in 1950. It was my own idea. The guy who'd grown up a hooligan on Henry Street wanted to prove to himself that he'd become an entertainer.

I hired two pianos and was in business. And I was scared to death. We opened, not in New York, not on Broadway where my material might have had some nostalgia for old-time theatergoers who'd known me as far back as the *Follies*. We opened on a college campus before audiences who had never seen me in their lives. It was "go for broke." I had no idea whether I could get across to the younger generation who hadn't been born when I was on Broadway and who hadn't been listening to radio or seeing pictures when those were my media, a generation sophisticated by television.

The acid test was opening night, a bitter stormy night at Orono, Maine, the University of Maine campus. So many tickets had been sold that I had to do two performances, each an hour and forty-five minutes long. I sang, I joked, I talked about people like Will Rogers and W. C. Fields and Fanny Brice—all just names to these kids—and it was one of the great nights of my life. We played other colleges after that: University of Arizona, William and Mary College, Oklahoma, A & M. Then Sol Shapiro of the Morris office talked me into something even more hazardous—he talked me into playing Carnegie Hall. This was a frightening thing. As the house got more sold out, it grew more frightening. When the big night finally came I was as nervous as the amateur who first walked out on stage at Miner's Bowery Theatre. Only this time the audience was waiting for me. There were three hundred chairs on the stage, and to get the show rolling I had stuffed the pockets of my dinner jacket with dollar bills. "I feel I owe an apology to you people sitting on the stage. Since you'll be seeing my back all evening, you shouldn't have to pay the same price as those people out front," and I started handing out the dollar bills.

Now I was more at ease; in ten minutes I was feeling fine. The nervousness of an entertainer melts once the audience starts to laugh and applaud. And the greatest tribute is when you want them to be silent and they are—when the silence is thunderous.

In my lifetime in show business I have only known seven or eight performers who have tried a one-man show and I wouldn't have missed them. So . . . now I had played Carnegie Hall to an ovation, but I wondered how much of the audience had been composed of friends, fans, and the curious. Maybe it was a freak success; I didn't know. I wasn't sure whether I'd proved I was an entertainer or not. I kept thinking about it while I played forty cities across America. I kept reading the notices:

N.Y. World-Telegram and Sun: "Broadway's week gave us Eddie Cantor in his own one-man show, and a rather wonderful show it is. I might even be inclined to vote for it as the best play of the season."

N.Y. Times: " 'The house was jammed' and it was not difficult to understand why. A few seconds after Mr. Cantor had sprinted to the center of the stage, he had the audience completely under his spell. His self-assurance, stage presence and timing, combined with humility are virtues that should be studied profitably by the neophytes of show business."

N.Y. Journal American: "A lesson in perfect showmanship to sit in Carnegie Hall and watch Mr. Cantor hold it and its contents by the magic of his craftsmanship. 'My Forty Years in Show Business' all by, all with and all about Eddie Cantor turned out to be one of the very best shows of the season."

Bob Considine: "A one-man 'South Pacific.'"

Had I really scored a hit? I went back to Carnegie Hall the next year to be *sure*. This time I knew the audience was anybody and this time I came off with a feeling of elation, of pride, and of proof.

"You satisfied?" Ida said. "Can you stop proving?"

She hadn't wanted me to try a one-man show. She's never wanted me to risk being hurt or disappointed. And I've tried to explain that if you don't go into the ring you don't get hurt but you're never a champion. An entertainer is no entertainer sitting on his patio in Palm Springs. He must have an audience. They make him come alive, God bless 'em!

19. Radio Audiences

To show you how important an audience is—what brought my first radio show to life (the Chase and Sanborn Hour) and took it to the top was the participation, for the first time, of a studio audience. There was an audience in the studio from the beginning; but during 1931 and the start of 1932 Jimmy Wallington would stand up before each broadcast and make a speech prepared by the J. Walter Thompson advertising agency:

"Ladies and gentlemen, you are here as guests of Chase and Sanborn. We ask you to co-operate with us in not applauding, not laughing, so that our listening audience can have the illusion of hearing a show without distraction."

If we were supposed to be at the North Pole, the advertising agency wanted those listening to think we *were* at the North Pole, not performing in a nice warm studio before nice warm people—and I mean *warm*. Studio audiences get their tickets free and they're with you every minute. But week after week these eager watchers couldn't laugh or applaud. So much as a snicker and an usher would come running to say "Shush!"

Now Jimmy and I are doing a scene in which women take over the jobs of men. What would happen if two lady truck drivers met in traffic? I was "Edwina" Cantor, he was "Jenny" Wallington. This is radio, we need no props, just speeches. But suddenly I can't resist . . . Ida and Mrs. Wallington are seated in the front row. They each have on hats and fur scarves in their laps. In the instant, I snatch the hats, clap them on Jimmy's and my heads, fling the furs around our necks and on with the show. The audience is howling and there's no stopping them as we two clowns mince around in our finery. They keep on laughing until the show is over. They're still laughing at a minute after nine when John Reber of J. Walter Thompson calls.

"Eddie, what happened?"

"John, forgive me, I'm impulsive, I got carried away."

"Well, let me tell you something. Your show's finally come alive! You have audience participation!"

It was this simple—the minute the studio audience began to laugh, the listeners laughed too. They were no longer alone in an empty living room, they were part of the show. And what a part! I didn't realize how vast until the mail began to pour in. I stayed up nights studying this mail that came from every conceivable spot in America, places no Ziegfeld show had ever played, places far from any movie theater.

To any ham who takes life from an audience, think what this type of mass communication means. Say you played in a Ziegfeld show at the New Amsterdam Theatre which seats 1600. In a week you play to 13,000 (including the standees). Play that Ziegfeld show for fifty weeks, you would play to 650,000. If you played for ten years, you'd play to six and a half million. In twenty years it would be thirteen million. And if you played for *forty years,* to packed houses, standing room only, you'd play to less people in forty years than you played to in *one night* on the Chase and Sanborn Hour!

I never thought of it then. If I'd thought I'd have been too scared to go on. Actually I didn't know much about radio until I was on it. Ida and I had come down to Florida in December 1930 because I had a chance to play a night club, for two weeks, and we'd never been to Florida before. Rudy Vallee was broadcasting from Miami Beach over an NBC station and he asked me to go on for a guest stint.

"Tell me more about radio, Rudy, advise me. What would be best for me to do on the show?" Rudy suggested that I sing, he suggested we clown around together and we did. An agent named Mort Millman caught the show and recommended me to Chase and Sanborn as a replacement for Maurice Chevalier, who was leaving for France. Chase and Sanborn offered me a four weeks' trial. Meanwhile I listened to radio until it was coming out of my ears. I listened to everything, every type of program, getting the feel of it—a medium where it wouldn't do you any good to roll your eyes or clap your hands or create perpetual motion.

J. Walter Thompson provided some writers and I gave them material, sure-fire things I'd proved already in the theater. The writers in those days had a steal. There'd be five or six writers to provide, say, fifteen minutes of dialogue and you couldn't get *that* until two and a half minutes before you went on the air. Later I got hold of talented David Freedman, and he wrote for me until the end of 1934. Our "cast" included announcer Jimmy Wallington, orchestra leader Rubinoff, and myself. Wallington doubled as straight man and I took all other parts—an Irish policeman, a Swedish cook, anything. I'd talk to myself in one dialect and then answer as me. And I also played the part of Rubinoff, asking him questions, then answering myself in a Russian accent.

After the first four weeks Chase and Sanborn gave me a year's contract with an option for another year. And then it got beyond anything that anyone had ever dreamed of. The rating climbed and climbed and stayed. During '32, '33 and '34 we had the biggest audience in America and sometimes there was as much as fifteen points difference between our rating and that of the second highest program. It was wonderful. It was also a great responsibility.

First of all I always believed in honesty in advertising. Don't oversell. But, of course, this wasn't my province, I was a comedian. One night, however, the show had been timed badly, something that *happens* in radio and in television. You're on from eight to nine, now it's eight fifty-five and you're saying your last lines while the guy in the control booth is fainting. He gives you a big motion with both arms that means "S-t-r-e-t-c-h!" and there's nothing to stretch, not another line of script.

"Ladies and gentlemen," I ad libbed, "it's nice to know that we come into your homes every Sunday night. It's nice to know that after these many months we're not only entertainers, we're part of your family, and it's nice to know you're not charging us board. Now I'd like to tell you something about Chase and Sanborn. Let's not kid ourselves, all coffee's good, ours just happens to be a little bit better. If you're drinking some other brand of coffee, nothing much can happen to you. Your teeth'll just come loose, your gums'll get flabby, you'll feel awful. That's all. But with Chase and Sanborn . . ." And I continued the pitch until our time was up.

Nothing of this kind had ever been done on the air before and John Reber now said we must always leave time at the end of the show for an impromptu little speech. That's how my closing lines originated. Sometimes I'd talk about something in the news, a bit of philosophy, anything. Sometimes I ad libbed, sometimes I'd have scribbled a few lines down on paper.

Later I went to Reber and discussed my ideas about honesty in advertising. He, in turn, went to the Standard Brands people. "Cantor wants to do a commercial which I think is negative selling, but he claims people will buy coffee on the strength of truth in advertising." This was my commercial:

"Ladies and gentlemen, I do *not* drink Chase and Sanborn coffee. The people who sponsor this program haven't enough money to make me say I do, because I don't. Now I often pick up friends from Broadway and bring them up to dinner without ever telling Ida. It's a dirty trick to play on the gal, but I do it. These guests have to take potluck. But no matter what we have for dinner they know they'll always finish with Chase and Sanborn coffee and everybody's happy. Ida likes it. My girls like it. So it must be good. And I believe if I *drank* coffee, I'd drink Chase and Sanborn's."

This commercial was not only successful, a group of men came to me from South America, trying to induce me to leave Chase and Sanborn and go on radio for them with "Eddie Cantor Coffee." All they asked was that I keep on with this type of underselling, honest commercial, stay on radio for them for five years, and I would be part owner of their company. I couldn't take the offer because I didn't think it ethical to my sponsors. But it was exciting to find that honest advertising could pay off. Department stores took it up and ran large ads in the same style. "Here's a dress we couldn't sell at $19.75 so we've marked it down to $15.00." Macy's immediately ran an ad on gloves. "These are some gloves we're offering at $3.50. We won't say they're worth $4.50 or $4.25, they're worth $3.50 and they *are* worth $3.50."

Our commercial attracted an enormous response of warm friendly letters. As a matter of fact, working on this program you had a feeling of being friends with almost everyone. On my fortieth birthday I mentioned that I was getting older, I was having a birthday.

"I'm not hinting about any presents," I gagged. "That would be cheap, not to say audacious. However, my shirt size is 15½, my socks, size 11; and if you're sending any kind of cake, make it chocolate because I could eat that the rest of my life!" (You know, I damn near did!)

It was all in fun—I thought. But within four days I must have received not less than fifteen *thousand* packages. So much that we had to call a committee to distribute the things, the cakes to orphanages, the shirts to needy unemployed, etc., etc. I was embarrassed and a little frantic; the sponsors were very pleased. Your success on radio can only be determined by the amount of produce you're selling and the amount of mail. We were certainly getting mail. When brochures were printed up on *Eddie Cantor at Home*, the printing order was for one hundred thousand and the requests in the first ten days were for a quarter of a million.

Gradually you became aware of what such an audience could mean, you had the ear of the nation. In March 1933 the National Safety Council had sent us some of their statistics on fatalities in traffic. You looked at the appalling figures and thought of the vast audience that listened every Sunday night, the audience you could reach. Maybe the public *could* be educated to more careful driving . . . maybe . . . I talked it over with David Freedman.

"But this is a serious spot, we've never done anything like it before," he said.

"It can be serious but it can start funny," I said. We talked it over and David came up with a great eight or ten minutes. It started with Jimmy Wallington getting a ticket for speeding. He came to me, wanted me to get the ticket fixed, and I explained why I wouldn't. For years we'd vacationed at a spot called Lucerne, New York. One year we came up to Lucerne and saw a sign, "Drive carefully. We love our children." I investigated and found that a lawyer and his wife had been happy residents of the community, they and their three children. One day the six-year-old had gone out to play, a few minutes later there was a screech of brakes and they ran out to pick up the lifeless body of their child. I told this story and warned the drivers of America that "Children should be seen and not hurt." So little time is saved by speeding. Driving from New York to Philadelphia, breaking all the speed laws, you'd get there eight minutes ahead of going sanely and obeying the laws.

When the script went in to J. Walter Thompson, John Reber blew his top. "You can't do this, you're a funny man, your business is to make people laugh."

"Can't I make them laugh harder if there's some contrast in my material?"

David Freedman agreed with me. I threatened not to go on unless I could do the spot. And of course J. Walter Thompson was stuck with me. The Chase and Sanborn Hour went on that Sunday night and within two days we'd heard from every insurance company in America with requests to reprint our speech. The National Safety Council checked traffic accidents throughout the country and proved that there was a definite drop in accidents the following week. A few hours later the man in charge of radio at J. Walter Thompson was telling his friends the trouble he'd had talking me into *doing* this!

From that night on I included a serious spot in every second or third broadcast. Sometimes it could be done with just a slogan: "Tomorrow is Flag Day. It's nice to hang out the flag, but why just on Flag Day? Why not give our flag a permanent wave?" . . . "Give. Keep the Red Cross out of the Red." . . . "Go to church. Why not put America on a *praying* basis?" . . . And for the blind, "Oh, say can you see? Then help someone who can't." We once discussed a family who'd been ruined by gossip and the tag, "God gives us two ears and one tongue so we can hear twice before we speak once." And concerning the importance of making your wife your partner: "I knew a fellow whose wife once told him, yes, he was doing all right in the stock market but he should put some of his money in irrevocable trust. He didn't listen, the stock market crashed . . ." Jimmy Wallington said, "I'll bet that guy's wife's really been riding *him!*" And I said, "Oh no, Ida isn't like that at all!"

For a long time we had a Night Court of the Air. As judge, I would try three or four comical cases and then a serious case. We had an instance of an attempted suicide. The fellow had pretty good arguments as to why he should take his life. He was fifty-five, he couldn't get a job, he felt it was not a cowardly but a brave thing to do. At least his family would benefit from his insurance money. But I reminded him of a man who at forty-eight had been considered a failure, who finally took a job clerking in his dad's leather store at eight hundred dollars a year—and eight years later was President of the United States! Ulysses S. Grant.

We got off the air and the phone calls started. A woman from Bridgeport, Connecticut, hysterical because her husband had committed suicide two weeks before and if he could have heard our broadcast, he would never have done it. Another woman from New Jersey thanking us. Her son had listened in and she was sure had been saved from such a possibility. We presented cases of child abandonment and juvenile deliquency, all sorts of things a comedian had never tried to talk about before. And it worked, it worked, we knew from the letters that poured in, from the rating, from the coffee we sold.

We'd started something that became a snowball. Comedians now pitch for money to combat all the serious diseases, they plug Community Chest and Red Cross and urge the public to vote and more power to them. We were able to start the snowball because our pattern was never to preach but to sneak in the serious stuff and always, primarily, to entertain.

It was never a matter of standing up before a cold mike wondering what kind of people were out there. I could see the Fort Worths and the San Antonios, the Kansas Citys, Omahas, Detroits and Clevelands, all the places I'd played on the road. And I met a cross section of Americans constantly at our preview broadcasts. This was a tryout broadcast I initiated in 1935, our regular show, before an audience but not on the air—a chance to try out the gags, time the laughs, test the show and the audience reaction. When the half-hour show was over, we'd stay with our studio guests for another half hour, or longer, letting them ask questions about anything. In Hollywood or New York we found that the audience represented a cross section of the country, visitors again from Des Moines and Tompkins Center. In the half hour after the broadcast they asked questions—about theatrical personalities, and Hollywood, yes, but about all sorts of other serious things, life, death, politics, religion, and taxes. We knew our audience, we had a sampling of them every week face to face, and they wanted a thought as well as a laugh.

The sponsors changed: Pebeco, Texaco, Camels; but always the audience was there, the great ear of America and you could *reach* it. In 1936, on the Texaco show, I started the first in an annual series of contests (essay and oratorical contests) with a college scholarship of five thousand dollars as the prize. I'd always regretted having had no education; at least I could give some boy or girl what I'd missed. And in each case the subject matter should be something of interest to the parents as well as the youth of the nation. Our first subject was "How Can America Stay Out of War?" This was 1936, but it didn't take a wizard to know that whatever happened in Poland or France or Germany must affect the whole world.

So that was the subject of the essay contest, and the American Legion was only too glad to sponsor it. Can you imagine the sort of response we got, plugging this over the air? Two hundred and fifty *thousand* high-school students submitted essays. Judges of the contest were Robert M. Hutchins, president of the University of Chicago; Ray Lyman Wilbur, president of Stanford University; Frederick B. Robinson, president of the College of the City of New York; and Henry Noble MacCracken, president of Vassar.

They awarded the prize unanimously to Lloyd Lewis, a Missouri farm boy. We brought him on to New York, we introduced him over the air, we turned his essay over to the newspapers. He was a hero, a country kid who'd never had a new suit of clothes before, but for his trip to New York the local townspeople had given him a suit of clothes and a suitcase. Then a terrible thing happened. The kid went to sleep a hero on Sunday night and woke up a bum Monday morning. A reporter on the Newark *News* phoned me early Monday. He'd discovered that the winning essay had been copied word for word from an article published by Dr. Frank Kingdon, president of the University of Newark. Word for word, even the punctuation marks. I don't know to this day what had been in the kid's mind. When I talked to him he said that no one had told him the essay had to be original. Bennie Holzman, my close friend and the public-relations man who had handled the contest, talked with the boy; I talked; we called his parents and explained the situation—that he could not win on this basis —and then we told the newspaper people. We pointed out that they could do one of two things: "You can ride this boy to the point where he'll jump out of a window—which we're sure you newspaper men don't want, even for the sake of a story—or you can say that this was an honest mistake. He's just a kid, he's had a big disappointment already." They were all magnificent about it. We put the unfortunate boy on a plane and sent him home. Before he left he looked down at his suit and said, "I guess I'll put this suit away when I get home. It doesn't belong to me and I'll never wear it again." I looked at Bennie Holzman and he looked at me. Bennie, who's been a newspaper man on Broadway all his life, had tears in his eyes. We both had to leave the room.

One radio editor and many program sponsors pointed out that I could have avoided a lot of embarrassment over the fake essay if we hadn't made public its text. But these contests weren't gags and we wanted them on the up-and-up. In this first instance the judges awarded the prize to the essay originally selected as second—by Owen W. Matthews III, a nineteen-year-old eagle scout who discussed the scout movement as an instrument toward world peace. He had attended an International Boy Scout Jamboree in Hungary, where he had lived with thirty thousand foreign brother scouts. His straight thinking became the basis for editorials in newspapers throughout the country.

And we continued with the contests for ten years, fifteen boys in all going to college and all of them turning out substantial citizens. I flew across the continent to attend the graduation exercises of Owen Matthews III at M.I.T.

In 1937 the head of the Americanization committee of the American Legion phoned me in California to tell me about the winner of our oratorical contest. "This seventeen-year-old boy quotes Hamilton, Lincoln, Roosevelt—he's an amazing boy, Eddie, I think you should have him come out to California and meet him." So the boy and his mother came out to California. And he was an exceptional extemporaneous speaker. He went with me to the Motor Vehicle group in Santa Monica, where I was speaking, and I introduced him. This boy made a speech about safety in driving that brought the house to its feet.

He stayed for about ten days, and the night before he left he and his mother were having dinner at our house. "Mr. Cantor," he said, "may I speak with you alone?" So we went into my den and for a moment he hesitated.

"For a guy who just won a prize for talking, I find myself at a loss for words," he said. "But there's something I have to tell you. I come from a town where we have five Jewish families. I don't know anything about them. I don't know anyone who's ever talked to them. We've regarded Jews as something less than human." He looked me in the eye. "I've spent some sleepless nights since we arrived here. I asked my mother, 'Isn't Eddie Cantor a Jew?' She said you are. 'But without him I could never have a college education. What does he get out of it?' We come to your house, we see your family life, and I've started thinking—there must be other Jews like you. Maybe a lot of them. Last night I decided that when we get home I'm going to every one of the Jewish families in our town and offer my hand in apology. I'm going to try all my life to tell people what I've learned—that they must not criticize or condemn any group by hearsay."

The boy went to Duke University, he's a lawyer now, and he's done even more than he dreamed in fighting intolerance.

Through radio you can do something like this. And the March of Dimes. I've told you about the March of Dimes and about the radio audiences that deluged the White House with dimes.

In 1942 I began thinking of the GIs scattered all over the country, all over the world, losing identity. A GI was just a number, he thought, far away from home, and what would be awaiting him when he got back? I talked with the War Department and dreamed up something that might help GIs feel they were not forgotten and could give one of them a start when he got home. On the air for Bristol-Myers, we announced a contest and put up five thousand dollars for the best letter that would identify and portray a typical GI. It could be written by his mother, his wife, himself, his commanding officer, anyone. We received forty thousand letters the first week, one hundred thousand letters the second week. It took a small army to read and analyze them.

The fellow who won was a GI in Italy, and it was his wife who'd written the letter. Their home was in the Kentucky hills. No electricity, no water, the most primitive sort of place. But one night this girl had visited friends and heard our broadcast. Her husband had so many dreams for their future, and they'd all been cut short by the war. Now he was in Italy and if he got back . . . She started her letter, then figured it didn't have a chance, blew out her kerosene lamp and went to bed. But she couldn't sleep. If there was a chance in a million, what right did she have not to take it—for him? So she lit the lamp again and wrote. And the letter was our winner. Years later, when I played the one-man show in Louisville, Kentucky, they came to see me. The ex-GI had put his money in a filling station. Now they own three of them.

And the next year, another GI idea. I'd been around in September and October, entertaining in the hospitals, and suddenly it occurred to me that these wounded GIs were the loneliest of all. They felt useless as well as forgotten, and if they felt forgotten now, how would they feel at Christmas time? Why not start something on radio that would bring them presents, from everywhere, from a whole nation who had *not* forgotten. *Give a Gift to a Yank Who Gave!*

First thing was to call my good friend Arthur Baer, of Stix, Baer and Fuller in St. Louis. He's a businessman, he knows what's practical, and he's always *with* me. Arthur not only thought it a good idea, he felt that the department stores would get behind it. He certainly did. Stix, Baer and Fuller had one window—at *Christmas time*—with nothing in it but a wounded veteran in a bed and a sign: GIVE A GIFT TO A YANK WHO GAVE.

I got in touch with all the veterans' organizations and they agreed to pick up the gifts in their trucks. Then we took to the air. We got two and a half million gifts, worth twelve and a half million dollars.

Newspapers picked up the chant editorially; department stores took full pages with nothing but the slogan and set up huge boxes into which the gifts could be dropped. The American Legion and the American Legion Auxiliaries and other veterans' organizations gave parties and hauled in hundreds of thousands of gifts. The next year we did it again, and the next. For five years. General Omar Bradley once called from Washington. "Eddie, we have so many gifts—would you mind if we sent some overseas?"

That's what mass communication can do. You stand in front of a little mike and suggest that America not forget its wounded soldiers, and Santa Claus rides as he never rode before. In five Christmases, ten million gifts worth fifty million dollars. The guys who thought they were forgotten found that they weren't. They're still getting gifts at Christmas from Americans who remember. That's the sort of an audience radio made possible.

You start as an entertainer, a guy who wants to make people laugh, and you fall into a privilege like this!

20. Jack Benny

At the Temple of Religion, the New York World's Fair, 1939, I made a speech that not only cost me $585,000 but threatened my radio career for good.

I'm standing before the mike, in my hands the photograph of a check the German-American Bund has presented to a so-called American who is playing footsie with the Nazis. Ida knows what's in my mind and she's begged me to be careful, to be prudent. But I speak as I feel I must about "The Enemy Within." I say, "Watch Father Coughlin, watch George Sylvester Vierick." I name names because it seems so important—the American public knows the enemies without, why shouldn't they know the enemies within. That night's headlines read: COMEDIAN BLASTS PRIEST. The next day, my thirty-nine-week radio program is canceled.

I didn't work in radio for a year, and the only reason I ever got back was—Jack Benny. We'd been friends for years. We were neighbors on Roxbury Drive. We dropped in on each other almost every day. More than anyone, Jack understood how depressed I was, an entertainer without an audience, a citizen who loved his country chastised for using the freedom of speech with which he'd meant to help her.

One night Jack paced up and down in his library, then went to the phone and called the head of Young and Rubicam in New York. "If radio's going to go on," he said, "Eddie Cantor must be part of it." Pause. "Yes, yes, I know. But why should he be punished just for having more guts than the rest of us?" Long pause while the advertising executive explained that sponsors were afraid of me, of what I might say next. "You can control that," Jack argued. "You can approve every script."

A few days later I was in New York talking with Young and

Rubicam, and almost at once I was back on the air for Bristol-Myers. I've tried to thank Jack many times. I've never made it. He's a guy who can't be thanked, it embarrasses him. He never realizes what he's given.

And let's say right here that the character of the miser is something Jack merely *plays*. He's the most generous man in the whole business, not only with money, but with his heart. He'll travel any number of miles, he'll raise huge sums because he says the right thing, he's a liberal thinker who makes no bones about it. He has never turned down a legitimate cause or let down a legitimate person. Let me show you what I mean . . .

During the first Israeli-Arab war, when money was so necessary for the fighting people of what was then called Palestine, Golda Meir (now Israel's Minister of Foreign Affairs) made a tour of America to raise money for the fighting forces of the young democracy. She was a guest at our home and we invited twenty of our friends to meet her. Jack had a radio rehearsal that night and couldn't come. In his place, he sent a fellow from the studio with a signed check and this note: "Eddie, fill in this check for whatever you need." I filled it in for twenty-five thousand dollars—the least Jack would have given. I know; we've had dealings with charity before. He's handed over more money to me for more causes than anyone I know. And he not only gives—but with joy.

This is the guy of whom I gag, "Jack's such a good friend I'd give him the shirt off my back. And you know what he'd do with it? He'd wash it, iron it, and charge me twenty-five cents."

The pose of being stingy has cost him a fortune. Where an ordinary person hands a train porter five dollars, Jack hands him twenty. Where a two-dollar tip would suffice in a restaurant, he hands out five, instinctively proving that the character of the miser is not the character of the man, as of course everyone knows who's ever known Jack.

I've known him for a long time. We met in 1918 when the cast of the *Follies* was asked to entertain at Great Lakes Naval Training Station. Jack was one of the gobs, at least he wore a sailor suit. He didn't look as if he could be second man in a rowboat. As a member of the reception committee, he helped welcome us that night and he put on his act as part of the show. It wasn't exactly a show stopper. While his violin wasn't good, his monologue was atrocious; but he had something, a happy faculty of relaxation, so that if the audience didn't scream with laughter, it didn't matter, he seemed to be making things up as he went along. I caught his single in vaudeville a number of times during the following years, and gradually the magic of the man began to appear.

He was an off-beat comedian, a man who had to educate the public to his pattern. Jack taught them to demand more than just a series of jokes. He created a comedy pattern for other comedians to follow in the radio years.

In 1927 I caught him at the L.A. Orpheum when he was emceeing the show. Most actors used to start a monologue with a stock line, "Ladies and gentlemen, on my way to the theater tonight a very funny thing happened . . ." and on to a joke. Jack got out there, looked his audience in the eye, and said, "Ladies and gentlemen, on my way to the theater this evening—nothing happened." He stared at them for a long moment. "So, good night," he said and walked off. The audience, including many picture stars, collapsed.

He never depended on a joke but on a character line. The longest laugh I ever heard on radio came during a scene where Jack was walking home late at night. You heard the voice of a hold-up man saying, "Stick 'em up!"

Jack says, "What?"

"Your money or your life," snarls the thug.

Then silence—a *whole minute* while the audience screams.

"Well?" barks the stick-up man.

Pause. Then Jack says, "I'm thinking, I'm thinking."

This is what I mean by a character line. It's uproarious not because of a joke but because of the character situation. Jack is never the effect of a situation but the creator of it.

There were years when he was a little discouraged—we all get discouraged along the way—but he had the courage of his convictions. He didn't want his writers going to a file of jokes and putting together a program, he wanted a program created for him. And once the public caught on, Jack's position has been immovable. Radio didn't mature him, he matured radio.

He took a writer, Harry Conn. With Jack, Harry created the characters of Jack Benny and Mary Livingstone; they created an

American stock company of the air. Each week you met players who played different parts in different situations, but you knew them. And the situations always had a basis of truth. This is Jack's format, take a basis of truth and exaggerate from there.

On a Sunday close to New Year's Day he'll start a scene by inviting Don Wilson to go with him to the Rose Bowl game. There *is* a game, everyone *knows* it and Jack *has* two tickets; but from then on, the exaggeration begins.

Watch Jack at rehearsals and you see him worrying at his best. He'll walk around suffering over some line or situation, wanting it just a shade better. Jessel once said, "Benny gets up so early, by nine o'clock he's worried two hours ahead of you already." When Jack first came on television he did a program with Fred Allen. The gimmick: Jack was trying to get his contract renewed and Fred Allen was trying to get to the sponsor before Jack did, in the hope of replacing him. It was a very funny program; still Jack wasn't quite satisfied. An hour before the show—live—Jack phoned me. I rushed over to Television City, no rehearsal, no preparation, and we finished the program with a scene where, with Fred Allen hiding in one closet, I hid in another closet, bounced out and was sitting on the sponsor's lap when Jack and Fred finally got to him. Now there was a double punch to the ending and Jack could worry a little less.

Actually Jack's worrying is a pleasure to those who work with him. It's the mark of a man who'll settle for nothing less than the best he can do. I've always enjoyed working with him and we've worked together many, many times.

Jack's "stingy" character may well have *begun* with the time he and I did a bit together at the Floridian Club in Miami Beach, December 29, 1930. This trip to Florida was almost like a vacation because Ida and I had asked Jack and Mary to go with us. Opening night, my party was sitting at a ringside table and I introduced Jack as a fellow they would know from vaudeville. We clowned around for a few minutes and I told the audience how we'd gone out to the dog track and here were all those people betting and losing their money, and we asked Jack what he's betting in the next race and he says he's betting two dollars on the rabbit—to *show*. The audience loved it.

The next night before I went to work I phoned Jack and asked if he wanted to come down to the club again and do the same bit. "Hey, wait a minute," he said, "aren't you the one who has the contract? What d'ya want to do, make this a nightly thing? Get a straight man for nothing?"

"Okay, Jack, forget it." I even felt a little hurt, but when I came on, there was Jack at the same table, ready. And the third night, I didn't even ask him, he was there. You couldn't keep him away.

Jack loves to entertain. No one in the business is more serious about it. It's his business and his hobby. He gets in a little golf, but his real hobby is show business. After a season of thirty-nine weeks he'll make a tour with his gang: Spokane, Vancouver, San Francisco. Ask him why and he says, "Eddie. I'm just a ham. To vacation you've gotta enjoy yourself. Where am I gonna have more fun than in a theater?"

Oh, and he has one other hobby, cards. We've played for years, gin rummy, casino; nobody can get hurt because the most we play for is a cent a point in gin or a dollar a game, casino. We play equally badly. On that trip to Florida we were playing casino. In the middle of the game my agent, Abe Lastfogel, called, offering me a fantastic amount to play the Paramount, New York. "Just a minute," I said, "I can't talk business. I'm concentrating," and went back to finish the game. Jack never stopped laughing. Abe was trying to give me twenty thousand dollars and I was worrying about winning a buck from Benny.

We had Jack's father along on that trip, the little tailor from Waukegan, and we took him out to the race track. Jack and I were making bets of two dollars or five dollars and the old man was betting twenty, sometimes fifty every race—in his *mind*. He wasn't risking cash. Before every race we'd ask him what he was betting and he'd tell us. Comes the seventh race, we say, "Dad, what'cha betting?" He says, "Nothing, I'm out too much already."

The poor little guy almost died once because he didn't understand Jack correctly over the phone. We were at my house playing gin and Jack said, "I'll play you this game for a telephone call to Waukegan to my dad." He won and he called his father. Mr. Kubelsky wasn't feeling too good; he said he had a cold. Jack said, "Take a bottle of magnesia, you'll feel fine." Two days later I had a call from Jack: "That damned phone call I won from you almost cost my father's life!" he said. "I meant citrate of magnesia. The poor guy drank a whole bottle of milk of magnesia!"

Jack's always been a family man, always worried about his family, always worried about his friends. But once when I was hospitalized and he came to visit me he took one look and burst into hysterical laughter. The sight of me lying quiet was more than he could bear. "You who jump up and down all the time like a frog."

Jack and I hit it off from the first. Every comedian loves him because he's a comedian's comedian, the best audience in the world. So, of course, you want to make him laugh. Jack is pretty rich and once, when he had just won a case from the government, giving him a capital gain on two million dollars, I phoned his house at once. "Jack, you may need some immediate money to eat and to pay your bills. If you'll tell me how much you need, and if you can't wait for it, I'll send it over by messenger."

A speaking engagement took us to San Diego. The next day when we were to leave, the hotel manager came to our luncheon table and asked if we'd drop by his office, he had a gift for each of us. The gifts turned out to be two hotel pamphlets with color photos of San Diego! Jack and I thought this was pretty funny. Then Jack went on to Oakland and I found his pamphlet left behind. I tossed it into my suitcase and wired Jack:

"*Notice you have forgotten pamphlet. Am arranging to have it forwarded.*"

Jack wired back: "*Don't know how this could have happened. Feel terrible going home to Mary without it.*"

The wires continued back and forth for weeks. Later when Jack made a tour I kept getting pamphlets not only from every city but from every hotel in that city!

Long ago we worked up a benefit act together. We both played so many benefits, why not play 'em together and have some fun? This was the time when Jeanette MacDonald and Nelson Eddy were a big hit and we worked up a take-off on them. The emcee would announce us as that noted team, Jeanette MacDonald and Nelson Eddy, and out we'd go—Jack very debonair in Eddy's evening clothes and wearing a blond wig, I in a remodeled gown of Jeanette's and red curls. We'd dance out to the strains of "Easter Parade"; no gags, just the song, with which we took dreadful liberties. We used to *hunt* for benefits just so we could have the fun of doing our act. We went all over the country with it. Sometimes we'd get through as many as eight bars before the audience knew exactly who we were.

We've had many exchanges, Jack guesting on my program, and I on his. Several times when I've needed Jack, the moment it got to a discussion of money he'd say, "I've got a notion to punch you in the nose." One time I sent him a television set as a small token of appreciation. He phoned me, he wrote me, met me, thanked me, until *I* was embarrassed.

He's got a sort of shyness and less pretense than any star I've known save Jimmy Durante. Jack has a staff of writers and he's the first to tell you that he doesn't make up lines, that he's no ad-lib comedian. I can only say—don't ever let him get you in a spot—he'll devastate you. He introduced me one night in San Francisco, where I was to be given a plaque.

"I can't get over how young Eddie Cantor looks," he said. "Look at him—not a gray hair in his head . . . tonight."

"Well, at least, Jack, this is my own hair."

"You shut up," he said. "I've got hair at home I haven't even used yet."

. . . And baby-blue eyes and thirty-nine years and all the rest of the Benny characterization.

As this is being written the London *Daily Express* writes of Jack's BBC-TV debut, "This was comedy de luxe—a superb exhibition of the art of comedy by a world master . . . I hope all the TV comedians of Britain were watching to see how it really can be done."

I hope the British comedians were watching, too; but it won't do them any good. We've *all* been watching for years; that's been one of the kicks of show business, to know Benny and to watch him in action. But the technique's all his. This fugitive from a violin is in a class by himself.

21. Radio Cast of Characters

Radio demanded variety, and the years 1931–52 gave me a chance to continually change format and to work with every name you can name from Rubinoff to John Barrymore. There was never a repertory company like it!

I've mentioned that Rubinoff didn't talk. I took his part at first, but after the first season I realized that it was silly to try to play a half dozen parts in each show, especially when there were available such competent radio actors as Alan Reed, Charlie Cantor, Betty Garde and others. But that doesn't detract from the personality of Rubinoff. He was and is one of the great showmen of the business—a good violinist rather than a great violinist, but a showman who gave the impression of being all the great violinists put together. He was a ham, publicity conscious, publicity wise, and publicity wild. When we went to the Mayflower Hotel in Washington, he actually *registered* as "Rubinoff and his Violin." He published his own little newspaper with stories about himself, which was sent to everyone who wrote him a letter, and his following was tremendous. His publicity paid off; for now, all these years later, he's still making a good living on the strength of those years.

But his fame in 1933 was such that one night when Yehudi Menuhin, with his violin case in tow, stepped into an elevator at NBC and said, "Can you take me right up? I'm in a hurry. I'm Yehudi Menuhin," the elevator operator said, "I don't care if you're *Rubinoff.*"

Dave Rubinoff was a riot conversationally. His brother Phil would come up to rehearsal and Rubinoff would say, "Pheel, how do you fill?" But when it came to business, he was conscientious and meticulous about everything he did. He'd stop in the middle of rehearsal and demand of the drummer, "What are you doing?"

"What 'm I doing, Dave? I'm chewing gum."

"Well, for God's sake, chew in tempo!"

Rubinoff, Wallington, and I were together and the format of the show changed very little. Occasionally we would introduce a guest. Just about the first was a little lady who'd never appeared on radio, but who was meant for it—Gracie Allen. I'd met her and Nat (George Burns) when we played the Palace together, and in 1932, when I was "running for President," I asked Nat to let Gracie come on the show as a newspaper reporter interviewing me. Just one show. Nat wasn't about to part with her for longer than that; and Gracie and George have been on the air ever since.

Then one day in 1934 I went to Boston to speak at a luncheon. A gentleman with the funniest Greek dialect I've ever heard, Parkyakarkus, was introduced as a member of the "Greek Embassy," and his serious talk in this funny dialect was a riot. "This guy ought to be in show business," I said. "Who is he?"

"He's Harry Einstein, he writes advertising copy for the Kane Furniture Company."

When the program was over I approached the advertising-copy writer. "How would you like to come on the Chase and Sanborn program?"

"When?"

"Next Sunday."

"It's a deal," he said. "You pay my expenses to New York and I'll be there."

He wouldn't consider salary. He said he was making a good salary, it would cost him fifty bucks to go to New York and that's all he wanted.

The next Sunday, Parkyakarkus showed up in New York and became famous overnight, one of the first big stooges in radio. We had a ball with him, paid him his fifty dollars, and he went back to Boston. A few days later he phoned. People had flocked into the store to see him in person, his bosses thought it would be just fine if he did another radio show next Sunday. After three or four Sundays I got ashamed and started paying Parky $250 a week; he gave up advertising-copy writing and became a part of our show. He was with us from 1934 until 1937 and his salary jumped to $600 to $1000 a week, the same salary whether he was working or not, fifty-two weeks a year, and sometimes he only worked thirty-five.

When I quit Chase and Sanborn to come out to the coast to make a picture for Goldwyn, Parky came with me. During *Strike Me Pink*, Ida rented us a house on Sunset, a huge place with a big marble staircase, three or four dining rooms, a dance hall, real cozy. It was so big we needed company and Parky practically lived there. Every time he got a pay check he felt, he said, like a burglar. But such a happy burglar! Finally I finished the picture and we went on tour. I thought it would be a thrill for Parkyakarkus to go back and play his home town, so we did and, of course, he tore down the house.

"Eddie," he said, after that, "I'm a big hit and I'm not getting enough money."

I laughed. "For the last seventeen weeks around the swimming pool you told me you felt like a burglar," I said. "But I don't want you unhappy, Parky. We have two more weeks to play. When we've finished we'll tear up your contract." I tore up the contract, handed Parky to my agent, William Morris, and he went on with Al Jolson for twice the salary he'd earned with us. He was miserable. He never got the laughs with Jolson, and finally he realized that the laughs meant more to him than the money.

One day I received this letter: "Dear Eddie, In 1934 when I was working for the Kane Furniture Store in Boston you invited me to come on your program. All I asked was fifty dollars. I would like to come back at the same price." Parky had become a wealthy man, he'd made shrewd investments and acquired plenty of good real estate. But he wanted to hear laughter again. At our preview broadcast when I ran across a line that would be funnier with Parky's accent I switched it to him. He heard his laughs and we've been friends ever since. Any time I need to raise money for some needy cause I send for Parky. He's a big fund raiser, a thoughtful and socially conscious man.

Parkyakarkus went with us to the Pebeco show in 1935 and shortly after, we were joined by Bert Gordon, whom we dubbed "The Mad Russian." When somebody asked him why he was the Mad Russian he'd say, "Take a look at my salary, you'll see why." He was a great natural comedian, hilarious without ever knowing what the words meant. After the show you'd have to explain the gags to him. One time he was fed a line:

"But you surely know Kipling!"

"I don't know, I never kippled," the Mad Russian said.

This got a big laugh and Bert wanted to know why, what was so funny. We explained to him who Kipling was. *Then* he laughed.

At this same time we had begun to use guest stars on the show and pitting Bert against anyone who had a certain amount of dignity was sure-fire—a Tallulah Bankhead, a Marlene Dietrich, a Lawrence Tibbett. He was the best anti-Communist propaganda on the air because he was constantly used for lines like this:

To Lawrence Tibbett: "Lawrence Kibbuts, I was an opera singer in Russia. It was there I developed my nose. In Russia you sing only through your nose."

Tibbett: "Through your nose? Why?"

Mad Russian: "In Russia, you can open your *mouth?*"

So far so good; we were still among the top ten after six years. But inasmuch as I wasn't the youngest fellow in the world, I began to think of surrounding myself with youth. In the back of my mind there was always the memory of Gus Edwards and what he had done for so many kids, including me. He'd found talent and given it a chance, and I thought I'd like to do that, too. Late in 1935 I auditioned thirty or forty children including a boy named Bobby Breen. The plan was to introduce a child on our Christmas broadcast and I had Bobby try a number—"Santa, Bring My Mommie Back to Me." It was the biggest tear-jerker you ever heard and Bobby jerked every tear. He sang to me in a small room at the studio until I cried, "Take him out, he's breaking my heart." That Sunday we went on with a program built around Bobby's song. I played Santa Claus coming to ask what the children wanted and Bobby asking for his Mommie in that clear child's treble was sensational. You never saw such a thing—men and women crying in the studio audience, ushers all but floating up and down the aisles. Bobby was *in*.

In the fall of '36 we went on for Texaco and added another youngster to our cast, lovely Deanna Durbin. We wrote in a romance between Bobby and Deanna. When they had a quarrel Bobby cried on my shoulder, "I gave this girl the best years of my life." He was nine. The audience loved it; he and Deanna attracted a whole new audience of listeners.

I have the late Rufus Le Maire, casting director at Universal, to thank for Deanna. He brought her to see me when she was thirteen, and we walked across the Goldwyn lot to Alfred Newman's bungalow to use his piano. I'll never forget this little girl, slipping her hand into mine as we walked along and saying, "I hope you aren't nervous, Mr. Cantor, because everything's going to be all right, I'm going to be with you."

Her poise amazed me, and oh, how she sang! She was with me all right; it was a thrill to present her. Several years later, we were playing a personal appearance at Keith's in Boston and a woman kept haunting the stage door all week, kept phoning the hotel, she wanted me to hear her daughter sing. I didn't want to hear any little girl sing, I had Deanna under contract. Besides, we were pressed for time doing five or six shows a day. So one day I come backstage and there is the woman and her daughter. She has bribed the stage doorman, obviously, and there is nothing to do now but hear her child sing. Deanna is sitting in the greenroom at this moment, reading a comic book, and as we pass through, the woman points at Deanna and says, "When my daughter gets through singing, you'll get rid of her."

Anyway, the daughter sings and she's not just fair, she's terrible. There are two things to do in a situation like this. You can say, "I have nothing to offer you now, but please leave your name and address and I'll get in touch with you." Or if you feel people are wasting precious money, you try to tell them the truth. This woman had told me that the girl's father is working in a garage and that every cent he makes goes into voice lessons for the kid, so I tell her the truth—the child has no talent, she's wasting money on lessons, she should save that money and let the child lead a normal child's life. You can see the fury rising in her face. For a moment I think she's about to slap me. Instead, she grabs the girl, rushes to the door, turns for an instant and yells, "*You* stink, *too!*"

Deanna Durbin is rolling on the floor. She never has laughed harder in her life! She's shaking every ribbon, every ruffle on her one and only stage dress. A few days later she was to lose that dress—and the story and its sequel are something O. Henry could have written.

We had Sunday off from Keith's theater to fly to New York for our Texaco broadcast. We chartered a plane and had a limousine meet us at the airport. During the day somebody broke into the limousine and stole Deanna's little suitcase with her stage dress.

"Deanna, don't cry," I begged. "We'll get you a dress."

"But, Uncle Eddie, it had such lovely ribbons."

The next day Ida went out on Boylston Street and bought Deanna a dress with a matching coat. On stage we kidded about it, I told the audience that Ida'd bought Deanna this new outfit, now if Deanna kept working for two more years she could pay off the dress and we'd start on the coat. She looked very sweet standing there in her new frock, her hair on her shoulders and that young face, the darling of our show.

Fade out; fade in, four years later. Deanna is now the darling of the world, the number-one star at Universal, more than that, the girl who has saved the studio from bankruptcy. On the strength of her contract after *Three Smart Girls*, Universal can go to the bank and borrow money to make as many pictures as they want. Deanna doesn't work for me any more. Once her first picture was released, she was dynamite. When it became obvious that rehearsals and broadcasts were interfering with what looked like a tremendous career in pictures, I'd given a little party for Deanna and torn up her contract. So now she is seventeen, the number-one American movie star in Europe, the second- or third-ranking star in South America, she's doing just great in America and she's showing me around her Beverly Hills mansion. There are closets filled with jackets, shoes, dresses, furs. Finally Deanna opens one closet and in it is nothing but one dress—the dress and matching coat Ida bought one day on Boylston Street, Boston. "Any time I feel I'm getting too cocky I open this door, Uncle Eddie, and remember the time I had just one stage dress."

There's nothing more exciting than to discover talent and nothing sadder than to see it wear itself out. Deanna's talent never wore out. She just fell in love too often, because as a girl she'd not been allowed to even talk to a boy. Her mother and her manager suppressed her too much and the minute she came of age, bing!—she married, three times. Luckily she's happy now. I phoned her a few years ago and asked her if she'd join us for a reunion show on TV. She said, "I'd love to, Uncle Eddie, but I'm so happy being a wife and mother, I don't want to have anything to do with show business ever."

The Bobby Breen story was a different matter. Bobby was with me for three years, happy years for us both. We complemented each other and the listeners took the childish voice to their hearts. Bobby's sister Sally watched over him, saw that he lived a balanced life, ate right and had the right clothes and knew his songs and was on time for our broadcast. Bobby did movies for Sol Lesser and, so far as our program was concerned, he never had to show up until the day of the broadcast. I only needed to know what song he was going to sing and in what key.

Then at the end of a new season Bobby's brother Mickey came to me about a further contract for the next year. To me it was just a formality. I was paying Bobby five hundred dollars a broadcast and expected to keep right on paying him until, heaven forbid, his voice should change. But when I met Mickey in Sol Lesser's office Mickey started walking up and down like a big impresario, like Sol Hurok.

"Uncle Eddie," he said solemnly, "speaking of next season, and representing Bobby Breen, and wishing to clarify our position, these are the things we want . . ." and he started on a list of what "we" wanted that went on for five minutes, and included Mickey's right to approve Bobby's material, select his songs, etc. "We want this, we want that . . ."

"Are you through, Mickey?" I said finally.

"Yes, Uncle Eddie, I'm through."

"Good. So is Bobby."

Mickey was flabbergasted. He started to compromise.

"You don't understand, Mickey. Up until now our relationship has been great. But with your present attitude, I don't want to haggle."

He wanted to approve Bobby's material. For all the time the lad had been on my program, whenever I thought a song didn't fit, or whenever I thought Bobby tired and not in good voice or otherwise not showing to advantage, I'd send him home and pay him. I was hurt and angry at Mickey's attitude and sorry that the fun of having Bobby on our show was over.

Two years later Bobby's sister Sally called me. "Uncle Eddie, Bobby has played some guest shots but they meant nothing. He wants to work and if only you would put him on just once . . ." So I put Bobby on, and again one time when I did a TV show and adopted a boy from an orphanage. That he didn't come back big isn't strange. If a child of six can spell well, you applaud; if he spells just as well at twenty, who cares?

At any rate, nothing can change the memories of young Bobby and the charm of the episodes that included him and lovely Deanna Durbin. And the show went on and we made new discoveries and changed the format.

In January 1939, when we needed a new announcer for the Camel Cigarette show, I heard an infectious voice one midnight on a radio show, emanating from the Cotton Club in Harlem. There was something about the voice and the laughter, the warm southern accent . . . I sent for Bert Parks. Just as Wallington had doubled as a straight man, now Bert Parks did. I started a running gag of trying to marry him to one of my daughters. I'd say,

"Bert, haven't I been treating you well on this program?"

"Yes, sir, Mr. Bossman. You've been like a father to me."

"That's it. I want to be more like a father-in-*law*. You've got to eat. Come on home and have dinner at our house."

Pause.

"You like good food, don't you, Bert?"

"Yes, it's, just . . . I'm afraid that dinner might turn out to be a wedding feast. I'm not quite ready, Mr. C."

We discovered that Bert had a nice voice and he began to sing. Then I doubled him up with another talented youngster, Kay St. Germain, and started a "romance" in that direction. Making the announcer part of the family, having him sing, involving him in a romance . . . all this was off-beat and new, and people tuned in for it. It's always the off-beat thing that attracts.

. . . Bringing Leslie Howard on the show, having him in tights, leaping up and down the stage, clapping his hands, rolling his eyes and singing in Shakespearean English, "If you knew Susan like I know Susan. Ah, me, Ah, what a wench!"

. . . Bringing Lauritz Melchior on the program (his first), weary of opera and pining to play Costello to my Abbott. With a big operatic introduction to *Aida*, he sings in that famous tenor, "Aida, sweet as apple cedar."

. . . Taking a Maurice Evans and having him do a modified strip tease as he sang "My Heart Belongs to Daddy." Evans made such a hit, he was the first guest star we ever held over. When he came on the following week he refused to talk to me. "Cantor, you superthyroid so and so, beforrrrrr I met you, I'd walk down the street and people would say, 'There goes Maurice Evans, the famous Shakespearean actor,' and now . . ." "Now, what, Maurice?" "Now they say 'There goes Hot Lips Evans.'"

. . . Getting the most famous doctor in the world, the doctor who'd just delivered the Dionne quintuplets. And what that had taken—telegrams, phone calls, pleading. Finally there was Dr. Allan Dafoe on our program and I introduced him to the Mad Russian.

"Russian, this is the person responsible for those five lovely girls."

"*This* is Ida?"

"No, no, he's the one who delivered the Dionne quintuplets."

"How do you like that?" the Mad Russian said. "The first stork I ever saw with glasses!"

It was while we were broadcasting for Camels that I made the speech at the Temple of Religion, my radio contract was canceled, and I was off for a year. When I came back in 1940 my announcer was Harry Von Zell, my orchestra leader, Edgar Fairchild. I'd been lucky in announcers, lucky in orchestra leaders. You can't always keep the same team. I'd lost Rubinoff when we started broadcasting from California, but Louis Gress was a fine musician and Jacques Renard replaced Gress when he had to go back East. Cookie Fairchild had enthusiasm and talent, so did Von Zell, and we needed that; for this time it was an uphill fight.

My program had always been in the top ten, but now after a year and a half off the air we had to start slowly. I was following Fred Allen on the show, and now Fred Allen was opposite us at the same time over CBS. He gave us some tough competition at first. To compete we used the biggest guest stars and started out to find a new girl singer. I heard about eighteen or twenty girls that time—never looking at them—if you look you may be swayed by a beautiful face or a charming manner, something the radio audience won't be seeing. (If I'd looked at Betty Hutton when she auditioned, her charm would've sold me. I just listened and turned her down because that razzamatazz voice wasn't for radio, where the audience only hears.)

So I'm listening this day, and all of a sudden there's a voice that I can say is the most natural feminine singing voice I've ever heard since Nora Bayes, a gal singing not because she's being paid for it—she'd pay you—but because she loves it. Dinah Shore. When she sang the first song I knew she was *in*, but I let her keep on singing. Producer Vic Knight, who was listening with me said, "What's the idea?"

"Vic, someday we'll pay a terrific cover charge to hear this girl. Let's enjoy it just this once for nothing."

This is the best singer in a period of twenty-five or thirty years because she breathes properly, she knows the proper phrasing, and she's intelligent—she knows what the words *mean*. During the war, when we went around to put on shows at the camps, it was nothing for Dinah to sing twenty songs, one or two on our broadcast and all the rest the minute we were off the air. In 1942 on a Marine base near San Diego many of the boys were getting ready to leave the next day. Dinah sang her heart out. As we walked away after the show I heard two Marines talking.

"Ain't she somethin'?" the one said. And the other answered with reverence . . .

"It makes no difference what happens to me now. Brother, I've lived!"

That's how the radio audiences felt about Dinah, too. And we were tricky. I'd find out the timing on the Fred Allen Show and at the moment of his commercial I'd put Dinah on the air. People turning their dials to avoid the commercial would get one earful of that and stay with NBC. So much so that Fred Allen demanded CBS change him from Wednesday to Sunday. From then on we had smooth sailing and Bristol-Myers kept us for six years.

When Dinah Shore started her own show we had other singers. One time my daughter Marilyn wrote to me, very excited. When I come back to New York I *must* hear a girl named Thelma Carpenter; she's a doll and she sings like mad. Believe me, I always listen to Marilyn; she has an eye for the spark of talent many people never notice until it flashes out into full fire. So I went to hear Thelma Carpenter and she *is* great and we sign her for the season, the first time a Negro girl singer has been on radio for other than just a guest appearance.

The afternoon before our first broadcast, *Time* magazine's representative phones and wants to know what I'm trying to prove. I wasn't trying to prove anything except that Thelma had talent. Was I going to announce her as a colored singer? I answered that

I didn't remember having introduced Dinah as a white singer. *Time* magazine ignored the whole thing. They'd been trying to make something out of it; if they couldn't, they didn't even care to review the show.

We had a great team during those years. When Cookie Fairchild suffered a heart attack one summer, I went to see him at the hospital and explained that I was depending on his coming back in September. He wouldn't have to conduct the orchestra; we'd have someone else do that, but I'd appreciate his being there to oversee everything and make sure the music was right. From that moment on, there was an improvement in Cookie's health. He knew he was *wanted*. This was something I only guessed at then. Now I know how important it is, when you're sick, to feel that you're wanted! Cookie went through rehearsals, and it was time for the show. Instead of sitting down and watching the broadcast, Cookie forgot and went right on conducting.

From 1946 until 1949 we were on for Pabst and the guest stars included all the greats. But of all the people we presented through the years, the one I myself got the top boot out of was John Barrymore. I had known Jack since 1917. We met at the old Knickerbocker Hotel where Caruso lived, where George M. Cohan would often lunch. Cohan knew I worshiped Barrymore, so he introduced us.

When Jack played *Hamlet* for Arthur Hopkins, he was to me just the greatest Hamlet. I saw the play four times, and Jack actually made me understand Shakespeare for the first time. And I wasn't the only fan! Jack had insisted on playing in London, despite Arthur Hopkins's warning that the British would be out to crucify him. Hopkins was right. For two months before the play opened the British press wrote about the great American actor who was going to interpret Shakespeare for them. There was almost a feeling of derision, the posters announcing JOHN BARRYMORE in big letters and *Hamlet* in small ones. The opening-night audience certainly didn't come with an open mind. And Jack scored a triumph. Some of the reviews ran on the front page instead of on the drama page and the critics accorded an ovation that had no London parallel at that time and has only been equaled since by the ovations given Danny Kaye at the Palladium.

Jack called Hopkins the next day and said, "Arthur, how many performances of *Hamlet* has anyone played in England?" Hopkins told him two hundred and ninety (or whatever the figure was) and Jack said, "We shall play two hundred and ninety-*one* —and then we shall close."

An assured artist—this was the man on our radio show in June 1938. When we met to discuss format Jack said:

"Eddie, let's have fun. Don't make me do the same dramatic stuff, let me do something different, something I've never done before."

"And what haven't you done?"

"Burlesque, a slapstick comedy, a table scene where we squirt Seltzer water. Remember the old Keystone comedies?"

So we did a slapstick comedy sketch that was a riot. We squirted Seltzer. At one point Jack dropped the script and, for the next three or four minutes, well, writers would love to write comedy the way he ad libbed it!

His eventual enemy was his drinking, and he drank because every waking moment of his life for more than twenty years, he was in pain. He had something wrong with his spine. It became a sad thing. I used to drop over to RKO where he was working and he was drinking so steadily that he couldn't learn his lines. So the words were printed on a big blackboard and one day Jack finally got off a perfect speech. He must have gone on for 275 feet of film and then, without a pause, he was saying, "And the goddamned blackboard is getting farther and farther and farther away!"

He was scheduled to do a show with us in February 1941, and everyone got scared that Jack would show up in no condition to do the show. George Gruskin of the William Morris Agency had booked him and wanted to protect both him and me, so he started following Jack everywhere he went. If he walked out of the studio for a drink of water, George shadowed him, and he felt very pleased with himself—he knew Jack hadn't noticed. The day of the show, we'd been rehearsing, there was a break, Jack started for the door, turned his head just slightly and said, "George, don't worry about John Barleycorn and John Barrymore today. I couldn't do that to this little owl—his eyes would haunt me." George stood flat-footed while Jack went out into the hall and dragged in a case of cokes, which he and I drank steadily until show time.

Radio Cast of Characters

Everyone from Rubinoff to Barrymore—those twenty years in radio were a memorable chunk of my life. (I'm still on radio but the shows are taped and the emphasis since 1950 has been on television.) What has stayed with me are the memories of the fun we all had and the thrill of discovering new talent. A guy who held onto the contracts of his finds would never've had to lift his finger again as an entertainer, he'd have been that rich. Imagine owning a per cent of Deanna Durbin then, of Dinah Shore, of Eddie Fisher now! But you don't hold onto talent, that's not the idea, you want it to be free.

And while I'm talking about new talent let me tell you about two other youngsters who weren't with me in radio but whom I probably recognized because radio'd sharpened my wits. While *Banjo Eyes* was on Broadway we needed a new leading lady.

In the show was an act called "Pansy the Horse," a fresh-faced blond girl put a dancing horse through its paces. You should have seen the men in the audience watching this girl! Me too, but for a different reason.

"How would you like to take over when our leading lady leaves?" I asked her.

"You mean it? Let me ask my brother-in-law"—who was the front end of the horse. The front of the horse said O.K., especially if we could still work in her routines with "Pansy"; so Virginia Mayo took over as heroine in *Banjo Eyes*. She was the cleanest, wholesomest bit of sex you've ever seen, always looked as if she were freshly scrubbed. The audience adored her; it was natural that she'd be signed for pictures.

She was my last discovery until 1949 when I went up to Grossinger's Catskill Mountain resort. I'd been there many times. Grossinger's has made it possible for me to raise close to a million dollars for various causes and when I played the one-man show there we raised a hatful for the Damon Runyan Memorial Fund.

So . . . I'm at Grossinger's and Milton Blackstone, the New York advertising man who's made this resort a national institution, told me I ought to put on a young singer who'd been working the place weekends. I had my show all put together, so I begged off. That afternoon we went for a walk and, just by chance, where do you suppose Blackstone walked me? To an auditorium where Eddie Fisher just happened to be rehearsing. He did have a nice voice and that night I introduced him on our show. He sang "You're Breaking My Heart," and how! As soon as the applause abated I said, "This boy doesn't know it, but from now on he's going to be with me." They applauded hard. I turned to Eddie and said, "Tomorrow we open at Convention Hall, Philadelphia."

"Does it have to be tomorrow?" he asked. "I have a date to audition for a job."

"You don't have to audition, young fellow, you have a job."

I wasn't *that* smart that I thought Eddie Fisher would be an immediate and sensational hit. Not at all. I had some trepidation that he might just be a local favorite; but our tour took us all over the country, and Eddie never failed to stop the show.

When we finished the tour I asked the Morris office to take Eddie from there. And to show you how much even the top agents know, the Morris office said, "These guys are a dime a dozen." So Eddie got another agent. He was always in good hands, because Milton Blackstone is one of the most farseeing, finger-on-the-public-pulse men I've ever met. When vaudeville died and the public was at its wake, he gave it artificial respiration and resurrected the whole business at Grossinger's. In twenty years Milt has booked 12,500 acts into this resort, introducing and including everyone you can mention: Sid Caesar, Jackie Gleason, etc.

And if anyone ever forced a fellow into discovering another fellow, Blackstone forced me. For which I'm grateful, because knowing Eddie Fisher has been a joy. He's this kind of guy . . . When Ida and I were celebrating our thirty-ninth wedding anniversary Eddie was closing at the Palladium, London. Our celebration took the form of a TV show at the El Capitan Theatre, Hollywood. A few days before came this cable: *"Understand you're celebrating your 39th wedding anniversary. May I fly on to California to the show and sing a couple of songs? Love to you and Aunt Ida. Eddie."* Like Dinah, Eddie loves to sing. He's in love with Debbie, his wife, he's in love with love, he's in love with life, and he shows it by singing.

If ever I did anything to help Eddie or Dinah or the others, they've all more than repaid me. It was stimulating to work with them and maybe I've been able to pay back in some small degree what Gus Edwards did for us.

22. Television

Show business is the tree, the trunk is the entertainer; and how you entertain—in musical comedy, on the concert stage, in radio, movies, television—these are all the branches. I always knew that whatever changes in show business, whatever the branch, I'd want to be part of it. In 1940 I already felt that television would be the greatest medium of communication, that the day would come when you'd pick up the phone in your own living room, call "New York 1971," and ask to be tuned in on *Pal Joey*, or call "Hollywood 2134," and see C. B. De Mille's *The Ten Commandments;* and at the end of the month the charge would merely appear on your phone bill. This not only would not kill the legitimate show or the movie, it would give that show or movie a fabulous additional monthly income. Instead of having one or two stars, a show could have six or seven stars and writers would thrive on the additional royalties, too.

I kept watching television, waiting for a full-scale audience. In 1947 and '48 TV sets were still a luxury. Sounds funny today, doesn't it, when a TV set is as great a necessity as a washing machine? I watched for several years, checking the number of sets sold, considering the type of material that would go—a combination of the theater and the movies. I felt definitely that weekly exposure would shorten the life of any comedian, that he'd reach a saturation point with the audience. There are isolated cases. Groucho Marx, for example, has managed to weather it; but your smartest comedians today, Dean Martin and Jerry Lewis, have made their appearances seldom enough to be a treat. If they'd stayed together, if they hadn't split up, in twenty years they'd still be going strong. Television is slow death to the comedian who goes on week after week; it exhausts his material, his body, his soul, and, alas, his audience.

Someone representing a network'll wander into a night club, see a fellow who has worked up (by the process of careful elimination) forty-five minutes of good punchy material; and he'll cry, "My God, how he makes them laugh!" So they put the comedian on television and he only has to do fifteen minutes; but that means in three weeks he's exhausted that carefully worked-up routine. What does he do the fourth week? It takes excellent writers, excellent management, to sustain a personality and make him stand out. In the last four or five years the only such personality—George Gobel. Just watch the ratings and see what happens from overexposure.

In 1950 I proposed to NBC that I'd be prepared to do a TV show once every four weeks, rotating with other comics. The idea was accepted as practical and it became the Colgate Comedy Hour: Fred Allen, Martin and Lewis, Abbott and Costello, Eddie Cantor. I opened the series in the fall of 1950 and with the exception of time out for my heart attack, was with them 1950-51, '51-'52, '52-'53, '53-'54.

Even once every four weeks was tough. What you're doing is a one-hour motion picture with no chance at a second take. It was all done live. Did I say "live"? It damn near killed me. When you're pushing sixty, running up and down stage, clapping your hands, taking pratfalls, keeping the thing paced, is not exactly a day in the country. But it was a great satisfaction. You love show business, you love to be in it, you want to make good. In those years the Colgate Comedy Hour was always among the top ten shows, usually among the top three or four. At that time we were still beating Ed Sullivan's Toast of the Town. Later, when the program had changed to the Comedy Hour and had gotten pretty smug, Sullivan outdistanced them at a walk—not only because he's a hard worker, not only because of his contacts as a newspaper man for getting guest stars, but because with Marlo Lewis, he's acquired a sense of showmanship second to no one in the business.

But in those first four years, we, too, were giving all we had—to the Colgate Comedy Hour. My format for the show was purely variety, with a slight theme to take it out of the realm of vaudeville. I had Al Goodman and his orchestra, I had Connie Russell,

I had Billy Daniels, who is a fine choreographer and dancer; the rest of the cast we'd pick up. We had one show that opened with a song, "If the USA Can't Get to Broadway, We'll Bring Broadway to the USA." We went to the opera and introduced Jan Peerce. We went to a burlesque show and Dorothy Lamour, Sidney Fields and I did a burlesque. We introduced a musical comedy, *Walkin' My Baby Back Home,* a ballet with Nanci Crompton, and then went to a night club where Sammy Davis, Jr., his father and his uncle took over.

In many shows we included a character whom I'd introduced years before in *Make It Snappy*—Maxie the Taxi, a comic-philosopher. This episode eased the hour strain; it gave me a chance to sit in a cab and gab with my passenger. No sooner did we get on the air than we were handed a suit by a New York taxi driver who claimed to have written a book about a taxi driver, a book never published, but which I must have read by "some devious means" and which must have given me the idea for Maxie. It was all silly. I'd never read his manuscript. Besides, he'd written it in the forties and I'd introduced Maxie in 1922. But he sued for more than a million dollars and I could only comment, "When you give a taxi driver a million bucks, how big should the tip be?"

We had new ideas, we used old ideas, too—a minstrel show, the famous skit "Joe's Blue Front," in which I played a tailor in a Seventh Avenue clothing store trying to sell a customer from the country. Each time it looked as though I had him sold he'd insist on a "suit with a belt in the back."

We had a lot of fun; we had a lot of fights. You see, if you're working in the theater for a man like Ziegfeld, you have Mr. Ziegfeld to cope with and no one else. If you're working in movies for Mr. Goldwyn, you have Mr. Goldwyn to cope with. In radio you have a sponsor. But in television you have a variety of bosses and the human equation is missing. Your main boss is the rating. Many of your other bosses don't actually know whether you have a good show or a bad until they *see* the next day's ratings. You may have a poor show, the public may not have liked it; but if the rating is good, on the strength of one rating a performer may be signed for five years! And one of the glaring faults in TV production is the lack of decision among the bosses: the sponsor, the advertising agency, the network representative, the executive producer and, as the King of Siam would say, "Etcetera, etcetera." A simple decision takes a week to achieve.

You rehearse all week, as contrasted to four or five hours for a radio show. Sometimes the executive producer comes on the set on Friday, the day before you shoot. And then the fun begins. "I wouldn't do this or I wouldn't do that." He's likely to tell Jascha Heifetz, "Why don't you bring in a saxophone? The audience has seen you with a violin a hundred times." Once we had a skit depicting Al Jolson and me playing a benefit. I was reminiscing; then fade out, and bring in a man in blackface who looked like Jolson who'd "sing" to a Jolson recording. Meanwhile I'd black up, come on, and we'd do a little dance together to finish the skit. On Friday the executive producer wandered in and turned thumbs down. He wouldn't say why, just "no."

I dropped out of the Colgate Comedy Hour when I realized that live shows, live song and dance and acting shows, were too tough for me, and then I promptly made an even bigger mistake. I signed a fabulous contract with Ziv for filmed shows. Fabulous so far as money was concerned, fatal so far as the last word on stories, casting, songs, and jokes. Supersalesmen, even within my own organization, assured me I'd have the last word but that they couldn't establish a precedent by putting that in my contract; and for once in my life I allowed my better judgment to be swayed by the money involved. I'd give all the money back if I could take back the shows, which are still running.

I was supposed to star in only thirteen productions; in the other twenty-six I was to act as host, introduce the people, come out at intermission, and again at the end of the show. The first show was O.K.; the second show had no story line at all and I started staying up nights to rewrite it. The battle began. My fight was, "Let's make it good." The producers' only consideration was, "Let's get it out. Finish this one, get on with the next one." In short, an assembly line, not a quality product. Of the starring shows, I wrote six; but the finished product wasn't worth the fight and I bowed out of a seven-year contract after one year, having learned a lesson.

My next television appearance had nothing to do with money. Oh, they paid me and paid me well, but comedy is what attracts the big money and I was making my debut, after almost fifty years in show business, in a straight dramatic part. It was on Matinee Theatre, an hour show over NBC, and was called *George Has A Birthday* by a new writer, Jean Clifford Raymond. George is a simple elevator operator whose ambition is to be the starter in the department store where he works. He is due to inherit five hundred thousand dollars but according to his father's will the fortune has been held until his fifty-fifth birthday. His two sisters, with whom he lives, have gone through their inheritance and are planning to murder George for his. They do, too, but the woman to whom he's secretly married discovers that he was murdered.

The author sent me the script. George was a whimsical character, a lovable character, and I suddenly decided I'd like a whirl at drama. This was a live show, we rehearsed for ten days, started work the day of the show at 5 A.M. It was nothing but enjoyable. Doing a serious piece is much easier than being a comedian, believe me. The audience plays a great part in your success. You can stand facing someone in a dramatic scene, turn away, drop your eyes, look down at your hands and the audience thinks, "Great acting," when all that's happened is—you've forgotten a line. Or you stutter a bit or splutter, and they attribute this to, "How emotional he is!" But you're not aware of the audience as you are in comedy. In comedy 98 per cent of the time you're playing directly to the audience. In a dramatic scene you're playing to whomever is in the scene.

And we couldn't have had a better cast. Madeleine Holmes and Mae Clarke played my sisters, Lillian Bronson, who has a sort of Lillian Gish quality, played my wife. We rehearsed for those ten days and we really rehearsed. They all knew it was my first dramatic show, they wanted it to be good, for themselves and for me. Mae Clarke called up a convent at five-thirty the day of the show. Five-thirty A.M., I mean. She wanted the sisters to offer a prayer for us, which I thought a very nice idea. The sister who answered the phone explained that it was so early they hadn't gone to Mass yet. "At this hour," I told Mae, "God isn't even up!"

It was a fascinating show to do. Albert McCleery, the producer, does the biggest job in television today, barring no one. He uses his scenery in cameo fashion. There is, within camera range, a fireplace, a couch, a chair, nothing more, but you have the illusion of a room. We have an automobile accident and a man is standing by to muss my hair and tie while the camera is moving a few steps, and I with it, to the next "set."

The main thing was the character of George. A good writer gives you a complete characterization, makes it easy. You yourself disappear, you slip into George, think like George, feel like George. Frankly I couldn't have done this thirty years ago, or twenty. I'd have put some Eddie Cantor into the part of George, I'd have had to show how smart I was at George's expense. He wasn't a hep guy, he was a guy, who, when the elevator starter said, "We certainly have our ups and downs," thought it the funniest thing he ever heard. Maybe the word "humility" is going a little too far, but let's say that, with the years, I've acquired some heart as well as some wit and I played George with heart.

Since then, I've had a chance to play a far meatier dramatic role, that of Morris Sizeman in *Sizeman and Son*, a ninety-minute live television show on Playhouse 90. Morris is a well-to-do businessman in New York's garment center and we meet him as he is eagerly awaiting the return from Korea of his son (Farley Granger), who returns with left-wing notions of how Dad should run that business. Elick Moll, who wrote the play, created wonderful characterizations: the pressers, salesmen, buyers, models, so familiar in the garment industry; he presented them with deep perception and humanity, avoiding all the clichés, the stereotypes into which they might have slipped. Peter Lorre played the presser, my lifelong friend; Mona Freeman, the model with whom my son fell in love.

It was a deeply moving and rewarding play, and not the least of the rewards were the press praises that poured in from all parts of the country. Jack O'Brian of the New York *Journal American*, who never has been a Cantor fan, wrote the review which pleased me most: "Most surprising to us was the fine, affectionate, dramatic fabric woven by Eddie Cantor. We've been reviewing Cantor for years in every medium and never gave him credit for depth. Ability, yes; aggressive drive, certainly; knowledge of the bombast and tricks of the clown's craft, of course; protecting himself in the clinches, always. But as an actor capable of disciplining his perfectly understandable ego . . . of sustaining a straight role with depth of characterization, well—that is something we never anticipated. At Eddie's age, it's hardly the time for such a gay old dog to learn new tricks, but Eddie has. Sizeman was an extra feather in his virtually Indian-headdress of comedy and variety awards . . . one of Cantor's finest hours."

I've had another fine hour recently, a fine hour to me personally, that is. Fifteen old friends and new friends showed up on my sixty-fifth birthday when we took over the Jackie Gleason show. Highlight of the evening for me was the very professional appearance of my daughter Marilyn who sailed through our song-and-dance number in a manner indicating she's well on her way. I don't know what I enjoyed most—Marilyn *on* the show or the rating *after* the show. With more than thirty million listeners, we beat Perry Como that night, only the second time anyone has beaten Como in a year. Variety is fun, but . . . I'd like to do more drama. I've never envied comedians, the people I've envied were the dramatic actors—John Barrymore, Orson Welles, Walter Hampden, Helen Hayes (I saw *Victoria Regina* ten times), Lunt and Fontanne in *There Shall Be No Night,* Henry Fonda in *Mister Roberts,* Lloyd Nolan in *The Caine Mutiny.* And there are many fine comedians who have the capacity to be good dramatic actors, because in understanding true comedy you have to be sincere, you have to make the audience believe. Chaplin is one of the finest dramatic actors who ever lived. Red Skelton is a fine actor, Jackie Gleason has the depth to be a completely legitimate actor. Mary Martin. Remember, in the middle of *South Pacific,* when she walked downstage and said, "Oh, God, please see that he's safe!"

You see, in baseball, when a pitcher loses the strength or a good part of the power he used to have in his pitching arm, he can still stay in the big leagues if he pitches with his head, knowing the idiosyncrasies of the various batters. Show business is no different. The physical end of comedy, the jumping, the dancing, is over for me. If I'm to spend the rest of my days in this business, I'm going to have to pitch with my head.

Take two of my contemporaries, Ed Wynn and Ted Lewis. Ed has given up some of his strenuous comedy for straight dramatic roles and has found a most responsive public. Ted Lewis, master showman, is taking it easier too. By sheer force of personality he's packing 'em in on the night-club circuit, doing a bigger business than ever. With an occasional television appearance, Ted could go on until he's a hundred.

I want to do more good theater, I'd like to do a spectacular once or twice a year—I'd trade in all of it for the chance to do a weekly filmed show that would be a public service, sponsored by some big firm that does institutional advertising. Instead of selling tooth paste or beer or soap, I'd like to sell Safety, the March of Dimes, Mental Health. Not preaching. You must always have a hootchy-kootchy dance to attract the people. You *must* have fun. The world starts the morning in tears, it wants laughter. That's why your comedians' ratings are high, why all the top comics are millionaires.

And if your Neilsen rating is forty or better—why not use that to do advertising of the most important sort? That's what I'd like to do with my life from here on. Be a comedian, a dramatic actor—for causes. It isn't a new idea with me, it's just something I believe in more all the time.

23. The Beggar

As far back as 1929 I had the same idea, this idea of public service. At that time I was playing in a show called *Whoopee*. Mr. Ziegfeld was paying me the top salary a comedian had ever earned, and on May 9 at a press conference I announced that when *Whoopee* closed I was retiring from show business.

The eyebrows went up. I was thirty-seven years old and not the type to sit around on park benches feeding the pigeons. I didn't intend to. I'd found that there were a lot of human beings in the world who needed help and that a clown, by virtue of his clowning, could help them. Benefits!

How could a guy like me not do benefits? To remember the squalid Henry Street basement and then look about at warmth and security, to have longed for a family and been blessed with one, to ride in a Rolls-Royce through streets where the pushcarts had run you down—you have to think, "Thank God, thank country, thank all the elements that made this possible." You know if you devoted the rest of your life to helping people you couldn't pay it back. Besides, there was my grandma who'd had nothing and always gave part of it to someone with less than nothing, who turned no one away.

That's why I wanted to retire from show business, to be free to help a Fresh Air Fund in Pittsburgh or flood victims in Missouri. And money was no object, I had all I'd ever need. From now on, I wanted my life to be one big benefit performance.

Six months later the only money I had in the world was in my pants pocket. Sixty bucks. I'd been wiped out in the stock-market crash and what I didn't even know—I owed $285,000 to the Manufacturers Trust Company, where the President had covered some of my calls for margin.

I'd wanted to *do* benefits? I needed one!

So I kept on in show business, luckily, for that has made me far more valuable to the causes I believe in. That's why I keep working today. Show business gives you a shine, like an electric torch; it gives you the opportunity you'd never have as a private citizen. And let me say right here that if actors did benefits just for the publicity involved, that still wouldn't detract from the results; but that isn't why they do it. Yes, in the beginning, back as far as 1917 when I was first asked to appear for charity, the ham in me was pleased.

But that feeling doesn't last. By 1929 fund raising had become a chore rather than an act. It was no longer fun to speak, you felt you had to do this, that if you failed to answer a request to raise money in Cleveland or Tulsa or Denver—and sometimes it was an effort to be there—it would be cheating, like a doctor who has his wife say he's not in when he doesn't want to make a night call. There's a combination of motives in everything we do, but basically I feel that this is the work I'm here for, and if the attendant publicity helps give others the idea to follow suit—good.

It all started with Surprise Lake Camp, the place where I was sent as a half-starved kid. Early in 1920 some of the fellows who'd gone to that camp formed a committee (later called the "Eddie Cantor Camp Committee") and started giving benefits to help build the camp. Between 1920 and 1930 we presented shows with Will Rogers, Fanny Brice, W. C. Fields, Clayton, Jackson and Durante, Gertrude Lawrence, Beatrice Lillie, the Astaires—there was no trouble in digging up stars. Show people are the only people in the world who give away that which they have to sell. We never needed publicity or advertising; a mere squib in the papers would draw a full house. Our audiences weren't just giving to charity, they were paying regular theater prices for great entertainment.

After ten years it got to the point where it was tough to get the theater, the stagehands, the electricians, the tickets and programs. So we decided to write our customers as follows: "Dear Charlie, What would you give not to have to get dressed up, leave your comfortable home, and come to town to see this benefit show? Is it worth fifty dollars to you?" We got more money for not giving the benefit than if we'd given one. We now have eight hundred

The Beggar

regular contributors we solicit by mail. The money has gone to build more than a hundred bungalows, provide larger kitchens, more toilets, more boats, and to accommodate more boys—always more boys. (A woman's auxiliary committee has raised hundreds of thousands of dollars for a girls' camp on the other side of the lake.)

Over the years, where once sixty boys went to camp this year there were twenty-four hundred. At times the camp has stayed open all year so that undernourished kids could stay three, four, six, eight months, until they were on their feet. On the spot where I first sang "Harrigan" before the campfire, the Eddie Cantor Playhouse has just opened, the gift of many friends of needy boys. It's a wonderful sight to visit this camp and see white boys, Negro boys, Mexican boys, all kinds of boys learning to live together. They learn things at camp they don't always learn at home. No boy is born a bigot; it comes from the family dinner table. At camp it's a different sort of dinner table. We try to give them the best in nourishment, physical, mental and spiritual.

But if I've given to Surprise Lake Camp—it has more than given back to me. . . . When the Stage Door Canteen opened in New York, Jane Cowl invited several of us down opening night. It was a great project. There was no problem with entertainment, but there was a problem about food, how to feed all these hungry guys. For the first few days I asked places like Reuben's and Lindy's and they each furnished a day's food. But the Canteen needed permanent sources of supply. I volunteered to furnish the milk. "You order it, I'll pay for it." Wow, how those corn-fed country guys could drink milk! The bills ran over six hundred dollars a month. I was playing in *Banjo Eyes* at the time, and for seven or eight months all was well. When the show closed and we took off for Hollywood, Ida explained to me that the time had come to get someone else to help. I couldn't just walk out on my milk bill so I tried to promote a milk company to replace me. Sheffield Milk Company said they'd donate for one day, Borden's said the same. I was coming away from my third turndown when a fellow stopped me in the corridor.

"Cantor," he said, "I was listening. Maybe I can help you. There's an organization in town known as the Independent Milk Owners. They're a bunch of small companies organized in opposition to the big companies. I know the head boy. Want to meet him?"

The next day at lunch I meet him, a big husky fellow who pumps my hand and says, "What do you want, boy?" "*Boy*," he says. I was old enough to be his grandfather.

"I want milk."

"O.K.," he says, "we'll supply the milk."

"But you don't understand. I mean for the duration of the war."

"O.K., boy, for the duration," he says. That floors me. He is a livin' doll, but it's been too easy.

"You didn't even give me a chance to make my pitch. Why're you doin' this?"

"Why? Well, boy, it's one small way of paying you back. I was the skinniest, most undernourished punk you ever saw, Eddie. I got my start when *you* sent me to camp."

That's how it goes. The mother of one of my closest friends had a brain tumor and needed a skilled surgeon who happened to be in the Navy. Secretary of the Navy Knox loaned me the sailor for a day or two and he saved the mother's life. As we said good-by and I thanked him, the surgeon said, "I was glad to come, Eddie. You know—I still have the card and the application—you sent me to camp when I was a kid."

Can you imagine the thrill when bread you've cast on the water comes back cake?

In the last twenty-five years I've raised about two hundred and eighty million dollars cash. This doesn't include the sale of bonds, which is only an exchange of paper (the customer is buying something, not giving). This two hundred and eighty million dollars came from Americans of all kinds and was given to a variety of causes—hospitals, orphans, veterans, Catholic and Protestant projects, the United Jewish Appeal. Sixty million was for the State of Israel, where I'm known as "The Schnorrer." Schnorrer means beggar; and they're right, I *am* a beggar, sometimes for human souls.

Making the Purple Heart Circuit of the hospitals one time, we hit the Veterans' Hospital in Kansas. The whole cast of our radio show was with me. The boys seemed to enjoy the show, all but one. While Nora Martin sang he read the newspaper. I questioned the nurse.

The Beggar

"He doesn't want to live," she told me. "He won't laugh, he won't cry, he won't take his medicine. He wrote to his girl this morning to tell her he doesn't love her, that she should find someone with better legs than his."

I can't get this boy out of my mind. We go from ward to ward. When we finish it is nine-fifteen, fifteen minutes before curfew. I ask the nurse if I can talk with the boy. She says I'll be wasting my time, but she lets me go over and sit down beside the bed.

"How are you, son?"

"Who wants to *know?*" He never lifts his eyes from the paper.

"Listen, mister," I say, "I'm not a young man any more. I have a home and family and I like to be with them. I don't have to go from hospital to hospital singing my lungs out, grabbing a sandwich, gulping a glass of milk, and trying to sleep on trains. None of these people has to do it. We come to cheer up boys like you, but you're a mean sourpuss!"

He looks up suddenly and starts to cry. "Yes, I am!" he says and tells me all about it, how bored he's been and how hopeless, and the girl . . .

"Look, son. Do one thing for me. Write your girl and tell her the truth, that you love her. We're making the rounds of forty hospitals, the trip'll be worth while if you'll do that. You get well and get out of here and I'll give you a wedding. You hear?"

He hears. As we leave, he's asking the nurse to bring him the medicine he'd refused to take.

A year and a half later I'm playing cards with Jessel when the bell rings at my house. Outside stands a good-looking fellow and a girl.

"O.K., Eddie, we're ready," the fellow says. I'm puzzled for a minute, not recognizing this husky guy until he tells me the story. What a wedding we had, complete with Burns and Allen, Jack Benny, Dinah Shore, and the Ritz Brothers. They live in El Paso now, have a little boy, and call him "Eddie."

And a time in San Diego four years ago. We go into the tuberculosis ward of a hospital and they try to put a mask on my face. I laugh. "How the hell can I sing 'Susie' through this thing?" So I sing without the mask and one of the kids calls me over to show me a letter from his dad. "So Eddie Cantor's coming to visit you," the letter reads. "What a strange world. In a tubercular ward in

Chelsea, Massachusetts, 1918, this same guy came and entertained us . . . and I'll bet you, with the same jokes!"

And Chicago. Buddy Clark has asked me to join him for a hospital show. We're doing the show and over the loud-speakers comes, "Eddie Cantor wanted in surgery, Eddie Cantor wanted in surgery." We think it's a gag. Until a nurse comes to say, "You really are wanted." Outside surgery is a cart with a boy. His spine is injured so that he's untouchable. The kid wants me to sing "Whoopee" before he's operated on. So there in the hall, no piano, no nothing, I sing "Whoopee."

The kid grins.

"O.K., Doc, let's go." And he goes. And he never comes back.

Always the human equation, always the miracle of helping to save a life or giving a moment's fun to someone who badly needs it. That's why Jolson and Benny and Hope . . . Look at the miles Bob Hope has traveled, more than any entertainer of the century. The guy deserves a medal for his service to the country and yet, like all of us, he'll tell you it's a privilege. As an elder statesman of the business, this is something I've been able to explain to a younger generation: the shows you do for free mean more than any shows you ever do for money. For once, you're more than a clown.

Five years ago President Harriman of the Red Cross came to me. The blood bank was in trouble and needed help. "Don't look at me," I gagged. "I'm anemic!" But in 1950 I'd done a one-man show, in the early days I'd been a singing waiter at Coney Island . . . I decided to try another one-man show: Admission—one pint of blood. I played ten cities, ten nights, and the box office yielded Mr. Harriman one hundred and ten thousand pints of blood. Maybe that blood saved a life. I hope so. Among the donors I ran across a little Jewish tailor, a refugee, who'd settled in Chicago. He gives blood six times a year. He's not allowed to donate that often in Chicago so he goes out of town, to Waukegan, to South Bend.

"Why?" I asked him. "Why so much blood?"

"Eddie Cantor, I'm surprised at you. Such a question. If I stayed in Germany, Hitler would have had it all in one day. No?"

People are wonderful, and in fund raising I've had a chance to meet them and know them as I never would staying behind the footlights. I knew no one when I arrived in Manchester, England. It was a Sunday afternoon in June 1938. I addressed a gathering at a country club, addressed a tea, a gathering at a railway station, now it was a hotel with a packed audience. The plea was for the refugee children who'd been separated from their parents in Germany. The first thing Hitler did, you remember, was separate the children from their mothers and fathers. The parents were now dead or in concentration camps and we were trying to transport the youngsters to Palestine. For $360 you could take one child out of Germany and give it a chance to grow up safely. Standing on the platform in Manchester that evening, I told of visiting one of the homes in Paris supported by the Joint Distribution Committee. There were sixty little orphans in this home, awaiting deportation. I'd brought with me a trunk of Oh Henrys and Hershey bars, but I noticed one little girl sitting there, candy in hand, not touching it. I went over and took her on my knee. "Little lady, what can I do for you?" She looked at me with that wan face and said, "Love me."

Since then I'd traveled twelve thousand miles for those children and the story of this little girl had raised many, many dollars for her fellow sufferers. So now, in Manchester . . .

When I finish there is a hush. Then a woman stands up in the audience, the tears streaming down her face. She starts toward the platform twisting a ring off her finger. "Mr. Cantor, your children need this ring more than I do. Auction it, please." I've never seen this woman in my life, I'm as surprised as she is. A beautiful, glittering diamond. I hold it up and invite bidding. The woman's husband offers a hundred pounds, another man bids a hundred and twenty. Others enter the picture, but these two bidders persist, the husband and the stranger, until the sum is far beyond the ring's value, seven or eight thousand dollars. The stranger outbids the woman's husband. Sold. He comes to the platform, writes a check, takes the ring and walking quickly to the lady's table, hands it to her without a word. Her husband jumps up now, rushes to the platform and makes out a check for *his* highest bid.

That ring took forty-one children out of tragedy-torn Europe and gave them a new start across the sea. People are wonderful.

Publisher Walter Annenberg wanted me to speak for one of his charities in Philadelphia—and what a great city that is, with what a great heart. I went through my song and dance at the Bellevue-Stratford Hotel, got a lot of laughs and a lot of money, and was ready to leave when someone yelled from the audience,

"What'll you take for your tie?"

"A hundred dollars," I said taking it off.

"How much for your coat?"

"What size shirt you wear, Eddie?"

And I took that off. And my trousers. Finally I was standing in shorts and undershirt and sold the shirt. They had to loan me a bathrobe and car to get across the street to my hotel. Minsky should have booked me. Gypsy Rose Cantor.

That's the only time I've used that technique, but other techniques you do use. You have to know when to stop talking; you can hurt a cause by overselling it. Mark Twain told the story of how, in church, hearing a minister talk, he was so moved he decided to put a dollar in the contribution. The minister kept talking. Twain decided fifty cents would be enough. The minister talked on and on. Maybe a quarter, Twain thought. By the time the collection plate came round he took out twenty cents. But you have to talk long enough; there are always those with a certain resistance, the wife who has said to Papa, "Don't you let that little beggar con you out of money you can't afford." For the first half hour I make 'em laugh. Then with one line I make a switch. Suddenly, instead of fun, I'm telling about needy children, and the line—"These children need you. They're orphans. *You* are their mothers and fathers."

But the actual appearance and pitch are only the last of it. First you have to investigate the cause to be sure it's worthy. Then you study the books to see who gave last year and how much, who are the givers and who the tightwads in the community. Often, the day before the formal meeting I call on one man, the leading tightwad, the one who could ruin the whole show by giving too little. I spend more time on him than on the final performance.

There isn't always time for this preliminary spadework. In a midwestern city, raising money for the United Jewish Appeal, I arrived just an hour before the cocktail party which customarily precedes these dinners. I went directly to the country club and sauntered into the bar. There was only one customer on hand, and he came up, introduced himself, and asked what I'd like to drink.

I hadn't caught his name but I thanked him kindly and ordered a Scotch old-fashioned. We started talking. He asked how I thought I'd do. I explained that in each community it all depends on the leading citizen. If he's liberal he sets the pace and others follow. If he's tough, raising money is tough. And according to my information the leader in this area was a bastard.

By this time the place had filled up, my acquaintance told me he didn't think I'd have too much trouble, and on this optimistic note we parted. At the proper moment, dinner ended, the leading citizen got up to introduce me—well, who else? the "bastard" I'd talked with in the bar! Luckily he had a sense of humor and his introduction was magnificent. "Eddie and I met in the bar an hour ago," he said, "and he told me what he thought of me." Then he started the donations with a check for fifty thousand dollars.

In another town, down South, I knew I couldn't raise peanuts. I'd been advised, but a guy who'll do a strip tease for money'll do anything. When we landed at the airport, the committee was waiting. I began to fret, I turned up my collar, pulled down my hat, headed for the hotel, and asked for a doctor, a friend of mine. The closer to "curtain time," the "sicker" I felt. At five-thirty my friend the doctor phoned the chairman of the committee and suggested they'd better get a pinch hitter for me. They were panic-stricken. The dinner was an hour and a half away! They couldn't get anyone to pinch-hit. This was no surprise. Finally, at seven, with the place packed, I had to face it. I arrived at the hall supported by the doctor on one side, a nurse on the other. I spoke in a weak voice but I spoke. And it worked. Where I'd have been lucky to raise one hundred and fifty thousand dollars I raised four hundred and fifty thousand dollars—only because they thought it was poor Cantor's last request.

And there was the night Ida read of the heroic death of an air-line stewardess, Mary Frances Housley, who saved ten passengers on her plane and died trying to save a child. Ida felt that for one day everyone would read of this girl and then she'd be forgotten. Ida wanted me to do something. The next morning I phoned Jacksonville, Florida, Mary Frances's home town, and asked what could be done in her memory. They reserved the ballroom of the George Washington Hotel for one performance. I flew down, worked two and a half hours, and we had fifteen thousand dollars to start an auditorium at the Hope Haven Home for Crippled Children, the auditorium to be named in Mary Frances's honor.

That night the laugh was on me. I had asked for questions from the audience and we were having fun with this sort of informal "conversation" when a card came up signed by Mrs. W. J. Johnson. "I am the mother of nine daughters," she wrote. "I came here tonight to meet a quitter."

From Jacksonville I went to Las Vegas to help the Right Reverend Monsignor Joseph J. Lambe raise thirty-two thousand dollars for his new school at Las Vegas—not by making any speeches either, but by making the rounds of the gambling casinos, putting the bite on the dealers, croupiers, crap-table operators, and their customers.

And there was the night we started the hospital in Denver to honor General Maurice Rose, the American general who was murdered in cold blood by the Nazis. We raised the money at a dinner, admission one thousand dollars a plate. After I'd sung, danced, and told stories, I jumped into a donor's lap and encored "If You Knew Susie" for another ten thousand dollars. We collected a half million dollars that night and Jack Benny and Martin and Lewis have since gone back to Denver to help raise the other half.

Little causes, big causes . . . some of them give you the thrill of a lifetime. Like the forty-three-million-dollar bond drive for which I went on the air for twenty-four hours at Station KPO, San Francisco. During the course of the broadcast a blind man came into the studio with ninety dollars. It was all he had, he wanted to convert it into bonds. "Mr. Cantor, I may be blind, but every day I see the wonders of America." He said this on the air, and on the strength of that one line within the next hour we sold a million and a half worth of bonds.

The thrill, too, of having been able to help the state of Israel, the youngest democracy in the world. When Ida and I were reviewing the Israeli Army in 1950 . . . here were these soldiers standing at attention and Director of the Army Dayan told us that more than a thousand of them were kids I had sent to Israel in 1938. We spoke of the Arab danger and when I questioned Dayan on how he thought the Israeli would make out in the next skirmish, he uttered a line I'll never forget.

"If we're outnumbered more than seven to one, we'll have to have ammunition."

The spirit of Israel has elicited a generous response from Americans and never more generous than on this past February 16 when a giant party was staged in honor of my sixty-fifth birthday at the Fontainebleau Hotel, Florida. Former President Harry S. Truman was speaker of the evening, the entertainment included Nat "King" Cole, Jimmy Durante, Georgie Jessel, Hal March, Georgie Price, Joe E. Lewis, Gloria DeHaven, and Jack Benny acted as program chairman. There have been few birthday parties like this in the world. Two thousand people from every major city in America attended the dinner at the Fontainebleau, others gathered at dinners in San Francisco, Chicago, Philadelphia, St. Louis, Newark, New York, Brooklyn, Boston, Detroit, Cleveland, Minneapolis, and Memphis to watch a television account (sent closed circuit) of festivities at the Fontainebleau. And each guest at each dinner pledged at least a thousand-dollar bond! The grand total—$16,450,000. At the Prospect Theatre, Long Island, people walked up to the box office, bought a thousand-dollar bond, and went into the theater to watch the televised show. Did you ever hear of anything like this? I felt honored indeed, as if this tribute were the very climax of my life. These people felt, with me, that we must help the professional and economic development of this young democracy.

My interest in Israel has nothing to do with religion. The only religion I've known is the Bible. To me Christianity and democracy go together, one can't live without the other. I've explained over and over to audiences—"Forget what Israel stands for, this hasn't anything to do with Jewishness, who is or who isn't. I raised money years ago for China and not one of Ida's relatives is Chinese. We'd help a pack of dogs if we saw them struggling in the mud, and these people are struggling. Because of immigration restrictions they cannot come into the country in any large numbers. Well, where else can they go? Israel is the only country with its gates wide open. God bless it and help it."

But often these rallies end up in a furor of nonsense. Selling Israeli bonds in Newark one time, a woman in the audience suddenly announced, "I'll buy a thousand-dollar bond if Mr. Cantor'll let me come up on the stage and kiss him."

"I've been had cheaper," I said, "but you're on."

She came up to the stage and gave me a good buss.

"Tell me," I said weakly, "how was it?"

"Not bad, but at this point I'd pay five thousand dollars to kiss Gregory Peck."

"Madam," I said, "I have everything Mr. Peck has, only I've had it longer."

I went on being kissed; we wound up selling nine hundred thousand dollars' worth of bonds.

En route to Washington to speak at a luncheon for the American Cancer Fund, the plane was late, so late that finally I realized I'd missed the luncheon meeting. I was bemoaning the whole thing, the Cancer people had counted on me. The man across the aisle leaned over.

"Mr. Cantor, could I help you out?" and he took out his checkbook. I promptly went into my act, sang, passed the hat, and arrived in Washington, late, but with forty-five hundred dollars from those generous people on the plane.

Such a wealth of memories. And the more you give to people, the more you get in return. I was asked to meet the first boatload of prisoners back from Bataan. It was a cold, rainy, misty San Francisco morning. We were ready at five. Pianist Bee Walker and I were out on the covered pier, watching a spectacle of happiness and heartbreak. How can you describe the waiting mothers, wives, and children . . . a mother catching sight of her son's face through a porthole, waving, waving, almost hysterical with happiness, then seeing him come down the gangplank—with no legs. I'm permitted to be the first to shake hands and say "welcome home." Then on the dock, while coffee and doughnuts are served, I sing song after song. Song hits of the moment. The boys look at you as if they don't see you. They're not listening. Suddenly it dawns on me—I swing into "Margie" and "Ida" and the other old ones and they start to cheer! This they recognize. This they know. This is home.

Later, in the hospital, a doctor asks if I'll go downstairs, twenty boys are down there, the mental cases. They lay sprawled on the floor on newspapers.

The Beggar

"O.K., boys, get up. Here's Eddie Cantor, he's going to sing for you." A few get up and shuffle forward. Some listen, some don't. One boy stands in the corner with his face to the wall. He's going to turn around if I have to sing two hundred songs to do it! He stands without moving. I sing and sing. Finally "Potatoes Are Cheaper," and he whirls around, the song has hit some spark, he stumbles forward, his face a normal face, the tears starting. Ida's crying, too. The doctor says the boy will return to sanity, they've been waiting for something to penetrate . . .

That night when she told me good night my wife said, "Eddie, if you'd never done anything but this, I'd be proud all my life."

A year ago she repeated herself. We were watching the Ed Murrow program with Dr. Salk and Dr. Francis reporting on the polio vaccine. We were both deeply moved, and to think that in an infinitesimal way I was part of this . . . the money came from the March of Dimes . . . and the March of Dimes . . .

24. The Men Behind the Beggar

No one accomplishes much alone. Behind any success I've had as a fund raiser stand five men: Jacob Holman, Emanuel Goldman, Bennie Holzman, Jack Crandall, Arthur Baer. These men have been my close friends for forty years, men of great heart, humanity, and shrewd business judgment; and our friendship is anchored in a need to give. They helped educate me to that need, they gave me the encouragement, the benefit of their know-how, they're the driving force behind the beggar.

Jack Holman and Mannie Goldman are the two who started the Eddie Cantor Camp Committee that's done so much for Surprise Lake Camp. It was Jack's idea and Mannie's been treasurer since the committee's inception in 1920. Mannie, who, with his brothers, runs the GGG Clothing Company, is the best possible choice for a treasurer because any time we're stuck for funds he digs into his own pocket to refill the treasury. He's the kind of man who wakes up in the morning and starts thinking what he can do for someone. He's been so busy doing, he's never gotten around to marrying and having a family of his own. He's part of my family, part of Jack's, part of all his friends' families.

Mannie, Jack, and I were together at Surprise Lake Camp when we were kids. Mannie lived on the East Side but in a *good* house; he dressed nicely, had spending money, and paid his way to camp; but he was one of us just the same. Jack was a little older, a camp counselor. There was something adult about his thinking even then. His brother Nat also went to our camp and grew up to be probably the best of all basketball players, a member of the Celtics. Jack grew up and went into the leather business, but needy boys were his real business and Surprise Lake Camp his focus. He and Mannie worked hard together on this; their work's been an inspiration to everyone who knows them. Jack, a kid from a poor family, Mannie a rich boy, they both felt the same debt to this country, Mannie because his family came here, poor immigrants from Russia, and America gave them a chance.

Mannie's so anxious to help a good cause that in 1938 when I went to Europe to raise money to get refugee children out of Germany—Mannie went too. We'd talked in New York about the devastation going on in Europe; Mannie was making my reservations to sail. Suddenly he said, "Eddie, this is going to be a tough trip. How can you make contacts, make all the speeches, and keep the books too? A lot of money'll be involved. I'd better go along as bookkeeper." He packed a couple of bags and sailed with us. His aid was invaluable. He arranged, for example, my meeting with Sir Montague Burton, the largest clothing manufacturer in the world, and we raised an enormous sum at this man's home in Leeds.

We "played" Manchester, Sheffield, Glasgow, Newcastle, Leeds, and London on this trip. In London we sat down with James G. McDonald, then representing the United States at the Avion Conference. We discussed the problems of evacuating the stricken people of Germany to other parts of the world. What McDonald told us only strengthened our determination. He told us that he had sat at the conference and actually cried, listening to representatives of the mighty nations of the world when they discussed the plight of these people. It was within the power of these nations to let down the bars a bit; they did nothing. Mannie and I looked at each other and went on, working as fast as we could. (McDonald worked too; he later became our ambassador to Israel.)

Every story you heard drove you harder. We went to the studio outside London where Elizabeth Bergner was working. Elizabeth talked with us about conditions in her native country. Her beautiful face clouded. "Eddie, you couldn't believe . . . I opened in a play in Berlin. I'll never forget the curtain calls and the flowers. The very next night I made my entrance on the same stage and someone from the audience yelled, 'Get off the stage, you Jewish pig!' They yelled, they threw things, I barely got off the stage. If it hadn't been for the loyal German woman who was my maid, I'd never have gotten out of Berlin that night alive."

I made more speeches, Mannie took in more money. When we were finally on the boat coming home Mannie said, "Eddie, let's relax and have fun. You ought to give a concert on board and let the money go to the Seamen's Fund." So we started looking around the ship for entertainment, and we heard that in second class there was a girl who played the piano. The girl's name was Hilda Somers, she was about seventeen. She'd been a concert pianist since she was twelve, traveling around to play in the capitals of Europe. We talked with Hilda and her mother and heard their story. When the Nazis came into Austria Hilda was forced to wash the streets with lye, and the tips of her fingers were so badly burned it took months to heal them.

I introduced her at the ship's concert and she played so well the audience wouldn't let her go. *Then* I told her story. Afterward she sat with Mr. and Mrs. McDonald and Mr. and Mrs. Darryl Zanuck and Mannie and me, and we talked of her plans. She was going with her mother to live with a relative in one room in the Bronx. How she was going to get a piano she didn't know. Mannie and I put our heads together. We got Hilda and her mother an apartment, a Steinway piano, a weekly allowance to live on. We sent her to Leopold Stokowski's wife, who's a great teacher of piano, and Mrs. Stokowski called me at the end of the first week. "Eddie, this girl is so good she could teach *me*. Eventually she should be able to make her debut at Carnegie Hall with the New York Philharmonic."

I told Mannie and I told him what Carnegie Hall would cost. "So what?" he said. So eventually we presented Hilda at Carnegie Hall with the New York Philharmonic and from there she went on to a series of concerts across the country, ending in a blaze of glory at the Hollywood Bowl. And she's still playing and she's happily married. A cheerful ending to the story that started so sadly in Austria. This is the sort of thing you do when you're palling around with Mannie Goldman.

Recently I sponsored Cantor Herskovits at Carnegie Hall, a man with a sublime voice. When you start something like this the first man you write to is Mannie Goldman; he'll buy two hundred tickets, give them to his employees, start the ball rolling. And he'll go to the concert himself. Mannie's a highbrow, his idea of entertainment is Toscanini. So you ask him how he liked your last television show and he'll say, "That dark blue suit looked wonderful, Eddie, such lapels!" The suit, of course, is always one his firm made.

Jack Crandall isn't so objective. He's one of the audience. "You must be right," he'll say, "you had me crying." Jack has a flair for investments and money matters, he's been my business manager for twenty-five years; but he has this warm heart too, and I met him first through the Solax Club, which was organized about 1916 to help keep kids out of trouble on the East Side streets. I don't ever remember anyone else being president of the club. Jack's scrupulously honest, everyone knows that, so let him *be* president and decide what to do with the funds. He's also been in on the Surprise Lake Camp project and has done more than anyone else save Holman and Goldman.

We've been closely associated, of course, for many years. I guess I'm one of his causes. Every comedian has a pal who will take practical jokes without hitting you on the head. Jack's my baby.

One time we were closing the season in Detroit. As always, the night we closed, I proceeded to indulge in some food that I wouldn't dare eat when I'm working—I might get sick. Season's end it didn't matter and I had a yen for hot dogs. The rest of the cast ate cold buffet, I ate hot dogs, and we finally went to bed about 5 A.M. The next night we left for New York, our musical director Louis Gress, Jack Crandall and myself, all in a drawing room. We had dinner on the train, came back, played cards until eight and turned in. But thanks to those hot dogs and the 5 A.M. party, I was overly tired and couldn't sleep. I lay there wide awake listening to Crandall snore, wondering if Louis was awake, and finally I whistled my special little whistle.

"What's the matter 'Kliener'?" whispered Louis.

"I can't sleep."

"Neither can I."

"And listen to that baboon in the upper berth—Crandall's a symphony of milk cans."

We lay for another fifteen minutes, talking in whispers. Then I said, "Louis, let's get up and dress, let's shave and get ready." Louis gave me a knowing wink. So we did. Now we're not more than four hours out of Detroit and I slap Crandall on the rump. "O.K., boy. Let's go!"

"What? Oh!" groaned Crandall. "What a sleep—the night just flew!" And he jumps up, puts on his clothes, shaves, and calls the porter.

"Take the bags, porter. How soon before we're in?"

"About nine-fifteen, sir," the porter says.

Jack looks at his watch and it is nine o'clock. "Fifteen minutes!" And he can't understand why the porter is reluctant to take the bags—at nine at *night!*

And another practical joke at Jack's expense I'm ashamed to even tell. One summer I was playing at the Earl Carroll Theatre in New York. Jack and I would commute back and forth to our summer place at Long Beach, Long Island. When we'd get home we'd play casino for an hour. We started playing for a dollar a game and worked up. Toward the end of the summer Jack owed me several thousand dollars because I always had eight cards hidden and among the eight cards, five or six spades including an ace. Jack was getting desperate. He wanted to raise the stakes, but I said no, I'd give him an easier way to win back his money. There was a hot-dog stand two blocks from the Long Beach station. We'd bet every night on how many hot dogs would be on the grill when we passed. The one nearest right would win and we set a high stake. By Labor Day, Jack was in debt almost ten thousand dollars. When he was on the verge of despair I called off the indebtedness and showed him my eight cards. He laughed till he cried. "But how about the hot dogs? How could you know the number of hot dogs?" It was easy; every night during intermission I'd phone the hot-dog stand and tell them how many dogs to put out. Jack is still laughing, and even better, he still takes care of my investments. Any time he wants, he can have the last laugh.

Interesting—I became deeply involved with all these men in each instance through some charity affair. Benjamin Franklin Holzman used to write "Up and Down Broadway" for the New York *Evening Mail* and he had the job of corralling stars to appear at the newspaper's annual benefit for its "Save a Home" fund. This fund took care of food, rent, and coal for distressed families in greater New York. The show was held at the Liberty Theatre in 1920, some of the stars were George M. Cohan, William Collier, and Will Rogers, and I was master of ceremonies. Bennie worked with us long and hard and we became friends. When the *Evening Mail* folded in 1924 I saw Bennie depressed for the first time. All my jokes failed to cheer him. He told me how he'd gone through the same ordeal when the New York *Press* had folded. Holzman had started on the *Press* in 1910. Munsey purchased that paper in 1916, and they called the undertaker promptly. Now that his second paper had folded, Bennie felt Munsey had made up his mind to chase him out of the fourth estate. He went to work for Ziegfeld as head of publicity, but eventually he went back to newspaper work as theatrical editor of the New York *Evening Journal*. Then, with Nat Dorfman, he opened the first independent press agent's office in New York, where they handled as many as ten shows simultaneously. He was (and is) a showman to the core. And he's made me do things I wouldn't have dreamed of. In 1920, for example, he had me emcee a show at the Palais Royal to raise money for his newspaper's camp. This thing went on from eight-thirty until two in the morning and you couldn't possibly prepare material—it had to be off the cuff. Bennie thought I could do it, so I did it.

During the years, he's been with me in every important cause. There were always columnists who yelled, "Get off the soapbox, Cantor, stop the flag waving." Bennie said, "Ignore them. I don't care what jokes you tell, I'll forget those and so will everyone else. They'll remember the serious things you've said. Keep saying 'em."

He's my kind of a guy; he and his wife and Ida and I can sit around and yak and enjoy every minute of it. I remember the New Year's Eve *Kid Boots* opened. It was a smash hit, the biggest night in my life until then. Bennie and Harriet, Ida and I picked up some delicatessen, some potato salad, a couple of bottles of beer, and celebrated. In the years he handled my publicity Bennie never went for phony gimmicks. Even when he had me run for mayor of Broadway, while it was all in fun, he gave me a platform that involved cleaning up Broadway. We asked that advertising be a trifle more dignified, that trash be picked up, and I *was* elected mayor and I think Broadway *was* cleaner—for about two days.

When Frank Fay was playing *Harvey* in Boston he denounced me as a communist. Again Bennie told me to ignore it. "Of course you're not a communist," he said, "but if you sue you only get more publicity and people misinterpret, they think where there's smoke, there must be fire. Everyone who's ever known you knows you aren't a communist. You know it. Hell, you're a plutocrat." Bennie was right. When a Boston newspaper approached someone like Charles Boyer, Boyer was indignant—"If Eddie's a communist, so am I"—and told how he and I had worked together during World War II. And one year later, when the Commonwealth of Boston presented their annual awards to an outstanding Catholic, Protestant, and Jew, they extended the honors to Frank Leahy of Notre Dame, to Eleanor Roosevelt, and to me.

Bennie never worried about my personal reputation as such; he didn't want my reputation damaged because it would hurt my strength as a "social worker." That's one of the things about these five friends of mine. They're all patriots, they're interested in their country and the people of that country, and no matter how good friends you are, if you ever went wrong, they'd be the first to tell you. If you're right, they'll fight for you. They came from far different backgrounds, but they have this basic purpose.

Arthur Baer, for example, was born with a golden spoon in his mouth, but from the beginning he was as concerned about the needs of fellow men as the kids who went hungry and *had* the need. We met when the *Follies of 1917* played St. Louis. Head of a big department store, he amazed me by his simplicity. I met his wife, we had dinner together, they drove me to the station the night we closed, and Arthur said, "Let's hear from you some time." I don't think he expected to, but I wrote to him as I had once written to Harry Ruby—because I liked him and respected him and wanted to know him better. When the *Follies of 1918* opened in Atlantic City, Arthur and his wife came and spent a lot of time with Ida and me. Arthur wanted to know, not about show business, but about my childhood, about the East Side, about the problems of people who live in the same country where he was born but in a different world. It didn't need a seer to see that this man was going to become the civic leader he is.

Like Mannie Goldman, he wants his money to work, and his generosity is strictly wholesale. When the crash came he flew to Atlantic City to meet me, opened up a suitcase, and offered me a hundred thousand dollars' worth of bonds, which I wouldn't take. But if he wasn't able to finance me he was able to donate large sums to Surprise Lake Camp, to boys who were kids like I had once been; to the Red Cross, and for a quarter of a century he has interested himself in the blind of Missouri. He got me actively interested too.

And I interested him in Israel. I'll never forget Arthur's face when I told him about the Catholic priest I'd met on board a plane from Lydda Airport to Paris, when Ida and I visited Israel in 1950. The priest said, "The finest Christians I have ever seen are the Jews in Israel. Who else has said, 'If you're homeless, here you shall have a home; if you're friendless, we will be your friends; if you're sick, we'll make you well. We'll feed you, clothe you, fight to get you in; if necessary we'll die to keep you here.'" That's what this priest said. I was just returning from Israel where I'd been summoned by Prime Minister Ben-Gurion. I had seen former businessmen, teachers and musicians there learning to till the soil. I had seen what progress was being made with what poor equipment. I had half realized what a home must mean to people who were refugees from gas chambers, but the words of the priest clarified the thing for fellows like me and Arthur Baer. Ben-Gurion had told me how much money was needed, he'd told me he expected me to raise one fifth of all that came from the United States. I covered forty-three states to raise the sum.

We've tried to bring Israel's situation to the attention of our State Department too. I ran an open letter to John Foster Dulles as a full-page ad in the New York *Times*. The gist of the letter: "If we Americans are honest in wanting to help democracies and in wanting to establish democracy as a way of life, how can we let down the youngest democracy in the world by handing arms to the Arabs?" Every cause that interests me I check first with Arthur and get his opinion. He's been with me on "Give a Gift to a Yank Who Gave," Cerebral Palsy, Cancer, Heart, Government bonds, everything.

His friendship, like that of these other men, taught me that show business is not everything in life. I've met Arthur's friends, doctors, professors, businessmen, and I've come to value what they do and how they think. They've shown me that whatever you have can be turned to use—that if you're a hootchie-kootchie dancer you can hootch and kootch for the big time, the causes that matter.

PART FOUR

The BEST of My Life

25. With Half a Heart

September 30, 1952. I was on stage at the El Capitan Theatre, Hollywood, my first television show of the season for the Colgate Comedy Hour. All summer I'd prepared for this, auditioning acts, working with writers, rehearsing songs, and the show was a complete success. Well, almost. Only one thing failed. My heart! Suddenly I had a swift sharp pain in my chest. When I came off stage, I felt weak and strange and asked for a drink of whiskey—the first time that had happened in all my years in the theater. But the show must go on and it did.

That was the night the ambulance came, the night I got a preview of my own funeral. For the next six weeks I lay in the hospital. Fanny Brice had died this way, Al Jolson had died, now . . . Ida stayed right with me, she never left the hospital, the girls were there, my three doctors were there—all *very* optimistic. The only one without cheer was the guy who'd once been billed as "the apostle of pep." I was depressed first because I thought I was dying, then because I realized I wasn't. How could I ever entertain again? How could I raise money or sell bonds if I couldn't get around to make people laugh?

I was having a chill. My teeth started chattering and they gave me a little brandy. It went down so fast it made me choke. "This is what Jessel *likes?*" I said. The doctors laughed. The next day a nurse walked in, tired, her feet hurt. "Lie down," I said, patting my bed, "there's room for both of us. Just don't expect to be paid for a full shift." The nurse laughed. I felt a little better. I woke up and started reading my mail. You've never read such mail.

There were letters from governors and mayors, a letter from Dwight Eisenhower aboard his campaign train; but that wasn't the half of it. There were hundreds of letters from servicemen and ex-servicemen. Like this . . .

"Dear Eddie: Please let me urge you to follow your doctor's orders so that you will quickly and completely recover from your illness. This country needs you, Eddie. We need your brand of humor to make us laugh during trying times. We need you as an exemplar of tolerance and good citizenship. We all have an abiding affection for you and speaking for myself and my family and my associates, we want you to get well and keep well and stay with us for a long long time. All best wishes . . .

PAUL F. MIELLY
Lt. Col. AUS

P.S. We've never met, I'm simply a well-wisher."

There were letters from people telling me that they'd just contributed to the blood bank because they knew I wanted that work to go on. There were letters advising me to take it easy, not to jump up and down when I came back. They were praying for me, they said. Ida heard from one church where a hundred people had that day lighted candles—for me. Can you imagine what this does for a guy who's flat on his back? Every letter was like a blood transfusion. I'd heard laughter and applause, sure, for forty-five years; but I hadn't realized that there was love behind the laughter.

Now that love came rolling in, and it was better than any medicine, it was something you had to repay. You wanted to get back on your feet and devote the rest of your life to doing as much for people as you could. Every week since I'd been in the hospital, there'd been a cake from a woman in Scranton, Pennsylvania. I sat up in bed and ate a piece of Scranton cake. Then I sent for my agent, Abe Lastfogel.

"Abe, tell the Colgate people I'll be back on the stage at El Capitan, January 18." Determination routed the blues; in nothing flat I began to recover.

Maybe it sounds farfetched to call a heart attack and after, "The Best of My Life." It's true. It's a privilege, in a way, to come close to death, because you come away with a new set of values. The small annoyances of the past become laughable: a columnist writing something untrue, a critic panning a show, someone turning you down for what you feel should be freely given. You used to get mad, now you shrug your shoulders, shrug it off.

Your attitude toward your work changes. You know you have to husband your energy, so you do only that which gives you the greatest pleasure, by which you're completely stimulated. You always loved to entertain but you also loved the pay check, the size of it was a measure of your success. Never again. What's important now—service is the rent we pay for our room on earth and I'd like to be a good tenant. You can't worry about the state of your health when you're worrying about the state of Israel or the people dying of cancer.

When you've plenty of time to reflect, you think out a lot of things you never had time to really think about before. Here are some of the things I've thought about:

THE WORLD. I believe that the cold war might be won if there were better relations between our people and the people of Russia, and this might be brought about by sending over, not just diplomats in frock coats and striped trousers, but entertainers, comedians, singers. Look what happened when the American company of *Porgy and Bess* went to Russia! They not only scored a big box-office hit, they scored a great hit outside the theater. Last Christmas, in a country whose policy is atheistic, the *Porgy and Bess* gang sang Christmas carols over the radio, in churches; the Russians accepted and applauded. Look what happened when Jan Peerce went over to do a concert tour a few months ago!

You can't hate people who make you laugh, who entertain you. You can't shoot them. I say, send Red Skelton, Harpo Marx, Danny Kaye, Sid Caesar to Russia; send them around the world and give people a view of a different American than they've been propagandized to believe exists—not bloated plutocrats but human beings with laughter and culture. Laughter and culture are good weapons; they're proven weapons.

I discovered that during the war when the government sent me to war plants whenever absenteeism was a problem. War workers weren't meaning to be unpatriotic, it was just that the girls wanted to get to a beauty shop or the men wanted to take a day off and do a little serious drinking. Mondays were the bad days, so on Mondays, there I'd be up on a platform in shipyards, plane plants, wherever the government sent me. I'd sing, dance, joke, then I'd get in a serious thought: "Any day you're not working for the man with the whiskers, you're working for the guy with the little mustache." "When you knock off, you may knock off the fellow next door." Often they'd start listening with a certain resentment; we Americans don't like to be told what to do. But I'd explain that I wasn't anti-union, I've been head of practically every theatrical union in this country, and pretty soon they'd begin joining in the chorus of "Margie." It worked. Absenteeism dropped off.

I saw it work in Europe when I went over to Paris to do some broadcasts on the Marshall Plan. We'd have entertainers from many countries, a singer from Italy, a dancer from France, a comedian from England; we did regular broadcasts. But instead of selling tooth paste or beer, we would tell people about the Marshall Plan. I acted as master of ceremonies, explaining what the plan was doing for them (tractors, railroads, etc.) and what they were expected to do for themselves. And *that* worked. You can sell the world iceboxes and washing machines by using entertainment—why *not* sell democracy the same way? The Mr. Dulleses yes, but a working gang of nonofficial ambassadors working too. The world needs laughter and music and culture—nothing could help more to make it *one world*.

And I've thought about . . . RELIGION. How wonderful it would be if people of all religions gave their religion a chance. Most of us don't think enough about plain everyday morality; we don't always stop and realize that no one flies alone, not even Lindbergh. You know the story about the guy who was at the race track, playing race after race and losing constantly. Finally, down to his last twenty dollars, he puts up his bet, the race starts, and the fellow prays, "God, help me! Bring this horse in and I'll be good the rest of my life." Now the announcer calls his horse. "He's third, he's second, he's leading by a length." In the stretch the horse is leading by two lengths and the praying one says, "Never mind, God, I'll take over from here."

I believe in all religions—but you have to practice them. Going to church doesn't make you good any more than a stadium makes a football player. You have to think, you have to feel, your daily relationships with people are the proof. If you believe in your fellow men, you have to stand on your two feet and speak up.

You can't trade the lives of people for oil. Hitler almost destroyed the world because not enough people had the courage to stop him, even without guns. You have to stand up for what you believe and not accept the slipshod nonreligious feeling that discriminates between man and man.

I first became aware of this working in the *Follies* with Bert Williams, the great Negro star. When we went on tour Bert couldn't live in the same hotel with the rest of us. In some towns where he could stay in the same hotel, he'd have to use the freight elevator. We'd ride up with him. Bert was very dear to me, a fine comedian, a loyal friend, a generous teacher. We were always together. One night we walked into a bar and ordered a scotch. The bartender looked at Bert and said, "That'll be fifty dollars." Bert opened his wallet, took out three hundred-dollar bills and said, "I'll take six, if you please." He never got angry, he kept his dignity—but why should he have been placed in such a position? There is, thank God, a democracy in show business. Sammy Davis, Jr., is honored at the Friars' dinner, but why can't it be practiced in all walks of life? Why should Nat King Cole be assailed on a concert tour? Or youngsters be assailed for going to school?

I recently conceived a story about a young Negro boy seated in his living room in the South, listening to the radio, to the Supreme Court ruling on segregation. The eleven-year-old boy asks his father, "What does it mean?"

"It means you can go to the white man's good school, son."

"I'd be afraid."

"You needn't be afraid, the Constitution says we're free and equal. The Supreme Court says all children may go to the same schools."

Comes the day. The child gets on the school bus, the others look at him as if he were a criminal. There are youngsters picketing in front of the school. It's an awful day; the Negro boy is frightened, he doesn't ride home on the school bus. He walks. A mile from home he's waylaid by picketeers. One of them throws a rock; the Negro child falls at the side of the road. He's dead. Now in heaven St. Peter is listing the newcomers. "George Thompson. Eleven years old."

"No, no," says St. Peter. "Fifty-six. He was supposed to die at fifty-six."

"George Thompson. Eleven years old."

St. Peter shakes his head sadly. "He was to die at fifty-six. He wasn't supposed to die until *after* he'd found the cure for cancer."

It isn't that I think I'm smart. Older people don't have to be smart, they've had a lifetime to experience, they've learned the hard way. And about themselves, frequently, they're not smart at all.

In the hospital I kept asking myself, "How did this happen to me?" Of course I was kidding myself. I *knew*. For a long time before the fateful night I'd been coming home tired, very tired. I should have taken a light bite and gone to bed. But there were benefits to play and dinners to attend and meetings where I was scheduled to speak. So I'd take a shower and have a drink and, temporarily refreshed, I'd get through. How happy I was to receive plaque after plaque for these extracurricular activities. I didn't realize that each one was a step closer to a plaque I wouldn't like at all: "DO NOT DISTURB" on a hospital door.

After that for a while it was tough to think straight. My family, frightened to death, used their visiting hours to beg me never to think of show business again. I almost agreed with them, especially the day the doctor said, "Good news, Eddie. Today you sit on the edge of your bed and dangle your legs." To a guy who was used to running up- and downstage a good two miles during a performance! I was frightened until I realized that fear could kill me quicker than my heart. I made up my mind to follow the doctor's orders, get well, and go back to work. I'd lick this disability if it meant learning to live all over again.

My whole life had been show business. Everything centered around the next broadcast, the next performance, a new song, a new gag, a new contract. Nighttime was playtime. I'd eat my big meal of the day at midnight, swapping stories with my pals. For twenty-five years, I never went to bed before 3 A.M. I never saw the sun rise except on my way home from a late party or a poker game.

Now it's early to bed and early to rise. I read the morning paper in the morning! By noon, I have almost a full day's work done. I've done 260 half-hour radio shows, recorded 17 songs for the film, *The Eddie Cantor Story*, done thirty-nine TV shows of my own, my first dramatic show, and a dozen guest appearances, made several short films for the American Heart Association (I was just named Heart Ambassador for 1957 and in the month of February alone, my voice was heard twenty thousand times on radio for Heart), I've stumped some twelve cities and raised over $15,000,000 for charity. So, you see, a heart attack is not a death sentence.

Some of you may be thinking, "Sure, Cantor got over his heart attack, he had all kinds of money to help him." Let me tell you something: whoever wrote "The Best Things in Life Are Free" must have had cardiac cases in mind, because the best medicine is free. It's rest, quiet, a philosophy without fear, regular exercise, a matter of keeping your weight down, *and* your emotions. A doctor can tell you, but once you leave his office you're your own best doctor.

And you can't cheat. If you're told a two-hour rest will do, don't cheat with one hour. If the doctor tells you to have a drink, that doesn't mean a drunk. It's better to eat four or five little meals a day than to have one big meal that'll overwork your heart. Weight must be kept down and that means counting calories. Avoid excess on the three Es—EATING, EXERTION, EMOTION. The toughest of these is emotion. I try to remember that there's no point in winning an argument if you lose your life. Even if you're right—the other guy has a weak argument, you have a weak heart!

But the important message I've tried to get over is to you people who haven't had a heart attack. You can avoid one if . . . you'll visit your doctor at least once a year. Pay attention to what he says or pay a lot more later. When you're tired, remember, a cocktail can't replace a pair of pajamas. And it's better to exercise ten minutes every day than to put in several hours on Sunday. We're inclined to live by the calendar. A man says, "I'm all right, I'm only forty." That's like looking at automobile tires and saying, "There's plenty of mileage left in this rubber," without giving a thought to the inner tubes. A blowout when you're going full speed can be very dangerous. Dangerous? It can be fatal!

We've all had friends die "suddenly" who've "never been sick a day in their lives." They lied, these people, the way I lied. Why? For the kick of hearing admirers say, "Look at that Cantor! Sixty years old and bouncing around like a boy. How does he do it at his age?" I wound up learning how to act my age.

So, to everyone everywhere who loves life and wants to keep on living it, I say, "Take a tip from an old liar and stop telling untruths. If you've had a tough day, don't try to bull your way through a tough evening. If your week ends in a headache, call off your weekend golf game. Eighteen holes may sound like fun, but the nineteenth hole could be the one they put you in."

Use your hearts, by all means, love with 'em and live with 'em. And if you have a heart attack or some other warning, come back from it knowing that it was a lucky break, a chance to learn, a chance to rearrange your values, to stop short and take stock.

When I was out walking one day, a woman did a double-take and said loudly to her friend, "Why there's Eddie Cantor, I thought he was dead!"

"Madam," I couldn't resist saying, "I not only am not dead . . . I have just begun to live."

26. With All My Heart

Let me say, too, that I didn't make it back alone. There was always someone with me—and I mean *with* me. Ida. Ida could write this book herself, she probably would if she weren't so busy with her painting; she's the Grandma Moses of Beverly Hills. My daughters say we're like a split personality, Ida and I, she's part of me and I'm part of her. It's not surprising. We've only been married forty-two years but we've known each other for fifty; and in those years she's been to me all women, the mother I never saw, the grandmother I lost, companion, friend, all women.

You will understand, then, why we're old-fashioned about marriage. Sometimes you hear people say, "Why do people in show business get married? Why don't they just have affairs and the public won't hear about it?" Ida and I disagree. Show business has nothing to do with it. When I was president of the Screen Actors' Guild, we made an extensive survey into the business of marriage in Hollywood and the list of people married twenty-five years would surprise you happily. It's people who get married, not places. There are just as many divorces in Newark but no one cares about Mr. and Mrs. Smith in Newark. If you'll look into it, you'll find it's the same people in show business who get married and divorced over and over. Take a fellow like Jack Benny. He's married to Mary Livingstone, but if he weren't he would still be married all his life to one woman. She'd have to leave him, he'd never leave her. The only way Ida could ever get rid of me would be to leave me.

And I don't know what I'd do. There have been times when we've been separated, when I've done a benefit and she hasn't been able to come along, or when I've come to California first and she's had to wait until the girls were out of school. I never liked it.

The house seems funny without Mother; empty. I want her there, the smell of her perfume in the bathroom, the sound of her hearty laugh, the snatch of song. She's always singing and she never knows the words. I kid her. I put down a twenty and say, sing the first eight bars and it's yours. I've had the same twenty for twenty years. And she kids me. I have a habit; when I'm not sure of a bit—I rub the back of my thigh while I'm on. Later I'll ask Ida how was it; she grabs her leg, rubs it, and says "Very good." She's a shrewd critic. She's shrewd period.

Once, in New York about 1934 I met a big businessman, very charming, a fast talker, he impresses me. After a week talking with this man I go home and tell Ida—this man is going to handle our business affairs, I am turning over everything, he'll give us an allowance . . .

Ida looks up from her knitting. "I've met him twice, how well do you know him?"

"*I know people*," I brag.

"Ask him to dinner, Eddie."

He comes to dinner. We sit and talk quietly. While Ida knits, she puts out enough needles to expose the man I knew as the man I don't know.

About the same time there's a chorus girl in the show who has a crush on me. It is embarrassing. She's just a kid. One night Ida rides up in the elevator with us and later she says, "Poor child, I feel so sorry for her. She's wilting."

"What can I do?"

"Be nice, dear, in a nice way."

The next night she brings Edna to the theater, and Natalie. We bring the chorine in and introduce her to my daughters. A thought has occurred. "Ida, doesn't this girl look like Edna, doesn't she, Edna?" That takes care of that.

Any woman whose husband is in show business could be jealous. Ida has too big a mind, too good a sense of humor. Only once did she ever suspect me. I was playing in *Kid Boots* and Ziegfeld called me to come to Long Island to sing for the Prince of Wales, now the Duke of Windsor, formerly the King of England. Because of various escapades he had promised his parents not to come to New York and he was staying with the Rodman Wanamakers. It was a memorable night that lasted until morning. The Prince said that if I ever came to London I should look him up. I told him not to worry, I'd be happy to stay at the palace. "I take breakfast out," I told him. "No need to wake your mother to make breakfast for me." A million laughs. I got home at 5 A.M. and Ida was pacing the floor.

"Where were you?"

"Ida, I'll explain everything. I was with the Prince of Wales."

"Go to sleep. Tomorrow you'll stay out till six and tell me you were with 'Coolidge.'"

I was saved; the morning papers carried a long story of the night before.

In marriage, companionship is the whole business. We discuss everything, every problem, mine in business, hers at home. The longest life in any relationship depends on this: if you don't get bored with each other, no matter how long you're with each other, no matter where you are . . . and if you can laugh! People who laugh together, live together.

How could you not laugh with Ida? There was a meeting one time at the Ambassador Hotel in Los Angeles, the National Conference of Christians and Jews, of which Nelson Rockefeller was the current head. I was one of the organizers of this group, with Dr. Everett Clinchy. Before we went down to dinner, we were in Nelson's suite at the hotel. Ida was in Palm Springs. I asked Nelson if I could use the phone and I called her.

"Where are you?" Ida asked.

"With Nelson Rockefeller."

"Who?"

"With Nelson Rockefeller. You know the Rockefellers."

"Don't you get in with any of their schemes, Eddie."

I told this to Nelson, and he opened his speech that night, quoting Ida. He's admired my wife a great deal. So did Maurice Chevalier. When Chevalier was out here we'd go to a restaurant. The waitresses would be dropping dishes, watching Maurice dunk his coffeecake—"Girls! He dunks!"—but he was oblivious, chatting with my wife. "How does a guy without talent get such a woman?" he said.

She was always looking out for me, always seeing that I got an occasional vacation. We'd fallen in love with Palm Springs in 1927 when I had pleurisy and she cured me with Janet. After that, we tried to come out to the desert every year. When Janet was two the nurse we left with the children was so determined to build them up, she stuffed Janet with milk. In between milk, milk. The baby got so fat by the time we got home, she said "Moo" instead of "Ma." In 1941 Ida decided to surprise me. We were going down to Palm Springs for a week and when we got in front of the usual hotel the car kept right on. It didn't stop until we drew up before a pretty cottage with a sign over the door "El Poonelo." Ida had bought the land, built the house, and arranged it to the last detail. When I walked in my clothes were in the closet, my toothbrush and shaving cream on the bath stand, even my pictures of the kids. We've spent our weekends there ever since.

We've lived very quietly since my heart attack in 1952. Ida adapts to the quiet life the way she has adapted always to everything. It was she who put her foot down on live television. "I want a live husband," was her answer. We still have a lot of fun, the girls are in and out of the house, and the grandchildren, and friends, and I'm still working like a son of a gun. The difference—Ida had a bell installed in her room with a button beside *my* pillow. If ever at night I should need her, all I do is push the button and she's right there. The bell is a symbol—Ida's always wanted to know when I'm in trouble, always wanted to be there to help.

For the last twenty-five years she has been as well known as any woman in this country, a fact of which she is equally proud and embarrassed. Embarrassed when she has to give her name in a department store, proud when it's something like this . . .

She was in an art gallery on Fifty-seventh Street in New York one day when a little old lady came up to her. "Aren't you Ida Cantor? Oh, Ida, we feel as if we all *know you*. My son does know your husband. And Sundays from eight to nine you can hear a pin drop while he and my grandsons listen to the Chase and Sanborn Hour." The little old lady was Sara Delano Roosevelt.

When we arrived in England in 1935, the newspapers merely captioned it "EDDIE AND IDA ARRIVE." And I'll never forget the Legion Convention in Chicago 1939, Mickey Rooney, Jack Benny, and I riding around Soldiers' Field in a jeep while one hundred and fifty thousand people shouted "We want I-da, we want I-da."

I didn't blame 'em. She's a great person, a good wife, and she can still do one hell of a Highland fling. They want her? I got her.

Addendum

Since the original publication of these books, new information has surfaced on the heritage of Eddie Cantor. It was my feeling not to alter any of the text of the original manuscripts, but to use this space to help clarify some situations that were not known to my grandfather in his lifetime. I must thank Russell Chase for his tremendous efforts in researching most of this information.

On June 20, 1894, Eddie's mother, Meta Iskowitz*, gave birth to a daughter, Lena. Sadly, Meta passed away at the age of 27 from tuberculosis on July 26, just a little over a month after becoming a mother for a second time. Because of her impoverished condition, she was buried in Silver Lake Cemetery on Staten Island with no headstone to indicate where the mother of the soon-to-be-celebrated Eddie Cantor was resting. If he had known, I am sure my grandfather would have put a large headstone with perpetual care in that spot, much as he did for his beloved Grandma Esther in 1917. On August 6, 1894, Eddie's newborn sister, Lena Ishkovitz*, died of gastroenteritis and was also buried at Silver Lake. Both Meta and Lena died at 39 Jackson Street on the Lower East Side of Manhattan.

Throughout this research, the name Max Itzkovitz* showed up as having passed away from tubercular meningitis at the age of 23 on March 22, 1896, with burial at Silver Lake. Although his address was no longer 39 Jackson but rather 3 Hester (still very near both Jackson and Henry), it seemed quite possible that this was the Michael Cantor that Eddie named in his books. On the death certificate it listed his occupation as tailor, which is what it said for Lena's father, a Max Ishkovitz.* The biggest clue was Max's mother's name—Leah. This would have been Jewish tradition to name his daughter after his

---

*There were often misspellings on these certificates, including many different spellings of Itskowitz.

mother. The American spelling for the Hebrew name of Leah is Lena!

So there you have it; perhaps we have helped to put some closure on my grandfather's tragic beginnings. I only wish he was here to learn of these findings . . . or maybe he knows anyway.

BRIAN GARI

Recording History (Songs)

Company	Date	Song		
Victor, NY	July 12, 1917	B-20216	The Modern Maiden's Prayer	18342
Victor, NY	July 12, 1917	B-20217	That's the Kind of a Baby for Me	18342
Aeolian, NY	November 1917	*	The Modern Maiden's Prayer	1220
Vocalian, NY	November 1917	*	That's the Kind of a Baby for Me	1220
Aeolian, NY	November 1917	*	Down in Borneo Isle	1228
Vocalian, NY	November 1917	*	Hello, Wisconsin	1228
Aeolian, NY	November 1917	*	Dixie Volunteers	1233
Vocalian, NY	November 1917	*	I Don't Want to Get Well	1233
Pathe, NY	August 1919	*	The Last Rose of Summer	22163
Pathe, NY	August 1919	*	We Don't Need the Wine to Have a Wonderful Time	22163
Emerson, NY	September 1919	4467	We Don't Need the Wine to Have a Wonderful Time	1071
Emerson, NY	October 1919	4508	Don't Put a Tax on the Beautiful Girls	1071
Emerson, NY	October 1919	4509	When They're Old Enough to Know Better	1094
Emerson, NY	November 1919	4629	I Used to Call Her Baby	10102
Emerson, NY	November 1919	4630	Give Me the Sultan's Harem	10105
Pathe, NY	November 1919	67953	When They're Old Enough to Know Better	22201
Pathe, NY	November 1919	67977	I've Got My Captain Working for Me Now	22201
Pathe, NY	November 1919	67979	Don't Put a Tax on the Beautiful Girls	22260
Emerson, NY	December 1919	4670	You'd Be Surprised	10102
Emerson, NY	January 1920	4734	The Last Rose of Summer	10134
Pathe, NY	January 1920	68091	At the High Brown Babies Ball	22260
Emerson, NY	February 1920	4759	When It Comes to Lovin' the Girls, I'm Way Ahead of the Times	10105
Emerson, NY	February 1920	4760	Come On and Play with Me, My Sweet Babee	10119
Pathe, NY	February 1920	68188	When It Comes to Lovin' The Girls, I'm Way Ahead of the Times	22318
Pathe, NY	February 1920	68189	I Never Knew I Had a Wonderful Wife	22318
Emerson, NY	March 1920	4779	All the Boys Love Mary	10119
Emerson, NY	March 1920	4780	You Ain't Heard Nothin' Yet	10134
Emerson, NY	May 1920	41171	The Argentines, the Portugese and Greeks	10200
Emerson, NY	May 1920	41172	Noah's Wife Lived a Wonderful Life	10200
Emerson, NY	June 1920	41207	The Older They Get, the Younger They Want 'Em	10212
Emerson, NY	June 1920	41208	Snoops the Lawyer	10212
Emerson, NY	July 1920	41239	She Gives Them All the Ha! Ha! Ha!	10292
Emerson, NY	August 1920	41375	Dixie Mad Us Jazz Band Mad	10263
Emerson, NY	August 1920	41376	When I See All That Lovin' They Waste on Babies	10263
Emerson, NY	October 1920	41453	I'd Wish I'd Been Born in Borneo	10301
Emerson, NY	November 1920	41494	Palasteena	10292
Emerson, NY	December 1920	41534	Margie	10301
Emerson, NY	December 1920	41551	You Oughta See My Baby	10327
Emerson, NY	January 1921	41632	I Never Knew	10349
Emerson, NY	January 1921		Timbuctoo	10352
Emerson, NY	January 1921		My Old New Jersey Home	10352
Emerson, NY	June 1921	41852	Anna in Indiana	10397
Emerson, NY	June 1921		Oh, They're Such Nice People	10397
Columbia, NY	April 28, 1922	80328	I Love Her, She Loves Me	A3624
Columbia, NY	May 10, 1922	80342	I'm Hungry for Beautiful Girls	A3624
Columbia, NY	July 5, 1922	80439	Oh, Is She Dumb!	REJECTED
Columbia, NY	July 5, 1922	80440	Susie	A3682
Columbia, NY	July 28, 1922	80439	Oh, Is She Dumb!	A3682
Columbia, NY	October 30, 1922	80636	Sophie	A3754
Columbia, NY	October 30, 1922	80637	He Loves It	A3754
Columbia, NY	December 13, 1922	80715	Joe Is Here	A3784

292 Recording History (Songs)

Company	Date		Song	
Columbia, NY	December 13, 1922	80716	How Ya Gonna Keep Your Mind on Dancing	A3784
Columbia, NY	May 4, 1923	81004	I Love Me (I'm Wild about Myself)	A3906
Columbia, NY	May 4, 1923	81005	Ritzi-Mitzi	A3906
Columbia, NY	June 12, 1923	81073	Oh! Gee, Oh! Gosh, Oh! Golly, I'm in Love	A3934
Columbia, NY	June 14, 1923	81076	Eddie (Steady)	A3934
Columbia, NY	July 26, 1923	81148	No, No Nora	A3964
Columbia, NY	July 26, 1923	81149	(I've Got the) Yes We Have No Bananas Blues	A3964
Columbia, NY	January 4, 1924	81459	O Gee, Georgie!	56D
Columbia, NY	January 4, 1924	81460	If You Do—What You Do	56D
Columbia, NY	April 4, 1924	81666	I'll Have Vanilla	120D
Columbia, NY	April 4, 1924	81667	On a Windy Day Down in Waikiki	120D
Columbia, NY	May 14, 1924	81779	Oh Papa	140D
Columbia, NY	May 14, 1924	81780	Monkey Doodle	140D
Columbia, NY	July 18, 1924	81878	Charley, My Boy	182D
Columbia, NY	August 8, 1924	81904	No One Know What It's All About	196D
Columbia, NY	September 12, 1924	140037	Doodle-Doo-Doo	213D
Columbia, NY	October 14, 1924	140106	How I Love That Girl	234D
Columbia, NY	November 17, 1924	140145	Those Panama Mamas (Are Ruinin' Me)	256D
Columbia, NY	December 29, 1924	140213	Goo-Goo-Goodnight Dear!	277D
Columbia, NY	January 6, 1925	140223	Laff It Off	283D
Columbia, NY	April 6, 1925	140499	If You Knew Susie	364D
Columbia, NY	April 27, 1925	140558	We're Back Together Again	REJECTED
Columbia, NY	June 1, 1925	140558	We're Back Together Again	379D
Columbia, NY	June 1, 1925	140641	Row, Row, Rosie	415D
Columbia, NY	September 10, 1925	140925	Oh Boy! What a Girl	457D
Columbia, NY	September 10, 1925	140926	Jake, the Plumber	REJECTED
Columbia, NY	September 10, 1925	140928	Eddie's Trip Abroad	REJECTED
Victor, NY	September 6, 1928	BVE-46989	Sonny Boy	REJECTED
Victor, NY	September 6, 1928	BVE-46990	It Goes Like This (That Funny Melody)	REJECTED
Victor, NY	September 28, 1929		Sonny Boy	TEST ONLY
Victor, NY	December 18, 1928	BVE-49001	Makin' Whoopee	21831
Victor, NY	December 18, 1928	BVE-49002	Hungry Women	21831
Victor, NY	January 28, 1929	BVE-49688	Eddie Cantor's Automobile Horn Song	21862
Victor, NY	January 28, 1929	BVE-49689	I Fall Down and Go Boom!	21862
Victor, NY	April 5, 1929	BVE-51610	Hello, Sunshine, Hello	21982
Victor, NY	April 5, 1929	BVE-51611	If I Give Up the Saxophone	21982
Victor, NY	October 29, 1929	BVE-57128	Does an Elephant Love Peanuts?	REJECTED
Victor, NY	October 29, 1929	BVE-57129	My Wife Is on a Diet	22189
Victor, NY	October 29, 1929	BVE-57130	Eddie Cantor's Tips on the Stock Market	22189
Victor, NY	August 23, 1931	PBVE-68306	There's Nothing Too Good for My Baby	22851
Hit of Week, NY	September 1931		Cheer Up (Ballyhoo)	K6
Columbia, NY	November 2, 1932	152316	What a Perfect Combination	2723D
Columbia, NY	November 2, 1932	152317	Look What You've Done	2723D
Monument, NY	April 16, 1934	15075	Over Somebody Else's Shoulder	M13001
Monument, NY	April 16, 1934	15076	The Man on the Flying Trapeze	M13001
Monument, LA	September 12, 1934	LA-204	Mandy	M13183
Monument, LA	September 12, 1934	LA-205	An Earful of Music	M13183
Monument, LA	September 12, 1934	LA-206	When My Ship Comes In	REJECTED
Monument, LA	September 12, 1934	LA-207	Okay Toots	M13184
Monument, LA	October 1, 1934	LA-206	When My Ship Comes In	M13184
Rex (GB) LO	December 1934	F-1117	That's the Kind of a Baby for Me	8389
Rex (GB) LO	December 1934	F-1118	Making the Best of Each Day	8389
Decca, LA	January 26, 1938	DLA-1152	Introducing Alexander's Ragtime Band	1887
Decca (GB), LO	July 23, 1938	DR-2822	Says My Heart/Little Lady Make-Believe	F6741
Decca (GB), LO	July 23, 1938	DR-2823	Lambeth Walk	F6741
Columbia, LA	November 26, 1939	LA-2049	The Only Thing I Want for Christmas	35325
Columbia, LA	November 26, 1939	LA-2050	If You Knew Susie	35325

Recording History (Songs)

Company	Date		Song	
Columbia, LA	February 26, 1940	LA-2171	Little Curly Hair in a High Chair	35428
Columbia, LA	February 26, 1940	LA-2172	Margie	35428
Decca, NY	May 6, 1941	69143	Makin' Whoopee	3798
Decca, NY	May 6, 1941	69144	Yes, Sir! That's My Baby	3798
Decca, NY	May 6, 1941	69145	Oh! Gee, Oh! Gosh, Oh! Golly I'm in Love	3873
Decca, NY	May 6, 1941	69146	They Go Wild, Simply Wild, over Me	3873
Decca, NY	March 19, 1942	70539	We're Having a Baby (with June Clyde)	4314
Decca, NY	March 19, 1942	70540	Now's the Time to Fall in Love	4314
Decca, LA	October 17, 1944	L-3648	Around and Around and Around (w/Nora Martin)	23529
Decca, LA	October 17, 1944	L-3649	You Kissed Me Once (w/Nora Martin)	23529
Decca, LA	October 31, 1944	L-3668	If You Knew Susie	23986
Decca, LA	October 31, 1944	L-3669	You'd Be Surprised	23987
Decca, LA	October 31, 1944	L-3670	Dinah	23988
Decca, LA	October 31, 1944	L-3671	Ma (He's Makin' Eyes at Me)	23723
Decca, LA	November 1, 1944	L-3673	Alabamy Bound	24597
Decca, LA	November 1, 1944	L-3674	Margie	23723
Decca, LA	November 1, 1944	L-3675	Ida (Sweet as Apple Cider)	23987
Decca, LA	November 1, 1944	L-3676	How Ya Gonna Keep 'Em Down on the Farm	23988
V-Disc	*	*	In My Arms	4
V-Disc	*	*	How Ya Gonna Keep 'Em Down on the Farm	258
Top Ten	1947	117	Hall of Records	*
Top Ten	1947	118	How Old Is Cantor?	*
Top Ten	1947	119	His School Days	*
Top Ten	1947	120	His Fool Days	*
Top Ten	1947	121	He Kills Vaudeville	*
Top Ten	1947	122	He Flunks His Physical (Part 1)	*
Top Ten	1947	123	He Flunks His Physical (Part 2)	*
Top Ten	1947	124	The Girls in Cantor's Life	*

*The above eight masters were released as the album "Eddie Cantor."

Company	Date		Song	
Pan American	*	St-71	One-Zy, Two-Zy	Pan036
Pan American	*	St-83	Josephine, Please No Lean on the Bell	Pan044
Pan American	*	St-84	Makin' Whoopee	Pan044
Victor	September 29, 1949	VB-1935	I Never See Maggie Alone	54-0005
Victor	September 29, 1949	VB-1946	Oh! Gee, Oh! Gosh, Oh! Golly, I'm in Love	30-0010
Victor	September 29, 1949	VB-1947	The Old Piano Roll Blues	30-0010
Victor	January 30, 1950	VB-3171	Enjoy Yourself	20-3705
Victor	January 30, 1950	VB-3172	I Love Her	20-3705
Victor	January 30, 1950	VB-3173	Now I Always Have Maggie Alone	Rejected
Victor	March 23, 1950	VB-3922	The Old Piano Roll Blues (with Lisa Kirk)	20-3751
Victor	March 23, 1950	VB-3923	Juke Box Annie (with Lisa Kirk)	20-3751
Capitol	April 2, 1954	12416	Maxie the Taxi (Part 1)	32159
Capitol	April 2, 1954	12417	Maxie the Taxi (Part 2)	32159

Recording History (LPs)

"Songs He Made Famous" . . . Decca DL 4431

Makin' Whoopee
Yes Sir, That's My Baby
Dinah
Oh! Gee, Oh! Gosh, Oh! Golly, I'm in Love
Ida, Sweet as Apple Cider
Now's the Time to Fall in Love
If You Knew Susie
Ma (He's Making Eyes at Me)
Alabamy Bound
Margie
They Go Wild Simply Wild over Me
How 'Ya Gonna Keep 'Em Down on the Farm

"The Eddie Cantor Story" (10") . . . Capitol L-467 (GB: Capitol LC 6652)

Now's the Time to Fall in Love
When I'm the President
If You Knew Susie
Ida, Sweet as Apple Cider
Josephine, Please No Lean on the Bell
(Pretty Baby)
(You Must Have Been a Beautiful Baby)
(Yes Sir, That's My Baby)
(Makin' Whoopee)
Ma (He's Makin' Eyes at Me)
Bye, Bye Blackbird
Margie
Row, Row, Row
How Ya Gonna Keep 'Em Down on the Farm

"The Best of Eddie Cantor" . . . RCA Victor VIX LX 1119, RCA Camden (8) 531. (GB RCA Camden SND 5005)

Yes Sir, That's My Baby	June 26, 1957
If You Knew Susie	June 24, 1957
Makin' Whoopee	June 25, 1957
How Ya' Gonna Keep 'Em Down on the Farm	June 26, 1957
Josephine, Please No Lean on the Bell	June 24, 1957
Ma (He's Makin' Eyes at Me)	June 26, 1957
Waiting for the Robert E. Lee	June 24, 1957
Margie	June 25, 1957
Ida, Sweet as Apple Cider	June 24, 1957
Ballin' the Jack	June 25, 1957

Ain't She Sweet	June 25, 1957
Baby Face	June 26, 1957

"A Date With Eddie Cantor" . . . Audio Fidelity AFLP 702

There's No Business Like Show Business
Tuesday Night at Carnegie Hall
Standing Outside of Lindy's
Josephine, Please No Lean on the Bell
Dinah
Is It True What They Say about Dixie
Ma (He's Makin' Eyes at Me)
Makin' Whoopee
There's No Business Like Show Business
Ida, Sweet as Apple Cider
Margie
If You Knew Susie

***This is a recreation of Eddie's 1950 Carnegie Hall concert, recorded in 1960.

Recording History (CDs 1992–2000)

(1992) A Centennial Celebration/The Best of Eddie Cantor . . . RCA/BMG 66033
(deleted)
(1992) Carnegie Hall Concert (2 cds) . . . OC 9217
(1993) The Show That Never Aired . . . OC 9347
(1994) Eddie Cantor Radio Show—1942–1943 (3 cds) . . . OC 9494
(1994) The Columbia Years: 1922–1940 (2 cds) . . . Columbia/Legacy C2K 57148
(1996) Cantor Loves Lucy/All Star Show . . . OC 9617
(1997) Cantor Meets Jolson (3 cds) . . . OC 9753
(1998) The Early Days (2 cds) . . . OC 9872
(1999) Pals . . . OC 9918
(1999) The Eddie Cantor Chase & Sanborn Radio Show 1931–1933 (4 cds) . . . OC 8715
(2000) I Remember Jolson . . . OC 2073
(2000) The Radio Songs Vol. 1, The 30s . . . Nostalgia Arts NOCD 3019
(import)

All CDs are produced by Brian Gari and released on Original Cast Records except where indicated.

Cantor on the Charts

Dated Charted	Peak Position	Weeks Charted	Artist/Record Title	Label and Number
			Eddie Cantor Born Eddie Israel Izkowitz in New York on 1/31/1892, Eddie Cantor became one of the most popular entertainers in vaudeville and musical comedy history. His brand of humor and inexhaustible energy catapulted him to stardom in the "Ziegfeld Follies of 1917," and Eddie remained a national figure for four decades—on stage, radio, movies, and even TV in the early 50s. Hollywood celebrated him with "The Eddie Cantor Story" in 1953; he died on 10/10/64.	
12/08/17	10	1	1. That's the Kind of a Baby for Me From "Ziegfeld Follies of 1917": orchestra directed by Rosario Bourdon	Victor
11/15/19	9	1	2. You Don't Need the Wine to Have a Wonderful Time	Pathe
2/14/20	8	7	3. You'd Be Surprised From "Ziegfeld Follies of 1919"	Emerson
3/27/20	9	2	4. When It Comes to Lovin' the Girls, I'm Way Ahead of the Times	Emerson
5/22/20	9	1	5. All the Boys Love Mary	Emerson
8/28/20	11	1	6. The Argentines, the Portugese, and the Greeks	Emerson
10/09/20	9	1	7. Snoops, the Lawyer	Emerson
1/05/21	1 (5)	12	8. Margie	Emerson
1/12/21	5	4	9. Palesteena	Emerson
8/12/22	3	5	10. I Love Her-She Loves Me (I'm Her He-She's My She)	Columbia
1/24/23	9	1	11. He Loves It	Columbia
10/06/23	7	3	12. Oh! Gee, Oh! Gosh, Oh! Golly I'm in Love From "Ziegfeld Follies of 1922"	Columbia
11/17/23	1 (2)	9	13. No, No, Nora!	*
11/17/23	2 (8)	6	14. I've Got the Yes! We Have No Bananas Blues	Columbia
11/15/24	3	6	15. Charley, My Boy	Columbia
12/20/24 +	5	3	16. Doodle-Doo-Doo	Columbia
7/18/25	195)	12	17. If You Knew Susie	Columbia
10/24/25	9	2	18. Row, Row, Rosie	Columbia
1/16/26	9	1	19. Oh Boy! What a Girl!	Columbia
2/09/29	15	2	20. Makin' Whoopee From the Broadway musical "Whoopee"	Victor
4/20/29	15	2	21. I Fall Down and Go Boom	Victor
11/28/32	7	5	22. What a Perfect Combination From the movie "The Kid from Spain"	Columbia
12/08/34	19	1	23. Okay Toots From the movie "Kid Millions"	*
8/24/50	27	1	24. The Old Piano Roll Blues Eddie Cantor & Lisa Kirk with Sammy Kaye & his orchestra featuring Stan Freeman (piano)	Victor

Filmography

In 1911 Eddie, George Jessel, and Truly Shattuck appeared in a Thomas Edison experimental sound short, *"Widow at the Races."*

In 1924 Eddie appeared in a Lee DeForest experimental one reel sound short, singing: *The Dumber They Come, The Better I Like 'Em* and *Oh Gee, Georgie*

1926 **Film:** *"Kid Boots"* (Paramount) 9 Reels/8565 feet. SILENT. With Clara Bow, Billie Dove, Lawrence Gray, Natalie Kingston, Malcolm Waite, William Worthington, Harry Von Meter, Fred Esmelton.

1927 **Film:** *"Special Delivery"* (Paramount) 6 Reels/5524 Feet. SILENT. With Jobyna Ralston, William Powell, Donald Keith, Jack Dougherty, Victor Posel, Paul Kelly, Mary Carr.

1929 **Short:** *"Ziegfeld's Midnite Frolics"* (Paramount) 2 Reel Short.

1929 **Short:** *"Getting a Ticket"* (Paramount) 1 Reel Short. 11 minutes. (no cast credit listed)
Featured song: *My Wife Is on a Diet*

1929 **Short:** *"That Party in Person"* (Paramount) 1 Reel Short. With Bobbe Arnst.

1929 **Film:** *"Glorifying the American Girl"* (Paramount) 9 Reels/8071 feet. Part Colour. With Mary Eaton, Edward Crandall, Olive Shea, Dan Healy, Kay Renard, Sara Edwards, and guest starring: Helen Morgan, Rudy Vallee, Adolph Zukor, Mr. and Mrs. Florenz Ziegfeld, Mayor and Mrs. James J. Walker, Texas Guinan
***Eddie performed his Tailor Shop sketch

1930 **Short:** *"Cock-Eyed News"* (Paramount) 1 Reel Short.

1930 **Short:** *"Insurance"* (Paramount) 1 Reel Short. 9 Minutes. (no cast credit listed)

Featured Song: *Now That the Girls Are Wearing Long Dresses*

1930 **Film:** *"Whoopee"* (Sam Goldwyn/United Artists) 94 minutes. COLOR. With Eleanor Hunt, Paul Gregory, John Rutherford, Ethel Shutta, Spencer Charters, Chif Caupolican, Albert Hackett, William H. Philbrick.

Featured Songs: *Makin' Whoopee!, A Girl Friend of a Boy Friend of Mine; My Baby Just Cares for Me.*

1931 **Film:** *"Palmy Days"* (Sam Goldwyn/United Artists) 80 minutes. With Charlotte Greenwood, Spencer Charters, Barbara Weeks, George Raft, Paul Page, Harry Woods, Charles B. Kiddlston.

Featured Songs: *There's Nothing Too Good for My Baby; My Honey Said Yes, Yes*

1932 **Film:** *The Kid from Spain"* (Sam Goldwyn/United Artists) 118 minutes. With Lyda Roberti, Robert Young, Ruth Hall, John Miljan, Noah Beery, J. Carrol Naish, Robert Emmet O'Connor, Stanley Fields, Paul Porcasi,

Featured Songs: *In the Moonlight, Look What You've Done* (with Lyda Roberti), *What a Perfect Combination.*

1933 **Film:** *"Roman Scandals"* (Sam Goldwyn/United Artists) 93 minutes. With Ruth Etting, Gloria Stuart, Edward Arnold, David Manners, Verree Teasdale, Alan Mowbray, John Rutherford, Grace Poggi, Willard Robertson, Harry Holman.

Featured Songs: *Build a Little Home; Keep Young and Beautiful; Don't Put a Tax on Love.*

1934 **Film:** *"Kid Millions"* (Samuel Goldwyn/United Artists) Part Colour. With Ann Sothern, Ethel Merman, George Murphy, Jesse Block, Eve Sully, Burton Churchill, Warren Hymer, Otto Hoffman, The Nicholas Brothers, and more.

Featured Songs: *When My Ship Comes In; Minstrel Routine* (includes *Mandy* sung by Eddie Cantor with cast); *Okay Toots; Ice Cream Fantasy* (with Ethel Merman)

1936 **Film:** *"Strike Me Pink"* (Sam Goldwyn/United Artists) 99 minutes. With Ethel Merman, Sally Eilers, Harry "Parkyakarkus" Einstein, William Frawley, Helen Lowell, Gordon Jones, Brian Donlevy, Jack LaRue, Bonnie O'Dea

Featured Songs: *The Lady Dances, Calabash Pipe* (with Ethel Merman)

1937 **Film:** *"Ali Baba Goes to Town"* (20th Century Fox) 81 minutes. With

Tony Martin, Roland Young, June Lang, John Carradine, Louise Hovick, Alan Dinehart, Virginia Field, Raymond Scott Quintet.

Featured Songs: *Laugh Your Way through Life; Swing Is Here to Sway; Vote for Honest Abe* (With Tony Martin)

1940 **Film:** *"Forty Little Mothers"* (MGM) 90 minutes. With Judith Anderson, Ralph Morgan, Rita Johnson, Bonita Granville, Diana Lewis, Martha O'Driscoll, Margaret Early, Louise Seidel, Charlotte Munier.

Featured Songs: *Little Curly Hair in a High Chair; Your Day Will Come*

1943 **Film:** *"Thank Your Lucky Stars"* (Warner Bros.) 127 minutes. With Humphrey Bogart, Bette Davis, Olivia De Havilland, Errol Flynn, Joan Leslie, John Garfield, Ida Lupino, Dennis Morgan, Dinah Shore.

Featured Song: *We're Staying Home Tonight*

1944 **Film:** *"Hollywood Canteen"* (Warner Bros.) 124 minutes. With Bette Davis, Joan Crawford, John Garfield, Sidney Greenstreet, Peter Lorre, Ida Lupino, Alexis Smith, Barbara Stanwyck, Jack Benny.

Featured Song: *We're Having a Baby* (with Nora Martin)

1944 **Film:** *"Show Business"* (RKO) 92 minutes. With Joan Davis, George Murphy, Nancy Kelly, Constance Moore, Don Douglas.

Featured Songs: *The Curse of the Aching Heart; Makin' Whoopee; Dinah* (With George Murphy, Joan Davis, and Constance Moore), *Alabamy Bound; I Don't Want to Get Well* (with George Murphy); *I Want a Girl* (with George Murphy, Joan Davis, and Constance Moore)

1948 **Film:** *"If You Knew Susie"* (RKO) 90 minutes.
With Joan Davis, Allyn Joslyn, Charles Dingle, Sheldon Leonard, Phil Brown, Bobby Driscoll.

Featured Songs: *If You Knew Susie; My, How the Time Goes By* (with Joan Davis); *What Do I Want with Money?*

1952 **Film:** *"The Story of Will Rogers"* (Warner Bros.) 109 minutes. COLOR. With Will Rogers Jr., Jane Wyman, Carl Benton Reid, James Gleason, Mary Wickes, Noah Beery Jr.

Featured Songs: *Ma (He's Makin' Eyes at Me)*

1953 **Film:** *"The Eddie Cantor Story"* (Warner Bros.) 116 minutes. COLOR. With Keefe Brasselle, Marilyn Erskine, Aline MacMahon, Marie Windsor, Alex Gerry, Will Rogers Jr., Arthur Franz, Greta Granstedt.

Featured Songs: *The World Is Mine* (with chorus); *Row, Row, Row; How Ya Gonna Keep 'Em Down on the Farm: If You Knew Susie; Bye Bye Blackbird/Pretty Baby/Yes, Sir, That's My Baby*

Index
by Vince Giordano and Brian Gari*

21 Club, the, 39

Abbott and Costello, 238, 246
Abby, Schroefel and Grau, 120
Abie's Irish Rose, 103
Actors' Equity, 208-211, 284, 125-126, 134, 169
Adamson, Harold, 169
Address of Regulus to the Roman, 26
Ager, Milton, 169
Ah, Wilderness!, 169
Aida, 238
Ain't She Sweet, 74, 169
Ain't We Got Fun, 166
Akst, Harry, 200, 73-74, 93
Alabama Bound, 169
Albany, NY, 189, 191
Albertina Rasch Ballet, 283
Alda, Delysle, 183, 72
Alexander's Ragtime Band, 69, 165
Alger, Horatio, 168
Alhambra, 142
Alice Blue Gown, 127
Allen, Fred, 83, 227, 246, 239-240
Allen, Gracie, 232
Ambassador Hotel, 161
Ambassador Hotel, Los Angeles, CA, 287
American Academy Of Dramatic Arts, 182-183
American Cancer Fund, 264
American Embassy, Rome, Italy, 192
American Express, 124
American Guild of Variety Artists, 184
American Heart Association, 283
American Legion, 220-221, 223
American, the, 105
Andersen, Hans Christian, 123
Andrews, Lois, 83
Anneberg, Walter, 259
Annie Dear, 119
Apollo Theatre, Chicago, IL, 226, 88

Apollo Theatre, St. Louis, MO, 226
Aquitania, The, 26
Ardmore, Jane Kesner, 179
Arlen, Richard, 268-269
Arrowhead, 92
Arthur, Roy, 116-117, 119, 65, 68
ASCAP, 75, 167
Astaire, Fred, 165, 254
Astor Hotel, 107
Astor, Lady, 110
Astors, 153, 118
Atkins, Ira, 24, 25, 115
Atlantic City, NJ, 103, 126, 176, 195, 200, 44-45, 71, 72, 77-78, 91, 102, 111, 125, 180, 272
Avion Conference, London, England, 267
Axelrod, George, 183

Babson, Roger, 112-113
Baby Snooks, 48
Back Home in Tennessee, 163
Bacon, Frank, 209
Baer, Arthur, 223, 266, 272-273
Baker, Newton, 109
Balfour, Lord, 109
Baltimore, MD, 109, 164, 198, 203
Banana Boat Song, 69
Banjo Eyes, 168, 209, 243, 255
Bank of America, 113
Bank of Manhattan, 137
Bankhead, Tallulah, 37, 234
Banky, Vilma, 262, 156
Barclay, Don, 205
Barney Google, 163
Barrymore, Ethel, 209, 37
Barrymore, John, 190, 231, 251
Barrymore, Lionel, 209
Barthelmess, Richard, 183
Barton, James, 210
Bassler's Saloon, 44, 45, 187
Bataan, 264

*Page numbers in bold indicate pages in second volume.

Battle Creek Sanitarium, 284–285, **134**
Bayes, Nora, **240**
BBC, **192**
Bedini and Arthur, 116–127, 133, 150, 212, **16, 25, 65–69, 77, 86**
Bedini, Jean, **78, 86**
Beery, Wallace, 269, 279
Behrman, S. N. (Sam), **50, 204**
Bellevue-Stratford Hotel, Philadelphia, PA, **260**
Belt in the Back (Joe's Blue Front), 216–218, 252–253, **73, 247**
Bendelbloom, Mrs., 36
Benedict Arnold the Traitor's Deathbed, 26, 34, **18**
Ben-Gurion, Prime Minister, **273**
Bennetti, Richard, **202**
Benny (valet), 268
Benny, Jack, 84, 92–93, 224–230, 258, 262–263, **285, 288**
Bergner, Elizabeth, **267**
Berk, Morris, 33
Berkeley, Busby, **153–154**
Berlin, Ellin (Mackay, Ellin), 75–76, **196**
Berlin, Germany, **267**
Berlin, Irving, 39, 98, 125, 183, 200–201, 281, **23, 48, 68–76, 165**
Berri, Beth, 236
Best's, **29**
Beverly Hills, CA, **111, 113, 236**
Beyond the Horizon, **202**
Big Brother, 291
Billboard, **162**
Billy the Kid, **19**
Biltmore Bowl, **93**
Biltmore Hotel, **32, 85**
Bird of Paradise, **103**
Blackstone, Milton, **243–244**
Block and Sully, **160**
Block, Paul, 260
Bloomer, Mrs., 36
Board of Aldermen, **188**
Bogart, Humphrey, **199**
Bolger, Ray, **78**
Bombo, 88
Borden Milk Company, **255**
Boston, MA, 89, **144, 203, 232, 236**
Bow, Clara, 263–266, **75, 150–152**
Bowery Savings Bank, **26**
Boyer, Charles, **272**
Bradley, General Omar, **223**
Brady, Diamond Jim, 154, **118, 121, 123**

Breen, Bobby, **234, 236–238**
Breen, Mickey, **237**
Breen, Sally, **237**
Brice, Billy, 48
Brice, Fannie, 4, 181, 205–206, 238, 241, **7, 30, 39, 41–50, 97, 105, 124–125, 141–142, 148, 208, 211, 254, 277**
Brice, Frances, 48
Brice, Lew, **43**
Brighton Beach Music Hall, **77**
Brisbane (Hearst writer), **112**
Bristol-Myers, **222, 225, 240**
Broadway Brevities, **212**
Bronson, Lillian, **249**
Brooklyn Chamber of Commerce, 297
Brooklyn Federation of Charities, 296
Brooklyn L, **55**
Buck, Gene, 182–183, **44, 72, 116–117, 123, 169**
Buffalo, NY, 161, **68, 143**
Buffano, Jules, **59**
Bumpity-Bumps, 220–221
Burke, Billie, **114, 118–119, 123–124, 130, 132, 138**
Burns and Allen, **205, 257**
Burns, George, **84, 232**
Burton, Sir Montague, **267**
Buzzell, Eddie, 3, 129, 131, **80**
By the Light of the Silvery Moon, 130
Bye Bye Blackbird, **277**
Byrd, Commander Richard, 260

CBS, **159, 239–240**
Caesar, Sid, **244, 279**
Cagney, James, 37, **190, 199**
Caine Mutiny, The, **251**
Calabasas, CA, **160**
Callahan, Marie, 236, **128**
Camel Cigarette Show, The, **238–239**
Camels, **219**
Camp Meeting Band, **163**
Camp Upton, **69**
Canary Cottage, 148–149, 151, 267, **27–28, 87, 99–102, 116**
Cantor and Jessel Tour (1933), **82–83**
Cantor and Lee, 144, **97–98**
Cantor Home for Girls, **300**
Cantor on the Sabbath, **206**
Cantor, Eddie (bicycle thief), **41**
Cantor, Eddie (birth of), **9**
Cantor, Eddie (blackface), 114, **102–103**
Cantor, Eddie (Dutch comedian), **64–65**

Index 305

Cantor, Eddie (first job), 47, **19**
Cantor, Eddie (first trip to California), **29–30, 285**
Cantor, Eddie (Heart Ambassador), 283
Cantor, Eddie (heart attack), 7, **246**, 277–284, **288**
Cantor, Eddie (home: Beverly Hills), 262
Cantor, Eddie (home: Bronx), 4, 148, 177, **108, 116–117**
Cantor, Eddie (home: Eldridge St.), 7, 9
Cantor, Eddie (home: Great Neck, LI, NY), 184, 287–288, 292–294, **31, 112, 180**
Cantor, Eddie (home: Henry St.), 44, **13, 15, 18, 22, 55, 253**
Cantor, Eddie (home: Madison St.), 17, 287
Cantor, Eddie (home: Market St.), 17, 18, **15–16**
Cantor, Eddie (home: Mount Vernon), 63, 177, 262, **28, 163**
Cantor, Eddie (home: Roxbury Dr.), **30, 224**
Cantor, Eddie (home: San Remo Apts. NY), **195**
Cantor, Eddie (home: Sunset Blvd., CA), **233**
Cantor, Eddie (insomnia), 63–68, 146
Cantor, Eddie (laryngitis), **33**
Cantor, Eddie (Long Beach, LI, NY), **270**
Cantor, Eddie (name change), **13–14**
Cantor, Eddie (pleurisy), 38, 164, 216, 279–280, 284, **30, 88, 133, 287**
Cantor, Eddie (purse thief), **19**
Cantor, Eddie (radio show), 303–309, **40, 148, 181, 191, 213–223, 282**
Cantor, Eddie (run for president), **114, 232**
Cantor, Eddie (sixty-fifth birthday), **263**
Cantor, Eddie (songwriter), **167**
Cantor, Eddie (television show), **282**
Cantor, Eddie (tonsils), 279, 293
Cantor, Eddie (wedding of), 140–141, **26**
Cantor, Edna (daughter), 176, 287–288, **28, 49, 175, 177–180, 182, 184–186, 286**
Cantor, Charlie, **231**
Cantor, "Edwina," **213**
Cantor, "Happy," **35**
Cantor, Gypsy Rose, **260**
Cantor, Ida (wife), 54, 56–62, 68–69, 71–74, 92–95, 105–111, 140–143, 158–159, 164, 170, 177–178, 185, 219, 260, 279–280, 283–284, 287, 292, **7, 13–14, 22–33, 48–49, 53, 62, 78, 87–88, 96, 101, 103, 111, 116–117, 126–128, 133, 137–138, 156, 160, 162, 166–167, 175–177, 180–184, 186, 191–192, 195–196, 204, 212–214,** 216, 224, 227, 233, 236, 239, 244, 255, 261–263, 265, 271–273, 278, 285–288
Cantor, Janet (daughter), 283, 287, **30–31**, 111, 167, 175, 181–182, 184–185, 287–288
Cantor, Maite (mother), 7, 8, 9, 11, 12, **12, 285**
Cantor, Marilyn (daughter), 219, 287, **29**, 166, 175–176, 179–180, 182–185, 240, **251**
Cantor, Marjorie (daughter), 4, 55, 148, 164, 220, 262, 268, 287–289, **23, 27–28, 163**, 175–176, 178–181, 184–185
Cantor, Michael (father), 6, 7, 8, 10, 11, 12, 13, 14, 151, **11, 12**
Cantor, Natalie (daughter), 4, 55, 151, 164, 287, **23, 27–29, 101, 116, 175, 177–180, 182, 185–186, 286**
Carnegie Hall, **211–212, 268**
Carolina in the Morning, **166**
Carpenter, Thelma, **240**
Carpentier, George, 131–132
Carr, Frank B., 88, **22**
Carr, Mary, 275–276
Carroll, Earl, 148–150, **96–103, 129, 131**
Carter, Allene, **121**
Carter, Frank, 185–187, 197, **35–36**
Caruso, Enrico, **90, 241**
Casino Theatre, NY, **120, 138**
Catherine St., **55, 187**
Catlett, Walter, 181, **125**
Caught Short, **31**
Cedars of Lebanon Hospital, **138, 184**
Celtics, the, **266**
Century Roof, **126**
Century Theatre, **89–90**
Cermak, Mayor, **83**
Chaplin, Charlie, 262, **153, 156–157, 251**
Charleston, The, **265**
Charley, My Boy, **166**
Charlot, Andre, 142, **27, 96**
Charters, Spencer, **135**
Chase and Sanborn Hour, 303, **32, 103, 163, 178–179, 184, 213–216, 218, 232–233, 288**
Chasen's, **83, 148**
Chayefsky, Paddy, **158**
Chazan ov Shabbas, **206**
Cheek to Cheek, **71**
Chelsea Yacht Club, 126, **77**
Chelsea, MA, **258**
Cherry St., **25**

Index

Chevalier, Maurice, 214, 287
Chicago Musical College, 119
Chicago World's Fair, 119–120
Chicago, IL, 83, 97–98, 126, 131, 258
Childs Restaurant, 38
Childs Restaurant, Cleveland, OH, 154
Childs Restaurant, Philadelphia, PA, 215
Childs Restaurant, St. Louis, MO, 204
China, 263
China Theatre, Stockholm, Sweden, 142
Chrysler, Walter, 32
Churchill, Sarah, 192
Churchill, Winston, 192
Ciano, Count, 193
Cincinnati, OH, 45–46, 50
Civic Repertory Theater, 297
Civil War, the, 119
Claire, Ina, 122
Clara (maid), 177
Clark, Buddy, 258
Clark, Thomas W., 18
Clarke, Mae, 249
Claudel, Ambassador France, 260
Clayton, Ida, 58
Clayton, Jackson, and Durante, 100, 56–58, 254
Clayton, Lou, 56–58
Clinchy, Dr. Everett, 287
Clinton Music Hall, 75–76
Club Durant, 56, 59
Club Richman, 240
Cohan Opera House, Chicago, IL, 171, 190
Cohan, George M., 61, 91, 56, 82, 169–172, 241, 270
Cohn, Irving, 165
Cohn, Lou, 59
Cole, Nat King, 263, 281
Coleman, Ronald, 156
Colgate Comedy Hour, 100, 246, 248, 277
College of the City of New York, 220
Collier, Constance, 50
Collier, William, 170, 270
Colonial Theatre, Boston, MA, 290, 140
Colonial Theatre, Chicago, IL, 145
Colonial Theatre, NY, 69
Comin' in on a Wing and a Prayer, 169
Commonwealth of Boston, MA, 272
Communist, 234
Community Chest, 219
Como, Perry, 251
Compton, Betty, 191

Coney Island, 95–96, 265, 53–54, 59, 62, 258
Congress Hotel, Chicago, IL, 127
Congressional Medal of Honor, 75, 170
Conklin, Chester, 269
Conn, Harry, 226
Conrad, Con, 163
Considine, Bob, 212
Continental, the, 163
Convention Hall, Philadelphia, PA, 244
Coolidge, Calvin, 5, 110, 287
Cooper, Lew, 101
Copley Plaza, Boston, MA, 145
Corthell, Herbert, 149
Cotton Club, Harlem, NY, 238
Coughlin, Father Charles, 224
Counselman, William, 154
Country Girl, The, (show), 176
Courtney, Florence, 82
Cowl, Jane, 138, 255
Crandall, Jack (Kreindel, Jack), 272–273, 266, 269–270
Crane Company, 102
Crompton, Nanci, 247
Crosby, Bing, 41, 76, 92, 198
Cruz, James, 276
Cukor, George, 50
Cunningham, Cecil, 39
Curtain Going Up, 183

Dabney, Ford, 116–117
Dafoe, Dr. Allan, 239
Damon Runyon Memorial Award, 243
Dandy Girls, 127
Daniels, Bebe, 269
Daniels, Billy, 247
Daniels, Josephus, 109
David Copperfield, 146
Davidson Theatre, Milwaukee, WI, 98
Davies, Marion, 181, 122
Davis Jr., Sammy, 247, 281
Davis, Benny, 163
Davis, Joan, 40–41
Davis, Owen, 285
Dayan, Moishe, 262
Dayton, OH, 163
De Sylva, Buddy, 91, 169
DeForest Phonofilm, 261
DeHaven and Sidney, 118
DeHaven, Gloria, 263
Delilah, 39
Delmar Racetrack, CA, 61

Index 307

Delmar, Ethel, 90
Demarest, William, 102
DeMille, Cecil, 245
Dempsey, Jack, 4, 131–132, 270, 283
Denver, CO, 262
Desert Inn, Palm Springs, CA, 178
Detroit Free Press, 113
Detroit, MI, 81, 113, 128, 130, 269–270
Diamond Tony's, 96, 53
Dickens, Charles, 140
Dietrich, Marlene, 234
Dillingham, Charles B., 36, 38, 154, 162, 118
DiMaggio, Joe, 164
Dinah, 74, 205
Dinty Moore's, 136
Dionne quintuplets, 239
Disreputable Insurance Company, 219
Divison St., 16
Divorce Question, The, 231
Dix, Richard, 269
Dixie Volunteers, The, 164
Dixon, Harland, 176, 236, 128
Dockstader, Lew, 86
Dolly Sisters, 72
Donahue, Jack, 202
Donaldson, Douglas, and Gumble, 167
Donaldson, Walter, 90, 155, 162, 166–167
Don't Sit under the Apple Tree, 168
Dooley, Johnny, 182–183, 208, 125–126
Dooley, Ray, 182–183, 208, 125–126
Dorfman, Nat, 271
Dorset Hotel, 81
Dove, Billie, 263, 265–267
Dowling, Eddie, 156, 181, 183, 125–126, 138
Down in Bom-Bom Bay, 147
Down Yonder, 163
Doyer St., 21
Dressler, Marie, 196
Du Barry, Mlle., 43
Duke of Windsor, 286
Duke University, 222
Dulles, John Foster, 273, 280
Dumas, Alexander, 230, 140
Duncan Sisters, 130, 78
Durando, 71
Durante, Jeanne, 57–58
Durante, Jimmie, 100, 53–61, 263
Durban, Deanna, 234–236, 238, 243

Earl Carroll Theater, The, 63, 245, 189, 270
Easter Parade, 71

Eaton, Mary, 236–237, 247, 38
Eddie Cantor at Home, 217
Eddie Cantor Camp, 37
Eddie Cantor Camp Committee, 254, 266
Eddie Cantor Coffee, 216
Eddie Cantor Playhouse, 255
Eddie Cantor Story, The, 282
Eddie, Behave, 261
Eddie, Steady, 133
Ederle, Gertrude, 190
Edgewater Beach Hotel, Chicago, IL, 167
Edison Hotel, NY, 205
Ediss, Connie, 142
Educational Alliance, 30, 20, 24
Edwards, Gus, 3, 126, 127–131, 133–134, 139, 150, 26, 33, 77–80, 96, 234, 244
Edwards, Mrs. Gus, 131
Einstein, Albert, 60
Einstein, Harry, 232
Eisenhower, Dwight, 277
El Capitan Theatre, Hollywood, CA, 244, 277–278
El Mirador Theatre, 59
El Paso, TX, 257
El Poonelo, Palm Springs, CA, 288
Elder, Ruth, 282, 190
Eliot, T. S., 140
Ella Cinders, 154
Enemy Within, The, 224
England (1935), 288
Erlanger, A. L., 180–181, 121
Ernst, Morris, 195
Errol, Leon, 226, 126, 159
Essex St. Dispensary, 20
Ethical Culture School, 297
Etting, Ruth, 37–38, 122, 135
Evans and Hoey, 120–121
Evans, Charley, 120
Evans, Maurice, 238–239
Evening Journal, 14–15, 271

Fairbanks, Douglas, 262, 278, 153
Fairchild, Edgar "Cookie," 239, 241
Fairfax, Beatrice, 72
Famous Film Corporation, 5
Famous Players-Lasky Corporation, 112, 263, 274
Fanya, 48–53, 56, 60–62, 65, 25
Fauntleroy, Little Lord, 75, 20
Fay, Frank, 210, 271
Federation, 291
Feltman's, 55

Fender, Harry, 236
Ferber, Edna, 132
Ferry the Frog, 118
Fields, Sidney, 247
Fields, W. C., xii, 4, 138, 161, 181, 195–205, 208–211, 7, 43–45, 47, 105–107, 110, 117, 124–125, 137, 139–149, 211, 254
Fine and Dandy, 154
Finkel, Mrs., 36
Fisher, Eddie, 243–244
Fitch, Dr., 251–252, 256–258, 129
Five O'Clock Girl, The, 237
Flash, Serge, 205
Floridian Club, Miami Beach, FL, 227–228
Folies Bergère, 121, 142, 197
Fonda, Henry, 251
Fontainebleau Hotel, Miami, FL, 263
Ford, Henry, 109
Fordham University, NY, 191
Fortescue's Pier, Long Beach, NY, 147
Forty-Five Minutes from Broadway, 169
Forty Little Mothers, 208
Fox Film Corporation, 5
Fox Theatre, San Francisco, CA, 204
Fox, William, 98
Foy, Eddie, 209
Francis, Dr., 265
Franklin, Sidney, 157
Fred Allen Show, The, 240
Freedman, David, 215, 217–218
Freeland, Thornton, 154–155
Freeman, Mona, 250
French, Minnie, 121
Fresh Air Fund, Pittsburgh, PA, 253
Friar's Club, 136, 170, 281
Friars Frolic, The, 170
Friend, Cliff, 168
Friganza, Trixie, 149–150, 267, 99–101
Frisco, Joe, 117
Frohman, 123–124
Fronde, 220

Gaine's Manhattan Theatre, 63
Garde, Betty, 231
Garden of Paradise, 123
Gari, Amanda (granddaughter), 175, 185–186
Gari, Brian (grandson), 175, 185–186
Gari, Roberto (son-in-law), 184–185
Garson, Greer, 60
Gartel, Mrs., 36
Gaxton, William, 204

Gedney Farms, 64
Gelles, Isaac Wurst Works, 21, 288, 15
Gents' Furnishings, 26
George Has a Birthday, 249–250
George Washington Hotel, Jacksonville, FL, 261
Georgian, the, 144
Gerard, Ambassador, 260
German-American Bund, 224
Gershwin, George, 39, 50
Gershwin, Ira, 50
Gest, Morris, 278
GGG Clothing Company, 266
Gilbert, L. Wolfe, 162–163
Gilmore, Frank, 208
Gilmore, Margalo, 204
Gimbel's, 63
Girl Crazy, 39
Gish, Lillian, 249
Give a Gift to a Yank Who Gave!, 223, 273
Glad, Gladys, 122
Gleason, Jackie, 244, 251
Gobel, George, 246
God Bless America, 75
Goddard, Dr., 283
Gold Diggers, 248
Goldman, Emanuel (Mannie Goldman), 266–269, 272
Goldstein, Jonah, 24, 25, 115
Goldwyn, Frances, 156
Goldwyn, Samuel, 32, 67, 87, 103, 136, 150–161, 177, 184, 233, 235, 247
Good Bad Woman, The, 231
Good Fellow Fund, 113
Good News, 240
Good Samaritan Dispensary, 20, 16
Good-By, Little Girl, Good-By, 130
Goodman, Al, 100, 246
Goodyear Rubber Company, 144–145
Gordon, Bert, 233
Gordon, Cliff, 77, 82
Grable, Betty, 154
Grady, Bill, 148
Grand Canyon scene, 123
Grand Opera House, 60, 61, 64–65
Grandma Esther. *See* Kantrowitz, Esther
Granger, Farley, 250
Grant, Ulysses S., 219
Great Lakes Naval Training Station, 225
Greek Embassy, 232
Green River, 174–175, 219
Green, Jane, 143

Greenwood, Charlotte, 99
Gress, Louis, 239, 269
Grey, Lawrence, 269
Griffith, Raymond, 149–150, 267, 269, 100–101
Grossinger's, 243–244
Grossmith, George, 142
Gruskin, George, 242

Halperin, Nan, 219
Ham Tree, The, 195, 139
Hamburg, Germany, 120
Hamilton, Alexander, 221
Hamlet, 241
Hammerstein, Oscar, 132
Hammerstein, William, 124–125
Hammerstein's Victoria Theatre, 116, 119, 120, 124–125, 212, 25, 65, 86
Hampden, Walter, 251
Harbach, Otto, 233–235, 127
Harding, Warren G., 4, 288, 110
Hardy, Sam, 144
Harlem, NY, 195
Harrigan, 169, 255
Harriman, President, 258
Harrimans, 153, 118
Harris, Elmer, 100–101
Harris, Sam H., 229, 172
Hart, Max, 134, 142, 144, 151–152, 153, 186, 96–103, 116, 124, 126
Hart, Moss, 42
Harvey (play), 271
Hay, Mary, 182–183, 72
Hayes, 71
Hayes, Brent, 97
Hayes, Helen, 251
Hearn, Lou, 216–219, 224
Hearst Papers, 101, 112
Hearst, William Randolph, 154, 15, 118
Hecht, Ben, 42, 156
Heifetz, Jascha, 146, 248
Heights, The, 231
Held, Anna, 20, 121, 123
Helene, Mme., 269–270
Hello, Frisco!, 169
Henderson's Theatre, 98
Henrici's, 37
Henry Street, 54, 56, 94, 106, 111, 113, 116, 118–119, 124, 163, 259, 261, 292, 16, 24–25, 62, 65, 150, 186–188, 204, 211
Henry, O., 235
Hepburn, Katharine, 42

Herbert, Victor, 120
Herskovitz, Cantor, 268
Higler, Mr., 98–99
Hildegarde, 78
Hillcrest Country Club, 84
Hillquit, Morris, 42, 43, 188
Hippodrome Theatre, 71
Hitchcock, Raymond, 162
Hitler, Adolf, 114, 193, 258–259
Hoctor, Harriet, 122
Hoffman, Gertrude, 123, 67
Hollywood Bowl, 268
Hollywood, CA, 255
Holm, Eleanor, 48
Holman, Jacob (Jack Holman), 266–267, 269
Holman, Nathan, 266
Holmes, Madeleine, 249
Holtz, Lou, 84, 204
Holzman, Bennie, 220–221, 266, 270–272
Holzman, Harriet, 271
Honolulu, America Loves You, 117
Hoover, Herbert, 110
Hope Haven Home for Crippled Children, 262
Hope, Bob, 41, 93, 258
Hopkins, Arthur, 241–242
Hopkins, Harry, 200
Hopkins, Miriam, 156
Hopkins, Peggy, 122
Hore-Delisha, Leslie, 192
Horowitz, Mrs., 17
Horowitz, Vladimir, 54
Hotcha, 138
Hotel Marlborough, 121
Hotel Wolverine, Detroit, 220
House That Ziegfeld's Jack Built, The, 300
Housely, Mary Frances, 261
How Can America Stay Out of War?, 220
How Deep Is the Ocean, 71
How Ya Gonna Keep 'Em Down on the Farm, 167
Howard, Frances, 156
Howard, Leslie, 238
Howard, Willie, 291
Howland, Jobyna, 236, 248, 251, 38–39, 129
Hugo, Victor, 140
Hunt, Eleanor, 154
Hurok, Sol, 237
Hutchins, A. (undertaker), 226
Hutchins, Robert M., 220
Hutton, Betty, 181, 239

I Got Rhythm, 39
I Just Can't Make My Eyes Behave, 20
I Love the Ladies, 142, 96
I Want To Be Glorified, 74
Ida, Sweet as Apple Cider, 162, 264
If the USA Can't Get to Broadway, We'll Bring Broadway to the USA, 247
If You Knew Susie (film), 40, 208
If You Knew Susie (song), 87, 169, 238, 262
I'll Marry No Explorer, 150, 100
I'm Always Chasing Rainbows, 127
I'm So Broken Hearted 'Cause I Haven't Got It, 75
I'm Sorry I Made You Cry, 164–165
Immerman, Hattie, 60
Imperial Theatre, 78
Independent Milk Owners, 255
Indian Maidens, 88, 22, 53
International Boy Scout Jamboree, Hungary, 221
International Rag, 71
Irene, 229, 127
Irving Berlin Music Company, 73
Isham, 85–86
Israel, 256, 262–263, 267, 273, 279
It All Belongs to Me, 74
It All Depends on You, 169
It Ruined Marc Anthony, 150, 100
It's a Boy, 231
It's up to the Band, 74

J. Walter Thompson Agency, 213–215, 218
Jackie Gleason Show, The, 251
Jackson, Eddie, 57–59
Jacksonville, FL, 261–262
Jannings, Emil, 267
Jardin De Paris, 121
Jazz Singer, The, 81, 91
Jefferson, Thomas, 194
Jessel, George, 3, 63, 129, 131–132, 158, 272–273, 77–87, 91, 162, 192, 205–207, 227, 263, 277
Jesus Christ, 195
Jewish Hospital of Brooklyn, 157, 296, 30
Jewish Theatrical Guild, 291
Jewish War Relief, 248
Joe Opp and Company, 73
Joe's Blue Front (Belt in the Back), 216–218, 252–253, 73, 247
John Barlycorn, 242
Johnson, Mrs. W. J., 262
Johnstone, Justine, 181, 122

Joint Distribution Committee, 259
Jolson Story, The, 93–94
Jolson, Al, 45, 212, 15–16, 39, 69, 73, 75–76, 80, 86–95, 167, 233, 248, 258, 277
Jolson, Erle, 94
Jolson, Henrietta, 87, 90–91
Jonas, Nathan, 166–172, 178, 292–297, 299, 190
Jonas, Ralph, 297
Judge, 97
Jungle Jingle, The, 74
Just You and Me, 44

Kahn, Gus, 90, 155, 162, 166–167
Kaiser, the, 109
Kalmar, Bert, 157–162, 164–165
Kalmar, Mrs. Bert, 164
Kane Furniture Company, 232–233
Kantrowitz, Annie, 17, 53, 167
Kantrowitz, Esther (Grandma), 2, 8–11, 13–20, 22, 28, 30, 35, 46, 48–53, 55, 65, 67, 68, 70, 76, 92, 138, 139, 157, 7, 11–25, 53, 106, 204, 285
Kantrowitz, Irwin, 17
Kantrowitz, Minnie, 17
Kathryn Perry and Company, 73
Kaufman, George S., 153, 160
Kaufman, S. Jay, 282
Kaye, Danny, 42, 84, 93, 159, 168, 241, 279
Kaye, Sylvia, 42
Keeler, Ruby, 90, 92–93
Keenan, Frank, 231
Keith Circuit, 122, 144, 96, 102
Keith's Theatre, Boston, MA, 235
Keith's Theatre, Louisville, KY, 125
Kelly, Gregory, 129
Kelly, Harry, 219
Kelly, Patsy, 102
Kelly, Walter, 83, 87, 144
Kelo Brothers, 224
Kern, Jerome, 132
Kessler, Sam, 142, 26–27, 43, 96
Keystone Comedies, 242
Khayyam, Omar, 197
Khonstamm, Dr., 234
Kid Boots, 63, 125, 183, 188, 191, 228, 231–234, 236–237, 239–241, 243, 245–248, 254, 257–259, 261, 263–268, 271–274, 278, 285, 29, 38, 73, 88, 98, 111, 119, 127–131, 133, 150, 163, 169, 178, 189, 271, 286

Index

Kid From Spain, The, 304, **155–157**, **159**, 193
Kid Kabaret, 3, 129–131, 137, 77, 79–80, 83, 86, **104**, **162**
Kid Millions, **39**, **160**
Kimel, 72, 73
King of England, **286**
King of Kings, 270
King of Siam, **248**
King, Allyn, **106**
King, Dennis, **138**
Kingdon, Dr. Frank, **220**
Kingston, Natalie, 263
Kipling, Rudyard, **233–234**
Kiraly, Victor, **117**, **124**
Kismet, **96**
Knickerbocker Hotel, NY, **241**
Knight, Vic, **240**
Knights of Columbus, **247**
Knott and Shott, 87–88
Knox, Secretary of the Navy, **256**
Knoxville, TN, **33**
Kohlmar, Fred, **160**
Korea, **94**
KPO, San Francisco, CA, **262**
Kreindel, Jack (Crandall, Jack), 272–273, **266**, **269–270**
Ku Klux Klan, **247**, **38**

La Marcheuse, **120**
LaGuardia, Fiorello, **195**
Laine, Frankie, **93**
Lake Charles, LA, 133
Lake Edwards, Canada, **133**
Lakeville Golf Club, 293–294
Lambe, Rt. Reverend Monsignor Joseph J., **262**
Lamb's Club, 232–233, **170**
Lamour, Dorothy, **247**
Lanza, Mario, **155**
Las Vegas, NV, **262**
Lasky, Jesse, 260–261, 271, 273, **133**
Lastfogel, Abe, **209–210**, **228**, **278**
Latin Quarter, **34**
Lawrence, Gertrude, **254**
Laye, Evelyn, **122**, **159**
Le Gallienne, Eva, **297**
Le Maire, Rufus, **234**
Leahy, Frank, **272**
Learn to Sing a Love Song, **74**
Lee, Al, 144–148, **278**, **55**, **97**, **99–100**
Lee, Leila, 3, **129**

Lefkowitz, Mrs. (neighbor), **19**
Lefty Louie, 39, **23**, **188**
Legion Convention, Chicago IL, **288**
Legs Legs Legs, **101–102**
Leipzig Conservatory of Music, **119**
LeMaire, George, 182–183, **72–73**, **125**
Lena From Palesteena, **163**
Leonard, Benny, 4, 143
Leonard, Eddie, **80**, **162**
Les Miserables, **140**
Leslie, Edgar, **164**
Lesser, Sol, **237**
Letters from a Self-Made Diplomat to His President, **110**
Levi Simpson's, **25**
Lew Dockstader's Minstrels, **86**
Lewis and Conger, **141**
Lewis, Al (producer), **229**
Lewis, Al (songwriter), **169**
Lewis, Jerry, **96**, **245–246**, **262**
Lewis, Joe E., **263**
Lewis, Lloyd, **220**
Lewis, Marlo, **246**
Lewis, Ted, **251**
Lexington Opera House, **209–210**
Liberty Bond Benefit, **89**
Liberty Theatre, NY, **169**, **270**
Lightnin', 209
Lillie, Beatrice, **254**
Lily of the Valley, **163**
Lincoln, Abraham, **163**, **194**, **221**
Lindbergh, Charles, **190**, **282**, **74**, **91**, **114**, **190**
Lindy's, **71**, **92**, **255**
Lipsky, Daniel, **24**, **25**, **28**, **29**, **30**, **31**, **35**, **37**, **53**, **60**, **75**, **115**, **127**, **141**, **165–172**, **176–177**, **17**, **20–21**
Literary Digest, **97**
Little Johnny Jones, **169**
Little Nellie Kelly, **169**
Little White House, **198**
Livingstone, Mary, **226–227**, **285**
Lloyd, Harold, 260, 268
Loesser, Frank, **70**
Loew, Marcus, 39, 112, 260, **64**
Loew's Avenue B Theatre, **76**
Loew's State Theatre, NY, **171**, **210**
London, England, **191–192**, **267**
London's Theatre, 80, 87
Long Island University, **297**
Long Island, NY, **111**
Longworth, Alice, **110**

Lorraine, Lillian, 181, **117**
Lorre, Peter, **250**
Louisville, KY, **223**
Love Me or Leave Me (film), **37**
Love Me or Leave Me (song), **135**
Lovin' Sam (The Sheik of Alabam), **169**
Low, Mayor, 296
Lucerne, NY, **217**
Lunt and Fontaine, **251**
Lyon's Corner House, **27**
Lyric Theatre, 179
Lyric Theatre, Brooklyn, NY, 112
Lyric Theatre, Hoboken, NJ, 112, 113, **64**

Ma, He's Making Eyes at Me, **163**
Macbeth, **72**
MacCracken, Henry Noble, **220**
Mackail, Dorothy, **122**
Macy's, **185, 216**
Mad Russian, The, **233–234, 239**
Madame X, 124
Madden, Owney, **56**
Madison Square Garden, **71**
Madison St., **187**
Mahoney, Will, **102**
Majestic Theatre Milwaukee, WI, **97**
Make It Snappy, 218, 222, 226, **126, 165, 247**
Makin' Whoopee, **135, 166, 192, 258**
Malitz, Joe, 95, 97–98, **53–54**
Mammy, **167**
Man in Evening Dress, The, 268
Manchester, England, **259**
Mandy, 183, **72, 125**
Manhattan Opera House, **170**
Manufacturers Trust Company, 165, 168–169, 171–173, 297, 299, **190, 253**
March of Dimes, 7, **198–200, 222, 251, 265**
March, Hal, **263**
Margie, **163, 264, 280**
Marlborough Blenheim Hotel, 200
Marshall Plan, the, **280**
Martin and Lewis, **96, 246, 262**
Martin, Dean, **96, 245–246, 262**
Martin, Mary, **251**
Martin, Nora, **256**
Martin, Tony, **165**
Marx, Groucho, **78, 84, 92, 184, 245**
Marx, Harpo, **84, 279**
Marx, Miriam, **184**
Master and Man, 144, **97, 99**
Matinee Theatre, **249**

Matthews III, Owen W., **221**
Maxie the Taxi, **247**
Maybe It's You, **74**
Mayfair Club, **270**
Mayflower Hotel, Washington, DC, **194**
Mayo, Virginia, **243**
MCA, **182**
McBride, Mr., **192–193**
McCarey, Leo, **157–158**
McCarthy Sisters, The, 225
McCarthy, Joseph, 183, 229, 232–234, 237, **72, 127, 169**
McCleery, Albert, **249**
McClellan, Mayor, 296
McCormack, John, **72**
McCree, Junie, 84
McDonald, James G., **267–268**
McGonigle, Clay, 201–204, **106–107**
McGuffey's Reader, **105**
McGuire, William Anthony, 229–235, 237, 241, 243, 285, **127, 134, 157, 166**
McHugh, Jimmy, **169**
McHugh, Judy (granddaughter), **175, 186**
McIntyre and Heath, 195, **139**
McIntyre, Marvin, **199–200**
McKibbon, **78**
Mechanicsville, NY, **64**
Meehan's Dogs, 90
Meir, Golda, **225**
Melancholy Baby, **54**
Melchoir, Lauritz, **238**
Mencken, Helen, 130
Mendelssohn's Spring Song, 123, **67**
Menjou, Adolphe, 184, 268–269
Menuhin, Yehudi, **231**
Merman, Ethel, **39–40, 160, 182, 208**
Meroff, Benny, **205**
Metro Goldwyn Mayer, 263
Metzger, Michael (grandson), **175, 182, 186**
Miami Beach, FL, **82, 214**
Midnight Frolics, The, 4, 152, 154–155, 162, 208, 211, **28, 69, 116, 123**
Midnight Rounders, The, 213, 215–216, 218, 221–222, 226, **81, 126, 163, 164, 202–203**
Mielly, Paul F., **278**
Mike's, **71**
Miller, Marilyn, 4, 181, 183, 185–186, 211, 226, **35–37, 72, 122, 125–126**
Millman, Mort, **214**
Milwaukee, WI, **97–99**

Index 313

Miner's Bowery Theatre, 78, 113, 137, 260, **21, 211**
Minsk, Russia, 7
Minsky, **260**
MIT, **221**
Mitchell Field Army Base, **191**
Mlle. Daisy, 123, **67**
Moanin' Low, 301
Mobile, AL, **94–95**
Molasso, 123, **66**
Moll, Elick, **250**
Monroe St., **187**
Monroe, Marilyn, **40**
Montgomery, Dave, **123**
Moore, Constance, **40**
Moore, Owen, **73**
Moore, Victor, 61, **25**
Morgan, Helen, **122**
Morning World, The, **105**
Morosco, Oliver, 148–149, 151, **96–103**
Morris Plan, the, 301
Morrison's Rockaway Theater, 127
Moter Vehicle Group, Santa Monica, CA, **221**
Muir, Lewis, **162**
Mule Train, 93
Munsey, Mr., **271**
Murphy, George, **40**
Murrow, Edward R., **265**
Mussolini, Benito, 110, **192–193**
My Baby Just Cares for Me, **155, 166**
My Baby's Arms, 183, **72**
My Best Girl, **167**
My Blue Heaven, **167**
My Dixie Pair o' Dice, **167**
My Fair Lady, **207**
My Forty Years in Show Business, **211–212**
My Heart Belongs to Daddy, **238**
My Man, **47**
My Mariuch She Took-a Da Steamboat, 56
My Sunny Tennessee, **164**

Naldi, Neita, **122**
Nat Lewis's Haberdashery, **26**
Nathan S. Jonas Hospital, 296
National Cloak and Suit Company, 70, **20**
National Conference of Christians and Jews, **287**
National Safety Council, **192, 217–218**
National Theatre Washington, D.C., **109**
Nature Boy, 30
Nazis, **262**
NBC, 303, **58, 94, 159, 214, 240, 246, 249**

Negri, Pola, 270
Neilson ratings, **252**
Nervous Wreck, The, 285, **134**
New Amsterdam Roof, 4, 152–153, **34, 116–117, 119, 136, 139, 169**
New Amsterdam Theatre, 194, 196, 208, 244, **74, 214**
New Faces, **183**
New Haven, CT, **111**
New Lyceum Theatre, Elizabeth, NJ, 112, **64**
New Orleans, LA, **83**
New Teacher, The, 77
New York Evening Mail, **270–271**
New York Journal-American, **212, 250**
New York Philharmonic, **268**
New York Press, **271**
New York Sun, **212**
New York Telephone Company, 265
New York Theatre, **121**
New York Times, The, 88, 105, **212, 273**
New York World's Fair, **224**
New York World-Telegram, **212**
Newark News, The, **220**
Newark, NJ, **203, 264**
Newman, Alfred, **235**
Next to Your Mother Who Do You Love, **68**
Night Court of the Air, **218**
Nineteenth Hole, 241, **256**
Nixon Theatre, Pittsburgh, PA, **106**
Nolan, Lloyd, **251**
Norchester House, **191**
Norma J. (yacht), **83**
North Africa, **94**
Not Likely, **27, 96**
Notre Dame, **272**
Now's the Time to Fall in Love, **169, 265**

Oakland, CA, **80, 86–87, 90–91**
O'Brian, Jack, **250**
O'Connor, Basil, **200**
Ode to the Electric Light, 147
Oh, How She Could Yacki Hicki Wicki Wacki Woo, **117–118**
Oh, Katharina, **163**
Oh. How I Hate to Get up in the Morning, **70**
Oklahoma University, **211**
Oliver St., **187**
Oliver Twist, **140**
Oliver, Vic, **192**
Olsen, George, 6, 238–240, 261, 274, 285, **90, 133**

O'Neill, Eugene, **158, 169, 202**
Opp, Joe, 216, **73**
Oriental Theatre, Chicago, IL, **145**
Orpheum Circuit, 90, 133, 238
Orpheum Theatre, **99–100**
Orpheum Theatre, Los Angeles, CA, **91, 226**
Orpheum Theatre, Oakland, CA, **87**
Orpheum Theatre, San Francisco, CA, **91**
Orpheum Theatre, Winnipeg, Canada, **104**
Ostenreider Advertising Company, 174–175
Osterman, Jack, 225
Osteroff, Eddie, **14**
Osteroff, Mamie, **13**
Over There, **170**
Oxford, The London, 142

Pabst Blue Ribbon Beer, **241**
Pal Joey, **245**
Palace Music Hall London, England, **120, 142**
Palace Theatre, 57, 92, 99, 86, 201, 204, 205
Palais Royal, **271**
Palestine, **259**
Paley, William, **159**
Palladium, London, England, **241, 244**
Palm Beach, FL, 83, **126–127**
Palm Springs, CA, 284, **30, 59–60, 87, 93, 154, 192, 212, 287–288**
Palmy Days, 303, **156–158**
Pansy the Horse, **243**
Papa's Wife, 179
Paradise Theatre, **81**
Paradise Theatre, Bronx, NY, **205**
Paramount Pictures, **207**
Paramount Studios, **150, 152**
Paramount Studios, LI, NY, 285, **153**
Paramount Theatre, **26**
Paris by Night, 123, **66**
Paris, France, **259, 280**
Parks, Bert, **238**
Parks, Larry, **93**
Parkyakarkus, **232–233**
Parlor Match, The, 179
Pasadena, CA, **196**
Pastor, Tony, 83
Pearl Harbor, **168**
Pebeco, **219, 233**
Peck, Gregory, **264**
Peerce, Jan, **247, 279**
Peg o' My Heart, 103
Penner, Joe, **198**

Pennington, Ann, 181, 183, **42–43, 72, 122, 125**
Pennsylvania Hotel, 63, **190**
People's Vaudeville Company, 112, **64**
Perlberg, Bill, **176–177**
Perry, Admiral Robert E. (née Peary), 82
Perry, Kathryn, **73**
Philadelphia, PA, **165, 259**
Pickford, Mary, 278, **153, 157**
Pierce, Betty, 130
Pig'n Whistle, **28**
Pike St. Synagogue, **19**
Pillsbury, Mr., 249, 253, **256–257**
Pincus, Mrs., 35, 91
Pittsburgh, PA, 90, 106, 109, **134–135, 189**
Playhouse 90, **250**
Plaza Hotel, **169**
Plymouth Park, Morristown, PA, 195
Pock Face Sam, 40
Polly, 247–248, 254
Poole, Bessie, **141–142, 144**
Poonelo (dog), **29**
Pope, the, **110**
Poppy, 195
Porgy and Bess, **279**
Porter, Cole, **70**
Portland, OR, **80**
Post, James H., **297**
Post, Wiley, **114**
Potatoes Are Cheaper, **169, 265**
Powell, William, **270**
Pretty Girl Is Like a Melody, A, 183, **72, 125**
Price, George, 3, 129, **263**
Price, Guy, **101**
Prince of Japan, **110**
Prince of Wales, 4, 5, 156–157, **110–111, 286–287**
Proctor's Fifth Aenue, **78**
Proctor's Theatre, NY, **25**
Producing Managers' Association, 207–208
Prospect Theatre, LI, NY, **263**
Proud and the Profane, The, **176**
P.S. 1, 54, 55, **13, 17, 150**
P.S. 177, 54, **24**
P.S. 2, **13**
Puck, **97**
Purple Heart Circuit, **256**
Put Both Hands Up, **53**
Put Your Arms around Me Honey, **34**

Radio City Music Hall, **142**
Ragtime Violin, 125, **68, 76–77**

Rainbow of Girls, 74
Ralston, Jobyna, 268–270
Rathskellar Trio, 118
Raymond, Jean Clifford, 249
Rea, Henry, 158
Reading, PA, 183
Reber, John, 214, 216, 218
Red Cross, 135, 141, 218–219, 258
Red Feather, The, 179
Reed, Alan, 231
Reed, Jack, 81, 203
Reed, Janet, 205
Reisenweber's, 34
Renard, Jacques, 239
Reuben's, 89, 255
Reynolds, Debbie, 244
Rhythm Boys, The (Tip, Tap and Toe), 205
Rialto Theatre, 125, 274
Ribbons And Bows, 74
Rice and Prevost, 118
Richards, Tom, 105
Rickenbacker (flyer), 114
Riegelmann, Edward, 166
Rin Tin Tin, 262
Ring, Blache, 105
Ringling Brothers, 120
Rio Rita, 74
Ritz Brothers, 257
Ritz Carlton, Boston, MA, 74
Rivoli Theater, 261, 26
R.K.O., 39, 242
Roberti, Lyda, 157
Robeson, Paul, 138
Robinson, Frederick B., 220
Robinson, J. Russel, 163
Rochester, NY, 99
Rockaway, 78
Rockefeller, Nelson, 287
Rockne, Knute, 114
Rogers, Betty (wife of Will), 135, 279, 108
Rogers, Charlie, 270
Rogers, Jimmy (son of Will), 135
Rogers, Will, xi, 4, 90, 134–138, 155, 156, 161–163, 181–182, 194, 196–199, 201–205, 211, 279, 290, 7, 43, 98, 104–115, 124–125, 137–139, 143–145, 147–148, 194, 207, 211, 254, 271
Rolls Royce, 136, 253
Roman Scandals, 26, 37, 138, 153, 160
Romanoff's, 83
Rooney, Mickey, 288
Roosevelt, Eleanor, 196, 272

Index   315

Roosevelt, Franklin Delano, 82–83, 110, 191, 194–200, 221
Roosevelt, Garner, and Me, 198
Roosevelt, Sara Delano, 288
Roosevelt, Theodore, 91
Rosalie, 231, 243, 134
Rose Bowl, 227
Rose o' Day, 168–169
Rose, Billy, 48
Rose, General Maurice, 262
Roseben's Pavilion, 53
Rosen, Max, 297
Rosen, Mr. (Loew's State manager), 210
Rosenbaum, Mr., 71
Rosenbaum, Pop, 160
Rosenthal murder, 23
Rosenthal, Sam (husband: Jennie Tobias), 62
Roses in December, 82
Rosner, Leo, 57, 92, 95, 25
Rosner, Louis, 57, 59, 60, 69, 73, 92, 95, 25
Roth, Jack, 59
Royal Family of England, 110
Royal Theatre, Brooklyn, NY, 112
Royal Vagabond, 236
Royce, Edward, 237, 239, 132
Rubinoff, David, 215, 231–232, 239, 243
Ruby, Harry, 64, 29, 157, 162–165, 272
Ruby, Toby, 29
Ruggles, Charles, 149, 151
Runyon, Damon, 56, 243
Russell, Connie, 246
Russell, Jane, 40
Russia, 234
Ruth, Babe, 160

Safety in Traffic, 192
Saks, 175
Salk vaccine, 200
Salk, Jonah, 265
Sally, 211, 226, 126
Salome, 123, 67
San Diego, CA, 150, 100, 137, 157, 240
San Francisco, CA, 80, 87, 264
Sander, Max, 66, 67
Sandow, Eugene, 120
Santa Barbara, CA, 158
Santa Claus, 234
Santa, Bring My Mommie Back to Me, 234
Santley, Joseph, 19
Saturday Evening Post, The, 107
Save a Home Fund, 270
Savoy, the (England), 192

Say It Isn't So, 71
Scandals, 208, 225
Schenck, Joseph, 112, 113, 271, **64–65, 84, 156**
Schenck, Nicholas, 112, **64, 210**
Schenectady, NY, **64**
School Days, 130
Schwartz, Ray, **24**
Schwartz, Mrs. Ray, 55
Schweitzer, Dr. Albert, **195**
Screen Actors Guild, **158, 192–193, 196, 285**
Seaman's Fund, **268**
See-Saw, 130
Seven Year Itch, The, **183**
Shakespeare, William, **202, 241**
Shaking the Blues Away, 74
Shannon, Marion, **122**
Shapiro, Bernstein and Company, **165**
Shapiro, Rose, **169**
Shapiro, Sol, **211**
Shea, Mike, **69**
Shearer, Norma, 262
Sheffield Milk Company, **255**
Sheik, The, **69**
Shenadoah, PA, **22, 53**
Sherman Hotel, Chicago, 146
Sherman, Al, **169**
Sherry Netherland Hotel, NY, **82, 93**
Sherwood, Robert, **153, 160**
Shore, Dinah, **93, 240–241, 243–244, 257**
Show Boat, 243, **119, 132, 134, 138**
Show Business, 40
Shubert Theatre, Philadelphia, PA, **203**
Shuberts, the, 210, 212–214, 219, 222, 224, 226, **47, 88, 103, 126–127, 150–161, 179**
Shulberg, Benny, 24, 25, 115, 261, 263, 271, 273, **150–161**
Shutta, Ethel, 261, 285, **90, 133, 208–209**
Sidman, Sam, **21**
Sidney (Ziegfeld's assistant), **138**
Silver, Frank, **165**
Silvers, Phil, **78**
Simon & Schuster, **31**
Sinatra, Frank, **197**
Singing Fool, The, **91–92**
Sinton Hotel, Cincinnati, OH, **205, 45**
Six Cylinder Love, 229, 231
Sixty Club, **123**
Sizeman and Son, **250–251**
Sizeman, Morris, **250**
Skelly Stadium, Tulsa, OK, **114**

Skelton, Red, **93–94, 165, 251, 279**
Sketch Book, **101–102**
Smith and Dale, **77**
Smith, Alfred E., 44, 45, 46, 260, 289, **110–111, 187–189, 194–195, 204**
Smith, Kate, **204**
Smith, Sammy, **189–190**
Snappy Stories of History, 241
Snyder, Colonel Gimp, **37–38**
Snyder, Ted, **68**
So Long Letty, 148, **99**
Sokolsky, Georgie, **18**
Solax Club, **34, 111, 269**
Soldier and the Cardinal, The, 230–231
Soldiers' Field, **288**
Somers, Hilda, **268**
Sonny Boy, **92**
Sons of Potash and Perlmutter, 133
Soul of the Violin, The, 26, 34, **17–18, 187**
South Pacific, **207, 251**
Spade, Mrs. (Will Roger's sister), **108**
Special Delivery, 112, 270, 275–279, **152**
Spellbinders' Club, 43
Springtime in Kalamazoo, **54**
Spur, Horton, 237
St. Denis, Ruth, 123, **67**
St. Germain, Kay, **238**
St. Louis, MO, **202, 272**
St. Moritz, Switzerland, **178**
St. Paul, The (ship), 143, **27**
Stage Door Canteen, **255**
Stamper, David, 103–104, 182–183, **44, 72, 169**
Standard Brands, **216**
Stanford University, CA, **220**
Stanley Theatre, Pittsburgh, PA, **159**
Star Theater, NY, 144, **97**
Steel, John, 182–183, **72, 126**
Sten, Anna, **156**
Stepp, Mehlinger, and King, 118
Sterling, Tom, 247–248, 254, 256
Stix, Baer, and Fuller, **223**
stock market crash of 1929, 301–303, 306, **31–32, 137, 146, 253**
Stokowski, Mrs. Leopold, **268**
Stotesburys, 4
Strand Theatre, **71, 164**
Strike Me Pink, **39, 160, 233**
Sullivan, Ed, **202, 246**
Sullivan, Jack "Twin," 161, **143, 148**
Sully, Eve, **160**
Sun Bonnet Sue, 130

Index 317

Surprise Lake Camp, 30, 31, 32, 33, 34, 35, 36, 37, 42, 55, 177, 278, 291, **18, 25, 57–58, 111, 113, 169, 254–255, 266, 269, 273**
Swanson, Gloria, 262

Talk of New York, The, 60, 61, **25**
Talmadge, Norma, 112, **84**
Tammany, 130
Tammany Hall, **188**
Tashman, Lilyan (Mrs. Al Lee), **98, 122**
Taxi Cab Skit, 281, **133**
Taylor, Estelle, 270
Television City, CA, **227**
Temple of Religion, **224, 239**
Ten Commandments of Show Business, **202**
Ten Commandments, The, **245**
Terris, Norma, **122**
Terry, Ethelind, 236
Texaco, **219, 234–235**
Texas A & M, **211**
Texas Jack, 194
Thalberg, Irving, 263, **150, 156**
Thanksgiving, **193–194, 198**
That's the Kind of a Baby for Me, 156, **75, 105, 125**
Thaw, Harry K., 268
There Shall Be No Night, **251**
Thinking of You, **164**
This Is the Army, **75**
Thomas, Danny, **84**
Thomas, John Charles, 209
Thompson, George, **281–282**
Thompson, Harry, 82, 87
Three Coins in the Fountain, **193**
Three Little Words (film), **165**
Three Little Words (song), **164**
Three Men on a Horse, **161**
Three Musketeers, The, 197, 208, 211, 230–231, 243, **119, 134, 137**
Three Smart Girls, **236**
Tibbett, Lawrence, **234**
Ticklin' the Ivories, **74**
Tierney, Harry, 183, 229, 233–234, 237, 72, **127, 169**
Tiffany's, 284
Timberg, Herman, 130
Time Magazine, **240–241**
Tin Pan Alley, **54, 68**
Tinney, Frank, 209, **97**
To Arms, **55**
Toast of the Town, **246**

Tobias brothers, **162**
Tobias, Charles, **162, 167–169**
Tobias, David (Ida's father), 92, 94, 107–109, 111, 139–140, **26, 28, 53, 204**
Tobias, Edna (Mrs. Charles Tobias), **168**
Tobias, Harry, **162, 167**
Tobias, Henry, **162, 167**
Tobias, Jennie (Ida's sister), 92, 94–95, 105, 107, 140, **27, 53, 62**
Tobias, Minnie (Ida's sister), 57, 95, 105–106, 140, **25, 62**
Toledo, OH, **163**
Tony Pastor's, 98, **19**
Toot, Toot, Tootsie, **166**
Torney General Hospital, 59
Toscanini, Arturo, **268**
Touraine Hotel, Boston, MA, **140**
Traubel, Helen, 60
Tribune, The, 105
Troy, NY, **64**
Truex, Ernest, 210
Truman, Margaret, 60
Truman, President Harry S., **84, 263**
Tucker, Sophie, 223, **33–35, 39–40, 209**
Tulip Time, 183, **72, 125, 169**
Turk St., San Francisco, CA, **87**
Tuttle, Frank, 263–267, **150–153**
Twain, Mark, **260**
Twentieth Century Fox, **84–85**
Two Little Girls in Blue, **35–36**
Tynan, Brandon, 209

UCLA, **182**
Ukelele Ike, **283**
Uncle Sam, **304–309**
Unholy Garden, The, **156**
United Artists, 112, **153**
United Jewish Appeal, **256, 260**
Universal Pictures, **234, 236**
University of Arizona, **211**
University of Chicago, **220**
University of Maine, **211**
University of Michigan, 240
University of Newark, **220**
Up and Down Broadway, **270**
Urban, Joseph, 183, **122–123, 132**

Valentine, **254–255**
Valentino, Rudolph, 223
Vallee, Rudy, **214**
Van and Schenck, 174–175, 181, 183, 204, 205, 208, **36, 72, 125**

Van Cortlandt Park, **29, 163**
Van, Gus, 174–175, 204–205
Vanderbilt home, 76
Vanderbilt, Mrs. W. K., **204**
Vanderbilts, 4, 153, 156, 158, **118**
Variety, **227**, 87–88, 101, 126
Vassar College, **220**
Veronica, **122**
Veteran's Hospital, Kansas, MO, **256**
Victor Company, 240, **125, 165**
Victoria Regina, **251**
Vidor, Florence, 269
Vierick, George Sylvester, **224**
Virginia Judge, The, 83
Vitaphone, 91
Viviani, M., **109**
Von Bulow, Hans, **120**
Von Zell, Harry, **239**

Wagner, Dr., 284
Waite, Malcolm, 271
Waiting for the Robert E. Lee, **162**
Waldorf Astoria, **35, 132**
Walker Boxing Bill, **190**
Walker, Bee, **264**
Walker, Herman, **20–21**
Walker, Jimmie Mayor, 98, 260, 281, **133, 166, 189–191, 194, 197**
Walkin' My Baby Back Home (show), 247
Wall St. Girl, The, **105**
Wallington, "Jenny," **214**
Wallington, Jimmy, **213, 215, 217–218, 232, 238**
Wallington, Mrs. Jimmy, **213**
Walls of Wall Street, 231
Walsh, Carey, 2, 96–100, 102–103, 105–106, 125, **53, 55, 61–62, 68**
Walter Reed Hospital, Washington, 143, **194**
Wanamaker, Rodman, 5, **286**
Wanger, Walter, 261
Warfield, David, 112, **162**
Warm Springs, GA, **197, 200**
Warner Brothers, the, **91, 171**
Warner, Jack, **91, 171–172**
Washington, DC, 83, **109, 194, 198, 264**
Washington, George, **194, 196**
Washington, Martha, **124**
Waterson, Berlin And Snyder, **69, 163–164**
Watson, Harry, **123**
Way of All Flesh, The, 267
Wayburn, Ned, 183, **44**

We Did It Before and We Can Do It Again, **168**
Weber and Fields Music Hall, 179
Weber, Joe, 179
Weiner, Jack, 78
Weir Brothers, 68, 70, **20**
Weir, J. C., **20**
Welles, Orson, **251**
Welsh, Joe, 75, **20**
West End Theatre, Harlem, NY, 112, **64**
West Point, NY, 18
West, Mae, **148**
Western Union, **102, 112**
Weston and Fields, 97–98
Whalen, Grover, **176**
When I Lost You, 71
When I'm Alone I'm Lonesome, **53**
When I'm the President, **169, 198**
When Ragtime Rosie Rags the Rosary, **162**
When Those Sweet Hawaiian Babies Roll Their Eyes, **164**
Where Did You Get That Girl?, **164**
White House, **84, 109, 110, 112, 171, 194, 197–199, 222**
White, Lee, 142
Whoopee!, 284–285, 302–303, **26, 31–32, 37, 87, 90, 101, 113, 122–123, 135–137, 153–155, 157, 166, 179, 189, 208, 253**
Who's Afraid of the Big Bad Wolf (skit), **163**
Wilbur, Ray Lyman, **220**
Wild Cherries, **53**
Will Success Spoil Rock Hunter?, 183
William and Mary College, **211**
William Morris Agency, **67, 83, 209, 211, 233, 242, 244**
William Penn Hotel, 204, **73**
Williams, Bert, 29, 158–162, 181, 183, 199, **44, 72, 105, 124–125, 139, 143–144, 281**
Williams, Harry (*Whoopee!* character), **209**
Wilson, Don, **227**
Wilson, Woodrow, 4, 155, **109–110**
Winchell, Walter, **56, 78**
Wings, 268, 270
Winter Garden, NY, 212, **34, 86, 89–92, 126, 163**
Winter Garden, Berlin, 196, **142–143**
Won't You Come and Play Wiz Me, **120**
Wood Wood Wood, 57
Wood, Georgie, **67**
Wood, Joe, **63, 67**
Woods Theatre, **88**

World Series, **144–145**
World's Fair, 179
Wynn, Ed, **209–210**, 97, **198**, **251**

Yankee Doodle Dandy (film), **171**
Yellen, Jack, **34**, **169**
Yes Sir, That's My Baby, **166–167**
Yes! We Have No Bananas, **165–166**
Yip, Yip Yaphank, **69**, **75**
YMCA, **70**
You Gotta Have It, **75**
You'd Be Surprised, **183–184**, **71–73**, **125**
Young and Rubicam, **224–225**
Young Love, **69**
Your Next President, **304**
You're Breaking My Heart, **243**
You're Laughing at Me, **48**
You've Got to Have It, **75**

Zanuck, Darryl, **91**, **268**
Ziegfeld Follies, xii, 29, 45, 70, 103, 136–138, 156–158, 162, 172, 174, 176, 180–183, 185–188, 194, 196–198, 200, 206, 208–209, 216, 236, 238, 240–241, 261, 265, 281–284, 7, 20, 23, **28**, 34–35, 37, 42–44, 46, **69**, 71–72, 74, **81**, 105–107, 109, 112–113, 116, 119, 121, 123–126, 130, 133, 137–141, 143, 145, 148, 152, **164**, 167, **169**, 178, 188, 190, 201–203, 211, 214, **225**, 247, **272**, **281**
Ziegfeld Sr., Dr. Florenz, **119–120**
Ziegfeld, Florenz, xii, xiii, 4, 21, 38, 45, 103–104, 152–153, 158, 162, 165, 171, 174, 182–184, 186–187, 190–193, 198, 206–209, 211, 216, 224, 226–227, 229–236, 238–245, 274, 281–284, 300, **28**, 32, 39–40, 42, 44, 46–47, 72–74, **88**, 90, **98**, 102, 105, 107–109, 114, 116–138, 140, 153–155, 157–159, 161, **164**, 166, 178, 201–202, 207, 253, 271, **286**
Ziegfeld, Patricia, **124**
ZIV, **248**
Zukor, Adolph, 112, 260, 271, **64**, **133**

www.ingramcontent.com/pod-product-compliance
Lightning Source LLC
Chambersburg PA
CBHW071710300426
44115CB00010B/1378